AMY VANDERBILT'S COMPLETE COOKBOOK

AMY

VANDERBILT'S

Complete Cookbook

DRAWINGS BY ANDREW WARHOL

DOUBLEDAY & COMPANY, INC., GARDEN CITY, NEW YORK

To my editor
Marion Patton
sine qua non

Introduction

I believe that the ability to prepare and serve good and attractive meals is a delightful feminine virtue. The importance of this and of being a good housekeeper were drilled into me from the time I could walk.

Like most Americans, I am a mixture. I am Dutch, French, English, Irish—but in appearance and personality, strongly Dutch and for six generations my Holland heritage has been preserved reasonably intact. On one hand, I had the influence of my mother, a third generation American of English and Irish descent, who strongly needed around her all of the aspects of gracious living but who found them difficult to achieve without servants. She loved to entertain and liked cooking if it was part of this entertaining.

On the other hand, in our household, almost from the time that I was born, was my aunt, brought up in the New York-Dutch-American tradition wherein a woman must know all of the household arts whether or not she has servants to instruct. My Aunt Louise was the best house-keeper I have ever seen and one of the finest cooks. Her bureau drawers were always ready for inspection and her closets a delight of organization. My handsome grandfather, who looked like Charles Evans Hughes and lived to the ripe age of ninety-five, was also a part of our household from my very early years. His very firm opinions and ukases in the matter of food and the running of a household impressed and almost terrified us all.

The men in our family were all quite sure of their roles as men, which in my opinion is the way it should be. My father and my grandfather were never to be found in the kitchen mixing a cake. They did, however, consider it their proper prerogative to purchase and carry home from the Washington Market every bit of meat the household consumed. The buying of meat, they held, was not a woman's business, any more than was the carving of it. I still think the art of carving belongs to the male, but I am willing to agree that women have had to learn how to buy meat, just as many of us have had to learn how to carve, either because the men in the family won't or because there are no men in the family.

When I was very young, about six, cooking was presented to me as a privilege. You had to be responsible and orderly to be allowed to proceed in the kitchen. I was permitted to prepare my own breakfast on Saturday mornings—but I had to clean up afterward.

My own three sons are given the same privilege, although they are not held to the rigorous cleaning up that I was held to—if they stack their dishes and put the pots in the sink, I'm satisfied. They lend me their masculine talents in many ways—by changing fuses, by running the tape recorder for my writing, by taking out the garbage. I taught them how to feed themselves well, but I don't want them to become unduly taken with their culinary skills to the neglect of such masculine ones as wood chopping, for which they are better adapted than am I.

Many people have said, since the publication of *Amy Vanderbilt's Complete Book of Etiquette* in 1952, that it should be followed by a complete cookbook. For, of course, I *can* cook. I enjoy preparing any kind of meal, but I prefer meals that have a special meaning—meals for guests. I even manage to feel a little guilty if I don't have some part in the preparation of *every* meal for guests. No matter how tired or how busy I may be, I always rise to the occasion when a party is in the offing.

Like my Dutch ancestors who daily went to market as European women do today, I, too, like to see the food I am buying for my household. Not for me, except in an emergency, is the telephoned order. I plan, of course, to use fruits and other foods in season to keep my food budget always at the proper point. When entertaining runs a little heavy, I counterbalance it with economy meals for the family. I am careful to see that leftovers are used, and perhaps because I have such a dislike of waste, I allow my considerable family of pets to consume the scraps which otherwise might go into the garbage pail in another family.

My children and I, despite my career, have a warm and loving relationship. This comes partly, I believe, because they know that their mother, when necessity arises—and it certainly does—is able to run the household and feed them good meals under cheerful, happy circumstances no matter what happens. Children get a great feeling of security knowing just this: that despite her necessary and often greatly enjoyed outside activities, a mother considers her children's welfare first and is willing to contribute to it with her own domestic talents.

The running of a home and the preparation of food is creative. This is something that too often is missed entirely in the education of our American girls. In our increasingly intellectualized society, there is too little stress on the sound satisfactions there are in being able to put on the table an attractive, nutritious meal without strain. Perhaps, however, it is encouraging to see that the kitchen, at one time compressed to a mere cubby hole, is now expanding warmly into the "family room" where the mother and the family are together in the preparation of meals. The mother is no longer isolated.

I have such a kitchen myself, where my children sit and do their homework, look at television, listen to records, read by the fire in an atmosphere free of "don'ts." Part of one wall is solid with cookbooks of every kind including some meant just for boys and girls.

My training in cooking began at about the age of six, but in my early teens, I was sent to school in Europe to the Institute Heubi in Lausanne, Switzerland. There at the graduate school, the Villa, I studied home economics under expert tutelage before going on to college preparation at the secondary school, the Chateau.

This was doing it the very hard way indeed, for in the graduate school all of the girls spoke excellent French. In fact we were not permitted to speak any other language. I began my culinary notebook in French not knowing what I was writing. My cooking classes thus greatly depended on my home-trained ability in the kitchen, for I was there for a good three months without being able to talk with my instructors or with my fellow pupils. It was the only three months in my whole life in which I knew what it must be like to be both deaf and dumb.

In my school I learned not only *haute cuisine,* but all the arts of housekeeping, even to the pleating of nightgowns with a pleating iron. For us there were no shortcuts, no scouring powders (we used brickdust), no canned, dehydrated, or frozen foods. Perhaps because of this training, I was once able to make a perfect zabaglione on a kerosene stove by the light of an oil lamp in a Virginia cabin!

We sometimes hear complaints that women spend too much time in the exchange of recipes, that this is a very trifling activity indeed. If this is so, then I am very guilty. Many of the recipes in this book came to me in exchange from friends all over the world and, have become part of my own cookery repertoire. When the routine of running house and office becomes irksome, I get out my recipe file and pull out one or more of these recipes that I have collected. As I knead my Irish soda bread (I often use the mix that is available—imported from Dunlaoghaire now), I recall the morning that I literally hung by my heels to kiss the Blarney Stone in Cork. When I serve our fresh sweet corn, I fill the little individual butter dishes that I bought at the Vista Alegre porcelain plant in Portugal. When we prepare Swedish smorgås-bord, my sons and I remember the lesson we learned in Stockholm—eat first the fish (herrings and seafoods), then the hot delicacies and meat, and finally the salads and cheese.

I know many people so frightened of entertaining that they have one or two standard company meals and these they serve forth every time they have guests. This sad poverty of cuisine is not for me. I like to adventure in the realm of food. I want my children to be able to accept a new dish, try it and, if possible, enjoy it as much as I do the serving of it.

Although I find the actual preparation of food—from scratch—interesting, creative, and challenging, I by no means, as you will see in the pages of this cookbook, spurn the use of quick methods. The commercial cake mixes are wonderful and in most cases can be enjoyed even by the calorie-watcher. I love the idea of being able to pick up from the freezer department at the supermarket fine sauces from Maxim's in Paris, baby brussels sprouts quick-frozen in Holland, or pastry quick-frozen in wonderful Copenhagen.

The United States is a fine place for gourmets—for anyone who likes good food with or without having the technical knowledge of preparing it. Or for anyone with a penchant for the exotic. I was pleased when my then twelve-year-old spent some of his allowance on a jar of chocolate covered bees!

I hope that as you work from these pages with me, you will travel to many of the places I have been and enjoy the specialties of some of the fine restaurants where I have been a guest. Often where there is a very personal reason for my including a recipe in this collection, I have told you why in a footnote to the recipe.

My own training as a cook has been technical in a different way than is the technical training of a home economist in this country. I was, however, for many years a food editor and am very familiar with American cookery methods and the development of food preparation in this country. However, I owe an enormous debt of gratitude to Miss Florence Brobeck who has tested these recipes in her capacity as a trained American home economist. A tyro in the kitchen can produce any recipe here successfully. The cooking time is exact and the number of portions are indicated. Possible difficulties in the more complex recipes are carefully described.

No cookbook fills all needs. If there were such a book I would have *it* and not the 300-odd books now in my collection. I have tried, however, in my own cookbook to compile one that will help the beginning cook and be of constant inspiration to the woman who must plan and produce three or more meals a day and meals for entertaining. There are things here that will challenge the very good cook indeed, but on the other hand there are many, many easy recipes for the cook who must hurry. The technical discussions on the purchase and preparation of certain foods are Miss Brobeck's, the result of her own fine professional background and experience. I have learned much from this contribution of hers.

Like my etiquette book, this book has taken years of preparation. Its production has given me much pleasure. I hope that you will enjoy it, too.

Amy Vanderbilt

"Daisyfields"
Weston, Connecticut

Contents

PART II   A WORD TO THE SUCCESSFUL COOK

PART I
Recipes and Menus

CHAPTER ONE

Appetizers

An appetizer, briefly described, is a refreshing, simple food or drink offered before the meal to the guest soon after he arrives.

The custom of serving appetizers is a boon to the maidless household, for the cook-homemaker-hostess can have ready a tray, around which the guests can find refreshment while she goes to the kitchen to put the final touches on the dinner. The tray, on the coffee table in the living room or on the porch, may hold a pitcher or shaker of iced fruit or vegetable juice and a plate of canapés, or a bowl of savory spread and crackers or toast for guests to make their own canapés. They can drink their appetizers, nibble a delicious mouthful of cheese or *pâté,* and entertain themselves while the first course of the dinner is being brought to the table. Then, their appetite whetted, but not dimmed by too many canapés, they can thoroughly enjoy a good dinner.

By planned shopping and preparation, canapés can be made in advance. The chafing dish is a great asset to the appetizer course and hot appetizers may be prepared ahead of time then reheated in the chafing dish at serving time. Some tidbits can be made days ahead and stored ready for use. Fruit juices may be mixed, vegetable juices blended, and all stored in the refrigerator to be taken out for final touches and garnishes at the last moment before guests arrive.

Tart shells, cheese straws, and similar pastry bits can be baked ahead of time. Let them cool and store in tightly covered containers in a cool spot in the kitchen. Before serving them, crisp 1 or 2 minutes in a hot oven. Then fill according to recipe and serve right away.

Small turnovers, filled straws, rolled cheese sandwiches, can be made the day before, refrigerated until needed, then baked quickly and served.

Dip, dunks, spreads, and mixes can be prepared a day ahead of time and kept in the refrigerator in tightly covered jars.

Raw vegetables can be prepared early on the day of the party, put in a bowl filled with cracked ice so that ice surrounds the vegetables, and stored in the refrigerator.

Hard-cooked eggs may be prepared a day ahead of time. Early on the day they are to be served, peel, halve, and stuff. Cover plate with foil or waxed paper loosely, then tuck ends of paper round and under the plate to cover thoroughly but not mash the eggs.

Deep-fried cheese balls, fish cakes, and similar tidbits can be fried in mid-afternoon of a party day and kept warm in a very low oven, with its door open. Reheat briefly by closing oven door and turning heat high for 2 minutes.

Hot canapés, snacks, and tidbits should be served hot, direct from a chafing dish, table grill, or electrically heated plate, or brought in hot from the kitchen.

Chilled canapés, dips, and other cold foods should be served very cold from a plate or bowl set on ice.

Crisp foods, such as crackers, toast, straws, fish sticks, should be crisped in the oven and served while slightly warm.

It is easy to overdo the appetizer habit. One or two delicious and exceptionally attractive foods, a small, icy-cold glass of well-seasoned tomato juice or mixed fruit juices, or a glass of dry sherry or dry champagne prepare the hungry guest for your dinner which follows. Too many canapés, too many glasses of juice or cocktails, dull the appetite and detract from the pleasure at the table.

Having the right size glasses, attractive serving platters, unusual and adequate bowls for dips, gay but serviceable napkins is essential to the eye appeal and enjoyment of the appetizers.

The number and style, kind and flavor of appetizers are determined by the menu which is to follow, and by whether you are serving drop-in guests on the porch or in the garden, or whether it is a long-planned occasion to which your husband's employer and his wife and other important guests are invited. Adjust the appetizers to the occasion.

Canapés and Crackers

BACON-AND-LIVERWURST CANAPÉS

½ pound liverwurst
2 tablespoons mayonnaise
¼ teaspoon thyme
1 tablespoon finely cut chives

18 2-inch rounds cut from thin bread slices
Softened butter
3 strips lean bacon

Blend together liverwurst, mayonnaise, thyme, and chives. Use cooky cutter to cut rounds from thin slices of bread. Spread rounds with softened butter, then with liverwurst mixture. Cut bacon strips crosswise in 6 pieces each. Lay piece of bacon on top of liverwurst. Chill until serving time. Broil canapés 2 inches from moderate broiler heat until bacon is crisp, browned, or curled. Serve at once. Makes 18 canapés.

BACON-CHUTNEY CANAPÉS

Broil lean bacon until crisp. Drain on paper towels. Crumble bacon fine. Combine with enough chopped chutney to make good spreading consistency. Spread on crackers. Lay crackers in broiling pan. Broil 2 or 3 minutes under moderate heat, until very hot. Serve hot. Delicious with salad, too.

This is a Weston, Connecticut, favorite from my neighbors, the Leon Dinels.

CHEESE-EGG PUFFS

16 crisp crackers
Commercial Cheddar cheese spread
1 egg

1 tablespoon mayonnaise
⅛ teaspoon salt
¼ teaspoon pepper

Start oven at moderate (350° F.).

Spread crackers with cheese mixture and arrange on baking sheet. Beat egg yolk until lemony. Mix with mayonnaise, salt, and pepper. Whip egg white stiff. Fold into yolk mixture. Heap on crackers.

Bake 13 minutes, or until top is set and lightly browning. Serve hot. Makes 16 puffs.

CALIFORNIA BITE TARTS

Rich pie pastry for 2-crust pie

1 ½ cups ground leftover roast beef

1 cup seedless raisins, soaked and drained

3 hard-cooked eggs, grated

½ cup sliced ripe olives

1 tablespoon prepared mustard

Mayonnaise or sour cream

Prepare pastry ahead of time and chill.

Combine beef, raisins, eggs, olives, and mustard. Moisten with enough mayonnaise or sour cream to hold together.

Start oven at moderate (350° F.). Lightly grease a baking sheet. Dust with flour.

Roll out pastry in a sheet about ¼ inch thick. Cut in 2½-inch rounds. Add spoonful of meat mixture to each round. Moisten edge and fold over to make half-moon shape. Press edges together with fork. Prick top with fork. Place on prepared baking sheet.

Turn oven to hot (450° F.). Bake 10 minutes, or until pastry is golden. Lower oven temperature to moderate (350° F.) again and continue baking another 5 minutes. These tiny pastries should be golden brown. Serve hot or cold. Makes 24 or more.

One of the best "finger" appetizers you can serve with champagne, fruit juice, any before-dinner drink. Also a fine idea with salad, soup, or for the buffet table when the main dish is creamed sea food or chicken.

CHEESE-BACON CANAPÉS

20 slices bread

2 tablespoons softened butter or margarine

3 slices lean bacon

2 egg whites

1 ¼ cups coarsely grated Swiss cheese

⅔ cup finely cut green pepper

1 teaspoon finely cut parsley

½ teaspoon salt

½ teaspoon orégano

¼ teaspoon pepper

Use 2-inch cooky cutter and cut 20 rounds from bread slices. Toast rounds on one side. Spread untoasted side with softened butter or margarine.

Cook bacon until half done. Drain. Chop or cut in fine pieces.

Start broiler at moderate (325° F.). Whip egg whites stiff. Fold cheese, green pepper, parsley, salt, orégano, and pepper into whites. Spoon onto buttered side of rounds. Sprinkle with bacon. Place on broiler pan.

Broil 4 or 5 inches from heat until cheese melts and bacon is crisp, about 10 minutes. Makes 20 canapés.

CHEESE-MUSHROOM CANAPÉS

1 tablespoon butter	2 ounces Old English processed
1 drop Tabasco sauce	cheese, grated (4 tablespoons)
1 tablespoon flour	36 narrow toast fingers
2 tablespoons cream	
1 (3-ounce) can chopped broiled mushrooms	

Place butter and Tabasco in saucepan over low heat. Stir in flour smoothly. Add cream and broth drained from mushrooms. Bring to boiling point, stirring constantly. Add cheese. Continue stirring until cheese melts. Remove from heat. Chop mushrooms very fine. Add to cheese mixture. Spread on toast fingers. Heat thoroughly under broiler just before serving. Makes 1 cup of spread—about 36 small canapés.

CRISP SESAME STRIPS

1 cup sifted all-purpose flour	1 egg yolk, lightly beaten
½ teaspoon salt	⅓ cup butter or margarine,
½ teaspoon powdered ginger	melted
½ teaspoon sugar	1 tablespoon water
1 cup grated sharp cheese	½ teaspoon Worcestershire sauce
¼ cup toasted sesame seeds	

Start oven at moderate (350° F.).

Sift dry ingredients together into bowl. Stir in cheese and mix well. Stir in sesame seeds. Combine remaining ingredients. Add to cheese mixture. Stir to form a ball. Roll out on lightly floured board to ⅛ inch thickness. Cut in strips 1 by 3 inches, or rounds. Place on ungreased baking sheet.

Bake 10 to 15 minutes. Let cool. Makes 48 strips or rounds.

Serve as canapé base for cheese or *pâté* mixtures or serve in place of crackers with various drinks, salads, and in lunch boxes.

CHEESED POTATO CHIPS

1 (4-ounce) package potato chips	1 tablespoon poppy seeds
½ cup grated cheese	½ teaspoon thyme

Start oven at moderate (350° F.).

Spread potato chips on baking sheets. Sprinkle with cheese, then with poppy seeds and thyme. Heat 5 to 8 minutes, or until cheese is melting. Serve hot. Makes 6 servings.

Vary the cheese for new flavors: use crumbled bleu cheese and finely diced olives together.

COCKTAIL PANCAKES

1 cup pancake mix	1 egg, beaten
¼ cup corn meal	1 tablespoon melted shortening
1 ½ cups milk	

Combine pancake mix with corn meal. Stir in milk. Beat in egg and shortening. Pour 1 tablespoon batter for each pancake onto hot, lightly greased griddle. Bake 2 or 3 minutes on each side, or until golden brown, turning cakes once. Makes 28 small pancakes.

Fill, and roll pancakes with:

Ham Filling

2 tablespoons mayonnaise	2 teaspoons prepared horse-radish
2 tablespoons cream cheese	2 cups chopped, cooked ham

Mix ingredients together. Spoon a little on each pancake. Roll and fasten with wooden pick. Heat under moderate broiler 2 minutes or sauté lightly in a little butter or margarine in chafing dish. Serve hot. Makes filling for 28 small pancakes.

This is an elaborate appetizer that may be prepared well in advance (even frozen) up to the final stage. May be brought to perfection in electric skillet, too, before the eyes of the guests and kept hot for late-comers.

CRAB-CHEESE CANAPÉS

1 cup crab meat	¼ teaspoon pepper
1 (3-ounce) package cream cheese	½ teaspoon curry powder
	¹⁄₁₆ teaspoon cayenne
½ cup commercial sour cream	1 tablespoon finely cut capers
½ teaspoon salt	1 tablespoon finely cut chives

Drain crab meat. Remove all fibers by flaking carefully through the meat with fork. Grind coarsely. Blend cheese and sour cream smoothly. Season with salt, pepper, curry powder, and cayenne. Combine with ground crab meat. Add more sour cream if needed for good consistency. Mix in capers and chives. Serve on toasted crackers or rounds of buttered toasted bread. Makes about 2½ cups of spread.

DAYTON CANAPÉS

Mayonnaise	Tiny rounds of bread cut with
Grated Parmesan cheese	1-inch cooky cutter
Onion, peeled and chopped	

Mix mayonnaise and cheese to consistency of softened butter. Place little chopped onion in center of each round of bread. Cover with mayonnaise-cheese mixture. Put under broiler until puffed and brown. Serve immediately.

These canapés can be prepared the day before and, covered with waxed paper, stored in refrigerator. They are broiled just before serving. This is a specialty of Mrs. Robert Hughes of the Dayton, Ohio, Junior League. She gave the recipe to me when I was lecturing there.

HOT CHEESE-BACON ROLLS

8 slices fresh bread	8 slices lean bacon
¼ pound (1 cup) shredded sharp American cheese	16 stuffed olives

Start broiler at moderately hot (400° F.).

Cut crusts from bread. Cut slices in half. Put about 1 tablespoon cheese on each strip. Roll. Cut bacon strips in half crosswise, wrap cheese roll with bacon strip and fasten with wooden pick. Place rolls on rack in shallow pan.

Broil about 8 minutes, or until bacon is cooked and crisp. Stick olive on end of pick. Makes 16 rolls.

CRUSTY CODFISH BALLS

1 ½ cups mashed potatoes	Salt and pepper to taste
1 cup flaked cooked codfish	Flour
2 eggs	Fine, dry bread crumbs
1 tablespoon chopped chives	Fat for deep frying
1 tablespoon sour cream	

Combine potatoes, fish, 1 egg, chives, sour cream, salt and pepper. Shape mixture into small balls about diameter of a quarter. Beat remaining egg. Dust fish balls with flour, dip into beaten egg, then roll in crumbs. Let stand at least 1 hour, so coating will become firm.

Fry in deep fat or bake in hot oven until fish balls are golden brown and crisp. Serve plain or with tartare sauce. Keep hot in chafing dish on buffet table. Makes about 30 codfish appetizers.

These will keep hot on a serving plate or an electric hot tray any place you wish to serve them.

HOT CRAB-MEAT BALLS

2 ½ tablespoons butter or margarine	2 cups crab meat
3 tablespoons flour	½ teaspoon finely cut tarragon
½ cup consommé or chicken stock	2 teaspoons finely cut parsley
½ teaspoon salt	1 (3-ounce) can chopped broiled mushrooms
¼ teaspoon white pepper	2 tablespoons butter or margarine
½ cup heavy cream	

Melt 2½ tablespoons butter or margarine in saucepan. Stir in flour smoothly until golden. Stir in consommé or stock, boiling 1 or 2 minutes. Add salt and pepper. Stir in cream slowly. Remove from heat. Flake crab meat lightly with fork. Remove all fibers. Add crab, tarragon, parsley, and mushrooms to cream sauce. Mix. Spread on platter to cool.

Form crab mixture into small balls. Refrigerate or freeze. At cocktail time sauté lightly in hot butter or margarine. Use chafing dish to keep balls hot. Serve each on wooden pick. Makes about 30 balls.

PASADENA CANAPÉS

1 (5-ounce) jar Cheddar cheese spread
1 cup sifted all-purpose flour
4 tablespoons butter

Have all ingredients at room temperature for at least 30 minutes. Blend all together smoothly. Form into roll. Wrap roll in waxed paper. Refrigerate 1 hour or longer.

To serve, start oven at moderate (350° F.).

Slice roll onto lightly floured baking sheet. Bake slices 20 minutes, or until puffed and browning. Serve hot. Makes 24 or more servings.

My friends the Frederick Wordens gave me this recipe on one of my California trips and it has become one of my stand-bys. Actually you can refrigerate it for a week or more or freeze it. A good thing to have on hand during heavy entertaining season.

PIROSHKI

1 recipe biscuit mix
½ cup commercial sour cream
1 cup finely cut cooked carrots
2 hard-cooked eggs, finely cut
1 tablespoon finely cut ripe olives
1 tablespoon finely cut parsley
½ teaspoon salt
¼ teaspoon pepper

Prepare biscuit dough according to directions on package. Roll pastry out about ¼ inch thick. Cut with round cutter. Brush each piece with sour cream.

Start oven at moderate (375° F.).

Combine carrots, eggs, olives, parsley, salt, and pepper. Place heaping teaspoon of mixture on each pastry round. Fold pastry over and pinch edges together. Prick pastry with fork. Place on baking sheet.

Bake 25 minutes, or until pastry is lightly browned.

Serve hot with soup, (especially borscht), salad, or as an appetizer with cocktails. Makes 24 or more, depending on size of cutter.

Delicious piroshki are made with filling of cooked fish, shrimp, turkey, chicken, or meat. Chop or grind filling fine and moisten with mayonnaise or Russian dressing. Add tang with chopped pickle, capers, or relish. Bake as described.

NOCHES

San Antonio spicy hot canapés

Fritos (or strips of homemade fried tortillas)
American cheese

Hot green pepper (available canned, called Zallentenos)

Lay strip of American cheese on each frito, then strip of hot green pepper. Place under moderate broiler heat until cheese melts. Serve hot.

I was introduced to these at the home of "O.P." Schnables the night I was made Honorary Mayor of San Antonio's La Ciudad de la Villita (the original city) and Honorary Citizen of Texas.

TOASTED CHICKEN CANAPÉS

1 cup ground cooked chicken
¼ cup finely cut celery
2 tablespoons finely cut black olives
¼ teaspoon salt

⅛ teaspoon pepper
¼ cup tartare sauce
12 thin slices bread
Butter or margarine, softened

Combine chicken, celery, olives, salt, pepper, and tartare sauce. Blend smoothly. Cut crusts from bread. Spread slices with softened butter or margarine. Spread with chicken mixture. Roll. Place seam side down in pan lined with waxed paper. Cover with waxed paper and damp towel. Chill in refrigerator 30 minutes or longer. Brush with melted butter. Broil under moderate heat until golden. Makes 12 canapés.

Add ¼ cup grated Cheddar cheese to this mixture for extra-good flavor.

Toasted Tuna Canapés or Toasted Salmon Canapés: Substitute flaked, cooked, or canned tuna fish or salmon for chicken. Add 1 teaspoon grated onion to fish mixture.

Dips and Spreads

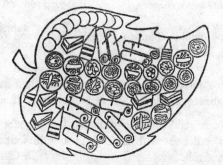

AVOCADO DIP

Guacamole

1 cup mashed avocado	1 teaspoon Worcestershire
1 tablespoon fresh lime juice	sauce
1 teaspoon salt	¼ cup crumbled Roquefort
1 ½ teaspoons grated onion	cheese

Blend all ingredients together smoothly by beating with spoon, or use blender. A chopped peeled tomato, or ½ pimiento, may be added for color. This recipe, which is Mexico's *Guacamole,* is a favorite spread for potato chips, Melba toast, and crisp crackers. Makes about 1¼ cups.

BLUE CHEESE-ALMOND SPREAD

1 cup (4 ounces) crumbled blue cheese	1 tablespoon Worcestershire sauce
½ cup crumbled soft Cheddar cheese	1 teaspoon paprika
1 cup commercial sour cream	½ cup chopped toasted almonds

Mash cheese. Blend with sour cream and seasonings with fork, or in blender, until smooth. Add almonds. Makes 2 cups.

Spread on toasted strips of raisin bread or toast triangles or fill tiny buttered biscuits with this spread. Delicious as a tea sandwich, too. Also try it on buttered rounds of Boston brown bread with hot or cold drink.

CHEESE-GARLIC DIP

2 (3-ounce) packages cream cheese
1 (6-ounce) roll smoky cheese
½ clove garlic, peeled and mashed
⅓ cup pineapple juice
¼ teaspoon Tabasco sauce

1 teaspoon Worcestershire sauce
1 tablespoon finely cut black olives
1 tablespoon finely cut green olives
Sour cream, if needed

Break up cheese. Add other ingredients. Use blender to make smooth paste. Or mash and beat with fork. Add a little sour cream if needed for smoothness. Chill.

Delicious with crisp potato chips, strips of pumpernickel, or toasted crackers. Makes about 1½ cups.

CHEESE-WALNUT DIP

1 (8-ounce) package cream cheese
1 (5-ounce) jar blue cheese
1 tablespoon grated onion
1 tablespoon capers, cut fine

1 teaspoon Worcestershire sauce
½ cup chopped California walnuts

Mash cream cheese with fork. Mix with blue cheese and remaining ingredients. Heap in bowl on cocktail tray. Serve with crisp potato chips or thin toast. Also good as tea sandwich filling. Makes 1⅔ cups.

CHICKEN-LIVER PÂTÉ IN ASPIC

1 (10½-ounce) can consommé
1 consommé can water
3 stalks celery, sliced
1 medium onion, peeled and sliced
1 tablespoon finely cut parsley
2 envelopes unflavored gelatin
½ cup cold water
¼ cup sherry

¼ cup cognac
1 pound chicken livers, cut in small pieces
2 (3-ounce) packages cream cheese
1 teaspoon Worcestershire sauce
1 teaspoon salt
Grind of fresh pepper

Combine consommé, water, celery, onion, and parsley in saucepan. Bring to boiling point. Lower to simmering temperature and cook slowly 20 minutes to half an hour. Taste for flavoring. Cook a little longer if vegetables have not become very soft. Strain.

Stir gelatin into ½ cup cold water. Let stand 5 minutes. Stir into strained hot broth until dissolved. Add sherry and cognac. Let stand a few minutes. Cover bottom of 6-cup or 2-quart mold with half of gelatin mixture. Let cool until fairly well set.

While gelatin cools, cook chicken livers in water to cover, 15 minutes or until done. Drain. Let cool. Mash cheese, adding Worcestershire, salt, and a few grains of pepper. Mash livers into cheese, mixing well. Taste for seasoning. Add more if needed. Add second half of gelatin to liver mixture. Stir well. Pour into mold on top of plain gelatin layer. Chill. Serve cold, sliced, with thin French or Italian bread. Makes 16 to 32 servings.

EMBASSY DIP

1 pound cream cheese
1 (10½-ounce) can condensed black bean soup
½ teaspoon orégano
⅛ teaspoon chili powder

1 teaspoon grated onion
1 teaspoon salt
2 tablespoons Worcestershire sauce

Combine all ingredients. Beat with spoon or in blender. Makes about 2½ cups.

Originally served by the wife of a U. S. Embassy official at her Paris cocktail parties. She uses black Mexican beans, soaks them overnight, then cooks them. When done, she sieves them, then makes this savory dip which always appears at her parties. Taste it for flavor. Add more orégano, if liked, or a little more chili. If condensed soup is too thick, use a little sour cream to thin mixture in blender.

SAGE-FLAVORED DIP

½ pound (2 cups) shredded sharp American cheese
1 (3-ounce) package cream cheese

⅜ cup light cream
½ teaspoon dry mustard
½ teaspoon grated onion
1 teaspoon crumbled sage

Combine all ingredients in blender or beat with spoon until smooth. Makes 1½ cups.

Lay rings of Bermuda onion on sliced pumpernickel. Spoon this delicious dip on top. Men like this with beer and other drinks. Tastes good, too, with potato chips, crackers, and French bread.

SARDINE-CHEESE SPREAD

2 (3¼-ounce) cans skinless, boneless sardines
1 cup cream-style cottage cheese
1 clove garlic, peeled and grated
2 tablespoons grated onion
½ teaspoon salt
¼ teaspoon celery seed
2 tablespoons Worcestershire sauce
6 drops Tabasco sauce
2 tablespoons lemon juice
1 tablespoon cognac

Drain sardines. Mash and flake with fork. Mix with remaining ingredients, blending thoroughly. Let stand at room temperature 30 minutes or so to blend flavors. Chill. Spread on hot buttered toast strips, on thin rounds of French bread, or on crackers. Makes about 2¼ cups.

SMOKED SALMON WITH CUCUMBER DIP

2 medium cucumbers
½ cup commercial sour cream
3 tablespoons cider vinegar
1½ tablespoons finely cut chives
¾ teaspoon crumbled fresh or dried dill
1 teaspoon salt
⅛ teaspoon pepper
½ pound smoked salmon
Pumpernickel bread

Wash and pare cucumbers. Slice thin. Combine sour cream, vinegar, chives, dill, salt, and pepper. Pour over cucumbers and mix. Cover and chill 2 or 3 hours.

Slice smoked salmon paper-thin. Place on thin rounds of buttered pumpernickel.

Serve cucumber mixture in a bowl as a dip, to which guests help themselves and spread on top of the salmon.

Or if served as a first-course appetizer with cocktails, serve cucumber mixture in sea-food cocktail glasses with salmon-and-pumpernickel strips around the glass. Makes 6 servings as first course.

YOGURT CHEESE DIP

¼ cup cottage cheese
¾ cup yogurt
⅓ cup finely cut celery
⅓ cup finely cut green pepper
3 tablespoons grated onion
1 tablespoon Worcestershire sauce
¾ teaspoon salt
Paprika

Combine all ingredients except paprika. Beat with spoon or in blender until smooth. Heap in serving bowl and dust lightly with paprika. Makes about 1⅔ cups.

Especially good with green salad or raw vegetables—cauliflower, cucumber, and carrot sticks. Or spread on crackers, toast, or pumpernickel. A godsend to the calorie-watchers.

Egg Appetizers

EGGS CARDINAL

12 hard-cooked eggs	1 tablespoon chopped ginger
1 quart very mild cider vinegar	root
1 cup juice from canned beets	1 tablespoon salt
1 teaspoon peppercorns	
1 tablespoon whole allspice	

Shell eggs and place in deep bowl or glass jar.

Combine vinegar, spices, and salt in enamel or glass saucepan. Simmer 5 to 10 minutes. Add beet juice and strain over eggs. Let cool. Cover bowl or jar and keep in refrigerator. Makes 12 servings.

Serve these eggs on appetizer tray or cut in slices or halves and use as garnish on salad platter.

My grandmother Vanderbilt used to consider these an essential part of Sunday-night supper. Men love them with cold beer or ale.

MUSHROOM-STUFFED EGGS

8 hard-cooked eggs	Pickle relish
1 (3-ounce) can chopped broiled	2 tablespoons finely cut ripe
mushrooms	olives
Mayonnaise	Salt and pepper

Shell eggs and cut in halves. Mash yolks in bowl. Add mushrooms and enough mayonnaise to blend smoothly. Add small amount of pickle relish and the olives. Blend with fork or spoon until fluffy. Stuff white halves. Chill 30 minutes or longer in covered dish. Makes 16 halves.

Serve 2 halves as appetizer, with or without dab of mayonnaise on top.

Garnish eggs with water cress, parsley, or other small green. Capers, sliced pickles, sliced olives, caviar are other good garnishes for stuffed eggs.

See also chapter on eggs (page 287) and use deviled eggs and other versions of stuffed eggs as appetizers.

PICKLED EGGS

12 to 16 hard-cooked eggs
2 cups cider vinegar
2 tablespoons sugar
1 teaspoon salt

1 teaspoon pickling spices (4 peppercorns, 1 clove, celery seed, mace, piece ginger root)
1 onion, peeled and sliced

Peel eggs and place in bowl or glass jar. Combine remaining ingredients in an enamel saucepan. Heat to boiling point. Reduce heat and simmer 8 minutes. Pour over eggs. Cover bowl or jar and let eggs stand in refrigerator several hours or overnight. Drain. Serve eggs halved or sliced as garnish for cold cuts or salads. Or serve as part of salad, or eat at picnics and barbecues.

RUSSIAN EGGS

Cut peeled hard-cooked egg in half lengthwise. Place halves on crisp lettuce on small salad plate. Spoon Russian dressing on halves. Add dab of black caviar as garnish. Makes 1 serving. Eggs, dressing, and caviar must be cold.

Russian Anchovy Eggs: Substitute curled anchovy fillet for caviar in above recipe.

Russian Smoked-Salmon Eggs: Place rounds or strips of smoked salmon on thin buttered toast. Slice hard-cooked egg on salmon. Top with dab of sour cream flavored with mustard, or with sour cream mixed with finely chopped cucumber. Add quick grind of black pepper to top.

Fruit and Vegetable Appetizers

FRUIT CUPS

Use various combinations of chilled fresh, quick-frozen, cooked, preserved, spiced, and brandied fruits in a chilled stem glass or dessert dish as a fruit cup. For instance:

Fresh orange and grapefruit sections, fresh pineapple cubes, pitted fresh oxheart cherries. Pour 1 tablespoon orange juice or cherry juice over the fruit in glass.

Thin slices red-peel apple, cubes fresh pear, melon balls, sections ripe apricot or orange. Top with mint leaf.

Sliced fresh strawberries, thin sticks ripe pineapple, sprig fresh mint.

Seedless white grapes, pitted sweet cherries, thin slices banana, and cubes of orange.

Pitted canned cherries, thin slices canned peaches, diced mint cherries, cubed apple or pear.

Cubed brandied peach, cubed fresh pineapple, thin sections grapefruit, brandied pitted oxheart cherry on top. Pour 1 tablespoon brandied cherry juice over fruit in glass.

Thin strips avocado, cubed fresh grapefruit, melon balls, cubed fresh pineapple, cubes lime gelatin. Pour 1 tablespoon grapefruit or pineapple juice over the fruit in glass, then add lime gelatin as garnish.

A fruit cup of one fruit only, such as cubed or sliced orange or grapefruit, should be garnished with a bright maraschino or mint cherry, or with a cube of bright jelly or gelatin. Pour 1 tablespoon grenadine or crème de menthe over the fruit in glass.

Avoid too-large pieces. A fruit cup is eaten with a spoon, and only fruits which are easily eaten from a teaspoon should be served.

Vary the fruit cups in your menus by using fruits and melons in season:

A few frosty-blue blueberries topping a mixture of orange, apple, and grapefruit.

Fresh red raspberries lightly combined with sliced banana and pineapple.

Sweet red currants with melon balls and a mild fruit, such as fresh pear.

Halved large grapes, seeds removed, with apple, pear, orange or grapefruit.

Sliced or halved strawberries combined with pineapple and orange.

Ripe persimmon, cubed, combined with pear, pineapple, avocado, with spoonful of pineapple juice poured over at the last moment before serving.

See also Fruit Desserts

HONEYDEW MELON PROSCIUTTO

To serve this delicious first course have melon chilled. Cut in slender pieces. Pare and remove seeds. Serve on chilled plates. Lay paper-thin slices of the Italian ham called prosciutto diagonally across the melon. Eaten with knife and fork, the two together are especially refreshing in flavor and delicious. Gourmets grind black pepper on melon and ham.

While this appetizer is familiar to diners in Italian restaurants, it need not be restricted to your Italian-style dinners at home. Serve it often when honeydew melons are in season.

OTHER MELON APPETIZERS

Any chilled, ripe melon may be served in appetizer cuts. When the melon is small, such as a honeyball, small cantaloupe, or small honeydew, a half melon is served as first course. Or serve a quarter or smaller section, depending on the menu and whether melon is to be merely a fresh, appetizing beginning or an important food contribution to the menu.

Fresh lime or lemon quarters, a shaker of powdered sugar or cinnamon, or both, are usually served with honeydew and honeyball melon, with some cantaloupes, and even with the more strongly flavored Spanish, Persian, and similar tropical melons. Watermelon is more often served as dessert or last course, but watermelon balls are popular in a mixed melon-ball cup or as a topping for fruit cups. Melon-ball cups and compotes are described in the chapters on fruit desserts and salads, as are additional ways of serving melons.

ARTICHOKES, GOLDEN HORN

8 small artichokes	½ cup white wine
Juice 2 lemons	¼ cup olive oil
4 small white onions, peeled	1 teaspoon salt
1 clove garlic, peeled and halved	Freshly ground black pepper

Select the smallest artichokes, bought at an Italian market if possible, since these markets specialize in fresh young artichokes. Rinse vegetables well under cold running water. Have ready 2-quart saucepan of cold water. Squeeze juice 1 lemon into the water. Pull off outer leaves of artichokes. Cut stem off and cut thorns at end of bud. Drop vegetables into lemon water.

When all are trimmed, drain. Pour boiling water over them and let stand 10 minutes. Drain. Add onions and garlic. Pour wine and olive oil over them. Add salt, pepper, and juice of remaining lemon. Add just enough boiling water to cover artichokes. Cover pan. Bring to boiling point and boil vegetables 10 to 15 minutes. Test with wooden pick at the stem end to see if vegetables are tender. Use wooden pick in place of fork to prevent any discoloring.

Place artichokes in serving bowl. Reheat liquid and boil down to half original amount. Let cool. Taste and add additional salt if needed. Pour over artichokes. Cover. Chill in refrigerator. Makes 4 servings.

ARTICHOKE HEARTS

Buy glass jars of artichoke hearts or quick-frozen hearts. Drain. Marinate canned artichokes in French dressing with lemon juice added. Let chill in marinade several hours. Drain. Spread rounds of toast with anchovy butter. Place artichoke heart on each and surround with border of whipped cream cheese and sour cream seasoned with paprika and onion salt.

Follow directions on package for defrosting and cooking quick-frozen artichoke hearts. Drain. Use as described above.

When you go to Spain, feast on artichokes during the spring season. I ate them daily at lunch in the garden of the Ritz in Madrid. The Spanish have seemingly hundreds of ways of preparing them, all delicious. Confession: I ate them twice a day for three weeks and never wearied of their infinite variety.

RUSSIAN ARTICHOKES

Cook, drain, and chill very small artichokes. Remove first two layers of leaves. Trim bottoms so artichokes stand firmly. Spread open remaining leaves, scoop out choke, add a little lemon juice or French dressing to cavity, then fill with caviar. Sprinkle with chopped hard-cooked egg, grated onion, and finely cut parsley. Serve very cold.

This is good as a first course, garnished with crisp lettuce, and French dressing or mayonnaise accompaniment. Or serve as garnish for cold meat platter or for salad tray.

BROILED STUFFED MUSHROOMS

1 (6-ounce) can broiled mushroom crowns
1 (3-ounce) can deviled ham
½ teaspoon prepared mustard
½ teaspoon grated onion
½ teaspoon finely cut parsley
1 tablespoon mayonnaise

Drain mushrooms. Save broth for soup or other uses. Scoop out stem ends of crowns with paring knife and cut fine. Mix with ham, mustard, onion, parsley, and mayonnaise.

Start broiler at moderate (350° F.).

Stuff mixture into mushroom crowns. Place on greased shallow baking sheet or pan to go under broiler. Broil 4 inches from heat about 5 minutes, or until thoroughly hot. Serve as hot canapé with drinks. Makes 4 servings.

Broiled Stuffed Mushrooms on Toast: Serve hot on toast with cream sauce as first course at luncheon. Or serve on top of scrambled eggs for brunch or supper dish.

CARROT CURLS

Cut washed and scraped carrots lengthwise into thin strips with a parer. Roll each strip and secure with wooden pick. Place rolls in bowl of cracked ice; chill 1 hour. Remove picks.

Use curls as appetizers with cocktails and fruit juices or as garnish for salads or cold meat platter.

CELERY PINWHEELS

1 (4½-ounce) can deviled ham	1 teaspoon Worcestershire sauce
1 (3-ounce) package cream cheese	1 tablespoon prepared mustard or sour cream
6 stuffed olives, cut fine	6 or 8 stalks celery

Combine all ingredients except celery. Beat smooth. Add seasoning if needed. Wash celery thoroughly. Trim extra leaves and coarse bottom edge. Stuff each piece with ham mixture. Press two filled stalks together, overlapping them, until all stalks are used. Wrap all together in waxed paper and secure with rubber bands. Chill 3 hours in refrigerator.

With sharp knife cut across each filled double stalk, making slices about ½ inch thick. Serve slices as appetizers with drinks or use as garnish on salad plates. Makes 20 or more pinwheels.

ITALIAN ZUCCHINI APPETIZER

1½ pounds very small zucchini	French dressing
1 teaspoon salt	6 scallions, cut fine
1 (10½-ounce) can consommé	2 tablespoons finely cut parsley
¾ cup dry white wine	Flat anchovy fillets

Scrub zucchini well. Cut off ends. Do not pare. Cook whole in saucepan containing salt, consommé, white wine, and additional water to make 1 inch liquid in pan. Cover tightly. Bring to boiling point. Boil 5 to 10 minutes. Vegetable should not be soft. Watch carefully after 5 minutes' boiling.

Drain vegetable. Chill. To serve, arrange vegetable in shallow serving dish. Mix French dressing, scallions, and parsley and pour over zucchini. Place drained anchovy fillet on each piece. Makes 6 or more servings.

Fruit and Vegetable Juices

APRICOT-AND-GRAPEFRUIT JUICE

1 (6-ounce) can frozen grapefruit concentrate

2 (12-ounce) cans (3 cups) apricot nectar

Add water to grapefruit concentrate, according to directions on can. Combine with apricot nectar. Chill. Serve in chilled glasses with cracked ice. Makes 6 to 8 servings.

Double recipe and make a tall-glass beverage for a summer cooler. Serve with sprig of mint or a minted green cherry.

APRICOT-PINEAPPLE JUICE

½ cup canned apricot halves and juice

1 cup finely cracked ice

1 cup pineapple juice

1 tablespoon lemon juice

1/16 teaspoon salt

Combine all ingredients in glass container of blender. Cover and blend about 30 seconds until contents are smooth. Serve at once in chilled glasses. Makes 6 small glasses.

FROSTY TOMATO APPETIZER

1 (No. 2) can (2 ½ cups) tomato juice

1 teaspoon sugar

1 teaspoon prepared horse-radish

1 teaspoon lemon juice

1/16 teaspoon Tabasco sauce

1 tablespoon grated onion

½ teaspoon celery salt

2 sprigs fresh dill

Sour cream or mayonnaise

Combine ingredients except dill and sour cream or mayonnaise. Mix well. Pour into refrigerator tray. Freeze firm. When ready to serve, let soften a little, break in chunks, and beat with electric or rotary beater until smooth. Serve in chilled bouillon cups. Garnish with small sprig of dill and dab of sour cream or mayonnaise. Makes 4 to 5 servings.

TOMATO JUICE REFRESHER

1 (No. 2) can tomato juice	½ teaspoon prepared horse-
⅛ teaspoon pepper	radish
¼ teaspoon salt	¼ teaspoon celery salt
1 tablespoon lemon juice	¼ teaspoon Worcestershire sauce

Combine all ingredients in mixer, or stir well. Chill. Serve in chilled glasses. Makes 2½ cups.

Mixed Juice Refresher: If your mixer or blender makes vegetable juice, combine equal amounts of fresh celery juice, or sauerkraut juice, with tomato juice; add seasonings. Mix well. Chill and serve.

Combine freshly washed water cress, parsley, carrots, celery, green peppers, and other favorite greens and raw vegetables in the mixer or blender. Serve freshly extracted juice mixtures of favorite greens very cold with thin fingers of Swiss cheese or crackers spread with cream cheese blended with horse-radish and crisp, crumbled bacon.

Hors d'Oeuvres

When a menu calls for hors d'oeuvres, you can simplify your shopping and preparation by buying one of the many varieties of Italian antipasto combinations now packed in flat glass plates for specialty grocers. Some of these include anchovies, sardines, pimiento, pickled mushrooms, and other pickled foods. To serve, remove the tin lid, drain off the olive oil, place the dish on a tray with other cold appetizers and you will please a good many of your guests.

The variety of foods in an offering of hors d'oeuvres is limited only by your imagination and budget. The famous international gourmet, André Simon, founder of the London Wine and Food Society, once listed his two favorite combinations of hors d'oeuvres, both of which I consider perfect. Here is his first:

liver sausage
pâté
sliced hard-cooked eggs with mayonnaise
radishes
sardines, drained (boneless, skinless)
a vegetable salad (that is, various cooked and raw vegetables in French
    dressing—no lettuce)

red cabbage slaw
pickled cauliflower
celery
sliced cucumbers in vinegar-and-black-pepper dressing
braised leeks in French dressing
potato salad
sliced tomatoes

M. Simon's second selection includes:
anchovies
shrimps in salad dressing
smoked eel
smoked trout
herring
artichoke hearts in French dressing
pickled mushrooms
tuna-fish-and-tomato salad
small canapés containing different savory mixtures

Such an array is possible only in a well-run restaurant or fairly formal home. But the appetizing flavor combinations in this gourmet's selections can guide us in making a more simple hors d'oeuvres tray. For instance, sardines, sliced eggs in mayonnaise, ripe olives, celery, for one assortment. On another occasion, potato salad, anchovies, sliced tomatoes, and artichoke hearts served as hors d'oeuvres.

To serve such assortments of appetizers attractively, use various small, shallow dishes. If you can find Chinese, Japanese, or other unusual pottery and chinawares, in graceful small shapes, your hors d'oeuvres tray will be all the more appealing. Place small forks or larger serving spoons and forks on each as needed.

Provide small plates for guests. Or if the hors d'oeuvres are served as a part of the meal—not just as an appetizer on the terrace or in the living room before the meal—let your guests help themselves at the table (with their dinner plates) to the hors d'oeuvres arranged on a revolving tray in the center or otherwise placed within reach of everyone.

This lends a buffet informality to the meal and makes serving easy and pleasant. As guests finish with their appetizers from this assortment, they help themselves to the hot dish. All dishes are taken to the kitchen afterward, and coffee and cheese, or other dessert, are brought in to a cleared table.

I prefer to use separate small plates for the hors d'oeuvres. Or for a summer supper on the terrace, try the new, colorful, treated paper plates, with matching small paper napkins, for this first pickup part of the dinner.

Quickies for the Cocktail Tray

Bologna Rolls: Place 1 tablespoon cream cheese mixed with finely cut chives in center of each thin slice of peeled bologna. Roll up. Chill 1 to 2 hours. Stick small piece of water cress in each end of roll; arrange rolls on serving plate.

Date-and-Bacon Idea: Remove seeds from large dried dates. Insert whole blanched or toasted almond in each date. Wrap in small piece lean bacon. Fasten with wooden pick. Cook in chafing dish until bacon is crisp, or cook in broiler. Drain on thick paper towel a moment or two before serving.

Deviled Pecans: 1 cup cooking oil, 1 pound shelled large pecans or almonds, 3 teaspoons salt, 2 teaspoons celery salt, 1 teaspoon garlic salt, ⅙ teaspoon cayenne. Heat oil. Add nuts. Fry 3 or 4 minutes until evenly browned. Drain on thick paper towels. Mix seasoning and sprinkle on warm nuts generously. Makes 1 pound cocktail nuts.

French Flute Slices: Buy the most slender French bread available (especially right for this appetizer are the double "flute" loaves in some bakeries and grocery shops). Slice these slender loaves very thin. Spread slices on baking sheet. Toast lightly under low broiler heat. Dip in melted herb butter. Return to broiler and heat 1 or 2 minutes. Serve hot.

Ham and Olives: 2 thin slices boiled ham cut in ½-inch strips, 2 tablespoons cream cheese, 12 stuffed olives. Strips of ham should be long enough to go around olives and lap over. Spread strips with cheese. Wrap around olives. Fasten with cocktail picks.

Stuffed Small Tomatoes: Scald and skin very small ripe tomatoes. Cut out stem end and hollow out center but do not break wall. Stuff with finely minced lobster salad. Chill thoroughly.

Whole Edam Cheese: Place a whole Edam (or Gouda) on a cheese board. Cut 1 or 2 thin wedges. Place good cheese knife on board.

Serve thin slices of buttered, crusty French bread with it or red apples or pears.

Salad Appetizers

Serve small portions of any salad as an appetizer. It must be well chilled, on crisp lettuce or water cress, or other garnish. Use decorative small plate, shell, or special appetizer dish. Green pepper, white turnip slices, capers, sliced olives, sliced pickled onions, and similar foods with appetizing tang make good garnish on salads served as first course.

Sea-food-and-vegetable salads, well-flavored vegetable or fruit-aspic salads are favorites as appetizers.

Tomato aspic, cut in cubes, combined with scallions, cucumber, green pepper, and a very small amount of Lemon French Dressing (page 518) is a favorite.

Lemon aspic, cut in cubes, combined with sections of avocado, orange, green pepper, with Lemon French Dressing (page 518) and a little freshly ground pepper is delicious served before a sea-food luncheon or dinner.

Very cold crab meat, shrimp, or lobster combined with Lemon Mayonnaise (page 523), capers, and green pepper, served in crisp lettuce cup, makes a savory appetizer salad before a luncheon at which ham or salmon soufflé is the featured dish.

Shellfish Appetizers

CLAM COCKTAIL

2 dozen cherrystone clams in shells
1 tablespoon lemon juice
½ teaspoon Worcestershire sauce
2 drops Tabasco sauce
¾ cup chili sauce or ketchup
1 tablespoon prepared horse-radish
⅛ teaspoon salt
4 small lettuce leaves

Clean and open clams. Cut clam meat loose from shells; chill thoroughly.

Cocktail Sauce: Blend lemon juice, Worcestershire, Tabasco, chili sauce or ketchup, horse-radish, and salt. Chill well.

To serve, line chilled sea-food cocktail glass with lettuce leaf. Spoon 6 shelled clams into each. Beat sauce to thoroughly mix. Spoon sauce onto clams or serve in bowl so guests may help themselves. Makes 4 cocktails.

Clams on Half Shell: Clean and open clams. Cut around clam through muscle. Remove top shell. Arrange bed of crushed ice in deep soup plate with small glass of chilled cocktail sauce in center. Arrange 6 chilled clams in their lower shells in circle around sauce. Serve additional sauce and lemon sections. Makes 1 serving.

For variation of flavor, add 1 tablespoon finely cut water cress, parsley, or fresh dill to the cocktail sauce.

Oyster Cocktail and **Oysters on Half Shell** are served in the same way. Serve only 4 oysters on half shell if they are extra large. Oysters must be iced or kept in very cold part of refrigerator until served.

See also chapter on fish and shellfish

CRAB-MEAT COCKTAIL

Freshly cooked and cleaned crab meat, or defrosted quick-frozen crab meat, or high-quality canned crab meat is served chilled as an appetizer. Look over meat before chilling. Remove all fibers and bones.

To serve 4 people, chill 1 pound cleaned and flaked crab meat.

Sauce

¼ cup mayonnaise	1 tablespoon lemon juice
2 tablespoons finely cut water cress	⅛ teaspoon paprika

Mix sauce ingredients. Chill. Beat well before serving.

Place crab meat in lettuce-lined sea-food cocktail glass or dessert dish. Sprinkle lightly with paprika; add spoonful of chilled sauce. Serve with section of lemon.

Various sauces for crab and lobster cocktails have been created by inventive cooks, but the flavor of these two shellfish is delicate. The sauce should have tang but not submerge the flavor of the sea food. Experiment with the sauce given above, adding finely chopped capers or olives, pickle relish, or parsley until you find the sauce which pleases you and your family. Tartare sauce, Russian dressing, and mixtures of mayonnaise with one of these dressings are restaurant specialties which are favorites with crab and lobster cocktails.

Lobster Cocktail: Substitute chilled lobster meat for crab in the above recipe. Freshly boiled and chilled, or defrosted quick-frozen lobster meat, or high-quality canned lobster is used in this service. Do not flake and mince lobster meat. Leave in small chunks.

About ½ to 1 pound cooked lobster meat makes enough for 4 lobster cocktails.

SHRIMP COCKTAIL

4 to 6 large, cooked shrimp
Crisp lettuce cup

2 tablespoons Cocktail Sauce
  (page 546)
Lemon quarter

Use deveined cooked, canned, or defrosted quick-frozen shrimp. Chill thoroughly. To serve, arrange small lettuce leaf in sea-food cocktail glass or dessert dish. Add 4 or more shrimp. Spoon chilled sauce over shrimp. Add section of lemon to plate. Makes 1 serving.

Capers, chopped pimiento-stuffed olives, pickle relish, fine cubes of avocado, finely cut parsley, thinly sliced gherkins, tarragon, and dill make good additions to cocktail sauce served with shrimp. Some prefer Tartare sauce or Russian dressing, or a sauce made by combining Cocktail Sauce with either of these mixtures, half and half. Have sauce very cold.

RICH MUSSELS

4 dozen mussels
1 bay leaf
1 medium onion, peeled and sliced
½ teaspoon salt

¼ teaspoon paprika
2 cups Hollandaise Sauce (page 550)
2 tablespoons finely cut fresh dill

Select large, fresh mussels with closed shells. Scrub shells well. Rinse thoroughly under cold running water. Discard any which have partly or completely opened.

Pour water into deep kettle to depth of 1 inch; add bay leaf, onion, salt, and paprika. Add mussels. Cover kettle tightly. Bring to a boil and let mussels steam 5 to 10 minutes, or until shells open. Remove kettle from heat. Strain broth and reserve it for soup or cocktail mixtures.

Remove mussels from their shells, chop off beard. Chill 3 or 4 hours in refrigerator. When ready to serve, mix mussels with cold Hollandaise Sauce into which the dill has been mixed. Serve as first course in seafood cocktail glasses set in cracked ice. Makes 8 or more servings.

We often gather mussels on the beaches around Weston and Fairfield, Connecticut, along with nearby Italian neighbors who know very well how to prepare them in a dozen delectable ways. If you gather your own, be sure to do so from approved waters. There are good canned mussels, too. Also you can quick-freeze your own when you gather a large supply.

CHAPTER TWO

Barbecues and Picnics

To cook successfully outdoors calls for as much planning and careful preparation as cooking in a kitchen. The abundance of barbecue tools, gadgets, utensils, and larger equipment available gives the outdoor cook a wide choice, whether he uses a small portable grill rolled out from the kitchen onto the terrace or into the back yard, or whether he has an elaborate barbecue setup of stone or brick.

Careful planning and preparation mean that much of the work is done ahead of time in the kitchen, so that semi-prepared dishes can be finished at the back of a large outdoor grill or carried ready-to-serve from the kitchen at the last moment. This advance preparation should include all foods on the menu, from the appetizer drinks and their canapés or crackers to the dessert and final hot and cold beverages.

The amount of preparation, as well as the kind of menu, depends on the type of equipment and on the manufacturer's instructions which guide your use of broilers and other tools and utensils.

Whatever fuel you use in a large barbecue fireplace—charcoal lumps, briquettes, or wood (oak, maple, hickory, or pine if very dry)— allow 1 hour for coals to form. When wood or charcoal is gray in color and gives off a ruddy glow, start cooking, but not until then.

Keep a well-built-up bed of coals near the front or at one end of the grill for cooking meats, and use the remaining portion of the grill for warming other food, making sauces, and cooking vegetables. A shallow bed of coals is adequate for chops and hamburgers. A deep bed is necessary for roasts and thick steaks.

Should the fire need freshening during cooking, place new fuel around the edges and push the entire bed of coals toward the center. Never add new fuel near the center of the fire.

After meat has cooked for a while, drops of fat will fall into the fire, making it flare up and setting the meat afire. These flames can be doused with a whisk broom dipped in water, or a clothes sprinkler. Keep one or the other handy, as well as a bucket of water or sand. Baking soda also acts as a fire extinguisher, as does salt, which makes it easier to salvage the food.

Menu suggestions given in this chapter are adaptable to large permanent outdoor barbecues and to portable table and pushcart barbecues on back porch and terrace. Your equipment will guide you in selecting dishes suited to your needs.

Poultry for Barbecuing

Poultry is one of the most satisfactory barbecue meats. Chicken and turkey—and, in some large-city markets, other birds—are available in convenient sizes, cut-to-order styles, as well as in parts such as breasts, legs, quarters, and halves.

Young chickens or squab chickens, weigh from 1¾ to 3 pounds ready-to-cook, a good size for barbecuing. Buy according to need, fresh-iced or quick-frozen. They require about 1 to 1½ hours cooking time outdoors.

Turkeys in the popular fryer-roaster size range from 4 to 7 pounds, ready-to-cook, and require about 1½ to 1¾ hours cooking time outdoors. Larger turkeys, of almost any marketable size, may be barbecued whole or in halves, but much cooking time is needed and almost continuous basting to prevent the meat drying out.

Ducklings barbecue well whole, or in halves or quarters. The outdoor cooking time is about 1¾ hours. They are cooked just like chicken; most large-city markets sell ducklings fresh-iced or quick-frozen. Be sure to pierce the skin only, not the meat, all over so as to achieve a crackling skin. Do this with goose also.

Goose may be barbecued for a big party. Weighing 10 to 14 pounds ready-to-cook, this bird should be cut in halves. Cookery time outdoors is about 3½ hours. Both duckling and goose are almost self-basting. I rub both with dry mustard, especially the cavities, and use a spicy barbecue sauce applied several times during the cooking period. Do not barbecue goose on a grill too near coals, since the fat will catch fire.

Advance preparation for poultry to be barbecued. Birds in most cases should be halved beforehand, washed, drained, kept chilled. To cook, brush with barbecue sauce; lay on grill skin side up. Use two long-handled forks or fork and large spoon to turn halves occasionally. Avoid piercing the meat, since this lets the juices drain away. Baste with brush or spoon. Keep fire or coals very low so birds won't scorch or cook too quickly. Place barbecue sauce near fire to keep warm.

Serve birds, cut according to size, on paper picnic plates or on warmed serving plates. Half an average chicken makes one serving, or a whole squab chicken or very small chicken is considered one serving for a barbecue meal. A quarter of a chicken is a child's serving.

Birds that weigh more than 3½ pounds may be quartered for serving to large parties. Ducks are served in halves or quarters. Small turkeys should be quartered. A goose, halved for barbecuing, should be disjointed by the barbecue chef, using a warmed board or platter and good carving knife and fork, then sliced for serving.

Barbecue sauce, served with birds and meats, should be warm.

Recipes which follow give instructions for advance preparation and cookery of meats, fish, and vegetables.

BARBECUE BURGERS

¾ cup Kabob Barbecue Sauce (page 558)
1 pound chuck steak, ground
½ cup diced celery
1 tablespoon finely cut parsley
¼ teaspoon marjoram
¼ teaspoon thyme
1 teaspoon salt
¼ teaspoon pepper
3 English muffins
3 tablespoons butter
1 large tomato, peeled

Make ½ recipe for Kabob Barbecue Sauce; keep it warm.

Combine meat, celery, parsley, herbs, and seasonings. Add ¼ cup barbecue sauce. Mix; shape into 6 patties.

Grill patties above glowing coals until done as desired, turning them once or twice. When patties go on the grill, split and toast muffins; butter them lightly. Cut tomato in 6 slices. Place 1 slice on each toasted and buttered muffin half. Top with hot burger patty. Add spoonful of barbecue sauce. Serve at once. Makes 6 servings.

BARBECUED FISH FILLETS

3 pounds fish fillets
3 tablespoons lemon juice
½ cup olive oil
½ teaspoon orégano
¾ teaspoon basil
¾ teaspoon celery salt
½ teaspoon salt
Fish Barbecue Sauce (page 558)

Buy either sole or flounder fillets. About 2 hours before you plan to barbecue the fish, place fillets in shallow glass dish. Mix lemon juice, oil, herbs, and seasonings. Pour over fish. Cover dish and place in refrigerator. Let fish marinate about 2 hours.

While fillets are in refrigerator, prepare barbecue sauce. Keep it warm until barbecue time, then set it at one side of the grill to reheat.

Drain fillets. Save marinade. Place fish in well-oiled, hinged double broiling rack. Brush with marinade. Grill close to coals 2 or 3 minutes. Turn and grill other side. Turn frequently until fish is cooked and golden. Serve immediately onto warmed plates, with hot Fish Barbecue Sauce. Makes 6 servings.

Barbecued Salmon Steaks: You can broil salmon or other fish steaks by this recipe. Fish should be cooked quickly, and just until tender. Have both fish and grill well oiled to prevent sticking. Brush fish steaks, or whole fish, with melted butter and lemon juice while cooking. Season with salt and pepper. Serve with or without barbecue sauce.

BARBECUE SANDWICH LOAF

1 loaf French bread, about 12
inches long
2 (4½-ounce) cans deviled ham

⅓ cup drained pickle relish
Soft butter or margarine
3 large tomatoes

Cut loaf diagonally in ½-inch slices, not quite through to bottom. Combine ham and pickle relish. Spread on one side of every slice. Spread butter or margarine on the other side of every slice. Scald and peel tomatoes. Cut in ¼-inch slices. Insert tomato slice on each ham-spread side. Wrap loaf in foil. Heat over coals about 25 minutes, or until very hot. Handle with barbecue gloves! Cut sandwiches apart and serve. About 10 servings.

If you heat this loaf in the kitchen oven, temperature should be very hot (450° F.). Place loaf on baking sheet. Heat 15 to 20 minutes.

BROILED BLUEFISH BARBECUE

1 or 2 bluefish
Olive oil
1 teaspoon salt
½ teaspoon pepper

Flour
Melted butter
Lemon quarters

Have fish cleaned and scaled. If good size, split down underside. Otherwise broil whole. Lay on hinged double broiler. Brush with olive oil. Sprinkle with salt, pepper, and a little flour. Close broiler. Cook fish over low coals, browning 1 side, then turning to brown the other. Brush fish frequently with oil. Fish is done when it flakes easily with fork. Have warm plates ready. Serve with melted butter and lemon juice, 1 small fish per person.

CHARCOAL-BROILED STEAKS

Start barbecue fire 30 to 40 minutes ahead of cooking time. Build fire so coals will be 5 to 7 inches below grill. When coals have burned down to hot glow with gray film on top they are right for cooking.

Have ready club, T-bone, porterhouse, or sirloin steaks cut 1½ to 2 inches thick. Rub hot grill or broiler with fat trimmed from meat. Brush steak with barbecue sauce or rub with cut clove of garlic.

Broil one side to a fine brown. Turn steak, but do not pierce with fork. If drippings flare up, quench flame with a sprinkle of water. Season browned side with salt and pepper or hickory-smoke salt or other favorite seasonings. Broil other side until done as you like it. Season second side. Serve steak sizzling hot on warmed platter with pat of butter under each serving.

CHINESE DUCK BARBECUE

2 ducklings, quartered
2 egg yolks
⅓ cup soy sauce
¼ cup honey

2 oranges
½ teaspoon sesame seed
1 tablespoon butter

Have meat dealer quarter the birds. When ready to cook on low barbecue fire, beat egg yolks with soy sauce and honey. Brush pieces on all sides. Broil cut side down, 45 to 60 minutes. Turn birds occasionally. Add little more of egg marinade from time to time. Bring pieces closer to fire for crisping as they near end of cooking time.

As birds finish, peel oranges, cut in slices, remove any seeds. Sauté slices in a pan with butter and sesame seed. Serve sautéed orange slices over and around duck. Makes 8 servings.

Portable Barbecue

FISHERMAN'S BARBECUE

6 freshly caught trout or other small fish

12 slices lean bacon
Seasoning

Fish must be cleaned, scaled, and drawn. Rinse cleaned fish and drain. Season inside lightly with salt and pepper. Wrap each fish in 2 strips bacon. Fasten with small metal skewers. Place in oiled, hinged double broiling rack. Broil slowly over glowing coals. When bacon is crisp and dark, fish is well done. Remove skewers. Slip fish onto warmed plates. Makes 6 servings.

GRILLED HAM STEAKS

2 ham steaks
4 tablespoons butter or margarine
1 cup dry white wine

2 tablespoons brown sugar
6 whole cloves

Brown steaks slowly, on both sides, on grill over glowing coals. Mix remaining ingredients and brush frequently during broiling. Heat any leftover marinade and pour over steaks when served. Makes 4 generous servings.

GRILLED VEAL IN FOIL

2 medium onions, peeled and cut fine
3 tablespoons butter or margarine
1 (3-ounce) can chopped mushrooms
1 teaspoon finely cut parsley
⅛ teaspoon thyme

1 teaspoon salt
Freshly ground pepper
¼ teaspoon powdered nutmeg
6 veal chops
Paprika
Cayenne
6 slices boiled ham

Cook onions in saucepan in 2 tablespoons butter or margarine until transparent, stirring constantly. Stir in mushrooms and their liquid, parsley, thyme, salt, pepper, and nutmeg. Cook few minutes over low heat, until almost dry.

Brown chops in remaining 1 tablespoon butter or margarine in a skillet, turning chops once or twice to cook nearly done. Season lightly with paprika and a very little cayenne. Place chop in center of heavy-duty foil, spoon a little of the mushroom mixture onto chop. Cover with slice of ham. Top with more mushroom sauce. Fold foil securely into tight package.

Grill over hot coals 20 minutes, or longer if chops are thick. Use pancake turner to slide hot package from grill to serving plates. Very hot! Use fork to pierce and open foil, or slit with paring knife. Makes 6 servings.

If cooked in the kitchen: Place browned chops in greased baking dish. Cover with half mushroom mixture. Lay ham slices over all. Spoon remaining mushroom mixture over ham. Cover casserole. Bake 30 minutes in moderate (325° F.) oven. Uncover and brown 5 to 10 minutes.

LAMB CHOP ROAST BARBECUE

Follow recipe for Steak Roast Barbecue (page 41), using one medium-thick lamb chop in place of small steak. For variety use 10 to 12 washed, drained green beans in place of carrots. Sprinkle about 1 tablespoon water over meat and vegetables before wrapping. Wrap as described. Place over hot coals. Cook 10 minutes. Turn package over and cook 10 minutes on opposite side, longer if chops are thick.

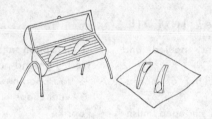

Pork Chop Roast Barbecue: If pork chops are used, cooking time must be extended to 30 minutes or longer. Pork must be well done. Should never be eaten pink.

I like garlic with both of these. I press out the juice in my indispensable garlic press or use powdered garlic. Sometimes I add a little extra nip of chili powder to the pork chops—but know your guests!

LONDON BROIL OVER THE COALS

2½ pounds top-quality steak, cut 1½ to 2 inches thick
3 tablespoons butter or margarine
1 (6-ounce) can sliced mushrooms
3 tablespoons lemon juice

½ teaspoon salt
Freshly ground pepper
¼ cup consommé
¼ cup dry red wine
1 teaspoon cornstarch
2 tablespoons grated lemon peel

Place steak on greased grill about 4 inches above hot glowing coals. Broil 4 to 5 minutes each side, longer if guests prefer medium or well-done meat. While steak cooks, melt butter or margarine in saucepan. Stir mushrooms and liquid in and sauté 1 or 2 minutes. Add lemon juice. Stir and cook 2 minutes. Add salt, pepper, consommé, and wine. Bring to a boil. Remove from heat. Stir cornstarch into about 1 tablespoon cold water until smooth, then stir into hot sauce. Return to heat and bring to a boil, stirring constantly. Boil 1 or 2 minutes, or until clear and thickened.

Use sharp, thin knife and cut steak diagonally in thin slices onto warm platter, overlapping the slices. Pour hot sauce over. Serve at once. Makes 6 servings.

Sauce may be made ahead of time and reheated at the barbecue.

MUSHROOMBURGERS BARBECUE

1 ½ pounds lean beef	1 (6-ounce) can sliced broiled
2 eggs, slightly beaten	mushrooms
¼ cup grated onion	Melted butter or margarine
¼ cup ketchup	6 large onion rings
1 ½ teaspoons salt	6 thin slices tomato
¼ teaspoon pepper	

Ask meat dealer to add about 3 ounces suet when grinding the beef. Combine meat, eggs, grated onion, ketchup, salt, and pepper. Mix thoroughly. Form 12 thin patties. Place mushrooms on 6 patties, leaving edge of meat all around. Cover with remaining 6 meat patties and press edges together well. Broil slowly over hot coals until done to order—rare, medium, well done. Add a little melted butter, an onion ring on top, and a slice of tomato. Serve on warmed plates. Makes 6 servings.

A seasoning and garnish tray is essential to enjoyment of these delicious burgers. Mustard, of course, a small bottle of soy sauce, jars of India relish, Major Grey's Indian Chutney, plum jam, chili sauce, ketchup are some of the favorites. And in place of buns, try chunky slices of fresh French bread or brush the top of the bun with melted butter and shake on sesame seed before heating.

PIMIENTO KABOB ROLLS

3 slices Swiss cheese
1 (4-ounce) can or jar whole
  pimientos
3 slices baked or spiced ham
2 or 3 frankfurters, cut in 1-inch
  pieces

Pimiento-stuffed olives
1 (3-ounce) can whole large
  mushroom crowns
Pineapple chunks
Melted butter or margarine
4 frankfurter buns

Lay drained pimientos between the 3 cheese slices, double-decker style, and cut "sandwiches" 1 inch square.

Slice each piece of ham into 3 strips and lay a length of drained pimiento along each. Fold strips lengthwise once or twice.

Thread the foods on skewers, alternating them as you like, a pimiento-and-cheese square, mushroom crown, olive, piece of frankfurter, pineapple chunk, and ham-and-pimiento foldover. Continue until skewers are filled. Brush foods with melted butter or margarine. Cook over barbecue grill until food is hot and cheese is melting. Split frankfurter buns, heat or toast them; push broiled kabobs off onto them. Makes 4 or more servings.

SCALLOPS-AND-BACON BARBECUE

2 pounds (1 quart) small scallops
1 egg, slightly beaten
2 tablespoons water
2 cups cracker meal
1 teaspoon salt

½ teaspoon pepper
1 teaspoon mixed herbs
10 strips lean bacon
Lemon quarters
Melted butter

Wash scallops, drain, dry on thick paper toweling. Mix egg and water. Dip scallops in egg, then in crumbs seasoned with salt, pepper, and herbs. Cut bacon strips crosswise in half. Fold pieces once. Arrange 5 or more scallops on each skewer, alternating with folded bacon. Brown lightly over hot barbecue grill. Turn skewers frequently for even cooking. Serve when bacon is crisp and done. Push scallops and bacon off onto warm plates. Serve lemon quarters and melted butter with scallops. Makes 6 to 10 servings.

STEAK ROAST BARBECUE

¾ pound steak
3 tablespoons butter or margarine
Salt and pepper
1 large potato, pared and sliced

1 medium onion, peeled and sliced
2 medium carrots, scraped and sliced

For each serving use piece of heavy-duty foil about 26 by 30 inches. Rinse steak and vegetables to increase moisture. Drain. Place 2 tablespoons butter in center of foil and lay steak on butter. Season lightly with salt and pepper. Spread potato over steak. Add remaining 1 tablespoon butter and season lightly. Spread onion slices on top of potato. Place carrots around meat. Fold foil lengthwise twice. Fold ends twice, then fold ends under package. Place package over hot coals. After 7 minutes turn package around, or slide to another place on grill, to give even cooking. Twenty minutes is sufficient cooking time if coals are really hot. Makes 1 serving.

To prepare dinner for 6 or more, make up packages so they are ready just as guests arrive. Have coals hot and ready in barbecue. While guests enjoy appetizer drinks, the dinner cooks.

Use pancake turner to slide hot packages onto warmed plates. Slit package with paring knife. Eat dinner out of foil envelope on plate.

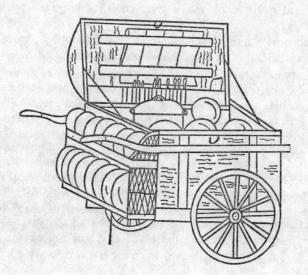

WEST-COAST BARBECUED STEAK

Large sirloin steak cut 2 inches
  thick
Clove garlic
2 or 3 tablespoons prepared mustard

2 cups soy sauce
2 tablespoons grated onion

Cut garlic in half, rub over both sides of steak. Spread mustard over steak and place steak in shallow glass dish. Cover with soy sauce, grated onion, and garlic halves. Cover dish. Let stand at room temperature 2 or 3 hours. Turn steak once or twice. Meat will darken. Oddly enough, rare-cooked steak will not be pink.

Remove steak from marinade. Place on greased grill or in hinged double broiling rack. Grill 4 inches from glowing coals, turning once. Use sharp, thin knife. Cut steak diagonally in strips onto hot plates. Serve hot. Makes 6 to 8 servings.

Remove garlic from marinade and store marinade in covered jar in refrigerator for future barbecue use.

Barbecued Vegetables

Vegetables are delicious cooked in foil, all seasonings added, over low coals, or at the back of the grill away from the high heat. Place partially defrosted lima beans, corn, peas, and other vegetables on heavy-duty foil. Add salt, pepper, butter. Wrap tightly, close ends well and fold under. Let cook slowly over coals, while meat, poultry, or fish is broiling.

Fresh corn with husks removed, fresh or canned mushrooms, whole peeled small onions, peeled and sliced potatoes, defrosted quick-frozen succotash are other favorites cooked this easy way.

Experiment before a party with vegetable cookery over your barbecue grill to determine necessary cooking time. Vegetables are usually better for long, slow cooking, which means that they should be started before the quick-cooking of chops and steaks but may be started at the same time the longer-cooked roasts and poultry go onto the grill or spit.

Tip: Mix seasonings for corn, adding paprika, salt, and pepper to the butter. Shape and chill. I have some individual butter dishes of Portuguese Vista Alègre porcelain I use for fancier parties. Pottery ones (or ceramic cheese jars) for the paper-plate kind of party. Decorate the butter mixture by pressing the blade of a knife clockwise around the mound. Guests help themselves when the hot corn is served.

ASH-ROASTED POTATOES

Scrub large baking potatoes thoroughly. Rinse. Let dry. Bury potatoes in hot coals 40 minutes. Test for doneness. Break open, add butter, salt, pepper. To prevent charring, wrap potatoes in heavy foil or rub unbaked potatoes thoroughly with olive oil.

Some barbecue chefs dip the oiled potato into salt until entirely coated. When baked, any remaining salt brushes off. Fine flavor results!

BARBECUED SWEET POTATOES

1 large sweet potato	¼ to ½ cup brown sugar, packed
2 tablespoons water	Salt and pepper

Wash and pare sweet potato. Slice thin, or cut into shoestring strips. Place in center of square of heavy-duty foil. Add 2 tablespoons water. Sprinkle with the sugar. Add a little salt and pepper. Fold foil over twice. Fold ends twice, then fold ends under package. Bake over hot coals 7 minutes. Turn package and bake 7 minutes longer. Makes 1 serving.

For 6 or more servings, prepare potato packages so they are ready to cook when the guests arrive.

Barbecued Acorn Squash: Follow recipe for sweet potatoes. Cut small squash in half. Remove seeds and fiber. Add butter, a little water, brown sugar, and seasoning to center of each half. Wrap and cook each half separately, as described for sliced sweet potatoes. One half squash makes 1 serving.

ROAST CORN ON THE COB

Buy the freshest possible sweet corn. Turn husks back. Strip off silk. Look over corn carefully. Cut away any bad parts. Lay husks back in position. Line ears up on grill over hot coals. Turn corn every few minutes, cooking about 20 minutes, or until husks are browned and dry. Roast to taste. Some prefer very brown corn.

To serve, break husks off. Serve on warmed plate with salt, pepper, and butter.

Plan for a Picnic

A barbecue cook-out is not necessarily a picnic. Often a barbecue and picnic are combined. Sometimes the old-fashioned basket-lunch picnic is the theme for a day in the country or at the shore. The meal carried in a hamper calls for special planning and certain specialized picnic accessories. First essential in the packed lunch is a bottle opener-can-opener gadget. Then at least two knives are needed for slicing bread or buns, cake, or other larger items, and a small knife for fruit, tomatoes, and for spreading butter or mayonnaise. *And* the bug-deterrents! Sprays and sticks of smudge-smoke, or ointment or cream sticks for bare legs.

If a picnic fire is to be built, add safety matches to the hamper. Take a small amount of kindling along for the fireplace at the picnic grounds, or a tube of the jelly compound packaged for the purpose of starting an outdoor fire easily and quickly.

Sandwiches, the mainstay of picnic spreads, can be made the night before if they are generously buttered, then wrapped individually in heavy waxed paper. They should be placed on a tray, covered with a damp towel, then with heavy foil, and stored in the refrigerator until time to pack the hamper next day. If possible, take the tray right along, damp towel and all. This insures fresher sandwiches. (See sandwich chapter.)

Wash celery, carrot sticks, green pepper sections, tomatoes, lettuce hearts. Chill in waxed paper or pliofilm bag in the refrigerator all night and take to picnic right in the wrappings. Open chilled olive jars or bottles at home. Drain. Close again, and add to the hamper.

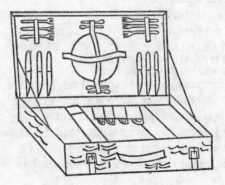

For young children in the picnic party provide a snack sandwich or some fruit to be served before the picnic lunch or supper is ready. Provide good-quality waxed-paper plates and cups. Use vacuum containers for hot and cold foods. For instance, a large vacuum jug should be chilled several hours by filling it with ice. Empty it. Fill with chilled salad. Or fill vacuum jug with warm water to heat it. Empty it. Fill with hot coffee or soup. New insulated containers for ice cubes will keep cubes several hours if packed just before leaving and kept tightly closed, with thick wrappings of newspaper all around them.

Small cakes, such as cupcakes, cookies, and poundcakes, travel better than layer cakes. Small pies, such as tarts and turnovers, travel better than a large pie.

Chilled fruits, especially melons, will remain cool 2 or 3 hours if you wrap them in foil as soon as they are taken from the refrigerator, then wrap thickly in newspaper and put more foil around that.

Take plenty of paper napkins along, and sipper straws for the long, cold drinks. Don't forget the salt and pepper, the sugar for the coffee, and the wooden, plastic, or silver knives, forks, and spoons which add so much pleasure to alfresco dining. Besides paper tablecloths for the picnic on the grass or beach, there are washable plastic cloths. Or use a length of matchstick bamboo window shade as a base on which to place plates of buns, sandwiches, and the other good things. Beach cushions or chairs and steamer blankets (mine are Irish) give something to sit on.

Menus for elaborate picnics, where well-equipped hampers include china and linen, may include a vacuum wine cooler containing a bottle with ice cubes around it, vacuum casseroles and containers of steaming soup and other delicacies. Plan your menu around your equipment and the appetites of your family and guests. Remember that picnic food—salads, sandwiches, deviled eggs, good pickles and olives, fruit, delicious cookies, cupcakes, doughnuts—tastes better outdoors than the dishes you are used to serving in your dining room. Plenty of hot coffee, plenty of chilled fruit juice add to this pleasure.

See also menu section for picnic menus.

CHAPTER THREE

Beverages

HOT CHOCOLATE, FRENCH STYLE

2½ (1-ounce) squares bitter choc- olate, grated	⅛ teaspoon salt
½ cup cold water	½ cup heavy cream, whipped
¾ cup sugar	4 cups hot milk

Combine grated chocolate and water in saucepan. Heat over direct heat, beating continually for 4 minutes. Add sugar and salt. Beat and cook 4 minutes longer. Let cool. Fold in whipped cream.

To serve, place generous tablespoon of chocolate mixture in each cup. Fill with scalding hot milk. Makes 8 small cups, 4 to 6 larger ones.

HOT COCOA

3 cups milk	Marshmallows or Whipped cream
¾ cup Chocolate Syrup (page 58)	

Heat milk and Chocolate Syrup together in upper part of double boiler over hot water. When boiling point is reached, remove from heat and from hot water. Beat with rotary beater until frothy. Pour at once into cups. Makes 3 large cups or 4 small ones. Serve topped with marshmallow or spoonful of whipped cream.

Properly speaking, this recipe makes hot chocolate instead of hot cocoa. Follow directions on packages of cocoa for various cocoa drinks. For economy, substitute hot water for part of milk called for, but for a creamy, better-tasting cup of cocoa use milk.

HOT CHOCOLATE, SOUTH OF THE BORDER

2 (1-ounce) squares bitter chocolate	⅛ teaspoon powdered cloves
2 cups milk	1 teaspoon vanilla
½ cup sugar	1 egg
1½ teaspoons powdered cinnamon	

Heat chocolate and milk together in top part of double boiler over hot water. Use rotary beater and beat until frothy. Beat in sugar, spices, and vanilla. Beat egg lightly with fork. Pour into hot chocolate. Beat with rotary beater until all is frothy again. Serve at once. Makes 3 large cups, 4 small ones.

Mexican cooks, and others in Spain and the Latin-American countries, use a carved wooden twirl stick for whipping the chocolate mixture. The stick is twirled rapidly between the palms, and its loose rings and moving sections—sometimes exquisitely and intricately carved—blend the chocolate mixture.

COFFEE

In general, the best coffee is made when you follow the rules worked out by the manufacturer for the particular coffee-maker you are using. For all methods use a standard coffee measure or its equivalent, which is 2 level tablespoons of coffee to each measuring cup of water for each serving of brewed coffee.

Start with a thoroughly clean coffee-maker. Rinse maker with hot water before using. Wash thoroughly after each use, and rinse with clean hot water. An electric percolator should be washed with cold water and baking soda occasionally.

Use fresh coffee and buy coffee in an amount which your household will consume within a week. Keep coffee in screw-top glass jar in the refrigerator. Buy the right grind for the maker you use.

Fresh water is important to flavor and body of coffee. Always make coffee with freshly drawn cold water. Use the full capacity of your maker. Never brew less than three quarters of its capacity. Follow manufacturer's directions, but after you find the exact timing to obtain the results desired, stick to it. Serve coffee as soon as made. Do not boil again. Hold freshly brewed coffee at serving temperature by placing the pot in a pan of hot water or over very low heat for a short time.

New coffee-makers are appearing from time to time. They are variations of the long-tried popular makes already on the market and are designed for the traditional methods: vacuum, drip, or percolator brewing. New devices from Europe and new versions of old ones are available in American housewares stores. Try various makers and methods until you find the one which seems easiest for you and which makes the kind of coffee you prefer.

If you do not serve your coffee in its maker, but prefer a coffeepot of silver, fine china, peasant pottery, or some other ware, be sure the pot is hot when you pour the freshly brewed coffee into it.

Rinse silver pots with boiling water. Never put a silver coffeepot or other piece of silver on the stove. Rinse china and other earthen pots with boiling water.

Arrange a coffee tray with the same care you give your most attractive tea service. Besides a bowl of lump sugar, a pitcher of light or heavy cream, the coffee tray, with its large or small cups, may include a small sweetmeat dish of ginger, nuts, or mints. For other suggestions see various coffee recipes which follow.

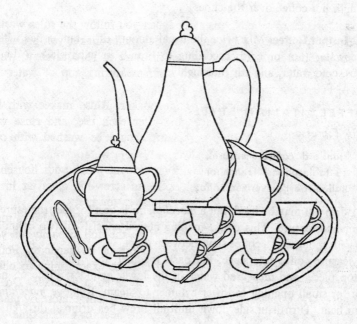

Leftover coffee: Many cooks who use glass coffee-makers have no qualms about reheating leftover coffee in them. Also, the manufacturer of one such coffee-maker has made a special glass storage container so that coffee for a party may be made in advance, then reheated at party time and served from the coffee-maker. I also freeze coffee essence and reconstitute it when needed. Leftover coffee makes fine coffee jelly. See recipe.

ICED COFFEE

Quick Double-Strength Way: Make hot coffee double-strength by using *half* the amount of water to the usual amount of coffee. Pour hot over ice cubes in tall glasses. The extra-strong coffee allows for dilution caused by ice.

Pre-Cooled Way: Make regular-strength coffee and cool in covered non-metallic container in refrigerator, no more than 3 hours before you plan to use it. Pour over ice in tall glasses.

Coffee-Ice-Cube Way: Brew extra breakfast coffee and freeze into coffee ice cubes. Then make iced coffee any time by pouring regular-strength hot coffee over the cubes.

Iced Instant Coffee: Mix *twice* the usual amount of instant coffee with a little water (hot or cold, according to brand) in each glass. Add ice cubes, cold water, and stir thoroughly.

COFFEE, ITALIAN STYLE

Caffè Espresso

4 standard coffee measures (8 tablespoons) French or Italian-roast pulverized coffee	1 ½ cups water

A drip pot may be used, but a *macchinetta* is best for the true espresso flavor and texture. This coffee-making utensil consists of two cylinders, one with spout, and a coffee sieve between them.

Measure coffee into sieve. Put parts together, the cylinder with spout as top piece, and measured water in the lower cylinder. Place on heat; wait for small opening in lower cylinder to steam. Remove *macchinetta* from heat. Turn it upside down until all brew has dripped through.

Serve in after-dinner coffee cups or coffee glasses with handles. A twist of lemon peel and sugar may be served with espresso—never cream. (In Italy they consider the lemon an American gilding.) Makes 4 demitasse cups.

COFFEE, SYRIAN STYLE
Café de la Syrie

Cardamom seeds   Hot coffee

Place 2 or 3 cracked cardamom seeds in the bottom of each after-dinner coffee cup. Fill cups with hot coffee. Sweeten to taste.

COFFEE, TURKISH STYLE

1 ½ cups water   4   teaspoons sugar
4   tablespoons finely pulverized
    coffee

Measure water into heavy saucepan or special Turkish coffee pan.

Turkish coffee pot

Add sugar. Bring to a boil. Stir in coffee. Bring to boiling point again and let brew froth up 3 times. Remove from heat. Add a few drops cold water. Spoon some of the foam into each cup. Pour in thick coffee. Makes 4 demitasse servings.

In the Near East, coffee brewed Turkish fashion is served in cups smaller than demitasses, so that each guest is sure to receive his share of the creamy foam from the pot. In Arabic this foam is called the face of the coffee, and a hostess is always careful to serve coffee with the foam on it.

51

COFFEE WITH MILK

Café au Lait

Café au lait is the favorite breakfast coffee of French households. To make it, use 1 pot of freshly brewed hot coffee and 1 pot very hot, rich milk. Take coffeepot in one hand, hot milk pot in the other, pour simultaneously into cups.

Coffee may be made in a variety of ways. Here are a few of the popular coffee-makers: Top—drip pot, old-fashioned coffee pot, glass filter; bottom—percolator, glass filter drip, and Italian macchinetta.

COFFEE WITH LIQUEURS

Coffee is sometimes served with cognac, as an after-dinner beverage. Or another liqueur is preferred in this tangy combination. Begin with strong, hot demitasse coffee and fill small (preferably hot) cup about ¾ full. Then add dash of cognac, or curaçao, kümmel, anisette, or Cointreau. Cognac in demitasse of coffee is called *Café Royale*.

IRISH COFFEE

Fine granulated sugar
Hot, strong black coffee

Irish whiskey
Softly whipped cream

Rinse a large wineglass with warm water. Add 2 teaspoons sugar. Fill glass about ⅔ full with hot coffee. Stir. Add about 2 tablespoons Irish whiskey. Top with spoonful of softly whipped cream. Makes 1 serving.

In Dublin I learned that it's a breach of etiquette to stir Irish Coffee—you drink it through the layer of cream on top.

LATIN-AMERICAN COFFEE

Spanish, Mexican, South American, and many Latin-American coffee drinkers make a blend of freshly brewed hot coffee and an equal amount of hot cocoa or chocolate. The two hot brews are mixed, never boiled together. They may be stirred with a wooden whirlstick or with a stick of cinnamon, or simply poured together into cups and served with or without topping of cream.

NEW ORLEANS COFFEE

Café Brûlot

1 orange peel, cut in thin strips	24 cubes sugar
1 lemon peel, cut in thin strips	¾ cup cognac
4 (1-inch) sticks cinnamon	1½ quarts freshly made hot
1 tablespoon whole cloves	coffee

Combine peels, cinnamon, cloves, and sugar in brûlot bowl or deep chafing-dish pan. Pour brandy over peels and sugar mixture. Ignite with match and let burn. Lift the flaming brandy in the brûlot ladle back and forth over the peels mixture. When flame burns out pour hot coffee slowly into brûlot bowl or chafing dish. Ladle at once into demitasses. Makes 12 or more demitasse servings.

For a brûlot ladle I often use a large silver spoon, my "Texas teaspoon," or a small soup ladle.

SWEET ITALIAN COFFEE

Caffè Cappuccino

Freshly made hot coffee   Powdered cinnamon
Scalding hot milk

Pour hot coffee and hot milk together into cups; dust generously with cinnamon.

A good drink for the rumpus-room crowd after an evening of cards and backgammon. Goes well with a fruit tart or big chocolate cake.

A brunch favorite too. Serve a delicate prune pastry with this, as a compromise breakfast bread-dessert.

You might approximate this Italian favorite by pouring hot milk and hot coffee together into a blender. Blend a few minutes. Pour, frothy and foaming, into cups. The question of sugar and cinnamon is up to the drinker. I've consumed gallons of this version of Italian coffee in Venice, Rome, Milan, Genoa, and elsewhere, without the sweetening.

VIENNESE COFFEE

Make fresh, hot coffee. Serve with hot milk and a little cinnamon, or serve sweetened with a spoonful of whipped cream on top (*Schlagobers*).

The cinnamon is optional. Demel's, the finest pastry shop in Vienna—and in the world, so far as I am concerned—serves coffee from 10 A.M., with brioches, croissants, or a fantastic array of hors d'oeuvres, such as smoked salmon on sweet-buttered bread or little finger rolls, stuffed eggs, caviar, and various *vol-au-vents*. The light-lunching American considers Demel's hors d'oeuvres quite sufficient and elegant for lunch and, thinking of the heavenly pastry she or he can't resist, leaves the whipped cream off the coffee. In fact, you may sit down at ten and eat right on through lunch. No one ever hurries you in a Viennese coffee-house, whether or not you have ordered.

TEA

Experiment with various teas on the market until you find one especially pleasing to your palate. Most tea bought today is a blend of twenty or thirty varieties, selected by tea experts for color, flavor, body, bouquet, and other qualities.

In general, the blends of these varieties are divided into three different types: black, green, and oolong. Black tea has undergone a special processing treatment which turns the leaves black. This gives the tea a rich, hearty flavor—preferred by most Americans, since 97 per cent of all tea consumed in America is black tea.

Green tea is prepared for market without the oxidation process which turns tea black. When green tea is brewed the color is light, the flavor more delicate.

Oolong tea is a compromise between black and green teas. It is tea which is semiprocessed, so its leaves are partly brown and partly green. When brewed, oolong is light in color.

These three types are made available to us by many importers. Variations in their flavor are created by adding an herb, as is the case of the famous Earl Grey mixture packed by certain English grocers, by adding dried blossoms and seeds or spices, and by various other additions found under many labels.

When you find a mixture especially pleasing to you, make it "your tea," and serve it as a *specialité de la maison,* as famous hostesses of the past have done. The great names of the social world in Europe and in America used to send to China, to Russia, and other distant places for a particular blend of tea which they had learned to prefer to all others. Charming glass, porcelain, and silver boxes, with lock and key, were seen on the tea tray in great households in the old days. They held the small, precious, and costly importations of tea, which were kept on hand for special guests and appeared on the tea table only when worthy guests sat around it. The hostess herself unlocked the box, spooned the tea into the heated teapot, and then locked the box again.

Whichever tea is served in your house, keep it in the tightly closed tin box in which it comes or in a glass jar with tight-fitting top. I like to keep on hand several kinds of tea, to please my guests with the blend of their choice.

I find that men who think they don't like tea need merely sample different varieties to find the kind or kinds that please their particular palate. I know a well-known surgeon who brews tea each busy afternoon in his office in an electric teapot, often selecting a spiced tea I send him as his pickup.

How To Make Good Hot Tea

Whether you use tea bags or loose tea from an airtight canister, there are a few simple rules for making hot tea taste right and look right.

Use your teapot, of heavy pottery, thin china, or earthenware. Even with a handsome silver tea service many hostesses prefer to use a china pot for tea, with boiling water in the silver kettle, and the silver pot full of piping-hot water on the tray. The pottery or china pot helps keep the tea hot while it brews.

Bring fresh, cold tap water to a rapid boil.

Use 1 teaspoon of tea, or 1 tea bag, per cup.

Rinse teapot with boiling water and drain. (Some sticklers even dry it, too.) Measure tea leaves or bags into the pot, allowing 1 teaspoon for each cup of beverage plus "1 for the pot."

Pour fresh, briskly boiling water over leaves or bag, allowing ¾ measuring cup of water for each cup of tea. Cover pot and let tea steep 3 to 5 minutes. Stir the tea in the pot once before pouring.

Pour tea hot and steaming into cups. Tea is at its best when sparkling amber in color. If steeped too long, it darkens and develops bitterness.

If you like weak tea, pour a little hot water into the cup. Serve tea with milk, lemon, or plain.

Hot tea for a large crowd: To prepare ahead of time for 40 to 50 cups of tea, bring 1½ quarts fresh, cold water to a rapid boil. Remove from heat and immediately add ¼ pound loose tea. Stir to immerse leaves and then cover. Let stand 5 minutes. Strain into teapot until ready to use. (Double recipe for 80 to 90 cups.)

To serve with this concentrate, bring out a pot of piping-hot water, fresh from the boiling teakettle. Pour about 2 tablespoons of concentrate from the teapot into each cup; fill up with piping-hot water. By varying the amount of concentrate, you can vary the strength of the tea.

GOOD ICED TEA

Follow the rules for making hot tea but add 50 per cent more tea to allow for melting ice. That is, use 6 tea bags, or 6 teaspoons of tea, for 4 glasses of iced tea.

An easy way to make iced tea ahead of time: Pre-measure ⅓ cup loose tea (or remove tags from 15 tea bags). Bring 1 quart freshly drawn cold water to a rapid boil in a saucepan. Remove pan from heat and, while water is still bubbling, add all tea at once. Stir. Let brew 5 minutes, uncovered. Stir again. Strain into pitcher holding an additional quart of freshly drawn cold water. Do not refrigerate. Serve in ice-filled glasses with lemon and sugar to taste. Refrigeration may tend to cloud tea, and while cloudiness does not affect the flavor, it makes a less attractive glass of tea. If a large pitcher of tea has clouded, dash a little boiling water into it, stir, and it will clear up.

Evening Tea

I often serve tea about 10 or 10:30 in the evening, Irish style. It's especially appreciated by guests who take no alcohol after dinner (most of mine). I serve it in the living room with simple sweets—small cookies, English biscuits, stuffed dates, etc.

Cold Summer Drinks
Non-Alcoholic

Dress up tall summer drinks with these ideas:

Watermelon-ball garnish: Spear watermelon ball with ice pick or a skewer; poke bright-colored sipper straw through the hole. Serve in tall glass of iced lemonade. Vary this garnish by adding to the sipper a ripe summer cherry or small cube of pineapple, peach, apricot, a seedless grape, or a fresh purple violet or a cowslip.

Garnish the block of ice: Top the block of ice in the summer punch bowl with a cool green grape leaf on which a bunch of ripe cherries or grapes rests. Be wary about adding flowers to the punch bowl. Some of them are poisonous. Arrange flowers around tray on which bowl stands.

Ice Cubes in Color: Freeze tea, fruit juice, coffee, and other summer beverages in ice trays. Use the cubes in tall drinks of tea, fruit, coffee.

Place a long-stemmed maraschino or mint cherry in each section of an ice tray. Fill with water. Freeze as usual. Serve these cubes in fruit drinks.

Wash limes, lemons, oranges, and other fruits. Chill. Slice very thin with thin-bladed sharp knife. Float a slice in a fruit drink or cut slice halfway through and perch it on rim of a tall drink.

Colored sipper straws add a gay note to the drink tray. Holders of fabric, plastic, and other materials around the glass prevent drip from moisture on the glass.

A charming hostess gift—or one for yourself—is a set of sterling ice-tea sipper-spoons (remarkably reasonable at even the most elegant jewelers such as Tiffany's).

CHOCOLATE MILK

For each glass of chocolate milk use 1 cup chilled milk and 1 tablespoon Chocolate Syrup (below). Beat with rotary beater or in blender. Pour into tall chilled glass. Makes 1 serving.

CHOCOLATE MILK SHAKE

1 cup milk	¼ cup Chocolate Syrup
½ cup ice cream	(below)
	Whipped cream if desired

Combine milk, ice cream, and Chocolate Syrup in blender. Blend 1 minute. Pour into tall chilled glass. Top with spoonful of whipped cream or serve plain. Makes 1 serving.

Vary the flavor by using vanilla, chocolate, coffee, or maple ice cream.

CHOCOLATE SYRUP

1 cup powdered cocoa	2 cups boiling water
2 (1-ounce) squares bitter chocolate	1 egg
	4 tablespoons butter
1 ½ cups brown sugar, packed	2 teaspoons vanilla
¼ teaspoon salt	

Combine cocoa, chocolate, sugar, salt, and water in saucepan. Stir and heat until sugar and chocolate are dissolved. Boil 3 minutes. Remove from heat and beat vigorously with rotary egg beater. Beat egg into mixture. Return to heat. Add butter, and beat again with rotary beater. Let simmer over lowered heat 10 minutes. Add vanilla. Let cool. Pour into quart jar and store in refrigerator for use in various chocolate drinks and as a dessert sauce. Makes about 1 quart syrup.

COFFEE FLOAT

Hot, freshly brewed coffee
Coffee ice cubes

Ice cream, vanilla or coffee flavor

Pour hot coffee over ice cubes in each tall glass and top with a generous spoonful of ice cream. Serve long-handled spoon and sipper straw with each glass.

Delicious as dessert-beverage for summer luncheon or supper. Serve cookies, cake, or small fruit tartlet with this drink. Or simply pass the sweetmeats tray with toasted almonds, candied orange peel, cool mints, and fresh cherries or strawberries (their stems left on) as the enticements.

EASY MOCHA SHAKE

1   pint chocolate ice cream
1   pint milk
2   tablespoons instant coffee
½   teaspoon powdered nutmeg

Whipped cream
Additional instant coffee or
   powdered nutmeg

Place first 4 ingredients in blender. Cover and blend about 1 minute or until smooth. Pour immediately into chilled glasses. Top each with a fluff of whipped cream and dust with a little instant coffee or nutmeg. Makes 4 servings.

ICED MOCHA

Chocolate Syrup (page 58)
Hot, freshly brewed coffee

Coffee ice cubes
Cream

Add spoonful Chocolate Syrup to each tall glass. Pour in a little hot coffee and mix. Add ice cubes and fill glass with coffee. Add topper of whipped cream or spoonful of plain cream. Serve glass stirring rod or long-handled spoon with each drink.

FROZEN STRAWBERRY DRINK

1 (10-ounce) package sliced
  quick-frozen strawberries
1 quart milk

1 pint strawberry ice cream
1 teaspoon grated lemon peel

Let strawberries thaw. Combine all ingredients in chilled bowl. Beat with rotary beater. Or combine half the ingredients at a time in electric mixer and beat at high speed 1 minute. Pour into chilled tall glasses. Makes 8 servings.

LEMON AND LIME JULEP

1 large bunch fresh mint
½ cup lime juice
  (about 3 limes)
3 tablespoons sugar

Cracked ice
2 (12-ounce) bottles lemon soda
4 slices fresh lime

Wash mint carefully and let drain. Break a few mint leaves into each of 4 chilled tall glasses. Add 1 tablespoon lime juice to each glass and about 2 teaspoons sugar. Stir, crushing the mint with the spoon to bring out the flavor. Fill glasses with cracked ice. Spoon remaining lime juice over. Fill with lemon soda water. Stick a lime slice and generous bunch of mint on top. Use green and yellow sipper straws. Makes 4 servings.

ORANGE SODA FLOATS

Orange juice
Sugar
Orange sherbet

Orange soda, chilled
Sliced oranges
Orange straws

For each serving, chill a tall soda glass and dip rim in orange juice, then in sugar. Let glass stand until sugar rim is set.

Scoop 2 balls of orange sherbet into each glass and fill with orange soda. Slip an orange slice onto glass rim. Serve at once.

TALL CRANBERRY COOLERS

2 (1-pint) bottles cranberry juice
  cocktail
4 tablespoons lemon juice
Cracked ice

1 pint lemon sherbet
Fresh mint sprigs, or
8 long lemon peels

Combine cranberry and lemon juice in chilled pitcher. Pack 8 tall glasses with cracked ice. Pour juice mixture over ice and top each with small scoop of lemon sherbet. Garnish with mint. Or insert lemon peel in cracked ice before pouring juice. Makes 8 servings.

Punches

Alcoholic and Non-Alcoholic

BACARDI PUNCH

5 oranges	½ cup granulated sugar
3 lemons	1 bottle (fifth) Bacardi rum
1 (No. 2) can unsweetened pineapple juice	1 quart ginger ale, iced
	Block of ice

About 1 hour before serving time squeeze 4 oranges and 2 lemons into a glass pitcher or bowl. Add pineapple juice and sweeten to taste. Add Bacardi. Slice remaining orange and lemon thin, then cut into small triangular pieces, stir well. Cover, let stand until serving time. Just before serving, place block of ice in punch bowl. Add ginger ale to juice mixture and pour over ice. Serve. Makes about 20 punch cups.

CHAMPAGNE PUNCH

¼ cup cognac	2 quarts champagne, iced
¼ cup curaçao	2 quarts carbonated water, chilled
¼ cup cherry brandy	
½ cup lemon juice	10 thin orange slices
¼ cup sugar	24 maraschino cherries
Large block ice	1 cup strawberries

Combine cognac, curaçao, cherry brandy, lemon juice, and sugar. Mix well and pour over block of ice in punch bowl, or over ice cubes in large pitchers. Add champagne and carbonated water. Stir lightly. Add fruit. Serve at once. Makes 20 punch cups.

Favorite for wedding receptions. The first five ingredients may be mixed the day before and allowed to mellow.

COGNAC-WINE PUNCH

3 tablespoons sugar
Juice 3 lemons
⅜ cup cointreau
⅜ cup cognac
Block of ice
1 quart claret, chilled

1 quart sauterne, chilled
1 quart carbonated water, chilled
Thin slices lemon
Small sprig fresh mint

Combine sugar, lemon juice, cointreau, and cognac. Stir to dissolve sugar. Place block of ice in chilled punch bowl. Pour cognac mixture over ice and add wines and carbonated water. Stir gently to mix. Float lemon slices and mint on punch. Serve at once in chilled punch cups. Makes about 20 to 24 punch cups.

CRANBERRY PUNCH

2 pint bottles cranberry juice cocktail
1 quart apple juice
1 (6-ounce) can frozen lemonade
1 (6-ounce) can frozen grapefruit juice

1 (6-ounce) can pineapple juice
Block of ice or ice cubes
2 (29-ounce) bottles carbonated water
12 orange slices, halved

Have all ingredients chilled. Pour juices over block of ice in punch bowl or over ice cubes in glass pitchers. Add carbonated water. Stir gently, just enough to mix. Add orange slices. Serve at once. Makes 24 or more punch cups.

FRUIT-CHAMPAGNE PUNCH

Place a few slices of apple, orange, grapefruit, banana, and pineapple in large chilled glass pitcher. Sprinkle lightly with sugar. Pour very cold champagne over all. Serve at once in chilled glasses or punch cups.

FRUIT-GINGER ALE PUNCH

1 (6-ounce) can frozen orange juice
1 (6-ounce) can frozen lemonade
1 (6-ounce) can frozen limeade

4 cups cold water
1 large bottle (3 ½ to 4 cups) ginger ale

Combine all ingredients except ginger ale. Pour over ice block in punch bowl or ice cubes in large glass pitcher. Add ginger ale just before serving. Makes 12 to 15 punch cups.

RHINE VALLEY PUNCH

¼ cup peach brandy
¼ cup Benedictine
2 oranges, sliced thin
1 lemon, sliced thin
2 sprigs fresh mint

Block of ice
1 cup washed, hulled strawberries
2 bottles Rhine wine, iced

Combine peach brandy, Benedictine, sliced fruit, and mint in small bowl. Mix and cover. Let stand 2 hours. Place block of ice in chilled punch bowl. Pour peach brandy mixture over ice and add strawberries. Pour wine in. Stir gently. Serve at once in punch cups. Makes about 15 cups.

WEDDING CUP

¼ cup cognac
¼ cup Triple Sec or curaçao
1 quart champagne, iced

1 quart carbonated water, chilled

Combine cognac and Triple Sec or curaçao in chilled glass pitcher. Immediately before serving, add champagne and carbonated water to pitcher. Stir gently once. Serve in punch cups or champagne glasses. Makes 12 to 18 servings.

If punch bowl is used, chill it by placing large block of ice in it. Scatter rose petals over the ice. Mix the brandies before pouring into bowl. Add carbonated water and champagne, stir once around, and serve at once.

MAY WINE

May Bowl

2 cups dried woodruff   Large block ice
  (Waldmeister)   3 bottles white wine, chilled

Tie woodruff tightly in small cheesecloth bag. Soak bag in bowl of cold water 30 minutes. Place block of ice in punch bowl. Lay soaked woodruff bag on the ice. Pour chilled wine over the herb and ice and let stand 5 minutes before serving. Delicious with fresh strawberries in it.

Remove woodruff bag after 15 minutes if all the wine has not been served. If fresh woodruff is used, it need not be soaked. Place sprigs of fresh herb, tied together, on the ice. Remove herb from punch after wine has taken on the flavor. Makes about 2½ quarts, 18 or more punch cups.

May wine—good, too—is available bottled. Nice to have on hand. Otherwise you might grow your own woodruff. You can buy the seeds at an herb shop or, possibly, given time, your druggist will oblige you by ordering it for you. Herb shops have it, too.

Try serving May wine instead of cocktails before a spring or summer dinner with delicate English biscuits or thin fingers of buttered fresh bread. Strongly flavored appetizers would kill the delicate woodruff.

Hot Punches and Cups

HOT CIDER CUP

1 ½ quarts cider   ⅛ teaspoon salt
¼ cup sugar   12 whole cloves
1 tablespoon grated orange   Cinnamon sticks
  peel

Combine all ingredients except cinnamon sticks in agate or enamel kettle over moderate heat. Bring to a boil and turn heat off. Let mixture stand 2 or 3 hours. Strain mixture and reheat. Serve for winter nightcap to departing guests. Add cinnamon stick to each mug. Makes 6 cups, or 12 small mugs.

HOT MULLED CIDER

1 lemon peel	¼ teaspoon salt
1 teaspoon whole allspice	½ cup brown sugar, packed
36 whole cloves	2 quarts fresh or bottled cider
3-inch stick cinnamon	Powdered nutmeg

Tie lemon peel, allspice, cloves, and cinnamon in small piece of cheesecloth. Combine salt, sugar, and cider in an enamel or agate saucepan over low heat. Stir until sugar dissolves. Add spice bag and bring mixture to a boil, then lower heat and simmer 10 minutes. Remove spice bag. Serve hot in mugs, topped with light sprinkling of nutmeg. Makes 2 quarts, 8 to 10 servings.

Hot Mulled Wine: Substitute a red wine for cider in above recipe.

HOT GRAPE PUNCH

4 cups bottled or canned grape juice	¼ teaspoon powdered nutmeg
	⅛ teaspoon powdered cloves
¼ to ⅓ cup sugar	⅛ teaspoon powdered ginger
1 teaspoon powdered cinnamon	5 long cinnamon sticks

Combine all ingredients except cinnamon sticks in enamel or agate kettle. Bring mixture slowly to a boil. Serve hot into mugs, with cinnamon stick in each. Makes 5 mugs.

HOT ORANGE PUNCH

4 cups orange juice	2 teaspoons whole cloves
⅓ to ½ cup sugar	2 teaspoons grated orange peel
6 (1-inch) sticks cinnamon	Few orange slices

Combine all ingredients except orange slices in agate or enamel saucepan. Bring to a boil, stirring only to mix. Let boil 1 minute. Reduce heat to simmering and simmer 5 minutes. Strain and pour into heated punch bowl or pitcher, or directly into mugs. Float orange slices on bowl or in pitcher, or add to mugs. Makes 8 servings.

To serve any hot punch in a glass bowl, first heat the bowl by pouring *warm, not hot,* water into it. Let stand until hot punch is ready. Pour water out. Pour hot punch in slowly.

NEW YEAR'S EGGNOG

1 dozen eggs	1 pint heavy cream, whipped
1 cup sugar, or more	1 bottle (3 ⅕ cups) cognac
1 ½ quarts milk	Powdered cinnamon or nutmeg

Separate eggs. Beat yolks until light in large bowl in which the nog is to be served. Add sugar, still beating. Stir milk and cream in. Pour brandy into this mixture very slowly, stirring to mix. Taste for sweetness. Add more sugar if needed.

Cover and let stand in refrigerator 1 or 2 hours.

Just before serving, beat whites of eggs stiff. Mix into the nog. Dust cinnamon or nutmeg over the top and serve. Makes about 2½ quarts, 20 or more servings.

NON-ALCOHOLIC EGGNOG

⅓ cup sugar	1 teaspoon vanilla or
2 eggs	2 tablespoons non-alcoholic
¼ teaspoon salt	sherry
4 cups milk, scalded	3 tablespoons sugar
	1 cup heavy cream
	Powdered nutmeg

Beat ⅓ cup sugar into egg yolks in upper part of double boiler. Add salt. Stir milk in slowly. Cook over hot, but not boiling, water until mixture coats spoon. Stir constantly. Let cool. Add vanilla or sherry. Beat egg whites until foamy. Gradually add the 3 tablespoons of sugar, beating until soft peaks form. Fold this meringue into the custard and mix thoroughly. Chill in refrigerator 3 to 4 hours in covered serving bowl. To serve, dot top with sweetened whipped cream and light sprinkling of nutmeg. Makes 6 to 8 servings.

CHAPTER FOUR

Breads

Yeast Breads

Ready-to-serve, heat-and-serve, ready-mix, and other modern forms of delicious time-honored yeast breads are widely available at bakery shops, grocers, and markets. Add to these the long-tested recipes for favorite breads of American homes and those of other countries and you can give delectable variety to today's meals.

In general, a freshly baked yeast bread calls for much more preparation time than baking-powder breads. Allow for this if you are planning to bake a loaf, or coffee cake, or a batch of rolls.

TO FRESHEN YEAST BREAD

Wrap leftover yeast bread in foil or waxed paper; store in deep freezer or coldest part of refrigerator. Such foil-wrapped bread and rolls may be reheated for about 20 minutes in their wrapping in a moderate (350° F. to 375° F.) oven. Or use Dutch oven, covered skillet, or heavy kettle. Place trivet in bottom, add 2 or 3 tablespoons water, place package of bread or rolls on trivet, cover pot tightly, and heat 10 minutes, or until bread is hot. The same idea works just as well in the top of a vegetable steamer or double boiler.

To freshen bakery rolls, sprinkle them lightly with water and heat in tightly closed paper bag or parchment paper in moderate (350° F.) oven about 15 minutes. Of course semi-prepared rolls and loaves are baked according to directions on their packages.

Many of my recipes which follow suggest delicious variations in flavoring and serving breads. They are good friends to young homemakers, saving cookery time and adding special interest to menus.

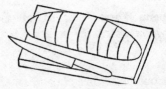

WHITE BREAD

1 cup milk, scalded	1 cup warm or lukewarm water
¼ cup sugar	6 cups sifted all-purpose flour
2½ teaspoons salt	Extra flour
6 tablespoons shortening	Extra shortening
1 package dry, or 1 cake compressed, yeast	Salad oil, or softened butter or margarine

Combine scalded milk, sugar, salt, and shortening in pan in which milk scalded. Let cool to lukewarm.

Crumble yeast into *warm* water in very large mixing bowl. For compressed yeast use *lukewarm* water. Stir until dissolved. Stir milk mixture into yeast. Add 3 cups flour. Beat until smooth. Stir remaining 3 cups flour in, beating and mixing to incorporate all flour.

Turn dough out onto lightly floured board. Knead until smooth and elastic. Grease mixing bowl well with shortening. Warm bowl slightly by setting it in warm water. Place dough in bowl and brush top with oil or softened butter or margarine. Cover with folded kitchen towel. Let rise in warm, but not hot, place (about 85° F.), free from drafts, until doubled in bulk. Punch dough down in bowl. Turn out onto lightly floured board.

With sharp knife cut dough in half. Cover the two pieces with towel and let rest 15 to 20 minutes. Grease two (9-by-5-by-3-inch) loaf pans. Shape each loaf with hands to fit length of pan and place in pans. Cover lightly with towel. Let rise in warm place about 30 minutes, or until center is slightly higher than edges.

Start oven at moderately hot (400° F.). Bake loaves about 50 minutes, or until crusty and browning and loaf has shrunk slightly from sides of pan. Remove loaves from pans as soon as taken from oven, turning out onto clean towel, then righting. Grease tops if soft, tender crust is preferred.

Let cool uncovered on cake racks; keep away from drafts. Makes 2 loaves.

Bread-making helpers: *Warm* water, to soften dry yeast, should be about 105° F. *Lukewarm* water, for moist or compressed yeast, about 95° F.

Temperature of surroundings while dough rises should be about 85° F., away from drafts, out of sunlight, away from range or any direct heat such as top of radiator. Warm bowl slightly before putting dough in it. If room is cold or cool, set dough bowl in deep pan of warm water. Add a little hot water to pan from time to time to keep its temperature gently warm, or about 85° F.

Time needed for dough to double in bulk depends on room temperature, size of bowl, and other influences. Test risen dough by pressing two fingers deep into dough. If dough has risen enough, holes should remain when fingers are withdrawn.

To punch down, pull edges of dough into the center and down into dough once. Turn dough over in bowl, leaving rounded side up. Follow recipe directions for next step.

Old-fashioned cooks did little to shape a loaf. Some modern cooks want a more commercial-looking baked loaf. To get this result, flatten each piece of dough slightly with fingers, then shape into an oblong roughly the size of the baking pan. Fold each end of oblong to the center, ends overlapping slightly. Press folds down firmly. Pinch center overlap together lightly. Narrow the sides slightly. Place the loaf, sealed edge down, in the greased loaf pan, brush with oil or fat, and bake as described.

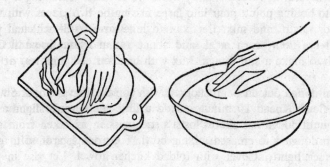

WHOLE-WHEAT BREAD

¾ cup scalded milk
4 tablespoons sugar
3 ½ teaspoons salt
6 tablespoons shortening
⅜ cup molasses
1 ½ cups warm or lukewarm water
2 packages active dry, or 2 cakes compressed, yeast

4 ½ cups whole-wheat flour
2 cups sifted all-purpose flour
Extra white flour
Extra shortening
Salad oil, or softened butter or margarine

Combine scalded milk, sugar, salt, shortening, and molasses in the pan in which milk scalded. Let cool to lukewarm.

Crumble yeast into *warm* water in very large mixing bowl. For compressed yeast use *lukewarm* water. Stir until dissolved. Stir milk-and-molasses mixture in. Add half of combined whole-wheat and white flours. Beat until smooth. Stir in rest of flour mixture, mixing to incorporate all flour.

Complete recipe as for White Bread (page 68). Makes 2 loaves.

PUMPERNICKEL

2 packages active dry, or 2 cakes compressed, yeast
3 cups water
1 ½ tablespoons salt
¼ cup molasses
1 cup unseasoned, freshly mashed potatoes (the dehydrated variety will do)

7 cups rye flour, stone-ground if possible
½ cup corn meal
2 cups whole-wheat flour
Milk

Soften yeast in ½ cup slightly warm water. Heat remaining 2½ cups water to boiling point; pour into large mixing bowl. Add salt, molasses, mashed potato, and mix. Let cool to lukewarm. Add softened yeast.

Add rye flour, corn meal, and about 1 cup whole-wheat flour, or enough to make a stiff dough. Mix with hands. Let dough rest 10 minutes.

Turn dough out on board floured with some of the remaining whole-wheat flour. Knead 10 minutes. Add a little more wheat flour as you knead until dough has almost lost its stickiness.

Turn dough into greased mixing bowl. Turn dough around to grease its surface lightly. Cover with folded kitchen towel. Let rise in warm place (80° to 85° F.) about 1½ hours, until dough has doubled in bulk and holds a depression when punched deeply with a finger.

Turn risen dough out on board lightly sprinkled with whole-wheat flour; knead 3 or 4 minutes. Let rise as before until half doubled, about 45 minutes.

Turn dough out again on surface sprinkled as lightly as possible with whole-wheat flour. Knead lightly into a ball. Cut ball in quarters. Shape each quarter into ball-shaped loaf or pulled-out longer loaf. Arrange loaves on baking sheet lightly sprinkled with corn meal. Brush tops of loaves with water. Let rise about 20 minutes in a warm place until loaves have increased about one quarter in size.

Start oven at moderate (375° F.). Brush risen loaves with milk. Bake about 1 hour and 15 minutes. For thick crust, brush with water several times during baking. Makes 4 loaves, each weighing more than 1 pound.

See temperature and rising directions under White Bread recipe (page 68).

CINNAMON RING

⅓ Basic Breakfast-Bread Dough (page 72)
½ cup melted butter or margarine
½ cup sugar
2 teaspoons powdered cinnamon
½ teaspoon powdered ginger
½ cup sifted confectioners' sugar
1 ½ teaspoons water

Place ⅓ basic dough on lightly floured board. Roll into rectangle about 10 by 16 inches. Spread with melted butter or margarine. Sprinkle with sugar, cinnamon, and ginger. Fold one long side to center. Fold other long side over, forming 3 layers; moisten long edge lightly. Press together to seal. Place on lightly greased baking sheet. Cut lengthwise through middle to within 1 inch of opposite end. Twist the two strips around each other to form braid; seal ends. Pick up one end of braid and make ring. Join ends and press firmly to seal.

Cover ring lightly with folded kitchen towel. Let rise in warm, not hot, place, away from draft, about 30 minutes, or until double in bulk.

Start oven at moderate (350° F.). Bake ring 20 to 25 minutes; place on wire rack to cool. Blend confectioners' sugar and water smoothly, drizzle over warm ring. Makes 6 or more servings.

BASIC BREAKFAST-BREAD DOUGH

¾ cup milk

4 tablespoons butter or margarine

⅓ cup sugar

1 teaspoon salt

¼ cup warm water

2 packages active dry, or 2 cakes compressed, yeast

2 eggs, beaten

4½ to 5 cups sifted all-purpose flour

Shortening

Scald milk. Pour over butter or margarine, sugar, and salt together in a large mixing bowl. Let cool to lukewarm. Sprinkle yeast on ¼ cup *warm* water in another bowl, or use *lukewarm* water for compressed yeast. Stir softened yeast into milk mixture. Add eggs. Stir a little flour in, beating until smooth. Add sufficient remaining flour to make soft dough, stirring until dough forms ball which leaves side of bowl.

Turn dough out onto lightly floured board. Press into flattened ball. Knead until smooth and elastic, adding only enough flour to keep dough from sticking. Grease mixing bowl. Return dough to bowl, turning dough once to grease its surface. Coat top of dough lightly with softened shortening. Cover with folded kitchen towel. Let rise in warm, not hot, place about 50 minutes, or until double in bulk.

Punch dough down and turn out onto lightly floured board. Cut into 3 pieces. Bake ⅓ as Cinnamon Ring (page 71), ⅓ as Pecan Roll (below), ⅓ as Sunday Brunch Buns (page 73).

If you like to bake, and your family prefers home-baked breads and breakfast pastries, this recipe will be your most popular one for quantity turnouts. Set aside time for this preparation and baking. The delicious results are worth the time and effort!

Also it's the perfect recipe for a church bazaar or church supper event.

PECAN ROLL

⅓ Basic Breakfast-Bread Dough (above)

1 (6½-ounce) package pitted dates

½ cup sugar

½ cup water

½ cup chopped pecans

¼ cup melted butter or margarine

Sifted confectioners' sugar

Let ⅓ basic dough rest a few minutes. Cut dates fine. Combine dates, sugar, and water. Bring to a boil. Lower heat and simmer 10 minutes, stirring constantly. Remove from heat. Stir in nuts. Let cool.

Place dough on lightly floured bread board. Roll into rectangle about 10 by 16 inches. Spread with melted butter or margarine and date-nut mixture. Fold one long side to center. Fold other long side over, forming three layers. Moisten long edge lightly and seal by pressing gently. Place on greased baking sheet.

Cut lengthwise through middle to within 1 inch of opposite end. Twist strips around each other to form braid. Seal ends. Pick up uncut end and make ring with braid. Seal ends. Cover lightly with folded kitchen towel. Let rise in warm, not hot, place away from drafts about 30 minutes, or until doubled in bulk.

Start oven at moderate (350° F.). Bake ring 20 to 35 minutes, or until browned. Let cool on wire rack. Sift confectioners' sugar over the roll as soon as placed on rack. Makes 6 or more servings.

SUNDAY BRUNCH BUNS

⅓ Basic Breakfast-Bread Dough (page 72)
½ cup dried currants

Milk for brushing tops
2 tablespoons sugar

Let dough rest a few minutes. Wash and drain currants; cover with cold water and soak 10 minutes. Drain. Grease 8-by-8-by-2-inch pan.

Place dough on lightly floured bread board. Knead currants well into dough. Shape dough into 9 balls. Place balls in greased pan. Cover pan lightly with folded kitchen towel. Let dough rise in warm, not hot, place away from draft, about 30 minutes, or until doubled in bulk.

Start oven at moderate (350° F.). Brush tops of rolls with mixed milk and sugar. Bake 25 to 30 minutes, or until browned. Serve warm. Makes 9 buns.

Various Coffee Breads

CALIFORNIA BREAKFAST PASTRY

1 package active dry, or 1 cake compressed, yeast	4 cups sifted all-purpose flour
¼ cup water	1 pound (about 4 cups) California walnut meats
1 cup milk	1 egg
½ cup butter or margarine	⅓ cup milk
2 eggs	½ cup sugar
½ cup sugar	½ teaspoon powdered cinnamon
Juice and peel ½ lemon	¼ teaspoon powdered ginger
½ teaspoon vanilla	Juice and peel 1 lemon
½ teaspoon salt	Melted butter or margarine

Sprinkle yeast in *warm* water to soften, or use *lukewarm* water for compressed yeast. Heat milk until film wrinkles over the top. Pour into mixing bowl. Stir butter or margarine in, mix and let cool to lukewarm. Beat eggs with sugar until smooth. Stir into milk mixture with juice and peel ½ lemon, vanilla, salt, and yeast. Beat flour in gradually. Cover with folded kitchen towel. Set bowl in warm, not hot, place until dough has doubled.

To make filling, chop walnuts with finest blade of food chopper. Beat egg and milk together. Stir into nuts with sugar, spices, peel, and juice of 1 lemon. Add a little more milk if too thick for spreading.

Grease two (11-by-7-by-1½-inch) baking pans. If dough is too soft to handle, chill a few minutes. Turn dough out onto bread board. Cut in half. Flour hands and pat one piece into a 12-inch square. Spread with ½ the nut filling; roll up as for jelly roll. Moisten edge and press to seal. Place roll in baking pan. Do the same with the remaining piece of dough and filling. Cover pans with folded kitchen towel. Let rise in warm, but not hot, place until doubled.

Start oven at moderate (350° F.). Bake 45 to 50 minutes. Brush tops with melted butter or margarine while still warm. Makes 8 or more servings in *each loaf*.

Serve warm for brunch, buffet luncheon or supper.

ORANGE-MARMALADE COFFEE CAKE

1 package active dry, or 1 cake compressed, yeast	1 ½ cups sifted all-purpose flour
2 tablespoons water	Extra flour
½ cup milk	1 egg
2 tablespoons sugar	Extra butter or margarine
½ teaspoon salt	½ cup orange marmalade
4 tablespoons butter or margarine	¼ cup sugar
	¼ teaspoon powdered cinnamon

Sprinkle yeast in *warm* water, or use *lukewarm* water for compressed yeast. Heat milk until film forms over surface. Pour into mixing bowl. Add sugar, salt, and butter or margarine. Stir. Beat ½ cup flour into milk mixture. Beat egg slightly. Stir into milk mixture with yeast. Add remaining 1 cup flour and beat hard. If a little more flour is needed, beat it in. It should not be more than 2 tablespoons extra. Grease larger bowl. Turn dough into it. Turn dough around once to grease its surface. Grease top lightly with softened butter or margarine. Cover bowl with folded kitchen towel. Let stand in warm, not hot, place about 1 hour, or until doubled in bulk.

Grease 9-inch cake pan. Punch dough down in bowl and turn it out into prepared cake pan. Spread dough lightly. Drop spoonfuls of jam on top and swirl it into dough with spoon. Sprinkle top with sugar and cinnamon. Cover pan lightly with towel. Let rise until doubled.

Start oven at moderate (375° F.) when coffee cake is about ready to go into oven. Bake 20 to 30 minutes, until lightly browned around edges. Remove from pan. Let cool slightly. Serve warm or cold. Makes 6 to 8 servings.

Perfect for brunch, and is so good cold that it makes a between-meals snack, with coffee or tea, for drop-in guests.

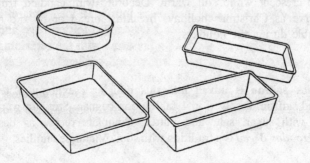

VIENNA BRAIDED CRESCENT

1 package active dry, or 1 cake compressed, yeast	1 egg, beaten
¼ cup water	3 cups sifted all-purpose flour
½ cup milk, scalded	2 teaspoons grated lemon peel
¼ cup sugar	½ cup finely cut mixed candied fruit (bought)
½ teaspoon salt	½ cup dried currants, soaked and drained
4 tablespoons softened butter or margarine	¼ cup chopped toasted almonds

Crumble dry yeast in *warm* water, or use *lukewarm* water for compressed yeast. Combine milk, sugar, salt, and butter or margarine in large mixing bowl. Let cool to lukewarm. Stir in egg and softened yeast. Add 2¾ cups flour, the lemon peel, candied fruit, currants, and nuts. Beat well.

Sprinkle about ¼ cup flour on bread board. Turn dough onto board. Knead 5 minutes. Grease mixing bowl. Return dough to bowl. Turn dough once to grease surface. Cover lightly with folded kitchen towel and let rise in a warm, not hot, place about 1 hour or until doubled in bulk. Punch dough down. Cover again and let rest 5 minutes.

Turn dough out on board. Cut into 3 equal parts. Shape each part on bread board into rope about 18 inches long. Place the 3 ropes parallel and close together on greased baking sheet. Starting at the middle of the strands, braid to the end. Again start at middle and braid to opposite end. Turn ends under and press to seal well. Form the braid into a crescent shape. Cover lightly with folded kitchen towel. Let rise in warm, not hot, place until doubled in bulk.

Start oven at moderate (350° F.). Bake crescent about 35 minutes. Remove from oven. Let cool. Makes 10 or more servings.

To ice this crescent for a holiday loaf, combine ½ cup confectioners' sugar, 2 teaspoons cream, ½ teaspoon vanilla. Beat together and drizzle over crescent while still warm. Decorate with candied fruits and nuts. Serve as Christmas holidays breakfast bread or on the tea and coffee table during the holidays.

Sometimes saffron is mixed into this dough: Use about 1 teaspoon powdered saffron dissolved in 1 tablespoon cognac. Stir into warm milk mixture with sugar, salt, and butter. Complete recipe as described. *Saffron Holiday Bread* is a tradition with some Viennese families.

Various Small Breads

BRIOCHE

1 package active dry, or 1 cake compressed, yeast	⅓ cup sugar
¼ cup water	½ teaspoon salt
½ cup milk, scalded	3 ¼ cups sifted all-purpose flour
½ cup butter or margarine	4 eggs
	1 tablespoon sugar

Soften dry yeast in *warm* water, or compressed yeast in *lukewarm* water. Let milk cool to lukewarm. Cream butter or margarine in very large mixing bowl. Add ⅓ cup sugar and the salt, creaming thoroughly. Add milk to creamed mixture. Stir in 1 cup flour. Add softened yeast, 3 beaten eggs, and I beaten yolk extra. Beat all well. Stir in remaining 2¼ cups flour. Beat 5 to 8 minutes longer.

Cover bowl with folded kitchen towel. Let rise in warm, but not hot, place until a little more than double, about 2 hours. Stir down. Beat well.

Cover bowl tightly with foil. Place in refrigerator overnight.

Next morning stir dough down. Turn out on lightly floured surface. Divide dough into 4 pieces. Set 1 piece aside. Cut the other 3 pieces in halves. Form each into 4 balls (24 balls in all). Form the reserved large piece into 24 smaller balls. Place large balls in 24 greased cups of muffin pans. Poke hole in top of each and moisten slightly with water.

Press small ball of dough into each hole. Cover pans with folded towel; let rise in warm place until double, about 1 hour. Beat remaining 1 egg white slightly with 1 tablespoon sugar. Brush tops of brioche with mixture.

Start oven at moderate (375° F.). Bake about 15 minutes, or until risen, browned, and done. Serve warm. Makes 2 dozen brioches.

ENGLISH MUFFINS, NEW STYLE

Shortening	1 package refrigerated pan-ready biscuits
1 tablespoon corn meal	

Melt enough shortening in heavy skillet to coat cooking surface; sprinkle corn meal over greased hot surface. Turn heat low. Arrange pan-ready biscuits in skillet. Cook uncovered. Turn biscuits occasionally. Should be done in 12 to 14 minutes. Serve hot, split and buttered. Makes 10 small muffins.

ENGLISH MUFFINS

1	cup milk, scalded	¼	cup warm water
1½	teaspoons salt	1	egg
2	tablespoons sugar	4	cups sifted all-purpose flour
3	tablespoons shortening	¼	cup corn meal
1	package dry yeast		

Combine milk, salt, sugar, and shortening in mixing bowl. Let cool to lukewarm. Dissolve yeast in ¼ cup warm water. Add to slightly cooled milk mixture. Beat egg and add. Blend well. Stir in 3 cups flour, beating until smooth. Turn out on floured board. Knead remaining 1 cup flour into dough. Grease bowl. Return dough to bowl. Cover lightly with folded kitchen towel and let double in bulk in warm, but not hot, place.

Turn out on lightly floured board and knead again. Let dough rest 1 minute. Roll dough ¼ inch thick; cut in rounds with 4-inch cutter. Sprinkle ½ corn meal evenly over baking sheet. Place rounds of dough on the corn-meal-covered sheet. Sprinkle remaining corn meal over tops of muffins. Cover lightly with towel. Let rise in warm, but not hot, place until well risen, approximately doubled in height.

Bake on greased griddle, moderate heat, 8 to 12 minutes on each side. Let cool on rack. Break open with fingers or fork. Toast and butter them to serve as breakfast or tea specialty. Makes 16 muffins.

STICKY PECAN ROLLS

1	package (12) brown-and-serve dinner rolls	¼	cup brown sugar, packed
4	tablespoons butter or margarine	24	pecan halves

Start oven at moderate (375° F.). Grease 12-cup muffin pan lightly.

Pull package apart. Place 1 roll in each muffin cup. With sharp paring knife cut X mark in top of each roll.

Melt butter or margarine and sugar together over low heat. Mix well. Spoon butter mixture over rolls. Tuck 2 pecan halves into top of each roll. Bake 15 minutes, or until browned. Makes 12 pecan rolls.

Our well-known "Red Barn" restaurant in Westport, Connecticut, makes a great specialty of these.

ORANGE SPIRAL ROLLS

1 package active dry, or 1 cake compressed, yeast
¼ cup water
1 cup milk, scalded
½ cup shortening
⅓ cup sugar
1 teaspoon salt

5 to 5½ cups sifted all-purpose flour
2 eggs
2 tablespoons grated orange peel
¼ cup orange juice
Orange Filling

Soften dry yeast in ¼ cup *warm* water, or compressed yeast in *lukewarm* water. Combine milk, shortening, sugar, and salt in mixing bowl. Let cool to lukewarm. Stir about 2 cups flour in and beat well. Add eggs, one at a time, beating well after each. Stir in softened yeast, orange peel, and juice. Add remaining flour, stirring to make a soft dough. Cover bowl with folded kitchen towel; let stand 10 minutes at room temperature.

Turn dough out onto lightly floured board, knead 5 to 10 minutes, or until smooth and elastic. Grease mixing bowl. Return dough to bowl, turning it once to grease its entire surface. Cover with towel. Let rise in warm, but not hot, place about 2 hours, or until doubled. Mix Orange Filling (see below).

Punch dough down. Turn out onto board. Cut in half. Cover with towel and let rest 10 minutes. Roll each half out lightly and quickly to a rectangle about 12 by 9 inches and ¼ inch thick. Spread with orange filling, roll up as for jelly roll, moisten edge and seal. Cut in 1-inch slices. Place cut side down in 24 cups of greased muffin pans. Cover with towel. Let rise in warm place about 45 to 60 minutes, until nearly double.

Start oven at moderately hot (400° F.). Bake rolls about 12 minutes, or until golden brown. Remove from pans. Serve warm. Makes about 2 dozen.

Orange Filling

½ cup sugar
½ cup chopped pecans

1 tablespoon grated orange peel
¼ cup melted butter or margarine

Combine all ingredients. Mix well. Use as described above in making orange-filled rolls.

Serve for buffet supper or carry out to a barbecue dinner on the terrace.

HOT CROSS BUNS

2 packages active dry, or 2 cakes compressed, yeast	3½ to 4 cups sifted all-purpose flour
⅓ cup water	1 teaspoon powdered cinnamon
⅓ cup milk scalded	
½ cup salad oil or melted shortening	3 eggs
	⅔ cup currants
⅓ cup sugar	3 tablespoons milk
¾ teaspoon salt	Confectioners' Topping

Soften active dry yeast in *warm* water, or *lukewarm* water for compressed yeast. Combine milk, salad oil or shortening, sugar, and salt in mixing bowl. Let cool to lukewarm. Sift 1 cup flour and the cinnamon into milk mixture. Add eggs. Beat well. Stir in softened yeast and currants. Add enough remaining flour to make soft dough. Cover bowl with damp cloth. Let rise in warm, not hot, place about 1½ hours, or until doubled.

Punch dough down. Turn it out on floured board. Roll it out lightly to about ½ inch thickness. Cut in rounds with 2½-inch biscuit cutter. Grease two (8-by-8-by-2-inch) pans; place 9 buns in each. Use scissors and snip top of each bun to form a cross. Cover pans with folded kitchen towel. Let rise in warm place about 45 minutes to 1 hour, or until almost double.

Start oven at moderate (375° F.). Brush tops of buns with milk. Bake 15 to 20 minutes, or until buns are lightly browned and shiny on top. Turn out on cake rack to cool. Drizzle tops with Confectioners' Topping. Makes 18 buns.

Confectioners' Topping: Combine 1½ cups sifted confectioners' sugar with warm water to make spreading consistency. Beat well.

SALLY LUNN

¼ cup milk, scalded	2 cups sifted all-purpose flour
6 tablespoons shortening	2 tablespoons sugar
1 package fresh dry, or 1 cake compressed, yeast	½ teaspoon salt
¼ cup lukewarm water	2 eggs, beaten

Combine milk and shortening. Let cool until lukewarm. Soften dry yeast in *warm* water, compressed yeast in *lukewarm* water. Let stand 5 to 10 minutes, or until well dissolved.

Sift flour, sugar, and salt together into large mixing bowl. Make well in center. Pour stirred-up yeast and shortening mixture in. Mix well. Let stand in warm place (80° to 85° F.), about 20 minutes. Stir 1 egg in. Mix well. Cover with folded kitchen towel. Let rise in warm place until double in bulk.

Grease two round 8-inch layer-cake pans.

Turn dough out onto lightly floured board. Knead lightly. Divide dough in half. Mold each into round, flat loaf. Place in prepared pans, pressing dough down with knuckles well into the pans. Cover pans with towel. Let rise in warm place until double in bulk.

Start oven at hot (425° F.). Brush tops of loaves with remaining egg. Bake 15 to 20 minutes, or until done. Serve hot, in wedges. Or next day split and toast wedges. Makes 2 loaves.

I'll always associate this with Colonial Williamsburg, where I first encountered it. The Sally Lunn pan there has a center hole and I make it that way too. A fine Sunday-night supper bread with cold roast beef or, maybe, chicken salad.

Quick Breads

Easily made biscuits, muffins, and rolls, made with your favorite recipes or from bought mixes, add good flavor and a special quality to any meal. Served hot, attractively presented in a napkin-lined basket, silver tray, painted box, or other favorite server, hot breads tell your family and guests that you gave special attention to planning and preparing the menu.

Delicious hot breads add a fillip to brunch, lunch, dinner, or supper. They are the high point of pleasure with tea served to a friend or to a large group. They add immeasurably to a coffee *klatsch* or any other hospitable occasion.

BAKING POWDER BISCUITS

2 cups sifted all-purpose flour	⅓ cup shortening
3 teaspoons baking powder	¾ cup milk
1 teaspoon salt	

Sift flour, baking powder, and salt together into mixing bowl. Cut shortening in with pastry blender until mixture is like coarse corn meal. Add milk, mixing lightly until dough holds together.

Start oven at hot (425° F.).

Transfer dough to floured board. Knead lightly. Roll dough ½ inch thick. Cut into large or small rounds or other shapes with floured cutter. Bake on lightly greased cooky sheet 12 to 15 minutes, until lightly browned. Serve at once. Makes 16 to 20 biscuits.

Biscuit Ideas

Canapés: Roll dough thin. Cut in fancy shapes. Bake 8 minutes. Spread while hot with any cheese mixture, or jelly, or fish paste. Serve as canapés with drinks or with soup or salad.

To top a meat or chicken pie: Roll biscuit dough thin. Spread with savory mixture of cheese and ketchup or deviled ham and ketchup. Roll up like jelly roll. Slice ½ inch thick. Lay slices on top of meat pie or casserole of stew or chicken. Heat in hot oven until Biscuit Wheels are done and browning.

Piroshki: The traditional recipe for these Russian filled rolls is given in the appetizers chapter. But an easy version is made with biscuit dough. Roll out as for biscuits. Cut in rounds. Spoon a little savory mixture of fish, meat, or chicken with egg and mayonnaise into center of each. Fold over and press edges together. Bake as for biscuits. Serve very hot, with appetizer drinks, soup, or salads.

Cheese Biscuits: Add ¼ cup grated Cheddar to dry ingredients. Complete recipe as described; sprinkle tops of biscuits on baking sheet with grated Parmesan cheese; bake as described. Serve hot.

Caramel Biscuits: Mix, roll, and cut biscuits as described. Rub muffin pans lightly with shortening. Place in each cup 1 teaspoon each butter, chopped nuts, and brown sugar. Place unbaked biscuit on top. Bake in hot oven 15 minutes or longer. Turn out upside down to serve. Specially nice for Sunday brunch.

Shortcake: The best shortcake dough is made with basic biscuit dough. Use Baking Powder Biscuit recipe. Add 2 tablespoons sugar to dry ingredients, 2 extra tablespoons shortening. Mix as described.

Cut with large biscuit cutter. Bake. Break open and spread rounds with butter while hot. Fill with sliced, sugared strawberries or other fruit. Serve with cream or whipped cream.

Biscuit Sticks: Mix biscuit dough. Roll out thin. Cut in sticks about 3 or 4 inches long, ½ inch wide. Place on baking sheet. Sprinkle sticks with salt, pepper, grated Parmesan cheese. Bake until browning, about 8 minutes. Serve with salads and drinks.

Or brush dough with milk. Sprinkle with onion salt, poppy or caraway seeds, and a light dusting of orégano. Bake as described.

Tiny Biscuits: Cut biscuit dough with very small floured cutter. Bake as described. Break open while hot and fill with jelly or finely minced salad mixtures, such as chicken with mayonnaise, lobster with mayonnaise, deviled ham with mustard and pimiento. Serve with salad or soup, or as appetizers with drinks.

Or brush unbaked tiny biscuits with milk. Sprinkle thickly with toasted sesame seeds or poppy seeds. Bake as described. Very small biscuits require shorter baking time.

CHEESE-PIMIENTO BISCUITS

2 cups sifted all-purpose flour	1 ½ cups grated Cheddar cheese
3 teaspoons baking powder	¼ cup finely cut drained,
½ teaspoon salt	canned pimiento
4 tablespoons shortening	1 tablespoon melted butter or
⅔ cup milk	margarine

Start oven at hot (425° F.). Grease baking sheet.

Sift flour, baking powder, and salt together into mixing bowl. Cut in shortening until mixture is like coarse crumbs. Add milk all at once. Stir just until dough follows fork around bowl. Turn out onto lightly floured board. Knead gently ½ minute.

Roll lightly into rectangle about ½ inch thick. Sprinkle with cheese and pimiento. Roll up as for jelly roll. Moisten edge and seal. Cut in 1-inch slices. Place slices cut side down on baking sheet. Bake 12 to 15 minutes, or until lightly browned. Serve at once. Makes 12 biscuits.

Perfect with salads.

CORN-MEAL BISCUITS

1 ½ cups sifted all-purpose flour	½ cup yellow corn meal
2 ½ teaspoons baking powder	⅓ cup shortening
½ teaspoon salt	⅔ cup milk

Sift flour, baking powder, and salt together into mixing bowl. Mix corn meal in. Cut shortening in until mixture is like coarse crumbs. Add milk, stirring lightly with fork, just enough to moisten all flour. Turn dough out on floured board. Knead lightly about ½ minute. Roll dough ½ to ¾ inch thick.

Start oven at hot (450° F.).

Cut dough with floured 2-inch cutter. Place on lightly greased baking sheet. Bake 12 to 15 minutes. Serve hot. Makes 12 biscuits.

This dough makes a delicious topping for meat pie, or stew, or casserole of chicken-and-leftovers. Add 1 or 2 tablespoons extra milk to dough when mixing. Drop by spoonful onto filled casserole. Bake in hot oven (450° F.) 12 to 15 minutes.

See suggestions for savory uses of Baking Powder Biscuits (page 82) and use Corn-Meal Biscuit dough in same recipes.

ONION BISCUITS

3 cups pancake mix	1 cup milk
3 tablespoons sugar	4 tablespoons melted butter
⅓ cup shortening	Onion salt

Start oven at hot (425° F.).

Combine pancake mix and sugar. Cut in shortening until mixture is in coarse crumbs. Add milk, stirring lightly only until mixture is dampened. Turn out on lightly floured board and knead gently a few seconds. Roll out to ¼ inch thickness. Cut with 3-inch round cutter.

Place rounds on lightly greased cooky sheet. Brush with melted butter. Sprinkle generously with onion salt. Fold over like pocketbook rolls. Brush top with melted butter. Sprinkle top with onion salt.

Bake 10 to 12 minutes, or until lighly browned. Makes 20 biscuits.

A delicious variation: Crisp a few canned or quick-frozen French-fried onions in the oven. Crumble. Add about 1 teaspoon crumbled onion to each buttered round. Fold over. Spread top with melted butter and sprinkle with onion salt. Bake as usual.

Delicious with salads, soup, or as a sprightly luncheon hot bread, or for a drawn-out Sunday breakfast with the Jewish specialty, lox (smoked salmon), cream cheese, and plenty of hot, strong coffee.

SOUTHERN BISCUITS

Substitute buttermilk for sweet milk in biscuit recipe, page 85. Use 2 teaspoons baking powder plus ¼ teaspoon baking soda. Add 2 tablespoons shortening to recipe. Follow biscuit recipe for mixing and baking.

Quick Loaves and Coffee Cakes

BANANA BREAD

2 eggs	1 ¾ cups sifted all-purpose flour
⅓ cup soft shortening	¾ teaspoon soda
2 ripe bananas, peeled and sliced	1 ¼ teaspoons cream of tartar
⅔ cup sugar	½ teaspoon salt

Start oven at moderate (350° F.). Grease 8-by-4-inch loaf pan.

Combine eggs, shortening, bananas, and sugar in glass container of blender. Cover and blend about 30 seconds, or until smooth. Sift dry ingredients together into mixing bowl. Pour blender combination over dry ingredients. Stir only until combined. Pour into greased loaf pan.

Bake about 45 minutes, or until lightly browned. Turn out of pan to cool on cake rack. When cool, wrap in waxed paper and chill several hours or overnight before slicing. Makes 1 loaf.

BLACK-WALNUT BREAD

2 ½ cups sifted all-purpose flour
3 teaspoons baking powder
1 teaspoon salt
½ cup sugar
4 tablespoons butter or margarine

1 cup chopped black walnuts
1 egg
1 cup milk

Start oven at moderate (350° F.). Grease loaf pan approximately 8½ by 4½ by 2½ inches.

Sift flour with baking powder, salt, and sugar into mixing bowl. Cut butter or margarine in until mixture is fine, then mix nuts in. Beat egg slightly. Combine with milk. Add dry ingredients all at once. Stir just enough to blend mixture. Pour into prepared pan.

Bake about 1 hour. Let cool. Remove from pan. Wrap in waxed paper for several hours or overnight before slicing. Makes 1 loaf, 10 or more servings.

At my grandfather's house on Staten Island the black walnuts came from his own tree, and the green outer shells, when dried, made a fine hot fire in the stoves of the old house. It's still fun to burn black-walnut shells—in your own fireplace!

COCONUT TEA LOAF

1 egg
1 ½ cups milk
½ teaspoon vanilla
¼ teaspoon almond flavoring
1 cup shredded coconut, toasted

3 cups sifted all-purpose flour
3 teaspoons baking powder
½ teaspoon salt
1 cup sugar

Start oven at moderate (350° F.). Grease 9-by-5-inch loaf pan.

Combine egg, milk, vanilla, flavoring, and coconut in glass container of blender. Cover and blend about 30 seconds, or until coconut is cut. Sift dry ingredients together into mixing bowl. Pour blender mixture over dry ingredients and stir only enough to combine. Pour into prepared pan.

Bake about 1 hour and 10 minutes, or until done. Turn loaf out of pan onto cake rack to cool. When thoroughly cooled, wrap in waxed paper and chill few hours in the refrigerator. Makes 1 loaf.

To toast coconut: Spread coconut thinly on baking pan. Set under low broiler and heat a few minutes, until edges are golden.

Why not double this recipe, bake in 2 pans, and put one loaf in the freezer or take one along to a city friend who hasn't time or talent for cooking (she imagines), or as a gift for a man—any nice man.

COFFEE CAKE WITH CHEESE TOPPING

1 egg, beaten slightly	1/16 teaspoon powdered allspice
2 tablespoons melted shorten-ing	1/2 cup brown sugar, packed
1/2 cup milk	1/4 cup all-purpose flour
1/2 cup sugar	2 tablespoons butter or marga-rine
1 cup sifted all-purpose flour	1/4 cup chopped almonds
1/2 teaspoon salt	1 cup cream-style cottage cheese
2 teaspoons baking powder	3/4 cup corn flakes, crushed
1/4 teaspoon powdered cinna-mon	

Start oven at moderate (375° F.). Grease 8-inch square pan.

Combine egg, shortening, milk, and sugar in mixing bowl. Add flour, salt, and baking powder sifted together. Mix well. Pour into prepared pan. Bake 20 minutes.

While cake bakes, mix topping: combine cinnamon, allspice, sugar, and flour in small bowl. Cut in butter or margarine with pastry blender. Add almonds and cheese. Mix well. Fold in corn flakes. Spread mixture on baked coffee cake. Broil 5 minutes under moderate broiler heat. Serve immediately. Makes 6 to 9 servings.

EASY RAISIN LOAF

2 cups pancake mix	4 tablespoons shortening
¼ cup brown sugar, packed	2 eggs, beaten
½ teaspoon powdered cinnamon	1 cup milk
¼ teaspoon powdered nutmeg	¾ cup seedless raisins
¼ teaspoon powdered allspice	

Combine pancake mix, brown sugar, and spices. Cut in shortening until mixture is coarse crumbs. Add eggs and milk, beating just enough to combine ingredients. Fold in raisins.

Start oven at moderate (350° F.). Grease 1-pound loaf pan. Line it with waxed paper and grease paper lightly. Pour batter into prepared pan.

Bake about 50 minutes. Let cool. Then store in bread box about 1 day before slicing. Makes 1 loaf.

Use as lunch or supper bread or make picnic and school sandwiches with it. Cut very thin, it makes a good tea sandwich with creamed butter or with jelly and cream cheese.

OATMEAL BREAD

1 cup seedless raisins	4 tablespoons shortening
2 cups sifted all-purpose flour	2 cups rolled oats
1 ½ teaspoons salt	½ cup molasses
4 teaspoons baking powder	1 ⅔ cups milk
⅓ cup sugar	

Wash and drain raisins, and soak few minutes. Drain. Sift flour, salt, baking powder, and sugar together into a mixing bowl. Cut shortening in until blended. Mix raisins and oats. Add to flour mixture. Stir molasses and milk in until blended.

Grease and flour loaf pan approximately 9½ by 5¼ by 2¾ inches. Pour dough into prepared pan. Cover lightly with folded kitchen towel and let stand 20 minutes before baking.

Start oven at moderate, (350° F.). Bake 1 hour. Remove loaf from pan. Let cool on rack. Makes 1 loaf.

This bread will always be associated in my mind with World War I and the wheat shortage. We baked our own oatmeal bread, and a delicious wartime "sacrifice" loaf it was. One of my earliest memories about cookery.

Corn Sticks, Muffins, Popovers, Scones, Spoon Bread

BLENDER CORN STICKS

1 cup sifted all-purpose flour	2 eggs
¾ cup yellow corn meal	1 cup milk
1 teaspoon salt	2 teaspoons sugar
3 teaspoons baking powder	4 tablespoons shortening

Start oven at moderately hot (400° F.). Grease 12-stick corn-stick pan or 9-inch square pan.

Sift flour, corn meal, salt, and baking powder together into mixing bowl. Combine eggs, milk, sugar, and shortening in glass container of blender and blend about 15 seconds, or until smooth. Pour blended mixture over dry ingredients. Stir lightly, only enough to combine mixtures.

Bake in stick pan or square pan 20 to 25 minutes, or until crisp and browned. Makes 12 corn sticks or 9 squares.

I have a fireplace in my kitchen in Weston where I hang some of my old bread molds and pans. It's a nice hobby to collect ancient kitchen utensils and pans and to use them as well as display them. I found my wooden Dutch speculaas molds in Hoorn and have brought out their beauty by waxing them carefully with ox blood shoe polish as I was advised to do by antiquarian Nicolas Kreuse of Amsterdam's "Five Flies" restaurant.

MUFFINS

1 ¾ cups sifted all-purpose flour	1 egg, well beaten
1 tablespoon baking powder	½ cup evaporated milk
2 tablespoons sugar	½ cup water
1 teaspoon salt	¼ cup melted shortening

Start oven at hot (425° F.). Grease 12-cup muffin pan.

Sift flour, baking powder, sugar, and salt together into mixing bowl. Mix egg, milk, water, and shortening. Add all at once to flour mixture. Mix quickly and thoroughly. Divide dough among 12 greased 2-inch muffin pans, filling each ⅔ full. Set pan in center of oven.

Bake 25 minutes, or until tops are browned. Makes 12 muffins.

Serve these warm. Break open with the fingers or fork, plop butter or a little jelly into each, or eat plain.

Blueberry Muffins: Add ½ cup of drained, cooked or canned blueberries to muffin batter.

Nut Muffins: Add ½ cup of chopped nuts to muffin batter.

ORANGE MUFFINS

1 ¾ cups sifted all-purpose flour	1 egg, well beaten
2 ½ teaspoons baking powder	¾ cup milk
2 tablespoons sugar	⅓ cup salad oil or melted
¾ teaspoon salt	shortening
3 tablespoons grated orange peel	12 sugar cubes
	Orange cubes

Start oven at moderately hot (400° F.). Grease 12-cup muffin pan.

Sift dry ingredients and orange peel together into mixing bowl. Make a well in center. Combine egg, milk, and salad oil or shortening. Add all at once to dry ingredients. Mix quickly, only until dry ingredients are moistened. Drop batter from tablespoon into muffin pans, filling each ⅔ full. Dip sugar cubes in orange juice until soaked. Place 1 cube on top of each muffin.

Bake about 25 minutes. Makes 12 muffins.

A good tea muffin, but equally popular as the bread for a light luncheon or for brunch.

SOUR-CREAM MUFFINS

1 ¾ cups sifted all-purpose flour	½ teaspoon soda
2 teaspoons baking powder	1 egg
¼ teaspoon salt	1 ½ cups commercial sour cream
3 tablespoons sugar	

Start oven at hot (425° F.). Grease 12-cup muffin pan.

Sift dry ingredients together into mixing bowl. Beat egg until foamy, add cream, and mix well. Stir into dry ingredients until just mixed. Pour into muffin pan.

Bake about 20 minutes. Makes 12 muffins.

COUNTRY CORN STICKS

⅓ cup butter or margarine	2 teaspoons salt
2 ¼ cups sifted all-purpose flour	¼ cup milk
2 tablespoons sugar	1 cup cream-style corn
4 teaspoons baking powder	

Start oven at hot (450° F.).

Melt butter or margarine in pan approximately 13 by 9 by 2-inches. Sift flour, sugar, baking powder, and salt together into a mixing bowl. Add milk and corn. Stir until soft dough is formed. Turn out onto well-floured board. Knead dough, fold, and knead about 15 times. Roll out in rectangle ½ inch thick. Cut into strips about 1 inch wide. Roll strips in melted butter or margarine in baking pan and arrange in the pan.

Bake 20 to 30 minutes, or until browned and edges are crisp. Makes 24 sticks. Serve warm.

Serve for lunch or supper or as accompaniment to soup or salad. Delicious cold, too, and appreciated in the lunch box if a little container of marmalade or apple butter is included for dunking.

GINGERBREAD

⅓ cup shortening	2 teaspoons baking powder
½ cup light-brown sugar (packed)	½ teaspoon soda
1 well-beaten egg	2 teaspoons powdered ginger
⅔ cup light molasses	1 teaspoon powdered cinnamon
2 cups all-purpose flour, sifted	¼ teaspoon powdered cloves
½ teaspoon salt	¾ cup buttermilk or sour milk

Start oven at moderate (350° F.). Line 9-inch square pan with waxed paper. Grease paper. Cream shortening and sugar together until light and fluffy. Stir egg and molasses in and beat well. Sift flour with salt, baking powder, soda and spices three times, then sift into egg mixture alternately with buttermilk or sour milk. Beat well. Pour into prepared pan. Bake in moderate oven 50 minutes, or until cake tester inserted deeply comes out clean. Leave plain, or top with any preferred icing. I like to serve it warm with mace-flavored, lightly sweetened whipped cream. Makes 16 or more squares.

POPOVERS

2 eggs	½ teaspoon salt
1 cup milk	1 tablespoon melted shortening
1 cup sifted all-purpose flour	

Start oven at very hot (475° F.). Grease 8 custard cups or an iron or heavy aluminum popover pan.

Break eggs into mixing bowl. Add milk, flour, and salt. Beat 1½ minutes with rotary or electric beater. Add melted shortening. Beat ½ minute. Don't overbeat. Fill 8 well-greased cups ½ full.

Bake 10 minutes. Reduce heat to moderate (350° F.). Continue baking about 25 to 30 minutes, until browned and firm.

A few minutes before removing from oven, prick each popover with a sharp prong of kitchen fork or large darning needle to let steam escape.

If you prefer popovers which are dry inside, turn off oven and let baked popovers stay 30 minutes, oven door ajar. Serve hot with plenty of butter. Makes 8 popovers.

This is a Sunday morning company breakfast treat served with apple butter, cottage cheese, scrambled eggs and sausages. (No Sunday dinner *chez nous*).

SCONES

2 cups sifted all-purpose flour	¼ cup dried currants, soaked and drained
½ teaspoon salt	
2½ teaspoons baking powder	1 egg, beaten
3 tablespoons sugar	¾ cup milk (a little less)
⅓ cup shortening	

Sift flour, salt, and baking powder together into mixing bowl. Add 2 tablespoons sugar. Cut shortening into dry ingredients until evenly mixed. Stir in currants. Combine egg and ½ cup milk. Add to flour mixture all at once. Stir lightly with fork, only until all flour is moistened. Turn dough out onto lightly floured board; knead gently about ½ minute.

Start oven at hot (450° F.).

Cut dough in half. Roll each piece into a round ¼ inch thick. Place rounds on lightly greased baking sheet. Cut each round with sharp knife into 6 pie-shaped pieces. Brush tops with remaining milk. Sprinkle with remaining 1 tablespoon of sugar.

Bake 10 to 12 minutes, or until well browned. Serve hot with butter and jam. Makes 12 servings.

This is the traditional Scotch bread for afternoon tea. The dough is sometimes cut with large, round cooky cutter and baked in rounds on a hot griddle with cover. The oven method, however, is the easiest.

It seems to me that I knew my way around London before I knew the streets of New York well, and teatime and Lyons (the famous tea shops of London) will ever be associated in my mind. Especially delicious were the scones with the bitter-sweet marmalade made from Seville oranges, and tea that was tea—properly made.

SPOON BREAD

3 cups milk
1 cup yellow corn meal
3 eggs
3 teaspoons butter or margarine

1 teaspoon salt
1 teaspoon baking powder
1 tablespoon softened butter

Combine 2 cups milk and corn meal in saucepan. Cook slowly until milk is absorbed. Stir frequently. Remove from heat. Beat egg yolks slightly. Add to corn-meal mixture with remaining 1 cup milk, 2 teaspoons butter or margarine, the salt, and baking powder. Mix well until smooth and evenly blended.

Start oven at moderate (350° F.). Grease 2-quart casserole.

Whip egg whites stiff. Fold into corn-meal mixture. Pour into casserole.

Bake 45 minutes. Serve hot in dish in which it baked; add spoonful softened butter to top of casserole. Makes 6 servings.

This is a favorite of mine for buffets. We use white or yellow corn meal, preferably stone ground. You can order it from various millers who advertise in the cookery and home-decorating magazines, and from the grocery departments of large-city department stores. Health stores have it, too, along with other delights you should investigate, such as cracked wheat, Roman meal, many beans such as soy and mung and spooning honeys by-the-can, jar and tube—Greek honey, for instance.

TOMATO-CHEESE SPOON BREAD

¾ cup sifted all-purpose flour	1 (19-ounce) can (2 ⅛ cups)
3 teaspoons baking powder	tomatoes, chopped
1 ½ teaspoons salt	⅓ cup melted shortening
2 tablespoons sugar	1 cup shredded Cheddar
1 cup yellow corn meal	cheese
2 eggs, slightly beaten	1 ½ tablespoons grated onion
1 ½ cups milk	

Start oven at moderate (325° F.). Grease 2-quart casserole.

Sift flour, baking powder, salt, and sugar together into mixing bowl. Stir in corn meal. Combine remaining ingredients; pour into flour mixture. Beat only enough to moisten all flour. Pour into casserole.

Bake about 1 hour and 10 minutes, or until set. Serve warm in dish in which it baked. Makes 6 servings.

Makes good supper dish for a cold night. Serve green salad, maybe a soup first, depending on family appetites. Just as good for guest luncheon; flavorful with salad, and gala dessert to follow—such as pecan pie, and coffee or tea.

Doughnuts

COUNTRY RAISED DOUGHNUTS

1 cup milk	1 egg
1 package active dry, or 1	2 tablespoons grated lemon
cake compressed, yeast	peel
¼ cup warm water	1 ½ teaspoons powdered nutmeg
¾ cup, plus 1 tablespoon sugar	1 teaspoon salt
4 ½ cups sifted all-purpose flour	Salad oil
3 tablespoons butter or marga-	Fat for deep-frying
rine	Confectioners' sugar

Scald milk. Pour into mixing bowl or large electric-mixer bowl. Let cool until lukewarm.

Soften dry yeast in *warm* water, compressed yeast in *lukewarm* water; stir until dissolved. Stir yeast into milk. Add 1 tablespoon sugar. Beat in 1½ cups flour, with electric mixer or by hand with egg beater, until smooth. Cover bowl with folded towel. Let rise in warm place, about 85° F., about 1 hour.

Cream butter or margarine with remaining ¾ cup sugar in small bowl of mixer or by hand. Add egg, lemon peel, nutmeg, and salt.

Continue to beat until fluffy. Beat sugar mixture into yeast mixture. Beat in remaining 3 cups flour.

Grease mixing bowl. Turn dough into bowl. Brush top with salad oil. Cover bowl with towel as before and let rise in warm place until doubled in bulk.

Turn dough out onto lightly floured board. Roll ½ inch thick. Cut with floured doughnut cutter. Place doughnuts on floured board. Let rise in warm place until doubled in bulk.

Heat fat (enough to make 1½ inches deep in frying kettle) to 370° F. on frying thermometer. Fry doughnuts until golden brown. Let drain on thick paper towels until cool, or sprinkle while warm with confectioners' sugar. Makes 2½ dozen.

If you have an electric deep-fat fryer, with its easily handled basket, all such frying jobs are so simple. And of course you can reuse the fat.

CHOCOLATE DOUGHNUTS

1 ⅓ cups sifted all-purpose flour	1 egg
½ teaspoon baking soda	½ cup granulated sugar
½ teaspoon baking powder	⅓ cup commercial sour cream
⅛ teaspoon powdered nutmeg	Fat for deep-frying
¼ teaspoon salt	Confectioners' sugar
¼ cup semi-sweet chocolate pieces, melted	

Heat fat (enough to make 1½ inches deep in frying kettle) to 370° F. on frying thermometer. Let fat heat slowly.

Sift flour, soda, baking powder, nutmeg, and salt together. Beat in chocolate. Beat egg and granulated sugar together in mixing bowl until light and thick. Beat in cream, then chocolate mixture.

Drop this dough by teaspoonfuls into hot fat. Turn nuggets as they fry, until browned and done. Let drain on thick paper towels until cool, or sprinkle while warm with confectioners' sugar. Makes about 2 dozen chocolate doughnuts.

To Glaze Doughnuts

1 cup sifted confectioners' sugar	2 tablespoons cold water

Beat sugar and water together until well blended. Using tongs, dip one side of doughnuts, while hot, into the mixture. Place glazed side up on cake rack to drip and cool. Substitute orange juice for water in this mixture for a delicious version of glazed doughnuts.

Pancakes

To make good pancakes you need special griddles and pans as well as sound, simple recipes. Flavor, shape, and texture of pancakes depend in part on the griddle or pan. Certain griddles must be properly seasoned for success. That is, used several times with generous coating of fat before you can bake good pancakes on them. *Never* scour them. I do wash mine (some cooks never do) but I am careful not to dry them out on a hot stove, which destroys their temper.

All griddles in housewares shops bear labels or tags which guide you in using them and caring for them. Today's cast iron, heavy aluminum, soapstone, and new metals such as stainless steel combine most of the virtues of the old-fashioned heavy-iron griddles, plus ease of handling and cleanability.

There are various specialty pancake pans, such as the *Swedish plättar pan,* having 4 to 6 small round indentions. And for *crêpes suzette* there is a special shallow pan with sloping sides, the handle set at a proper angle for convenient grasping. Under the crêpes pan a candle, alcohol flame, or small electric unit is used for the final steps in preparing these dessert pancakes. And of course a chafing-dish pan is used for crêpes, the pancakes more often than not prepared in the kitchen or bought in a jar, then given the final heating in butter with jam and a liqueur in the crêpes pan or chafing dish at the table.

German pancakes should be made in a large, light-weight frying pan with sloping sides and easily grasped handle. Electric frying pans may be used for pancakes: read the label instructions before buying such a pan for your utensil cupboard, and make sure it is usable for pancakes as well as for the many other kinds of skillet cookery.

BLINTZES

1 cup sifted all-purpose flour	½ cup cream-style cottage cheese
½ teaspoon salt	½ cup apricot jam
3 eggs	Fat for deep-frying
1 cup water	Sifted confectioners' sugar

Sift flour and salt together into mixing bowl. Beat eggs. Combine with water. Add to flour mixture. Beat lightly until smooth. Pour 2 to 4 tablespoons of batter into lightly greased frying pan. When batter draws away from side of pan, turn pancake and bake 1 minute on other side. Lift it out to thick paper toweling. When all blintzes are baked, spoon 1 tablespoon mixed cottage cheese and apricot jam into center of each. Fold cake over filling. Lay filled pancakes in frying basket. Lower into deep hot fat. Fry until lightly browned. Drain 1 minute. Serve hot with light sprinkling of confectioners' sugar. Makes 4 to 6 blintzes.

Russian Blintzes: Omit apricot jam. Fill with cheese; fry as described. Top with red caviar, sour cream, and chopped chives.

I sometimes serve them this way on our cool Connecticut summer nights to a small crowd after the theater or Pop concert. Hot tea, Russian style, in thin glasses, with lump sugar and clove-stuck lemon slices, goes with the blintzes. This is a good freezer recipe. Of course you can buy very good ready-frozen blintzes, too. Your own or ready-made ones are good Sunday night fare in front of TV. I always have them on hand.

FILLED PANCAKES

2 cups canned berries	1 cup pancake mix
1 cup sugar	2 tablespoons melted butter or
2 eggs, beaten	margarine
1 ½ cups milk	

Combine berries and sugar. Bring to a boil, lower heat and cook 10 minutes. Keep berries warm while pancakes are made.

Combine beaten eggs, milk, pancake mix, and 1 tablespoon butter or margarine, stirring until smooth. Place remaining 1 tablespoon butter or margarine in small frying pan and heat until fat bubbles. Pour in enough batter to coat bottom of pan with a thin layer. Bake until delicately browned on under side; turn cake and bake on other side. Stack hot cakes in pan in hot oven with its door left open.

To serve, place 2 tablespoons warm berries on each pancake. Roll up jelly-roll fashion. Serve at once. Makes 6 servings.

Plättar, Swedish Pancakes: For small dessert pancakes, bake cakes in greased plättar pan. Or for each cake pour about 2 teaspoons of batter on hot greased griddle. Plättar should be about 2½ inches in diameter. For each serving use 4 to 6 little cakes sprinkled with powdered sugar and a spoonful of canned lingonberries in center of plate.

My youngest ate *forty* of these at one sitting aboard the youth hostel ship, "Af Chapman", in Stockholm harbor one lovely summer.

BLUEBERRY PANCAKES

2 cups pancake mix
2 cups milk
1 egg, slightly beaten
2 tablespoons melted shortening or butter

1 cup drained blueberries (fresh, frozen, or canned)
Butter and syrup, or
Cinnamon and sugar

Add milk, eggs, and melted shortening or butter to the mix, stirring lightly. Fold in drained blueberries. Bake on hot, greased griddle. Turn cakes once. Serve hot with butter and syrup or cinnamon and sugar. Makes 14 to 16 pancakes.

We love these for a leisurely Saturday or Sunday breakfast. We gather our own blueberries in a wild shooting preserve near us, quarts and quarts of berries in June and July. I make and freeze blueberry muffins and pies and freeze containers of blueberries for winter pancakes. How good they taste on a bitter January day. The children remember our summer blueberrying as they trudge through the snow to Sunday school after a pancake breakfast.

CORN-MEAL PANCAKES

1 cup yellow corn meal
1 cup sifted all-purpose flour
1 tablespoon baking powder
1 tablespoon sugar
1½ teaspoons salt

2½ cups milk
2 eggs
4 tablespoons melted butter or margarine

Sift first 5 ingredients together into mixing bowl. Combine milk, eggs, butter or margarine. Stir into dry ingredients. Beat 1 or 2 minutes, until just blended. Pour batter on hot griddle by ¼ cup for large cakes, or pour 2 or 3 tablespoonfuls for each smaller cake. Makes 10 or more pancakes.

Serve with butter and syrup or honey, or with crisp bacon.

These are fine, too, for lunch Southern style, with leftover stew, beef or lamb, creamed chicken, turkey, or oysters. A specialty of the famous Argyl in San Antonio is served this way.

GERMAN PANCAKES

Pfannkuchen

5 or 6 eggs	Powdered cinnamon
1 ½ cups sifted all-purpose flour	Sugar
¼ teaspoon salt	Lemon juice
2 tablespoons sugar	Cooked apples, or
1 cup light cream	Blueberries, or
1 cup milk	Currant jam
½ pound butter or margarine	

Beat eggs lightly. Beat in flour, salt, sugar, cream, and milk. Beat 5 minutes to make batter smooth and light.

Use large light frying pan with high sides. Melt enough butter in pan to coat bottom and sides by tilting pan. When hot, pour in about ½ cup batter. Turn pan and tilt it so batter spreads to form large, thin pancake reaching a little up pan sides. Cook until pancake begins to look a little dry and golden brown around the edge. Turn it and brown other side quickly. Slip cake onto large warmed platter. Sprinkle lavishly with cinnamon and sugar, add squeeze of lemon, spoonful of apples, blueberries, or jam. Fold and cut in half, making 2 servings out of each large cake. Recipe makes 4 to 6 cakes, depending on size of pan used. Serve pancake as soon as baked; other guests must wait for theirs.

A puffy pancake is preferred by chefs in old-time German restaurants. To get this result, as soon as pancake is browned on one side the skillet is set in a very hot oven (550° F.) for 3 to 4 minutes. Cake puffs and browns delicately. It is then sprinkled with cinnamon, sugar, and any one of several sweet jams or cooked fruits added to center, then served at once, 1 huge cake to a person.

COUNTRY PANCAKES

1 cup sifted all-purpose flour	1 cup buttermilk
1 tablespoon sugar	2 tablespoons melted butter or
½ teaspoon salt	margarine
½ teaspoon baking powder	Syrup
½ teaspoon baking soda	Butter
2 eggs	

Sift dry ingredients into mixing bowl. Beat egg whites until stiff but not dry. Beat egg yolks until thick and lemon-colored. Stir buttermilk and butter or margarine into yolks. Pour yolk mixture over dry ingredients and stir only until blended. Fold in egg whites.

Heat griddle or heavy frying pan very slowly. Test temperature by sprinkling a few drops of water on it. When drops bounce about, temperature is right. Grease lightly or not, according to kind of griddle.

Ladle or pour batter onto heated griddle, using about ¼ cup for each cake. Bake until bubbles appear on top and begin to break and edges of cake are dry; turn cake; brown other side. Keep cakes hot on pan in hot oven with its door open, until all are ready.

Serve hot with syrup and butter. Makes 12 pancakes.

FRENCH DESSERT PANCAKES

Crêpes Suzette

1 cup sifted all-purpose flour	2 eggs, slightly beaten
¼ teaspoon salt	1 cup apricot jam
2 tablespoons sugar	Confectioners' sugar
½ teaspoon powdered cinnamon	2 tablespoons butter or margarine
1 ¾ cups milk	1 tablespoon cognac or cointreau, optional
2 tablespoons melted butter or margarine	

Sift flour, salt, sugar, and cinnamon together into bowl. Add milk and butter or margarine to eggs. Stir into flour mixture. Beat with a rotary beater until smooth. Grease 5-inch skillet. Heat, then pour in 3 tablespoons of batter. Tilt pan quickly until batter covers bottom. Bake until pancake is brown on bottom. Turn pancake and brown other side. Keep crêpes warm on pan in hot oven with its door open.

When all is ready, place 2 teaspoons of jam in center of each pancake. Roll. Dust with confectioners' sugar. Heat butter or margarine in chafing dish with remaining ½ cup jam and cognac or liqueur.

Place rolled crêpes in chafing dish. Spoon hot sauce over them for 1 or 2 minutes, while sauce bubbles around them. Serve on warmed dessert plates. Makes 12 crêpes, 6 to 12 servings.

The crêpes may be served flambé: Fill large serving spoon with cognac. Ignite it with match. Stir into remaining sauce in chafing dish. Quickly spoon sauce, while still flaming, onto the rolled crêpes.

Waffles

CHOCOLATE NUT WAFFLES

2 cups pancake mix	½ cup chopped nuts
2 cups chocolate milk (bought)	1 ½ pints vanilla ice cream
⅓ cup melted shortening	Chocolate Syrup (page 58)
2 eggs	

Combine pancake mix, chocolate milk, shortening, and eggs in mixing bowl. Beat with rotary beater until fairly smooth. Stir in nuts. Bake on hot waffle iron until steam stops. Serve hot with vanilla ice cream and Chocolate Syrup. Makes 5 servings.

Teen-agers' delight: Makes a popular dessert for a school club meeting at your house or a party in the rumpus room. Batter can be mixed ahead of time, kept in refrigerator, and beaten again just before baking.

CORN-MEAL WAFFLES

1 cup sifted all-purpose flour	1 cup yellow corn meal
2 teaspoons baking powder	2 eggs, beaten
1 teaspoon baking soda	2 cups buttermilk
1 teaspoon sugar	4 tablespoons shortening,
½ teaspoon salt	melted

Sift flour, baking powder, soda, sugar, and salt together into mixing bowl. Stir in corn meal. Combine eggs, buttermilk, and shortening. Stir into dry ingredients. Mix only enough to moisten all flour. Bake in hot waffle baker. Makes 3 to 4 large waffles. Especially good with simple butter-and-molasses topping.

A winter Sunday breakfast favorite with sausages or bacon. Equally popular at Daisyfields as a Sunday supper waffle. Corned-beef hash, or creamed lamb hash or creamed chipped beef is served with the waffles.

DIXIE WAFFLES

2 eggs	3 teaspoons baking powder
1 ½ cups milk	1 teaspoon sugar
¼ cup salad oil or melted shortening	¼ teaspoon salt
2 cups sifted all-purpose flour	½ cup pecan halves

Place eggs, milk, and salad oil in blender. Cover. Run at high speed about 30 seconds, or until creamy. Add remaining ingredients, except pecans. Mix at high speed about 1½ minutes, or until smooth. Scrape mixture from sides of container with rubber spatula during blending.

If mixed by hand, beat thoroughly but quickly.

Pour batter onto hot waffle iron. Sprinkle batter with pecans. Bake until golden brown. Makes 6 medium or 12 small waffles.

Serve with any favorite syrup or dusted with powdered sugar and a little melted butter. Or serve as dessert or as a brunch bread.

CHAPTER FIVE

Cakes, Cupcakes, Cookies, Frostings

Cake making is not a magic art to be enjoyed by only a few home-makers. It is one of the most rewarding branches of home cookery. But it is an exacting kind of cookery: the recipe must be accurate and it must be followed exactly in measuring, mixing, and in all procedures. Pans, mixing bowls, blender, and other equipment must be those specified in the recipe. Oven temperature should be even and thermometer-controlled.

Cakes made with shortening are mixed differently from the non-shortening cakes—the sponge and angel cakes. When baked, the cake made with shortening is different in texture, appearance, and flavor from the non-shortening cake. Some cake recipes are adaptable to baking in layer pans or loaf or sheet pans. Some specify tube pan or mold. In many of the following recipes the batter may be baked in cupcake pans, instead of the layer pans for variety.

The ingredients for a cake must not only be those called for in the recipe, but they must be of the best quality: fine-grained sugar, fresh fats softened at room temperature, cake flour or all-purpose flour sifted before measuring, then sifted again with dry ingredients. Eggs must be of fresh and of finest quality, with a thick white and a yolk that does not spread when the egg is broken. If you have access to fresh-laid eggs, keep them for three days before using in cakes. Remove eggs from the refrigerator thirty minutes before using in a cake recipe.

The electric mixer is not essential to good cake making but it is a time-and-labor-saving helper. The electric-mixed cake can be smoother and lighter than the hand-beaten cake when the mechanical beating instructions are followed exactly. Read the manufacturer's leaflet which came with your mixer or blender for guidance in using the appliance for cake mixing as well as for its many other uses. Many of my cake recipes call for electric beating. These give exact time and speed instructions as well as exact hand-mixing instructions.

Oven temperature and baking time are given in all recipes. Place cake pans near center of oven, but not touching each other. Do not place one cake pan directly over another on a lower shelf. A good batter, properly mixed, in an oven of right temperature should give you a cake which rises a little during the first quarter of its baking time, then continues to rise and brown slightly during the next quarter. The browning continues in the third quarter, and the cake finishes baking and shrinks slightly from the sides of the pan in the last quarter of the specified baking period.

Use a thin metal cake tester. Insert it near the center of the cake or layer. If tester comes out clean, the cake is done. Also, a cake when done springs back when pressed lightly with finger. Always test cake for doneness.

Read your cake recipe carefully. Assemble all ingredients and have them ready at room temperature for at least fifteen minutes before mixing. If boiling water is called for, put fresh water on to boil. If scalded milk is an ingredient, put milk on to scald so it is steaming hot just as you are ready to use it. Follow recipe instructions as to when to start the oven and how to prepare baking pans. Use pan of right size, the pan called for in the recipe. Measure all ingredients exactly, using standard measuring spoons, cups, and other utensils. Follow mixing instructions and all others to last detail.

When baked layers or larger cakes have cooled, make filling and frosting. Brush any loose crumbs from cake. Place layers together with filling or frosting according to recipe. Cover sides of cake with frosting, then frost top, spreading frosting out to the edge with light swirling motion of spatula unless frosting is the poured-on variety.

Serve cake the day it is baked, or keep it in a cool place, not the refrigerator, in tightly covered container. Some cakes can be frozen. Recipes for such cakes include freezing instructions. Some cakes, such as poundcake and fruitcake, may be wrapped and stored for several days, or, in the case of fruitcake, several weeks or months, with good results. Follow recipe suggestions on serving and storing.

If you live in a high-altitude state or move to a place which is 2,000 feet or higher above sea level, write to the Home Economics Department of the local state university or to the Bureau of Home Economics, Department of Agriculture, Washington, D.C., for help in changing your favorite cake recipes, and other baking recipes, over to high-altitude measures for the baking powder, liquid, sugar, shortening, and the oven temperature.

When using commercial cake mixes, follow the manufacturer's directions exactly for best results. These wonder cakes are time-savers. Many of the mixes, worked out with care and emphasis on texture, flavor, and appearance, make delicious eating. Filling, frosting, and other ingredients may be included in the package. Keep your favorite cake mixes in your kitchen for ready baking when the menu calls for cake, cupcakes, and cookies.

The causes of failure in cake baking can be eliminated if you follow recipes exactly, as I suggested at the beginning of the cake chapter.

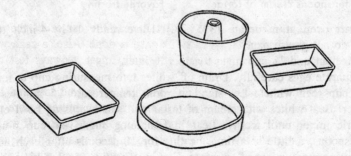

This means, of course, that you are using standard measuring cups and spoons and using them *level full,* not heaping—using them exactly as the recipe suggests.

In recipes your friends give you, or others which you try when you may not be sure of amounts and methods, remember that a *coarse-textured cake* may result from too much leavening or not enough liquid. Or maybe you did not cream the butter and sugar and dry ingredients together smoothly. Also, too slow an oven can coarsen a cake, as can too much shortening and sugar.

A dry cake can come from too much flour, not enough shortening and sugar, overbeaten egg whites, or too-long baking.

Too hot an oven can hump the cake up in the middle and crack the crust as well. *A soggy streak* through the cake can mean either too much liquid or not enough mixing to smoothly blend and integrate all ingredients.

Too much sugar will make a *sticky crust* on the cake. *Use the size of pan called for,* because too-large a pan makes a thin, undersized layer.

Too-small a pan will cause batter to flow over the sides when baking begins. *The too-slow oven* may cause the same sad mess and so will too much sugar or shortening.

It's best to compare a new recipe, or one which doesn't look right, with a similar recipe you have made in the past with success.

My Favorite Cakes

ANGEL CAKE

1 cup sifted cake flour	¼ teaspoon salt
1 ⅝ cups sugar	1 ½ teaspoons vanilla
12 egg whites	½ teaspoon almond flavoring
1 ½ teaspoons cream of tartar	Favorite frosting

Start oven at moderate (375° F.). Have ready 10-by-4-inch tube pan; do not grease pan.

Sift flour and ¾ cup sugar together 3 times.

Separate eggs carefully. Drain off whites into measuring cup to make 1½ cups egg whites. Let stand at room temperature 15 minutes or longer. Beat whites with cream of tartar and salt in mixing bowl or in electric mixer until frothy. Beat in remaining sugar, ¾ cup plus 2 tablespoons, a little at a time, beating for 10 seconds after each addition using medium speed on mixer. Continue beating, now at high speed on mixer, until meringue is firm and holds stiff points when whip is pulled out. Fold in flavorings.

Sift flour-sugar mixture, about 3 tablespoons at a time, over meringue. Cut and fold gently with wire whip until flour-sugar mixture disappears each time. Use rubber scraper and push batter from mixing bowl into tube pan. Spread and level batter against tube and sides of pan. Cut through batter gently with a knife.

Bake 30 to 35 minutes or until no imprint remains when finger lightly touches top of cake. Invert cake immediately, placing tube over upturned funnel on kitchen table. Let hang until cold. Remove cake from pan. Frost as preferred. Makes 8 or more servings.

Delicious with a rich dark chocolate frosting. Handsome with white boiled frosting or a lemon- or orange-flavored pour-on frosting. Try serving it with old-fashioned wine jelly.

DEVIL'S FOOD CAKE

1 ½	cups sifted all-purpose flour	½	cup shortening
1 ½	cups sugar	1	cup milk
1 ¼	teaspoons baking soda	1	teaspoon vanilla
1	teaspoon salt	3	eggs
¼	cup powdered cocoa		
¼	cup finely grated sweet chocolate		

Start oven at moderate (350° F.). Grease two round 8-inch cake pans; dust lightly with flour.

Sift dry ingredients together into bowl. Add shortening, milk, and vanilla. Beat 2 minutes, medium mixer speed, or 300 hand strokes. Scrape sides and bottom of bowl constantly. Add eggs. Beat 2 minutes more, scraping constantly. Pour into prepared pans.

Bake about 38 minutes. Let cool in pans a few minutes, then turn out on cake rack. Frost with dark or light icing. Makes 8 servings.

The *absolute* favorite of my three sons and, I suspect, of small boys everywhere.

CHOCOLATE GOLD CAKE

2 eggs	⅓ cup cooking oil
1 ½ cups sugar	1 cup milk
2 ¼ cups sifted cake flour	1 ½ teaspoons vanilla
2 teaspoons baking powder	Soft Chocolate Frosting
1 teaspoon salt	(page 130)

Start oven at moderate (350° F.). Grease two round 8-inch layer pans or one oblong pan 13 by 9½ by 2 inches. Dust lightly with flour.

Beat egg whites until frothy. Beat in ½ cup sugar until stiff and glossy.

Sift remaining sugar, flour, baking powder, and salt together into another bowl. Add oil, half of milk, and the vanilla. Beat 1 minute medium speed in electric mixer or 150 strokes by hand; scrape sides and bottom of bowl constantly. Add remaining milk and the 2 egg yolks. Beat 1 minute as before, scraping bowl constantly. Fold in meringue. Pour into prepared pans.

Bake layers 30 to 35 minutes, oblong pan 40 to 45 minutes. Let cakes cool in pans few minutes, then turn out onto cake rack.

When layers are cold, put together with thick coating of Soft Chocolate Frosting; cover top and sides with remaining frosting. For oblong cake, make ½ frosting recipe. Layer cake makes 8 servings, oblong cake 12 squares.

BRIDE'S CAKE

¾ cup shortening	6 egg whites
2 cups sugar	½ cup chopped blanched
1 teaspoon vanilla	almonds
3 cups sifted cake flour	¼ cup chopped mixed candied
½ teaspoon salt	fruit
4 teaspoons baking powder	Bride's Cake Frosting (page 125)
1 cup milk	

Start oven at moderate (350° F.). Grease two round 10-inch layer-cake pans. Line with waxed paper. Grease paper.

Cream shortening and sugar together thoroughly in mixing bowl. Add vanilla. Sift flour, salt, and baking powder together; add alternately with milk to shortening and sugar.

Whip egg whites stiff. Fold into batter. Add nuts and fruit. Pour into prepared pans.

Bake 30 minutes or until cake tester inserted in center of each layer comes out clean. Let cool few minutes in pans, then turn out on cake rack to cool.

Put cooled layers together with a little Bride's Cake Frosting. Cover top and sides lavishly with remaining frosting. Decorate with frosting flowers, if desired, or place small bridal dolls and spray of orange blossoms on top.

For very large 3-tier cake increase recipe one half. Use one round 10-inch pan, one 9-inch pan, and one 7- or 8-inch pan. Make frosting recipe twice.

The 2-layer cake serves 8 or more. The 3-tier cake makes 12 or more servings.

To include the "lucky" favors which are sometimes baked in the Bride's Cake, wrap the traditional thimble, tiny horseshoe, ring, button, or any other favorite silver charms separately in waxed paper. Make small cuts in baked cake, at random; insert one charm in each cut. Frost as described.

The lucky pieces of cake mean an early engagement, happy life, spinsterhood for the thimble finder, and other amusing nonsense which you may or may not want to introduce at the bridal reception.

LORD BALTIMORE CAKE

1 cup shortening	2 teaspoons cream of tartar
1 ¾ cups sugar	½ teaspoon powdered nutmeg
7 egg yolks	1 cup milk
3 ¼ cups sifted all-purpose flour	½ teaspoon lemon flavoring
¼ teaspoon salt	Lady Baltimore Filling (page 111)
1 teaspoon baking soda	Seven-Minute Frosting (page 129)

Start oven at moderate (350° F.). Grease two round 9-inch layer-cake pans. Line with waxed paper. Grease paper.

Cream shortening and sugar together thoroughly in mixing bowl. Add egg yolks, one at a time, beating well after each addition. Sift dry ingredients together. Add to shortening bowl alternately with milk and flavoring. Pour into prepared pans.

Bake 35 to 40 minutes or until done when cake tester inserted in center of each layer comes out clean. Let cakes cool several minutes in pans, then turn out onto cake rack to cool completely.

Fill layers with Lady Baltimore Filling. Frost top with remaining Seven-Minute Frosting. Makes 8 or more servings.

Some cooks like to decorate Lord Baltimore cake with chopped fruit and nuts.

COCONUT CHOCOLATE CAKE

2 eggs
1 ½ cups sugar
1 ¾ cups sifted cake flour
¾ teaspoon baking soda
¾ teaspoon salt
⅓ cup cooking oil

1 cup milk
2 (1-ounce) squares unsweetened chocolate, melted
Chocolate Frosting (page 126)
⅔ cup moist shredded coconut

Start oven at moderate (350° F.). Grease two round 8-inch layer pans or one oblong pan 13 by 9½ by 2 inches. Dust lightly with flour.

Beat egg whites until frothy. Beat in ½ cup sugar gradually. Continue beating until very stiff and glossy.

Sift remaining sugar, flour, soda, and salt into another bowl. Add oil and ½ cup milk. Beat 1 minute medium speed in electric mixer or 150 vigorous strokes by hand. Scrape sides and bottom of bowl constantly. Add remaining ½ cup milk, the 2 egg yolks, and chocolate. Beat 1 minute, as before, scraping bowl constantly. Fold in meringue; pour into prepared pans.

Bake layers 30 to 35 minutes, oblong pan 40 to 45 minutes. Let cool few minutes in pan, then turn out on cake rack. When layers are cold, put together with about ⅓ of the chocolate frosting. Spread top and sides of cake with remainder. Sprinkle top and sides thickly with coconut. Let stand 30 minutes or longer before serving. Makes 8 layer-cake servings, 12 servings or more from oblong cake.

For oblong cake, make up half Chocolate Frosting recipe; cover cake with frosting; sprinkle thickly with coconut.

DARK CHIFFON CAKE

2 eggs
1 ½ cups sugar
2 ¼ cups sifted cake flour
3 teaspoons baking powder
1 teaspoon salt
½ cup milk

½ cup cold, strongly brewed
   coffee
⅛ teaspoon baking soda
⅓ cup cooking oil
2 teaspoons vanilla
Fluffy Coffee Frosting (page 127)

Start oven at moderate (350° F.). Grease two deep 8-inch layer-cake pans; dust lightly with flour.

Beat egg whites until frothy. Gradually beat in ½ cup sugar. Continue beating until very stiff and glossy. Sift remaining sugar, flour, baking powder, and salt into another bowl. Combine milk, coffee, and baking soda. Pour oil into flour mixture with half coffee mixture and vanilla. Beat 1 minute, using medium speed on electric mixer, or 150 strokes by hand. Scrape sides and bottom of bowl constantly. Add remaining coffee mixture and egg yolks. Beat 1 minute longer, scraping bowl constantly. Fold in egg-white mixture lightly but thoroughly. Pour into prepared pans.

Bake 30 to 35 minutes.

Remove from pans. Let cool. Use thin, long-bladed knife and split each layer into two layers. Put all together with Fluffy Coffee Frosting and cover top and sides with frosting. Makes 8 or more servings. Let stand in cool place.

LADY BALTIMORE CAKE

¾ cup shortening	¾ teaspoon vanilla
2 cups sugar	½ teaspoon lemon flavoring
3 cups sifted cake flour	6 egg whites
¾ teaspoon salt	Lady Baltimore Filling
3 teaspoons baking powder	Seven-Minute Frosting (page 129)
1 cup milk	

Start oven at moderate (350° F.). Grease two round 9-inch layer-cake pans. Line with waxed paper. Grease paper.

Cream shortening and sugar together in mixing bowl until light and fluffy. Sift dry ingredients together into shortening, alternately with milk. Beat smooth after each addition. Add vanilla and lemon flavorings. Whip egg whites until they stand in points. Fold into batter. Pour into prepared pans.

Bake 30 minutes or until done when cake tester inserted near center of each layer comes out clean.

Let layers cool several minutes in pans, then turn out onto cake rack and let cool completely. Put layers together with Lady Baltimore Filling. Frost top and sides with remaining Seven-Minute Frosting.

Lady Baltimore Filling: Make up Seven-Minute Frosting. To ⅓ of frosting add ¼ cup each finely cut dried figs, seedless raisins, candied cherries, and chopped pecans. Use between layers. Cake makes 8 or more servings.

Southern cooks prefer this cake plainly frosted with Boiled or Seven-Minute Frosting. Other cooks decorate the top with leaves and flowers made of butter icing, adding a colorful nosegay of fresh flowers to the center of the top.

MRS. MOLNAR'S MOCHA TORTE

6 eggs	½ cup sifted cake flour
1 cup sugar	2 teaspoons baking powder
Grated peel and juice ½ lemon	¼ teaspoon salt
5 tablespoons strongly brewed	2 cups heavy cream
coffee, or 2 teaspoons coffee	⅓ cup powdered sugar
essence	1 cup finely chopped walnuts

Start oven at moderate (350° F.). Grease two round 8-inch cake pans; dust lightly with flour.

Beat egg yolks slightly. Mix sugar, lemon peel, juice, and 2 tablespoons coffee or 1 teaspoon coffee essence into yolks. Sift flour, baking powder, and salt together 4 times. Add little at a time to yolk mixture, beating well. Whip egg whites until they stand in stiff points when beater is removed. Fold whites into mixture. Pour batter into prepared pans.

Bake 20 minutes, or until torte has pulled away a little from side of pan. Let cool.

Whip cream, combine with powdered sugar, walnuts, and remaining 3 tablespoons coffee or 1 teaspoon coffee essence. Put torte together with cream filling and cover top lavishly. Refrigerate several hours before serving. Makes 6 or more servings.

Coffee Essence: Coffee essence may be bought bottled, ready for use. Or make it at home by combining 1 cup strongly brewed coffee with *1 cup ground coffee*. Bring to a boil. Boil 2 minutes. Strain. Use as described.

This was the torte I learned to bake when I was thirteen years old. Mrs. Molnar, a Staten Island neighbor, was a fabulous Hungarian cook and she taught me how to make this and other specialties of the Hungarian kitchen.

OLD-FASHIONED BURNT SUGAR CAKE

½ cup shortening	1 cup milk
1 ½ cups sugar	3 tablespoons caramelized
2 eggs	sugar
1 teaspoon vanilla	Burnt Sugar Frosting (page 129)
2 ½ cups sifted cake flour	Hickory-nut halves, or ½ cup
¼ teaspoon salt	chopped mixed nuts
2 ½ teaspoons baking powder	

Start oven at moderate (350° F.). Grease two round 8-inch layer-cake pans. Line with waxed paper. Grease paper.

Cream shortening and sugar together thoroughly in mixing bowl. Add egg yolks and vanilla. Beat well until light. Sift dry ingredients together. Add alternately with milk, beating well after each addition. Add caramelized sugar and beat well. Whip egg whites stiff; fold into batter. Pour into prepared pans.

Bake about 30 minutes or until cake tester inserted in center of each layer comes out clean. Let cakes cool several minutes in pans. Turn out on cake rack to cool completely. Put together with burnt sugar frosting. Frost tops and layers with the same. Arrange hickory-nut halves on top or sprinkle thickly with chopped nuts. Makes 8 or more servings.

Caramelized sugar: Melt ½ cup granulated sugar in heavy skillet over low heat until brown. Remove from heat. Add ½ cup boiling water; return to heat. Stir rapidly until like molasses. Use as described in recipe.

RICH FUDGE CAKE

2	cups sifted cake flour	3	(1-ounce) squares unsweetened chocolate, melted
1	teaspoon salt		
1 ½	teaspoons baking soda	1 ⅓	cups milk
½	teaspoon baking powder	3	eggs
1 ⅔	cups sugar	1	teaspoon vanilla
½	cup shortening		Soft Chocolate Frosting (page 130)

Start oven at moderate (350° F.). Grease two round 9-inch cake pans. Line pans with waxed paper. Grease paper.

Sift flour, salt, soda, baking powder, and sugar together into mixing bowl. Add shortening, chocolate, and ⅔ cup milk. Beat vigorously by hand until smoothly combined. Set the mixer medium speed for 2 minutes, scraping bowl often. Add eggs, remaining ⅔ cup milk, and vanilla. Beat 2 minutes by hand or mixer. Pour into prepared pans.

Bake 35 to 40 minutes. Let cool about 10 minutes in pans. Remove to cake rack to finish cooling.

Put cooled layers together with Soft Chocolate Frosting. Cover top and sides with remaining frosting. Makes 8 or more servings.

SUNDAY-NIGHT CAKE

3 eggs	¾ cup scalded milk
1½ cups sugar	3 tablespoons cognac
¼ teaspoon almond flavoring	½ Almond Custard recipe
1½ cups sifted all-purpose flour	(page 237)
1½ teaspoons baking powder	Almond Frosting (page 124)
¼ teaspoon salt	Nuts or chopped candied fruit

Start oven at moderate (350° F.). Grease two round 9-inch layer-cake pans. Line with waxed paper. Grease paper.

Beat eggs until light. Add sugar gradually, beating until thick and fluffy. Add flavoring.

Sift dry ingredients and fold in alternately with hot milk until blended. Pour into prepared pans.

Bake 25 to 30 minutes or until cake tester inserted near center of each layer comes out clean. Let pans stand on cake rack 5 minutes. Loosen cake from sides of pans with spatula. Turn out on rack. Let cool.

Make Almond Custard and use as filling, and Almond Frosting.

Sprinkle bottom layer of cake with cognac. Cover with Custard Filling. Top with second layer. Spread with Almond Frosting. Decorate with nuts and fruit. Makes 8 or more servings.

OLD FRENCH CAKE

½ cup butter	1 teaspoon powdered mace
1 cup sugar	¼ teaspoon salt
3 eggs, well beaten	¼ cup milk
2 cups sifted all-purpose flour	1½ cups chopped raisins
2 teaspoons baking powder	Flour

Start oven at slow (250° F.). Grease 9-by-9-inch pan. Dust lightly with flour.

Cream butter. Add sugar gradually. Beat eggs in gradually until mixture is light. Mix and sift dry ingredients. Sift into egg mixture alternately with milk, blending carefully. *Do not beat.* Sprinkle raisins lightly with flour; shake in sieve, then add to batter. Pour into prepared pan.

Bake 1 hour or until cake tester shows cake is done and it has shrunken slightly from sides of pan. Let cool in pan few minutes, then turn out and let cool on rack. Frost with special butter frosting.

Special Butter Frosting for this cake: Combine 3 tablespoons butter with 2 cups confectioners' sugar, beating until well creamed. Add 3 tablespoons milk or strongly brewed coffee and 1 teaspoon vanilla. Beat all until smooth. Or use 3 tablespoons lemon juice and grated peel 1 orange or lemon in place of milk and coffee.

Be sure not to use an overly refined cake flour for this. It is supposed to be of coffee-cake texture. Its long baking in a slow oven approximates the Dutch-oven baking of the French farm kitchen. We have this often with evening tea and there is never any left to grow stale.

Cupcakes

HONEY ORANGE CUPCAKES

1 ½ cups sifted cake flour	¼ cup sugar
¾ teaspoon baking soda	2 teaspoons grated orange peel
¾ teaspoon salt	1 teaspoon vanilla
5 ½ tablespoons butter or margarine	2 eggs
½ cup strained honey	3 tablespoons cider vinegar

Start oven at moderate (375° F.). Grease 18 (2½-inch) muffin-pan cups.

Sift flour, soda, and salt together. Cream butter or margarine, honey, sugar, orange peel, and vanilla together thoroughly in mixing bowl. Add eggs. Beat until fluffy. Add dry ingredients and vinegar alternately, beginning and ending with dry ingredients. Beat well after each addition. Pour into prepared muffin pans.

Bake about 20 minutes. Frost as desired. Makes 18 cupcakes.

FRUIT CUPCAKES

½ cup seedless raisins
½ cup chopped dates
½ cup chopped candied citron
½ cup chopped assorted candied
   fruit
½ cup chopped nuts
1 cup sifted all-purpose flour
½ teaspoon baking powder
½ cup light corn syrup
8 tablespoons softened shortening

¼ cup brown sugar, packed
2 eggs
2 tablespoons orange juice
¼ cup sifted all-purpose flour
½ teaspoon salt
½ teaspoon powdered cinnamon
¼ teaspoon each, powdered
   cloves, allspice, nutmeg
1 egg white
Additional chopped candied fruits
and nuts

Cut all fruit in very fine pieces with kitchen scissors dipped in hot water. Combine with nuts in mixing bowl. Sift flour and baking powder together over fruit and nuts. Toss lightly to coat evenly. Put remaining ingredients, except egg white and extra fruit, in glass container of blender. Cover and blend until smooth, about 1 minute, stirring mixture down continually. Pour blended mixture over fruit and nut mixture and mix well.

Start oven at moderately slow (300° F.).

Place 18 fluted paper bake cups in muffin pans. Pour batter into cups.

Bake 1 hour. Remove pans from oven. Brush tops of cakes lightly with egg white. Garnish with candied cherries, slivered almonds or pecans. Return to oven for 15 minutes. When done, remove pans. Let cool. Makes 18 cupcakes.

ICED SMALL CAKES

Petits Fours

4 tablespoons butter or margarine
4 tablespoons shortening
1 cup sugar
½ teaspoon vanilla or other
   flavoring
2 cups sifted cake flour
¼ teaspoon salt

3 teaspoons baking powder
¾ cup milk
¾ cup egg whites
¼ cup sugar
Petits Fours Frosting (page 128)
Silver candies, coconut, pistachio
nuts

Start oven at moderate (350° F.). Grease 9-by-12-inch pan. Line with waxed paper; grease paper.

Cream butter or margarine and shortening together in mixing bowl until fluffy and light. Beat in 1 cup sugar smoothly. Add flavoring. Sift dry ingredients together into sugar mixture alternately with milk, beating well after each addition. Whip egg whites stiff with the ¼ cup sugar added. Fold into batter. Pour into prepared pan.

Bake 40 minutes or until cake tester inserted near center of pan comes out clean. Let cake cool few minutes in pan. Turn out carefully onto cake rack to cool.

When cool, cut in small shapes, such as triangles, rounds, squares, and oblongs. Frost with Petits Fours Frosting. Decorate with silver candies, pistachio nuts, or coconut; or with rosebud of colored butter frosting or whirls and stripes of chocolate frosting. Makes 10 to 12 or more little cakes.

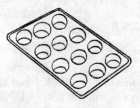

NEW ORLEANS CUPCAKES

5½ tablespoons butter or margarine	¾ cup milk
2 cups sifted cake flour	1 egg
1 cup sugar	1 teaspoon lemon flavoring
2 teaspoons baking powder	½ cup chopped pecans
½ teaspoon salt	Brown Sugar Topping

Start oven at moderate (375° F.). Place 18 fluted paper bake cups in muffin pans.

Cream butter or margarine in mixing bowl. Sift flour, sugar, baking powder, and salt together into fat. Add half the milk. Add egg. Mix until all flour is dampened, then beat vigorously 2 minutes. Add remaining milk and flavoring. Beat 1 minute. Stir in nuts. Pour into paper-lined pans, filling ½ full.

Bake 25 minutes or until done.

Brown Sugar Topping: A few minutes before cakes are done, mix topping:

¼ cup melted butter or margarine   18 pecan halves
¾ cup brown sugar, packed

Combine butter or margarine and sugar, beating until smooth. When cakes are done, remove pans. Spread brown sugar mixture quickly on tops, place pecan half on each. Return pans to hot oven for 5 minutes. When done, let cakes cool in pans. Makes 18 cupcakes.

Fruitcakes

HOLIDAY FRUITCAKE

1 ½ cups seedless raisins, soaked and drained
1 ½ cups chopped candied cherries
½ cup quartered dates
¾ cup chopped candied pineapple
¾ cup slivered blanched almonds
1 cup chopped pecans
6 tablespoons butter or margarine

½ cup sugar
3 eggs
¾ cup sifted all-purpose flour
¾ cup uncooked oatmeal
¼ teaspoon salt
¼ teaspoon powdered cloves
¼ teaspoon powdered nutmeg
½ teaspoon powdered cinnamon
1 tablespoon orange juice

Mix fruits and nuts together in large bowl. Beat butter or margarine in mixing bowl until soft. Cream with sugar. Add eggs, one at a time, beating well. Mix dry ingredients together. Gradually add all but about ¾ cup dry ingredients to butter mixture, mixing well. Add orange juice. Mix the ¾ cup dry ingredients with the fruits and nuts. Pour batter over fruit, mixing well.

Start oven at slow (275° F.). Grease 1-pound coffee can or mold and small loaf pan. Line pans with waxed paper. Grease paper.

Pour cake batter into prepared pans. Bake coffee-can loaf 3 hours and small loaf pan about 1½ hours. Let cool thoroughly in pans.

To store, remove from pans, brush with brandy or orange juice, and wrap tightly in foil or heavy waxed paper. Keep in cool place, but not in refrigerator. Total weight, about 2¾ pounds; 20 to 30 servings.

Use round cake for your holiday tea table or give as gift.

Serve smaller cake throughout holidays for dessert or with coffee and tea, and also as dessert in lunchboxes.

WEDDING FRUITCAKE

Sometimes called Groom's Cake

1 cup shortening	1 ¼ cups chopped candied pine-
1 cup sugar	apple
5 eggs	½ cup chopped dates
2 cups sifted all-purpose flour	½ cup chopped dried apricots
1 teaspoon salt	½ cup chopped figs
1 ½ teaspoons baking powder	½ pound white raisins
¼ cup pineapple juice	2 cups sliced blanched almonds
¼ pound (½ cup) chopped	½ cup chopped pecans
mixed candied fruits	2 (4-ounce) cans moist
¼ pound each, chopped	shredded coconut
candied orange peel and	
lemon peel	

Start oven at slow (275° F.). Grease two loaf pans measuring about 3½ by 7½ inches, or use five 1-pound loaf pans. Line pans with paper. Grease paper.

Cream shortening and sugar together in very large mixing bowl. Add eggs, one at a time, beating well. Sift together flour, salt, and baking powder. Add all but about ½ cup flour mixture alternately with pine-apple juice to shortening. Mix well. Sprinkle the ½ cup flour mixture over combined fruit and nuts. Mix. Stir into batter. Add coconut. Stir just enough to mix. Pour into prepared pans.

Bake about 1½ hours. Let partially cool in pans. Turn out on rack to finish cooling.

Serve some of this cake at wedding reception. Cut remainder into small pieces for guest boxes. Makes 5 pounds. Forty or more servings or gift boxes.

Loaf Cakes

APPLESAUCE CAKE

½ cup shortening	½ teaspoon soda
1 ½ cups sugar	¼ teaspoon powdered nutmeg
2 eggs	1 teaspoon powdered cinnamon
1 cup thick, unsweetened applesauce	
	½ teaspoon powdered cloves
2 cups sifted all-purpose flour	1 cup dried currants, soaked and drained
¼ teaspoon salt	
1 teaspoon baking powder	

Start oven at moderate (350° F.). Grease 8-inch-square baking pan. Line with waxed paper. Grease paper.

Cream shortening and sugar together in mixing bowl until light and fluffy. Add eggs and beat well. Add applesauce and mix. Sift dry ingredients together. Beat into batter until smoothly combined. Add currants. Pour into prepared pan.

Bake 45 to 60 minutes or until done. Let cool in pan. Makes 8 or more servings.

A good brunch cake.

CHOCOLATE POUNDCAKE

3 (1-ounce) squares unsweetened chocolate	1 ¾ cups sugar
	½ pound butter or margarine
2 ½ cups sifted all-purpose flour	⅔ cup milk
¾ teaspoon cream of tartar	1 teaspoon vanilla
½ teaspoon baking soda	3 eggs and 1 extra yolk
1 ½ teaspoons salt	

Start oven at moderate (350° F.). Grease bottom of 10-inch tube pan; line with waxed paper. Grease paper.

Melt chocolate over hot (not boiling) water. Sift flour, cream of tartar, soda, salt, and sugar together. Cream butter or margarine until soft. Beat in dry ingredients thoroughly until mixture is crumbly. Stir in milk and vanilla. Beat 300 strokes by hand, or 2 minutes at low speed in electric mixer. Add unbeaten eggs and extra yolk to batter. Beat 150 strokes, or 1 minute longer in mixer. Pour into prepared pan.

Bake 60 to 70 minutes or until cake tester comes out clean inserted near center of cake. Let cool in pan 15 minutes, then loosen sides carefully with spatula, invert pan on a cooling rack to remove cake, and let cool completely. Makes 10 or more servings.

If frosting is desired, use Soft Chocolate Frosting (page 130).

CHOCOLATE REFRIGERATOR CAKE

18 ladyfingers (36 halves)	3 eggs
1 (6-ounce) package, or 1 cup, semi-sweet chocolate pieces	1 cup heavy cream
1 tablespoon instant coffee	1/16 teaspoon salt

Arrange 6 whole, or 12 halves ladyfingers in bottom of an 11-by-7-by-1½-inch baking pan.

Melt chocolate pieces over hot water. Stir in coffee. Let cool. Beat egg yolks into chocolate one at a time. Beat egg whites until they stand in peaks, then gently mix into chocolate mixture. Whip cream, with salt added, until stiff. Mix carefully into chocolate combination. Pour half chocolate mixture into prepared pan. Place layer of ladyfinger halves over the chocolate. Pour in remaining chocolate. Cover with remaining ladyfinger halves, pressing them lightly into the chocolate. Chill in refrigerator 1 hour or longer. Makes 6 to 8 servings.

TEXAS CHOCOLATE CAKE

1 cup sliced dates	3 tablespoons powdered cocoa
¼ teaspoon soda	1 teaspoon salt
1 cup boiling water	1 teaspoon vanilla
½ pound butter or margarine	1 (6-ounce) package chocolate bits
1 cup sugar	
2 eggs	Powdered sugar
1¾ cups sifted all-purpose flour	

Start oven at moderate (350° F.). Grease 6½-by-10½-inch pan.

Sprinkle soda over dates in small saucepan. Add boiling water; bring to a boil over direct heat and let boil 1 or 2 minutes. Set aside to cool.

Cream butter or margarine in mixing bowl. Beat in sugar. Add eggs, one at a time, beating well after each addition. Sift flour, cocoa, and salt together. Add alternately with drained dates to butter mixture. Add vanilla. Pour into prepared pan. Cover top with chocolate bits.

Bake 45 minutes. Remove pan from oven. While cake is still warm sprinkle with powdered sugar. Makes 12 squares.

DAISYFIELDS MARBLE LOAF CAKE

⅓ cup shortening
1 cup sugar
1 teaspoon vanilla
2 cups sifted cake flour
¼ teaspoon salt
2 teaspoons baking powder
⅔ cup milk

3 egg whites
1 (1-ounce) square unsweetened chocolate, melted
2 tablespoons hot water
¼ teaspoon baking soda
Soft Chocolate Frosting (page 130)

Start oven at moderate (350° F.). Grease loaf pan measuring about 5½ by 10½ inches. Line with waxed paper. Grease paper.

Cream shortening and sugar together thoroughly in mixing bowl. Add vanilla. Sift dry ingredients together. Add alternately with milk to shortening. Whip egg whites until they stand in points. Fold into batter.

Combine chocolate, water, and soda in smaller mixing bowl. Pour about half cake batter into chocolate mixture, stirring until completely mixed. Spoon remaining light batter and chocolate mixture alternately into prepared pan. Do not mix or stir together in pan.

Bake about 60 minutes or until cake tester inserted in center comes out clean. Let cool in pan several minutes. Turn out on cake rack to completely cool. Leave plain, or frost (as we like it at my home) with a soft, creamy chocolate frosting. Makes 10 servings.

To keep this cake, do not frost cooled cake but wrap it in foil or waxed paper. Keep in cool, not cold, place several days. Frost just before serving. Makes wonderful lunchbox cake too.

I remember my wonder as a child at a cake that could incorporate two different colors and flavors in the batter. It was fun to lick the chocolate bowl!

FRENCH YULE LOG

6 eggs
½ cup sugar
½ cup sifted all-purpose flour

2 teaspoons baking powder
2 tablespoons cognac
Granulated sugar

Start oven at moderate (375° F.). Butter 12-by-15-inch baking sheet or jelly-roll pan. Line with heavy waxed paper. Butter paper lightly.

Beat yolks and sugar together in mixing bowl until light and fluffy. Sift flour and baking powder together into egg mixture. Add cognac. Whip egg whites until they stand in points. Fold into yolk mixture. Spread batter on prepared baking sheet or jelly-roll pan.

Bake about 6 minutes or until cake is done. Remove from oven. Immediately turn cake out onto a towel sprinkled generously with granulated sugar. Roll cake up with towel. Let cool.

While cake cools, prepare frosting:

1 cup butter or margarine	2 (1-ounce) squares unsweetened
2 egg yolks	chocolate, melted
4 cups confectioners' sugar	

Beat butter or margarine until creamy. Stir in egg yolks. Beat sugar in a little at a time. Beat in slightly cooled melted chocolate smoothly.

Unroll cooled cake. Remove towel. Spread cake with about half the frosting. Roll cake up firmly. Place on board or platter. Cover top and sides with remaining frosting. Use fork to draw design resembling surface of log in frosting. Decorate top with sprig of holly. Makes 8 or more servings.

I have included this recipe especially for your holiday parties.

RAISIN ORANGE CAKE

2 cups sifted all-purpose flour	1 unpeeled seedless orange, diced
1 teaspoon soda	1 cup seedless raisins
1 teaspoon salt	1 cup sugar
1 teaspoon baking powder	1 cup sour milk or buttermilk
2 eggs	Uncooked Orange Frosting (page
8 tablespoons soft shortening	129)

Start oven at moderate (350° F.). Grease baking pan measuring about 7 by 11 inches. Have all ingredients at room temperature for 15 minutes before mixing. Sift flour, soda, salt, and baking powder together into mixing bowl.

Pour eggs, fat, orange, raisins, sugar, and sour milk or buttermilk into glass container of blender. Cover and blend until orange is well cut, about 30 seconds. At end of first 10 seconds, stop blender. Stir mixture down. Start blender and run 20 seconds. Stop blender. Stir mixture down.

Pour blended mixture over flour in mixing bowl. Stir lightly until flour is just mixed in. Pour batter into prepared pan.

Bake about 45 minutes or until cake tester inserted in center comes out clean. Let cool in pan. Frost with Uncooked Orange Frosting. Makes 8 or more servings.

SHAGGY-TOP CAKE

4 tablespoons butter or margarine	1 teaspoon baking powder
4 tablespoons shortening	1 teaspoon baking soda
1 ½ cups sugar	2 teaspoons powdered nutmeg
½ teaspoon vanilla	¼ teaspoon salt
3 eggs, beaten	1 cup buttermilk
2 cups sifted all-purpose flour	Broiled Coconut Frosting

Start oven at moderate (350° F.). Grease pan measuring about 13 by 9 by 2 inches; dust lightly with flour.

Cream butter or margarine and shortening together in mixing bowl until like thick cream. Add sugar gradually, beating until light and fluffy. Add vanilla and eggs. Beat until light and fluffy. Sift dry ingredients together. Add to creamed mixture alternately with buttermilk, beating after each addition. Pour into prepared pan.

Bake 40 minutes, or until cake tester inserted in center comes out clean.

Broiled Coconut Frosting: When cake has been in oven 35 minutes, prepare frosting:

4 tablespoons butter or margarine	1 cup flaked or shredded coconut
1 cup brown sugar, packed	
2 tablespoons light cream	

Cream butter or margarine and sugar together until light and fluffy. Add cream. Mix well. Stir in ½ cup coconut.

As soon as cake comes from oven, spread frosting over it. Sprinkle remaining ½ cup coconut on top. Place in broiler about 4 to 5 inches from heat. Broil 4 minutes or until top browns lightly. Let cool in pan to slightly warm. Cut in squares and serve warm. Makes 12 or more servings.

Fillings and Frostings

ALMOND FROSTING

2 egg whites	⅔ cup almond paste
1 cup sifted confectioners' sugar	or finely ground almonds

Beat egg whites until they stand in points. Combine with almond paste and sugar, beating until smooth and of spreading consistency. Makes about 2 cups of frosting.

Thin with a little heavy cream or undiluted evaporated milk if necessary.

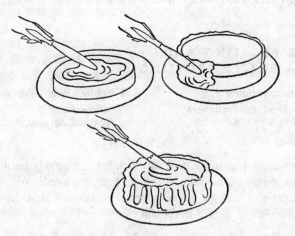

BRIDE'S CAKE FROSTING

2 cups sugar	⅛ teaspoon salt
½ cup water	2 egg whites
⅛ teaspoon cream of tartar	1 teaspoon vanilla

Cook sugar, water, and cream of tartar in saucepan to soft-ball stage, or 236° F. on candy thermometer. Add salt to egg whites in upper part of double boiler. Beat until frothy. Place over hot water and gradually add sugar syrup, beating constantly. Continue beating until mixture forms peaks. Add vanilla. Use as filling for Bride's Cake (page 108) and to cover top and sides. Double recipe for a 3-tier cake.

For floral decorating, with pastry tube and frosting, follow directions which come with tube set.

BROWN SUGAR FROSTING

¼ cup butter or margarine
½ cup brown sugar, packed
3 cups sifted confectioners' sugar

¼ cup cold, strongly brewed coffee

Cream butter or margarine. Add brown sugar and continue creaming until smooth. Add confectioners' sugar and coffee alternately, beating constantly. Spread on homemade or bought baker's cakes, or on gingerbread, cupcakes, and cookies. Makes about 4 cups of frosting.

BUTTER FROSTING AND MOCHA BUTTER FROSTING

3 tablespoons butter
2 cups sifted confectioners' sugar
⅛ teaspoon salt

3 tablespoons milk or strongly brewed coffee
1 teaspoon vanilla

Beat butter, 1 cup sugar, and salt together thoroughly until light and fluffy. Use mixer at medium speed or beat by hand. Add remaining cup of sugar and milk or coffee alternately, beating until very smooth. Add vanilla. Frosts 9-by-9-by-2-inch cake.

When coffee is used the frosting is Mocha Butter Frosting.

CHOCOLATE FROSTING

2½ cups sifted confectioners' sugar
1 egg
2 tablespoons water
¼ cup granulated sugar
¼ teaspoon salt

½ cup butter or margarine
1 teaspoon vanilla
2 (2-ounce) blocks unsweetened chocolate or 4 (1-ounce) squares, melted

Combine confectioners' sugar and egg in mixing bowl. Beat until smoothly blended and light. Mix water, granulated sugar, and salt in saucepan. Bring to a boil over medium heat and boil vigorously 1 minute. Pour hot syrup slowly into egg mixture, beating constantly. Add butter or margarine, vanilla, and melted chocolate. Beat until creamy and of spreading consistency. Makes enough to frost tops and sides of two round 8-inch layers.

EASY RUM-RAISIN FROSTING

3 cups sifted confectioners' sugar
2 tablespoons cream
3 tablespoons rum

½ cup seedless raisins, soaked and drained
4 tablespoons softened butter or margarine

Sift 2 cups sugar into bowl. Combine remaining ingredients in glass container of blender. Cover and blend 1 minute. Pour blended mixture into sugar and stir until of right consistency to spread. Makes enough frosting for top and sides of two round 8-inch layers.

FLUFFY COFFEE FROSTING

1½ cups butter or margarine
1 cup sugar
½ teaspoon salt

¼ cup cold, strongly brewed coffee
1 teaspoon vanilla
2 eggs

Combine all ingredients in small mixing bowl or beat at high speed with electric mixer 2 or 3 minutes, or with rotary hand beater about 10 minutes, until smooth and fluffy. Use on Dark Chiffon Cake (page 110), gingerbread, and on white cake. Makes about 2¾ cups of frosting.

ORANGE CUSTARD FILLING

⅓ cup sugar
¼ cup flour
¼ teaspoon salt
1½ cups milk

2 egg yolks, slightly beaten
2 tablespoons grated orange peel
½ teaspoon orange flavoring

Combine sugar, flour, and salt in upper part of double boiler. Stir in milk, blending smoothly. Set pan over hot water. Cook until thickened, stirring constantly. Cover pan. Let cook 5 minutes longer, stirring occasionally. Add small amount of mixture to beaten yolks, stirring constantly. Then stir yolks into milk mixture. Cook 2 or 3 minutes, stirring constantly. Remove from heat and let cool. Add flavoring and peel. Chill. Makes about 2 cups of filling.

PETITS FOURS FROSTING

2	cups granulated sugar	1½	cups sifted confectioners'
⅛	teaspoon cream of tartar		sugar
1	cup hot water	Pure-food coloring	
½	teaspoon vanilla		

Combine granulated sugar, cream of tartar, and hot water in saucepan; stir to mix well. Let come to a boil. Boil until thin syrup forms, or 226° F. on candy thermometer. Let cool to lukewarm (110° F.). Add vanilla. Beat in confectioners' sugar until right consistency to pour, usually about 1¼ to 1½ cups sugar. Pour a little frosting into another pan or bowl. Tint pale pink, green, or yellow with 1 or 2 drops of food coloring. Pour frosting on cakes.

Decorate with small candies, coconut, or nuts, or frost half-and-half with colored frosting and white.

Make small amounts of coffee or maple frosting, burnt sugar, mocha, orange, or other favorite frostings when baking petits fours. When frosted cakes are glossy, use butter frosting, squeezed on with pastry decorating tube, to make rosebuds, dots, stripes, and other small decoration which add to the professional look of your tray of petits fours.

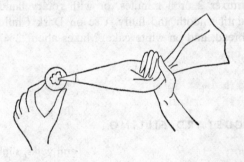

POUR-ON FROSTING

½	cup granulated sugar	¼	teaspoon salt
4	tablespoons butter or marga-	½	teaspoon vanilla
	rine	1½	cups confectioners' sugar
¼	cup milk		

Combine granulated sugar, butter or margarine, milk, and salt in saucepan. Bring to a boil over moderate heat, stirring constantly. Boil vigorously 1 minute. Remove from heat. Add vanilla and confectioners' sugar. Mix. Let cool 3 to 4 minutes, until frosting is right consistency for pouring. Pour frosting slowly over top of cooled cake. Let frosting run down sides. Do not move cake until frosting is firm. Makes enough for 2-layer cake or large loaf cake.

Can be used as filling between layers. Pour a little frosting on layer. Let stand until it begins to set. Place layer on top, then pour frosting on as described above.

SEVEN-MINUTE FROSTING

2 egg whites
½ cup light corn syrup
½ cup sugar

⅛ teaspoon salt
1 teaspoon vanilla

Combine egg whites, syrup, sugar, and salt in upper part of double boiler. Beat with rotary beater until partially mixed. Set pan over rapidly boiling water. Cook 3 to 4 minutes, beating constantly with rotary beater until frosting stands in peaks. Remove pan from hot water. Continue beating about 1 minute more. Add flavoring. Beat in to mix well. Makes enough to cover top and sides of two round 8- or 9-inch layers.

Butterscotch Seven-Minute Frosting: Substitute dark corn syrup for the light, and brown sugar for the white sugar.

Burnt-Sugar Frostings: Substitute 2 tablespoons Caramelized Sugar Syrup (page 113) for corn syrup.

See also Brown-Sugar Topping (page 118).

UNCOOKED ORANGE FROSTING

1 cup heavy cream
Sugar

1 (6-ounce) can frozen orange concentrate, thawed but not diluted

Whip cream stiff, beating in orange concentrate as you whip. Sweeten to taste.

Makes enough to generously frost a 13-by-9-by-2-inch loaf cake or one round or square layer.

SOFT CHOCOLATE FROSTING

6	(1-ounce) squares unsweetened chocolate	1 ½	tablespoons butter or margarine
3	egg yolks	¹⁄₁₆	teaspoon salt
1 ¼	cups sugar	2	teaspoons vanilla
¾	cup milk		

Melt chocolate in saucepan over hot water. Beat egg yolks in heavy saucepan until very thick. Add sugar and beat smoothly together. Add milk and butter or margarine, stirring well. Cook over very low heat, stirring constantly. Bring to a boil and boil 1 minute only. Remove from heat, stir in chocolate, add salt and vanilla. Beat until it will spread nicely.

Makes enough to use between two layers and to frost top and sides. This frosting has gloss, stays soft.

Cookies

BROWNIES

⅓	cup shortening	⅔	cup sifted all-purpose flour
2	(1-ounce) squares unsweetened chocolate, grated	¾	teaspoon salt
½	cup brown sugar, packed	¼	teaspoon baking soda
½	cup granulated sugar	½	cup chopped nuts
2	eggs	1	teaspoon vanilla

Start oven at moderate (325° F.). Grease 9-inch square pan.

Combine first 4 ingredients in saucepan. Place over low heat. Stir occasionally until shortening and chocolate melt. Remove from heat, add eggs, and beat until well blended. Sift dry ingredients together. Beat into egg mixture. Stir in nuts and vanilla until smooth. Pour into prepared pan.

Bake about 25 minutes or until done. Set pan on cake rack to cool. Cut into squares or bars. Makes about 2 dozen brownies.

Good brownie mixes are on the market. Follow directions on the mix package.

BROWN-SUGAR OATMEAL COOKIES

1 ¼ cups sifted all-purpose flour	1 egg
¾ teaspoon baking soda	2 tablespoons milk
¾ teaspoon salt	1 teaspoon vanilla
½ cup shortening	1 ½ cups uncooked oatmeal
¾ cup dark brown sugar, packed	

Start oven at moderate (350° F.). Grease two cooky sheets.

Sift flour, soda, and salt together into mixing bowl. Combine shortening and sugar, beating until smooth. Beat into dry ingredients with egg, milk, and vanilla. When smoothly combined, beat in oats. From the stiff dough, form balls about 1 inch in diameter. Place balls of dough on cooky sheets 2 inches apart. Flatten each a little with spatula.

Bake 12 to 15 minutes.

Remove cookies from cooky sheets. Let cool on cake rack. Makes 3½ dozen cookies.

COCONUT MACAROONS

2 egg whites	¾ cup sugar
⅛ teaspoon salt	1 (4-ounce) can moist shredded coconut (1 ½ cups)
⅛ teaspoon cream of tartar	
1 teaspoon vanilla	

Start oven at slow (300° F.). Cover cooky sheets with waxed paper.

Beat egg whites, salt, and cream of tartar together until soft peaks form. Beat in vanilla and sugar until peaks are stiff when beater is removed. Fold in coconut. Drop mixture from teaspoon, about 1 inch apart, on prepared cooky sheets.

Bake about 25 minutes. Let cool slightly before removing from paper. Makes about 2 dozen macaroons.

My children enjoy cooking, too, and find the macaroon recipe on the condensed milk can delicious and easy to make. Not too much cleaning up necessary, either. The macaroons are good with tea or as an after-school snack with milk or cocoa.

BROWN-SUGAR PECAN COOKIES

3 tablespoons butter or margarine

1 cup brown sugar, packed

1 egg

1 cup pecan halves

¼ cup flour

1 teaspoon vanilla

Start oven at moderate (350° F.). Grease two cooky sheets well. Dust lightly with flour.

Melt butter or margarine in saucepan and stir in sugar. Beat egg and add with nuts, flour, and vanilla. Mix thoroughly. Drop from teaspoon onto prepared cooky sheets, about 5 inches apart, to allow for spreading.

Bake 8 to 10 minutes. Remove from oven. Let cookies stand just 1 minute. Use wide spatula to remove to cake rack to cool. Makes 3 to 4 dozen cookies.

CHOCOLATE OATMEAL BARS

⅓ cup melted butter or margarine

2 cups uncooked oatmeal

½ cup brown sugar, packed

¼ cup dark corn syrup

½ teaspoon salt

1½ teaspoons vanilla

1 (6-ounce) package semisweet chocolate pieces

¼ cup chopped nuts

Start oven at hot (450° F.). Grease 7-by-11-inch pan.

Pour melted butter or margarine over oats in mixing bowl. Stir well. Add brown sugar, syrup, salt, and vanilla. Mix thoroughly. Pack firmly into prepared pan.

Bake 12 minutes, or until rich brown color. Let cool in pan. Turn out of pan. Melt chocolate, spread over cake, and sprinkle with nuts. Let stand until chocolate is set. Cut in bars. Makes 2 dozen bars.

COUNTRY CRISP SUGAR COOKIES

½ cup butter or margarine

1 cup sugar

1 egg

1 tablespoon heavy cream

1 teaspoon vanilla

2 cups sifted all-purpose flour

½ teaspoon salt

1 teaspoon baking powder

Extra sugar for tops

Cream butter or margarine with sugar in mixing bowl until light and fluffy. Add egg, cream, and vanilla. Beat well. Sift flour with salt and baking powder. Add to creamed mixture, beating until well combined. Chill dough overnight.

When ready to bake, start oven at moderate (350° F.). Grease two or more cooky sheets lightly. Dust lightly with flour.

Roll out small amount of dough at one time, very thin, on lightly floured board. Cut with scalloped cutter. Sprinkle cookies lightly with sugar. Place on prepared cooky sheets.

Bake 5 minutes or until done. Makes about 36 to 50 large cookies, 6 dozen or more small cookies.

DATE SQUARES, HOLT-WILSON

½ pound (1 cup) dates	1 cup brown sugar, packed
½ cup granulated sugar	1 ½ cups sifted all-purpose flour
2 tablespoons cornstarch	½ teaspoon salt
1 cup water	½ teaspoon baking soda
3 tablespoons lemon juice	1 ¾ cups uncooked oatmeal
¾ cup butter or margarine	
½ teaspoon powdered mace or anise	

Pit and shred dates. Place them in small saucepan with granulated sugar. Stir cornstarch into a little water, then into 1 cup water, and add to dates. Add lemon juice. Cook, stirring constantly over low heat 5 minutes or until thickened. Remove from heat.

Start oven at moderately hot (400° F.).

Combine butter or margarine, mace or anise, and brown sugar in a mixing bowl. Cream smoothly together. Sift flour, salt, and soda together into creamed mixture. Mix well. Add oats. Mix and rub together until of crumblike consistency.

Spread half the oatmeal crumbs in greased 9-by-13-by-2-inch baking pan. Pour date filling on top. Cover with remaining half of crumbs. Press down lightly.

Bake 25 to 30 minutes or until lightly browned on top. Near end of baking time watch carefully that top does not brown too quickly. Let cool. Cut in squares. Makes 24 or more pieces.

These are a specialty of some of my favorite cousins who live in a lovely old pre-Revolutionary house outside Philadelphia. I often make them as gifts from my own kitchen and you can too.

Raisin Squares: Use same recipe with 2½ cups seedless raisins, soaked and drained. Use only ¾ cup water, no mace, increase flour to 1¾ cups and reduce oats to 1½ cups.

FRENCH ALMOND-CRESCENT COOKIES

1 cup sifted all-purpose flour	1 egg
⅓ cup sugar	½ teaspoon lemon flavoring
¼ teaspoon salt	½ cup slivered toasted almonds
⅔ cup ground blanched almonds	Light corn syrup
½ cup butter or margarine	Sliced candied cherries or angelica

Start oven at moderate (350° F.).

Combine flour, sugar, salt, and ground almonds in mixing bowl. Cut in butter or margarine until mixture is in coarse crumbs. Beat egg yolk slightly. Add with lemon flavoring to mixture. Blend smoothly. Divide dough into thirds. Form each portion into a long strip ½ inch wide and ½ inch thick. Cut strips in 2-inch lengths. Shape into crescents. Flatten slightly and taper ends. Place on ungreased cooky sheet. Brush tops of crescents with egg white. Press toasted almonds lightly in surface of crescents.

Bake 15 to 20 minutes or until lightly browned. Let cool slightly. Remove to rack to be glazed and decorated. While still warm, brush lightly with a little hot corn syrup. Sprinkle with pieces of cherry and angelica. Makes about 2 dozen small crescents.

GINGERBREAD MEN

3 cups sifted all-purpose flour	½ cup shortening
½ teaspoon baking soda	½ cup sugar
½ teaspoon each, powdered cinnamon, ginger, cloves, and mace	1 egg
	½ cup light molasses
¼ teaspoon salt	1 ½ teaspoons vinegar
	Dried currants for decoration

Sift flour, soda, spices, and salt together. Cream shortening and sugar together in mixing bowl until light and fluffy. Add egg and beat. Blend in molasses and vinegar. Stir in dry ingredients until lightly blended. Chill several hours or overnight.

When ready to bake, start oven at moderate (350° F.). Dust cooky sheets lightly with flour.

Roll dough out on lightly floured board to ⅛ inch thickness. Cut with gingerbread-man cutter. Transfer men to cooky sheets. Use currants to form features and buttons.

Bake about 10 minutes. Use wide spatula and remove men from cooky sheets promptly. Let cool on cake rack. Makes about 3 dozen.

Use cutters of various shapes, such as animals and trees, Santa Claus, and wreaths. For more elaborate decoration use Confectioners' Frosting (page 80) to make hat, trimmings, and detail on cookies.

The children love to bake these at Christmas to hang on the tree. They give them to visiting children as gifts from the tree.

SPICE COOKIES

½ cup shortening	½ teaspoon baking powder
½ cup butter or margarine	½ teaspoon salt
1½ cups sugar	½ teaspoon powdered cinnamon
2 eggs	
2 tablespoons milk	¼ teaspoon powdered allspice
½ teaspoon vanilla	¼ teaspoon powdered ginger
2½ cups sifted all-purpose flour	

Cream shortening and butter or margarine, sugar, and eggs thoroughly in mixing bowl. Stir in milk and vanilla. Sift dry ingredients together. Stir into creamed mixture until well blended. Wrap dough in foil and refrigerate until ready to bake.

Start oven at hot (425° F.).

Pat cooky dough out on lightly floured board. Roll dough about ⅛ inch thick. Cut with cooky cutters of various shapes. Arrange cookies on cooky sheet. Bake about 6 minutes or until done. Makes about 8 dozen small cookies.

To vary cookies, sprinkle some with a little granulated sugar before baking, and others with chopped almonds or peanuts.

To add to spiciness, mix a little cinnamon with sugar and sprinkle cookies just before removing from oven.

Let cool before storing in covered glass jar or in tin box lined with waxed paper.

HOLIDAY FRUIT COOKIES

1 ¼	cups sifted all-purpose flour	2	cups finely cut dates
½	teaspoon salt	1	cup chopped mixed candied
½	teaspoon powdered cinnamon		fruits
½	teaspoon baking soda	1	cup chopped pecans
1	cup sugar	1	cup chopped filberts
½	cup butter or margarine		Confectioners' Topping
2	eggs		(page 80)
3	tablespoons water		

Start oven at moderate (350° F.). Grease two or more cooky sheets.

Sift flour, salt, cinnamon, and soda together. Cream sugar, butter or margarine together until light, in mixing bowl. Add eggs, beat lightly. Add flour mixture and mix thoroughly. Stir in water, fruits, and nuts. Mix well. Drop by tablespoonful onto prepared cooky sheets.

Bake 15 to 17 minutes.

To frost, dribble icing over warm cookies. Makes about 5 dozen cookies.

JELLY-SLICE COOKIES

½	cup raspberry jelly	1	(13 ½-ounce) package plain
¼	cup finely chopped pignolia		cooky mix, plus flour and water
	nuts		

Combine jelly and nuts in bowl. Make up cooky dough according to directions on package for rolled or pressed cookies. Divide dough in half. Roll each half out ⅛ inch thick on lightly floured board into rectangle 8 by 14 inches. Spread ½ jelly-nut mixture over each rectangle of dough, not quite to edges. Roll each up like jelly roll. Chill.

When ready to bake, start oven at moderate (375° F.). Grease two cooky sheets.

Cut rolls in ¼-inch slices. Place cut side down on prepared cooky sheets.

Bake 8 to 10 minutes or until golden brown. Remove from cooky sheets immediately. Let cool on rack. Makes 7½ dozen slices.

SCOTCH SHORTBREAD

1	cup butter or margarine	2 ½	cups sifted all-purpose flour
½	cup sugar		

Cream butter or margarine with sugar in mixing bowl until light and fluffy. Sift in flour, mixing well. Chill 1 hour or longer.

Start oven at moderately slow (300° F.).

Roll dough out ¼ to ½ inch thick on lightly floured board. Cut with 2-inch round cutter or in diamonds or strips. Place on ungreased baking sheets.

Bake 25 to 30 minutes or until lightly browned. Remove from pan to cool. Makes 2 to 3 dozen pieces.

Scotch and English cooks spread shortbread dough in a round pan and mark the dough in pie-shaped wedges before baking. Use round layer-cake pans. Roll dough about ½ inch thick. Spread evenly in pan, smoothly to the sides. Mark 8 wedges in each pan.

LEMON-CHEESE COOKIES

1 (3-ounce) package cream cheese	½ teaspoon lemon flavoring
½ cup butter or margarine	1 cup sifted all-purpose flour
½ cup sugar	2 teaspoons baking powder
2 tablespoons grated lemon peel	¼ teaspoon salt
	1½ cups corn flakes, coarsely crumbled

Mash cheese. Cream together with butter or margarine, sugar, lemon peel, and flavoring in mixing bowl. Sift flour, baking powder, and salt together. Add to creamed mixture gradually, beating smoothly. Chill dough about 1 hour.

When ready to bake, start oven at moderate (350° F.).

Shape dough into small balls. Roll each in corn flakes. Place 1½ inches apart on ungreased cooky sheets.

Bake 12 to 15 minutes. Remove from pan to cool on rack. Makes about 3 dozen cookies.

QUICK COCONUT MACAROONS

1 (8-ounce) package shredded coconut (3 cups)	1 teaspoon vanilla or lemon flavoring
½ (15-ounce) can sweetened condensed milk (⅔ cup)	

Start oven at moderate (350° F.). Grease cooky sheets lightly.

Combine coconut and condensed milk. Mix well. Add flavoring.

Drop from teaspoon about 1 inch part onto prepared cooky sheets.

Bake 8 to 10 minutes or until delicately browned. Remove from cooky sheet immediately. Let cool on cake rack. Makes about 2½ dozen macaroons.

SPIKED CLOVE COOKIES

1 pound butter or margarine	1 teaspoon vanilla
1 egg yolk	1 cup ground or grated walnuts
¼ cup sugar	6 cups (about) sifted cake flour
2 tablespoons cognac or whiskey	Whole cloves

Cream butter or margarine until soft, fluffy, and light. Use electric mixer if possible. Beat egg yolk into creamed fat. Add sugar, brandy or whiskey, and vanilla, beating well. Beat in walnuts and flour thoroughly. Dough should be heavy, moist, but not sticky.

Start oven at moderate (325° F.).

Shape balls of dough about the size of a walnut. Stick 1 clove in top of each.

Bake on ungreased cooky sheets 15 to 20 minutes. Let cool before removing from pan. Makes about 7 dozen cookies. Try these as a gift for a man.

CHAPTER SIX

Candies and Sweetmeats

A candy thermometer is essential to successful home candymaking. The familiar temperatures *soft ball, hard ball, brittle,* etc., have their corresponding thermometer gradings. Here they are for your guidance:

Fudge, panocha, and similar candies	Soft Ball	234° to 238° F.
Fondant	" "	238° to 240° F. and higher
Taffies	Hard Ball	265° to 270° F.
Brittles	Hard Crack	300° to 310° F.
Clear hard candy	" "	310° F.

APRICOT-COCONUT BALLS

1 cup (8-ounce) dried apricots
1 cup shredded coconut
¾ cup pignolia or pistachio nuts
1 teaspoon grated lemon peel
1 teaspoon lemon juice

1 tablespoon orange juice
2 tablespoons confectioners' sugar
Granulated sugar

Steam apricots in top part of double boiler over boiling water 10 minutes. Put apricots, coconut, nuts, and peel through food grinder together twice, using fine blade. Add juices and confectioners' sugar. Stir well. Shape into small balls. Roll in granulated sugar. Let dry several hours before using or storing in airtight container. Makes 2 dozen balls.

These delicious confections may be dipped in chocolate coating. Let dry on waxed paper until chocolate is cold and firm. Try serving as a "little sweet" for dessert with demitasse.

CANDIED GRAPEFRUIT, LEMON, AND ORANGE PEEL

2 grapefruit, or	½ cup water
4 oranges, or	2 tablespoons light corn syrup
8 lemons	Extra granulated sugar
1 cup sugar	

Strip peel from washed grapefruit, oranges, or lemons in lengthwise sections. Put peel in saucepan with cold water to cover. Bring to a boil, reduce heat, and simmer 10 minutes. Drain peel. Cover with fresh cold water, bring to a boil, and boil 40 minutes. Drain peel. Remove pith from inside peel with spoon. Cut peel in even strips with kitchen scissors.

Combine sugar, water, and syrup in saucepan. Boil until thick or 228° F. on candy thermometer. Add peel. Cook until it becomes transparent. Drain peel in coarse sieve. Spread on plate or waxed paper to cool. Roll cooled peel in sugar. Store in airtight container. Makes about ¾ pound.

I make frequent small batches at Christmas time for gifts.

Chocolate Lemon and Orange Peel: Dip candied peel in melted chocolate. Let dry on waxed paper in cool place until chocolate is firm.

CANDY APPLES-ON-A-STICK

You can make professional-looking apples-on-a-stick by this recipe. Select firm, red apples. Wash and polish. For the sticks use wooden meat skewers or swab sticks bought at the drugstore.

8 medium-size red apples	1 cup water
2 cups sugar	½ teaspoon cinnamon flavoring
⅔ cup light corn syrup	Red pure-food coloring

Grease cooky sheet lightly. Remove stems from washed and polished apples. Insert wooden sticks firmly in stem end.

Stir sugar, syrup, and water together in medium-size saucepan over moderate heat until sugar almost dissolves. Cover pan and bring slowly to a boil. Remove cover and boil rapidly without stirring until 1 teaspoon of syrup dropped into cold water separates into hard, brittle threads, or to 300° F. on candy thermometer.

During cooking, wipe inside of pan often with wet cheesecloth wrapped around a fork. At 300° F. add flavoring and enough coloring to tint syrup bright red. Remove at once from heat. Stir only until color is evenly distributed.

Tip saucepan. Dip apples, twisting in syrup until covered. Let extra syrup on apples drain back into saucepan. Work quickly, placing saucepan over boiling water, if necessary, to keep syrup thin enough to coat apples easily. Save any excess syrup to help stick decorations (small candies and cutouts of candied fruits) on apples. Place coated apples, stick up, on prepared cooky sheet to harden. Makes 8 apples-on-a-stick.

CARAMEL NUTS

1 cup brown sugar, packed	1 tablespoon butter or margarine
½ cup granulated sugar	1 tablespoon vanilla
½ cup light cream	2 cups walnut halves
2 tablespoons light corn syrup	

Combine sugars, cream, and syrup in saucepan. Cook until a little dropped in cup of cold water forms soft ball, or 236° F. on candy thermometer. Add butter or margarine and vanilla. Let cool at room temperature without stirring until lukewarm (110° F.). Beat just until mixture begins to lose gloss. Add nuts and stir until nuts are well coated. Turn out on waxed paper. Separate nuts with spoon or two forks. Let stand until cool and firm. Makes about 1 pound.

DEVILED NUTS

1 pound shelled pecans, walnuts, or filberts	½ teaspoon Tabasco sauce
	¼ teaspoon pepper
⅓ cup melted butter or margarine	1 teaspoon salt
1 tablespoon Worcestershire sauce	

Start oven at moderately slow (300° F.). Place nuts in shallow baking pan.

Combine remaining ingredients. Pour over nuts. Stir well.

Bake 20 minutes, stirring several times. Let cool on thick paper towels. Store in airtight jar.

If you prefer top-of-the-stove cookery, use heavy skillet with tight cover over very low heat, or use electric skillet. Stir several times during heating period. A very nice hostess or Christmas gift.

Also see appetizer chapter for deviled nuts.

GLAZED NUTS

⅓ cup New Orleans molasses
⅓ cup light corn syrup
2 cups sugar

1 cup water
1 pound shelled almonds, walnuts, pecans, or mixed nuts

Combine molasses, syrup, sugar, and water in saucepan. Cook slowly, stirring constantly until sugar is dissolved. Then cook without stirring until small amount dropped into cup of cold water forms very brittle ball, or to 300° F. on candy thermometer. Remove from heat at once.

Using slotted kitchen spoon, dip nuts quickly into syrup. Spoon out onto waxed paper to drain until coating is cold and hard.

Makes 1 pound glazed nuts.

These make a delicious Christmas gift for people who "have everything."

CHOCOLATE-CARAMEL TURTLES

1 pound package (54) caramels
2 tablespoons water
¾ pound salted cashew nuts

1 (6-ounce) package semi-sweet
chocolate pieces

Heat caramels and water in top part of double boiler over boiling water about 5 minutes. Stir occasionally until evenly melted.

Grease baking sheet. Arrange 36 groups of 4 cashews each, about 2 inches apart on sheet. Drop melted caramels by teaspoon on each group of nuts. Let turtles cool 15 minutes. Reheat caramel over boiling water if necessary.

Melt chocolate pieces over hot, not boiling, water. Drop by teaspoon on top of each caramel turtle; spread chocolate if necessary with spatula. Set in cool, dry place until firm. Makes 36 turtles.

All children love to make and eat these.

CHOCOLATE COATING

Professional coating chocolate is especially prepared for wholesale candymakers, and it must be bought from caterers and candymakers, usually in 10-pound cakes. Simple substitutes, however, can give satisfaction in the home kitchen.

Many of the chocolate bars found on candy counters may be melted over hot water and used for dipping home-made fondant centers as well as caramels, nut clusters, and other sweetmeats. Experiment with a small amount of dipping with such available chocolate until you find one which gives you good results.

A few tips from the professional candymaker: for a large assortment of candies to be chocolate-dipped, buy 1-pound cake of your favorite chocolate, either bitter or semi-sweet. Leftover chocolate can be melted again and used for another batch.

You need a double boiler, fork, or dipper, boards or trays covered with waxed paper on which the chocolates dry. The room should be cool, 60° to 65° F., and if the candymaking is done in the kitchen, there should be no steam or other moist cookery going on. Have centers to be dipped ready on tray at left of bowl of dipping chocolate, and drying trays or boards at right.

Break chocolate in small pieces into upper part of double boiler. Place over hot water at not more than 130° F. on the candy thermometer. Do not have heat under water. To avoid overheating chocolate, stir chocolate constantly while it melts, so that chocolate in the bottom of the pan, next to hot water, does not become too hot.

Remove about 1 cup of melted chocolate to a bowl set in warm water at about 85° F. Stir and work chocolate with spoon until right consistency for dipping, about 83° to 88° F. Dip one or two pieces as trial chocolates. Drop center into chocolate. Cover completely and lift from bowl. Drop onto waxed paper. When placed on board or tray, the coated candy should be perfectly smooth except for the finial, the little string of chocolate on the top left by the twist of the spoon. The coating should harden quickly.

Dipped chocolates should cool quickly also, to prevent light spots appearing on the surface. If room is not cold, set trays in refrigerator to cool dipped chocolates.

Never add water to dipping chocolate. If it becomes too thick it must be remelted carefully.

For raisin and nut clusters and similar pieces, dipping chocolate should be cooler than for fondant centers. Drop nuts or clusters into chocolate, lift out with spoon, and drop onto waxed paper.

Fondant centers (see recipes) should be dipped as soon as possible after shaping. If they become too dry before dipping, they will never soften to a delicious creamy consistency. Fondants may be colored. Caramels, nougat, butter crunch, preserved fruits, stuffed fruits, fruit peels are favorites for coating with chocolate for the home sweetmeat tray.

CHOCOLATE CLUSTERS

1 (6-ounce) package semi-sweet chocolate pieces	1 tablespoon water
¼ cup light corn syrup	2 cups crisp rice cereal

Combine chocolate pieces, syrup, and water in top part of double boiler. Cook over hot, not boiling, water until melted and mixed together. Remove from heat. Stir in cereal. Drop from teaspoon onto waxed paper. Let chill until firm.

Store between sheets of waxed paper in airtight container. Makes 2½ to 3 dozen pieces.

Other good flavors: Use recipe above, but use 3 tablespoons light corn syrup instead of ¼ cup. Add any one of following to chocolate mixture: 1¼ cups chopped candied lemon or orange peel; 1½ cups shredded or flaked coconut; 1½ cups seedless raisins; or 1 cup pistachio, pino nuts, or chopped hazelnuts.

CREAM TAFFY

2 cups sugar	½ cup light cream, mixed with
¼ cup light corn syrup	½ cup heavy cream
¾ cup water	1 teaspoon vanilla

Grease shallow pan.

Combine sugar, syrup, and water in saucepan. Cook, stirring until sugar is dissolved. Continue cooking to firm ball stage or 250° F. on candy thermometer. Add cream. Cook slowly, stirring constantly to prevent burning, until hard ball stage, not quite brittle, or 260° F. is reached. Let cool.

When cool enough to handle, pour the vanilla into center of the mass. Gather corners toward center so that flavoring will not be lost. Remove from pan, and pull. Grease your hands lightly with butter or margarine.

When firm, and light buff color, stretch out in long rope. Cut into pieces. Wrap pieces in waxed paper. Makes about 1 pound. Cuts into 80 or more pieces.

My children like to make this for Christmas. It's a wonderful old-fashioned candy that can't be bought except, maybe, at church fairs. We pack it in small glass apothecary jars which we decorate with red ribbon and green pine from our own woods. Wonderful for token gifts and for the children's teacher. Men friends anticipate it annually.

HONEY TAFFY

1 cup sugar	½ cup water
3 tablespoons cornstarch	⅔ cup honey
⅛ teaspoon salt	

Grease large platter.

Combine sugar, cornstarch, and salt in saucepan. Stir in water and honey. Cook over medium heat until taffy forms heavy, hard thread when a drop is tested in cold water, or 266° F. on candy thermometer.

Pour onto platter. Let cool until taffy can be handled. Butter your hands. Pull taffy until milky-looking. Shape into a long rope and cut into pieces about 1½ inches long. Let cool on platter or waxed paper.

Tastes better after 24 hours. Wrap pieces in waxed paper to store, or use in boxes of mixed candy. Makes about 40 pieces.

Fudge

DELUXE BROWN-SUGAR FUDGE

1 cup brown sugar, packed	2 (1-ounce) squares chocolate, broken
1 cup granulated sugar	
⅓ cup milk	2 tablespoons butter
⅓ cup light cream	1 teaspoon vanilla

Combine sugars, milk, cream, and chocolate in saucepan. Cook slowly, stirring constantly until soft ball stage, or 236° F. on candy thermometer.

Remove from heat at once. Add butter without stirring. Set pan aside to cool at kitchen temperature. Grease two shallow square pans. When candy has cooled to lukewarm, add vanilla and begin beating. Continue beating until fudge has lost shiny look and a small amount dropped from spoon onto a plate or saucer holds its shape.

Pour into prepared pans. Let cool. Cut into squares. Makes about 1¼ pounds, or 36 pieces.

This is our very favorite fudge, often made on long, dark winter afternoons over the weekend—especially when we have male guests. It goes into Christmas goodie boxes, too. I make it for our church fair.

SOUR-CREAM FUDGE

2 cups sugar
½ teaspoon salt
1 cup commercial sour cream
2 tablespoons butter or margarine

½ cup broken pecans or other
   nuts

Combine sugar, salt, and sour cream in saucepan. Cook, stirring occasionally, until a little dropped in cup of cold water forms soft ball,
or 236° F. on candy thermometer. Add butter or margarine. Let cool
at room temperature, without stirring, until lukewarm (110° F.). Beat
until mixture loses gloss, then add nuts. Spread in buttered 8-inch square
pan. When firm, cut into squares. Makes about 24 pieces.

Nuts may be omitted and shredded or flaked coconut substituted for
them. Or use puffed rice cereal in place of nuts.

DIVINITY

2 cups light brown sugar, packed
½ cup light corn syrup
½ cup hot water

¼ teaspoon salt
2 egg whites, beaten stiff
1 teaspoon vanilla

Combine sugar, syrup, water, and salt in saucepan. Cook until a little
dropped in cup of cold water forms hard ball or to 248° F. on candy
thermometer. Remove from heat. Pour syrup in thin stream slowly over
stiffly beaten egg whites, beating constantly. Beat until mixture holds its
shape. Stir in vanilla. Drop from tablespoon onto waxed paper, lifting
and twirling spoon to form peak on top of each mound.
    If divinity becomes too stiff for twirling, add few drops hot water
to bring back desired consistency. Makes about 1½ dozen pieces.

Nuts may be added to this candy. A good combination of flavors
results when chopped pistachio nuts are added. It is also good with
pecans, filberts, or black walnuts.

WHITE FONDANT

The home candymaker who likes to create professional-looking
chocolates and other candies must be able to make good fondant. This

recipe is simplified from a commercial formula. The fondant remains creamy and workable. It may be shaped and dipped in chocolate. Some may be colored with pure-food coloring. Some may be combined with nuts, coconut, chopped candied fruits or combined in layers with fudge, caramels, and other mixtures to make logs, squares, and various decorative pieces for the sweetmeat tray.

This recipe makes 1 pound of fondant, an amount easy for the beginner to handle. (Note: It must be ripened before using. See below.)

2 cups sugar
1 ¼ cups water
2 tablespoons light corn syrup

1 teaspoon vanilla or lemon flavoring

Place a large platter in refrigerator to chill.

Combine sugar, water, and corn syrup in saucepan. Cook, stirring constantly, until sugar is dissolved. Remove spoon. Do not stir candy again during cooking.

When candy begins to boil, cover saucepan tightly and let boil 3 minutes; the steam formed washes down any sugar crystals. Remove cover; continue cooking. From time to time, wash away sugar crystals which now appear on the sides of the uncovered saucepan. For this, use a fork wrapped in a piece of cheesecloth and dipped in cold water.

Cook to soft ball stage, and 1 minute longer, or 240° F. on candy thermometer, for firm fondant for molding. (At 238° F., which is soft ball, fondant is suitable for coconut drops, layers in fudge, et cetera.)

At 240° F. remove pan from heat; pour fondant at once onto cold, wet platter. Let fondant cool to lukewarm. Add flavoring. Beat with fondant paddle, spatula, or wide, flat wooden spoon until fondant becomes white and creamy. Knead until the mass is smooth and no lumps remain.

Put fondant away in covered glass bowl or jar to ripen for 2 or 3 days before using. It may be kept longer if tightly covered. Use fondant as suggested in various recipes.

Chocolate Fondant: Add 1½ (1-ounce) squares chocolate, or 3 tablespoons dry cocoa, to sugar mixture in above recipe before cooking. Cook as described, but only to 238° F.

COFFEE FONDANT

2 cups sugar	1 teaspoon vanilla
1 ¼ cups strongly brewed coffee	1 teaspoon coffee essence
2 tablespoons light corn syrup	

Combine sugar, coffee, corn syrup, vanilla and coffee essence in saucepan. Cook, following directions for making and storing Fondant.

Lemon Fondant: Prepare basic Fondant as described, but cook to 248° F. Spread grated peel of ½ lemon and 3 tablespoons lemon juice on cold, wet platter just before pouring fondant on platter. Do not stir. Let cool to lukewarm.

Add flavoring. Beat long and steadily until fondant is thick enough to be handled, then knead as described above. Fruit juice does not always blend well with sugar mixture, and long beating is necessary. Store and use like basic fondant.

Orange Fondant: Prepare Fondant as described, but cook to 252° F. Mix grated peel of 1 orange, 3 tablespoons orange juice, 1 tablespoon lemon juice. Spread on cold, wet platter. Pour fondant over fruit mixture. Do not stir. Let cool to lukewarm. Beat, knead, and store as described for basic Fondant.

CREAMY FONDANT

2 cups sugar	1 tablespoon butter
¾ cup milk or light cream	1 teaspoon vanilla
1 tablespoon light corn syrup	

Place platter in refrigerator to chill.

Combine sugar, milk or cream, and syrup in saucepan. Cook, stirring until sugar dissolves. Continue cooking to soft ball stage, or 238° F. on candy thermometer. Stir occasionally to prevent scorching. Remove from heat and add butter. Let stand until butter is melted. Stir only enough to mix the butter through the fondant. Pour onto cold, wet platter.

When cooled to lukewarm, add vanilla and begin beating with fondant paddle, spatula, or wide, flat wooden spoon.

Follow general directions for beating and kneading as given in recipe for basic Fondant (page 146).

This rich, creamy fondant makes delicious centers for chocolate coating, pecan rolls, and other pieces. Makes about 1 pound.

HAZELNUT CRUNCH

1 cup butter or margarine
1⅓ cups sugar
1 tablespoon light corn syrup
3 tablespoons water
1 cup coarsely chopped hazelnuts, toasted

4 (4½-ounce) bars milk chocolate, melted
1 cup finely chopped hazelnuts, toasted

Melt butter or margarine in large saucepan. Add sugar, syrup, and water. Cook, stirring occasionally until a little dropped in cold water hardens and cracks, or 300° F. on candy thermometer. Remove at once from heat. Stir in coarsely chopped nuts. Spread in ungreased pan measuring about 13 by 9 by 2 inches. Let cool completely.

Turn out on waxed paper. Spread top with half the chocolate. Sprinkle with half the finely chopped nuts. Cover with waxed paper and invert. Spread other side with remaining chocolate. Sprinkle with remaining finely chopped nuts. Let stand until chocolate is firm. Chill if necessary. Break into pieces. Makes about 1½ pounds, 24 or more pieces.

MOLASSES POPCORN BALLS

1 cup molasses
1 cup sugar
1 tablespoon butter or margarine

4 quarts unsalted freshly popped corn

Combine molasses, sugar, and butter or margarine in saucepan over low heat. Stir until sugar dissolves. Cook over medium heat until little syrup dropped into cup of cold water separates into threads which are hard but not brittle or candy thermometer reads 270° F.

Pour syrup over popcorn, stirring to coat all. When cool enough to handle, rub palms with butter or margarine, shape corn into balls. Let them cool on waxed paper. When cooled, wrap each ball in waxed paper, then in colored cellophane. Makes about 2 dozen balls.

Christmas Popcorn Balls: Add ¼ cup finely chopped candied red cherries, ¼ cup finely chopped candied green cherries or angelica, 2 cups chopped cashew or pignolia nuts to popcorn in bowl. Mix. Make balls as described in Molasses Popcorn Balls.

MARZIPAN FRUITS

2 egg whites	Pure-food coloring
2 cups almond paste	Cocoa
Confectioners' sugar	

Whip egg whites until stiff. Add almond paste and enough confectioners' sugar to make mixture easy to shape. Form into small pears, apples, cherries, and other fruits. Brush some very lightly with food coloring. Roll others in cocoa. Wrap and store in cool place until wanted. Makes about 2 pounds, 30 to 50 pieces.

Almond paste can be bought at pastry shops and confectioners. Usually texture and flavor are better in marzipan when paste is mixed with an equal amount of freshly made White Fondant (page 146).

Pecan Twins: Put 2 large pecan halves together with small amount of colored marzipan.

Marzipan Stuffed Dates: Remove pits from large dried dates. If very sticky, rinse dates in cold water and let them dry. Fill with marzipan mixed with fondant.

While we associate marzipan with Christmas stockings (absolutely essential!), it is, of course, a delightful sweetmeat for any time of the year. In Toledo, Spain, I lunched in the warm sun at a hotel restaurant which features marzipan made by nearby nuns. This delicacy, made in your kitchen, is a conversation piece as an after-coffee sweet or featured on the tea tray assortment.

PEANUT BRITTLE

2 cups sugar	$\frac{1}{16}$ teaspoon salt
1 cup roasted peanuts	

Heat sugar in heavy skillet. Cook and stir constantly 5 minutes or until a thin syrup forms. Add nuts and salt. Stir until nuts are coated. With greased spatula spread in thin layer on well-greased baking sheet or waxed paper. When nearly cold, crack into pieces. Makes about 1 pound.

If made in electric skillet, set control at 300° F. or follow manufacturer's directions.

RUM SQUARES

Cut fruitcake into 1-inch cubes. Sprinkle lightly with rum. Roll in sifted confectioners' sugar. Store in airtight container 1 or 2 days.

Bourbon Squares: Use bourbon whiskey in place of rum in above recipe. Bought fruitcake may be used, or your favorite homemade cake.

STUFFED DATES

30 large dried dates	½ teaspoon powdered cinnamon
4 figs	¼ teaspoon powdered cloves
6 prunes	Orange juice
¼ cup broken pecans	Granulated sugar

If dates are very sticky, rinse in cold water. Drain and let dry. Make side slit in each and remove pit.

Wash figs and prunes, drain, and steam over rapidly boiling water 5 minutes. Remove stones from prunes. Put figs, prunes, and nuts through food chopper. Add spices to ground mixture. If too dry, add few drops orange juice. Mix well. Stuff dates. Roll dates in sugar. Makes 30 stuffed dates.

Vary this filling by using pistachio nuts and a few washed, soaked currants. Walnut and Brazil-nut flavors are delicious, too, in this stuffing.

BLACK BOTTOMS

Dip bottoms of large red and green gumdrops into melted semi-sweet chocolate pieces. Let cool and harden on waxed paper.

CHERRY ROSETTES

Cut candied cherries in quarters, almost through. Place a tiny ball of fondant or marshmallow in center. Press together. Use for decorating cakes and candy assortments.

SUGARED MARSHMALLOWS

Dip tops of marshmallows in water, then in red sugar. Let stand on waxed paper until dry. Use to decorate birthday cakes and candy assortments.

Red sugar: Add 1 or 2 drops red pure-food coloring to 1 cup granulated sugar, stirring continually. Mix and stir until well colored. This can also be used on Christmas cookies.

CHAPTER SEVEN

Casserole Meals

A casserole in your kitchen, or kitchenette, makes meal planning and preparation easy. It makes service in dining room or living room, in the patio or on a terrace, on back porch or garden flagstones a pleasure. It takes the worry out of being a hostess because the food stays hot, looks appetizing, tastes the way food should taste.

A stack of casseroles, from the big three-quart models down to very small individual-serving size, can give variety to the presentation of your menus. In earthenware, glazed pottery, flameproof (that is, metal-base ware) pottery, and glass, these cooking-serving dishes may be kept warm on an electric-wired wheeled table or tray, or over canned heat, a candle warmer, or an alcohol burner on the buffet table, insuring the hot, flavorful dish which adds so much to any menu.

A pastry crust on the casserole, or a crisp, crusty pastry shell filled with a casserole mixture, can take the place of bread in the menu. Cutouts of pastry, biscuits, and strips of pastry baked on top of a casserole add considerable food value to the dish. And while most of my menus mention bread of some kind, it may certainly be omitted in many casserole meals (as it is in some European countries, Norway and Sweden, for example), the nourishing bread-topped casserole supplying all that is needed in flavor and food value.

For additional casseroles see chapters on cheese, chicken, eggs, fish, and vegetables.

THOMPSON STREET FISH-AND-RICE

2 cups water	½ teaspoon salt
1 teaspoon salt	Freshly ground black pepper
1 cup uncooked rice	1 pound fresh or quick-frozen
2 tablespoons butter or marga-	flounder or sole fillets
rine	1 teaspoon paprika
1 large Bermuda onion, peeled	1 tablespoon lemon juice
and sliced	1 (8-ounce) can tomato sauce
¾ teaspoon orégano	8 thin slices processed American
6 large peeled tomato slices	cheese

Combine water, 1 teaspoon salt, and rice in 2-quart saucepan. Bring to a vigorous boil. Turn heat as low as possible. Cover pan and simmer about 14 minutes. Remove pan from heat, but leave lid on for 10 minutes.

Start oven at moderate (350° F.). Grease shallow 10-by-6-by-2-inch casserole.

While rice cooks, melt butter or margarine in skillet. Cook onion in it until soft but not brown. Arrange cooked onion slices in prepared casserole. Pour rice over onion. Sprinkle with orégano. Top with tomato slices. Season slices lightly with salt and pepper. Cut fish fillets into serving-size pieces. Spread over tomato layer. Sprinkle fish with salt, a grind of black pepper, paprika, and lemon juice. Pour tomato sauce over fish. Cover with cheese slices.

Bake about 30 minutes or until cheese bubbles and top is browning. Makes 6 servings.

This approximates a dish I used to enjoy in a Thompson Street restaurant, part of New York's Little Italy. It lay across the park from my home on Washington Square. There were green dandelions in the salad and sawdust on the floor. We finished dinner with zabaglione.

BAKED NOODLES-AND-CORNED BEEF

1 (8 or 9-ounce) package	1 (8-ounce) can tomato sauce
noodles	¼ cup chili sauce
1 onion	¼ cup water or bouillon
1 green pepper	1 teaspoon prepared mustard
2 tablespoons butter or marga-	1 teaspoon Worcestershire sauce
rine	¼ cup grated Cheddar cheese
1 (1-pound) can corned beef	

Start oven at moderate (350° F.). Grease 1½-quart casserole or baking dish.

Cook noodles until tender, according to directions on package. Peel and dice onion. Cut green pepper fine. Cook onion and green pepper in butter or margarine about 5 minutes or until tender. Break corned beef into small chunks with fork. Add to onion mixture. Stir. Add tomato sauce, chili sauce, water or bouillon, mustard, and Worcestershire sauce. Stir and heat 1 minute. Pour noodles into prepared baking dish. Make depression or well in center and fill with meat combination. Sprinkle top with cheese.

Bake 30 minutes. Makes 4 or more servings.

BEANS FOR EVERYBODY

⅓ cup butter or margarine
½ cup minced peeled onions
1 clove garlic, peeled and sliced
2 teaspoons brown sugar
1 teaspoon dry mustard
2 (No. 2) cans kidney beans, drained

1 (No. 2) can green limas, drained
1 (1-pound) can Boston-style baked beans
¼ cup ketchup
2 tablespoons vinegar
Salt and pepper

Start oven at moderate (350° F.).

Heat butter or margarine in skillet. Sauté onions and garlic together 5 minutes, or until onions are tender. Stir brown sugar, mustard, kidney beans, limas, and baked beans, ketchup, and vinegar in. Mix well. Taste for seasoning. Add salt and pepper as needed. Pour into 2-quart casserole.

Bake, covered, 25 minutes. Uncover and let brown 5 minutes. Makes 8 servings.

BEEF PIE

3 pounds beef, cut in small cubes
3 tablespoons butter or margarine
2 cups stock or bouillon
12 small whole onions, peeled
4 carrots, scraped and diced
1 (3-ounce) can sliced mushrooms

½ teaspoon freshly ground pepper
¾ cup red wine
1 sprig thyme
¼ teaspoon crumbled leaf sage
1 tablespoon dry parsley
Pastry for top

Start oven at moderate (325° F.).

Melt butter or margarine in 3-quart flameproof casserole. Add beef, stir, and cook 15 minutes. Add stock or bouillon. Cover and cook slowly in oven 1 hour. Add onions, carrots, mushrooms. Season with pepper. Cover and cook slowly ½ hour longer, or until vegetables are cooked and meat nearly done. Add wine, and let sauce cook down, uncovered if too much remains. Add herbs and stir. Remove casserole. Cover top with pastry. Trim edge and press edge of pastry to rim of casserole with fork. Gash pastry top in small leaf-and-stem pattern in center to allow steam to escape. Turn oven up to hot (425° F.).

Bake 15 to 20 minutes until crust is golden. Makes 8 servings.

BROCCOLI MORNAY

2 (9-ounce) packages quick-frozen broccoli
Chicken à la King

3 tablespoons grated Parmesan cheese

Cook broccoli as described on package. While broccoli cooks prepare chicken recipe, using chicken breasts or leftover roast chicken.

Drain cooked broccoli. Place in buttered 1½-quart baking dish. Pour Chicken à la King over broccoli. Sprinkle with Parmesan cheese.

Brown under medium broiler heat. Makes 6 servings.

BISCUIT-TOP TUNA CASSEROLE

1 onion, peeled
1 green pepper
3 tablespoons butter or margarine
⅜ cup sifted all-purpose flour
3 cups milk
1 teaspoon salt

⅛ teaspoon pepper
2 (7-ounce) cans tuna
1 cup biscuit mix
⅓ cup milk
½ cup grated Cheddar cheese
1 slice canned pimiento

Start oven at moderate (375° F.). Grease 2-quart shallow baking dish.

Chop onion and green pepper coarsely. Cook in butter or margarine about 5 minutes or until tender. Stir in flour smoothly. Add milk gradually. Season with salt and pepper. Cook, stirring constantly, until sauce bubbles. Mix in drained and flaked tuna. Pour into prepared baking dish.

Combine biscuit mix and milk according to package directions. Turn dough out on lightly floured board. Pat about ½ inch thick in rectangular shape. Sprinkle dough with cheese and fine slivers of pimiento. Roll as you would jelly roll. Cut in 8 slices. Arrange slices on top of casserole mixture.

Bake 30 minutes or until biscuit tops are done and browning. Makes 6 servings.

CHEESE-TOP GREEN BEANS

1 (9-ounce) package quick-frozen green beans French cut	⅛ teaspoon pepper
	¼ teaspoon thyme
1 small onion, peeled and chopped	¼ teaspoon savory
	½ teaspoon of Accent
3 tablespoons butter or margarine	1 tablespoon finely cut parsley
	6 hard-cooked eggs
¼ cup flour	½ cup grated Swiss or processed cheese
2 cups milk	
2 teaspoons salt	¼ cup bread crumbs

Start oven at moderate (350° F.).

Cook frozen beans as directed on package. Drain, and set aside. Cook onion in 2 tablespoons butter or margarine until golden. Stir in flour smoothly. Add milk gradually, stirring. Cook, stirring constantly until bubbly. Season with salt, pepper, herbs, Accent and parsley. Remove from heat.

Cut eggs in slices. Mix with green beans in 1½-quart baking dish. Pour parsley sauce over mixture. Sprinkle with cheese and crumbs. Dot with remaining 1 tablespoon butter or margarine.

Bake 30 minutes or until brown. Makes 4 servings.

CHICKEN OR TURKEY SCALLOP

⅓ cup uncooked rice	2 finely diced canned pimientos
2 cups chicken consommé or dissolved bouillon cubes	2 eggs, beaten
	¼ cup heavy cream
2 ½ cups diced cooked chicken or turkey	¾ teaspoon salt
	⅛ teaspoon poultry seasoning
⅓ cup chopped celery	¼ cup buttered crumbs

Start oven at moderate (325° F.). Grease 10-by-6-by-1½-inch baking dish.

Cook rice, covered, in chicken broth or consommé about 10 minutes, or until almost tender. Combine with remaining ingredients except crumbs. Pour into prepared baking dish. Sprinkle crumbs generously over all.

Bake 45 to 50 minutes or until hot and browning. Makes 6 servings.

CORN-TOMATO CASSEROLE

2 cups whole-kernel corn, fresh, frozen, or canned	2 medium tomatoes
	1 teaspoon salt
1 small onion	1 teaspoon sugar
½ green pepper	⅛ teaspoon pepper
3 slices bacon	¾ cup coarse cracker crumbs

Start oven at moderate (375° F.). Grease 2-quart casserole.

Cut fresh corn from cob or drain canned corn or thaw frozen corn. Peel and dice onion. Dice green pepper. Cook bacon in skillet until crisp. Remove slices to thick paper towels to drain. Cook onion and pepper in bacon fat about 5 minutes. Scald and skin tomatoes. Cut in slices. Pour corn into prepared casserole. Sprinkle with half of salt and sugar. Cover with onion mixture. Place tomato slices over this. Season with remaining salt and sugar and pepper.

Crumble drained bacon. Mix with crumbs. Sprinkle over top of casserole.

Bake 25 to 30 minutes. Makes 4 or more servings.

COUNTRY POTATO SUPPER

6 or 8 potatoes	⅛ teaspoon pepper
½ pound thinly sliced boiled ham or 1 ¼ cups shredded baked ham	2 tablespoons grated onion
	2 tablespoons butter or margarine
2 tablespoons flour	1 ¾ cups milk
1 teaspoon salt	

Start oven at moderate (350° F.). Grease 2-quart casserole.

Wash, scrub, pare potatoes. Slice enough to make 1 quart. Arrange layer of potatoes and one of ham in prepared casserole. Sprinkle with half the flour, salt, pepper, onion, and dabs of butter or margarine. Add second layer of potatoes, second layer of ham, then remaining potatoes as top layer. Sprinkle remaining flour, seasoning, and butter or margarine over all. Pour milk over contents of casserole and cover dish.

Bake 30 minutes. Uncover dish and bake 30 minutes longer or until potatoes are done and top browning. Makes 6 servings.

CZARDAS CASSEROLE

1 large onion, peeled and chopped	⅛ teaspoon pepper
1 tablespoon fat	1 bay leaf
2 teaspoons flour	4 cups cubed roast beef
1 (No.2) can tomatoes, chopped	12 large pitted prunes
½ teaspoon salt	6 or 8 very small boiled potatoes

Start oven at moderate (375° F.).

Cook onion in fat in 2-quart metal-base casserole until golden. Blend in flour. Add tomatoes, seasonings, and beef. Stir to mix well. Let simmer slowly 10 minutes.

Stuff 6 prunes with pieces of boiled potato. Add remaining potatoes and remaining prunes to beef mixture. Top with stuffed prunes. Cover casserole.

Bake 30 minutes. Uncover dish and bake 10 minutes longer. Makes 6 servings.

DE LUXE BEAN CASSEROLE

1 large onion, peeled and chopped

½ garlic clove, peeled and mashed

2 tablespoons bacon fat

1 (1-pound) can baked beans in tomato sauce

2 cups good-sized pieces cooked turkey, chicken, or veal

¼ pound sliced salami, cut in thin strips

2 tablespoons finely cut parsley

½ cup red wine, or

¼ cup sherry or vermouth

Start oven at moderate (350° F.). Grease 2-quart casserole.

Sauté onion and garlic in bacon fat 5 minutes. Remove garlic and discard. Pour beans into prepared casserole. Add chicken, turkey, or veal, and salami and parsley. Add onion and bacon fat. Stir just enough to combine flavors. Pour wine, sherry, or vermouth over all. Cover casserole.

Bake 25 minutes. Uncover casserole and let bake 5 minutes longer. Makes 6 servings.

DEVILED CRAB BAKE

1 cup (1 9-ounce package) frozen Alaska king crab meat

¾ cup milk

1 tablespoon butter or margarine

15 round salty crackers

1 teaspoon dry mustard

1 minced onion

½ teaspoon salt

½ teaspoon prepared horse-radish

1 teaspoon soy sauce

½ teaspoon pepper

12 large canned mushroom caps

Melted butter or margarine

Parsley

Drain crab meat. Break up coarsely, look over carefully for fibers and bones.

Heat milk and butter or margarine together in large saucepan. Crumble crackers into milk. Add crab meat to milk and crackers. Combine mustard, onion, salt, horse-radish, soy sauce, and pepper. Add to crab mixture and mix well.

Start oven at moderate (350° F.).

Place mushroom caps in four buttered individual baking dishes. Heap crab mixture in mushrooms. Spoon a little melted butter or margarine over tops.

Bake 20 minutes. Garnish with parsley. Serve hot. Makes 4 servings.

GARLIC-SHRIMP CASSEROLE

4 pounds cooked fresh or quick-
frozen deveined shrimp
1 cup butter or margarine,
melted
2 cloves garlic, peeled and
minced

⅓ cup finely cut parsley
½ teaspoon paprika
⅛ teaspoon cayenne
½ cup sherry
2 cups soft bread crumbs
Extra parsley, finely cut

Remove shells and dark veins from freshly cooked shrimp. If quick-frozen deveined shrimp are used, cook as described on package. Let cool.

Start oven at moderate (325° F.). Grease 2½-quart casserole.

Combine melted butter or margarine, garlic, parsley, paprika, cayenne, and sherry. Mix and add crumbs. Pour shrimp into prepared casserole. Spoon butter mixture over all.

Bake 20 to 25 minutes or until crumbs are browned. Sprinkle with additional parsley to serve. Makes 8 servings.

HAM-AND-EGGS CASSEROLE

2 to 3 cups diced cooked ham
6 hard-cooked eggs, sliced
1 (6-ounce) can mushroom caps,
drained
1 (10½-ounce) can condensed
cream-of-celery soup
½ cup milk
2 cups grated sharp process
cheese

2 teaspoons Worcestershire
sauce
½ teaspoon Tabasco sauce
¾ cup dry bread crumbs
3 tablespoons melted butter or
margarine
2 tablespoons finely cut chives

Start oven at moderate (325° F.). Rub 2-quart casserole with butter.

Make alternate layers of ham, eggs, and mushrooms, starting and ending with ham in prepared casserole. Combine soup and milk in saucepan. Add cheese, Worcestershire, and Tabasco. Heat, stirring until cheese melts. Pour over mixture in casserole. Mix crumbs and butter or margarine. Sprinkle over top.

Bake uncovered about 25 minutes or until hot through and crumbs are golden. Sprinkle top with chives just before serving. Makes 6 servings.

HERBED LAMB CHOPS

1 tablespoon cooking oil	4 thin slices lemon
4 thick shoulder lamb chops	1 teaspoon sugar
¼ teaspoon salt	⅛ teaspoon basil
⅛ teaspoon pepper	¼ teaspoon thyme
4 thick slices peeled onion	½ teaspoon marjoram
4 thin rings green pepper	1 cup chopped canned tomatoes

Heat oil in a large metal-base casserole over moderate heat. Brown chops well on both sides. Season with salt and pepper. Place slice of onion, green pepper ring, and lemon slice on each chop.

Stir sugar and herbs into tomatoes. Pour over chops. Cover dish tightly with foil. Store in refrigerator until about 1 hour before dinner. Remove casserole from refrigerator. Let stand at kitchen temperature until chill is off dish. Remove foil.

Start oven at moderate (350° F.). Cover casserole with its own lid. Bake 1 hour or until chops are tender. Makes 4 servings.

If you are calorie-conscious omit the oil. Turn chops frequently to prevent burning or sticking.

HUNGARIAN CASSEROLE

½ cup butter or margarine	1 teaspoon paprika
4 large onions, peeled and sliced	½ teaspoon powdered nutmeg
1 clove garlic, peeled	¼ teaspoon powdered mace
2 pounds veal, cut in serving pieces	1 tablespoon sugar
1 teaspoon salt	1 (No. 2) can tomatoes, chopped
½ teaspoon freshly ground pepper	1 cup commercial sour cream
	2 tablespoons flour
	4 cups hot cooked rice, noodles, or macaroni

Start oven at moderate (325° F.).

Melt butter or margarine in 2-quart metal-base casserole. Add onions and garlic. Cook until onions are soft, about 5 minutes. Remove garlic and discard it. Add veal. Cover and cook 20 minutes. Add seasonings and tomatoes, and cover.

Cook in oven until veal is tender, about 1 hour. When almost done, add sour cream. Stir. Mix 1 tablespoon flour with a little sauce in the casserole, then stir into casserole. Let boil 2 or 3 minutes to thicken. Use more flour if necessary. Serve hot, over rice, noodles, or macaroni. Makes 8 servings.

KRAUT-AND-HAM CASSEROLE

3 slices ham, ¼-inch thick
1 (No. 2) can (2½ cups) sauerkraut
¼ cup brown sugar, packed
3 tablespoons fine, dry bread crumbs

3 tablespoons butter or margarine
3 medium-sized apples, cored and sliced

Start oven at moderate (350° F.).

Cut ham slices in half. Cook over low heat about 10 to 15 minutes, until lightly browned on both sides. Then arrange the ham in 8-by-12-by-2-inch baking dish. Top with undrained kraut. Sprinkle brown sugar and bread crumbs over all.

Bake 25 to 30 minutes.

Melt butter or margarine. Add apples and sauté 5 to 7 minutes, until lightly browned. Drain apples and add as garnish to casserole. Makes 4 to 6 servings.

MACARONI-AND-SARDINE CASSEROLE

6 hard-cooked eggs
5 tablespoons mayonnaise
½ teaspoon salt
½ teaspoon prepared mustard
⅛ teaspoon pepper
2 (8-ounce) cans tomato sauce
1 cup water
1 cup grated processed American cheese

1 tablespoon grated onion
½ teaspoon Worcestershire sauce
⅛ teaspoon orégano
4 cups drained cooked elbow maccaroni (8-ounce package)
1 (3¼-ounce) can boneless, skinless sardines

Shell eggs. Cut in half lengthwise. Remove yolks. Put through coarse sieve into bowl. Blend in mayonnaise, salt, mustard, and pepper. Stuff white halves.

Combine tomato sauce, water, ¾ cup grated cheese, onion, Worcestershire sauce, and orégano in saucepan. Cook over low heat until cheese melts. Combine with macaroni in bowl.

Start oven at moderate (350° F.). Grease 13-by-9-by-2-inch baking dish.

Pour macaroni mixture into prepared baking dish. Arrange deviled eggs and drained sardines on top. Sprinkle with remaining ¼ cup cheese.

Bake 20 minutes or until top is browning and bubbly. Serve hot. Makes 6 servings.

MEAL-IN-ONE CASSEROLE

1 pound sliced cooked ham
8 to 12 slices cooked chicken
½ cup chopped peeled onion
½ cup chopped celery
4 tablespoons butter or margarine
¼ cup all-purpose flour
1 cup light cream
1 cup chicken broth, or
2 chicken bouillon cubes in 1 cup boiling water

½ teaspoon salt
⅛ teaspoon pepper
1 (3-ounce) can broiled sliced mushrooms, drained
Melted butter or margarine
1 package refrigerated ready-to-bake biscuits

Start oven at moderately hot (400° F.). Grease 10-by-6-by-1½-inch baking dish.

Make alternate layers of ham and chicken in prepared baking dish. Cook onion and celery in butter or margarine 8 minutes, or until celery is tender but not brown. Blend in flour, mixing smoothly. Stir in cream and broth gradually. Cook, stirring constantly until thick. Add salt and pepper. Pour sauce over ham and chicken in casserole. Arrange mushrooms around edge of casserole. Brush them with melted butter or margarine.

Bake uncovered 12 to 15 minutes. Place ready-to-bake biscuits in oven with casserole. Bake 12 to 15 minutes or until biscuits are golden brown. Arrange biscuits in ring on casserole mixture. Serve hot. Makes 6 servings.

MEAT-SPAGHETTI CASSEROLE

1 pound pork sausage meat
⅓ cup chopped peeled onions
⅓ cup chopped celery
½ cup coarsely chopped green pepper
1 (6-ounce) can tomato paste
1 (8-ounce) can tomato sauce

¼ teaspoon orégano
¾ teaspoon salt
2 teaspoons sugar
1 cup water
1 (8-ounce) package spaghetti
3 tablespoons grated Parmesan cheese

Break up sausage meat with fork in heavy skillet or Dutch oven. Add onions, celery, and green pepper. Stir over medium heat until meat is browned and crumbly. Add tomato paste, sauce, orégano, salt, sugar, and water. Mix, cover skillet, and simmer about 30 minutes. Stir frequently.

Start oven at moderate (375° F.). Grease 1½-quart baking dish.

Cook spaghetti according to package directions. Place alternate layers of drained spaghetti and meat sauce in prepared baking dish. Sprinkle top with cheese.

Bake about 20 minutes or until top is browning and bubbly. Makes 4 to 6 servings.

MUSHROOM-AND-ONION PIE

4 tablespoons butter or marga- rine	1 (3-ounce) can chopped broiled mushrooms
6 cups sliced peeled onions (about 2 pounds)	¼ pound processed American cheese, diced
2 teaspoons Kitchen Bouquet	2 eggs
1½ teaspoons salt	3 cups seasoned mashed
¼ teaspoon pepper	potatoes
¼ teaspoon thyme	

Start oven at moderate (350° F.). Grease 8-by-12-inch baking dish.

Melt butter or margarine in large frying pan over moderate heat and add onions. Cover and cook 10 minutes, stirring occasionally. Remove from heat. Stir in Kitchen Bouquet, salt, pepper, thyme, mushrooms, and cheese. Mix well.

Beat eggs. Stir into onion mixture. Pour into prepared baking dish. Spoon mashed potatoes over top.

Bake about 45 minutes or until potato topping is lightly browned. Serve immediately. Makes 6 servings.

TUNA-RICE CASSEROLE

1 (8-ounce) jar soft cheese spread	1 tablespoon grated peeled on- ion
½ cup milk	⅛ teaspoon pepper
¼ teaspoon Worcestershire sauce	3 cups hot cooked rice
1 (7-ounce) can tuna	½ cup crumbled thin pretzel sticks
1 tablespoon lemon juice	

Start oven at moderate (350° F.). Grease 1½-quart baking dish.

Combine cheese, milk, and Worcestershire sauce in top of double boiler. Cook over hot, not boiling, water 5 minutes, or until smooth. Stir in drained, flaked tuna. Add lemon juice, onion, and pepper, and mix well. Stir into rice and toss to mix. Pour into prepared baking dish. Sprinkle with pretzel pieces.

Bake 20 minutes or until top is browned. Makes 4 or 5 servings.

RICE PILAU CASSEROLE

1 cup uncooked rice
2 tablespoons butter or margarine
1 pound chicken livers, fresh or quick-frozen
1 (3-ounce) can sliced mushrooms
1 (10½-ounce) can condensed cream-of-mushroom soup
⅓ cup milk
⅛ teaspoon pepper
2 tablespoons finely cut parsley
2 tablespoons white wine
¼ cup chopped pistachio or pignolia nuts

Start oven at moderate (350° F.). Grease 2-quart casserole.

Cook rice until tender, according to package directions, and all water is absorbed. Melt butter or margarine in skillet. Sauté chicken livers 5 minutes or until lightly browned. Add mushrooms and their liquid, soup, milk, pepper, parsley, and wine. Cook until hot and smooth. Mix with rice. Pour into prepared casserole. Top with nuts.

Bake 30 minutes. Makes 4 to 6 servings.

SALMON PIE

3 cups mashed potatoes
½ cup shredded Cheddar cheese
1 egg yolk
4 tablespoons butter or margarine
¼ cup chopped peeled onions
3 tablespoons flour
1 tablespoon lemon juice
1 cup evaporated milk
½ teaspoon salt
⅛ teaspoon pepper
1 canned pimiento, shredded
1 (1-pound) can salmon

Start oven at moderate (325° F.). Grease 1½-quart baking dish.

Combine potatoes, cheese, and egg yolk. Press mixture in prepared baking dish, covering bottom and sides. Make thick ruffled edge of potato-cheese mixture around top.

Cook onions in butter or margarine 5 minutes. Stir in flour smoothly. Add lemon juice and continue to stir to smooth paste. Add milk. Stir and cook until sauce is smooth. Add salt, pepper, and pimiento. Break drained salmon into large pieces. Add to sauce. Pour into potato-lined casserole.

Bake about 25 minutes, or until potato edge is browned. Makes 4 to 6 servings.

SAVORY BAKED STEAK

2-pound flank steak
3 tablespoons flour
1 teaspoon salt
⅛ teaspoon pepper
3 tablespoons cooking oil

¼ cup hot water or bouillon
⅓ cup French dressing
⅓ cup crumbled bleu cheese
¼ cup light cream
½ teaspoon Worcestershire sauce

Start oven at moderate (350° F.).

Score steak with knife. Mix flour, salt, and pepper. Rub into meat on both sides. Brown steak on both sides in hot oil in heavy metal-base casserole. Pour hot water or bouillon and French dressing over meat. Cover dish.

Bake 1 hour. Combine cheese, cream, and Worcestershire. Pull baking dish out to edge of oven shelf. Spread cheese mixture over steak. Return to oven uncovered. Bake 30 minutes longer, or until tender. Baste occasionally with juices in casserole or with mixture of French dressing and a little added Worcestershire. Serve in baking dish. Slice steak diagonally. Makes 4 to 6 servings.

SAVORY CHICKEN CASSEROLE

2 ½-pound frying chicken, dressed
    and cleaned
½ cup all-purpose flour
1 ½ teaspoons salt
¼ teaspoon pepper
½ teaspoon paprika
¼ cup cooking oil

1 (10 ½ -ounce) can condensed
    cream-of-mushroom soup
1 cup hot water
1 large onion, peeled and
    sliced
¼ cup sliced stuffed green olives

Cut chicken into serving pieces. Mix flour, salt, pepper, and paprika together in paper bag. Shake chicken pieces in tightly closed bag to coat evenly.

Heat oil in heavy skillet. Cook chicken over moderate heat until well browned on all sides. Place chicken in 2-quart casserole. Stir soup and hot water into skillet drippings. Cook and stir until smooth. Pour over chicken. Spread sliced onion over all. Cover dish. Store in refrigerator 1 hour or longer.

About 1 hour before dinner, remove casserole from refrigerator and let stand at kitchen temperature until chill is off dish.

Start oven at moderate (375° F.).

Bake casserole, covered, 1 hour. Uncover dish. Sprinkle chicken with olives. Cover and bake 15 minutes longer, until chicken is tender. Makes 4 servings.

SAVORY ONION PIE

¾ cup salty-cracker crumbs	2 eggs
¼ cup melted butter or marga-rine	1 cup milk
	1 teaspoon salt
2 cups thinly sliced peeled on-ions	¼ teaspoon pepper
	¾ cup grated Cheddar cheese
2 tablespoons butter or marga-rine	½ cup ground boiled or baked ham

Prepare crumb crust by combining crumbs and melted butter or margarine. Press evenly in bottom and sides of 9-inch pie plate or shallow baking dish.

Start oven at moderately slow (300° F.).

Cook onions in butter or margarine 5 minutes. Let cool slightly. Spread in crumb-lined dish. Beat eggs slightly, mix with milk, and add seasonings. Combine cheese and ham and add to milk mixture. Pour over onions in crumb crust.

Bake 35 to 40 minutes, until set. Makes 4 to 6 servings.

SEATTLE STUFFED PEPPERS

4 large green peppers	¼ teaspoon salt
1 (1-pound) can salmon, drained, boned, flaked	⅛ teaspoon pepper
	1 (15-ounce) can spaghetti with tomato sauce and cheese
1 tablespoon grated onion	
1 teaspoon lemon juice	¼ cup grated Swiss cheese

Cut peppers in half lengthwise. Cut out cores and seeds. Drop peppers into boiling water. Remove from heat. Let stand 10 minutes. Remove peppers and drain.

Start oven at moderate (375° F.).

Combine salmon, onion, lemon juice, salt, and pepper in large bowl. Add spaghetti mixture and toss to combine well. Spoon into pepper halves. Place heaped-up peppers in 11-by-7-by-2-inch baking dish. Pour few tablespoons boiling water into dish.

Bake 25 minutes. Add a little hot water to dish from time to time to prevent burning pepper bottoms. Remove dish from oven. Top peppers with grated cheese. Bake 5 minutes longer or until cheese melts slightly. Makes 8 servings.

When I had this dish of stuffed peppers in Seattle it was followed by enormous strawberries from Alaska. It was such a surprise to me that summertime Alaska is Seattle's truck farm. Try this colorful combination.

SHRIMP-AND-SPAGHETTI CASSEROLE

1 (9-ounce) package spaghetti	1 teaspoon salt
1½-pound ham steak	½ teaspoon pepper
1 (12-ounce) package quick-frozen, deveined shrimp	3 cups milk
	¼ cup sherry
3 tablespoons butter or margarine	¼ cup grated Swiss cheese
2 tablespoons flour	¼ cup grated Parmesan cheese

Cook spaghetti according to directions on package. Drain.

Start oven at moderate (350° F.). Grease 2-quart casserole.

Cut ham in 1-inch cubes. Separate shrimp. Combine spaghetti, ham, and shrimp in prepared casserole. Melt butter or margarine in saucepan. Stir in flour smoothly. Add salt and pepper. Stir in milk slowly. Cook and stir until slightly thickened. Stir in sherry slowly. Pour sauce over casserole mixture. Sprinkle cheese on top.

Bake 40 minutes. Serve hot. Makes 6 servings.

SHEPHERD'S PIE

2 cups cubed cooked beef	¼ teaspoon pepper
1 cup mixed cooked green vegetables	¼ cup finely cut parsley
	2 cups mashed potatoes
1 bay leaf	1 egg
¼ cup light cream	Melted butter or margarine
½ teaspoon salt	Paprika

Start oven at moderately hot (400° F.). Grease 1½-quart casserole.

Pour beef into prepared casserole. Drain vegetables and add to meat. Crumble bay leaf and add to dish. Mix cream, salt, pepper, and parsley into the mashed potatoes. Beat egg until light. Fold into potato mixture. Spread over meat and vegetables. Brush top with melted butter or margarine. Sprinkle lightly with paprika.

Bake 20 minutes or until top is browned. Makes 4 or more servings.

This is an English specialty, of course, and one of the best. Sometimes we make it with leftover lamb, an obvious Monday dinner. In a pinch we use those convenient dehydrated potatoes (always in our cupboard) or quick-frozen mashed potatoes, good to have on hand, too.

SWEETBREAD-AND-OYSTER PIE

Puff paste, or regular pastry for 2-crust pie
1 pair sweetbreads
1 teaspoon salt
1 tablespoon lemon juice or vinegar
1 pint shelled oysters
2 tablespoons butter or margarine

1 tablespoon flour
1 cup heavy cream
3 egg yolks
½ teapoon salt
¼ teaspoon pepper
Paprika

Prepare pastry and store in refrigerator.

Cover sweetbreads with boiling water, add 1 teaspoon salt and the lemon juice. Bring to a boil, reduce heat, and cook slowly 20 minutes. Remove from heat and drain. Plunge sweetbreads into cold water. Let stand until cool, then drain. Remove skin and membrane with short, sharp paring knife. Cut sweetbreads into 1-inch cubes. Set aside in refrigerator until ready for use.

Heat oysters in their liquor in 1-quart saucepan. Boil only 1 or 2 minutes, or until edges curl. Mix butter or margarine and flour smoothly together. Add to oysters. Stir cream and slightly beaten egg yolks together. Add, stirring slowly, to oysters. Add salt and pepper. Stir gently only until sauce thickens. Remove from heat.

Start oven at hot (450° F.). Line deep oval 1½-quart baking dish with pastry, making thumb-crimped edge all around.

Fill prepared dish with alternate layers of oyster mixture and sweetbread cubes. Place top pastry on dish, crimping it all around to the pastry edge of the lower crust. Cut 2 or 3 decorative gashes in pastry top. Sprinkle top lightly with paprika.

Bake 20 to 25 minutes or until crust is golden. Serve hot. Makes 4 to 6 servings.

SWEET-SOUR HAM ROLLS

¾ pound ground cooked pork
½ pound ground cooked ham
1 cup cracker or bread crumbs
1 egg
¾ cup milk
½ teaspoon salt

½ cup brown sugar, packed
½ teaspoon dry mustard
¼ cup vinegar
¼ cup hot water
2 tablespoons seedless raisins or currants

Start oven at moderate (325° F.). Grease shallow 1-quart baking dish.

Mix together meats, crumbs, well-beaten egg, milk, and salt. Shape into 4 serving-size rolls. Place in prepared baking dish.

Mix remaining ingredients in glass or enamel saucepan. Heat, stirring until sugar dissolves. Spoon about half of the sauce over rolls.

Bake 50 minutes. Baste frequently with sauce. Serve hot with any remaining hot sauce. Makes 4 servings.

S.J.'S FAVORITE

1 (1-pound) can baked beans	4 thick slices canned luncheon
1 onion, peeled and diced	meat
3 tablespoons New Orleans mo-	¼ cup coarse bread crumbs
lasses	Extra molasses
1 teaspoon prepared mustard	

Start oven at moderate (350° F.). Grease 1-quart casserole.

Mix beans, onion, molasses, and mustard together. Pour into prepared baking dish. Lay meat slices on top. Sprinkle with crumbs. Dribble a little molasses over all.

Bake 25 minutes, until browned and bubbly. Makes 4 servings.

PAUL'S FAVORITE FRANKFURTER CASSEROLE

8 medium-sized new potatoes	½ tablespoon prepared mustard
6 frankfurters	8 boneless anchovy fillets
6 tablespoons butter or marga-	
rine	

Start oven at moderate (375° F.). Grease shallow 2-quart casserole.

Scrub potatoes. Slice, but do not pare. Pour half the potatoes into prepared casserole. Place franks on potatoes. Cover with remaining potatoes. Melt butter or margarine. Add mustard and pour over franks and potatoes. Cover dish.

Bake 35 minutes. Uncover casserole and garnish top with anchovy fillets. Continue baking, uncovered, 10 minutes, or until potatoes are done. Makes 6 servings.

TURKEY OR CHICKEN LEFTOVER PIE

1 (9-ounce) package quick-frozen broccoli	1 ½ tablespoons flour
	1 ½ cups milk
3 thin slices baked or boiled ham	1 teaspoon salt
	½ teaspoon pepper
3 large, thin slices cooked turkey	⅓ cup each grated Swiss and Parmesan cheese
4 tablespoons butter or margarine	Cayenne

For Chicken Leftover Pie substitute cooked chicken for the turkey in above recipe. Or use leftover duck, goose, or a mixture of roast fowl in this recipe.

Cook broccoli according to directions on package until pieces are just separated, then drain. Place in bottom of 2-quart casserole. Add layer of ham slices and top with turkey or chicken.

Start oven at moderate (350° F.).

Melt 2 tablespoons butter or margarine in saucepan. Stir in flour smoothly. Add milk slowly, stirring and cooking until slightly thickened. Season with salt and pepper. Reduce heat. Add remaining 2 tablespoons butter or margarine and stir. Add Swiss cheese, stirring to mix well. Pour over contents of casserole. Sprinkle top with Parmesan cheese.

Bake 25 minutes or until bubbly. Makes 4 to 6 servings.

HALIBUT-AND-POTATO SUPPER

6 halibut steaks	Freshly ground pepper
6 potatoes	1 tablespoon finely cut parsley
2 small onions	6 anchovy fillets, cut fine
Sliver of garlic	½ cup olive oil
½ teaspoon salt	

Dip steaks into cold salted water. Drain. Dry on paper toweling.

Start oven at moderately hot (400° F.). Butter large shallow baking dish.

Scrub, rinse, and pare potatoes, and dice fine. Peel and dice onions. Cut garlic fine. Mix potatoes, onions, garlic, salt, a quick grind of pepper, parsley, anchovies, and olive oil. Spread half the mixture in prepared baking dish. Lay halibut on top. Cover fish with rest of potato mixture.

Bake 15 minutes with casserole covered. Remove cover and bake 20 minutes or until top is lightly browned. Makes 6 servings.

Any fish steak may be used in this recipe. The dish is especially good with hot corn bread or corn muffins fresh from the oven.

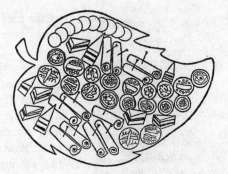

CHAPTER EIGHT

Use Your Chafing Dish

Adaptable table-cookery devices, electrical and nonelectrical, add much pleasure to present-day hospitality. Family and guests like to participate in the preparation of a dish—at least participate in watching *you* do the work. Also they enjoy the savory cooking odors which rise from a chafing dish.

For best results, ease of handling, and pleasure to you as well as to guests, plan any chafing-dish cookery well ahead in the kitchen. Assemble all needed foods and seasonings on a tray, which you bring to the table and place within easy reach of the chafing dish. Have the chafing dish ready on its alcohol burner, canned heat, or electrical unit.

Some recipes may be prepared ahead of time in the kitchen and simply reheated in the chafing dish at serving time. Or part of the dish may be completed ahead of time and the dish finished at the table. The recipes which follow indicate the procedures.

Almost any recipe for skillet or top-of-the-stove cookery found in this book can be prepared in a chafing dish. Try it on the family first before cooking a guest meal at the table.

In recent years, with the revival of the chafing dish, a number of cheap models have come onto the market. Some made for low-priced selling include copper-lined cookery pans. After sad experiences on the part of many young homemakers, these are gradually finding their way to the discard pile, because cookery in a copper-*lined* utensil is poisonous. European cooks know how to handle these safely, scouring after each use to prevent formation of verdigris. But for us they are unsafe. If you do collect them in Europe, have them lined by a tinsmith here before using.

Many handsome copper chafing dishes, *with nickel or aluminum or other white-metal linings in the cook pan,* are, of course, in use. So are silver chafing dishes and others with enamel-lined pans. The latter are recommended for any mixture containing tomatoes or other acid juices.

See also chapters on chicken, eggs, fish, and pastas.

BUFFET PARTY SEA FOOD

½ cup butter or margarine
2 onions, peeled and diced
2 green peppers, cut fine
1 (6-ounce) can sliced mushrooms
⅔ cup sifted all-purpose flour
2 teaspoons salt
½ teaspoon pepper
4 cups milk
1½ cups shredded sharp American cheese
1 tablespoon lemon juice
1 teaspoon dry mustard

½ teaspoon Worcestershire
   sauce
1 (12-ounce) package quick-
   frozen lobster meat
1 (12-ounce) package quick-
   frozen crab meat
1 (8-ounce) can deveined
   shrimp, or 1 cup cooked or
   quick-frozen shrimp
1 pound small macaroni shells,
   hot, freshly cooked
4 or 5 tablespoons finely cut
   parsley

Melt butter or margarine in large (about 3-quart) chafing dish pan over moderate heat. Stir in onions, green peppers, and mushrooms. Cook about 10 minutes, stirring occasionally. Remove from heat. Blend in flour, salt, and pepper smoothly. Stir in milk gradually. Return pan to heat. Cook, stirring constantly until thickened. Stir in cheese, and mix. Add lemon juice, mustard, and Worcestershire. Cook until cheese melts.

Break defrosted lobster and cleaned crab meat into serving pieces. Add with drained shrimp to sauce. Mix, and let mixture heat to a boil. Serve on generous mounds of hot macaroni. Add parsley as garnish. Makes 8 to 10 servings.

CHAFING-DISH MEAT BALLS

20	salty crackers	½	pound ground beef
1½	cups milk	½	pound ground cooked pork
1	small onion, peeled and diced	1	egg
1	tablespoon butter or margarine	2	teaspoons salt
		½	teaspoon pepper
		Extra butter or margarine	

Crumble crackers into milk. Let stand 5 minutes. Sauté onion in butter or margarine about 5 minutes, or until golden. Combine crackers, milk, onion and remaining ingredients, and mix well. Shape into 24 small balls. Sauté in frying pan in butter or margarine until well browned on all sides and cooked through.

Sauce for meat balls:

Pan drippings from meat balls		1	tablespoon prepared horse-radish
1	tablespoon flour	½	teaspoon salt
1⅓	cups milk	¼	teaspoon pepper

Blend pan drippings and flour smoothly together in frying pan. Stir in milk gradually. Mix in horse-radish, salt, and pepper. Cook and stir over medium heat until mixture thickens and boils. Pour over meat balls.

At serving time, reheat balls and sauce together in chafing dish at table. Makes 6 servings.

CHERRIES FLAMBÉ

¾	cup currant jelly	1½	quarts vanilla ice cream
1	(No. 2) can pitted Bing cherries drained	½	cup cognac

Melt jelly in chafing dish pan over direct heat, and stir gently. Add drained cherries. Mix, and heat slowly.

Spoon ice cream into 8 dessert dishes.

Pour almost all of brandy into center of cherries. Do not stir. Pour rest of brandy into large spoon. Ignite it with match, then pour flaming brandy into brandy in chafing dish to ignite.

Spoon flaming cherries over ice cream in dessert dishes. Makes 8 servings.

177

CHAFING-DISH PAELLA

1 ½ cups quick-cooking rice	1 cup cooked deveined shrimp
1 ¾ cups water	1 cup crab meat, all bones re-
¾ teaspoon salt	moved
½ teaspoon saffron	½ cup cooked peas
⅛ teaspoon black pepper	1 (3-ounce) can chopped mush-
½ bay leaf, crumbled	rooms
Small sliver garlic	
1 can chicken fricassée with gravy, or 1 cup creamed chicken	

Cook rice with water, salt, saffron, pepper, bay leaf, and garlic in 2-quart chafing dish pan. Bring to a boil. Cover tightly. Let boil rapidly 8 to 10 minutes. Mix in remaining ingredients. Place pan over hot water. Cover pan. Let mixture heat 10 minutes or until thoroughly hot and flavors well mixed. Makes 6 or more servings.

This dish may be prepared ahead of time in kitchen, kept hot in double boiler, then transferred to warmed chafing dish and brought in to the table. Let stand covered over hot water for a few minutes before serving.

CHICKEN À LA KING

2 chicken breasts	1 canned pimiento, cut fine
2 cups Thick White Sauce (page 557)	¼ cup dry sherry
	½ teaspoon salt
4 tablespoons butter or marga- rine	¼ teaspoon white pepper
2 green peppers, cut fine	
1 pound mushrooms, sliced, or 2 (6-ounce) cans sliced mush- rooms	

Heat about 2 cups water in saucepan to a simmer. Add chicken. Cover, and simmer about 20 minutes or until chicken is done. Drain, and cut meat in bite-size pieces.

While chicken cooks, prepare White Sauce.

Then heat butter or margarine in saucepan or chafing dish. Add peppers and mushrooms, and sauté 10 minutes. Add chicken, White Sauce, pimiento, sherry, salt, and pepper. Mix and heat to boiling point. Serve on toast, split toasted English muffins, biscuits, or corn bread. Makes 6 servings.

Turkey à la King: Use same recipe, substituting turkey for chicken. Omit pimiento and add ¼ cup diced black olives or cooked peas. Sprinkle top with ½ cup slivered toasted almonds for *Turkey à la King Amandine.*

These time-tested favorites fit into almost any menu from brunch to midnight supper. I like them especially for Sunday-night supper or for an unplanned Sunday luncheon when I suddenly decide it would be fun to have guests.

CHICKEN, NEW JERSEY

2 broilers, about 3 pounds each	1 tablespoon finely cut parsley
Salt and pepper	1 teaspoon thyme
¼ pound butter or margarine	½ cup cider
¼ cup best applejack	½ cup heavy ceam
6 scallions or shallots	

Have chickens cut in serving pieces. Sprinkle all sides with salt and pepper. Brown lightly in butter or margarine in chafing dish pan, about 15 minutes. Lower heat, cook chicken 15 minutes longer, turning pieces often.

Push pieces aside in pan. Pour almost all of the applejack into pan. Pour rest of applejack into large cooking spoon and ignite with match. Pour the flaming brandy over the chicken and spoon the brandy in the pan up onto the chicken. As flame dies down add scallions or shallots, parsley, thyme, and cider, stirring into the pan sauce. Rearrange chicken in the sauce. Cover pan and cook 20 minutes or longer, until tender.

To serve, place chicken on warmed plates. Stir cream into skillet, mix with sauce, heat, and pour over chicken. Makes 6 servings.

CHINESE HAM-AND-GREEN BEANS

2 tablespoons butter or margarine	1 (9-ounce) package quick-frozen French-style green beans
1 teaspoon curry powder	
1 drop sesame oil, or ¼ teaspoon crushed sesame seeds	1 tablespoon cornstarch
	½ cup orange juice
1 cup diced celery	2 cups thin strips cooked ham
1 large onion, peeled and diced	1 (5-ounce) can water chestnuts, drained and sliced thin
1 (9-ounce) can pineapple tidbits	

Melt butter or margarine in large chafing dish pan. Add curry powder and sesame oil or seeds. Stir until curry is very hot. Add celery and onion; stir and cook 5 minutes.

Drain syrup from pineapple. Add water to syrup to make 1 cup. Stir syrup mixture into curry mixture. Add beans and cook 10 minutes, over moderate heat.

Blend cornstarch with orange juice. Stir into curry mixture. Cook, stirring constantly, until mixture thickens and sauce is clear. It should boil 2 minutes. Add pineapple, ham, and chestnuts. Simmer 2 or 3 minutes, until very hot. Makes 4 to 6 servings.

CREAMED DEVILED CRAB MEAT

3 tablespoons butter or margarine	1 (3-ounce) can chopped broiled mushrooms
1 tablespoon minced peeled onion	1 teaspoon lemon juice
	½ teaspoon Worcestershire sauce
3 tablespoons flour	2 hard-cooked eggs, cut coarsely
½ teaspoon salt	
½ teaspoon dry mustard	1 (6½-ounce) can crab meat, flaked and bones removed
¼ teaspoon paprika	
⅛ teaspoon pepper	4 slices toast or crackers
1 cup milk	

Melt butter or margarine in chafing dish pan. Cook onion 5 minutes. Stir in flour and seasonings smoothly. Stir in milk gradually. Cook, stirring until slightly thickened. Add mushrooms and their liquid. Stir in lemon juice and Worcestershire. Add eggs and crab meat. Mix and let heat thoroughly. Serve on toast or crackers. Makes 4 servings.

CREAMED HAM ON TOAST

2 tablespoons butter or margarine	⅛ teaspoon pepper
3 tablespoons flour	1 (4½-ounce) can deviled ham
2½ cups milk	6 slices buttered toast
	3 hard-cooked eggs, sliced

Melt butter or margarine in chafing dish. Stir in flour smoothly, and cook 1 or 2 minutes. Add milk gradually. Continue to stir and cook until thickened. Add seasoning and deviled ham, and mix well. Serve hot creamed mixture over buttered toast. Garnish with sliced egg. Makes 6 servings.

DAISYFIELDS CREAMED EGGS

2 tablespoons butter or margarine	1 teaspoon cognac
2 tablespoons flour	4 slices hot toast, spread with butter and liver pâté
½ teaspoon salt	4 hard-cooked eggs, sliced
¼ teaspoon pepper	8 anchovy fillets
1 cup milk	

Melt butter or margarine in chafing dish pan, top of doubleboiler or in copper-clad saucepan. Stir in flour, salt, and pepper smoothly. Let cook 1 or 2 minutes. Add milk gradually. Stir and cook until slightly thickened. Stir in brandy. Arrange toast on serving plates. Cover with sliced egg. Spoon hot sauce on top. Crisscross 2 anchovy fillets on each serving. Makes 4 servings.

FISH PILAU

1½ cups milk	¼ teaspoon Tabasco sauce
1 (3-ounce) can chopped broiled mushrooms	¼ teaspoon marjoram
½ teaspoon Kitchen Bouquet	1 cup quick-cooking rice
½ teaspoon salt	1½ cups cooked fish
⅛ teaspoon pepper	Tomato or curry sauce (page 549)

Combine milk, mushrooms and their liquid, Kitchen Bouquet, seasonings, and herb in top pan of chafing dish. Heat to scalding over boiling water, stirring occasionally. Add rice, cover, and cook 8 to 10 minutes or until rice is tender. Add fish and mix with rice and mushrooms, using fork. When hot through, serve with tomato sauce, or the curry sauce. Makes 4 servings.

CRAB MEAT À LA KING

2 tablespoons butter or marga-
    rine
1 tablespoon flour
½ teaspoon salt
¼ teaspoon pepper
¼ teaspoon celery salt
1 cup heavy cream

2 hard-cooked eggs, chopped
1 tablespoon finely cut chives
1 pound cooked crab meat, all
    bones removed
¼ cup sherry
Buttered toast
1 teaspoon paprika

Heat butter or margarine in chafing dish pan over hot water. Stir
in smoothly flour, salt, pepper, and celery salt. Add cream and stir until
mixture is hot and beginning to thicken. Add eggs, chives, and crab
meat. Mix, and let heat thoroughly. Add sherry a little at a time, stirring
gently into mixture. Serve on buttered toast. Add sprinkling of paprika
to each serving. Makes 4 to 6 servings.

CURRIED TUNA ON RICE

2 medium onions, peeled and
    diced
3 tablespoons butter or marga-
    rine
½ garlic clove, peeled and
    mashed
2 tablespoons curry powder
1½ tablespoons flour

¾ cup milk
2 (7-ounce) cans tuna, drained
    and broken
2 cups commercial sour cream
½ cup white raisins, soaked and
    drained
5 cups hot buttered rice

Sauté onions in butter or margarine 5 minutes in chafing dish pan.
Add garlic and curry powder. Heat and stir until very hot. Remove
garlic and discard it. Stir in flour smoothly. Add milk, stirring constantly.
Cook 1 or 2 minutes, until bubbly. Add tuna and mix over low heat
about 5 minutes. Stir in sour cream. Let stand until hot and sauce is
well blended. Combine raisins and hot rice. Serve curried tuna on generous portions of rice. Makes 4 servings.

PEARS LUXURO

4 ripe pears
1 cup water
½ cup sugar

1 quart vanilla ice cream
Luxuro Sauce

182

Pare, halve, and core pears. Combine water and sugar in saucepan; bring to a boil, stirring constantly until sugar dissolves. Let boil 5 minutes. Simmer pears in syrup, covered pan, 10 to 15 minutes or until tender. Chill pears in syrup.

To serve, spoon ice cream into serving dish. Top with pear half. Add spoonful of hot Luxuro Sauce. Makes 8 servings.

Luxuro Sauce

1 package semi-sweet chocolate pieces	3 tablespoons water
	¼ teaspoon vanilla
2 tablespoons butter	2 tablespoons pistachio nuts

Use small chafing dish; combine chocolate pieces, butter, and water in chafing dish pan over hot water; cook, stirring frequently, until smooth and well blended. Add vanilla. Mix. Add nuts. Serve warm over pear dessert.

LEFTOVER DUCKLING IN WINE GRAVY

2 cups cubed roast duckling	2 tablespoons finely cut parsley
Duck liver	¾ teaspoon salt
6 tablespoons butter or margarine	¼ teaspoon cayenne
Juice ½ lemon	1 cup leftover pan gravy from roast duckling
½ cup Madeira or sherry	Toast strips

Cut leftover roast duckling in bite-sized pieces. Cook duck liver 5 minutes in 1 tablespoon butter or margarine in chafing dish. When cooked through, mash liver with fork. Add lemon juice and remaining 5 tablespoons butter or margarine. Mix and cook 1 or 2 minutes over low heat. Add wine and parsley. Stir and add seasonings and pan gravy (with its fat skimmed off). Heat and mix 1 or 2 minutes until well blended and hot. Add diced duckling meat. Mix and continue to heat until mixture is very hot. Serve on toast. Makes 4 servings.

If there is less than 1 cup of leftover pan gravy from roast duck, skim fat from gravy and add enough consommé or bouillon to make 1 cup.

HOT DEVILED SHRIMP

1 (12-ounce) package quick-frozen, deveined shrimp or 1½ cups cooked fresh shrimp	1 teaspoon curry powder
	½ teaspoon Tabasco
	½ teaspoon salt
4 tablespoons butter or margarine	¼ teaspoon pepper
	½ teaspoon celery salt
1 teaspoon Worcestershire sauce	

Break shrimp apart, let partially defrost. Melt butter or margarine in chafing dish over direct heat. Stir in Worcestershire and curry powder. Continue to stir until very hot. Add remaining seasonings, and mix. Add shrimp. Sauté about 5 minutes, until cooked and well seasoned with butter mixture.

Serve hot in scallop shell as appetizer. Makes 8 or more appetizers. Or serve on slices of buttered toast, with rice or noodles, as entrée. Makes 4 entrée servings.

DAISYFIELDS WELSH RABBIT

4 tablespoons butter or margarine	1 (12-ounce) can V-8 vegetable juices
¼ cup sifted all-purpose flour	½ pound processed American cheese, grated
½ teaspoon salt	
¼ teaspoon pepper	Crackers or toast
¼ teaspoon dry mustard	

Melt butter or margarine in chafing dish pan. Stir in flour smoothly. Add salt, pepper, and mustard. Mix, and add vegetable juices gradually, stirring constantly. Bring to a boil, stirring continually. Cook 2 minutes. Add cheese, and stir until melted. Serve at once on crackers, toast, or split and toasted English muffins. Makes 4 or 5 servings.

SUNDAY-SUPPER SCRAMBLED EGGS

1 tablespoon olive oil	½ teaspoon pepper
2 onions, peeled and sliced	½ teaspoon brown sugar
1 cup chopped, drained, canned tomatoes	¼ teaspoon orégano
	6 eggs
½ teaspoon salt	4 English muffins or toast slices

Heat olive oil in chafing dish pan. Sauté onions over moderate heat, 5 minutes or until tender. Add tomatoes and seasonings. Stir 1 or 2 minutes. Beat eggs slightly. Pour into pan. Cook over low heat until almost set. Stir gently 1 or 2 minutes, until scrambled. Serve at once on split and toasted English muffins or on toast. Makes 4 servings.

VEAL KIDNEYS FLAMBÉ

3 veal kidneys
3 tablespoons butter or margarine
1 (3-ounce) can sliced mushrooms
½ teaspoon salt

Quick grind black pepper
1 tablespoon chopped shallots
⅓ cup cognac
¾ cup light cream
½ teaspoon dry mustard
Thin toast

Remove fat and membranes from kidneys. Rinse, drain, and cut crosswise in slices. Sauté slices in butter or margarine in chafing dish pan with mushrooms, seasoning, and shallots. Stir occasionally. Cook 8 minutes or until kidneys are done and lightly browned. Pour most of the brandy over the mixture. Pour the rest of brandy into heavy cooking spoon, ignite with match, and pour flaming brandy over mixture in chafing dish to ignite it. When flame dies down, stir cream and mustard into mixture. Mix, and let heat thoroughly. Serve at once on toast. Makes 4 servings.

CHAPTER NINE

Cheese

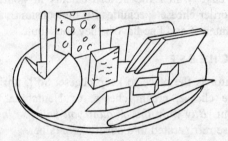

The serving of cheese with fresh fruit as a dessert has grown in popularity in our homes in recent years. For this pleasant finish to a meal, you may serve one delicious cheese or an assortment. A well-ripened Camembert calls for a fragrant summer pear, or a fine McIntosh apple, or seedless grapes, with, of course, good crackers or toasted French or Italian bread. The crackers should be crisped a few minutes in a hot oven. They are even more appetizing if you brush them lightly with butter and sprinkle them with paprika or celery salt before heating them in the oven.

A cheese tray might include good American Cheddar in one large piece from which guests cut as much as they want, or an Edam or Gouda into which guests may cut, serving themselves as generously as they like. A square of cream cheese is welcome on a cheese tray, especially if you provide guava jelly or currant jam to go with this mild favorite. Or serve a block of fine Swiss cheese or any other of your delights. Usually three kinds of cheese, appropriate knives for cutting, a small knife or spreader for each guest, crackers, and possibly jam, complete a cheese tray offering.

Another alternative is to serve one rare and spectacular cheese—perhaps an elegant Brie—alone or as the center of interest on the cheese tray, or a fine Italian cheese, a New York State Cheddar, a Canadian Oka, or a gift from someone in Wisconsin or elsewhere. Or serve something as unusual as the cheese called La Grappe, which comes from France and has a thick crust of grape seeds on it. The mild, pale, creamy interior is delicious, but the French eat the coarse crust too.

Study the cheese chart on pages 197–200 for varieties which you may not know at the present and which you will want to try for future menus. There are many unusual cheeses made in this country. Others are imported from South America, Mexico, Canada, as well as from countries across the two oceans. They add variety to our menus and pleasure to our palates. Visit foreign food shops, especially the cheese stores in your city. Watch the advertisements in gourmet and home magazines and order cheese specialties for the constant variation of your menus and the interest and fine flavors they contribute.

CARE OF CHEESE

The refrigerator is the place to keep cheese. Soft, unripened cheeses, such as cottage cheese, cream cheese, or Neufchâtel, quickly spoil, mold, or dry out. *Buy only the amount you will use in a day or two.* Keep such cheese refrigerated in a covered container.

Packaged cheeses should be refrigerated in their containers; if they are strong-odored, use additional waxed paper or foil to wrap them, because the odor comes through the package and perfumes the refrigerator.

Unpackaged cheese should be tightly wrapped in heavy waxed paper or foil before refrigerating.

Cheese with a strong aroma, such as Limburger, should be refrigerated, after wrapping, and placing in a tightly covered container. *Use within a few days after purchasing.*

Cover cut surfaces of a large cheese with coating of melted paraffin, then wrap tightly and refrigerate. Warning: melt paraffin in top of double boiler. Flammable! In general, don't buy a large cheese unless you are going to share it with neighbors and friends; buy only what you can use up quickly. However, a gift of a large cheese can be appreciated if this paraffin method is used to protect it.

Mold which develops on some cheese is not harmful. Cut it off and use the cheese beneath it.

Processed cheese spreads in glass jars need not be kept in refrigerator until opened. Once opened, however, refrigerate them tightly covered. *Do not store cheese in the freezer;* freezing damages cheese texture and flavor. Cheese experts say the exceptions to this rule are Camembert and Liederkranz, which may be frozen for several months, but they must be served promptly after thawing.

In general, to serve cheese, remove from refrigerator 30 minutes to 1 hour before serving time. A large piece needs an hour to mellow. Cut off the amount needed and return the rest to the refrigerator.

See chapters on appetizers, casseroles, chafing dish cookery, and desserts for additional cheese recipes.

BAKED FONDUE

1 ½ long loaves French bread	5 cups hot milk
½ cup butter or margarine	1 ½ teaspoons Worcestershire
½ cup prepared English mustard	sauce
1 ½ pounds sharp Cheddar	1 teaspoon salt
cheese, sliced ¼ inch thick	⅛ teaspoon cayenne
4 eggs	Paprika

Prepare this dish the day before serving.

Slice French bread ½ inch thick. Spread slices generously with butter or margarine blended with mustard. Make alternate layers of bread and cheese in 4-quart casserole.

Beat eggs well. Combine with milk, Worcestershire, salt, and cayenne. Pour over bread and cheese layers. Sprinkle top lightly with paprika. Cover dish and refrigerate until next day.

About 1 hour and 45 minutes before serving, start oven at moderate (350° F.). Remove casserole from refrigerator and let stand at kitchen temperature 15 minutes to take chill off dish.

Bake fondue, uncovered, 1 hour and 30 minutes. Serve as soon as removed from oven. Makes 8 servings.

BRANDIED EDAM CHEESE

Let an Edam cheese stand at room temperature 1 hour or longer. Cut top from Edam. Cut cheese out of its red shell, being careful not to break outside wall. Place cheese in electric blender bowl with a little cognac. Blend to smooth paste, adding more brandy if needed. Fill Edam shell. Put top in place and wrap Edam in heavy waxed paper or foil. Place in cool, not cold, part of refrigerator for 24 hours. Remove paper or foil. Let stand at room temperature about ½ hour. Place on cheese tray with knife and crisp crackers.

Serve with coffee after luncheon or dinner, or serve on cocktail buffet table or with salad. Makes 20 or more servings. This is a luxurious gift from your kitchen, by the way.

CHEESE-AND-JAM TARTS

Pastry for 2-crust pie	2 tablespoons sugar
Plum jam	½ teaspoon salt
1 (8-ounce) package creamed cottage cheese	2 eggs
	Milk
½ cup commercial sour cream	Powdered cinnamon

Prepare pastry according to your favorite recipe, or use mix and follow directions on package. Line small or medium-sized muffin pans with pastry, leaving generous overlapping edges. Add a scant teaspoon of jam to each pastry-lined pan.

Start oven at hot (425° F.).

Combine cheese, sour cream, sugar, and salt smoothly. Beat egg yolks. Stir into cheese mixture. Beat egg whites until they stand in stiff points when beater is removed. Fold into cheese mixture. Add about 1 tablespoon cheese mixture to each pastry-lined muffin pan. Fold pastry over, bringing edges together on top, and pinch edges together. Brush lightly with milk. Sprinkle lightly with cinnamon. Bake 10 minutes. Reduce heat to moderate (350° F.). Bake 20 minutes longer or until pastry is done and browning. Makes 12 tarts.

These hearty tarts may be served as a dessert after a light luncheon, for afternoon coffee or tea, or as a brunch dish.

CHEESE BLINTZES

Russian Pancakes

1½ cups cream-style cottage cheese	2 tablespoons butter or margarine
¼ cup commercial sour cream	2 eggs
1½ tablespoons sugar	1¼ cups milk
½ teaspoon salt	Extra butter or margarine
1½ cups sifted all-purpose flour	Strawberry jam or stewed berries
3 tablespoons sugar	Sour cream
½ teaspoon salt	

Mix filling ahead of time to chill in refrigerator: combine cottage cheese, ¼ cup sour cream, 1½ tablespoons sugar, and ½ teaspoon salt. Beat smooth. Pile in glass bowl, cover, and chill.

To make blintzes, sift flour, 3 tablespoons sugar, and ½ teaspoon salt together into mixing bowl. Melt butter or margarine. Beat eggs until thick and lemony. Combine with butter or margarine. Add milk, and beat into flour mixture with rotary beater until smooth.

Grease small frying pan lightly with butter or margarine. For each pancake pour just enough batter to coat pan thinly. Tilt skillet at once, back and forth, to spread batter evenly. Cook pancake over medium heat 2 minutes, or until lightly browned on bottom and firm on top. With wide spatula remove pancake to warm plate, brown side up. Stack pancakes as they are baked.

As soon as all are baked, spoon about 1½ tablespoons of chilled cheese filling onto center of the brown side of one pancake. Fold two opposite sides of the pancake to the center. Begin with one of the open ends, roll up, and press the edges to seal. Repeat until all are rolled.

Complete blintzes in a chafing dish or skillet. Melt 1 tablespoon butter or margarine. Arrange several folded blintzes in the hot fat. Brown on all sides over medium heat. Turn carefully with tongs or use two spoons. Remove browned blintzes to warm serving plates. Serve with jam or stewed berries, and sour cream. Or dash them with powdered sugar and top with sour cream. Makes 12 blintzes. (See also appetizer chapter and pancakes.)

Try this recipe on the family before you make it for guests. Delicious, but to make sure of timing, practice once or twice before adding blintzes to a guest menu. The blintzes are so rich and good that you can serve them as a main dish, with either hot tea or coffee, for lunch or casual supper. Or start with fruit cup and let your guests enjoy that while you finish making blintzes. There are good frozen blintzes on the market and of course you can freeze your own.

QUICK TOMATO RABBIT

½ pound processed American cheese, grated
½ teaspoon salt
1 teaspoon dry mustard
1 (10½-ounce) can condensed tomato soup
6 slices hot toast or 6 English muffins, split and toasted

Cook cheese and seasonings together in upper part of double boiler or chafing dish over simmering water. Stir until cheese melts. Add enough tomato soup to thin mixture to right consistency to pour over toast. Makes 6 servings.

The first Sunday-night supper dish I learned to make as a child. We often served it on pilot crackers, too.

CHEESE CROQUETTES, BEEBE

4 egg whites	1 tablespoon water
1 pound processed American cheese, shredded	1½ cups fine, dry crumbs
	Fat for deep-frying
1 egg	Tomato sauce

Beat egg whites until they stand in stiff points when beater is removed. Carefully fold cheese into whites. Shape into 10 or more croquettes. Chill in refrigerator 30 minutes.

Beat egg. Combine with 1 tablespoon water. Dip croquettes into egg-and-water, then into crumbs. Let dry 15 minutes. Fry in deep, hot fat at 375° F. on frying thermometer until brown on all sides. Let drain on thick paper towel. Serve hot with Tomato Sauce. Makes 5 or more servings.

Flavor of these delicious croquettes may be varied by using ⅔ American cheese and ⅓ grated Swiss (Emmentaler) cheese. Add about 1 teaspoon finely cut fresh parsley. Combine cheese and parsley. Use as described in recipe.

This is a recipe of one of the best men cooks I know—Ralph Beebe, a man who has perfectly equipped his country kitchen for serious male cookery.

CHEESE RAVIOLI

Kreplech

1 recipe noodle dough	½ teaspoon salt
2 (8-ounce) packages creamed cottage cheese	½ teaspoon powdered cinnamon
	Grated peel 1 lemon
2 tablespoons melted butter or margarine	1 quart water
	1 quart milk
1 egg	Butter or margarine
1 teaspoon sugar	

Roll out noodle dough and cut into 2-inch squares.

Mix all remaining ingredients except water, milk, and extra butter or margarine. Place 1 teaspoon cheese mixture on each square of noodle dough. Fold over. Wet edges. Press together with tines of fork or fingers. When ravioli are all ready, combine water and milk. Bring to a boil. Drop a few ravioli into rapidly boiling liquid. They rise to the top as soon as lightly cooked. Remove with skimmer or slotted spoon. Keep them warm, until all are cooked, on serving dish in a warm oven with its door left open. Serve hot with sprinkle of paprika, grated Parmesan, and melted butter or margarine. Makes 4 servings.

CHEESE SPOON BREAD

3 cups milk
1 cup yellow corn meal
1 ½ teaspoons salt
½ teaspoon dry mustard
⅛ teaspoon cayenne

3 eggs
1 cup grated sharp Cheddar
cheese
Paprika

Scald milk in upper part of double boiler over hot water.

Start oven at moderate (350° F.). Grease 2-quart deep baking dish.

Combine corn meal, salt, mustard, and cayenne. Beat egg yolks until thick and lemony. Blend with dry mixture. Stir into scalded milk gradually, to avoid lumps. Cook, stirring, until mixture thickens. Remove from heat. Add cheese and stir until melted. Whip egg whites until they stand in stiff points when beater is removed. Fold cheese mixture into whites. Pour at once into prepared baking dish. Sprinkle top with paprika.

Set dish in shallow pan of hot water. Bake 35 to 40 minutes. Serve hot in the dish in which it baked. Makes 4 to 6 servings.

FRENCH CREAM-CHEESE DESSERT

Petit Coeur à la Crème

3 (3-ounce) packages cream cheese
¼ cup commercial sour cream
1 tablespoon powdered sugar

⅛ teaspoon salt
Cognac or a fruit brandy such as
cherry or apricot

Beat cheese and sour cream together until soft. Add sugar and salt. Continue to beat. Add few drops brandy or as much as 1 or 2 teaspoons if cheese mixture is too thick.

Mold in heart-shaped wicker basket lined with damp cheesecloth. These little baskets are sold at fancy housewares stores and by importers of French cookery utensils. Or use small heart-shaped gelatin mold of aluminum. Use 4 small, individual molds or 1 large mold. Recipe makes 4 servings. *Petit Coeur à la Crème* is served with fresh strawberries, ripe summer currants, currant jelly, or any stewed fruit.

A wonderful dessert after a meager luncheon! Makes a whole luncheon for someone who eats little at noon—*Petit Coeur à la Crème*, fresh berries, small, hot, toasted rolls, hot coffee or tea.

MANICOTTI

1 tablespoon butter or margarine	1 tablespoon cognac
1 cup sifted all-purpose flour	½ teaspoon salt
1 cup milk	2 eggs
	Olive oil

Make pancake batter. Melt butter or margarine. Stir in flour smoothly. Stir in milk gradually to avoid lumps. Add brandy, salt, and slightly beaten eggs. Mix well. Cover bowl and let stand at kitchen temperature about 1 hour before using.

Filling:

½ pound ham	¼ pound grated Romano or Parmesan cheese
3 tablespoons finely cut parsley	
2 eggs	
1 pound ricotta or cottage cheese	

Chop ham into fine cubes. Add parsley, slightly beaten eggs, and all cheese. Mix well.

Sauce:

1 (8-ounce) can tomato sauce	Grated Romano or Parmesan cheese

Start oven at moderate (350° F.).

Add about 1 tablespoon olive oil to 6-inch frying pan. Let heat. Beat pancake batter a few seconds. Add 2 or 3 tablespoons of batter to pan, tip until batter covers bottom. Cook to delicate brown. Turn pancake. Cook second side until brown. Bake 12 pancakes.

Spoon filling onto each cake. Roll. Place in shallow baking dish. Pour tomato sauce over all. Sprinkle with Romano or Parmesan cheese.

Bake 15 to 20 minutes, until bubbly hot. Makes 4 to 6 servings.

Double or triple the recipe for a large buffet. You can do this early in the day, adding the finishing touches while the guests are having cocktails. I have a friend with four children under eight and she manages to entertain beautifully without help. This is one of her one-dish specialities.

GNOCCHI

1 ½ cups milk
1 ½ cups water
1 cup farina or Cream of Wheat
1 ½ teaspoons salt
3 tablespoons butter or margarine

2 cups grated Parmesan cheese
3 eggs
4 tablespoons butter or margarine
Freshly ground pepper

Combine milk and water in 1½-quart saucepan. Bring to a boil. Stir in cereal gradually. Add salt. Continue to stir to avoid lumps and cook until thick. Remove from heat. Beat in 3 tablespoons butter or margarine, ½ cup cheese, and the eggs. Mix well. Spread mixture about ¼ inch thick on platter or in shallow pan. Let cool.

Start oven at moderate (350° F.). Grease 2-quart baking dish.

Cut cold cereal mixture into small squares or other shapes. Make layer in prepared baking dish. Sprinkle generously with some of the remaining cheese and dabs of butter or margarine. Repeat layers of gnocchi, cheese, and butter or margarine. Top layer should be cheese with dabs of butter or margarine. Add light sprinkling of pepper.

Bake about 30 minutes or until top is browned. Makes 4 to 6 servings.

In northern Italy gnocchi often replaces spaghetti. When dough is made into a roll (instead of being spread on a platter) it is usually sliced with a string to prevent breaking.

SWISS BAKED-CHEESE CUSTARD

2 cups heavy cream
1 cup grated Swiss cheese
4 egg yolks

½ teaspoon salt
1 teaspoon Tabasco sauce

If you have a blender-mixer, combine all ingredients in container. Blend 1 minute.

Start oven at moderately slow (300° F.). Butter 4 large custard cups. Pour mixture into cups. Set cups in shallow pan of hot water.

Bake 25 minutes, or until set. Serve warm. Makes 4 servings.

If you have no blender, combine cream and cheese in saucepan. Cook over low heat until cheese is melted. Beat egg yolks until thick. Pour cream and cheese mixture over egg yolks. Mix thoroughly. Add salt and Tabasco. Pour into prepared custard cups. Bake as described.

SWISS CHEESE PIE

Quiche Lorraine

Pastry mix for 1-crust 9-inch pie	⅛ teaspoon sugar
18 small slices lean bacon	1/16 teaspoon cayenne
4 eggs	⅛ teaspoon pepper
2 cups heavy cream	1 tablespoon butter or margarine
¾ teaspoon salt	
⅛ teaspoon powdered nutmeg	¼ pound Swiss cheese, grated

Prepare pastry according to directions on package. Roll dough out on lightly floured board into circle 1½ inches wider all around than inverted 9-inch pie plate. Fit pastry into pie plate. Flute edge with fingers. Place in refrigerator to chill about 30 minutes.

Start oven at hot (425° F.).

Fry bacon until crisp. Drain on thick paper towels. Crumble all but 6 strips. Beat eggs with cream, salt, nutmeg, sugar, cayenne, and pepper. Rub chilled pie shell with softened butter or margarine. Sprinkle crumbled bacon and cheese into pie shell. Pour cream mixture over all.

Bake 15 minutes. Reduce oven temperature to moderately slow (300° F.) and bake 40 minutes longer, or until knife inserted in center comes out clean. Remove from oven. Garnish with remaining 6 cooked bacon strips. Let stand 5 minutes. Carry to table. Cut into 6 wedges and serve at once. Makes 6 servings.

This is the recipe all visitors to France and Switzerland wish they had upon their return home. Well, here it is. Try it for spring or summer guest luncheons on the terrace. We like it for Sunday nights, too.

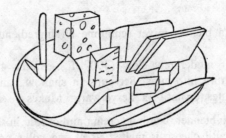

CHEESE CHART

CHEESE	ORIGIN	CHARACTERISTICS	USE
American Cheddar	Originally made in England, now made in U.S.	Waxed yellow-brown or black surface. Cream to deep orange inside. Mild flavor when fresh. Sharper the more cured and aged.	Eating Cooking Processing
Asiago	Italy	Dark surface, creamy inside. Hard, granular texture. Piquant flavor.	Eating when fresh Grating when old and drier
Bel Paese	Italy	Gray-brown surface. Light yellow inside. Soft texture, delicate flavor.	Eating
Blue or Bleu	France Denmark South America Switzerland U.S.	Usually foil-wrapped. White interior with blue veins. Semi-hard. Piquant flavor that gets stronger with age.	Eating Cooking
Brie	France	Russet-brown surface, creamy yellow inside. Soft, creamy. Resembles Camembert. Mild to pronounced flavor. Crust is eaten.	Eating
Caciocavallo	Sicily	Light brown glossy surface, yellowish inside. Solid body and texture, rather hard. A slightly salty, smoked flavor.	Eating, sliced Grating when aged and dry
Camembert	France	Gray-white mold surface, soft inside. Before serving, store at room temperature until runny. Eat crust. Ammonia flavor if too ripe.	Eating
Cottage Cheese	Unknown Very old	Soft, white. Pleasantly sour flavor. Made from skim milk. Either crumbly, or very smooth when cream is added.	Eating Cooking

CHEESE	ORIGIN	CHARACTERISTICS	USE
Cream Cheese	Europe Asia United States	Made from cream and milk. White, delicate. Slightly acid taste.	Eating Cooking
Edam	Holland	Red waxed surface, yellowish inside. On the hard side. Mild, Cheddarlike flavor.	Eating Cooking
Gammelost	Norway	Hard. Golden brown, with a strong flavor.	Eating
Gjetost	Norway	Hard. Dark brown, with a sweet, uncheese-like flavor. Made from goat's milk.	Eating
Gorgonzola	Italy	Clay-colored surface, white inside with green veins. Piquant flavor. Pungent.	Eating, sliced or crumbled on salad
Gouda	Holland	Usually red surface. Semi-hard texture, yellow inside. Edamlike flavor if imported. Domestic Gouda is softer and may have a slightly sour flavor.	Eating
Gruyère	Switzerland France	Hard, with holes. Tastes like Swiss. In the U.S. Gruyère means a processed cheese that is foil-wrapped and light yellow.	Eating Cooking
Incanestrato	Sicily	Dry, hard. Pale yellow.	Eating grated
Liederkranz (Trade-mark name)	United States	Russet surface, creamy inside. Soft, with robust flavor and odor.	Eating
Limburger	Belgium	Grayish-brown surface, creamy-white inside. When fresh it is white, tasteless, and without odor. Cured, it is soft, with a full, aromatic flavor.	Eating

CHEESE	ORIGIN	CHARACTERISTICS	USE
Manteca	Italy	Pale. Pronounced flavor. Add black pepper.	Eating
Monterey Jack	California	Semi-hard when fresh. Hardens with age. Mild flavor when new.	Eating Cooking Grating
Mozzarella	Italy	Mozzarella is the fresh variety of Provolone. It is white, tender, with a moderately sharp taste.	Eating, sliced Cooking Grating
Münster	Germany	Yellowish-tan surface. When fresh, white inside. Turns yellow with curing.	Eating Cooking
Mysost	Scandinavian Countries	Light brown. Sweetish flavor. Imported is made from goat's milk. Domestic from cow's milk.	Eating
Neufchâtel	France	Mild cream cheese made of milk and cream.	Eating
Oka	Canada	Russet surface, creamy inside. Semi-hard.	Eating
Parmesan or Parmigiano	Italy	Dark green or black surface, whitish inside. Hard, granular texture. Flavor gets stronger with age.	Eating when fresh Grating
Pecorino	Italy	Medium sharp, goats' cheese.	Eating, grated
Pineapple	United States	A Cheddar type shaped like a pineapple.	Eating Cooking
Port du Salut	France	Mild flavor sometimes resembling Cheddar or the stronger Limburger.	Eating
Pot Cheese	America	A form of cottage cheese with a dry curd. Not creamed.	In salads, sauces, etc.
Primost	Norway	Soft, light brown. Mild flavor. Unripened. Made from whey.	Eating

CHEESE	ORIGIN	CHARACTERISTICS	USE
Provolone	Italy	Provolone is hard with a yellow-brown surface and yellowish inside. Sharp, smoky flavor. Link-shaped or round, and hangs from strings. Good with green salads.	Eating Cooking Grating
Ricotta	Italy	White, soft, like cottage cheese.	Eating Cooking, also grating
Romano	Italy	Greenish-black surface, whitish inside. Granular and hard texture. Sharp flavor.	Grating
Roquefort and Roquefort-type	France	Foil-wrapped, green mold veins inside. Semi-hard texture. On the crumbly side. Sharp flavor. Made from ewe's milk. Only genuine Roquefort is allowed to have the name Roquefort. Imports are marked Roquefort-France.	Eating Cooking
Sap Sago	Switzerland	Green throughout. Hard and pungent-flavored with herbs. Small, conical shape.	Eating Grating
Scamozza	Italy	Smooth white, unsalted.	Eating, sliced
Stilton	England	Wrinkled surface. Creamy with green mold veins inside. Semi-hard texture. Sharp flavor.	Eating
Strachino	Italy	Very sharp, light yellow goats' milk cheese.	Eating, sliced
Swiss and American Swiss	Switzerland and America	Brownish-yellow surface with thick rind. Light yellow interior with regular holes. Semi-hard. Nutty flavor.	Eating Cooking Grating
Tilsit	East Prussia Germany	Yellowish outside, white to yellow inside.	Mostly eating, sometimes cooking

CHAPTER TEN

Chicken and Other Poultry Dishes

Buy fresh-dressed or quick-frozen poultry by brand name to be sure of highest quality. So much has been done by poultry marketing experts to give us cleaned, dressed, kitchen-ready chicken, turkey, duck, and other birds that most of the trouble and hard work of preparation no longer exist. You have only to travel abroad a little to see how superior our scientifically raised and fed poultry is. In fact, American growers are beginning to produce for European markets. This is especially true of ready-to-cook birds. They are convenient, economical, and, as a rule, of better quality than poultry in other forms. Here are some points to remember about chicken:

Choose the type of chicken called for in the recipe, or the parts which are preferred by your family.

Keep quick-frozen chickens and chicken parts on hand for drop-in guest meals or other convenient cookery.

Store iced fresh chicken, loosely wrapped, in coldest part of refrigerator. Store quick-frozen chicken in frozen food compartment of refrigerator or in freezer. After chicken is thawed, use at once. Do not refreeze.

Do not let cooked chicken stand at room temperature. Refrigerate covered, and use within 3 days or less. *It is particularly important to cool stewed chicken and broth quickly.*

Freeze cooked chicken, if desired. Use within 1 month for best flavor qualities.

The recipes indicate size or weight of bird and how poultry dealer should cut bird for convenient handling in the kitchen. Study packaged quick-frozen poultry and other forms of marketed poultry to aid in selecting the birds most useful in your cookery. Food packers are constantly improving their variety and packaging.

BAKED STUFFED CHICKEN BREASTS

Make up one half or less of your favorite poultry stuffing. Select large chicken breasts at poultry dealer's. Have dealer split the breasts just enough to fold.

Season breasts with salt and pepper. Squeeze orange or lemon juice over them. Stuff. Fold and hold stuffing in place with skewers. Dip stuffed chicken in melted butter or olive oil and place in baking dish.

Bake uncovered in moderate oven (325° F.) 45 minutes. Turn pieces. Bake 45 minutes longer. During baking baste two or three times with melted butter and orange juice. When browned and tender, remove skewers. Serve hot with your favorite green vegetable or salad. Serve one to each guest or cut with sharp knife and serve one half with half of the stuffing to each person.

A few chopped mushrooms added to the stuffing give good flavor. An herb stuffing, or rice-and-orange-peel stuffing, is well suited to this recipe. For dessert, a compote of black cherries, and for those who enjoy a sweet, serve paper-thin crisp cookies with the compote.

BARBECUED CHICKEN IN THE KITCHEN

3 broiling chickens, 1 ½ to 2 pounds each	1 small onion, peeled and minced
Cooking oil	1 ½ tablespoons Worcestershire sauce
¼ pound butter or margarine, melted	2 teaspoons salt
1 ½ cups ketchup	1 ½ teaspoons dry mustard
¾ cup water	1 teaspoon paprika
⅓ cup cider vinegar	⅛ teaspoon cayenne
3 tablespoons brown sugar	

Have poultry dealer split birds into halves and remove backbone, neck, and keel bone. Bring wing tips back under the shoulder joints.

Grease grill in broiler pan lightly with oil. Brush chicken all over with melted butter or margarine. Arrange halves skin side up on grill, about 8 inches from heat. Grill, turning frequently, 30 to 45 minutes or until drumstick twists easily out of thigh joint.

While chicken cooks, mix ketchup and remaining ingredients in a 1-quart enamel or glass saucepan. Bring to a boil, lower heat, simmer 15 minutes. During cooking brush chicken several times with this hot sauce. Chicken should be brown, with crisp crust, when done. Makes 6 servings.

Reheat any remaining sauce and serve with chicken.

Can be cooked on outdoor grill. Served indoors or on the terrace, this chicken calls for a bowl of tossed green salad, Italian bread, and a finger dessert such as fresh fruit, cupcakes, or small fruit tarts.

Or, for another dinner, complete the menu with au gratin potatoes crisply topped with crumbs and cheese, hot rolls, and fruit salad served in cantaloupe ring.

BROILED CHICKEN HALVES

2 broiler-fryers, 1½ to 2 pounds each	1 teaspoon salt
Soft butter or margarine	½ teaspoon pepper

Have chickens cut in halves. Place in broiler pan, not on rack. Bring wing tips onto back, to expose thick breast meat to heat. Brush generously with butter or margarine. Season halves with salt and pepper. Flatten halves, skin side down.

Place pan under broiler heat so that chicken is 7 to 9 inches from heat. Chicken should just begin to brown after 15 minutes. Broil slowly. Turn pieces after 30 minutes. Baste frequently with butter or margarine. Broil skin side up 20 to 25 minutes or until drumstick twists easily out of thigh joint. Makes 4 servings.

Anchovy-Broiled Chicken: Combine 1½ tablespoons anchovy paste and 2½ tablespoons softened butter or margarine. Brush this mixture on chicken two or three times during broiling. Good for the chicken you cook on an outdoor grill, too.

French Broiled Chicken: Use 1 cup French dressing plus 1 teaspoon paprika in place of butter or margarine in recipe for Broiled Chicken Halves. Makes 4 servings.

Lemon-Broiled Chicken: Rub chicken halves with 2 cut lemons. Coat with melted butter or margarine. Sprinkle with mixture of 2 teaspoons each salt and sugar, 1 teaspoon paprika, and ½ teaspoon pepper. Broil as described in Broiled Chicken Halves. Makes 4 servings.

When to serve broiled chicken? At any meal of the day. A wonderful idea for spring breakfast, or brunch, with new asparagus, tiny creamed potatoes, warm brioches, and coffee. Equally good at luncheon any day. Delicious for dinner or a supper. Sometimes served with mixed green salad, and a strawberry shortcake for dessert. Sometimes served cold, with salad and an ice-cream pie, on a holiday. Fine, cold, for a late snack.

BROILED CHICKEN, HONOLULU STYLE

½ cup salad oil	1 teaspoon orégano
⅓ cup lemon juice	1 teaspoon salt
¼ cup soy sauce	¼ teaspoon pepper
1 clove garlic, peeled and minced	2 broiler chickens, about 2 pounds each, split in half

Combine all ingredients. Pour over chicken halves in a bowl. Cover and let marinate in refrigerator 4 to 5 hours.

To cook, drain chicken. Place on greased broiler rack skin side down, about 7 inches below heat. Broil 20 minutes or until lightly browned on one side. Brush with marinade. Turn chicken. Broil 10 minutes. Brush with marinade and continue broiling 10 minutes longer or until chicken is done. During final 10 minutes of cooking brush once or twice with remaining marinade. Makes 4 servings.

A fine idea for summer luncheon on the porch. Serve a fresh garden salad, such as tomatoes and cucumbers with water cress or lettuce. Cheese rolls or loaf. For dessert strawberries and ice cream. Iced tea, or demitasse of hot coffee, makes a good finale.

A variation of the sauce: Combine 1 cup olive oil, ½ cup cider vinegar, 1½ teaspoons dried thyme, 1½ teaspoons orégano. Mix well. Use as marinade and brush chicken as described above.

CHICKEN-AND-HAM SHORTCAKE

1 (12-ounce) package corn-muffin mix	1 (3-ounce) can sliced mushrooms, drained
2 cups prepared biscuit mix	12 slices (¾ pound) cooked chicken or turkey
1 egg	
1½ cups milk	12 slices (¾ pound) cooked ham
2 (10½-ounce) cans condensed cream-of-mushroom soup	1 cup grated sharp Cheddar cheese

Start oven at moderately hot (400° F.). Grease 13-by-9-by-2-inch pan.

Combine muffin and biscuit mixes in bowl. Stir in egg and milk. Mix well. Spread in prepared pan.

Bake 10 to 12 minutes, or until done.

Blend soup and ½ cup mushroom liquid until smooth. Stir in mushrooms. Heat until steaming hot. Do not boil.

As soon as shortcake is done, remove from oven. Let stand 2 or 3 minutes. Cut in 12 rectangles. Place on baking sheet. Cover each rectangle with piece of ham and chicken. Spread mushroom sauce over. Sprinkle generously with cheese. Broil under moderate heat until bubbly and browned. Makes 12 servings.

When there is leftover chicken or turkey this combination makes a fine spur-of-the-moment lunch or supper dish for family and guests. Or if you plan the dish ahead, a good delicatessen shop can supply chicken or turkey as well as the ham.

To complete the menu, a salad, ice cream or sherbet, and hot coffee.

CHICKEN BREASTS, AMANDINE

2 breasts chicken, cut in half
5 tablespoons butter or margarine
3 tablespoons cognac
1 small clove garlic, peeled and crushed
½ cup blanched almond halves
1 mushroom, chopped fine, or
1 tablespoon chopped canned mushrooms

1 teaspoon cornstarch
½ cup dry white wine
½ cup bouillon or hot water
Salt and pepper
Paprika

Brown chicken breasts slowly in 3 tablespoons butter or margarine. Pour brandy into large kitchen spoon. Ignite with match. Pour over chicken. When flame dies down, remove chicken from skillet. Add 1 tablespoon butter or margarine, the garlic, ¼ cup almonds, and the mushroom or chopped mushrooms. Cook 3 or 4 minutes. Remove garlic and discard it. Remove pan from heat. Stir in cornstarch. Mix well. Add wine and bouillon or hot water, stirring well. Return to heat and stir until sauce boils 2 or 3 minutes. Taste for seasoning and add salt and pepper if needed. Return chicken breasts to skillet and cook 20 to 25 minutes or until chicken is done.

Brown remaining ¼ cup almonds in remaining 1 tablespoon butter or margarine. Serve chicken on warmed platter. Pour pan sauce over. Sprinkle top with almonds. Makes 4 servings.

May be prepared in chafing dish at table, or start dish in kitchen, prepare sauce in chafing dish, add browned chicken breasts, and heat at table.

CHICKEN CURRY

1 ½ - to-2-pound chicken	2 tablespoons butter or marga-
4 peppercorns	rine
2 whole cloves	1 teaspoon curry powder
1 bay leaf	2 cups chicken broth
Salt	2 tablespoons cornstarch
1 chili pepper from mixed-pickle spice	1 egg yolk, beaten
2 onions, peeled and sliced	

Have poultry dealer cut chicken in serving pieces. Place chicken in small kettle. Add peppercorns, cloves, bay leaf, salt, chili pepper, and enough hot water to cover. Bring to a boil. Reduce heat and let simmer 2 hours or until chicken is tender. Drain chicken. Save broth.

Sauté onions 5 minutes in butter or margarine in large, deep frying pan. Skim out onions. Brown chicken in same fat. Sprinkle chicken with curry powder. Add chicken broth. Cook 5 minutes. Push chicken to one side in pan. Make a paste of cornstarch with 3 tablespoons water. Stir into pan. Cook and stir until sauce is thickened. Let boil 1 or 2 minutes. Stir in egg yolk. Cook 1 minute longer. Spoon sauce over chicken.

Serve hot with border of hot rice and curry condiments, such as chopped green pepper, chopped peanuts, chopped orange peel, and Serundang (see recipe, page 555). Makes 6 servings. I sometimes add 1 tablespoon of orange marmalade and a tablespoon of diced apple to the curry sauce.

CHICKEN, FRENCH RESTAURANT STYLE

4-pound roasting chicken, ready for cooking	1 bay leaf
	2 cloves
Salt and pepper	⅛ teaspoon mace
3 tablespoons butter	2 sprigs parsley
½ pound sliced ham, cut in strips	1 shallot, sliced
⅛ teaspoon thyme	

Have poultry dealer cut chicken in serving pieces and remove bones carefully. Season chicken lightly with salt and pepper.

Melt butter in deep skillet or saucepan. Stir in remaining ingredients. Mix. Let cook 1 or 2 minutes over low heat. Place chicken pieces in mixture, turning chicken to coat well. Cover pan. Cook slowly about 1 hour or until chicken is tender and done. Stir frequently. Uncover pan for last few minutes of cooking. Place cooked chicken on warmed serving dish. Makes 6 servings. I am not a thyme enthusiast and substitute marjoram in the recipe.

Sauce Ninon: In French restaurants a sauce is usually poured over this flavorful chicken. To make it, use:

3 tablespoons tarragon vinegar
1 teaspoon sugar
¼ cup chopped mushrooms

1 cup Onion-seasoned Cream
   Sauce (page 557)
2 egg yolks

Mix vinegar, sugar, and mushrooms into cream sauce over hot, not boiling, water. Stir slowly until blended. Beat egg yolks slightly. Stir into sauce. Pour very hot over chicken. Serve at once.

This dish can be made in the early hours of a hot or busy day and finished at dinner time in the chafing dish or electric skillet at the table.

CHICKEN, HUNTER'S STYLE

Chicken Cacciatora

4-pound roasting chicken, ready
   to cook
2 tablespoons butter or margarine
2 tablespoons olive oil
1 stalk celery, sliced thin
1 carrot, scraped and sliced
   thin

1 onion, peeled and diced
1 tablespoon finely cut parsley
1 teaspoon salt
½ teaspoon freshly ground
   pepper
1 tablespoon tomato paste
¾ cup dry sherry

Have chicken cut into serving pieces. Heat butter and olive oil together in heavy skillet. Brown chicken on all sides. About 20 minutes. Add all vegetables and salt and pepper. Cover. Simmer 10 minutes or until vegetables are partially cooked. Mix tomato paste and sherry. Stir into vegetables. Cover skillet. Let cook slowly, stirring occasionally to prevent burning. Let simmer about 30 minutes or until chicken is done. If more liquid is needed from time to time, add a little hot water or consommé mixed with sherry. Serve very hot. Makes 4 to 6 servings.

This is the famous Italian dish which is usually served after antipasto and with a small order of spaghetti and a large green salad. An herb dressing on the salad will add to the mingling of good flavors. *Caffè espresso* is called for at the end of this meal. If anyone wants a dessert, it should be fresh fruit with a mild Italian cheese or a small rum cake.

CHICKEN IN WINE

Coq *Au Vin*

3½- to-4-pound roasting chicken, cut in serving pieces	3 pieces parsley, tied together
Flour	6 small white onions
¼ pound butter or margarine	1 (6-ounce) can mushrooms
⅜ cup cognac	6 slices lean bacon, partially cooked
1 clove garlic, peeled	1 cup red wine
1 bay leaf	½ cup large croutons, fried in butter or bacon fat
⅛ teaspoon thyme	

Dredge chicken in flour. Heat butter or margarine in large skillet or flameproof casserole. Brown chicken well on all sides. Pour all but a large cooking spoonful of the brandy over the chicken. Ignite the spoonful with a match and pour into the skillet to flame the rest of the brandy. Let blaze a few seconds. When flame dies down add garlic, bay leaf, thyme, parsley, onions, mushrooms, a little salt and pepper. Cut up bacon and add to skillet. Pour wine over chicken. Cover pan.

Cook slowly 25 minutes or longer, until chicken is tender and done. Remove parsley and garlic and discard. If sauce is too thin, add 1 tablespoon cornstarch or flour and butter smoothed together. Stir into pan sauce, pushing chicken to one side. Cook and stir until sauce boils at least 2 minutes. Pour sauce over chicken and croutons over the top. Makes 6 servings.

This dish may be prepared in the morning of the day on which it is served. Keep covered in refrigerator until 30 minutes before cooking time. Then reheat in moderate (350° F.) oven about 25 minutes or until bubbly and very hot. Add croutons and serve.

Coq au Vin makes a dinner in itself. With it serve chunky French bread, a simple salad, and that wonderful dessert called Philadelphia Peaches (page 268). Or if that seems too elaborate for the occasion, serve quick-frozen red raspberries, defrosted and spooned over poundcake.

CHICKEN TARRAGON

2 tablespoons dried, or 4 tablespoons fresh, tarragon	¼ pound butter or margarine
1 cup white wine	Salt and pepper
2 young broilers, 1½ to 2 pounds each	10 shallots, or green onions, cut fine
	2 tablespoons finely cut parsley

If fresh tarragon is used, strip leaves from stem. Discard stems. Add tarragon to wine. Let stand 1 hour.

Cut chickens in serving pieces. Melt butter or margarine in skillet. When quite hot, brown chicken, 20 to 25 minutes. Season with salt and pepper. Add shallots or green onions. Cover skillet and cook slowly 20 minutes longer or until chicken is tender. Add strained wine. Increase heat. Cook briskly to reduce sauce. Sprinkle with parsley. Serve at once. Makes 4 servings.

This is a flavorful chicken dish, especially good with rice or noodles, or plain boiled very small new potatoes. Avoid serving herb-flavored salad or a highly seasoned appetizer with it. A chocolate soufflé for dessert will make your guests appreciate your imagination and skill as a menu maker.

Serve this with a dry white wine, perhaps a Muscatel, a Sancerre or a Beaujolais Blanc.

CHICKEN SAUTÉE, ITALIANO

2 broiler-fryers, about 1½ to 2 pounds each, ready to cook	3 tablespoons finely cut parsley
5 tablespoons olive oil	¼ teaspoon thyme
2 tomatoes, skinned and chopped	Salt and pepper
	¾ cup white wine
1 clove garlic, peeled and mashed	1 cup sliced ripe olives
	⅛ teaspoon cayenne

Cut chicken in serving pieces. Heat oil in large skillet. Brown chicken 20 minutes. Turn pieces to cook evenly. Add tomatoes, garlic, parsley, thyme, salt, and pepper. Blend well to coat chicken. Pour wine over all. Cover skillet. Lower heat.

Cook 25 minutes or until chicken is almost done. Stir sauce frequently and spoon over chicken. Add olives. Mix. Cook 10 minutes longer or until chicken is done. Sprinkle cayenne lightly over all. Serve at once. Makes 4 servings.

Can be made in a casserole. Use flameproof metal-base type of casserole. Put casserole in oven for final 30 minutes of cooking, at moderate (350° F.) heat. Bring casserole to table.

This makes a fine dish for a buffet meal. Green salad and either spaghetti or noodles go well with this Italian favorite.

CHICKEN PAPRIKA

2½ to 3½ pounds chicken, cut in serving pieces	2 medium onions, peeled and chopped
1 teaspoon salt	Paprika
½ teaspoon pepper	¼ cup water
¼ cup flour	1 (3-ounce) can sliced mushrooms
4 tablespoons butter or margarine	1 cup commercial sour cream

If frozen chicken is used, thaw as described on package. Combine salt and pepper with 3 tablespoons flour in paper bag. Shake chicken in bag until pieces are well coated with flour mixture. Melt butter or margarine in heavy skillet. Cook chicken over medium heat until browned on all sides. Add onions, 1 teaspoon paprika, water, mushrooms and their liquid. Cover.

Cook over low heat about 30 minutes or until chicken is tender and done. Remove chicken to hot platter.

Stir remaining 1 tablespoon flour into mixture in skillet until smooth. Add sour cream. Stir over low heat 1 or 2 minutes until hot and bubbly. Pour over chicken. Sprinkle lightly with paprika. Serve hot. Makes 4 to 6 servings.

This Hungarian dish should be served with small dumplings or noodles, or small boiled potatoes. New green peas make a delicious accompaniment. Serve Hungarian Peach Pastry (page 469) for dessert.

CHICKEN SUPREME, MARJOLAINE

Suprême de Poulet Marjolaine

Breast of 3½-pound roasting chicken cut in half	12 tablespoons sweet butter (1½ sticks)
Powdered nutmeg	¼ cup sherry
Salt and pepper	Extra herbs
1½ teaspoons mixed dried herbs (crumbled rosemary, bay leaf, thyme, marjoram)	

Season the two pieces of chicken with a little nutmeg, salt, pepper, and the mixed herbs. Heat 4 tablespoons butter in skillet. Cook chicken 10 or 15 minutes. Turn pieces and cook 10 minutes more or until delicately browned and done. Cooking time depends on thickness of meat. Remove chicken to pan and keep hot in oven with its door open, or place chicken in chafing dish pan over hot water.

Add sherry to skillet in which chicken cooked. Simmer until sauce is reduced a little. Remove from heat, gradually add remaining butter and enough additional mixed herbs to suit taste. Pour herb-butter sauce over chicken in chafing dish. Heat and serve. Makes 2 servings.

If chafing dish is not used, place chicken in warm serving dish and pour hot herb-butter over. Serve at once.

CHICKEN WITH RICE

Arroz con Pollo

3-pound frying chicken, cut in serving pieces

6 tablespoons butter or margarine

3 onions, peeled and chopped coarsely

2 green peppers, cut fine

½ clove garlic, peeled and chopped

1 (19-ounce) can tomatoes

1 (10½-ounce) can condensed chicken consommé

½ teaspoon salt

¼ teaspoon pepper

1 bay leaf

1 cup uncooked rice

1 teaspoon saffron

1 (9-ounce) package quick-frozen peas, defrosted

Sauté chicken in about 3 tablespoons butter or margarine 25 minutes or until browned on all sides.

While chicken cooks, melt remaining 3 tablespoons butter or margarine in another large heavy skillet over moderate heat. Add onions, green peppers, and garlic. Cook until soft. Stir in tomatoes. Add consommé, salt, pepper, bay leaf, rice, and saffron. Mix. Cover skillet and let cook about 20 minutes over low heat. Stir in peas. Cook 5 minutes longer.

Start oven at moderate (350° F.). Place browned chicken in 2-quart casserole. Pour rice mixture over. Cover and bake 15 to 25 minutes or until chicken is done. Makes 6 servings.

This savory combination of chicken, rice, and vegetables makes a good winter dinner. Try with it a mixed green salad with herb dressing, and baked caramel custard for dessert.

You may eat your way through Spain, Mexico, and Latin America with this classic. Its genesis is Spanish, hence it is not "hot." Appeals to lovers of *non*-chilied, Spanish-style cooking.

CURRY-BAKED CHICKEN

2½-to-3-pound chicken, ready to cook
1 cup sifted all-purpose flour
1½ teaspoons curry powder
1 teaspoon salt
½ teaspoon pepper
4 tablespoons butter or margarine
½ cup chicken consommé

Have chicken cut in serving pieces. Combine flour, curry powder, salt, and pepper in paper bag. Shake chicken pieces in bag until well coated.

Start oven at moderately slow (300° F.).

Melt fat in flameproof casserole. Brown chicken on all sides about 20 minutes. Pour consommé over chicken. Cover casserole.

Place in oven and bake 25 minutes or until chicken is tender and done. Makes 6 servings.

A good conversation piece for a buffet meal. With this chicken dish serve hot saffron rice and Major Grey's chutney. The garnish tray should include chopped green pepper, chopped peanuts, shredded coconut, chopped orange or grapefruit peel, and Bombay duck, if your specialty grocer or a Chinese grocer can supply you. This "duck" is salty, crumbled, dry fish and a perfect addition to any curry dish. Guests help themselves to one or more of these garnishes. This is another menu which should end with a cooling sherbet, a compote of fruit, sautéed bananas, or any melon in season.

Note on this and other curries throughout the book: I never serve curry to guests whose food preferences I do not know. When in doubt I ask before planning the menu. If I know my guests like curry, I may make it hair-raising hot, otherwise I'm cautious.

HERB-FRIED CHICKEN

3-to-3½-pound chicken, cut for frying
Juice ½ lemon
¾ cup sifted all-purpose flour
1 teaspoon salt
¼ teaspoon freshly ground pepper
½ teaspoon each dried thyme, marjoram, basil
Fat
¼ cup finely cut fresh parsley
½ teaspoon dried rosemary
1 (10½-ounce) can condensed consommé

Sprinkle pieces of chicken with lemon juice. Combine flour, salt, pepper, thyme, marjoram, and basil in paper sack. Shake to mix well. Then shake one or two pieces of chicken at a time in bag. Place chicken on rack to dry few minutes. When all chicken is coated, empty paper bag into a bowl and save mixture for gravy.

Melt enough fat in large skillet to make ¼ inch deep. When very hot, add large pieces of chicken and brown slowly. Add smaller pieces. When all are lightly browned remove to 2-quart shallow baking dish. Sprinkle chicken with parsley and rosemary. Heat ½ can consommé in chicken skillet, stirring well. Pour over chicken in casserole.

Start oven at moderate (375° F.).

Bake chicken uncovered 45 minutes or until tender and done. Makes 6 servings.

Gravy for Herbed Chicken: Stir 2 tablespoons butter or margarine into chicken skillet. Stir 2 tablespoons of remaining herb-flour mixture slowly into melted fat. When smooth, add 1½ cups milk mixed with remaining half can of consommé. Cook slowly, stirring, until gravy thickens and boils about 3 minutes. Serve with chicken.

Whatever happened to mashed potatoes? Don't hesitate to serve the dehydrated or quick frozen variety if time presses—or if it doesn't, for that matter. So good with this chicken dish. So is baked green or yellow squash. This might be the day to serve warm corn bread, blackberry jam, and for dessert a deep-dish pear pie.

New Fried Chicken Flavor: The next time you fry chicken, cook the pieces only until browned. Then brush them on all sides with honey, place in baking dish, and bake in moderate oven (350° F.). Bake 30 minutes or until chicken is done. Baste twice during the 30-minute period with honey mixed with a little warmed wine. Serve hot or cold.

Delicious with Almond Rice (page 449) and a mixed green salad. Fruit sherbet or a slice of honeydew melon is a perfect finish for this Sunday luncheon or supper.

MILDRED LANGROCK'S CHICKEN FRICASSEE

4-to-4½-pound fowl, cut in frying pieces	1 to 1½ cups water
Flour	1 cup commercial sour cream
Salt, pepper, paprika	3 eggs
2 tablespoons butter	1 cup sifted all-purpose flour
1 onion, peeled and minced	1½ quarts boiling salted water
1 clove garlic, peeled and mashed	

Rinse chicken in cold running water, drain, and pat dry with paper towel. Sprinkle pieces with flour, salt, pepper, and paprika. Heat butter in Dutch oven or heavy kettle. Brown chicken, onion, and garlic together lightly. Add 1 to 1½ cups water, just enough to cover. Cover pot and simmer about 2 hours or until chicken is tender. Add more water if needed. Add sour cream, stir into pan juices. Add dumplings and serve.

Make these special dumplings while chicken cooks. Break eggs and beat slightly. Use half eggshell as measure and add 3 half-shells of water to beaten eggs. Add flour, mixing steadily, until mixture is soft dough, just right for dropping from spoon. Drop by spoonful into rapidly boiling water. Let cook 3 to 5 minutes or until dumplings are done. Test for doneness. Remove dumplings from boiling water with slotted spoon. Drain and add to chicken pot. Spoon some of sauce in pot over dumplings and serve. Makes 6 servings.

PATTY QUINLAN'S DRUNKEN CHICKEN

2½-to-3½-pound fryer	3 tablespoons shortening, butter or cooking oil
3 tablespoons flour	
1½ teaspoons salt	¼ cup cognac
1 teaspoon pepper	⅓ cup sauterne wine

Have chicken cut in serving pieces. Combine flour, salt, and pepper in a paper bag. Add chicken pieces, close bag tightly, and shake it until chicken is well coated. Heat fat or oil in flameproof casserole. Fry chicken 40 minutes or until about ⅔ cooked. Pour brandy into very large cooking spoon. Ignite and pour over chicken while aflame. When flame dies out, add wine to casserole. Cover tightly and cook over moderate heat about 20 minutes. Serve in casserole. Makes 4 to 6 servings.

Perfect go-withs for this chicken dish are wild rice, with sautéed chicken livers and Richelieu spiced grapes in clusters as garnish for the chicken. A mousse, sherbet, or jellied fruit makes a fitting dessert.

I "swapped" this recipe and the next one in the Bahamas, and it is a great favorite with us as an easy guest dinner. The children are very amused by its title and know that alcohol in cooking adds flavor only, so they may enjoy it with the grownups.

PATTY QUINLAN'S ROCK CORNISH HEN

½ large Rock Cornish hen per person, or 1 small whole hen
Salt
Pepper

Bread crumbs
4 tablespoons butter or margarine

Start oven at moderately hot (400° F.).

Season hen with salt and pepper. Sprinkle with crumbs lightly. Dot heavily with butter or margarine. Place each small whole bird, or half of large bird cut side down, in brown unglazed paper bag. Gather each end of the bag tightly and tie with string so bag will retain steam. Place bags on cooking sheet. Turn oven down to moderate (375° F.); bake 45 minutes.

Immediately on taking bags out of oven, slit paper and let steam escape. Serve at once, or preheat under moderate broiler heat.

If ordinary broiler chickens are used, split a 2½-pound broiler for 2 people.

TIMETABLE FOR ROASTING CHICKEN

READY-TO-COOK WEIGHT	OVEN TEMPERATURE	APPROXIMATE TIME STUFFED BIRD	APPROXIMATE TIME UNSTUFFED BIRD
1½ to 2½ pounds	325°F.	1¼ to 2 hours	1 to 1¾ hours
2½ to 3½ pounds	325°F.	2 to 3 hours	1¾ to 2¾ hours

Test for doneness: Chicken leg moves easily in thigh joint, and drumstick meat feels soft when pressed between fingers. Protect fingers with folded waxed paper when making these tests.

ROAST CHICKEN WITH STUFFING

¼ onion, peeled and minced	½ teaspoon poultry seasoning
1 cup diced celery	½ to 1 cup consommé or water
4 tablespoons fat	1 roasting chicken, 3 to 4
4 cups bread cubes, firmly	pounds, ready to cook
packed	Salt for cavity
1 teaspoon salt	Fat
¼ teaspoon pepper	Milk or consommé

Cook onion and celery in fat over low heat, stirring occasionally until onion is soft but not browned. Blend seasonings with bread cubes. Add onion, celery, and fat to bread. Pour consommé or water over surface, and stir lightly. Add more seasoning if desired. Rub cavity of chicken with ½ teaspoon salt. Stuff wishbone and body cavities lightly.

Close bird by placing skewers across body opening and tying shoelace fashion with string. Tie drumsticks to tail. Fasten neck skin to back with skewer. Shape wings akimbo style: bring tips onto back.

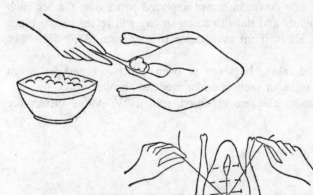

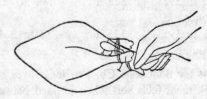

Start oven at moderate (325° F.).

Place bird breast up on rack in shallow open pan. Brush skin with fat. Cover top of chicken with piece of folded cheesecloth dipped in melted fat. Roast according to timetable (page 215), 2 to 3 hours. Do not sear, do not add water to pan, and do not cover. Baste chicken 2 to 4 times with drippings from pan, or mixture of melted fat and milk or consommé.

Chicken Giblet Gravy

When roast chicken is done, pour off all pan drippings except 3 table-spoons fat and the brown residue. Blend in 3 tablespoons flour, stirring until smooth. Cook, stirring until frothy. Add 2 cups warm water or consommé all at once, stirring until evenly thickened and smooth. Boil gently 5 minutes. Season to taste. Add chopped cooked giblets and 2 chopped hard-cooked eggs. Makes 3 cups gravy. (See Cooked Giblets recipe, page 228.)

WINE-BAKED CHICKEN BREASTS

1 cup red wine	1 teaspoon powdered ginger
¼ cup soy sauce	¼ teaspoon orégano
¼ cup salad oil	1 tablespoon brown sugar
2 tablespoons water	3 chicken breasts, split in halves
1 clove garlic, peeled and sliced	3 or 4 cups cooked wild rice

Start oven at moderate (375° F.).

Combine all sauce ingredients and mix well. Place chicken in large casserole. Pour mixture over all and cover dish.

Bake about 1½ hours or until chicken is tender and done. Uncover for last 15 minutes of baking, unless pan juices have cooked down to almost nothing. Serve at once, surrounded by mounds of hot cooked wild rice. Makes 6 servings.

Duckling

DUCK BIGARRADE

4-to-5-pound duckling, ready to cook
1 teaspoon Worcestershire sauce
1 teaspoon Kitchen Bouquet
1 tablespoon sherry
1 tablespoon port
⅓ cup duck fat
¼ cup minced, peeled onion
⅓ cup flour
1 teaspoon salt
1 cup giblet broth
1 (3-ounce) can sliced broiled mushrooms
1 (6-ounce) can condensed frozen orange juice
¼ cup currant jelly

Skin duck and cut in serving pieces. (Be polite to your meat dealer and he'll do this for you.) Cook neck, skin, giblets, and backbone in 3 cups water with 1 teaspoon salt, about 45 minutes. Place pieces of duck in a bowl. Sprinkle on all sides with Worcestershire, Kitchen Bouquet, sherry, and port.

Measure 1 cup broth in which giblets cooked. Heat fat in Dutch oven. Brown drained seasoned duck lightly over moderate heat. Remove pieces to shallow baking dish. Add onion to fat in Dutch oven. Cook about 1 minute. Stir in flour and salt smoothly. Add 1 cup broth from giblets, add mushrooms with their liquid. Cook, stirring constantly, until sauce thickens. Add orange juice and jelly, stirring until jelly dissolves. Pour over duck. Cover baking dish.

Start oven at moderate (350° F.). Let heat 10 minutes.

Cook duck about 1 hour. Makes 4 servings.

DUCK, FRENCH COUNTRY-HOUSE STYLE

4-to-5-pound duck, ready for cooking
2 tablespoons butter or margarine
3 or 4 large mushrooms, sliced
Finely shredded peel 1 orange
1 small clove garlic, peeled and crushed
3 teaspoons cornstarch
¼ cup dry sherry
¼ cup cognac
½ cup cointreau
½ cup orange juice
1 tablespoon red currant jelly
1 tablespoon chopped truffle
Salt and pepper
2 oranges
2 tablespoons butter
2 tablespoons sugar

Start oven at moderate (350° F.).

Truss duck and place on back in roasting pan. Roast until tender and browned, allowing 20 to 25 minutes per pound. Remove duck when done.

Pour fat off pan juices. Melt butter or margarine in the pan. Add mushrooms, orange peel, and garlic. Cook slowly 2 minutes, stirring a little. Remove from heat and discard garlic. Stir in cornstarch smoothly. Add sherry, cognac, cointreau, and orange juice. Return pan to heat and stir until sauce begins to boil. Add jelly and truffle. Stir and heat until jelly melts and blends with sauce. Taste and add salt and pepper if needed.

Cut duck into serving pieces. Reheat in sauce a few minutes. Do not boil. Slice unpeeled oranges. Sauté in butter and sugar 5 or 6 minutes or until they begin to brown. Arrange pieces of duck in warmed serving dish. Pour hot sauce over them and garnish with cooked orange slices. Makes 4 servings.

French bread and pâté served with a glass of champagne first, then only one delicately flavored vegetable, such as braised celery-with-almonds, new peas, asparagus, or artichoke hearts. For dessert a lime sherbet or fresh strawberries.

I like to serve duck because many people, unfamiliar with its versatility, are surprised and pleased to find it in a guise other than roasted. It can be used in any chicken or turkey recipe. Interesting cold, served either with hot orange sauce and gravy or with cold relishes and salad dressing. It makes a fine aspic—in place of the chicken called for in the aspic recipe. If ducklings are plentiful at your market, buy them and enjoy them. Cold duck salad, made like turkey or chicken salad, is delicious. Add sliced orange or apple, or both, to the mixture.

Goose

Three kinds of goose are available at poultry markets: young goose of either sex, which is tender-meated. Mature goose of either sex, which is less tender-meated. Wild goose.

Since age and sex are not readily apparent, the goose grower, retailer, or label information on individual packaged geese, should be relied upon in selecting the bird. A young, quality goose is the usual choice.

They are marketed either as ready-to-cook—that is, fully drawn and ready for cooking, fresh or quick-frozen—or as dressed—goose not drawn, head and feet on, and only feathers removed.

The popular sizes vary from 6 to about 10 pounds, ready-to-cook weight. About 1 pound, ready-to-cook weight, per serving is a good allowance in choosing size or quantity.

CARE OF COOKED GOOSE

Do not, under any circumstances, allow goose meat, stuffing, or gravy to remain out of the refrigerator after the meal is served. (It is a fallacy to believe that placing warm foods in the refrigerator causes them to spoil.)

Refrigerate leftover goose and gravy, well covered, as soon as possible after the meal. Remove any stuffing from stuffed birds and refrigerate it *separately,* well covered. Use this food within 2 or 3 days, before it dries out and loses flavor. Stuffing should be *thoroughly* reheated for service.

Meal-size units, properly wrapped, may be frozen. Serve them within a month, while the flavor and moistness are at their best.

Goose Stuffings: In preparing domestic goose for roasting it, you may or may not stuff it. Stuffings that have little or no added fat are definitely preferred. Celery, onion, apple, cranberry, dried fruit stuffings (apricots, currants, prunes, raisins), sauerkraut, and mashed potato are among the favorites. Time-saving packaged stuffings may also be used. Follow package suggestions for lean or rich stuffings.

If sauerkraut is used, roast the goose about ⅔ done. Remove from oven, drain any fat from cavity, stuff with heated and drained sauerkraut, and complete the roasting. When mashed potatoes are used, they should be slightly dry. Herb seasoning may be added—basil, poultry seasoning, rosemary, sage, or thyme.

As for me, I just stuff a goose with sliced unpared apples, which I discard before serving the bird. The apples flavor it and help soak up the fat. If I do decide on stuffing, I bake it separately.

Also, I prick the goose skin all over—but not the flesh. As fat collects in the pan, I spoon it off into an oven-glass bowl which can stand the heat of the fat.

Goose fat or grease is considered a great delicacy in German cookery. I reheat it, strain, and keep in a covered bowl or lard can in refrigerator for use from time to time as called for in German dishes. Or I mix it with seed for winter bird feeding.

ROAST WILD GOOSE

1 young wild or domestic goose, 6 to 8 pounds dressed weight	2 tart apples, cored and chopped coarsely
Juice 1½ lemons	1 cup chopped dried apricots
Salt	3 cups soft bread cubes
Pepper	½ teaspoon salt
4 tablespoons butter or margarine	¼ teaspoon pepper
	4 to 6 slices lean bacon
¼ cup diced peeled onions	Melted bacon fat

Rinse goose in warm water, inside and out, and drain. Sprinkle inside and out with lemon juice, salt, and pepper. Melt butter or margarine in large saucepan. Add onions and cook until tender. Stir in apples, apricots, bread cubes, salt, and pepper. Mix well and cook 1 or 2 minutes.

Start oven at moderate (325° F.).

Spoon stuffing lightly into cavity. Close opening with skewers and string. *If goose is wild and lean,* cover breast with bacon slices and cheesecloth soaked in melted bacon fat. *If plump domestic goose* is to be roasted, omit bacon slices and melted fat. Place goose breast up on rack in roasting pan.

Roast 20 to 25 minutes per pound or until tender and done.

For wild goose, baste frequently with bacon fat and drippings in pan. For plump domestic goose, insert fork once or twice in breast and thighs to let fat drain off. Baste domestic goose with mixture of lemon juice and hot water.

For large, older goose, add about 1 cup hot water to pan and cover pan for last hour of roasting. Then uncover, remove bacon and cheesecloth, and let brown about 15 minutes.

Remove skewers and string. Place goose on large warmed serving platter. Serve with or without gravy. Makes 6 to 8 servings.

Gravy can be made in pan on top of the stove. Skim off excess fat. To about ¼ cup pan drippings, add 3 tablespoons flour, mixing until smooth. Stir in 2 cups milk slowly. Bring to a boil and boil 2 or 3 minutes, stirring continually. Makes about 2 cups of gravy.

Cook young green cabbage to serve with goose. Boil or steam small new potatoes and sprinkle with freshly cut chives, dill, or parsley. Port served with open-face plum tart makes a perfect finish to this dinner.

Guinea Hen

BAKED GUINEA HEN

1 plump guinea hen, medium size, ready to cook	1 tablespoon tomato sauce
4 tablespoons butter or margarine	1 cup dry white wine
	Salt
4 strips fat bacon	Paprika

Start oven at moderate (350° F.).

Leave guinea hen whole. Do not stuff. Heat butter or margarine in medium-size flameproof casserole. Brown bird well on all sides. Turn bird on back. Lay bacon strips over breast. Mix tomato sauce and ¾ cup wine. Pour into casserole around bird. Season bird lightly with salt and paprika.

Cover casserole and roast 50 minutes. Baste frequently with juices in casserole. After 50 minutes, stir remaining ¼ cup wine into casserole juices. Baste bird. Remove bacon. Increase oven heat to hot (425° F.). Roast about 10 minutes longer. Serve with wine sauce from casserole. Makes 2 generous servings.

If sauce cooks away, continue to add wine, ¼ cup at a time, always mixing it with juices in the casserole. There should be more than 1 cup gravy in casserole when bird is done.

With guinea hen, as with duck, goose, and game, a tart, well-flavored jelly, such as red or black currant, raspberry, or cranberry, adds much to the enjoyment of the meat.

Serve wild rice or a delicate saffron or curry-flavored rice, or small rice croquettes with jelly. A delicate apple soufflé or apple meringue makes a perfect dessert after this roast fowl.

Guinea Hen with Wild Rice: Prepare guinea hen as described above. When done, and bacon is removed, use thin, sharp knife to quickly cut hen into serving pieces. Return to casserole. Surround with cooked wild rice mixed with white raisins, orange peel, and mushrooms.

1 cup wild rice	3 mushrooms, sliced thin
¾ cup large white raisins	2 tablespoons grated orange peel
½ cup white wine	

Wash rice thoroughly through three waters. Drain and cook in three cups water or diluted chicken consommé 35 minutes or until tender. If all liquid is not absorbed, drain. While rice cooks, let raisins soak in wine. When rice is done, drain raisins, saving the wine. Mix raisins, mushrooms, and orange peel into rice.

Pour off pan juices from casserole into small saucepan. Surround pieces of guinea hen with rice. Spoon raisin wine over all. Reheat pan juices 1 or 2 minutes. Pour over guinea hen, scattering a very little on top of rice. Return casserole to oven for 10 to 15 minutes, until top of rice browns a little. Serve hot. Makes 4 to 6 servings.

Squabs

SQUABS ALEXANDRA

2 large squabs, or squab chickens, or small rock hens, ready to cook	2 tablespoons finely cut parsley
6 tablespoons butter or margarine	½ teaspoon thyme
	½ cup dry white wine
8 shallots, or young green onions, cut fine	Salt and pepper
	¾ cup commercial sour cream
1 small tomato, peeled and chopped	Paprika

Have birds split and breastbones removed. Heat butter or margarine in skillet until very hot. Brown birds well all over. Add shallots or onions, tomato, parsley, and thyme, and blend well. Add wine, salt, and pepper. Cover skillet and cook over low heat 45 minutes to 1 hour. Turn birds frequently.

Just before serving add sour cream, mixing with sauce in skillet. Heat just to boiling point, but do not boil. Remove birds to hot serving dish. Pour sauce over them. Dash with paprika. Serve at once. Makes 2 to 4 servings.

May be served on hot toast strips on luncheon plates. Wild rice, cooked in orange juice with chopped mushrooms added, makes a fine flavor contrast to these small birds. Or serve herbed lima beans or small French peas in lemon butter. Toast and tart jelly and a baked custard or floating island for dessert, or if you had custard yesterday and have some left over, try Ceil Chapman's Dessert (page 239) and delight your guests.

Turkey

Fresh Turkey. If whole, refrigerate promptly at 36° to 38° F., loosely wrapped in aluminum foil, parchment, or waxed paper. Use turkey within 2 or 3 days. If cut up, use within 1 or 2 days. Just before cooking, wash turkey in cold water, drain, and pat dry. If whole turkey is purchased dressed style, draw promptly and refrigerate as directed above.

Quick-Frozen Turkey. Keep turkey frozen until it is to be cooked— allowing sufficient time before cooking for defrosting. Properly packaged quick-frozen ready-to-cook turkey stored at 0° F. or lower may be kept for several months.

Defrosting Quick-Frozen Turkey. Follow package directions or use one of these two methods or a combination of both:
Leave bird in original body wrap. Place on shelf in refrigerator. Allow 2 to 6 hours to defrost.
Place bird, still in original body wrap, under running cold water. Allow 2 to 6 hours to defrost.

As soon as turkey is sufficiently pliable, remove giblets and neck, usually wrapped together in parchment. They will be found in body cavity and wishbone pocket just underneath the skin. Their removal speeds defrosting too. Fresh and defrosted quick-frozen turkeys are cooked by the same methods.

Turkey Giblets. Giblets include gizzard, heart, and liver. When whole turkey is purchased, giblets and neck are usually included. Fresh or defrosted, giblets and neck should be promptly cleaned and cooked. Any blood vessels of the heart and any gall stain on liver should be cut away. Be sure gizzard has been split open and inner sac removed. The lining of gizzard should be scraped with sharp knife. After cooking, remove giblets from broth. Cool and refrigerate giblets and broth promptly until giblets are to be chopped or ground (meat removed from neck bones) for adding to stuffing, gravy, or other dishes.

To Broil Turkey. All sizes of tender fryer or roaster turkey may be broiled. The 4-to-5-pound ready-to-cook weight is a popular size. Quarters make suitable servings. The turkey is split in half lengthwise. Backbone, neck, keel bone, and wing tips should be removed. Turkey may be cut into quarters before or after broiling.

Place halves or quarters in bottom of broiling pan—do not use rack. This helps to keep turkey moist in the juices.

Brush thoroughly with butter, margarine, or any desired fat.

Season with 1 teaspoon salt and ¼ teaspoon pepper for each half. Flatten halves skin side down in pan.

Place pan in broiler so that surface of turkey is 7 to 9 inches from heat.

Broil slowly 40 to 45 minutes, until surface is nicely browned and takes on a well-cooked appearance. Baste with butter, margarine, or other fat as it cooks.

Turn turkey skin side up. Broil an additional 30 to 40 minutes, basting several times, until turkey is done. If surface becomes brown but turkey is not done, it may be turned again. *When done, drumstick should twist out of thigh joint readily.* Allow 1¼ to 1½ hours total cooking time for a 4-to-5-pound ready-to-cook weight turkey.

Serve on warm platter skin side up. Pour any pan drippings over turkey. Garnish and serve.

Piquant Broiled Turkey: Rub favorite herbs or spices—cinnamon, ginger, marjoram, nutmeg, poultry seasoning, thyme, et cetera—into surface before brushing with fat.

Barbecue Broiled Turkey: Marinate young turkey cut in serving pieces in barbecue sauce or French dressing 1 to 3 hours. Drain. Broil as described. The drained marinade may be used for basting.

Lemon-Broiled Turkey: Add 1 teaspoon sugar with salt and pepper for seasoning each half. Drizzle lemon juice over turkey during the broiling.

To Fry Turkey: Young turkey, 4-to-5-pound ready-to-cook weight, is best for frying. Turkey should be disjointed and cut up to give 11 or 12 pieces—2 drumsticks, 2 thighs or second joints, 2 or 3 pieces of breast, 2 wings, 2 or 3 pieces of back, the neck and giblets. By-the-piece young turkey is available in some markets, permitting selection of favorite pieces.

Coat turkey before frying to prevent drying out, to aid in browning, and to help give desirable crispness. Common coatings are flour and egg-and-flour—both with added seasoning.

Heat ½ inch of cooking fat in heavy kettle or skillet until a drop of water just sizzles. Start browning meaty pieces first, slipping less meaty pieces in between as turkey browns. Do not crowd pieces. Turn, as necessary, to brown and cook evenly. Use tongs or two spoons to avoid piercing coating, which causes spattering and loss of juice. When turkey is *lightly* browned, about 20 minutes, reduce heat, cover pan tightly, and cook 50 to 60 minutes slowly until tender, depending on size and thickness of pieces. Light browning is important since turkey will continue to brown during this slow cooking. Turn occasionally to assure uniform cooking and attractive color. Cook until thickest pieces are fork-tender. Test a breast and thigh piece. Avoid overpricking with fork.

If kettle or skillet cannot be covered tightly, add 1 to 2 tablespoons water. The steam hastens cooking. Avoid adding more water since turkey may lose coating and color, become too moist, and lack desirable crispness. Uncover last 5 to 10 minutes to recrisp coating. Lift turkey to a warm platter. Prepare gravy with pan drippings.

If the giblets are to be fried, coat liver and *precooked* gizzard, heart, and neck and cook with turkey last 20 minutes of frying.

Fried Turkey Variations: Marinate turkey pieces in buttermilk or sweet milk overnight. Pour enough milk over turkey, placed 1 layer deep in pan, to just cover. Drain thoroughly, coat, and pan fry or oven fry.

Add a favorite herb such as thyme or orégano to coating mixture.

TIMETABLE FOR ROASTING TURKEY

A timetable serves as a guide to the total roasting time. The timetable below gives the *approximate* time to roast *stuffed* ready-to-cook-weight turkeys. Differences among individual birds may necessitate a slightly increased or descreased total time. *To judge doneness* of meat, drumstick should twist out of joint easily, or meat thermometer should register 190° to 195° F.

When turkey is desired at a *definite* time, start bird 30 minutes earlier than time prescribed for roasting. This will avoid delay should turkey take longer to cook than suggested in timetable. It allows time to make gravy, remove trussing cord and skewers, and arrange bird attractively on platter. It is always best to plan the roasting schedule so that turkey is out of oven 20 to 30 minutes before it is served. This period gives the meat a chance to absorb the juices. It will carve more easily and attractively.

READY-TO-COOK WEIGHT	OVEN TEMP.	TOTAL TIME APPROX. HOURS	INTERNAL TEMP. ° F.
Whole Birds		**Stuffed Bird**	
4 to 6 lbs.	325° F.	3 to 3¾	190–195
6 to 8	325	3¾ to 4½	190–195
8 to 10	325	4 to 4½	190–195
10 to 12	325	4½ to 5	190–195
12 to 14	325	5 to 5¼	190–195
14 to 16	325	5¼ to 6	190–195
16 to 18	325	6 to 6½	190–195
18 to 20	325	6½ to 7½	190–195
20 to 24	325	7½ to 9	190–195
Half and Quarter Turkey			
3½ to 5	325	3 to 3½	190–195
5 to 8	325	3½ to 4	190–195
8 to 12	325	4 to 5	190–195

To Make Turkey Gravy: The pan drippings are important to good gravy for color, flavor, and richness. Pour these drippings into a heat proof bowl or measuring cup, leaving the brown residue in the pan. For each cup of gravy desired, use *1½ tablespoons each of fat and flour and 1 cup of liquid.* The liquid may be a combination of the meat juice under the fat layer of drippings, giblet broth, water, or milk. For 2 cups of gravy, use 3 tablespoons fat, 3 tablespoons flour, and 2 cups liquid. The finished gravy may appear slightly thin, but it will thicken and be an excellent consistency when served. Allow ¼ to ⅓ cup gravy per serving.

Skim fat layer from drippings. The meat juices below the fat layer should be used as part of the liquid. Measure quantity of fat needed for the gravy back into roasting pan. Set aside any extra fat for other cooking. Add measured flour to fat. Blend thoroughly. Place pan over low heat. Cook slowly until frothy, stirring constantly. If desired, brown the fat and flour mixture slightly, at this point in the cooking, to give more color and flavor to the gravy. *Add the cool or lukewarm, not hot, liquid—all at once.* Cook, stirring constantly, until uniformly thickened. While stirring, scrape the brown residue on the sides and bottom of the pan into the gravy. Simmer about 5 minutes. Season to taste. Serve very hot.

To Cook Giblets: The giblets (gizzard, heart, and liver) and the neck are usually included when a whole fresh or quick-frozen chicken or turkey is purchased. They are also available in some markets fresh or quick-frozen.

Giblets should be cleaned and cooked promptly after purchasing. When they are added to gravy, sauces, or stuffing or served with broiled and fried chicken or turkey, the giblets and neck must be pre-cooked by simmering in seasoned water until gizzard is fork-tender, 2 to 3 hours. To season the water, add 1 teaspoon salt, 2 or 3 pepper-corns, 1 or 2 cloves, a tip of bay leaf, and a little carrot, celery, and onion. Gizzard and heart always remain slightly firm.

Refrigerate giblets and the strained broth separately. When chicken or turkey is braised or stewed, the gizzard, heart, and neck may be cooked with the bird. Liver, on the contrary, is very tender and requires only 10 to 15 minutes cooking at low temperature. It is so tender that it may be broiled or fried without the preliminary cooking required for gizzard, heart, and neck. It may be simmered with the other giblets 10 to 15 minutes before they are done. Overcooking makes liver dry and hard.

To Refrigerate Leftover Turkey: Cool leftover turkey meat or meat cooked in advance of service as rapidly as possible (running cold water around a kettle). Wrap closely or place in suitable container with tight lid. Refrigerate at 36° to 38° F. without any broth. Include in meals within next 2 or 3 days, before it dries out and loses its fine flavor. Small meal-size units, properly wrapped, may be deep-frozen and held up to 1 month before serving.

As soon as possible remove every bit of stuffing from wishbone and body cavities. Cool stuffing, meat, and any gravy promptly. Refrigerate, each wrapped separately, at 36° to 38° F. Use gravy and stuffing within 1 or 2 days and *heat them thoroughly for service.*

Do not deep-freeze an uncooked stuffed turkey or a roast stuffed turkey.

Giblet broth, broth resulting from simmered turkey, poached turkey, turkey cooked in aluminum foil, or it may be drippings, should be cooled rapidly to 50° F. (a kettle may be set in sink with running cold water around it). A practical procedure is to cool the broth and meat separately at room temperature—not over ½ hour—and then place in refrigerator. Refrigerate promptly at 36° to 38° F. Do not hold longer than 2 days. Bring broth to a full rolling boil before it is served or used in combination with other ingredients.

Note: It is true that commercially frozen meat, chicken, and turkey pies probably remain in freezers longer than one month. However, they contain some preservative. Also, the best brands in the commercially frozen meat pies are delivered in small quantities to grocers and usually go out of the grocers' freezers to customers within a week or a few days.

CHAMPAGNE-BASTED TURKEY

1 tablespoon salt	2 onions, peeled and sliced
¾ teaspoon freshly ground pepper	½ teaspoon thyme
	½ teaspoon marjoram
1 teaspoon celery salt	2 tablespoons finely cut parsley
12-to-15-pound turkey, ready to cook	1 cup consommé
	1 pint champagne
4 tablespoons butter or margarine	1 tablespoon flour

Start oven at hot (425° F.).

Mix salt, pepper, and celery salt. Rub into turkey thoroughly, inside and out. Place bird in roasting pan. Rub 3 tablespoons butter or margarine over breast and down sides. Roast 30 minutes. Combine onions, thyme, marjoram, parsley, and consommé. Pour over turkey. Reduce heat to moderate (325° F.) and continue roasting another hour. Pour champagne over turkey. Continue roasting an additional 2½ hours or until turkey is done (see chart, page 227). Baste frequently.

Remove turkey to warmed platter. Let stand in warm place. Strain pan gravy. Melt remaining 1 tablespoon butter or margarine in saucepan. Stir in flour smoothly. Add strained pan gravy gradually. Stir and let boil 5 minutes. Serve in warmed gravy boat. Makes 10 or more servings.

Garnish turkey with mounds of hot shoestring potatoes and crisp water cress, or freshly cooked brussels sprouts, or artichoke hearts in lemon butter sauce.

Any favorite dressing may be baked separately and served warm with this turkey.

Serve with the traditional holiday accessories or as the featured dish on a holiday buffet. Squash pudding or hot corn pudding, sweet potatoes, or a casserole of scalloped potatoes is a homey addition much appreciated by men guests.

A tomato aspic, pickle relishes, small buttered rolls add to the menu. Tiny hot mince tarts to be picked up in the fingers make a practical as well as savory dessert for a buffet party.

TURKEY MORNAY

1 (9-ounce) package quick-frozen broccoli spears	½ cup shredded sharp American cheese
3 tablespoons butter or margarine	1 teaspoon lemon juice
2 tablespoons flour	⅓ cup sherry
¾ cup milk	4 thick slices roast turkey breast
¼ teaspoon salt	2 tablespoons grated Parmesan cheese
⅛ teaspoon pepper	
2 egg yolks, beaten	

Cook broccoli as described on package, and drain.

Make sauce: melt 2 tablespoons butter or margarine in saucepan over low heat. Stir in flour smoothly. Add milk gradually. Cook, stirring constantly, until smooth and thickened. Stir in salt, pepper, egg yolks, and American cheese. Cook until cheese melts, then remove from heat.

Arrange drained broccoli in greased shallow flameproof baking dish. Sprinkle broccoli with remaining 1 tablespoon melted butter or margarine, lemon juice, 1 tablespoon sherry, and salt and pepper to taste. Lay turkey slices over broccoli. Stir remaining sherry into cheese sauce. Pour over all. Sprinkle top with Parmesan cheese.

Broil 3 inches from heat 6 to 8 minutes, until hot and sauce is browning. Makes 4 servings.

Chicken Mornay: In the above recipe substitute thick slices roast chicken meat for turkey.

This dish makes a perfect luncheon or supper main dish. Serve hot rolls and a tart jelly, such as grape. Forget dessert, unless perhaps you have quick-frozen or fresh peaches or raspberries, and light cookies.

Leftover Turkey and Chicken Ideas

Make creamed turkey or chicken. To creamed turkey or chicken add a few chopped, lightly sautéed oysters. Serve hot on toast points. Garnish with finely cut celery tops.

Of course creamed chicken may be made in a chafing dish, and for a *de luxe* flavor addition combine few tablespoons diced roast ham to plain creamed chicken or to the turkey and oyster mixture.

Cut leftover turkey in slices. Heat slices in chicken consommé or bouillon to cover. Add 1 teaspoon orégano, cover saucepan, and bring to a boil. Lower heat and let simmer until turkey or chicken is hot. Serve with chutney, heated shoestring potatoes, and toasted roll as a luncheon menu during holidays. Tiny mince or apple tarts and tea or coffee complete this.

See also chapters on casseroles and chafing dish.

Stuffings

APRICOT STUFFING

7 cups dry bread cubes	⅓ cup melted butter or marga-
1 ½ cups sliced dried apricots	rine
2 small onions, peeled and	1 (10 ½-ounce) can condensed
chopped	cream-of-celery soup
¼ teaspoon powdered nutmeg	

Combine bread, apricots, onions, nutmeg, and butter or margarine. Dilute soup according to directions on can, and stir soup until smooth. Mix with other ingredients, using only enough soup to moisten and combine mixture. Stuff bird. Or bake stuffing in 1½-quart casserole in moderate oven (350° F.) about 45 minutes. Serve hot with bird. Makes enough to stuff 6-pound turkey or large capon.

CARAWAY BREAD STUFFING

1 ½ quarts soft bread cubes	¼ cup diced peeled onions
1 teaspoon caraway seeds	¼ cup diced celery
½ teaspoon salt	1 egg
½ teaspoon pepper	½ cup milk
4 tablespoons butter or marga-	
rine	

Combine bread, seeds, salt, and pepper. Toss lightly to mix. Melt butter or margarine in skillet, and add onion and celery. Cook over low heat until onion is tender. Stir frequently to mix. Beat egg slightly, add to milk, and stir into bread cubes. Add celery and onion with butter or margarine in which they cooked and mix well. Stuff large chicken, capon, or small turkey. Makes 1½ quarts stuffing.

CORN-BREAD STUFFING FOR TURKEY

1½ cups corn meal	1 pound link sausage
2 cups sifted all-purpose flour	4 onions, peeled and diced
2 tablespoons sugar	4 stalks celery, thinly sliced
1 teaspoon salt	½ teaspoon sage
4 teaspoons baking powder	½ teaspoon thyme
2 eggs	1 teaspoon salt
2 cups milk	⅛ teaspoon pepper
4 tablespoons bacon drippings	

Start oven at hot (450° F.). Grease two square 9-inch pans.

Sift dry ingredients into bowl. Stir in lightly beaten eggs. Add milk and bacon drippings. Beat until well mixed. Spread in prepared pans. Bake 30 minutes. Let cool. Crumble into coarse pieces.

Fry sausage over low heat until browned, then cut into ½-inch slices. Toss into crumbled corn bread and mix lightly together. Cook onions in sausage fat until tender. Pour onions and fat into corn-bread mixture. Add celery and all remaining ingredients, and mix together lightly. Stuff loosely into cavity of 12-to-15-pound turkey. Roast as described (on page 227), 5¼ to 5½ hours.

FRUIT-NUT STUFFING

1 box Triscuit wafers, crumbled	3 tablespoons butter or margarine
½ pound prunes, cooked and pitted	1 (6-ounce) can chopped salted almonds
1 cup juice from cooked prunes	½ teaspoon thyme or savory
2 onions, peeled and diced	1 teaspoon pepper
2 green peppers, diced	2 teaspoons salt
1 cup diced celery	
½ cup finely cut parsley	
1 (3-ounce) can chopped mushrooms	

The day before roasting turkey, capon, or large chicken, make this dressing. Soak crumbled Triscuit in juice from cooked prunes. Sauté onions, green peppers, celery, parsley, and mushrooms in butter or margarine until soft but not too brown. Stir in almonds. Blend herb, pepper, and salt into mixture. Cut up prunes and mix in. Stir soaked Triscuit crumbs and juice into prune mixture. Store in covered bowl overnight in refrigerator.

When bird is ready for cooking, stuff this flavorful mixture loosely in neck and cavity. Roast at once. Makes enough for large capon or roasting chicken, or small (6-to-8-pound) turkey. Double recipe for large turkey.

OYSTER STUFFING

1 ½ quarts coarse dry bread crumbs
3 teaspoons salt
¼ teaspoon pepper
4 tablespoons butter or margarine

4 tablespoons sausage fat
¼ cup milk
3 cups shucked small oysters

Combine crumbs and seasoning. Add melted butter and sausage fat. Brown mixture about 5 minutes, stirring occasionally. When lightly browned throughout, combine with milk and oysters. If oysters are large, chop before mixing with crumbs. Makes almost 2 quarts stuffing. If crumbs are very fine, mixture shrinks to about 1½ quarts.

Sage may be added, or other seasoning. But the delicate flavor of oysters is better left alone in this mixture. A touch of mace does enhance it—but be cautious.

SAUSAGE STUFFING

½ pound pork sausage meat
½ cup diced peeled onions
2 quarts soft bread cubes
3 cooking apples, pared, cored, chopped coarsely

½ teaspoon sage
½ teaspoon pepper
1 egg
½ cup milk

Heat skillet. Cook sausage meat, breaking it up with fork, until lightly browned. Add onions and cook, stirring occasionally until meat is done, 20 to 25 minutes. Combine bread cubes, apples, sage, pepper, and sausage-onion mixture. Beat egg and mix with milk. Add to sausage mixture and mix well. Stuff large capon or medium-size turkey. Makes about 2 quarts stuffing.

Note: I always keep packaged, herb-flavored stuffing on hand and vary the mixture by adding chopped livers or cooked chestnuts, pecans, currants, sliced water chestnuts, oysters, and other good things.

RICE-ALMOND STUFFING FOR ROAST CHICKEN

4 tablespoons butter or margarine	1 ½ cups cooked rice
½ cup finely chopped celery	½ teaspoon salt
1 small onion, peeled and chopped	2 teaspoons sugar
¼ cup chopped almonds	¼ teaspoon thyme
	2 tablespoons grated orange peel

Melt butter or margarine in skillet. Add celery, onion, and almonds. Mix, cooking and stirring over low heat about 15 minutes. Add rice, salt, sugar, thyme, and orange peel. Mix and stir. Makes stuffing for large capon or roasting chicken. Fill bird lightly to allow for expansion.

An orange glaze for this roast adds to the good flavor. Combine 1 cup orange juice, 2 teaspoons grated peel, ¼ cup honey, ¼ cup salad oil. Mix well and brush over stuffed chicken when it goes into oven. Bake at moderate (325° F.) 2½ hours or until tender and done. Every 15 minutes during roasting pour little of orange juice mixture over roast, until all is used up. Baste bird at same time with drippings in pan.

This is a delicacy among roast chicken dishes. Surround it with your most delicious vegetable dishes. I like small creamed onions and baked zucchini with it. Also a gelatin dessert, such as port-wine jelly with whipped cream, for the non-calorie counters at the party. Or use a low-calorie whip all may enjoy.

CHAPTER ELEVEN

Desserts

Cheesecakes

BEST CHEESECAKE

1 ½ cups finely crushed graham-cracker crumbs	1 pound cream cheese
¼ cup melted butter or margarine	2 tablespoons flour
	¼ teaspoon salt
¾ cup sugar	1 ½ teaspoons vanilla
¼ teaspoon powdered cinnamon	4 eggs
	1 cup light cream

For crust, combine crumbs, butter or margarine, ¼ cup sugar, and cinnamon. Mix thoroughly. Press mixture evenly in bottom of well-buttered 9-inch spring-form pan.

Start oven at moderate (325° F.).

Mash cheese. Add flour, remaining ½ cup sugar, salt, and vanilla. Beat with spoon, or electric mixer at medium speed, until smooth and fluffy. Add egg yolks 1 at a time. Beat well after each addition. Stir in cream. Whip egg whites until stiff but not dry. Fold cheese mixture into whites. Pour into crumb-lined pan.

Bake 1 hour or until center is set. Let cake cool completely. Cut around edge of pan and remove rim of pan. Chill cake. Serve plain, or decorate top with border of graham-cracker crumbs mixed with butter, raspberry jam, and cinnamon. Makes 8 to 10 servings.

In my years of entertaining I've never found a man who didn't consider a fine homemade cheesecake on a par with superior homemade apple pie. No greater accolade!

CONNECTICUT CHEESECAKE

2 (8-ounce) packages cream cheese	1 cup sugar
	¼ teaspoon salt
5 eggs	2 cups commercial sour cream
1 teaspoon vanilla	9-inch graham-cracker crust
2 tablespoons lemon juice	spring-form pan

Start oven at moderate (350° F.).

Beat cheese, egg yolks, vanilla, lemon juice, sugar, and salt together until smooth. Use large electric-mixer bowl with mixer at medium speed, or use hand beater. Add sour cream. Continue beating until well mixed. Beat egg whites until they stand in stiff points when beater is removed. Fold cheese mixture into whites. Turn into crumb-lined pan.

Bake 1 hour.

Then turn heat off. Let stand in oven 1 hour longer. Remove pan from oven and place on cake rack away from drafts. Let stand another hour. Then use spatula to loosen cake from sides of pan. Remove cake carefully, leaving it on flat insert of pan. Let stand 2 hours. Makes 10 to 12 servings.

Refrigerate any leftover cheesecake and serve next day. Or heat leftover cheesecake on cooky sheet in moderately hot oven (400° F.) about 15 minutes.

This is a little richer, a little more "cheesy," because of the sour cream. Sometimes I add a tablespoon of grated lemon peel.

REFRIGERATOR CHEESECAKE

1 recipe Special Crumb Pastry	½ cup milk
2 tablespoons unflavored gelatin	2 cups cottage cheese, sieved
½ cup cold water	1 lemon, grated peel and juice
2 eggs	1 teaspoon vanilla
1 teaspoon salt	1 cup heavy cream, whipped
½ cup sugar	

Mix Special Crumb Pastry, line pan and chill, as described in recipe. Soften gelatin in cold water about 5 minutes. Beat egg yolks lightly. Combine with salt, sugar, and milk in top of double boiler over hot water. Stir until sugar is dissolved. Cook, stirring constantly, until mixture thickens. Remove pan from hot water. Add gelatin and mix well to dissolve gelatin. Place pan in cold water to cool. Mix in cheese, lemon peel and juice, and vanilla.

Whip egg whites until they stand in stiff points when beater is removed. Whip cream stiff. Fold cheese mixture into egg whites and cream. Pour into chilled crumb-lined pan. Scatter the remaining crumbs from pastry recipe in border around cheese or evenly over top. Chill until set. Makes 6 to 8 servings.

This is very different from the best baked cheesecake, but there are times when I prefer it. It's particularly good for summertime, when you don't want to start the oven yet want a rather elaborate dessert to complete a fairly simple and easy-to-get meal. I like it, too, because you can never buy this kind of cheesecake, even at the famous cheesecake restaurant, Reuben's, in New York.

SPECIAL CRUMB PASTRY

5 cups corn flakes, or 10 pieces zwieback

4 tablespoons butter or margarine

2 tablespoons sugar

½ tablespoon powdered cinnamon

Roll or grind corn flakes or zwieback fine. There should be about 2 cups very fine crumbs. Melt butter or margarine in 9-inch spring-form pan. Add sugar, cinnamon, and crumbs. Mix thoroughly. Remove about ⅓ of mixture and save for topping. Press remaining crumbs evenly and firmly around sides and in bottom of pan. Chill. Makes one (9-inch) shell.

Custards

ALMOND CUSTARD FOR DIETERS

2 eggs

1½ cups skim milk

¼ cup sugar

1½ tablespoons flour

⅛ teaspoon salt

¼ teaspoon almond flavoring

4 almond halves

Beat eggs thoroughly in top of double boiler. Add milk, stirring constantly. Combine sugar, flour, and salt. Add to egg mixture and mix well. Cook over hot water, stirring constantly until mixture coats spoon and is slightly thickened. Remove from hot water at once and add almond flavoring. Let cool, then chill. Garnish with almonds before serving. Makes 4 servings.

BAKED CUSTARD

3 eggs, slightly beaten	2 cups milk, scalded
¼ cup sugar	½ teaspoon vanilla
¼ teaspoon salt	

Start oven at moderate (325° F.).

Combine eggs, sugar, and salt. Add milk and vanilla slowly. Pour into 6 (5-ounce) custard cups. Set cups in shallow pan containing about 1 inch hot water.

Bake 40 to 45 minutes, or until knife inserted in center of cup comes out clean. Serve warm or chilled. Makes 6 servings.

Baked Custard with Coconut Topping: Combine ¼ cup shredded coconut, 2 tablespoons brown sugar, 1 tablespoon soft butter or margarine. Sprinkle on top of warm or chilled custards. Place cups on cooky sheet. Broil 3 to 4 inches from heat about 5 minutes or until tops are golden.

CHARLOTTE RUSSE

Ladyfingers	¼ teaspoon powdered mace
2 tablespoons unflavored gelatin	4 eggs
¼ cup cold water	2 tablespoons sherry
2 cups milk, scalded	⅛ teaspoon salt
½ cup sugar	1 pint heavy cream

Line 2-quart mold with ladyfingers.

Soften gelatin in cold water about 5 minutes or longer. Stir into hot milk in saucepan. Continue to stir until gelatin is dissolved. Add sugar and mace. Beat egg yolks slightly and add. Place saucepan over low heat. Cook and stir until slightly thickened, then let cool. Add sherry. Whip egg whites with salt until they remain in stiff points when beater is removed. Fold custard into whites. Whip cream until stiff. Fold into mixture. Pour into prepared mold. Chill until firm. Unmold onto chilled platter. Makes 10 servings.

Garnish servings with additional sherry-flavored whipped cream or leave plain. Some cooks prefer a light sprinkling of powdered nutmeg on top.

CUSTARD-AND-FRUIT DESSERT

Ceil Chapman's Dessert

Baked Custard (page 238)   Sugar
Sliced fresh strawberries   Powdered nutmeg
Fresh blueberries

When you make baked custard for the family, bake it in a large, shallow dish instead of in custard cups. Set dish in pan of hot water. Follow recipe directions. Keep leftover custard covered in refrigerator until next day. Otherwise it liquefies.

For dinner, cut generous squares of custard, place in wide, shallow dessert dishes. Cover with few spoonfuls of chilled strawberries and blueberries. Add light sprinkling of nutmeg, unless nutmeg was used in flavoring the custard. Delicious dessert!

FRENCH CHOCOLATE CUSTARDS

Petits Pots de Crème au Chocolat

2 cups milk   6 egg yolks
½ pound sweet chocolate   Whipped cream

Combine milk and broken chocolate in small saucepan. Stir constantly over low heat until chocolate is melted and mixture reaches boiling point. Remove from heat at once. Beat egg yolks quickly until thick and lemon-colored. Pour chocolate into yolks and mix. Pour into small custard cups. Let cool. Chill. At serving time add whirl of whipped cream to top of each. Serve in the baking cups. Makes 6 servings.

French cooks usually pour the hot chocolate-and-egg mixture through a fine "hair" sieve into the "little pots." This pouring aerates the mixture, giving it lighter, more delicate texture. Few American kitchens include these French sieves. Actually, the mixture does not require sieving.

If you collect old china, it's fun to find pot de crème dishes and to use them for individual service of this favorite. Or buy French modern ones—in white or "chocolate" pottery.

MUTTI'S CHOCOLATE MOUSSE

Mousse au Chocolat

½-pound cake Baker's bitter
    chocolate
½ cup sugar
½ cup water

5 eggs
1 teaspoon vanilla
½ teaspoon pulverized coffee

Combine chocolate, sugar, and water in upper part of 1-quart double boiler over hot water. Stir until smooth. Set aside to cool, stirring occasionally. Beat egg yolks. Add vanilla and coffee. Stir into chocolate mixture which should not be too smooth.

Whip egg whites until they stand in points when whip is removed. Blend gently into chocolate-egg mixture. Spoon into individual mousse or custard cups. Chill. Makes 6 to 8 servings, depending on size of cups. Serve with whipped cream or plain, since this mixture is very rich.

I sometimes make this with ½ pound of chocolate bits, no additional sugar, no vanilla, but otherwise following the recipe. It is a favorite recipe for large buffet suppers, for which I double or triple the recipe, as needed. It may be made the day before or on the morning of the party day. The whipped cream, of course, should be put on at the last minute before serving. It is well to know that the whipped cream bought in "spritzer" cans must always be added at the last minute, as it collapses on standing.

FLOATING ISLAND WITH SHERRY

1 egg white
Salt
⅜ cup sugar
2 cups milk

2 eggs
1 egg yolk
Milk
2 tablespoons sherry

Make meringue toppings first. Beat egg white with 1/16 teaspoon salt until soft peaks form. Add 2 tablespoons sugar gradually, beating until stiff peaks form when beater is removed. Heat 2 cups milk in skillet. When simmering, place meringue on milk by tablespoonfuls. Cook slowly, uncovered, about 5 minutes, or until meringues are firm. Lift meringues from milk with spatula or wire whisk to thick paper toweling. Let drain. Reserve milk for custard.

Beat eggs and yolk slightly in upper part of double boiler. Add remaining ¼ cup sugar and 1/16 teaspoon salt. Stir in the slightly cooled 2 cups of milk from meringues, adding extra milk if needed to make the 2 cups. Cook over hot, not boiling, water, stirring constantly until mixture coats metal spoon. Remove from hot water at once. Let cool slightly, then add sherry. Pour into serving dish. Top with meringues. Chill. Makes 4 servings.

Peach Floating Island: Place 1 cup thinly sliced ripe peaches in bottom of serving dish. Pour slightly cooled custard over. Top with meringues. Chill.

Strawberry Floating Island: Place 1 cup hulled red-ripe berries in serving dish. Pour slightly cooled custard over. Top with meringues. Chill.

MILDRED LANGROCK'S CRÈME BRULÉE

1 ½	quarts heavy cream	7	tablespoons granulated
1	teaspoon vanilla		sugar
12	egg yolks	6	tablespoons brown sugar

Start oven at moderately slow (300° F.).

Heat cream with vanilla, but do not let it boil. Beat egg yolks with granulated sugar until smooth and thoroughly blended. Add hot cream to sugar-yolk mixture. Pour into 2 shallow baking dishes. Set dishes in very shallow pans of warm water.

Bake 30 to 45 minutes or until set. When done, paring knife inserted in center of custard should come out clean. Let custards cool, then cover lightly with waxed paper and chill 4 hours in refrigerator.

To serve, sprinkle brown sugar over top of each casserole. Place under broiler until sugar melts. Be careful it does not burn. Let casseroles cool, then put back in refrigerator until melted sugar forms a crust. Serve very cold. Makes 8 servings.

This is very rich, very elegant. An appropriate *finis* for an important dinner party.

SABAYON

also Zabaglione and Weinschaum

4 egg yolks	5 teaspoons lemon juice
¾ cup sugar	¾ cup sherry or Marsala wine
2 teaspoons grated lemon peel	

Use large glass or enamel double boiler. In lower part heat enough water to almost touch bottom of top part. Set top part in place. Beat yolks lightly in it. Beat in remaining ingredients gradually. Continue to beat with rotary egg beater over boiling water until mixture is as thick and fluffy as whipped cream. Remove from water at once.

Serve immediately in parfait or sherbet glasses.

Or chill and serve in dessert glasses or as topping for spongecake or fruit. Makes 4 servings.

A dessert to capture a man's heart. Takes a little practice, though.

Frozen Sabayon: Set control of freezer in refrigerator at lowest point. When Sabayon is made, turn into freezer tray. Freeze about 3 hours or until firm.

Éclairs and Puffs

CHOCOLATE ÉCLAIRS

1 cup water	5 eggs
½ cup butter or margarine	Éclair Rum Filling
1 cup sifted all-purpose flour	Éclair Chocolate Frosting

Start oven at moderate (375° F.). Grease baking sheet.

Combine water and butter or margarine in small saucepan. Bring slowly to a boil. When mixture is boiling add flour, all at one time. Stir over low heat until smooth ball of dough is formed and mixture clears sides of pan. Transfer to electric beater bowl. Add 4 eggs, one at a time, beating well after each addition.

Force dough through pastry bag onto prepared baking sheet to form 16 éclairs, oblongs 1 by 4 inches. Beat remaining egg. Brush lightly over éclairs.

Bake 45 minutes or until golden brown and firm and dry to the touch. Let cool. Slit with sharp knife. Fill with Éclair Rum Filling. Frost with Éclair Chocolate Frosting. Makes 16 éclairs.

Éclair Rum Filling

1 egg plus 1 extra yolk	2 tablespoons strongly brewed coffee
3 tablespoons sugar	
3 tablespoons flour	1 egg white
1 teaspoon unflavored gelatin	5 tablespoons heavy cream, whipped
¾ cup hot milk	
4 (1-ounce) squares sweet chocolate	2 tablespoons rum or 1 teaspoon vanilla

Beat egg and extra yolk smoothly with sugar in upper part of double boiler. Add flour and gelatin. Continue beating until light and fluffy. Pour hot milk slowly into egg mixture, stirring constantly. Place over simmering, not boiling, water until mixture just comes to boiling point, and stir constantly. Remove from hot water and add chocolate which has been melted with coffee over hot water. Stir over cracked ice until mixture cools. Whip egg white stiff. Fold into mixture. Fold in whipped cream. Flavor with rum or vanilla. Fill éclairs. Makes enough for 16 éclairs.

Éclair Chocolate Frosting

1 ½ (1-ounce) squares bitter chocolate	1 egg yolk, slightly beaten
¼ cup milk	½ teaspoon vanilla
1 teaspoon melted butter	2 ½ to 2 ¾ cups sifted powdered sugar

Stir chocolate, milk, and butter together in saucepan over low heat until chocolate melts. Beat until smooth. Pour over slightly beaten egg yolk and add vanilla. Add powdered sugar gradually until of spreading consistency. Spread over filled éclairs. Let stand until chocolate is firm. Makes enough for 16 éclairs.

Éclairs, if you follow directions carefully, are *not* difficult. If I had a daughter I'd let her try her hand on éclairs fairly early in her cookery instruction, as I did. I filled my first éclairs with cocoa-flavored sweetened whipped cream and iced them with chocolate. They—and I— were a great success.

243

CREAM PUFFS

½ cup butter or margarine	¼ teaspoon salt
1 cup boiling water	4 eggs
1 cup sifted all-purpose flour	Cream-Puff Custard Filling

Start oven at hot (450° F.). Grease cooky sheet.

Melt butter or margarine in boiling water. Add flour and salt all at once. Stir vigorously. Cook, stirring constantly, until mixture forms ball that doesn't separate. Remove from heat and let cool slightly. Add eggs one at a time, beating vigorously after each addition until mixture is smooth.

Drop dough by heaping tablespoonfuls 3 inches apart on prepared cooky sheet.

Bake 15 minutes. Reduce oven to moderate (325° F.) and bake 25 minutes longer. Remove from oven. Split puffs in half. Turn oven off and put cream puffs back in oven to dry out, about 20 minutes. Let cool on cake rack. Fill centers with Custard Filling. Replace tops. Makes about 10 large puffs. Very good filled with hot, creamed seafood, fish, meat or chicken, too.

For Tiny Puffs (to fill with appetizer mixtures): drop dough from teaspoon about 1½ inches apart on greased cooky sheet. Bake in hot oven (425° F.) 10 minutes, then in moderate oven (325° F.) 10 minutes. To crisp, cut tops from puffs. Turn heat off. Let puffs stay in closed oven 10 minutes to dry out. Let cool on cake rack. Fill with turkey, chicken, seafood salad mixtures. Makes 5 to 6 dozen tiny puffs.

Cream-Puff Custard Filling

¾ cup sugar	3 cups milk
3 tablespoons cornstarch	2 egg yolks, slightly beaten
3 tablespoons all-purpose flour	1 cup heavy cream, whipped
¾ teaspoon salt	2 teaspoons vanilla

Combine sugar, cornstarch, flour, and salt in saucepan. Stir in milk gradually. Bring to a boil over moderate heat, stirring constantly. Cook and stir until thickened. Remove from heat. Stir a little of hot mixture into egg yolks, then add yolks to saucepan. Return to heat and bring to a boil, stirring constantly. Remove and let cool. Beat well with rotary beater. Stir in vanilla. Fold in whipped cream. Fills 10 large cream puffs.

SWEDISH CORNETS

2 eggs	1 cup heavy cream
⅝ cup sugar	1 cup raspberry or strawberry
¼ cup sifted all-purpose flour	jam
¼ teaspoon powdered cinnamon	

Start oven at moderately hot (400° F.).

Beat eggs with sugar until light. Stir in flour and cinnamon. Blend smoothly together. Place tablespoon of batter on greased baking sheet. Spread it into 5-inch round. Repeat until all batter is used. Bake rounds 5 to 10 minutes or until delicate brown.

As soon as pan is removed from oven, loosen rounds, remove, and shape each into a cone or cornucopia. Let cool. Fill with whipped cream or with whipped cream mixed with jam. Makes about 20 cornets.

When you are in Stockholm you might look for these on the tea menu aboard the fabulous youth hostel ship, Af Chapman.

Fritters

FRUIT FRITTERS

6 ripe nectarines or peaches	Fat for deep frying
Grated peel 1 lemon	Fritter Batter
3 tablespoons sugar	Confectioners' sugar
½ cup Madeira	

Wash and peel nectarines or peaches. Cut in half and remove stone. Place fruit in glass bowl. Sprinkle with lemon peel, sugar, and wine. Cover and let marinate about 3 hours.

Put fat on to heat in frying kettle.

Drain fruit. Dip into batter. Fry a few at a time in deep hot fat at 370° F. on frying thermometer. Drain fritters on thick paper towels. Sift confectioners' sugar over them and serve hot. Makes 6 or more servings.

Fritter Batter

¾ cup sifted all-purpose flour	2 tablespoons cognac
1 tablespoon sugar	⅛ teaspoon salt
1 tablespoon melted butter	1 egg
¼ cup lukewarm water	

Sift flour and sugar into bowl. Stir in melted butter and water to make smooth batter. Stir in brandy. Add salt and beaten egg yolk. Batter should be consistency of thick cream. If too heavy, thin with a little of the wine in which the fruit marinated. Whip egg white stiff. Fold into batter just before using.

Apple Fritters: Pare and core apples, cut in eighths, and cover with water. Add 1 tablespoon sugar. Cook 10 minutes, then drain. Substitute for nectarines or peaches in above recipe.

You may use other fresh fruits, such as apricots, to replace nectarines in above recipe.

BANANA FRITTERS

Fat for deep frying	¾ teaspoon baking powder
2 eggs	2 tablespoons brown sugar
2 tablespoons melted shortening	6 bananas
½ teaspoon salt	½ cup flour
1 cup milk	Sifted confectioners' sugar
1 cup sifted all-purpose flour	1 cup commercial sour cream

Put fat on to melt in deep-frying kettle.

Beat egg yolks. Add shortening, salt, and ½ cup milk. Sift together flour, baking powder, and sugar. Add to yolk mixture. Beat until smooth. Beat in remaining ½ cup milk. Whip egg whites stiff. Fold batter into whites.

Peel bananas, cut in half lengthwise, and roll each piece in flour. Dip in batter. Fry in hot fat (375° F. on frying thermometer) about 5 minutes or until golden brown. Drain few seconds on thick paper towels.

Lay warm bananas on dessert plates, sprinkle with confectioners' sugar, and serve with sour cream. Makes 6 servings.

Small boys, and their fathers, love this dessert. This variation is very popular with us.

SPANISH FRITTER CRISPS

Fat for deep frying
1 teaspoon salt
1 ½ cups water

2 cups sifted all-purpose flour
Confectioners' sugar

Heat fat for deep frying.

Add salt to water, bring to a boil, remove from heat, and let stand 1 or 2 seconds. Pour all at once into flour. Stir vigorously to form smooth paste. Spoon into pastry tube with star end which feeds batter in about ½-inch swirls.

When fat is hot, about 375° F. on frying thermometer, squeeze batter into the fat in a loop so ends cross. Fry 2 or 3 minutes or until lightly browned and cooked through. Turn loops once. Lift fried loops out onto thick paper towels. Let drain. Sprinkle with confectioners' sugar. Serve warm or cold. Makes about 12 crisps.

This fried crisp is served with hot coffee or tea, as a light pastry with ice cream or fruit salad, or with the delicious Spanish thick, hot chocolate you drink in Madrid at the cafés until 3 A.M.

Ice Cream and Frozen Puddings

To make ice cream at home the modern homemaker has a choice between the relatively simple method of letting the automatic refrigerator do the work and the old-fashioned hand freezer or motor-turned crank freezer method for family fun in making this great American dessert.

Many of my recipes are intended for refrigerator freezing, but nearly all of them can be adapted to the crank-turned can freezer and I also give crank-freezer directions. Follow freezing directions which your refrigerator recipe booklet may include or the leaflets which came with your crank-turned freezer.

In general, for the crank freezer about 12 pounds of ice are needed for freezing and packing 2 quarts of ice cream. The ice should be put in a canvas or burlap bag and pounded very fine, or use an electric ice crusher.

Use 8 parts crushed ice to 1 part rock salt for freezing. Use 4 parts ice to 1 part rock salt for packing the can of ice cream after freezing. To pack a mold (or mould) containing mousse, parfait, or frozen pudding (ice cream containing candied fruits), use 3 parts ice and 1 part rock salt.

The hand-cranked freezer can and dasher must be washed and scalded each time just before using. Place can in freezer tub. Adjust dasher and cover so handle will turn easily.

Fill tub with alternate layers of ice and salt, 8 parts ice to 1 part rock salt, to within 3 inches of top.

Wipe cover and remove. Wipe edge of can. Pour ice-cream mixture into can. Can should not be more than ⅔ full. Adjust cover and fasten crank. Let stand 5 or 10 minutes to chill cream mixture.

Turn crank slowly, then increase speed. Continue to turn crank until it can no longer be turned easily.

Remove can from freezer. Wipe cover carefully. Open and remove dasher. Beat ice cream with spoon a few times if it is slightly soft. Cover top of can with layers of heavy waxed paper. Replace cover of can.

Empty freezer tub. Replace can. Repack around can, using 4 parts ice to 1 part salt, until can is covered. Let stand 2 hours. If ice cream must stand longer, use 8 parts ice to 1 part salt for packing.

To serve, remove ice from top of can and from well down into tub. Wipe can carefully. Remove lid and waxed paper.

Freeze ices and sherbets in same way. See recipes for these and for refrigerator-tray freezing.

PISTACHIO ICE CREAM

½ cup sugar
1 tablespoon cornstarch
1 cup light cream
½ cup milk
2 eggs, slightly beaten
⅛ teaspoon salt

1 teaspoon vanilla
½ teaspoon almond flavoring
½ teaspoon pure-food green coloring
1 cup heavy cream, whipped
½ cup finely chopped pistachio nuts

Set temperature control on refrigerator at lowest.

Mix sugar and cornstarch in top part of double boiler. Add light cream and milk, stirring smoothly. Bring to a boil, stirring constantly. Stir a little into eggs mixed with salt. Return mixture to double-boiler top. Set pan over simmering water. Cook, stirring until mixture thickens. Let cool. Add flavoring and coloring.

Pour into freezing tray. Freeze until firm. Turn out of freezing tray into chilled bowl. Beat with electric or hand beater until soft but not mushy. Beat in whipped cream and nuts. Return to freezing tray.

Freeze until firm, 4 hours or longer, according to directions with your freezer. Makes 6 servings.

If this mixture is frozen in hand freezer or automatic crank freezer, add nuts when mixture is opened and stirred.

For a gala buffet party, fill a large oval crystal dish with pistachio ice cream heaped in one end and raspberry sherbet in the other. Delicious combination of flavors. Or make a pretty parfait of alternate layers of pistachio ice cream and raspberry sherbet. Top with a few chopped pistachio nuts.

RAISIN ICE CREAM

1   cup seedless raisins
⅓   cup sugar
1   tablespoon cornstarch
½   teaspoon powdered cinnamon
¼   teaspoon powdered cloves
¼   teaspoon powdered nutmeg
⅛   teaspoon salt
1   cup milk

2   eggs, beaten
½   teaspoon vanilla
1   (6-ounce) can (⅔ cup) evaporated milk, chilled and whipped
¼   cup chopped California walnuts

Set refrigerator control at freezing.

Mix raisins, sugar, cornstarch, spices, and salt together in saucepan. Stir in milk. Cook, over moderate heat, stirring constantly until mixture thickens. Add to eggs gradually, beating well. Add vanilla.

Pour into refrigerator tray. Freeze until mushy. Turn out into chilled bowl and beat thoroughly. Fold whipped evaporated milk in with nuts. Return to tray. Freeze firm, 3 hours, or according to directions for your refrigerator. Makes 6 servings.

VANILLA ICE CREAM

1   quart light cream
¼   teaspoon salt

¾   cup sugar
1   tablespoon vanilla

Combine ingredients and stir until sugar is dissolved. Pour into hand or electric freezer can. Freeze according to directions on page 247 or directions with freezer. Makes 1½ quarts, 6 to 8 servings.

This version of vanilla ice cream can be frozen in an automatic refrigerator also. Follow directions for tray freezing as described in preceding ice-cream recipes.

Banana Ice Cream: Mash 4 ripe bananas. Add to cream mixture before freezing.

Burnt-Almond Ice Cream: Add 1 cup chopped, toasted, blanched almonds to recipe for vanilla ice cream. Substitute light brown sugar for granulated in recipe.

Coconut Ice Cream: Add 1 cup toasted shredded coconut to recipe for vanilla ice cream.

Chocolate Ice Cream: Add 2 (1-ounce) squares sweet chocolate to 1 cup cream. Heat over hot water until chocolate is melted. Beat thoroughly. Combine with remaining 3 cups cream and other ingredients and freeze as vanilla ice cream.

Coffee Ice Cream: Scald ⅓ cup ground coffee with 1 cup cream. Strain and let cool. Combine with remaining 3 cups cream and other ingredients in vanilla ice cream recipe.

Peppermint-Candy Ice Cream: Omit sugar and flavoring in vanilla ice cream recipe. Crush ½ pound peppermint molasses kisses or peppermint stick candy. Combine with cream and salt in the vanilla ice cream recipe.

Tutti Frutti: Add 2 tablespoons sherry, ½ cup mixed chopped candied fruits, ¼ cup chopped nuts to vanilla ice cream recipe.

Bisques, Creams, Mousses, Parfaits

BISQUE TORTONI

⅓ cup sifted confectioners' sugar	1 pint heavy cream, whipped
1 teaspoon vanilla	2 egg whites
3 tablespoons sherry	2 tablespoons granulated sugar
¼ teaspoon salt	1 cup fine dry macaroon crumbs
	¼ cup chopped, toasted almonds

Turn temperature control of refrigerator to coldest setting.

Fold confectioners' sugar, vanilla, sherry, and salt into whipped cream.

Whip egg whites until foamy. Add sugar, 1 tablespoon at a time. Continue to whip until whites stand in stiff peaks when beater is withdrawn. Fold cream mixture and macaroon crumbs into egg whites. Spoon into 4-ounce pleated paper cups. Sprinkle tops with almonds.

Freeze in freezer or refrigerator tray until firm. Makes 8 to 10 servings.

If they are to be kept in a freezer, package as usual for freezing. Use within two weeks. For refrigerator freezing, turn temperature control to coldest.

FROZEN CANDY CREAM

Crush ½ pound peanut or almond brittle. Fold into 2 cups heavy cream whipped stiff.

Pour into 1-quart refrigerator tray. Set temperature control at coldest. Freeze until firm. Do not stir. Makes 6 to 8 servings.

Teen-agers love this. It is a good frozen dessert for parties.

FROZEN CREAM CHEESE

1	(8-ounce) package soft cream cheese	⅛	teaspoon salt
⅔	cup canned sweetened condensed milk	1 ½	teaspoons vanilla
½	cup cold water	1	cup heavy cream
			Strawberries or sliced peaches

Turn temperature control of refrigerator to coldest setting.

Combine cheese with milk, using electric mixer or hand beater. Mix in water, salt, and vanilla. Beat until smooth. Place in refrigerator to chill. Whip cream to custard-like consistency. Fold into chilled cheese mixture.

Turn into freezing tray. Freeze until frozen 1 inch in from edge of tray. Turn mixture into chilled bowl. Beat with egg beater or electric mixer until smooth but not melted. Return mixture to freezing tray. Freeze about 1 hour or until just firm enough to spoon out.

Serve like ice cream, spooned into dessert dishes. Top with crushed sugared strawberries or sliced sugared peaches. Makes 4 servings.

FROZEN CUSTARD FOR DIETERS

2 teaspoons sucaryl solution or	2 eggs
16 tablets sucaryl, crushed	2 teaspoons vanilla
1 ½ tablespoons cornstarch	½ teaspoon powdered nutmeg
1 ½ cups skim milk	⅓ cup evaporated milk

Blend sucaryl, cornstarch, and ½ cup cold milk in upper part of double boiler. Add egg yolks and mix well. Scald remaining 1 cup milk. Stir into cornstarch mixture gradually. Cook over boiling water until thickened, stirring constantly. Let cool. Add vanilla and nutmeg.

Whip egg whites until stiff. Fold cooked mixture into whites.

Whip evaporated milk until thick. Add to mixture.

Pour into ice-cube tray. Set temperature control at coldest. Freeze until frozen. Remove to chilled bowl, break up, and beat with spoon until creamy. Pour back into freezing tray. Freeze until firm, with control set for normal freezing, about 4 hours overall, or follow directions given with your freezer. Remove from refrigerator a little while before serving. Spoon into chilled dessert dishes. Makes 6 servings.

To whip evaporated milk, chill it in refrigerator until ice crystals form around edge, then beat with rotary beater until stiff.

APPLESAUCE MOUSSE

1 cup applesauce	¼ teaspoon powdered nutmeg
6 tablespoons sugar	1 cup heavy cream, whipped
1 ½ teaspoons grated lemon peel	

Turn temperature control of refrigerator to coldest setting.

Mix applesauce, sugar, lemon peel, and nutmeg. Fold into whipped cream. Pour into freezing tray of refrigerator. Freeze 2 hours. Turn out into chilled bowl. Beat thoroughly and return to freezer tray. Freeze about 2 hours or until firm. Makes 4 or more servings.

CHOCOLATE MOUSSE

½ pound sweet chocolate	5 eggs
6 tablespoons strongly brewed coffee	1 tablespoon cognac

Melt chocolate with coffee in small saucepan over low heat. Add egg yolks, one at a time, beating well after each addition. Remove from heat. Add cognac. Beat egg whites until they stand in stiff peaks when beater is withdrawn. Fold chocolate mixture into whites.

Pour mixture into refrigerator tray. Set temperature control at coldest. Freeze until almost firm. Turn out into chilled bowl. Beat thoroughly. Return to tray. Freeze until firm, total time 3 to 4 hours. Or follow directions given with your refrigerator. Serve in dessert dishes. Makes 6 or more servings.

Chocolate Almond Mousse: Add ½ cup chopped toasted almonds to mousse when beating frozen mixture.

CHOCOLATE SABAYON MOUSSE

4 egg yolks
2 tablespoons sugar
1 tablespoon cold water
½ cup Marsala or port wine
2 (1-ounce) squares semi-sweet
   chocolate, grated

1 pint heavy cream, whipped
1 cup chopped pistachio or pignolia nuts

Stir egg yolks, sugar, and water together in saucepan. Set over low heat. Beat in wine 2 or 3 minutes or until mixture is thick and creamy. Remove from heat. Stir in chocolate. Pour into mixing bowl. Let cool quickly over cracked ice. Fold in whipped cream and nuts.

Pour into freezing tray. Set temperature control at coldest.

Freeze almost firm, about 3 hours. Turn out into chilled bowl. Beat thoroughly, return to tray, and freeze until firm, about 4 hours in all. Or follow directions for your refrigerator. Makes 8 servings.

See also Frozen Sabayon (page 242).

MAPLE MOUSSE

4 eggs
1 cup maple syrup

2 cups heavy cream
1 teaspoon vanilla

Turn temperature control of refrigerator to coldest setting.

Beat egg yolks lightly. Heat maple syrup in upper part of double boiler over hot, not boiling, water. Stir in yolks. Cook and stir constantly until thickened, about 2 or 3 minutes. Remove pan from hot water and set in cold water to cool.

Whip egg whites stiff. Whip cream stiff. Combine whites, cream, and vanilla. Beat maple mixture into whites and cream. Pour into chilled refrigerator tray. Freeze 1 hour. Turn mixture out into chilled bowl and beat. Pour back into tray and freeze again 3 hours or until thick enough to serve. Makes 8 to 10 servings.

MAPLE MOUSSE FOR DIETERS

2 teaspoons sucaryl solution or 16 tablets sucaryl, crushed	1 cup skim milk
2½ tablespoons flour	2 eggs
¼ teaspoon salt	1 teaspoon maple flavoring

Combine sucaryl, flour, and salt in top part of double boiler. Stir in milk gradually. Set over hot water and cook, stirring constantly, until consistency of thick sauce. Beat egg yolks until thick and lemon-colored. Add a little of the hot milk mixture slowly to the yolks, stirring. Return to double boiler. Cook until mixture mounds when dropped from spoon. Add flavoring and let cool.

Spoon into refrigerator tray. Turn temperature control to coldest. Freeze ½ hour. Turn mixture out into chilled bowl. Break up and mash with fork or beat with spoon. Whip egg whites stiff. Add maple mixture slowly to whites, beating with rotary egg beater or electric mixer at slowest speed. Spoon into sherbet glasses. Chill thoroughly in freezing compartment. Makes 4 to 6 servings.

COFFEE PARFAIT

3 cups milk	3 tablespoons instant-coffee powder
1½ cups sugar	
6 eggs	2 cups heavy cream

Heat milk in saucepan to boiling point, but don't let it boil. Stir in sugar until dissolved. Add a little hot milk mixture to slightly beaten egg yolks and mix well. Then stir yolks into hot milk in saucepan. Cook over low heat, stirring constantly, until mixture is smooth and coats metal spoon. Stir in coffee until dissolved and evenly blended. Remove from heat. Let cool.

Beat egg whites until they stand in stiff points when beater is removed. Mix cool coffee custard gently into whites. Pour into 3 refrigerator trays.

Set temperature control at coldest point.

Freeze mixture until almost firm. Scrape into chilled bowl. Beat with rotary beater until smooth. Return to refrigerator trays. Freeze until firm, about 3 to 4 hours total time, or follow directions given with your refrigerator.

At serving time, whip cream stiff. Spoon alternate layers of parfait and whipped cream into tall parfait glasses. Makes 8 parfaits.

Decorate this luxurious dessert with a sprig of angelica or piece of candied orange peel on top of each parfait.

COFFEE SPUMONI

8 egg whites	¼ cup water
¾ cup sugar	1 ¼ cups heavy cream
2 tablespoons instant-coffee powder	

Set temperature control on refrigerator at coldest.

Beat egg whites until foamy. Add sugar gradually and beat until meringue stands in stiff points. Dissolve coffee in water. Blend with meringue. Whip cream not quite stiff. Fold into coffee mixture. Turn into freezer tray. Freeze until firm. Makes about 2 quarts, 8 servings.

Italian Spumoni: Line chilled spumoni mold with thick layer of slightly softened Bisque Tortoni (page 250). Fill center with Coffee Spumoni or Coffee-Chocolate Ice Cream. Cover mold with waxed paper. Cover with lid. Freeze 2 or more hours until firm. To serve, turn out mold onto chilled dessert platter. Cut mold into 6 or 8 sections, from top to bottom.

Another version of this Italian favorite is to add chopped almonds to rich custard-vanilla ice cream for lining the mold. Fill center with heavy cream, whipped stiff and mixed with chopped candied cherries, candied orange peel, and 1 tablespoon sherry.

Italian restaurants use individual molds, and dark and light layers of spumoni vary according to the chef's preferences. Usually Chocolate Sabayon (page 253) is frozen for center and Bisque Tortoni (page 250) without macaroon crumbs as lining of the mold.

RUM FRUIT MOLD

½ cup canned pineapple cubes	1 cup heavy cream, whipped
½ cup sliced candied cherries	¾ cup powdered sugar
½ cup diced candied-fruit mixture	½ cup chopped pecans
	1 quart chocolate ice cream
Rum	

Drain pineapple. Combine with other fruits. Pour rum over to moisten well, cover, and let soak several hours.

Whip cream stiff, then stir in sugar. Add fruit mixture and nuts.

Line 2-quart melon mold with chocolate ice cream. Fill center with whipped-cream mixture. Cover with waxed paper, then with mold cover. Place in deep-freeze or freezer of your refrigerator overnight. Remove from freezer 20 minutes before serving. Unmold on platter or tray. Serve at table. Makes 8 servings.

Ices and Sherbets

RASPBERRY ICE

2 cups hot water	2 cups mashed, strained fresh,
2 cups sugar	canned, or quick-frozen red
	raspberries
	¾ cup raspberry juice

Combine hot water and sugar in saucepan. Stir over heat until sugar dissolves. Boil 5 minutes without stirring. Let cool. Add mashed berries and ¾ cup juice. Pour in freezer tray or ice cream freezer. Freeze according to directions given with refrigerator or crank freezer. Makes about 1⅓ quarts, 6 to 8 servings.

Black Raspberry Ice: Substitute fresh or canned black raspberries for red berries in above recipe.

Blackberry Ice: Substitute cleaned blackberries for raspberries in above recipe.

Cranberry Ice: Substitute cooked, slightly sweetened cranberries for raspberries in above recipe. Use bottled cranberry juice cocktail for part of the juice.

GINGERED-GRAPEFRUIT SHERBET

1 envelope unflavored gelatin
¼ cup cold water
¾ cup sugar
1 tablespoon finely chopped candied ginger
½ cup hot water
1 (No. 2) can unsweetened grapefruit juice

Few drops yellow pure-food coloring
2 egg whites
⅛ teaspoon salt
¼ cup sugar

Turn temperature control of refrigerator to coldest setting.

Soften gelatin in cold water. Combine ½ cup sugar, candied ginger, and hot water in saucepan. Boil 2 minutes. Remove from heat. Add gelatin and stir until dissolved. Add grapefruit juice and food coloring. Mix.

Pour into refrigerator tray. Freeze until partially frozen. Beat egg whites with salt until soft peaks form. Gradually add remaining ¼ cup sugar and beat until stiff peaks form. Scrape grapefruit mixture into chilled bowl. Fold in meringue. Return to tray. Freeze firm, 3 or more hours, or according to directions given with your freezer. Makes 1½ to 2 quarts, 6 or more servings.

PINEAPPLE SHERBET

1 (9-ounce) can crushed pineapple
⅔ cup sugar
⅛ teaspoon salt

2 cups buttermilk
2 teaspoons vanilla
1 egg white

Turn temperature control of refrigerator to coldest.

Combine pineapple, sugar, and salt in medium-size bowl. Beat well. Stir in buttermilk and vanilla.

Pour mixture into cold, dry freezing tray. Freeze until firm about 1 inch around edge.

Beat egg white until stiff but not dry. Scrape mushy sherbet into chilled bowl. Beat with rotary beater until smooth but not melted. Fold beaten egg white into sherbet. Return to freezer tray. Freeze until firm, 3 to 4 hours, or according to directions given with your refrigerator. Makes about 1 quart, 6 to 8 servings.

LEMON-ORANGE SHERBET

½ cup orange juice
⅓ cup lemon juice
¾ to 1 cup sugar

1 cup milk
1 (6-ounce) can (⅔ cup) evaporated milk, chilled very cold

Turn temperature control of refrigerator to coldest setting.

Combine orange and lemon juices, then add sugar. Gradually stir in milk.

Pour into refrigerator tray. Freeze until mushy. Turn out into chilled bowl and beat thoroughly. Whip evaporated milk until stiff. Fold into frozen mixture. Return to tray. Freeze firm, 3 or 4 hours, or according to directions given with your refrigerator. Makes 6 servings.

Lime Sherbet: Substitute ½ cup fresh lime juice for orange juice in above recipe. Add 1 teaspoon grated lime peel. *Use 1 cup sugar.*

Mint Sherbet: When Lemon-Orange Sherbet is mushy, turn out into chilled bowl. Mix ¾ teaspoon mint flavoring and 2 tablespoons finely cut fresh mint leaves into mixture. Add 1 or 2 drops green pure-food coloring. Beat thoroughly. Return to refrigerator and freeze as described.

Or substitute ½ cup crème de menthe for orange juice in Lemon-Orange Sherbet. Complete recipe as described.

Sherbet Ring: To make a sherbet ring in which to serve fresh fruits, make or buy 3 pints of sherbet. Cut 6 strips waxed paper 1 inch wide and 12 inches long. Lay strips in 5-cup ring mold crosswise with ends of strips hanging over edge of mold. Pack sherbet in mold tightly. Freeze firm in freezing compartment of refrigerator. About 10 minutes before serving time, dip bottom and sides of mold quickly in warm water. Run knife around edge. Turn out upside down on a baking sheet so that ends of waxed paper are out from under mold. Strip them off. Slip mold onto chilled serving platter. If necessary, let mold stand few minutes until it begins to soften. Then fill center of ring with 1 quart washed, hulled, and sweetened strawberries or mixed fresh berries and cut fruits. Serve at once. Makes 6 to 8 servings.

Fresh mint leaves are a pretty garnish for this ring.

Desserts Made with Ice Cream

ALMOND-COCONUT ICE CREAM

¼ cup chopped toasted almonds
⅓ cup toasted shredded coconut

½ teaspoon almond flavoring
1 quart vanilla ice cream, softened

Combine almonds and coconut. Reserve 2 teaspoons for topping. Fold remaining nuts, coconut, and almond flavoring into slightly softened ice cream. Spoon into 8 (4-ounce) paper cups. Sprinkle with topping.

Place in freezer 1 hour or longer. Keep in freezer until serving time. Makes 8 servings.

QUICK ICE-CREAM PIE

4 cups corn flakes
7 tablespoons melted butter
⅓ cup brown sugar, packed
4 (1-ounce) cakes bittersweet chocolate, melted

1 quart vanilla or raisin-rum ice cream
Grated or shaved sweet chocolate
½ cup coarsely chopped pecans

Combine corn flakes, butter, sugar, and chocolate in large mixing bowl. Mix well. Line 10-inch pie plate evenly with mixture. Make smooth edge around top. Let cool and become firm in refrigerator.

Fill chilled crust with ice cream. Sprinkle with sweet chocolate and pecans. Cut in wedges to serve. Makes 6 servings.

This pie may be prepared ahead of time. Wrap in foil. Place in freezer or in very cold freezing compartment of refrigerator.

Let teen-agers of the family make this for their parties.

BAKED ALASKA

5 egg whites
⅛ teaspoon cream of tartar
⅛ teaspoon salt
1 cup sifted confectioners' sugar

1 round 6-inch angel-food cake
1 round pint strawberry ice
cream, frozen hard
Fresh whole strawberries

Start oven at hot (450° F.). Use board about 9 inches square. Lay strip of brown paper on board.

Make meringue. Whip egg whites until frothy. Add cream of tartar, salt, and continue whipping until stiff but not dry. Add sugar, 2 tablespoons at a time, whipping after each addition. Continue to whip until meringue stands in stiff peaks when beater is withdrawn.

With sharp knife enlarge center hole in cake enough to hold roll of ice cream. Place cake on prepared board. Run spatula inside ice cream carton. Slide ice cream into hole in cake. Quickly cover cake and ice cream with meringue, swirling thickly on top and sides. *Cake and ice cream must be completely and thickly covered all over.*

Set board in oven 5 minutes or until meringue is golden brown. Remove immediately to serving platter. Pull Alaska on strip of brown paper onto serving platter. Pull paper off platter and discard. Garnish Alaska quickly with berries. Serve at once. Makes 6 servings.

Use any other favorite ice cream, such as peach, pistachio, mocha, chocolate, or maple. Garnish Alaska on platter as desired, with fruits or candied fruits or small squares of frosted cake. *But serve immediately.*

A shipboard favorite. Fun to surprise guests with at home. This was a dessert that impressed me unforgettably on my first trip to Europe on the Holland-American Line, where it is still a *pièce de résistance.*

CAKE-AND-ICE-CREAM LOAF

Angel cake, 10 by 4 by 2 inches
1 pint brick green mint or pistachio
ice cream
1 pint brick strawberry ice cream
1 tablespoon sugar

1 teaspoon vanilla
2 cups heavy cream, whipped
1 (4-ounce) can (1½ cups) moist
shredded coconut

Rub brown crumbs from cake. Cut cake lengthwise in 3 even layers. Cut ice cream bricks in thirds lengthwise. Cover bottom cake layer with the mint ice cream. Add second cake layer. Cover with the sliced strawberry ice cream. Add last layer of cake. Blend sugar and vanilla into whipped cream. Spread over top and sides of loaf. Sprinkle with coconut.

Place in freezer or freezing compartment of refrigerator until whipped cream is firm. Serve immediately. Makes 8 to 10 servings.

Fruit Desserts

ALMOND-BAKED APPLES

6 large baking apples	Butter or margarine
½ cup bread crumbs	1 cup hot water
1 cup chopped, toasted almonds	Juice and grated peel 1 lemon
1 cup brown sugar, packed	

Start oven at hot (425° F.). Grease 2-quart baking dish.

Wash, pare, and core apples. Mix crumbs, almonds, and ¼ cup sugar. Roll apples in mixture. Pat mixture on with little butter or margarine to make it stick. Place coated apples in prepared baking dish. Fill centers with remaining crumb mixture and ½ cup brown sugar. Mix water, juice, peel, and remaining ¼ cup sugar. Pour into dish and cover.

Bake 20 minutes. Uncover, and baste apples with juices in dish. Cover. Continue baking until apples are almost tender. Uncover, baste again, and finish baking with dish uncovered. Baste apples well when done. Serve warm or cold, with or without cream. Makes 6 servings.

CARAMEL BAKED APPLES

4 to 6 tart apples, cored	3 tablespoons butter or margarine
½ cup seedless raisins	
3 tablespoons flour	¼ cup chopped California walnuts
⅓ cup light brown sugar, packed	
½ teaspoon powdered cinnamon	½ cup water
	½ cup orange juice

Start oven at moderate (325° F.).

Core apples. Pare strip off around top of each. Place in baking dish and fill centers with raisins. Combine flour, sugar, and cinnamon in small mixing bowl. Cut butter or margarine in with pastry blender or fork until crumbly. Add nuts. Sprinkle mixture over apples. Pour water and orange juice over.

Bake uncovered 1½ hours or until done, basting occasionally with syrup in dish. Makes 4 to 6 servings.

APPLE CHARLOTTE

3 pounds apples
1 stick butter (8 tablespoons)
½ cup brown sugar, packed
¼ teaspoon powdered nutmeg

⅛ teaspoon powdered cloves
Juice 1 lemon
1 loaf day-old sandwich bread

Wash, pare, core, and quarter apples. Combine with ½ butter, all sugar, nutmeg, and cloves in saucepan. Cook gently until apples are soft and thick. Add lemon juice.

While apples cook, prepare charlotte mold, or use 1½-quart casserole. Cut bread in thin slices. Remove crusts, then cut in strips about 1½ inches wide and as long as the mold or casserole is deep. Cut additional pieces of bread into triangles to cover bottom of mold or casserole. Grease inside of mold with 1 tablespoon remaining butter. Melt remaining 3 tablespoons butter. Dip strips and triangles of bread in butter, then line mold or casserole with strips, overlapping pieces of bread to make lining complete.

Start oven at hot (425° F.).

Fill center of lined mold or casserole with thick cooked apple mixture. Set on baking sheet.

Bake 40 to 45 minutes or until bread is golden brown. Serve in casserole, with or without cream, or with sauce such as apricot sauce. Makes 6 servings.

BLUEBERRY-AND-PEACH SHORTCAKE

1 package piecrust mix
2 cups fresh blueberries
4 ripe peaches, peeled and sliced,
   or 1 package quick-frozen
   peaches, thawed and drained

1 cup commercial sour cream
2 tablespoons brown sugar

Start oven at hot (450° F.).

Prepare piecrust mix according to directions on package. Cut dough in half. Roll out each half in circle about 9 inches across. Trim edge smoothly with pastry wheel. Cut each circle in 6 wedges with sharp knife or pastry wheel. Slip wedges onto baking sheet with wide spatula.

Bake 7 minutes or until golden brown. Let cool enough to handle.

While pastry bakes, set aside few blueberries and 6 peach slices for garnish. Combine remaining berries, ¾ cup sour cream, and brown sugar in bowl.

To serve, put 1 warm pastry wedge on each dessert plate. Add berry-sour-cream mixture and peaches. Top with pastry wedge. Garnish with remaining sour cream, a few berries, and peach slice. Makes 6 servings.

Strawberry Shortcake: Use above recipe. Substitute 4 cups red-ripe strawberries. Wash and hull berries. Slice all but about 12. Sprinkle with ½ cup sugar. Use sugared berries in place of blueberries and peaches. If preferred, use sweetened whipped cream.

Or make Baking Powder Biscuits (page 82). Split and butter warm biscuits, place on serving plates, fill with sugared strawberries. Top with biscuit halves, berries, and whipped cream, or with berries alone. Serve whipped or plain cream with this version.

BROILED GRAPEFRUIT

Wash heavy juice-filled grapefruit. Cut in halves crosswise. Remove seeds and with sharp knife cut around each section to free it from membrane.

Sprinkle each half with 1 tablespoon light brown sugar and dot with little butter. Cover and store in refrigerator until ready to broil.

Broil 10 minutes, or until golden brown, under moderate heat. Serve hot. Just before serving pour 1 teaspoon sherry or rum over broiled surface.

Serve as first course or dessert.

Molasses-Broiled Grapefruit: Pour about 2 teaspoons New Orleans molasses over each prepared half. Sprinkle lightly with cinnamon. Dot with butter. Broil under moderate heat few minutes or until browning and bubbly. Serve at once.

DRUNKEN FIGS

1 (No. 303) can figs in syrup (about 3 cups)	¼ cup Bourbon whiskey ½ cup heavy cream

Add whiskey to figs and their syrup. Chill in covered bowl until very cold. Whip cream. Two or 3 figs and syrup to cover make a serving. Add whipped cream as garnish. Makes 6 or more servings.

Broken walnut meats may be added to the whipped cream for novel flavor combination with the figs.

Not for the little ones, this. But the big ones do enjoy it. A good company dessert when time is limited and help nonexistent.

EASY PEACH DESSERT

Swirl currant or red raspberry jam through whipped cream. Serve on sliced ripe, canned, or defrosted quick-frozen peaches.

CHERRIES JUBILEE

1 (No. 2) can Bing cherries	½ cup cognac
2 tablespoons sugar	1 quart vanilla ice cream

Heat cherries and juice in chafing dish. Sweeten with sugar. When hot (do not boil) add almost all of brandy. Put remaining brandy in large spoon. Ignite with match. Pour over cherries and let blaze. When flame goes down, spoon hot cherries over ice cream. Makes 6 or more servings.

Fruit Flambé: Dissolve 1 cup sugar in 1½ cups water. Bring to a boil in chafing dish and boil 10 minutes. Add 6 peeled fresh peaches or nectarines, or drained canned fruits, such as 1 cup drained Bing cherries and 6 brandied peaches. Add ¼ cup Cointreau and ignite. Let flames die down. Spoon fruit into dessert dishes or onto sliced poundcake. Makes 6 servings.

If fruit and liquid are slow to flame, fill large cooking spoon or silver ladle with Cointreau or brandy, light with match, and pour flaming liquid into chafing dish. This will ignite the Cointreau-fruit syrup.

This is definitely a dish to prepare in full view of the guests. A well-known writer I know does it with great pyrotechnics on the sideboard. His wife encourages such culinary conceits. She can forget the dessert course.

See also chafing dish chapter.

GREEN GAGE PLUMS DE LUXE

1 (No. 2) can large green gage plums	½ cup thick cold Custard Sauce (page 565)
¼ cup slivered blanched almonds	

Chill plums thoroughly. Place 2 or 3 plums and a little of their syrup in each of 4 dessert dishes. Sprinkle with slivered almonds. Top with 2 tablespoons thick cold Custard Sauce. Makes 4 servings.

This is a superior dessert if you will take the trouble to find top quality canned plums, such as those sold at specialty food shops. Leftover custard also makes a fine combination with these plums. When using yesterday's custard instead of Custard Sauce, spoon firm custard into serving dishes first, garnish with 2 or 3 large green gage plums, sprinkle with almonds, add a very little syrup over the plums, and serve.

I associate this with Staten Island Sunday night suppers when I was a child—but the plums were home-canned.

MELONS

Wash melons. Chill. Cut just before serving. Remove seeds and fibers of honeydew, honey ball, cantaloupes, Persian melons, and similar melons. Cut in halves, quarters, or smaller sections.

Watermelon may be served in slices or sections. Some hostesses like to cut the pink melon out of the rind and serve it in wedges or smaller pieces.

A section of fresh lemon or lime is usually served with cantaloupe, honeydew, and similar melons. Both salt and powdered sugar should be available also. A pepper mill is much appreciated by some guests. A light sprinkling of freshly ground black pepper on honeydew melon is delicious.

A spoonful of crushed red raspberries on a thin new-moon slice of honeydew is another favorite combination. Or garnish this delicate melon with paper-thin slices of the Italian ham called prosciutto.

Another good flavor combination is a light sprinkling of powdered ginger on honeydew and cantaloupe.

Why not pass a tray of sliced pared melon—honeydew, cantaloupe, Persian melon, and watermelon—and let guests serve themselves to their favorites. Then pass an assortment of seasonings and garnishes, such as quarters of fresh limes, lemons, sticks of fresh pineapple, fresh cherries, raspberries, or blueberries, a pepper mill, a silver shaker filled with cinnamon and another with powdered ginger. This makes a dramatic finish to your terrace luncheon on a lovely summer day, or for dinner on a hot night.

See also appetizers chapter.

MELON-BALL COMPOTE

1 cup sugar
1 cup water
¼ teaspoon salt
3 sprigs fresh mint

1 cup watermelon balls
1 cup cantaloupe balls
1 cup honeydew balls

Combine sugar, water, salt, and mint in saucepan. Boil 15 minutes or until temperature of syrup reaches 220° F. on candy thermometer. Let cool. Remove mint, pour syrup over melon balls, and cover bowl. Chill 2 or 3 hours.

To serve, arrange few balls of each melon in stemmed fruit cup or dessert dish. Garnish with fresh mint leaf. Makes 4 or more servings.

Melon Ball Fruit Cups: Cut balls from chilled melons. Combine 2 or 3 kinds of melon balls in chilled stemmed dessert dish. Garnish with fresh mint leaf.

For another interesting flavor, mix 1 cup orange juice with 1 tablespoon grenadine or crème de menthe. Or use maraschino liqueur. Pour over 3 cups chilled melon balls. Serve as first course or for dessert.

MOLASSES APPLE CRISP

6 cups sliced, tart cooking apples (4 large apples)
½ cup sugar
¼ teaspoon powdered nutmeg
⅛ teaspoon salt

½ teaspoon powdered cinnamon
5 tablespoons molasses
3 tablespoons butter or margarine
¾ cup sifted all-purpose flour

Start oven at moderate (375° F.). Grease a 6-by-10-by-2-inch baking dish.

Pare and core apples. Slice about ⅛ inch thick. Mix together ¼ cup sugar, nutmeg, salt, and ¼ teaspoon cinnamon. Alternate apples and sugar mixture in prepared baking dish. Spoon 4 tablespoons molasses over top. Mix together remaining ¼ cup sugar, 1 tablespoon molasses, ¼ teaspoon cinnamon, butter or margarine, and flour to a crumb consistency. Sprinkle evenly over apples.

Bake uncovered 50 minutes or until apples are done. Serve warm with cream or Molasses Hard Sauce (page 566). Makes 6 servings.

PEACHES MARION

Serve quick-frozen peaches, half thawed, topped with some of their own syrup and grated coconut or finely chopped candied ginger. Two large peach halves make 1 serving.

TIPSY PEACHES

Arrange a layer of ladyfingers in flat glass dish. Cover with layer of sliced fresh or thawed quick-frozen peaches. Sprinkle lightly with sugar. Cover peaches with another layer of ladyfingers. Add 1½ teaspoons cognac to about ¾ cup peach juice. Pour over ladyfingers to moisten well. Cover dish. Chill 1 hour or longer.

To serve, cut peach combination in squares. Lift squares into dessert dishes. Top with vanilla ice cream or with whipped cream flavored with little cognac.

VENETIAN PEACHES

2 cups sugar	Sabayon dessert (page 242)
2 cups water	1½ pints lemon ice cream
1 teaspoon vanilla	½ cup chopped pignolia nuts
6 ripe peaches, peeled	or slivered almonds

Dissolve sugar in water, add vanilla, and boil 10 minutes. Add peeled peaches to syrup. Cover saucepan and simmer 5 minutes or until peaches are tender.

Prepare Sabayon dessert (page 242). Let cool.

To serve, arrange portions of ice cream in dessert dishes. Top each with peach. Pour spoonful of sauce over fruit. Sprinkle top with nuts. Makes 6 servings.

PEARS COINTREAU

6 firm ripe pears
1 tablespoon lemon juice
2 cups water

¾ cup sugar
1 cup Cointreau

Pare, quarter, and core pears. Cover at once with cold water to which lemon juice has been added to prevent discoloring.

Combine 2 cups water and sugar. Boil 5 minutes. Drain pears, add to syrup, and cover pan. Simmer 5 minutes or until pears are tender and transparent but not mushy. Turn pears and syrup into glass serving dish. Let cool few minutes. Pour Cointreau over them. Let cool, spooning syrup over fruit several times. Serve chilled. Makes 6 servings.

PEARS IN WINE

6 winter pears
2 cups red wine
2 cups water
1 cup sugar

1 clove
1-inch piece cinnamon stick
1 lemon, sliced

Wash pears. Pare but leave stems on. Combine with wine, water, sugar, clove, cinnamon, and lemon in large glass or enamel saucepan. Cover and cook over low heat 30 minutes or until pears are tender and done. Remove pears to serving dish. Reheat juice and boil uncovered to reduce about half. Pour over pears. Chill. Makes 6 servings.

This is a winter stand-by. Sometimes to be a little fancy I serve the pears with whipped cream, passed in a silver bowl, so guests may help themselves or resist, as they please.

PHILADELPHIA PEACHES

6 peach halves
½ cup chopped, toasted almonds
1 cup seedless white grapes,
   stems removed

¼ cup seedless raisins
6 rounds toasted spongecake
Hot Raspberry and Currant Sauce

Use fresh, canned, or quick-frozen peaches for this delicious dessert. If peaches are fresh, dip them in boiling water quickly. Remove skins, cut in halves, and remove stone. If quick-frozen, let defrost. Mix almonds, grapes, and raisins. Place a peach half on a round of toasted cake. Fill center of peach with nut mixture, top, with spoonful of hot sauce. Makes 6 servings.

Raspberry and Currant Sauce: Use 1 package quick-frozen red raspberries. Let thaw. Add berries and juice to about ½ cup (1 small jelly glass) currant jelly. Heat slowly. While warm spoon over stuffed peaches. Sweeten sauce if needed.

PRUNE WHIP

3 egg whites
1 tablespoon grated lemon peel
2 tablespoons lemon juice
2 tablespoons prune juice
⅛ teaspoon salt

⅓ cup sugar
1 cup finely chopped cooked prunes
Light cream or
Custard Sauce (page 565)

Combine egg whites, lemon peel, lemon juice, prune juice, salt, and sugar in upper part of double boiler. Set over boiling water. Beat with rotary beater 10 minutes or until mixture holds its shape. Remove pan from boiling water. Fold in prunes. Let cool. Chill. Serve in dessert glasses with a little cream or Custard Sauce. Makes 6 servings.

This is a glamourized version of the prune dish which is the delight of the tea shoppe. This delicious prune whip is fit to appear at your most toiled-over dinner party for Very Important People.

Quick and Easy Fruit Desserts

Apricots: Drain canned apricots. Serve with spoonful of whipped cream mixed with shredded almonds.

Figs: Drain canned figs. Combine with spiced Seckel pears in the spicy liquid from the pears. Let chill overnight. Drain and serve with cream cheese and crackers.

Peaches: Combine brandied peaches with drained canned Bing cherries. Chill. Serve with poundcake.

Pears: Drain canned pears. Serve topped with thawed quick-frozen blueberries and softened vanilla ice cream.

RICE MELBA

⅔ cup packaged precooked rice
2 cups milk
⅓ cup sugar
½ teaspoon salt
⅛ teaspoon powdered nutmeg
⅛ teaspoon powdered cinnamon

½ cup heavy cream
1 (No. 2½) can cling-peach halves, drained
⅓ cup red currant or raspberry jelly

Combine rice and milk in saucepan. Bring to a boil and boil gently, loosely covered, 15 minutes, fluffing rice occasionally with fork. Remove rice from heat. Stir in sugar, salt, nutmeg, and cinnamon. Let cool 5 minutes, then chill rice in freezing compartment of refrigerator 20 minutes but do not let it freeze.

Whip cream. Fold chilled rice into cream. Heap in dessert dishes. Lay drained peach half on top, cut side down. Melt jelly over hot water. Pour a little jelly over peach. Makes 6 servings.

A hearty dessert to serve after a light luncheon.

SPICED PEARS COMPOTE

Heat spiced Seckel or summer pears in their own spicy juices. Add 1 or 2 teaspoons grated orange peel or chopped candied orange peel. Serve warm in dessert dishes, 2 small pears or 1 large one for each serving.

STRAWBERRIES CHANTILLY

Wash, hull, and cut red-ripe strawberries in half. Stir them into whipped cream which has been slightly sweetened with powdered sugar and flavored with few drops of vanilla. Chill 2 hours or longer. Serve heaped in dessert glasses.

Red Raspberries Chantilly. Apricots Chantilly. Peaches Chantilly.
Follow above recipe. Use fresh, ripe fruit or defrosted quick-frozen
fruits. Served chilled in dessert dishes after simple luncheon or supper.

STRAWBERRIES ROMANOFF

1 quart red-ripe strawberries	1 cup heavy cream, whipped
½ cup sugar	Sugar
½ cup orange juice	Additional curaçao, or Cointreau
½ cup curaçao	

Wash and hull berries. Sweeten with sugar to taste. Combine orange
juice and liqueur. Pour over berries. Chill in covered bowl 1 hour or
longer. Whip cream, sweeten with little sugar, and flavor with a little
liqueur.

At serving time heap berries in serving dish. Garnish with flavored
whipped cream. Makes 6 or more servings.

If quick-frozen sliced strawberries are used, omit sugar from above
recipe.

This is so easy and *so* impressive. I am always amazed that few
hostesses use imagination when serving it. I serve mine from an antique
porcelain bowl onto white porcelain plates.

WINTER COMPOTE

12 dried prunes	1 orange, juice and peel
12 dried apricots	Juice ½ lemon
3 fresh or canned pears	1 cup canned Bing cherries,
½ cup sugar	pitted
1 cup water	½ cup cognac

Wash dried fruits. Cover with cold water and cook about 15 minutes,
until softened. Drain. Wash pears. Pare, core, and quarter, or core and
quarter canned pears.

Combine sugar and water in saucepan and bring to a boil. Boil 5
minutes. Add orange and lemon juice.

If fresh pears are used, place them in syrup and add strips of orange
peel. Simmer until pears and peel are tender. If canned pears are used,
simmer orange peel until tender, then add pears. Add cherries and their
juice and cooked fruits. Heat together about 5 minutes. Add brandy,
then let cool a little. Serve warm. Makes 6 servings.

Gelatin Desserts

APRICOT BAVARIAN

½ cup sugar
1 envelope unflavored gelatin
⅛ teaspoon salt
1 (12-ounce) can apricot nectar
3 tablespoons lemon juice

1 egg white
½ cup heavy cream
12 canned apricot halves, drained

Combine sugar, gelatin, and salt in upper part of double boiler. Add apricot nectar and stir. Heat and stir over hot water until gelatin dissolves. Remove from heat. Pour into small mixing bowl. Add lemon juice. Let cool at room temperature. When cooled, stir unbeaten egg white into mixture. Place in refrigerator. Chill until partially set, about 1½ hours.

Whip partially set gelatin until light and fluffy with soft peaks. In another bowl, whip cream stiff. Fold cream into gelatin mixture.

Pour into 1-quart melon mold. Cover mold with waxed paper. Chill in refrigerator 2 or 3 hours or until firm. Unmold onto chilled platter. Garnish with apricot halves. Makes 6 servings.

CHAMPAGNE-FRUIT DESSERT

2 envelopes unflavored gelatin
½ cup cold water
1 cup canned apple juice, or apricot or peach nectar
3 tablespoons cognac

2 cups champagne
1½ cups canned fruit salad, drained (remove any pineapple sections)

Soften gelatin in water. Place over hot water and stir until dissolved. Let cool. Add apple juice, or apricot or peach nectar, mix, and chill 30 minutes. Beat until thick and syrupy. Add cognac, champagne, and well-drained fruit, and mix.

Pour into lightly oiled 2-quart mold. Cover with waxed paper. Chill 2 to 3 hours or until firm. Unmold carefully on chilled platter. Serve with whipped cream or plain. Makes 6 servings.

COFFEE BAVARIAN

2 envelopes unflavored gelatin	¼ teaspoon salt
¼ cup cold water	6 tablespoons sugar
3 eggs	Whipped cream or
1 ¾ cups milk	Custard Sauce (page 565)
2 tablespoons instant coffee	
½ teaspoon powdered cinnamon	

Soften gelatin with cold water in mixing bowl. Beat egg yolks slightly. Combine with milk, coffee, cinnamon, salt, and 3 tablespoons sugar in upper part of double boiler. Cook, stirring over boiling water until mixture coats metal spoon. Remove from hot water. Pour hot egg mixture over gelatin, stirring until dissolved. Let cool, then chill until slightly thickened.

Beat egg whites until foamy. Add remaining 3 tablespoons sugar gradually, beating until stiff peaks remain when beater is withdrawn. Fold gelatin mixture into egg whites.

Pour into 1-quart mold. Let chill until firm, about 2 hours. Serve with whipped cream or Custard Sauce, or plain with chocolate cookies. Makes 6 servings.

COFFEE JELLY

1 envelope unflavored gelatin	⅓ cup sugar
½ cup cold water	⅛ teaspoon salt
1 cup boiling-hot strong coffee or 1 cup boiling water and 1 tablespoon coffee concentrate	2 tablespoons chopped walnuts
	½ cup heavy cream
	Extra cream for garnishing

Soften gelatin in cold water, then dissolve in hot coffee. Stir in sugar, salt, and walnuts. Set in cold place to thicken. When stiff, break gelatin up with fork or rotary egg beater. Whip cream stiff and fold into jelly. Serve with additional whipped cream or plain cream. Makes 4 to 6 servings.

This was my mother's favorite dessert and one of my favorites. Few hostesses seem to know it.

ORANGE CHARLOTTE

2 envelopes unflavored gelatin	1 cup cold water
½ cup cold water	⅓ cup lemon juice
¾ cup hot water	2 egg whites
1½ cups sugar	1 cup heavy cream, whipped
1 (6-ounce) can frozen orange-juice concentrate	

Soften gelatin in cold water. Stir into hot water until dissolved. Combine sugar, orange-juice concentrate, 1 cup cold water, and lemon juice. Stir in gelatin mixture gradually. Stir in unbeaten egg whites and mix well. Chill until partially set. Beat mixture until fluffy and soft peaks form. Fold in whipped cream.

Pour into 2-quart mold. Chill until set, 1½ to 2 hours. Unmold on chilled serving platter. Serve plain or garnished with coffee-flavored whipped cream and almonds. Makes 6 to 8 servings.

SUNDAY-NIGHT WINE JELLY

4 envelopes unflavored gelatin	3 lemons, grated peel and juice
1 cup cold water	2 cups Madeira or sherry
1 quart boiling water	1 cup cognac
1½ cups sugar	

Soak gelatin in cold water until softened. Stir into boiling water to dissolve. Add sugar, lemon juice, and peel. Mix. Let cool. Add wine and cognac.

Pour into 2½-quart mold. Chill until firm, 2 to 3 hours. Unmold on chilled dessert platter. Serve with cream or whipped cream—and poundcake, for those who aren't counting calories. Makes 6 to 8 servings.

This is the jelly I like to serve with angel cake.

WINE-CHERRY MOLD

1 (1-pound 13-ounce) can Bing cherries	½ cup sherry
¾ cup hot water	½ cup chopped filberts
1 package black-cherry or cherry-flavored gelatin	1 cup commercial sour cream
	Powdered nutmeg

Drain cherries, reserving juice. Add hot water to gelatin in bowl, and stir until dissolved. Stir in sherry and ¾ cup juice from cherries, and mix. Chill until partially set. Stir in cherries and nuts.

Pour into 1½-quart mold. Chill until firm, 2 to 3 hours. Unmold on chilled platter. Serve with sour cream, sprinkled lightly with nutmeg. Makes 6 servings.

Puddings

APPLE CRISP

4 cups pared, cored cooking apples	½ cup brown sugar, packed
1 tablespoon lemon juice	½ teaspoon salt
⅓ cup sifted all-purpose flour	1 teaspoon powdered cinnamon
1 cup oatmeal, uncooked	⅓ cup melted butter or margarine

Start oven at moderate (375° F.). Grease shallow 1½-quart baking dish.

Pour apples into prepared dish. Sprinkle with lemon juice. If tart apples are used, add light sprinkling brown sugar. Combine dry ingredients. Add melted butter or margarine. Mix until like coarse crumbs. Sprinkle crumb mixture over apples.

Bake 30 minutes or until apples are done. Serve warm or cold, with top milk or light cream. Makes 6 servings.

RICH DATE PUDDING

3 tablespoons shortening	1 teaspoon grated lemon peel
1 (6½-ounce) package pitted dates, chopped	1½ cups sifted all-purpose flour
1 cup boiling water	1 teaspoon salt
1 egg	1 teaspoon baking soda
1 cup brown sugar, packed	½ cup chopped walnuts

Start oven at moderate (325° F.). Grease 1½-quart baking dish.

Combine shortening and chopped dates in large bowl. Pour boiling water over and let cool slightly. Stir in egg, sugar, and lemon peel. Sift flour, salt, and soda together. Add to date mixture and mix well. Stir in nuts. Pour into prepared baking dish.

Bake uncovered 55 minutes or until done. Serve hot with Hard Sauce (page 566) or Sherry Cream Sauce (page 568). Makes 8 servings.

BANANA-CUSTARD PUDDING

¾ cup sugar	3 eggs
1 tablespoon flour	1 teaspoon vanilla
¼ teaspoon salt	Vanilla wafer cookies
2 cups milk	6 bananas

Combine ½ cup sugar, the flour, and salt in top part of double boiler. Stir in milk. Cook over hot water, stirring constantly until thickened. Cook, uncovered, 15 minutes longer, stirring occasionally.

Beat egg yolks. Stir a little of the hot mixture into yolks. Then stir yolks into rest of mixture in double boiler. Cook 5 minutes, stirring constantly. Remove from hot water and add vanilla.

Start oven at hot (425° F.).

Line 1½-quart casserole with vanilla wafers. Top with sliced bananas. Pour some of custard over bananas. Continue layers of wafers, bananas, and custard, ending with custard on top.

Beat egg whites stiff. Add remaining ¼ cup sugar gradually and continue beating until whites stand in stiff points when beater is removed. Pile on top of pudding in casserole.

Bake 6 to 8 minutes or until meringue is delicately browned. Serve warm or chilled. Makes 6 servings.

BLUEBERRY COBBLER

Blender

2 cups blueberries	1 egg
⅓ cup sugar	⅔ cup sugar
⅛ teaspoon powdered cinnamon	¼ cup shortening
1 cup sifted cake flour	½ cup milk
1 teaspoon baking powder	½ teaspoon vanilla
1 teaspoon salt	

Start oven at moderate (350° F.). Grease 8-inch square baking dish.

Wash and drain berries. Look over for discards. Combine berries with ⅓ cup sugar and cinnamon. Spread evenly in prepared baking dish.

Sift flour, baking powder, and salt together into mixing bowl. Combine remaining ingredients in glass container of blender. Cover and blend thoroughly about 1 minute. Pour over sifted flour mixture. Stir lightly until just smooth. Spread this batter over berries in baking dish.

Bake about 35 minutes or until cobbler is done. Serve warm with top milk, cream, or ice cream. Makes 6 servings.

Cherry Cobbler: Substitute 2 cups drained canned or quick-frozen sweet cherries for blueberries in above recipe.

Peach Cobbler: Substitute 2 cups sliced fresh, canned, or defrosted quick-frozen peaches for blueberries in above recipe.

Plum Cobbler: Substitute 2 cups halved ripe or canned sweet plums for blueberries in above recipe. Add more sugar if plums are tart.

Strawberry Cobbler: Substitute 2 cups defrosted sliced quick-frozen strawberries for blueberries in above recipe.

CINNAMON FLUFF

Topping

½ cup sugar
1 tablespoon butter or margarine

1 tablespoon powdered cinnamon

Fluff

½ cup butter or margarine
⅔ cup sugar
2 eggs, well beaten
1½ cups sifted all-purpose flour
1 teaspoon baking soda

1 teaspoon baking powder
1 tablespoon powdered cinnamon
1 cup sour milk

Mix topping ingredients together smoothly.

Start oven at moderate (350° F.). Butter 1½-quart baking dish.

Mix fluff ingredients. Cream butter or margarine and sugar smoothly together. Stir in eggs. Sift flour with remaining dry ingredients. Add these alternately with sour milk and beat 1 minute. Pour batter into prepared baking dish. Spread with topping.

Bake about 1 hour or until tester comes out clean. Serve warm with cream or any preferred fresh fruit sauce. Makes 6 servings.

This is so unusual, so good, we turn to it again and again, especially in winter.

BROWN-RICE HONEY PUDDING

1 cup brown rice	1 teaspoon butter or margarine
2 ¼ cups boiling water	1 teaspoon powdered cinnamon
1 teaspoon salt	
¾ cup honey	1 teaspoon lemon juice
½ cup seedless raisins	¾ cup heavy cream

Combine rice, boiling water, and salt in 1-quart saucepan. Cover pan tightly. Cook over low heat 25 minutes or until all water is absorbed and rice grains feel soft between your fingers.

Start oven at moderate (325° F.). Butter 1-quart casserole.

Pour honey into 1-quart saucepan. Boil until lightly browned. Stir in cooked rice. Add raisins, butter or margarine, cinnamon, and lemon juice. Pour into prepared casserole.

Bake 20 minutes or until top is lightly browned. Serve with plain or whipped cream. Makes 4 servings.

A queen of rice puddings! Not just another "rice pudding again!"

CHOCOLATE-ALMOND PUDDING

¼ cup butter or margarine	2 cups sifted cake flour
¾ cup sugar	1 ½ teaspoons baking powder
1 egg	¼ teaspoon salt
½ teaspoon vanilla	1 cup milk
2 ½ (1-ounce) squares bitter chocolate, melted	Sauce

Cream butter or margarine smoothly with sugar. Add egg, vanilla, and melted chocolate, and beat well. Sift flour with baking powder and salt. Add alternately with milk to butter mixture.

Pour into well-greased pudding mold, filling it half full. Cover tightly. Steam in covered steamer 2 hours. Keep water boiling rapidly throughout steaming period.

Unmold on warm serving dish. Serve hot with cream, Chocolate-Almond Sauce (page 564), or Sherry Cream Sauce (page 568). Makes 8 servings.

If served with sauce, make the sauce while pudding steams and have ready when pudding is done.

FROSTED RICE PUDDING

1 quart milk	2 teaspoons lemon juice
½ cup rice	1 teaspoon vanilla
½ cup seedless raisins	½ teaspoon salt
4 eggs	¼ teaspoon cream of tartar
½ cup granulated sugar	¼ cup sifted confectioners' sugar

Combine milk, rice, and raisins in 2-quart saucepan. Cover and cook slowly over low heat until rice is tender, about 40 to 50 minutes. Stir occasionally.

When rice is done, start oven at moderate (375° F.). Grease 1½-quart casserole.

Beat egg yolks lightly with granulated sugar. Add lemon juice and vanilla. Stir into hot rice mixture. Pour into prepared casserole.

Whip egg whites until foamy, then whip salt in with cream of tartar and confectioners' sugar until stiff. Spoon this meringue over top of rice pudding.

Bake 20 minutes or until meringue is golden. Serve warm or cold. Makes 6 servings.

My very best rice pudding recipe. I gave a prize for it years ago when I was a food editor, and the talented originator's name is now lost to me. But her recipe is part of our kitchen regulars, bless her!

JELLY-ROLL PUDDING

4 eggs	1 teaspoon vanilla
⅓ cup sugar	6 slices jelly roll, ½ inch thick
¼ teaspoon salt	Sweetened whipped cream
3 cups milk, scalded	

Start oven at moderate (350° F.). Butter 10-by-6-by-1¾-inch baking dish.

Beat eggs slightly, add sugar and salt, and mix well. Add milk gradually, stirring vigorously. Add vanilla. Pour just enough of this custard mixture into prepared baking dish to cover bottom. Lay jelly-roll slices in custard in dish. Pour remaining custard over slices. Slices will begin to float to top.

Bake 45 minutes or until knife inserted in center comes out clean. Let cool at room temperature. Chill. Cut in squares to serve. Add dab of whipped cream to each piece. Makes 6 servings.

FARINA PUDDING

1 quart milk	½ cup farina, plus 1 tablespoon
½ cup sugar, less 1 tablespoon	

Combine milk and sugar and bring to a boil. Gradually stir in farina. Cook 5 to 10 minutes or until well thickened, stirring to prevent lumps.

Pour cereal into a mold and chill until firm. Turn out onto chilled platter. Surround with Thompson seedless grapes, canned red plums, and Red Plum Sauce. Makes 6 servings.

Red Plum Sauce

2 tablespoons sugar	½ cup light corn syrup
1½ tablespoons cornstarch	1 teaspoon butter or marga-
⅛ teaspoon salt	rine
1 cup plum juice, drained from canned plums	Few drops almond flavoring

Mix sugar, cornstarch, and salt in small saucepan. Add plum juice gradually, stirring well. Add corn syrup. Cook over medium heat, stirring constantly, until sauce thickens and boils. Boil 3 minutes, stirring constantly. Remove from heat. Add butter or margarine and flavoring. Makes about 1½ cups syrup.

This is one of my French recipes. I learned to make it at the Institute Heubi in Lausanne. I had never seen farina used as anything but a breakfast cereal, and I was fascinated—and still am—by the idea of the pudding. Highly recommended.

STEAMED MOLUCCA PUDDING

1⅓ cups sifted all-purpose flour	⅔ cup whole-wheat or graham flour
½ teaspoon baking soda	
1 teaspoon baking powder	1 cup sliced pitted dates
½ teaspoon salt	⅓ cup shortening or margarine
¼ teaspoon powdered cloves	1 cup brown sugar, packed
½ teaspoon powdered cinnamon	1 egg
	½ cup sour milk
¼ teaspoon powdered nutmeg	

Sift flour, soda, baking powder, salt, and spices together. Add whole-wheat or graham flour and dates and mix well. Cream shortening or margarine and sugar together thoroughly. Add unbeaten egg to sugar mixture and beat 2 minutes. Add sour milk alternately with dry ingredients. Pour into 6 buttered custard cups. Cover each with doubled piece of waxed paper. Tie tightly with string. Set cups in steamer above boiling water. Steam 1 hour. Serve warm with or without cream or a fruit sauce. Makes 6 servings.

SWEDISH MERINGUE APPLE PUDDING

6 cooking apples	¼ cup boiling water
1 cup light brown sugar, packed	3 egg whites
¼ teaspoon powdered cloves	⅛ teaspoon salt
½ teaspoon powdered cinnamon	½ cup sugar
¼ teaspoon powdered nutmeg	1 tablespoon grated lemon peel
1 tablespoon melted butter or margarine	⅓ cup slivered blanched almonds

Start oven at moderate (350° F.). Butter shallow 2-quart baking dish.

Wash, pare, and core apples, and slice thin. Pour into prepared baking dish. Combine brown sugar, spices, and melted butter or margarine. Sprinkle over apples. Add boiling water. Bake about 20 minutes or until apples are tender. Let cool slightly.

Beat egg whites until foamy. Add salt and sugar, 2 tablespoons at a time. Continue beating until the meringue is satiny and stands in peaks. Fold in lemon peel. Spread over apples. Sprinkle with almonds.

Return to oven and bake 15 minutes longer or until meringue is golden brown. Serve warm or cold. Makes 6 servings.

The 3 egg yolks will make a Custard Sauce (page 565), which Swedish hostesses chill and serve with this pudding.

SUET PUDDING

1 ½ cups sifted all-purpose flour	½ cup seedless raisins
1 ½ teaspoons baking powder	½ cup ground suet
½ teaspoon salt	½ cup molasses
½ teaspoon powdered cloves	¾ cup milk
¾ teaspoon powdered cinnamon	

Mix and sift flour with baking powder, salt, and spices. Stir in raisins. Combine suet, molasses, and milk. Add dry ingredients to suet mixture and blend well. Pour into greased 1-quart mold, cover tightly with lid or cover with metal foil held in place by tightly tied string. Set mold in steamer over lively boiling water. Cover steamer. Steam 3 to 4 hours. Serve with Nutmeg Sauce (page 567) or Hard Sauce (page 566). Makes 6 servings.

Now this is a dish that makes a man reminisce about his mother's— or his grandmother's—cooking. In fact, this recipe is one from *my* grandmother Vanderbilt's collection. A dessert for a cold winter day.

Tortes

CHOCOLATE JAM TORTE

8 eggs	¾ cup raspberry jam
1 cup sugar	Double recipe for Soft Chocolate
¼ teaspoon salt	Frosting (page 130)
¼ pound filberts, grated	Pistachio nuts
¼ pounds walnuts, grated	

Start oven at moderate (350° F.). Grease two (9-inch) layer-cake pans. Line with waxed paper and grease paper.

Beat egg yolks until thick and lemon-colored. Beat ½ cup sugar in gradually. Add salt to egg whites. Beat until stiff but not dry. Beat remaining ½ cup sugar gradually into whites, until they stand in stiff peaks when beater is removed. Fold egg-yolk mixture into egg-white mixture. Fold in nuts. Pour into prepared cake pans.

Bake 30 minutes. Loosen sides, turn cakes out on rack. Remove waxed paper. Let cool. When cold, split each layer, making 4 layers in all.

Spread layers, except the top one, with jam, then with Soft Chocolate Frosting. Put layers together. Spread top and sides with Frosting. Garnish with chopped pistachio nuts. Let stand until chocolate is firm. Makes 12 servings.

LINZERTORTE

1 cup butter	⅛ teaspoon powdered cloves
1 cup sifted all-purpose flour	⅛ teaspoon powdered cinnamon
1 tablespoon cocoa powder	2 egg yolks
1½ cups grated almonds	½ to ¾ cup raspberry jam
½ cup sugar	1 egg white

Chop butter into flour and cocoa in mixing bowl. When crumbly add almonds. Use pastry blender to mix.

Combine sugar, cloves, and cinnamon. Beat yolks and add to sugar mixture. Stir into flour mixture. Knead in bowl until smooth and well blended.

Turn ⅔ of dough into an ungreased 9-inch cake pan with removable bottom. Press dough over bottom and up sides to form pie shell. Pour jam into shell.

Roll remaining dough lightly to ¼ inch thickness. Cut in strips about ½ inch wide and 9 inches long. Place strips on pan or tray and chill in refrigerator until firm.

When strips have chilled, start oven at moderate (325° F.). Remove strips from tray with spatula one at a time, and place lattice-fashion over jam pie. Crimp ends of each strip to dough rim by pressing lightly. Brush strips with egg white.

Bake on lower shelf of oven about 1 hour and 15 minutes or until pastry is browned.

Let pan cool on cake rack before removing rim of pan. Makes 10 or more servings.

COFFEE TORTE

2 tablespoons unflavored gelatin

½ cup cold, strongly brewed coffee

1½ cups hot, strongly brewed coffee

1 cup sugar

2 cups heavy cream

1 cup broken pecans

1 tablespoon vanilla or rum

2 dozen ladyfingers

½ (3-ounce) package semi-sweet chocolate pieces, melted

3 teaspoons sugar

1 teaspoon instant-coffee powder

Whipped cream

Sprinkle gelatin on cold coffee. Let stand 5 minutes. Add hot coffee and sugar. Stir until sugar and gelatin dissolve. Chill until consistency of unbeaten egg white.

Whip chilled gelatin mixture until light and fluffy. Whip cream and fold into gelatin with nuts and flavoring. Spoon into 9-inch spring-form pan to a depth of about ½ inch.

Split 9 or 10 ladyfingers. Dip one end of each piece in melted chocolate. Stand chocolate-tipped ladyfingers upright around edge of pan, chocolate tips uppermost. Add about ⅓ remaining gelatin mixture, then layer of split ladyfingers, then another ⅓ of remaining gelatin mixture, another layer of ladyfingers. Make top layer gelatin. Chill until firm. Remove pan rim just before serving. Sprinkle with mixture of sugar and instant coffee. Garnish with whipped cream. Makes 12 servings.

LEMON-CREAM TORTE

Meringue Shell (page 460)

4 egg yolks

½ cup sugar

⅛ teaspoon salt

3 tablespoons grated lemon peel

3 tablespoons lemon juice

1 cup heavy cream

Prepare Meringue Shell. Let cool.

Make lemon filling: beat egg yolks in top part of double boiler until thick and lemon-colored. Beat in sugar gradually. Add salt, 1 tablespoon lemon peel, and all lemon juice. Cook over simmering water, stirring constantly until thickened. Let cool.

Whip cream stiff. Spread half of whipped cream in Meringue Shell. Pour cooled lemon filling on top of cream. Spoon remaining whipped cream on top. Sprinkle with remaining 2 tablespoons grated lemon peel. Chill 5 hours. Makes 8 servings.

VIENNA SACHERTORTE

5½ tablespoons softened butter
6 tablespoons sugar
3 (1-ounce) squares semi-sweet
   chocolate, melted
4 egg yolks

9 tablespoons sifted all-purpose
   flour
5 egg whites
2½ tablespoons apricot jam
Torte Frosting

Start oven at moderate (325° F.). Grease deep 8-inch round cake pan with removable bottom. Dust pan lightly with flour.

Beat butter and sugar together smoothly in mixing bowl until light and fluffy. Add chocolate and mix thoroughly. Add egg yolks, one at a time, beating well after each. Stir in flour until well combined. Whip egg whites until they stand in stiff points. Gently fold batter into egg whites. Pour into prepared pan.

Bake on lower shelf of oven about 1 hour and 15 minutes or until cake shrinks from sides of pan and cake tester inserted near middle comes out clean.

Let cake stand about 10 minutes on a cooling rack before turning out of pan. Turn cake out on rack. Turn right side up and let cool completely. When cold, place on platter and spread with apricot jam.

Torte Frosting

½ cup sugar
⅓ cup water

3½ (1-ounce) squares semi-sweet
   chocolate

Combine sugar and water in a small saucepan and bring to a boil. Turn down heat and simmer 2 or 3 minutes, stirring until sugar dissolves. Remove from heat, add chocolate, and stir until chocolate melts and mixture is smooth. Bring to a boil, stirring constantly. Remove from heat. Stir until frosting begins to thicken. Pour at once over cake. Let stand until frosting is set. Makes 8 to 10 servings.

The first time I had real Sachertorte in the place of its origin, the restaurant of the great Hotel Sacher, in Vienna, I was so impressed. Perhaps too impressed. Can it ever taste as good as it is supposed to taste? When you go to Vienna, remember you can order it from the finest pastry shop in the world, Demel's. They will make one for you to ship home. I ordered mine with St. Stephen's Church outlined in white icing on the shiny chocolate frosting, with "Grüsse von Wien" as a further reminder of its source. It was then packed tenderly in a wooden box and shipped air mail to the States, arriving almost immediately, fresh and unmarred. Total cost at the time, about $5.00.

CHAPTER TWELVE

Eggs

The eggs you buy should be freshly gathered farm eggs, or eggs from your own hens, or fresh eggs from the grocer, *eggs which he keeps in a refrigerator,* not stacked in cartons on the counter. For from the time the egg leaves the nest, it should be kept chilled until the cook breaks it into a bowl or puts it in a pan of water to cook.

The U. S. Department of Agriculture has established strict standards according to which eggs are judged for size and quality in labeling for the market. There is no nutritional difference between brown and white eggs.

Size ratings are established by weight per dozen, as follows:

Jumbo	Extra-Large	Large
30 oz.	27 oz.	24 oz.

Medium	Small	Peewee
21 oz.	18 oz.	15 oz.

Quality rating is determined by the appearance of the egg when taken out of its shell:

Grade AA: Egg, when broken, covers small area. White is thick, stands high. Yolk is firm and high.

Grade A: Egg covers moderate area. White is reasonably thick, stands fairly high. Yolk is firm and high.

Grade B: Egg covers a wide area. Has small amount of thick white. Yolk is somewhat flattened and enlarged.

Grade C: Egg covers very wide area. White is thin and watery. Yolk is flat, enlarged, breaks easily.

Grade AA and A eggs have a delicate flavor and are good for all purposes, especially poaching, frying, boiling, shirring, and for meringue and cake baking.

Keep eggs in the refrigerator or in a cold, airy place. Take them out of the cold 30 minutes to 1 hour before using for cake and other recipes in which the white is to be stiffly whipped. Do not wash eggs before storing.

BAKED CHEESE-EGGS

⅔ cup mayonnaise
¼ teaspoon salt
⅛ teaspoon pepper
1 teaspoon Worcestershire sauce
¼ cup milk

1 cup grated processed American cheese
6 eggs
3 tablespoons grated Parmesan cheese

Start oven at moderate (350° F.).

Combine mayonnaise, salt, pepper, and Worcestershire in saucepan. Add milk gradually, stirring until smooth. Add cheese. Cook over low heat, stirring constantly until cheese melts and mixture is thick and smooth, about 5 minutes.

Put 2 tablespoons cheese mixture in each of 6 custard cups. Break an egg into a saucer, slip egg into each cup. Add another 2 tablespoons cheese mixture to each cup. Sprinkle ½ tablespoon Parmesan on top of each. Set cups in shallow pan containing a little water.

Bake 25 to 30 minutes. Serve at once. Makes 6 servings.

A brunch favorite. Serve toasted scones or English muffins with these eggs. Canadian bacon and baked apple or half a grapefruit complete this menu.

CHAFING-DISH EGGS

3 cooked or canned artichoke bottoms
5 tablespoons butter or margarine
½ clove garlic, mashed

6 eggs
Salt and pepper
2 tablespoons cream
3 slices thick toast, buttered
Anchovy paste

Heat artichoke bottoms in chafing dish with 4 tablespoons butter or margarine and garlic. Discard garlic as soon as butter is very hot. Beat eggs slightly. Add to chafing dish. Season lightly with salt and pepper. Cook, stirring gently until eggs begin to set. Add cream and remaining 1 tablespoon butter or margarine. Cook 1 minute longer. Spread toast with anchovy paste. Serve eggs on toast at once. Makes 3 to 4 servings. Delicious Sunday morning—or night.

DEVILED EGGS

2 tablespoons prepared mustard
1 tablespoon sugar
1 tablespoon cream
1 tablespoon vinegar
½ teaspoon salt
8 hard-cooked eggs
Paprika
Finely cut parsley

Combine mustard, sugar, cream, vinegar, and salt in bowl. Beat until fluffy. Cut eggs in halves lengthwise. Remove yolks and mash with fork. Combine with mustard mixture to make smooth paste. Refill egg whites. Garnish with a little paprika and finely cut parsley. Makes 16 halves.

See Pickled Eggs, Stuffed Eggs, and appetizer chapter.

DEVILED EGGS-FOR-LUNCH

12 deviled stuffed-egg halves
1 (3-ounce) can chopped mushrooms
½ cup mayonnaise
¼ cup milk
6 tablespoons buttered crumbs

Start oven at moderately hot (400° F.).

Place stuffed eggs in lightly greased casserole. Drain juice from mushrooms, saving ¼ cup juice. Blend juice with mayonnaise and milk in saucepan over low heat and stir until smooth. Add mushrooms and mix. Pour over eggs in casserole. Sprinkle with crumbs.

Bake 10 minutes or until crumbs are browning. Makes 6 servings.

When buttering crumbs, add light sprinkling of orégano or sweet basil, a delicious variation which I call *Herbed Deviled-Egg Luncheon Dish*.

EGGS À LA FLAMENCA

Huevos a la Flamenca

Canned tiny peas
Eggs, 2 per person
Boiled ham, 2 small pieces per
  person

Mild tomato sauce
1 teaspoon butter or olive oil
  per person
Sliced canned pimiento

In individual casseroles arrange a bed of drained canned peas. Break over them 2 eggs, side by side. Add 2 pieces boiled ham, one at each side, so they do not cover eggs. Pour 2 or 3 tablespoons tomato sauce over all. Add butter or olive oil. Decorate with strips of pimiento. Cook under moderate broiler heat until eggs are set or cooked as much as each person likes them.

I enjoyed this dish at the Café Varela in Madrid. It is a wonderful, spacious old place, a favorite of artists, writers, and the intellectuals who like good food but have little money to spend on it.

EGGS BENEDICT

6 English muffins
6 small slices boiled ham
1 tablespoon butter
6 eggs
¾ cup mayonnaise

⅓ cup milk
½ teaspoon salt
¼ teaspoon pepper
1 teaspoon lemon juice
Paprika

Split muffins ready for toasting. Sauté ham lightly in butter a few minutes, just to heat through and brown lightly. Poach eggs.

Combine mayonnaise, milk, salt, and pepper in upper part of double boiler over hot water. Stir and cook 5 minutes, then add lemon juice. Toast muffins and place on warmed plates. Lay ham slice across muffin halves. Place poached egg on ham and spoon hot sauce over eggs. Sprinkle lightly with paprika. Serve at once. Makes 6 servings.

Hollandaise-Eggs Benedict: Omit sliced ham from above recipe. Spread toasted muffins with deviled ham, top with poached egg, and spoon Hollandaise Sauce (page 550) over egg. Drizzle with browned butter.

Some restaurants decorate the top of the egg with a small bit of canned truffle, sliced ripe olive, or finely cut parsley.

This is a gourmet dish the most overworked mother can manage, and children accept it as a fine supper dish, which, indeed, it can be. Good for Sunday brunch, too.

EGG BURGERS

6 hard-cooked eggs	½ teaspoon pepper
1 ½ cups cooked rice	1 cup bread crumbs
⅓ cup mayonnaise	Tomato Barbecue or Mushroom
2 teaspoons grated onion	Sauce (pages 558 and 553)
1 teaspoon salt	

Start oven at hot (450° F.). Grease baking sheet.

Chop or cut eggs coarsely. Combine with rice, mayonnaise, onion, salt, and pepper. Shape into 6 flat cakes. Coat well with crumbs. Place on prepared baking sheet.

Bake 15 minutes or until lightly browned. Serve hot with Tomato or Mushroom Sauce. Makes 4 servings.

Serve these burgers as main dish for luncheon or supper. The family's favorite mixed green salad goes well with them, or serve a salad of onion rings, green pepper, and grapefruit. A simple dessert, such as brownies or a warm fruit pudding, and coffee afterwards.

EGG CURRY

2 tablespoons butter or margarine	½ teaspoon salt
2 tablespoons flour	1 ⅓ cups milk, scalded
1 teaspoon curry powder	4 hard-cooked eggs
⅛ teaspoon paprika	1 cup cooked rice
½ tablespoon grated peeled onion	6 crisp patty shells

Cream butter or margarine and flour together in saucepan. Add curry powder, paprika, onion, and salt, and stir well. Add scalded milk. Cook and stir until mixture thickens. Chop or cut whites of eggs coarsely. Add with rice to sauce. Serve hot in patty shells. Garnish with grated yolks of eggs. Makes 6 servings.

An easy and delicious luncheon dish. For variation, omit patty shells, serve egg curry on saffron rice, garnish with scallions and green pepper rings. Serve toast or hot rolls with this, and fruit for dessert.

EGGS IN ASPIC

1	teaspoon salt	⅔	cup water
1	teaspoon vinegar	1⅓	cups consommé
4	eggs	2	tablespoons sherry
½	tablespoon unflavored gela-	1	tablespoon lemon juice
	tin		Fresh tarragon or dill

Fill heavy frying pan about ⅔ full of water. Add salt and vinegar. Let come to a boil, then reduce heat. Break eggs, one at a time, into saucer. Slip each carefully into simmering water, using egg poacher to keep eggs in even rounds, or trim eggs after poaching. The whites should be firm, yolks creamy soft. Remove eggs carefully from water with buttered skimmer. Set aside to cool at room temperature.

Soften gelatin in ⅔ cup cold water. Heat consommé and add softened gelatin, sherry, and lemon juice. Pour a layer of gelatin mixture into an oiled shallow pan and chill. Let remaining gelatin mixture cool at room temperature. When refrigerator aspic is almost firm, place eggs carefully in aspic. Sprinkle with finely cut tarragon leaves or dill. Cover eggs with slightly jelled aspic at room temperature. Let chill in refrigerator. To serve, cut out eggs in rounds, place on small chilled plates, garnish with remaining firm aspic cut in tiny cubes. Makes 4 servings.

A favorite for hot-weather buffet luncheon or supper. Can be made early in the day and kept in refrigerator.

EGGS IN SHELLS

Place eggs in saucepan and cover with cold water to at least 1 inch above eggs. Bring to a boil. Reduce heat at once.

For Medium-Soft Eggs, leave eggs in simmering water 2 to 4 minutes, depending on firmness desired.

For Hard-Cooked Eggs, put eggs in saucepan. Cover with cold water and cover pan. Bring water to a boil rapidly, then turn heat off. Remove saucepan from stove. Let eggs stand, covered, 20 minutes, then let cold water run over them 3 to 4 minutes. Drain, crack shells, and roll eggs between hands to loosen shells. Let cool. Remove shells. Use as called for in recipes.

Breakfast Tray

FRIED EGGS

Sunnyside Up

Use just enough butter, margarine, or fat to grease skillet. Heat until hot enough to sizzle a drop of water. Break eggs into saucer, one at a time. Slip each carefully into skillet. Lower heat when eggs are in skillet.

When white is set and edges cooked, add ½ teaspoon water per egg to skillet. Cover and cook until done as you like them. Season with salt and pepper. Serve at once.

Country-Fried Eggs: Use more fat in skillet. When eggs are set and edges browning, turn each egg with greased pancake turner. Cook lightly on other side. Serve hot with crisp bacon.

Eggs fried country-style make fine teen-ager sandwiches. Use thick slices of whole-wheat or white bread, buttered. Have prepared mustard, ketchup, and chili sauce at hand. A popular way to satisfy hunger after games or skating.

MRS. MCLENNAN'S SCOTCH EGGS

6 hard-cooked eggs, shelled	¼ cup water
1 ½ cups bread crumbs	1 pound sausage meat
1 egg, slightly beaten	Fat for deep-frying

Roll hard-cooked eggs in crumbs, then dip in beaten egg which has been mixed with water. Dip into crumbs again. Let stand 15 minutes at kitchen temperature to dry slightly. Divide sausage meat into 6 portions. Wrap each crumbed egg with sausage. Cover evenly and retain shape of egg. Roll again in beaten egg and crumbs. Let dry about 15 minutes.

Fry in deep, hot fat (375° F.) about 5 minutes or until sausage is cooked and browning. Drain on thick paper towels. Chill. Serve whole or cut in half with salad. Makes 6 or 12 servings.

These are quite good hot, but this would be sacrilege in Scotland! Their real advantage is that they may be made ahead of time and will keep several days in a covered dish in the refrigerator.

PICKLED EGGS

12 hard-cooked eggs	⅛ teaspoon celery seeds
1 ½ cups vinegar	3 peppercorns
½ cup water	2 whole cloves
2 tablespoons brown sugar	Small piece mace
1 teaspoon salt	Extra cloves for garnish
½ clove garlic, mashed	

Combine pickling ingredients in 1-quart enamel or glass saucepan. Bring to a boil over medium heat. Reduce heat and simmer 5 minutes. Strain.

Place 6 shelled eggs each in 2 glass jars or bowls. Pour hot pickling mixture over them. Cover, let cool, and set in refrigerator. Let chill several hours or overnight.

Poke whole cloves in each before serving, or cut eggs in halves and decorate each half with a thin ring of onion or black olive. Serve as appetizer or salad garnish. Makes 12 pickled eggs.

See also Deviled Eggs (page 289), Mushroom Stuffed Eggs (page 17), and appetizer chapter.

POACHED EGGS

Pour water about 2 inches deep in shallow wide saucepan or skillet. Heat water to boiling point. Break eggs into saucer one at a time. Slide one at a time into barely boiling water. For round shape use muffin rings or egg-poacher rings. Keep water simmering but not boiling. When eggs are cooked, 3 to 5 minutes, remove with slotted spoon or buttered pancake turner. Drain. Serve on toast on warmed dish. Season with salt and pepper. One or 2 eggs makes 1 serving.

One teaspoon of cider vinegar in the water is a good, old-fashioned way to keep whites intact.

SCRAMBLED EGGS

6 eggs	¼ teaspoon Worcestershire sauce
⅓ cup light cream	⅛ teaspoon pepper
¾ teaspoon salt	4 slices buttered toast

Beat eggs, then beat in cream and seasonings. Cook in upper part of double boiler over hot water until just set, stirring frequently. Serve at once on toast. (Foolproof. Super!)

Or eggs may be scrambled in small amount of fat in skillet or chafing-dish pan over direct heat. Stir frequently until set. Serve on toast. Makes 3 to 4 servings.

Cottage Scrambled Eggs: Use recipe above. When eggs are partially set, stir ½ cup large-curd cottage cheese into them. Cook only until eggs are set but still moist. Remove from heat at once. Serve on toasted English muffins or on buttered toast. Makes 4 servings.

To either cream scrambled or plain scrambled eggs various additions may be made for good flavor. Add 2 tablespoons finely cut chives or parsley, or add the same amount of finely cut green pepper or onion.

Just Plain Scrambled Eggs: Many men prefer this version. Use 2 eggs per person, salt, and freshly ground pepper. Beat eggs lightly. Pour into butter- or bacon-greased heavy skillet. Cook over low heat, stirring until desired consistency, firm or soft. Serve with crisp bacon or pan-fried potatoes with onion. I use about ¾ teaspoon salt to 6 eggs, and light grind of pepper.

SHIRRED EGGS

For each serving of shirred eggs, melt 1 teaspoon butter in an individual fireproof baking dish. Break 2 eggs into a saucer. Slip eggs into the melted butter and sprinkle with a little salt. Cook 1 minute over low heat.

Then pour about 1 tablespoon melted butter over egg. Set baking dish in moderate (350° F.) oven. Cook until whites are milky. Serve at once in baking dish or cut out and serve on buttered toast.

Shirred Eggs with Cream: Prepare as described. Substitute 2 or 3 tablespoons hot heavy cream for 1 tablespoon melted butter when egg goes into oven.

Shirred Eggs with Cheese Sauce: Spoon 2 or 3 tablespoons Cheese Sauce (page 546) over eggs when they go into oven for finishing.

Shirred Eggs with Shrimp Sauce: Spoon 2 or 3 tablespoons Shrimp Sauce (a few chopped shrimp added to Cream Sauce) over eggs when they go into oven for finishing.

Other variations: use Tomato Sauce, or Cream Sauce (page 557) with crumb topping, or chopped onion or chives in Cream Sauce.

TOASTED EGG CUPS

6 slices bread	¼ cup milk
2 tablespoons melted butter or margarine	1 teaspoon salt
6 eggs	¼ cup grated sharp processed cheese

Start oven at moderate (350° F.).

Remove crusts from bread. Brush both sides of slices with melted butter or margarine. Gently press each slice into a large custard cup or muffin-pan cup. Beat eggs slightly. Combine with milk, salt, and cheese. Divide egg mixture equally between bread cups. Set custard cups or muffin pan in shallow pan containing a little water. Bake 30 minutes. Makes 6 servings.

A brunch favorite, especially good with sausage or broiled ham.

Omelets

PLAIN OMELET

6 eggs
⅓ cup milk
¼ teaspoon salt

⅛ teaspoon freshly ground pepper
1 tablespoon butter or margarine
Parsley or water cress

Beat eggs slightly. Beat in milk and seasonings. Heat butter or margarine in 10-inch skillet. Tilt skillet so fat covers whole cooking surface. Pour in omelet mixture. Cook slowly. Run spatula around edge, lifting to let uncooked portion flow underneath. When egg is just cooked, loosen edge. Roll omelet or fold half over. With wide spatula, lift quickly to warm platter. Garnish with parsley or water cress. Makes 3 to 4 servings.

Extra good when served as base for creamed chicken or Chicken Sauce (page 548), Tomato Sauce, Curry Sauce (page 549).

An omelet is served at breakfast, brunch, luncheon, or supper. The various omelet recipes which follow make main dishes for many occasions.

CHINESE OMELET

Egg Fooyoung

8 eggs
1 cup finely cut celery
1 cup sliced canned mushrooms
1 cup finely cut string beans
1½ cups shredded cooked chicken

1 cup finely cut peeled onions
1 teaspoon salt
½ teaspoon white pepper
Peanut oil for cooking

Beat eggs slightly in large bowl. Mix remaining ingredients (except oil) into eggs. Divide into 8 portions. Grease hot skillet or chafing dish with a little peanut oil. Sauté "omelets" on one side until golden brown. Turn and sauté other side. Makes 8 small omelets, 4 servings.

Lobster Egg Fooyoung, Shrimp Egg Fooyoung: Substitute 1½ cups shredded cold boiled lobster or shrimp for chicken. Add ¼ cup finely cut green pepper or scallion tops to mixture.

This omelet is popular for teen-ager parties and also for any buffet or serve-yourself meal on the terrace or in the house. It is hearty and filling, delicious and easily made.

BAKED OMELET WITH AVOCADO SAUCE

4 eggs
½ teaspoon salt
¼ cup cold water
Quick grind black pepper
1 tablespoon butter

1 cup hot Medium White Sauce (page 557)
⅓ cup grated processed American cheese
1 cup diced avocado

Start oven at moderate (350° F.).

Beat yolks slightly. Beat whites until they stand in stiff points when beater is removed. Blend salt, cold water, pepper, and egg yolks into whites. Cook 2 to 3 minutes in butter in heavy frying pan. Set pan in oven 15 minutes.

While omelet bakes, make White Sauce. Stir cheese in until melted. Add avocado.

Remove omelet pan from oven. Spread a little avocado sauce over it. Fold omelet over and serve right from pan onto warmed plates at table. Top each serving with more sauce. Makes 4 servings.

Baked Omelet with Glazed Apples: Make omelet as described above, finishing in oven 12 to 15 minutes. Loosen, slide onto warmed plate. Sprinkle with confectioners' sugar and cinnamon. Cut in wedges quickly and lightly with 2 forks. Serve with sautéed sliced apples.

When sautéeing apples for this omelet, cook 2 pared, quartered, sliced apples in a little butter. Sprinkle with 2 tablespoons brown sugar, ½ teaspoon salt, and lightly with cinnamon as they cook. They should be glazed, soft, but not mushy, cooking 10 to 15 minutes.

PUFFY OMELET

4 eggs
2 tablespoons water
½ teaspoon salt

2 tablespoons flour
⅛ teaspoon pepper
1 tablespoon butter or margarine

Start oven at moderately slow (300° F.).

Beat egg whites until frothy. Add water and salt, then beat until stiff but not dry.

Combine yolks with flour and pepper. Beat until thick and lemon-colored. Fold yolks into whites.

Heat butter or margarine in 10-inch skillet. Pour omelet mixture in. Level it gently, leaving slightly higher around outside edge. Cook over low heat about 5 minutes, until puffy and lightly browned on bottom. Set pan in oven to finish, 8 to 10 minutes.

Omelet is done when knife inserted in center comes out clean. Loosen, fold, serve at once on warm plates. Makes 2 to 3 servings.

Jelly Omelet: Tart jelly, such as cranberry, is especially good with this omelet. Apple jelly is another favorite. Add jelly to omelet just before folding.

Tomato Omelet: Tomato Sauce or heated and seasoned chopped canned tomatoes may be served over a puffy omelet.

Spanish Omelet: Add chopped green pepper and onion to the tomatoes in above recipe.

RUM SOUFFLÉ OMELET

2 egg yolks
¼ cup sifted confectioners' sugar
1 tablespoon rum
4 egg whites
⅛ teaspoon salt
1 ½ tablespoons butter or margarine
Sifted confectioners' sugar for topping
Rum for flaming

Beat yolks until light and lemony. Beat in sugar gradually, then beat in rum. Whip egg whites stiff with salt added. Fold yolk mixture into whites.

Melt butter or margarine in 8-inch omelet pan. Tilt pan to spread fat. Pour in egg mixture. Cook over low heat. After 5 minutes loosen omelet gently around edge with spatula. Continue cooking 3 minutes or until golden on bottom and top is glazed. Tilt pan and, using spatula, fold over. Holding pan in one hand, rest it against edge of heated platter. Slip omelet onto platter with spatula. Sprinkle lightly with confectioners' sugar. Pour about 3 tablespoons rum into large cooking spoon. Ignite with match. Pour flaming rum over omelet and serve at once. Makes 2 servings.

Serve as main dish for luncheon or supper. A fine flavored soup first, this omelet, buttered toasted rolls with it, plenty of hot coffee, and chocolate cake for dessert make a Sunday luncheon.

SOUR-CREAM OMELET

5 eggs	2 tablespoons butter or margarine
1 cup commercial sour cream	Strawberry preserves or cranberry
1 teaspoon salt	jelly

Start oven at moderate (325° F.).

Beat egg yolks until thick and lemon-colored. Beat ½ cup sour cream into yolks with salt. Beat egg whites stiff. Fold yolks into whites. Heat butter or margarine in 10-inch skillet. Pour in omelet mixture, leveling gently. Cook over low heat about 5 minutes, until fluffy and lightly browned on bottom. Set pan in oven about 12 to 15 minutes or until top is golden. Loosen and slide onto warmed plate. Cut in wedges quickly with 2 forks. Serve at once with dab of remaining sour cream and either strawberries or cranberry jelly. Makes 3 to 4 servings.

A good brunch omelet. Have fresh brioche ready, coffee, and a fine melon.

SPAGHETTI LUNCHEON OMELET

3 eggs	2 tablespoons butter or marga-
¼ teaspoon salt	rine
⅛ teaspoon pepper	¾ cup grated processed Ameri-
1 can spaghetti in tomato-cheese	can cheese
sauce	2 tablespoons grated Parmesan

Start oven at moderate (375° F.).

Mix egg yolks, salt, and pepper with spaghetti and its sauce. Beat egg whites until they stand in stiff points when beater is removed. Fold spaghetti mixture into whites.

Melt butter or margarine in medium-size heavy skillet. Pour in omelet mixture. Cook over medium heat about 10 minutes or until brown around edges when lifted with fork. Sprinkle top with mixed cheese. Set pan in oven. Bake 10 minutes or until cheese is melted and top is browning. To serve, cut in 4 large wedges. Makes 4 servings.

Serve as supper dish too. It calls for an herb-dressed green salad and whole-wheat rolls. To finish this menu, a warm brandied fruit compote and coffee.

CHAPTER THIRTEEN

Fish and Shellfish

Fish and shellfish must be cooked as soon as caught. If you live too far from the sea or a well-stocked lake or stream, then buy from a reliable fish dealer and refrigerate your purchase until ready to cook, which should be very soon after your catch leaves the market man's iced counters.

Fresh fish should be just that—with bright, clear eyes full and moist. The flesh should be firm but elastic, moist and odorless, except for fresh fish odor. Gills should be red and fresh in color, not gray. Scales should cling tightly.

The recipes tell you how much to buy and what kind of fish. The fish dealer will draw and clean fish for you. Some dealers will bone shad and other sea food. On the dealer's counters the fresh fish are classed as *whole,* which means as caught, or *drawn,* which is fish eviscerated but head and tail left on. Small fish are sold drawn—they are ready to cook. *Dressed* fish means fish which have been scaled, eviscerated, head and tail removed, and any large, coarse fins cut off. *Pan-dressed* means ready for the pan, without further cleaning. And of course fish fillets, the joy of modern cooks, need no further attention from the fish dealer. These, sold fresh cut or quick-frozen, are the meaty sides of fish cut lengthwise away from the backbone. They are single, or butterfly—that is, unseparated sides of a fish—and sticks, which some dealers cut lengthwise or crosswise in uniform size.

Ask the fish dealer for his freshest and best. Substitute whatever he has for whatever fish you may have planned for that night's dinner. Ask for the newest in quick-frozen fish and shellfish and for new developments in canned sea food. Always have such specialties in your freezer and on the pantry shelf. They make up into delicious spur-of-the-moment meals, and they belong in your menu plans for day-to-day cookery.

One of the essentials of good fish cookery is fish stock. Make stock up whenever you buy whole fish. Keep stock in the freezer or refrigerator a few days only. Then use up. Make fresh stock when you buy whole fish again.

Lemon Garnishes for Fish

FISH STOCK

2 tablespoons butter	6 peppercorns
1 pound fresh fish trimmings and bones	3 cups water
	3 cups dry white wine
1 onion, peeled and sliced	¼ teaspoon salt
4 sprigs parsley	

Melt butter in 2-quart saucepan. Tilt pan to coat bottom and sides. Chop fish trimmings and bones. Add with onion, parsley, and peppercorns. Add about ½ cup water. Cover pan and simmer 20 minutes. Add remaining 2½ cups water, the wine, and salt. Cover and simmer gently 30 minutes longer. Strain stock. Use as described in recipes.

Fumet of Fish: Another name for highly seasoned fish stock. Usually contains bay leaf, few slices carrot, 1 or 2 stalks celery cut fine, added to above stock recipe. After stock is strained the fumet is cooked down, reduced a little. Use in making fish sauces and poaching fish.

FISH FORCEMEAT
Mousseline

Mousselines are small mousses, feathery, light mixtures cooked to garnish fish dishes. Also, mousseline forcemeat is used as the base of gelatin rings and various recipes.

Mild-flavored fish, such as halibut, sea bass, cod, haddock, sole, and shellfish, are used in making fish forcemeat or mousseline.

1 pound raw fish or shellfish	¼ teaspoon white pepper
2 egg whites	2 to 2½ cups heavy cream
½ teaspoon salt	

Free fish or shellfish of skin, shells, bones. Put flesh through finest cutter of food chopper. Beat in wooden bowl with heavy spoon or potato masher, working vigorously until smooth. Work egg whites into mixture. Add salt and pepper, beating or pounding until silky smooth. Force mixture through fine sieve into saucepan. Set pan in bowl of cracked ice. Continue to work or beat vigorously with wooden spoon, gradually adding cream to make a very smooth mixture. Makes about 3½ cups forcemeat to use in recipes.

QUENELLES

Shape mousseline forcemeat into small ovals with teaspoon or tablespoon. Use second spoon the same size to round off top. Dip second spoon into warm water and gently slide the quenelle off the first spoon, one by one, into shallow, well-buttered pan.

Add enough Fish Stock (page 302) to barely cover. Bring liquid slowly to a boil. Poach quenelles over low heat about 10 minutes, until they are firm.

Remove quenelles from stock with perforated spoon. Drain on thick paper towel or cheesecloth. Serve on heated platter with any fish sauce. Garnish platter with hot cooked shrimp, oysters, or mussels.

A delicacy for a guest luncheon. With it serve a Belgian endive salad, tiny rolls, honeydew melon or other fresh fruit. Champagne makes the perfect appetizer beverage before this luncheon. Delicate celery crackers with caviar its accompaniment.

THYRA SAMTER WINSLOW'S BOUILLABAISSE

Heads and tails 6 pounds cleaned fish
2 ½ quarts water
1 ½ teaspoons salt
½ teaspoon pepper
2 small onions, peeled and sliced
2 (No. 2 ½) cans tomatoes or 6 large tomatoes peeled and chopped fine
6 to 10 medium onions
2 green peppers
¾ cup olive oil
6 cloves garlic
1 teaspoon powdered allspice
3 tablespoons finely cut parsley
1 teaspoon thyme
1 bay leaf crumbled

¼ teaspoon cayenne
1 teaspoon salt
¼ teaspoon pepper
½ cup flour
6 pounds cleaned fish, assorted kinds, all mild-flavored
8 cups tomato-and-fish stock
½ teaspoon saffron
2 pounds canned, cooked, or quick-frozen shrimp, cleaned and deveined
2 lobsters, cooked and cut in pieces
1 pint dry white wine
1 lemon, sliced
8 to 12 thick slices toast or fried bread

Start this gigantic and delicious dish by making the necessary well-flavored fish stock. Place fish heads and tails in 3- or 4-quart kettle. Cover with 2½ quarts water. Add 1½ teaspoons salt, ½ teaspoon pepper, 2 small peeled and sliced onions. Bring to a boil, cover, and let simmer 1 hour or longer. Strain stock, then add tomatoes. Let boil and stir until slightly thickened. Remove from heat.

Peel and chop the 6 to 10 onions. Slice peppers, discarding stem end, seeds, and fiber. Chop and combine with onions in deep 1½-gallon kettle. Add olive oil. Let cook slowly until onions begin to turn yellow.

Peel and chop garlic very fine. Mix with spice, herbs, cayenne, salt, pepper, and flour. Cut fish into generous bite sizes. Rub fish on all sides with garlic mixture. Lay coated fish on the simmering onions and green peppers in large kettle. Cover and let cook 10 minutes. Turn fish carefully, stirring onions so they don't burn. Cook 8 to 10 minutes longer. Add tomato-fish stock. Stir saffron into a little of the stock, then stir into the kettle.

Add shrimp and lobsters. Cover and let boil 8 minutes. Add wine and lemon slices. Let come to a boil again.

Place a slice of toast in each large soup plate. Serve fish, shrimp, and lobster onto toast. Ladle bouillabaisse over all. Serve very hot. Makes 8 to 12 servings.

What to serve with bouillabaisse? A green salad topped with crumbled *bleu* cheese, coffee, fruit or fruit tart.

Thyra Samter Winslow once entered this recipe in a cookery contest I organized and won first prize. It's been my standard bouillabaisse recipe ever since—expensive but really memorable. A real winner of male hearts, by the way. Good for the career-girl cook, too, because it's even better made the night before it is to be served. Make up, except for wine and lemon slices. Refrigerate until just before serving time. Reheat to boiling point. Add wine, lemon, and serve in hot soup plates as described. Very nice served from a heated tureen. If there's any left over, it's even better the next day.

CODFISH CAKES

1 ½ cups or ½ (1-pound) package shredded salt cod
2 potatoes
1 tablespoon butter or margarine
1 teaspoon anchovy paste
2 eggs
Fat for deep-frying

Cover fish with cold water and bring to a boil. Remove from heat and let cool in the water 2 hours, then drain. Cover fish with fresh cold water and bring to a boil again. Boil gently 15 to 20 minutes or until fish is cooked. Drain and let cool. Remove all bones. Flake fish fine with fork, searching carefully for bones.

Scrub potatoes, rinse, and cover with water. Boil 20 to 30 minutes or until done, then drain. Scrape skins off. Put potatoes through ricer. Add fish and beat to combine evenly. Add butter or margarine and anchovy paste. Beat eggs, then mix into fish thoroughly.

Heat fat for frying to 375° F. on frying thermometer. Drop fish mixture by heaping tablespoonful, a few at a time, into hot fat. Fry 3 to 4 minutes or until cakes are browned on both sides. Drain on thick paper towels on pan in hot oven with door left open. Reheat fat slightly after each batch is fried. Serve hot with ketchup, chili sauce, or well-seasoned tomato sauce. Makes 4 to 6 servings.

CARP IN PAPRIKA SAUCE

1 ¼ pounds carp, cleaned, heads and tails removed
2 large yellow onions
1 teaspoon butter or margarine
2 cups water
1 teaspoon paprika
1 teaspoon salt

Slice fish in 6 pieces. Wash, peel, and chop onions. Cook in fat in a kettle until lightly browned. Add water and bring to a boil. Lower heat and let simmer 30 minutes. Add paprika and salt and stir well. Put in fish, cover kettle, and simmer 45 minutes. If additional liquid is needed, add a little bouillon or consommé. Makes 6 servings.

CRUSTY-TOPPED BAKED FISH

1 pound fish fillets
3 tablespoons flour
½ teaspoon salt
⅛ teaspoon paprika
⅛ teaspoon celery salt
½ tablespoon finely cut parsley
1 cup milk
4 tablespoons butter or margarine, melted
1 cup cracker crumbs or dry bread crumbs

Start oven at moderate (375° F.). Butter 1½-quart shallow baking dish.

Place fish in buttered baking dish. Sprinkle with flour, seasonings, and parsley. Combine milk, butter or margarine, and crumbs. Spread over fish.

Bake 25 minutes or until top is browned. Serve in baking dish or on warmed platter. Makes 3 or 4 servings.

This simple fish dish is quickly put together for luncheon or supper. With it serve buttered carrots, apple, orange, and green-pepper salad, and a chocolate meringue pie or tarts for dessert.

SUNDAY-BRUNCH FINNAN HADDIE

2 pounds finnan haddie
2 cups water
2 cups milk
1 green pepper, cut fine
8 onions, peeled and chopped
½ cup butter or margarine
½ cup flour
2 ½ cups light cream
2 cups poaching liquid
White pepper
½ cup buttered crumbs

Soak finnan haddie in combined water and milk for about 2 hours. Simmer fish gently in same liquid 15 minutes. Drain fish and save poaching liquid.

Start oven at moderately hot (400° F.).

Sauté green pepper and onions in butter or margarine in 2-quart saucepan until onion is transparent. Stir flour in slowly until smooth. Add cream, stirring constantly. Add 2 cups poaching mixture. Cook, still stirring, until sauce is smooth and thick. Add flaked fish and a quick grind of pepper. Pour mixture into 2½-quart baking dish. Cover with crumbs.

Bake about 20 minutes or until top is browned. Serve hot. Makes 6 servings.

Start brunch with broiled grapefruit. Serve the hot creamed haddie on thin toast. Hot coffee and warm blueberry cobbler to finish.

My father was no man for brunch. He was a man who expected—and got—three meals on Sunday. But finnan haddie was his favorite Sunday breakfast, running neck and neck with buckwheat cakes-with-sausages.

FLOUNDER OR SOLE, AMANDINE

4 fresh or quick-frozen flounder or sole fillets	3 tablespoons lemon juice
Salt and pepper	¼ cup slivered almonds
¼ cup flour	4 sprigs parsley
⅓ cup cooking oil	4 lemon wedges

Dip slightly thawed fish in lightly salted cold water. Dry on paper towel. Sprinkle lightly with salt and pepper, then coat with flour. Pan-fry in hot oil about 6 minutes or until cooked and browned on both sides. Remove fish to warmed platter.

Add lemon juice to oil in pan. Heat and pour over fish. Brown almonds quickly in same pan. Sprinkle over fish. Garnish with parsley and lemon wedges. Makes 4 servings.

A simple Friday luncheon or dinner dish. Serve new potatoes dressed with butter, broccoli or asparagus, corn bread or whole-wheat rolls, a lemon-meringue tart or raisin pie for dessert.

When I took my middle son, Paul, to New Orleans at the age of five, he lunched on this daily at Antoine's, the only place he deemed fit. A born gourmet, alas!

FLOUNDER WITH CHINESE SAUCE

1 ½	pounds fresh or quick-frozen flounder fillets		Pepper
½	cup cooking oil	2	tablespoons cornstarch
½	teaspoon garlic salt	1	cup cold water
2	tablespoons butter	2	onions, peeled and sliced thin
½	cup vinegar	2	tablespoons diced stem ginger
⅔	cup sugar	1	lemon peel, cut fine
2	teaspoons soy sauce	4	slices lemon

Sauté fish in oil 8 to 10 minutes. Keep fish hot on warmed platter. Mix garlic salt and butter in glass or enamel saucepan. Add vinegar, sugar, soy sauce, a quick grind of pepper, and mix well. Heat slowly. Stir cornstarch into 1 cup cold water. Add to butter mixture and bring to a boil. Add onions, ginger, and lemon peel. Cook 5 minutes. Pour over hot fish on platter. Garnish with lemon slices. Makes 4 or more servings.

Add hot rice to the menu when you serve this savory fish. Fresh fruit or sherbet or a fruit pie makes a good dessert.

STUFFED FLOUNDER FILLETS

1	pound spinach	1	teaspoon Kitchen Bouquet
2	tablespoons dry bread crumbs	1	(3-ounce) can sliced broiled mushrooms
½	teaspoon salt		
⅛	teaspoon pepper	1	teaspoon cornstarch
1	teaspoon prepared mustard	¼	cup finely cut peeled onions
4	flounder fillets	2	tablespoons finely cut parsley
2	tablespoons butter or margarine	¼	cup commercial sour cream

Wash spinach thoroughly. Do not drain. Cook in own moisture in covered saucepan about 20 minutes. Drain and chop fine. Combine with crumbs, salt, pepper, and mustard.

Place a portion of spinach mixture on broad end of each fillet. Roll up and fasten with wooden pick. Blend butter or margarine and Kitchen Bouquet. Brush over rolled fillets. Arrange fish in shallow casserole.

Start oven at moderate (350° F.).

Combine mushrooms and their liquid with cornstarch in small sauce-pan. Bring to a boil, and stir constantly. Pour over fish rolls. Sprinkle with onion and parsley.

Bake about 30 minutes or until fish flakes easily. Remove from oven. Remove wooden picks. Top rolls with sour cream. Place casserole under broiler just long enough to brown slightly, about 5 minutes. Serve at once. Makes 4 servings.

Many cooks make their own version of stuffed, rolled fillets, using whatever green vegetable is in the kitchen. Finely chopped broccoli or asparagus stalks are delicious in this recipe. It makes a perfect luncheon dish but is much appreciated as a dinner entrée too. Serve crisp shoe-string or French-fried potatoes with it (oven-warmed, quick-frozen potatoes) and small hot rolls with jelly. Orange layer cake or custard for dessert.

SAVORY HALIBUT STEAKS

6 halibut steaks	2 tablespoons bread crumbs
2 tablespoons butter	½ cup white wine
2 small onions, peeled and grated	½ cup consommé
2 tablespoons finely cut parsley	½ cup croutons
1 tablespoon each chopped pecans, almonds, hazelnuts	3 tablespoons butter

Dip steaks in cold salted water. Drain, and dry on paper towel. Melt 2 tablespoons butter in shallow pan with tight cover. Place steaks in butter and spread with onions and parsley. Add enough water to pan to cover bottom and make steam. Heat to boiling point, cover pan, and simmer 15 minutes or until fish is done and water cooked away.

Put nuts and crumbs in small saucepan. Shake over low heat about 3 minutes or until crumbs are browned. Stir from time to time. Add wine and consommé, mix, and bring to boiling point.

Brown croutons in 1 tablespoon butter in shallow baking dish. Lay fish and onion-parsley mixture from fish kettle on croutons. Pour nut sauce over all. Add dabs of butter. Brown under broiler heat 3 to 5 minutes. Serve hot. Makes 6 servings.

SAVORY BAKED HADDOCK

2 (12-ounce) packages quick-frozen haddock fillets	2 tablespoons chili sauce
1 onion, peeled and sliced	½ clove garlic, mashed
1 tablespoon butter or margarine	½ teaspoon prepared mustard
	½ teaspoon salt
1 (10-ounce) can tomato sauce	¼ teaspoon thyme
1 tablespoon Worcestershire sauce	½ teaspoon basil
	2 teaspoons sugar

Let fillets thaw slightly. Cut each block into 4 pieces. Place in large casserole.

Start oven at moderately hot (400° F.).

Sauté onion in butter or margarine until tender. Add tomato sauce, Worcestershire, chili sauce, garlic, mustard, salt, thyme, basil, and sugar. Mix and simmer gently 8 minutes. Remove garlic. Pour sauce over fillets in casserole.

Bake 20 to 30 minutes or until fish flakes easily. Makes 4 servings.

This is a hearty dish. Brown rice or mashed potatoes goes well with it and so does tossed green salad. Keep dessert simple, such at a warm compote of mixed fruits with cooky, and coffee.

Cheese Baked Haddock: Use above recipe to prepare haddock for baking. Cover thawed fish in casserole with Cheese Sauce (page 546) and top with crumbs. Bake about 20 to 30 minutes or until top is browned. Makes 4 servings.

Cheese-and-Macaroni Haddock: For variety, add a layer of cooked and drained macaroni or pasta shells to the thawed fillets in casserole. Cover with cheese sauce. Sprinkle top with grated Parmesan cheese mixed with buttered crumbs. Bake 25 to 30 minutes. Makes 4 servings.

HALIBUT FILLETS WITH ONION AND ALMONDS

1 ¼ pounds fresh or quick-frozen halibut fillets	2 tablespoons boiling-hot bouillon, consommé, or fish stock
2 scallions, sliced thin	1 chicken bouillon cube
2 tablespoons slivered almonds	1 ½ teaspoons lemon juice
2 tablespoons butter or margarine	

Start oven at moderate (350° F.).

If frozen fish are used, thaw as directed on package. Place fish in greased baking dish. Top with scallions. Sauté almonds in butter or margarine in saucepan until lightly browned. Stir in remaining ingredients until bouillon cube is dissolved. Pour over fish in casserole.

Bake 20 to 30 minutes, until fish flakes easily. Makes 4 servings.

DEEP-DISH HERRING PIE

From an 1805 recipe

Pastry for top crust
2 fresh herring
1 blade mace
½ teaspoon pepper
¾ teaspoon salt
3 tablespoons butter or margarine

2 apples, pared, cored, and diced
2 onions, peeled and sliced
6 to 8 tablespoons water or milk

Prepare pastry for top crust. Start oven at hot (425° F.).

Clean herring and rinse. Cut in pieces. Remove fins and tail. Season fish with beaten mace (or use ½ teaspoon powdered mace), pepper, and salt. Put about 1 tablespoon butter or margarine in 1½-quart baking dish. Place herring in dish. Add apples and onions. Add dabs of remaining 2 tablespoons butter or margarine. Pour a little water or milk over all.

Cut pastry to cover dish. Pierce with fork to allow steam to escape. Fit pastry over top and crimp edge to rim of dish.

Bake 45 minutes, or longer if fish are large and thick. Makes 4 to 6 servings.

One or 2 small potatoes may be pared, sliced, and added with apples and onions and an additional 2 tablespoons water or milk. Another version of this dish is made with *smoked herring*. Soak herring overnight, drain, and remove all bones. Baking time is then reduced to about 30 minutes.

BAKED MACKEREL WITH TOP DRESSING

1 mackerel	1 teaspoon finely cut parsley
1 medium onion, peeled and cut fine	1 (No. 2) can tomatoes
	1½ teaspoons salt
1 green pepper, cut fine	½ teaspoon pepper
2 tablespoons oil	Paprika
2½ cups soft bread crumbs	

Select 3-pound mackerel. Have fish cleaned and split by fish dealer. Start oven at moderate (350° F.). Lay fish in oiled baking dish, flesh side up.

Cook onion and ½ of green pepper in 1 tablespoon oil until soft but not brown. Mix with crumbs and add parsley. Drain tomatoes and moisten crumb mixture with tomato juice. Season with salt and pepper. Mix well and spread on top of fish. Cover top of dressing with whole, drained tomatoes. If tomatoes are very large, quarter them before placing on fish. Scatter remaining green pepper on top. Add light sprinkling of salt, pepper, and paprika. Add remaining 1 tablespoon oil.

Bake 45 minutes. Serve in baking dish. Makes 6 servings.

This is a hearty fish dish, good at any time of the year. I like to serve spoon bread with it, and for dessert, a deep-dish plum pie. I once caught fifty-two young mackerel! When mackerel are running they'll take *any* bait, including a bit of red flannel. This can mean fish for the whole neighborhood. This is a fine recipe to bring out if you have eager deep-sea fishermen—or maybe just dock fishermen—around.

BROILED MACKEREL, MAÎTRE D'HÔTEL

1 whole mackerel or 1½ pounds fillets	½ teaspoon salt
	¼ teaspoon pepper
2 tablespoons cooking oil	Cayenne
2 tablespoons butter or margarine	1 tablespoon lemon juice
	2 tablespoons finely cut parsley

Select 3-pound mackerel. Have fish dealer clean and split it for broiling. Or buy fillets.

Start broiler at hot (450° F.).

Brush fish with oil on all sides. Place on greased broiler rack, skin side down, 2 inches below heat. Broil 5 minutes, then turn fish and broil on other side 3 minutes.

While fish broils, melt butter or margarine. Mix with salt, pepper, a few grains of cayenne, the lemon juice, and parsley. Place fish on warmed serving platter, pour butter sauce over it, and serve at once. Makes 4 to 6 servings.

Boiled new potatoes or succotash taste good with this fish. Toast small rolls. Serve your best peach or apple pie for dessert.

BROILED MACKEREL WITH MINT

1 whole mackerel or 1 ½ pounds fillets	¾ teaspoon salt
	1 teaspoon finely cut fresh mint
4 tablespoons butter or margarine	

Select 3-pound mackerel. Have fish dealer clean and split it for broiling. Or buy fillets.

Start broiler at hot (450° F.).

Melt 2 tablespoons butter or margarine, add salt. Brush on all sides of fish. Place on greased broiler rack skin side down 2 inches from heat. Broil 5 minutes. Turn fish and broil 3 minutes.

While fish broils, melt remaining 2 tablespoons butter. Mix with mint. Place fish on warmed serving platter. Pour mint butter over fish and serve. Makes 4 to 6 servings.

A delicate fish dish which is better for a spring luncheon than for any other occasion. New asparagus or parsleyed very small new potatoes go with this fish. Serve a delicate orange or lemon soufflé for dessert.

HERBED SALMON STEAKS

2 salmon steaks about ¾ inch thick	Juice 1 lemon
	½ teaspoon thyme
1 clove garlic, peeled and mashed	½ teaspoon salt
	3 tablespoons finely cut parsley
¼ cup salad oil	

Dip steaks in slightly salted water. Dry on paper towel. Remove center bone and long bones from steaks. Place steaks in shallow dish. Combine remaining ingredients, pour over fish, and cover dish. Let marinate in refrigerator 1 hour. Turn steaks occasionally.

Preheat broiler 10 minutes. Broil drained steaks 2 inches from heat about 3 minutes on each side or until easily flaked with fork. Brush once or twice with remaining marinade during broiling. Divide to make 4 servings, or, if steaks are small, serve whole to 2 persons.

Baked or scalloped potatoes are a good accompaniment to this fish. Serve a salad of sliced cucumbers and tomatoes, toasted small rolls, and homemade ice cream with lemon cake.

MACKEREL PIE WITH HERBS

1 ½	pounds mackerel fillets	⅓	cup crumbs
1	teaspoon salt	¼	cup lemon juice
¼	teaspoon pepper	4	egg yolks
½	teaspoon thyme or orégano	2	tablespoons cider vinegar
¼	teaspoon marjoram		Pastry for 1 crust pie

Start oven at hot (450° F.).

Season fillets with salt, pepper, and herbs. Butter shallow baking dish. Line bottom with crumbs. Place fish on crumbs. Pour lemon juice over fish. Beat yolks, mix with vinegar, and pour over fish.

Roll pastry ⅛ inch thick. Cover dish, trim edges, and press pastry to dish with tines of fork. Pierce in several places with fork to let steam escape.

Bake 10 minutes. Reduce heat to moderate (350° F.) and bake 30 minutes longer. Makes 6 servings.

Small baked potatoes, new green peas, and a tomato-aspic salad are good menu companions for this fish pie. A fruit sherbet, such as pineapple or raspberry, makes a refreshing dessert.

SALMON MOLD

1 ½	tablespoons unflavored gelatin	1	teaspoon Worcestershire sauce
½	cup cold water		Pepper
1	cup boiling water	½	cup finely diced celery
1	chicken bouillon cube	1	(7 ¾-ounce) can salmon
½	teaspoon salt		Water cress
¼	cup lemon juice		
3	tablespoons finely cut peeled onion		

Soak gelatin in cold water, then dissolve in boiling water with bouillon cube. Add salt, lemon juice, onion, Worcestershire, and quick grind of pepper. Chill until it begins to set. Then add celery and salmon, which has been drained and flaked, all skin and bones removed. Transfer mixture to mold. Chill until set.

Unmold on chilled platter, garnish with water cress. Serve with mayonnaise or Tartare Sauce (page 524). As part of buffet vegetable salad platter, especially good with romaine, Belgian endive, and green pepper rings. Makes 4 servings.

Delicious as a luncheon main dish for a summer day. Small hot rolls, cold green salad, tea or coffee, and strawberry shortcake make a guest menu with the salmon.

SALMON WITH SHRIMP SAUCE

1 quart dry ginger ale or champagne	4-pound salmon, cleaned, ready to cook
2 cups water	2 tablespoons butter or margarine
2 stalks celery, cut fine	
1 onion, peeled and sliced	2 tablespoons flour
1 tablespoon salt	2 egg yolks
½ teaspoon pepper	2 cups heavy cream
1 bay leaf	1 pound small shrimp, cleaned and cooked, or deveined quick-frozen shrimp
3 peppercorns	
3 cloves	

Combine champagne or ginger ale with water, celery, onion, salt, pepper, bay leaf, peppercorns, and cloves in saucepan. Bring to a boil. Wrap salmon carefully in 2 thicknesses of wet cheesecloth and place in boiling stock. Cover, and cook over lowered heat about 1 hour. Remove salmon, unwrap carefully, and place fish on warmed serving platter, and keep it warm.

Strain stock. Measure 1 cup. Melt butter or margarine in saucepan. Stir in flour smoothly. Add the 1 cup stock, stirring constantly until boiling. Reduce heat. Cook, stirring, 5 minutes. Beat egg yolks in bowl. Add cream. Slowly add a little of the hot sauce, beating constantly to prevent curdling. Return mixture to saucepan, mix, and add shrimp. Reheat slowly over low heat. Do not boil. Serve with salmon. Makes 8 to 10 servings.

Cold Boiled Salmon: Cook salmon as described in above recipe. Unwrap, let cool few minutes, then chill in covered dish in refrigerator. Serve very cold with cold mayonnaise mixed with finely chopped cucumber and water cress. Makes 10 servings.

MRS. RODRIGUEZ' SALMON WITH SHRIMP AND MUSHROOMS

Saumon à la Brantôme

1 (7 to 8-pound) salmon	½ teaspoon salt
1 bottle dry white wine	¼ teaspoon pepper
6 onions, peeled and sliced	15 raw shrimp, shelled and cleaned
6 carrots, scraped and sliced	
1½ teaspoons mixed herbs: basil, orégano, thyme, marjoram	

Have salmon cleaned but leave head and tail on. Place in a kettle large enough to cook the fish whole. Add wine, onions, carrots, herbs, salt, and pepper. If more liquid is needed, add a little hot water or consommé mixed with white wine. Heat until boiling. Reduce heat, cover kettle, and let fish simmer slowly. When simmering begins add shrimp. Cover again, let simmer 1 hour.

While fish is cooking make the sauce:

1 onion, peeled and minced fine	2 cups fish stock or consommé
3 tablespoons butter	½ bottle white wine
3 tablespoons flour	1 cup cognac

Brown onion in butter. Add flour, stir, and brown thoroughly. Add stock or consommé, stirring until it boils about 4 minutes and is thickened. Remove from heat.

In another (2-quart) saucepan combine the half bottle of wine and the cognac. Set over heat, add onion sauce at once, stirring and blending. Cover pan. Turn heat down, and let sauce reduce about 1 hour or until it measures about 2½ to 3 cups. Watch carefully, stirring frequently. Do not let it boil. It should simmer. Strain and reheat to serve.

Prepare the mushrooms which are to garnish the fish:

12 mushrooms	Few drops herb vinegar
1 tablespoon olive oil	1 tablespoon minced parsley
½ teaspoon essence garlic	

Wash, drain, and dry mushrooms. Sauté in oil in frying pan. Add garlic essence, parsley, vinegar. Mix and stir about 5 minutes.

When ready to serve fish, remove salmon and shrimp from pot in which they have cooked. Place salmon on a warmed platter. Surround with alternating mounds of shrimp and mushrooms. Serve strained onion-and-wine sauce separately with the fish. Makes 8 or more servings.

The foregoing mushroom garnish recipe is from the Chilean Embassy in Washington given to me years ago but still a favorite whenever I want to prepare a memorable fish dish.

SALMON CROQUETTES

3 tablespoons butter or margarine
3 tablespoons flour
½ teaspoon salt
¼ teaspoon pepper
1 cup milk
2 cups finely flaked cooked or canned salmon
1 tablespoon finely cut parsley
1 tablespoon finely cut peeled onion
2 hard-cooked eggs, diced
2 eggs
2 tablespoons heavy cream
1 teaspoon lemon juice
1 cup fine bread crumbs
Fat for deep frying

Melt butter or margarine in saucepan over low heat. Stir in flour, salt and pepper. Add milk gradually, stirring constantly. Cook sauce, stirring constantly until smooth and thick. Add salmon, parsley, onion, hard-cooked eggs. Cook over low heat 4 or 5 minutes, stirring occasionally.

Beat 1 egg lightly with cream. Stir into salmon mixture. Cook, stirring 1 or 2 minutes. Remove from heat and add lemon juice. Let mixture cool few minutes, then pour into buttered shallow dish or pan. Let cool completely.

Shape into croquettes. Roll each in crumbs. Beat remaining egg lightly with 2 tablespoons water. Dip crumbed croquettes into egg and again into crumbs.

Heat fat to 390° F. on frying thermometer.

Fry croquettes, a few at a time, until delicately browned. Drain on thick paper towels in pan in hot oven with door left open. Serve with any fish sauce or with chili sauce. Makes 6 servings.

SALMON FOR THE CHILDREN'S LUNCH

2 cups peas, 1 pound fresh or 1 (12-ounce) package quick-frozen
½ cup milk
1 (10½-ounce) can condensed cream-of-chicken soup
1 (8-ounce) can salmon, drained
5 or 6 pieces buttered toast

Cook peas in small amount of salted water until tender, then drain. Combine milk and soup in upper part of double boiler over hot water. Stir to mix well. Add peas and flaked salmon, and heat thoroughly. Serve on toast. Makes 5 to 6 servings.

SALMON SCALLOP

1	(12-ounce) package quick-frozen peas	1½	cups milk
1	(1-pound) can salmon	½	teaspoon salt
1	small onion, peeled and sliced	¼	teaspoon pepper
		1	bay leaf
4	tablespoons butter or margarine	2	bouillon cubes
		½	cup sliced ripe olives
4	tablespoons flour	¼	cup dry bread crumbs
		½	cup grated Cheddar cheese

Cook peas according to directions on package, then drain. Drain and flake salmon. Sauté onion in butter or margarine 2 or 3 minutes. Stir in flour smoothly. Stir in milk, cooking over moderate heat until smooth and thickened. Add salt, pepper, bay leaf and bouillon cubes. Cook, stirring frequently, until sauce is bubbly.

Start oven at moderate (350° F.). Butter 1½-quart casserole lightly.

Combine peas, salmon, and olives in prepared casserole. Remove bay leaf from sauce. Pour sauce over salmon combination. Sprinkle top with crumbs and cheese.

Bake 30 minutes or until top is browned. Makes 4 to 6 servings.

A simple dish for luncheon or supper. Makes a good Sunday-night supper dish. Tossed green salad or an aspic ring filled with vegetable salad goes well with the salmon. Serve strawberry preserves, creamed cheese, crackers, and coffee afterwards.

BATTER-FRIED SARDINES

For an easy and good supper, open a can of boneless, skinless sardines and drain them. Dip each in batter. Coat with thick layer of crushed corn flakes. Sauté in butter or margarine about 5 minutes or until golden brown on all sides. Serve with new potatoes, string beans, an onion-and-tomato salad, buttered toast or toasted rolls, and coffee.

SEA BASS IN CHINESE SAUCE

1½	cups uncooked rice	3	tablespoons soy sauce
3	pounds sea-bass fillets	¼	cup white wine
3	tablespoons peanut oil	1	tablespoon chopped preserved ginger
Drop or two of sesame oil			
6	scallions, sliced thin	1	cup water

Cook rice according to directions on package.

While rice cooks, dip fish in cold salted water. Drain and wipe dry on paper towel. Heat oil and drop of sesame oil in skillet with tight cover. Add scallions and cook 2 minutes, stirring. Add fish, pour soy sauce and wine over all, and add ginger and water. Cover skillet. Bring to a boil, then lower temperature and simmer 15 minutes. Test fish for doneness; should flake easily with fork. Cook uncovered a few minutes longer if necessary. Serve hot on hot rice. Makes 6 servings.

Canned Chinese fried noodles may be substituted for the rice. Crisp the noodles in hot oven few minutes. Spoon onto hot serving platter. Spoon fish mixture on top. Serve at once.

DELICIOUS, DELICATE SOLE

1	cup champagne or dry ginger ale	2	teaspoons finely cut parsley
2	tablespoons butter	2	tablespoons heavy cream
2	tablespoons grated peeled onion	4	sole fillets
1	bay leaf	2	teaspoons salt
¼	cup chopped mushrooms	1 ½	teaspoons pepper
		2	tablespoons grated Gruyère or Parmesan cheese

Start oven at moderate (375° F.). Butter shallow casserole.

Combine champagne or ginger ale, butter, onion, bay leaf, mushrooms, and parsley in saucepan. Bring to a boil, reduce heat, and cook slowly until reduced by half. Remove bay leaf, add cream, and mix. Remove pan from heat.

Dip fillets in slightly salted water. Drain and wipe dry with paper towel. Sprinkle fish with salt and pepper. Place in baking dish. Pour sauce over them. Sprinkle with cheese.

Bake 25 minutes or until top is browned. Makes 4 servings.

Start this luncheon or dinner with champagne. Serve with it pâté and chunky French bread. Give your guests a first course of Boola-boola soup, then the sole garnished with water cress, braised celery with almonds, and small dinner rolls. For dessert, baked gingered peaches.

SEA BASS MOUSSE

Mrs. George Washington Kavanaugh's Recipe

1	pound cooked sea-bass meat	1	teaspoon Worcestershire
¾	tablespoon plain gelatin		sauce
2	tablespoons water	1	tablespoon dry mustard
2	egg yolks	1	teaspoon grated onion
1 ½	tablespoons soft butter	⅛	teaspoon cayenne
½	tablespoon flour	¼	cup cider vinegar
1 ½	teaspoons salt	¼	cup lemon juice
2	teaspoons sugar	¾	cup milk

The cooked fish should be free of all bones. Use fork to flake it smoothly.

Soak gelatin in 2 tablespoons water. Beat egg yolks in upper part of 1-quart double boiler over hot water. Stir in butter and flour smoothed together, salt, sugar, Worcestershire sauce, mustard, onion, cayenne, vinegar, lemon juice, and milk. Stir steadily until thickened. Remove from heat. Add softened gelatin and stir until dissolved. Let cool until slightly set.

Use 1½-quart ring mold rubbed with cooking oil. Pour ⅓ gelatin mixture into mold. Let set 5 minutes. Add ⅓ fish. Repeat with gelatin and fish until all is used. Pour last of gelatin on top. Chill until firm, about 3 hours. Garnish with water cress. Serve with Cucumber Sauce (page 548). Makes 6 servings.

A delicate dish for a guest luncheon. Serve hot tomato bouillon first. Add toasted rolls or small hot biscuits, and a hearty dessert such as pecan pie or parfait and cake.

Mrs. Kavanaugh was a famous New York hostess, whose East Sixty-Second street house was a center of social entertaining. Her beautiful buffet tables (this was often a feature) were as much a trademark as her famed emeralds.

BAKED SHAD WITH STUFFING

	4-pound shad, cleaned and boned by fish dealer	1	tablespoon finely cut peeled onion
	Salt and pepper	1 ½	tablespoons flour
2	(12-ounce) packages quick-frozen chopped spinach	½	cup commercial sour cream
		1	tablespoon lemon juice
5	tablespoons butter	¼	cup dry white wine

Dip shad in slightly salted water. Wipe dry with paper towel. Season inside with salt and pepper. Cook spinach according to directions on package, then drain. Melt 3 tablespoons butter in saucepan. Sauté onion until tender. Stir in flour smoothly. Blend until bubbly. Add spinach and cook, stirring constantly until thickened. Remove from heat. Add sour cream, lemon juice, ½ teaspoon salt, and ¼ teaspoon pepper. Mix well.

Start oven at moderate (325° F.). Rub shallow oblong baking dish lightly with butter.

Stuff head and body of shad with spinach mixture. Tie in shape and place in prepared baking dish. Add wine to dish. Sprinkle lightly with salt and pepper and dot with remaining 2 tablespoons butter.

Bake uncovered about 45 minutes. Baste frequently with wine in dish, and add more wine if needed. Test for doneness: fish should flake easily with fork. Serve immediately. Makes 6 servings.

A spring dinner favorite. Serve new asparagus or broiled mushrooms with it, or new peas and tiny new potatoes cooked together, and fresh strawberries for dessert. I serve this to foreign guests. So American.

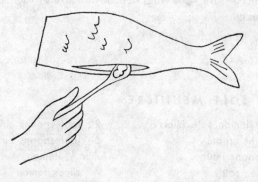

SHAD ROE

Rinse fresh roe in slightly salted water. Drain on thick paper towels or gently wipe dry. Do not break roe skin. Cover with lightly salted water. Add 1 tablespoon lemon juice or cider vinegar. Bring to a boil, lower heat, and simmer 5 to 10 minutes, depending on thickness of roe Drain. Use in baked and broiled recipes.

Baked Roe: Place parboiled roe in lightly greased baking dish. Baste with melted butter. Bake 5 to 8 minutes in moderate (350° F.) oven. Turn roe carefully with buttered pancake turner to brown both sides. Baste with butter once or twice during baking. Roe should be baked through but not hard anywhere. Serve with garnish of lemon wedges or crisp curls of bacon, or both.

Broiled Roe: Place parboiled roe in greased shallow pan. Broil under moderate heat, basting once or twice with melted butter. Turn roe carefully, using buttered pancake turner, to brown both sides. Or broil bacon in pan under high broiler heat until bacon is half done, lower heat, and place parboiled roe in same pan. Let roe broil as bacon finishes. Turn roe so it is cooked through but not hard. Drain roe and bacon and serve on warmed platter.

Pan-Fried Roe: Sauté parboiled roe in frying pan with very little butter. Turn roe once or twice to cook through and brown lightly. Add a little more butter for last 2 or 3 minutes of cooking. Place cooked roe on warmed platter. Add juice of ½ lemon to butter in pan. Stir and pour over roe on platter. Delicious with au gratin potatoes as luncheon feature.

Amount needed for 4 servings depends on size of roe. Ask fish dealer when in doubt.

ENGLISH SOLE MEUNIÈRE

1 ½ pounds lemon sole fillets	2 tablespoons olive oil
1 cup light cream	6 tablespoons butter
3 tablespoons flour	Juice ½ lemon
1 teaspoon salt	4 slices lemon
½ teaspoon pepper	

Dip fillets in slightly salted water. Drain, and wipe dry on paper towel. Pour cream into deep plate. Dip fillets in cream, then into flour mixed with salt and pepper. Sauté fillets in olive oil until brown on one side. Turn fish carefully and brown other side.

Melt butter in small saucepan. Combine with lemon juice. Pour over fish on warmed serving platter. Serve at once, garnished with lemon slices. Makes 4 servings.

Good flavor combinations with this dish: parsleyed new potatoes and asparagus Hollandaise. Fresh fruits for dessert.

Flounder Meunière: Use flounder fillets in recipe for English Sole Meunière.

FILLETS OF SOLE, BONNE FEMME

2 pounds sole or flounder fillets	1 teaspoon finely cut parsley
¾ cup dry sherry or white wine	½ teaspoon salt
Juice 1 lemon	2 cups Medium Cream Sauce
1 small onion, peeled and cut fine	(page 557)
	¼ cup heavy cream
1 (6-ounce) can sliced mushrooms	1 egg yolk
	4 to 8 whole broiled mushrooms

Start oven at moderate (325° F.).

Dip fillets in slightly salted water. Drain, and wipe dry on paper towel. Place fish in buttered shallow baking dish. Pour sherry or wine, lemon juice, onion, mushrooms, parsley, and salt over fish.

Bake 20 minutes or until fish is done.

While fish bakes, prepare Cream Sauce. Also whip cream and beat egg yolk. Combine sauce, cream, and yolk. Spread over cooked fish. Add mushrooms. Brown under moderate broiler 3 or 4 minutes. Serve at once in baking dish. Makes 6 servings.

A delicious fish for guest luncheon. Especially liked by men, and a recipe you will use many times after the family once samples the dish.

BAKED SOLE MOUSSE

Turn prepared Mousseline Forcemeat (page 303), made with sole, into well-buttered charlotte or ring mold. Cover mold with buttered waxed paper. Set mold in shallow pan containing a little hot water.

Bake mousse in moderate oven (350° F.) 15 to 18 minutes or until knife inserted in center comes out clean. Unmold mousse on warmed serving dish. Serve with any preferred fish sauce. Makes 4 to 6 servings.

SUNDAY-SUPPER SOLE

8 sole or flounder fillets	½ teaspoon chopped scallion
1 cup Medium Cream Sauce (page 557)	¾ pound crab meat
	3 hard-cooked eggs, chopped
½ cup mayonnaise	½ teaspoon salt
1 teaspoon dry mustard	¼ teaspoon pepper
½ teaspoon prepared mustard	3 tablespoons grated Parmesan cheese
1 teaspoon chopped pimiento	
½ teaspoon Worcestershire	

Start oven at moderately hot (400° F.). Butter deep casserole lightly.

Dip fillets in slightly salted water. Drain, and wipe dry on paper towel. Place 4 fillets in prepared casserole. Heat cream sauce in top of double boiler over hot water. Add mayonnaise and mix thoroughly. Add mustards, pimiento, Worcestershire, and scallion. Stir slowly until well mixed. Fold crab meat and hard-cooked eggs into sauce. Add salt and pepper. Cover fillets with about half of sauce. Lay remaining 4 fillets on top. Cover with remaining sauce. Sprinkle with cheese.

Bake 20 minutes or until top is browned. Makes 4 to 8 servings.

Begin supper with melon or fresh berries and sliced peaches. Then serve oven-heated, quick-frozen shoestring potatoes with the casserole, crisp celery hearts and radishes, whole-wheat rolls, and sherbet and cake with coffee to finish.

BAKED WHITEFISH WITH OYSTERS

2 pounds fillets whitefish	Juice 1 lemon
¾ teaspoon salt	3 tablespoons flour
½ teaspoon pepper	1 cup milk
1 cup small drained oysters	½ teaspoon salt
6 tablespoons butter or margarine	¼ teaspoon pepper
	1 tablespoon finely cut parsley

Dip fillets in lightly salted water. Dry on paper towel. Lay fillets in buttered shallow baking dish. Season with salt and pepper.

Start oven at moderate (375° F.).

Heat oysters in small saucepan 2 or 3 minutes or until they are scalding hot. Drain, and save liquid. Melt 4 tablespoons butter or margarine. Add oyster liquid and lemon juice. Pour over fish in baking dish. Bake 15 minutes.

While fish bakes, melt remaining 2 tablespoons butter or margarine in small saucepan. Stir flour smoothly into it. Add milk gradually, stirring steadily. Let boil 1 or 2 minutes. When slightly thickened, add seasonings and oysters.

Place baked fish on warmed platter. Add sauce from baking pan to milk sauce. Mix and pour over fish. Sprinkle with parsley. Serve at once. Makes 6 servings.

I like potatoes or rice with this fish dish. Fried mashed-potato cakes or parsleyed tiny new potatoes or small rice croquettes, and either asparagus or string beans with lemon butter sauce. Dessert? An ice, pineapple or mint for coolness.

CURRIED SKATE OR WHITEFISH

2 tablespoons grated onion
1 apple, pared, cored, and diced
1 teaspoon finely cut parsley
2 medium tomatoes, peeled and quartered
2 tablespoons butter or margarine
1 to 1 ½ tablespoons curry powder
½ cup dry white wine
2 cups shredded, lightly steamed skate or whitefish
2 cups Fish Stock (page 302)
2 tablespoons flour
1 tablespoon lemon juice
1 teaspoon salt
½ teaspoon black pepper

Sauté onion, apple, parsley, and tomatoes in butter or margarine 5 minutes. Mix curry powder to smooth paste with a little of the wine. Stir into remaining wine. Add to onion mixture with fish and stock. Stir well. Mix flour with little stock until smooth. Stir into hot fish mixture. Bring to a boil, stirring occasionally until sauce boils 4 or 5 minutes. Add lemon juice, salt, and pepper.

Serve hot over rice with a sprinkling of chopped sautéed peanuts or almonds, if desired. Makes 4 to 6 servings.

This simple curry is served as a supper dish. In place of rice, serve a casserole of baked macaroni with crumbs and butter sauce. A green salad or a fruit salad goes well with it also.

Shellfish

Shellfish in any form except quick-frozen spoil very quickly. Buy fresh, live shellfish and cook immediately. Or, if bought cooked, serve as quickly as possible. Keep in coldest part of refrigerator or for a short time in the freezer. When serving canned shellfish and other sea food, use as soon as can is opened. *Do not let fish and shellfish salads stand on a buffet table except in bowl of crushed ice. Do not make fish and seafood sandwiches for lunchbox or picnic basket.*

BAKED SHELLFISH, CHILEAN STYLE
Chupe de Mariscos

1 pound live lobster	¼ cup grated Parmesan cheese
6 clams	3 eggs
8 shrimp	1 teaspoon salt
4 crabs, or ½ pound crab meat	½ teaspoon white pepper
½ cup bread crumbs	½ teaspoon chili powder, or to
1 cup milk	taste
1 cup shellfish stock	4 or 5 thin slices soft cheese

Add live lobster, scrubbed and rinsed clams, shrimp, and cleaned crabs all together to salted boiling water in large kettle. Boil 8 minutes, counting time when water starts to boil again after sea food is added. Drain shellfish and save stock. Cut and clean lobster. Shell and devein shrimp. Remove meat from crabs. Place all sea food in well-buttered 3-quart baking dish.

Heat crumbs in milk in 1½-quart saucepan. Add 1 cup shellfish stock. Mix and let boil down to slightly thickened sauce. Let cool 20 minutes at room temperature.

Start oven at moderately slow (300° F.).

Add grated cheese to crumb sauce. Beat egg yolks with seasoning and add to sauce. Whip egg whites stiff, then fold into sauce. Pour over sea food in baking dish. Lay slices of soft cheese on top.

Bake 30 minutes or until cheese has melted and dish is bubbling. Makes 6 servings.

Preparation of this delicious dish can be simplified by using quick-frozen lobster meat and other sea foods. Simmer together 5 minutes in seasoned water or Fish Stock to cover. Complete recipe as described.

This is one of my party specialties. The recipe was given to me by Chilean friends. Easier than Bouillabaisse, almost as effective.

Clams

Both hard-shell and soft-shell clams are available in our sea-food markets as well as at shore markets on both coasts. *Hard-shells* abound along the Atlantic Coast southward to Florida and all the way to the Gulf. Sometimes called quahaug or quahog, the small hard-shell cherry stones are eaten raw or cooked. Their large brother is a favorite for chowder. Some hard-shells, called Littlenecks, Mud, and Rock clams, are found on the West Coast. They are used locally for chowders, also are canned and frozen for market. In general, these sea delicacies are marketed in the Eastern and Far Western ports live in shells or shucked. And of course the canned and quick-frozen clams are widely distributed throughout the country.

Soft-shell clams, usually found near Cape Cod and north of it in colder waters, are longer than the hard-shells. The soft-shell clam burrows in the mud and is the favorite of local clam diggers in search of a good supper.

In fall, winter, and spring the freshly marketed hard-shells are served as a first course, and otherwise used in many delicious dishes. From about May to October the freshly marketed soft-shells or steamers are available for chowder and clam bake.

Pacific Coast clams, from little hard-shell butter clams to huge geoducks, are available all year round.

Buy live clams by the dozen or quart. *Shells should be tightly closed, not gaping.* Or buy them shucked (shelled) or minced, by the quart, or in vacuum-sealed cans, or quick-frozen.

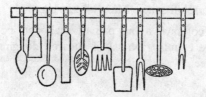

CLAMS BAKED IN SHELLS

2 dozen hard-shell clams	Butter
Salt	Finely cut fresh parsley
Black pepper	Lemon wedges

Start oven at hot (450° F.).

Scrub shells thoroughly under cold running water. Drain. Place in shallow baking pan. Bake until shells open, usually 5 to 7 minutes. Remove pan from oven. Take top shells from clams. Season clams in their lower shells with salt, quick grind of pepper, dab of butter, and a little parsley. Garnish with lemon wedge. Makes 4 servings.

Another good topping is a dab of Tartare Sauce (page 524) or mayonnaise mixed with chopped ripe olives.

CLAM PATTIES

1 pint fresh or quick-frozen shucked clams or canned minced clams	½ teaspoon sweet basil
	¼ teaspoon thyme
	2 tablespoons minced fresh parsley
½ cup cracker crumbs	
½ teaspoon salt	4 tablespoons butter
¼ teaspoon pepper	¼ cup ketchup or chili sauce
2 eggs, well beaten	

Scrub clams under cold running water. Open and remove all black. Mince clams fine. Or buy canned or quick-frozen minced clams and drain them.

Combine crumbs, seasonings, eggs, and herbs in mixing bowl. Add clams, mix well, and shape into round patties. Melt butter in skillet. Sauté patties until golden brown, about 3 minutes on each side. Drain on thick paper towels in pan in warm oven with door open. Serve hot with ketchup or chili sauce. Makes 4 servings.

These call for colesaw, a big pan of scalloped potatoes, a tossed green salad. In the country a bowl of sugared doughnuts goes on the table with the coffee.

FRIED CLAMS

3 or 4 dozen small hard-shell clams	½ cup cracker crumbs
	¼ pound (1 stick) butter
Salt	4 tablespoons finely cut chives
½ cup flour	1 lemon, cut in quarters
1 egg, well-beaten	

Scrub clam shells thoroughly under cold running water. Rinse and drain. Remove clams from shells by inserting short, thin knife blade between shells and cutting around clam muscle. Cut black off clams.

Sprinkle clams lightly with salt. Coat with flour. Dip into beaten egg, then into cracker crumbs.

Heat butter. Fry clams quickly, 3 minutes on one side, 2 minutes on other, or until golden brown. Drain on thick paper towels in pan in warm oven with door left open. Serve very hot on warmed plates. Garnish with fresh chives and quarter of lemon or with mayonnaise mixed with chives and lemon juice.

Serve coleslaw, chili sauce or ketchup, an assortment of pickles and olives as additional garnish for this dish. Warm corn bread, a pot of baked beans, are other favorites when fried clams are served. Makes 4 to 6 servings.

MINCED-CLAM CASSEROLE

2 (6½-ounce) cans minced clams
¼ cup flour
1 (10½-ounce) can cream-of-mushrooms or cream-of-chicken soup
1 (12-ounce) can whole-kernel corn
1½ cups soft bread crumbs
½ cup finely chopped peeled onions
3 tablespoons chopped green pepper
Garlic salt
Pepper
Buttered bread crumbs

Start oven at moderate (375° F.). Butter 5-cup baking dish.

Drain clams. Combine juice with flour in 1½-quart saucepan, stirring over low heat until smooth. Stir in soup, drained corn, 1½ cups crumbs, onions, green pepper, and seasonings until well combined. Add clams. Pour into prepared casserole. Cover top with buttered crumbs.

Bake 25 to 30 minutes. Makes 4 to 6 servings.

This clam-and-corn pie is a good casserole to serve for a terrace supper. Crisp bacon as garnish adds good flavor. Sliced tomato-and-lettuce salad, biscuits and jelly are favorites with this country dish. For dessert serve warm pear pie with cheese.

STEAMED CLAMS

4 dozen soft-shell clams
Bay leaf
1 to 2 cups boiling water
½ pound butter
Juice 1 lemon

Paprika
Freshly cut chives
Garlic salt
Celery salt

Scrub clams thoroughly under cold running water to remove all sand. Drain. Put bay leaf in bottom of large pot. Pour boiling water in to cover bottom and add clams. Cover pot tightly. Steam about 8 minutes or until shells open. Do not overcook. Remove pot from heat. Place clams in shells in warmed deep soup plates. Serve melted butter, lemon sections, paprika, chives, garlic salt, and celery salt for each guest to use as preferred.

Strain broth from steamer. Reheat and serve lightly seasoned with paprika in warmed bouillon cups. Makes 4 servings of clams and bouillon.

Steamed Clams, Little Italy: Add 1 mashed clove garlic, 2 tablespoons olive oil, 2 tablespoons finely cut fresh parsley to pot in which clams are to steam. Heat 3 minutes. Add ½ cup water, ½ teaspoon salt, ¼ teaspoon black pepper. Add scrubbed clams as described. Steam as in above recipe. Serve hot with melted butter and with clam broth on the side.

Steamed Clams with Pastas: Steam clams as described for the Italian recipe. Remove clams from shells, cut in small pieces, and add to freshly cooked spaghetti, macaroni, noodles, or other Italian pastas. Dress with melted butter and seasonings or favorite sauce.

Crabs

Crabs are in season in all Eastern coastal areas the year round; and crab meat, canned and quick-frozen, is available for delicious cookery wherever a modern grocer sets up shop.

All crabs are hard-shell unless very young. The young soft-shells are available mostly from April to October, with the peak of their season in July and August. Large Pacific crabs, both hard-shell and soft-shell, from Oregon, Washington, and California coasts, are summer delicacies which may be enjoyed all over the country, thanks to modern air shipping and quick-freezing. Quick-frozen king crab from the Oregon coast is now an all-season specialty in many parts of the country.

Sweet-water crabs, found in North Carolina and Chesapeake Bay, are favorites for flavor and tenderness. These also are shipped live by air to all parts of the country or frozen at the fishing docks.

Buy live soft-shell crabs by the dozen, or buy crab meat canned or quick-frozen. Much of the canned meat from Pacific and Alaskan coast fisheries is large Dungeness crab. All crab meat must be looked over for small gristle-like fibers or bones which resemble the meat and are hard to find; use two forks to toss. Flake crab meat before using in any recipe or serving it iced as an appetizer. Watch carefully for the thin white fibers and remove all of them.

CHESAPEAKE BAY CREAMED CRAB MEAT

1 ½ cups Cream Sauce (page 557)	½ teaspoon salt
2 hard-cooked eggs, diced	½ teaspoon celery salt
1 tablespoon finely cut chives	¼ teaspoon pepper
1 pound cleaned cooked or quick-frozen crab meat	Buttered toast points
2 tablespoons Worcestershire sauce	Water cress

Prepare Cream Sauce in saucepan or chafing dish. Add eggs and chives and continue to heat 5 minutes, stirring constantly. Add crab meat. Continue to heat until mixture is very hot but do not boil. Remove from heat. Stir in Worcestershire and seasonings. Serve on toast points. Garnish with cress. Makes 4 to 6 servings.

This makes a good chafing dish for supper or terrace luncheon. Serve cold baked Virginia ham, buttered rolls, a lemon aspic salad, Lady Baltimore cake, and homemade sherbet.

CHESAPEAKE BAY DEVILED CRAB MEAT

3	cups cleaned cooked or quick frozen crab meat	¼	cup lemon juice
⅛	teaspoon mace	½	cup melted butter
1½	teaspoons dry mustard	1	egg yolk, beaten
½	teaspoon salt	2	egg whites
¼	teaspoon pepper	½	cup sherry or Madeira
1	teaspoon Worcestershire	½	cup buttered crumbs

Flake crab meat in mixing bowl; remove all bones. Combine seasonings, Worcestershire and lemon juice, mix with crab meat.

Start oven at moderate (350° F.). Butter 1½ quart baking dish. Combine melted butter, beaten egg yolk, add wine a few drops at a time, then combine with crab mixture. Whip egg whites stiff, fold crab mixture into whites. Pour into buttered baking dish. Top with crumbs. Bake 30 minutes, or until top is browning. Makes 4 to 6 servings.

Serve this casserole as the hot dish in a cold buffet menu. A salad, beef-tongue sandwiches of beaten biscuit, stuffed celery, ice-cream pie, and hot coffee will please guests and family.

CRAB MEAT ON RICE

4	tablespoons butter	½	teaspoon salt
2	(8-ounce) cans crab meat, cleaned, or 1 pound fresh, cleaned crab meat	3	tablespoons finely cut parsley
		4	cups hot saffron rice
		4	tablespoons toasted slivered almonds
⅓	cup heavy cream		

Melt butter in chafing dish or saucepan. Heat crab meat, lifting and turning lightly with fork until hot and beginning to brown. Add cream, salt, and parsley. Heat only 1 or 2 minutes. Spoon onto saffron rice; top with almonds. Makes 4 to 6 servings.

For lunch, a green-pepper and grapefruit salad tastes good with this. Add a lime chiffon pie for dessert, with coffee.

Crab Meat in Shells: Use above recipe for creamed crab meat. Use 1 cup cream, 2 tablespoons minced scallions or onion, ¼ teaspoon grated lemon peel, 1 tablespoon lemon juice, ½ teaspoon mixed basil and thyme. Divide in 6 or 8 decorative sea-food "shells" made for oven cookery or into small individual baking dishes. Top with crumbs and almonds. Bake in moderately hot (400° F.) oven 10 to 15 minutes. Serve hot as appetizer course or as main dish.

Note: For calorie watchers whole evaporated milk can be substituted for cream.

CRAB CAKES

1 pound freshly cooked crab meat or 2 (8-ounce) cans crab meat	3 eggs
	1 teaspoon salt
	1 teaspoon dry mustard
1 medium onion	2 tablespoons finely cut parsley
½ cup butter or margarine	2 tablespoons cream
1 cup fine dry bread crumbs	Flour

Remove all fibers from crab meat. Flake meat lightly. Peel onion. Grate or dice fine. Cook in half the butter or margarine until tender. Add crumbs and mix well.

Beat eggs. Add to crab meat with crumb mixture, salt, mustard, parsley, and cream. Mix. Shape into 8 flat cakes. Coat lightly with flour. Fry in remaining 4 tablespoons butter or margarine, on both sides, until lightly browned. Makes 4 servings.

Serve any sauce you prefer with these good cakes. Tartare Sauce (page 524) is a favorite of many. A sauce made by combining equal amounts of mayonnaise and chili sauce or ketchup is liked by others.

HOT CRAB PIE

Pastry for 1-crust pie	½ teaspoon salt
1 ½ cups cleaned cooked or canned crab meat	¼ teaspoon pepper
	¼ teaspoon celery salt
2 tablespoons finely cut parsley	6 eggs
1 tablespoon finely cut chives	1 ½ cups milk
2 tablespoons dry vermouth or white wine	1/16 teaspoon cayenne
	Paprika

Prepare pastry. Line deep 9-inch pie dish. Trim and crimp edge. Chill 1 hour.

Start oven at hot (450° F.).

Combine crab meat, parsley, chives, vermouth or wine, and seasonings. Brush chilled pastry shell lightly with 1 beaten egg white. Pour crab mixture into shell. Beat 5 eggs and the 1 extra yolk slightly. Combine with milk and cayenne. Pour over crab in pie shell.

Bake 10 minutes. Reduce oven heat to moderate (350° F.). Continue baking 20 to 30 minutes or until knife inserted in center comes out clean. Serve hot as main dish for lunch, dinner or supper. Makes 6 servings.

CRAB MEAT WITH LOUIS SAUCE

1 small onion
3 sprigs parsley
1 cup mayonnaise
¼ cup chili sauce
¹⁄₁₆ teaspoon cayenne
⅓ cup heavy cream

1 head lettuce
1 pound cooked crab meat or 2 (8-ounce) cans, cleaned and chilled
4 hard-cooked eggs, grated
4 tablespoons finely cut chives

Make the Louis Sauce first. Wash, peel, and grate onion. Cut parsley as fine as possible. Mix both with mayonnaise, chili sauce, and cayenne. Whip cream stiff. Blend into seasoned mayonnaise. Chill in refrigerator while arranging the crab plates.

Wash lettuce. Discard soft outer leaves. Cut lettuce crosswise in four thick slices. Place on chilled plates. Spoon generous mound of crab meat on lettuce. Add spoonful of grated egg around crab meat. Sprinkle with chives. Spoon sauce lavishly over crab meat. Makes 4 servings.

PANCAKES WITH CRAB-AND-SHRIMP SAUCE

Your best pancake recipe, or use mix
Cream Sauce (page 557)
¼ teaspoon dry mustard
¼ teaspoon black pepper
1 cup cooked deveined shrimp

½ cup cooked, cleaned crab meat
¼ cup grated Swiss cheese
¼ cup grated Parmesan cheese
¼ cup heavy cream, whipped

Prepare pancake batter.
Start oven at moderate (375° F.).

Prepare Cream Sauce. Add mustard and pepper, and mix. Add shrimp and crab meat. Combine cheese with whipped cream.

Make 4 large pancakes. Place in greased wide shallow pan. Add generous spoonful of sea-food mixture on each cake. Fold over and top with spoonful of whipped cream and cheese.

Bake 10 minutes or until top is browned. Serve at once. Makes 4 generous servings.

Both pancake batter and topping can be prepared ahead and the recipe may be finished at the time of serving.

A guest supper favorite. Needs only fruit or a gelatin mold and coffee to complete the menu.

DEVILED CRABS

4 tablespoons butter or margarine
3 tablespoons flour
2 tablespoons prepared mustard
½ teaspoon paprika
⅛ teaspoon powdered nutmeg
⅛ teaspoon cayenne
1 cup milk
2 cups flaked, cooked, cleaned
  crab meat

½ teaspoon salt
2 tablespoons finely cut parsley
1 tablespoon lemon juice
8 scrubbed crab shells
½ cup buttered cracker crumbs
Pepper
Extra parsley for garnishing

Melt butter or margarine in saucepan. Add flour and seasonings,
stirring to smooth paste. Add milk, stirring. Cook, stirring constantly
until sauce thickens and boils 1 or 2 minutes. Remove from heat. Add
crab flakes, salt, parsley, and lemon juice. Mix well. Spoon mixture
into crab shells. Sprinkle each with buttered cracker crumbs and a little
pepper.

Start oven at moderate (350° F.). Place filled shells on baking
sheet or in shallow pan.

Bake about 15 minutes or until lightly browned. Garnish with parsley
and serve hot. Makes 8 servings.

A good dish for buffet supper. Or feature it at Sunday luncheon.
Potatoes au gratin go well with the crabs, and most people like a mixed
green salad with this menu. Sherbet, especially pineapple, is a suitable
dessert after the rich crabs.

Seafood Steamer

FROGS' LEGS SAUTÉ SALONAISE

10 cleaned frogs' legs
½ cup heavy cream or whole evaporated milk for the calorie watchers
1 teaspoon salt
½ teaspoon pepper
¼ cup flour
3 tablespoons olive oil

1 onion, peeled and cut fine
½ small eggplant, pared and cut fine
1 tomato, peeled and cut fine
1 clove garlic
½ tablespoon butter or margarine
Lemon quarters

Rinse frogs' legs and wipe dry. Dip each in cream. Sprinkle with seasoning and roll in flour. Fry legs in olive oil in large skillet until golden brown. Remove to pan and keep hot in oven with its door open.

Sauté onion, eggplant, and tomato together 10 minutes in the skillet in which frogs' legs cooked. Peel garlic, slice it. Cook in butter or margarine in small pan 3 minutes. Add to vegetables and mix. Pour over frogs' legs on warmed serving platter. Serve garnished with lemon quarters. Makes 3 or 4 servings.

Serve frogs' legs sauté as the main dish of lunch or dinner. A green salad and fresh fruit go well with their rich texture and flavor.

Lobsters

HOW TO BOIL A LOBSTER

The average weight of live lobsters sold in East Coast markets is 1½ to 2½ pounds. As a rule, the smaller lobsters are more tender, with juicier meat.

Boil one lobster at a time, unless you have a very large kettle. For each lobster, use 3 quarts water in a large kettle. Add about 3 tablespoons salt, 2 outside stalks celery with their leaves, 1 bay leaf, 2 cloves, 6 peppercorns, ¼ cup wine vinegar. Let water boil rapidly 5 minutes. Then hold lobster behind its head and plunge it head first into the water. Cover kettle and reduce heat. When water begins to simmer, start to time the cooking. Simmer 5 minutes for the first pound, 3 minutes more for each additional pound; for example, simmer a 1½- to 2-pound lobster 8 to 10 minutes. Shell should be bright red.

Remove from water. Lay lobster on its back until cool enough to handle. Take a large knife and split from head to tail right through the hard back shell. Cut off claws. Remove long black vein, the small sac at base of the head, and the green spongy lungs, and discard. Keep the green liver and roe or lobster coral. Remove meat from halves or leave in shells for various recipes. Or serve at once, cut side up, as *Boiled Lobster,* with melted butter.

Use nutcracker or lobster cracker to break claws; serve cracked claws with boiled lobster. Or remove claw meat and use in various recipes; *pull* claw meat out and remove center fiber. Keep lobster meat covered in refrigerator until used in recipes.

Chilled Lobster in the Shell is served garnished with mayonnaise and capers or sour-cream horse-radish dressing. Allow one small to medium lobster as one serving.

CHAN-FAMILY LOBSTER

4 quick-frozen lobster tails	¼ teaspoon salt
½ pound lean pork	⅛ teaspoon pepper
1 tablespoon peanut oil	4 tablespoons cornstarch
6 scallions	2 tablespoons soy sauce
1 carrot	¼ cup water
1 stalk celery	1 (1-pound) can Chinese bean
2 cups chicken consommé or Fish Stock (page 302)	sprouts
	4 cups hot rice

Cook lobster tails according to directions on package. Let cool slightly. Remove all meat from shells and cut into chunks. Cut pork into cubes. Brown pork in hot oil in skillet. Chop scallions, carrot, and celery fine, and add to pork in skillet. Cook until vegetables are limp but not brown. Pour in consommé or stock. Season with salt and pepper and cover. Cook slowly 10 minutes. Mix cornstarch, soy sauce, and water smoothly together. Stir into pork mixture. Stir and boil until sauce thickens and is clear.

Start oven at moderate (350° F.).

Add lobster meat and drained bean sprouts to pork mixture. Pour into 1½-quart casserole.

Bake 20 minutes. Serve with hot rice. Makes 4 servings.

Serve this savory dish for dinner or a supper, or for a buffet meal, keeping it hot on the buffet table. Rice and oven-crisped canned Chinese noodles go with it. Water cress and romaine salad, a sweet, such as a custard with fresh strawberries, round out a delicious menu.

BROILED LOBSTER

Freshly boiled lobsters
Butter
Salt and pepper

Paprika
Lemon wedges

Split freshly boiled lobsters and clean.

Start broiler at moderate (350° F.).

Place halves of lobster, meat side up, on broiler rack. Brush generously with melted butter. Season lightly with salt, pepper, and paprika. Broil 3 to 4 minutes or until lobster is hot and butter has been absorbed. Brush with more butter.

Serve on hot plates with lemon wedges. Allow one half lobster as one serving. If lobsters are small, count two halves as a serving.

If lobster seems a little dry, serve additional lemon butter with broiled halves. Melt butter, stir lemon juice into it, add dash of paprika. Pass with broiled or boiled lobster.

CURRIED LOBSTER, VANDERBILT

4 quick-frozen lobster tails
6 tablespoons butter
4 shallots or scallions
1 tablespoon curry powder

1 cup light cream
⅜ cup cognac
Thin buttered toast

Cook lobster tails according to directions on package. Let cool slightly. Remove all meat from shells and cut in thick slices.

Melt 4 tablespoons butter in saucepan. Add sliced shallots or scallions. Sauté and mix with butter 3 minutes. Stir in curry powder, and mix well. Add cream, stirring constantly. Let cook until very hot but do not boil. Remove from heat but keep hot over hot water.

Melt remaining 2 tablespoons butter in another saucepan. Add lobster and heat slowly over low heat. When hot, pour brandy over lobster. Remove from heat. Ignite brandy with match and let flame about 20 seconds. Pour lobster into warmed serving dish. Pour hot sauce over brandied lobster. Serve at once on thin toast. Makes 4 servings.

LOBSTER NEWBURG

1 pound fresh lobster meat or 2 (7¾-ounce) cans
2 egg yolks
½ cup cream
¼ cup butter or margarine

2 tablespoons sherry
½ teaspoon salt
⅛ teaspoon cayenne
¼ teaspoon powdered nutmeg
Thin buttered toast

Break any large pieces of lobster into small chunks. Beat egg yolks slightly and mix with cream. Melt butter or margarine in upper part of double boiler or chafing dish over hot water. Stir in egg mixture and sherry a little at a time over low heat. Cook, stirring constantly until sauce thickens. Add seasonings and lobster. Stir and heat 1 or 2 minutes. Serve on toast points or into toast cases. Makes 4 servings.

This old favorite is easily made today with lobster tails and lobster meat available in cans and quick-frozen. Serve as luncheon dish, with asparagus salad, fresh fruit, and coffee. Or for supper.

LOBSTER THERMIDOR

2 large boiled lobsters or 4 cooked lobster tails or 2 (7¾-ounce) cans lobster
3 tablespoons butter or margarine
3 tablespoons flour
1½ cups milk
1 (3-ounce) can chopped mushrooms
⅛ teaspoon paprika
⅛ teaspoon dry mustard
½ teaspoon salt
2 tablespoons finely cut parsley
¼ cup sherry
½ cup light cream
½ teaspoon chopped chervil or dried tarragon
¼ cup grated Gruyère or Parmesan cheese
¼ cup toasted bread crumbs

Cut lobsters in half lengthwise. Remove all meat from body and claws. Break meat into chunks.

Melt butter or margarine in saucepan. Stir in flour smoothly. Add milk gradually, stirring constantly over low heat until sauce thickens slightly and boils. Remove from heat.

Drain mushrooms. Combine with lobster, seasonings, parsley, and sherry. Pour into hot sauce, stirring constantly. Add a little cream, if needed, and the chervil or tarragon.

Start broiler at moderate (350° F.).

Spoon lobster mixture into lobster shells. When canned lobster is used, complete this dish in 1-quart shallow casserole. Sprinkle surface of filled shells or casserole with crumbs and cheese. Broil 4 or 5 minutes or until mixture is bubbly and lightly browned. Makes 4 servings.

As a de luxe first course, bake Lobster Thermidor in individual shallow casseroles. Bring to table with garnish of red lobster shell.

LOBSTER STEW

2 ½ cups milk
2 cups light cream
2 tablespoons butter or margarine

1 ½ cups lobster meat
Salt and pepper
Celery salt

Combine milk and cream in 2-quart saucepan. Heat until a light film forms over surface but do not boil. Heat butter or margarine in another saucepan. Add lobster, and cook over low heat 4 or 5 minutes. Stir lobster and butter into milk mixture. Season with dash of salt, pepper, and celery salt. Cook slowly 1 or 2 minutes, until steaming, but do not boil. Serve in warmed bowls. Makes 4 servings.

Family and guests may not want anything but toasted French bread or crackers with this stew, with melon or wine-flavored compote afterwards, and coffee.

MY LOBSTER À L'ARMORICAINE

4 (1 ¼-pound) live lobsters
4 tablespoons butter
¼ cup cognac or armagnac
1 clove garlic, peeled and mashed
8 shallots, sliced
1 small celery heart, sliced
1 small carrot, sliced
1 leek, sliced
6 small tomatoes, peeled and chopped

1 teaspoon finely cut parsley
1 teaspoon chervil
½ teaspoon thyme
1 bay leaf
½ teaspoon salt
Pepper
1 pint dry white wine
2 cups Fish Stock (page 302)
Parsley for garnish
Thin buttered toast

Cook and clean lobsters. Cut meat in bite-size pieces. Sauté in butter in 2-quart saucepan 2 or 3 minutes. Pour brandy over and ignite with

340

match. When flame dies down add garlic, chopped vegetables, herbs, salt, and pepper. Add wine and Fish Stock, and cook 20 minutes. Remove garlic and discard. Remove lobster and keep it hot. Cook sauce until reduced by half. Add lobster and reheat just to boiling point. Sprinkle with little finely cut parsley. Serve at once on toast. Makes 4 to 6 servings.

This may be made in advance. Add lobster to carefully reheated (but not boiled) sauce when ready to serve.

A luxurious specialty which should be served with rice, a salad, and coffee, as a special guest supper.

LOBSTER TURNOVERS

1 (10½-ounce) can condensed cream-of-mushroom soup	½ teaspoon Worcestershire sauce
1 (7¾-ounce) can lobster meat	⅛ teaspoon cayenne
¼ cup mayonnaise	1 package pastry mix

Combine ½ cup soup with lobster, mayonnaise, and seasonings.
Prepare pastry according to package directions. Roll out 4 (6-inch) circles about ¼ inch thick. Place ¼ of lobster mixture on each circle. Fold over to form turnover. Seal edges with fork, and prick in several places to let steam escape.
Start oven at hot (450° F.).
Place turnovers on greased baking sheet. Bake 15 to 20 minutes or until pastry is browning. Serve with Mushroom Sauce (page 553) or Shrimp Sauce (page 315), or hot spicy mustard. Makes 4 servings.

Make very small turnovers and serve hot with sauce as appetizer course. Or serve hot, without sauce, as finger food at buffet supper or with soup and salad.
Turnovers can be prepared ready for baking ahead of time, then frozen and baked at serving time for 15 to 20 minutes or until the pastry is browned.
These may be served with hot, spicy mustard or Duck Sauce now available in jars practically everywhere.

STUFFED LOBSTER

4 lobsters	1 tablespoon capers, drained
2 cups mayonnaise	1 teaspoon paprika
½ cup heavy cream, whipped	

Boil lobsters. Let cool 20 minutes in liquid in which they cooked. Remove lobsters. Strain liquid and measure ½ cup. Split lobsters carefully. Remove meat and save shells. Cut meat into cubes and chill in refrigerator 1 hour or longer.

Mix mayonnaise with the ½ cup lobster stock. Fold in whipped cream. Add to lobster meat with capers. Mix lightly. Fill lobster shells with mixture. Sprinkle with paprika. Serve at once. Makes 4 servings.

Serve as cold entrée for luncheon or dinner. Fresh fruit salad afterwards, with thin nut-bread sandwiches and hot tea or coffee, make a good luncheon. Or serve a hot potato puff, or peas soufflé, rolls, cheese tray, brandied cherries-and-peaches, with *caffè espresso*.

Mussels

In many parts of the country a good supply of fresh mussels is available from October to April and they are much cheaper than clams and oysters. They are marketed as small, medium, and large mussels. The small ones are preferred for service in the shell, the large ones for chowders, stews, fritters, creole dishes, and other recipes.

Buy fresh mussels in the shell by the pound. They average 15 to 20 a pound. *All shells must be tightly closed.* The shells are thin and mussels large, averaging more food per pound than in the same weight of oysters or clams.

In general, mussels are prepared like clams and oysters. Scrub well under cold running water. Use as described in various clam and oyster recipes.

Mussels are also available canned. In my supply closet there are always 10-ounce cans of Norwegian mussels packed in wine, and Dutch mussels smoked and in tomato sauce for quick hors d'oeuvres service.

ITALIAN FISHERMAN MUSSELS

3 to 4 dozen small mussels	½ cup sherry or dry white wine
2 onions, peeled and chopped	½ teaspoon thyme
1 bay leaf	¼ teaspoon chopped dill
2 tablespoons finely cut parsley	4 tablespoons butter
⅛ teaspoon cayenne	Salt and pepper

Place scrubbed and rinsed tightly closed mussels in large kettle. Add onions, bay leaf, parsley, cayenne, wine, and herbs. Cover tightly, and steam about 15 to 20 minutes or until shells open. Remove mussels and strain broth. Remove meats from shells. Cut dark beard from each.

Pour broth into saucepan. Bring to a boil and reduce heat. Simmer 2 minutes, add butter, season with little salt and freshly ground pepper. Add mussels. Heat just to boiling point. Serve mussels in deep soup plates, with small dish of the sauce with each plate. Dip mussels in sauce to eat. Makes 4 or more servings.

Use chopped cooked mussels in macaroni, spaghetti, noodles, and other pasta dishes, either with simple butter sauce or combined with pasta sauces; top mixture with buttered crumbs for *Scalloped Mussels*.

See also appetizers chapter.

Oysters

Many kinds of oysters are available in American markets. They vary in size and flavor and are menu favorites as raw oyster appetizers or cooked in a great many delicious dishes.

Today fish dealers call an oyster a Blue Point if it is from 2 to 4 inches long and about 2 inches wide, no matter where it grew; and Lynnhaven now means the larger, angular oysters. These names once indicated the source of the sea food.

Some specialties still remain in spite of the trend toward standardization of names and uses. Local gourmets on the West Coast prefer their Olympias, the tiny oysters which average 100 to a pint, or they will insist on having the huge Northwest Coast oysters. Many knowledgeable oyster lovers demand Chincoteagues, which are so large that one mid-westerner I know thinks they should be eaten with a knife and fork. Not so—though they are a mouthful. Use scissors to cut them for cooking.

A woman can learn how to open oysters without necessarily losing a finger. An excellent method I have often demonstrated is the one recommended by the Fishery Council, illustrated below.

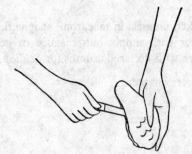

Insert the upraised tip of a beer can opener into the hinge of the oyster and press down. The hinge is then loosened. Insert a thin-bladed knife to separate the muscle of the oyster from the upper shell. Sever the muscle from the lower shell—and there you have it, ready for serving or cooking.

Fresh oysters are in all markets from September through April (the R months). Besides the popular raw oyster cocktail, this sea delicacy may be steamed, fried, stewed, and combined with other foods to make main dishes.

Buy oysters alive, in their shells, by the dozen, or shucked (shelled) by the pint, quart, or pound. Or buy quick-frozen oysters. Follow recipe directions for preparation and cooking. The oyster flavor is delicate, the texture easily spoiled by overcooking.

BAKED OYSTERS IN SHELL

2 dozen large oysters in shell	1 lemon
1 cup butter or margarine	1 ½ cups buttered bread crumbs
2 tablespoons finely cut parsley	1 ½ teaspoons salt
Freshly ground pepper	

Scrub oyster shells thoroughly. Rinse under cold running water. Open oysters using the method recommended by the Fishery Council. See illustration, page 344. Discard flat shell. Keep deep halves for use.

Start oven at moderately hot (400° F.).

Melt butter or margarine. Season with parsley and a quick grind of black pepper. When butter is slightly cooled, roll each oyster in it, barely coating oyster. Return oyster to shell. Squeeze lemon juice over oysters and cover each with crumbs. Place filled shells in shallow baking pans. Bake 5 minutes. Add light sprinkling of salt to oysters and continue baking 3 minutes. Serve hot in shells. Makes 4 to 6 servings.

Broiled Oysters: Instead of cooking in the oven, use preheated broiler. Place oysters 3 inches below heat. Broil 3 minutes. Add sprinkling of salt and broil 1 or 2 minutes longer. Serve at once.

Serve as hot appetizer for a special guest dinner, or serve as main dish, with au gratin potatoes, green beans with almonds, warm corn bread. Deep-dish plum pie or apple pie tastes good with these.

BAKED OYSTERS, PARMESAN

1 quart shelled oysters	½ cup cracker crumbs
½ clove garlic	½ teaspoon salt
½ cup olive oil	¼ teaspoon pepper
¾ cup grated Gruyère or Parmesan cheese	¼ teaspoon paprika

Start oven at hot (450° F.). Grease 1½-quart shallow baking dish.

Drain oysters. Peel garlic, dice fine, and add to olive oil. Mix cheese, crumbs, salt, pepper, and paprika together. Dip oysters in oil, then into cheese mixture, coating well on both sides. Arrange in baking dish. Sprinkle any remaining cheese mixture over top.

Bake 12 to 15 minutes or until top is delicately browned. Makes 4 servings.

Tastes delicious outdoors, too. If your barbecue includes an oven, serve these at a backyard picnic.

BROILED OYSTERS ON SKEWERS

Thread long broiling skewers with squares of green pepper, stuffed green olives, onion triangles, and oysters. It is a good idea to sauté green pepper and onion lightly before using on skewer. Brush all with mixture of 4 tablespoons melted butter or margarine, 2 tablespoons lemon juice, 1 tablespoon soy sauce, and 2 drops Tabasco sauce. Place filled skewers in preheated broiler about 3 inches from heat.

Broil 12 to 15 minutes, turning skewers and brushing with butter mixture 2 or 3 times. Serve hot onto hot saffron or brown rice or wheat pilaf. Each skewer makes 1 serving.

Do as the Syrians do with a skewer of lamb and green pepper: serve a compote of dried apricots cooked with honey and pignolia nuts for dessert, and a delicate, very sweet paper-thin pastry and mild white cheese, such as cream cheese, with coffee.

Syrian and Armenian restaurants often sell their pastries to take out. Cream cheese to top it is only a mild approximation of their thick, solid cream topping which is quite delectable.

FRIED OYSTERS

3 dozen shelled oysters	1 cup very fine cracker crumbs
2 eggs	Fat for deep frying (peanut oil
½ cup oyster liquid	adds a delectable flavor)
1 teaspoon salt	Tartare Sauce (page 524)
¼ teaspoon pepper	Lettuce

Drain oysters and save about ½ cup liquid. Beat eggs slightly. Stir oyster liquid, salt, and pepper into eggs. Dip oysters into egg mixture. Coat with cracker crumbs. Let dry a few minutes.

In heavy kettle heat fat for deep-frying (to 375° F. on frying thermometer or until 1-inch cube of bread browns in 1 minute). Lower few oysters at a time in frying basket into hot fat. Fry 3 to 4 minutes or until golden. Drain on thick paper towels in pan in warm oven with its door open. When all are fried, serve on hot platter with garnish of small lettuce cups filled with Tartare Sauce. Makes 6 servings.

To save time when preparing guest dinner, crumb and coat oysters in advance. Keep on covered platter in refrigerator until ready to fry.

More Fried Oyster Ideas

Drain shelled oysters, save liquor, and remove all bits of shell. Sprinkle oysters with pepper and salt and set in cool place 10 to 15 minutes. If oysters are small, pour them into a pan of fine cracker crumbs. Add oyster liquor, mix well, and let stand 5 minutes. *Mold into small cakes* with 2 or 3 oysters in each. Roll again in dry cracker crumbs until thickly coated. Fry in mixture of hot lard and butter, or beef drippings. Serve hot.

Or, dip drained oysters in beaten egg yolks. Season with salt and pepper. Dip in corn meal into which a teaspoon of baking powder has been mixed. Fry in deep, hot lard.

Or, drain oysters thoroughly. Place in lightly greased hot (heavy) frying pan. Turn oysters quickly, letting each side brown lightly. They cook this way in a few minutes and the delicious flavor of the oysters is well preserved. Serve in hot covered dish with butter, pepper, and salt. Or add a little cream to the oysters just before serving and spoon them onto hot buttered toast.

Or, roll oysters in 2 parts fine cracker crumbs and 1 part corn meal, mixed together. Fry in mixture of hot lard and butter or margarine. Season with salt and pepper.

OYSTERS CARIBBEAN

From the Pontchartrain, New Orleans

4 shallots	2 teaspoons Worcestershire sauce
4 tablespoons butter	2 cups Medium Cream Sauce
1 quart oysters, drained	(page 557)
1 tablespoon finely cut parsley	6 cups hot steamed rice

Sauté washed, drained, and sliced shallots in butter 8 minutes. Brown oysters in lightly greased, very heavy skillet or griddle. Heat only until edges begin to curl. Add to shallots. Sauté over low heat 2 minutes. Add parsley, Worcestershire, and sauce. Let simmer 5 minutes or until steaming hot. Serve at once on hot rice. Makes 6 servings.

This is a popular dish of the Pontchartrain's excellent buffet suppers. Delicious combined with rosy slabs of cold roast beef. A masculine favorite.

WALLED OYSTERS

3 or 4 cups freshly cooked mashed potatoes*	2 tablespoons flour
2 eggs, beaten	¼ teaspoon pepper
1 quart shelled oysters	½ teaspoon salt
Salt and Pepper	1 cup heavy cream
2 tablespoons butter or margarine	Buttered toast strips

Start oven at moderate (325° F.).

Make a wall of seasoned mashed potatoes 1½ inches high and ¾ inch thick just inside rim of medium-sized heatproof platter or deep soup plate. It's fun to do this with a pastry tube—and decorative. Glaze potatoes by brushing with beaten egg. Place platter in hot oven for few minutes. Then turn off heat. Let platter keep warm, with oven door open.

Drain oysters. Heat oyster liquor in saucepan and skim well. Season oysters lightly with salt and pepper. Add to hot liquor and let boil 1 or 2 minutes, only until oyster edges begin to curl. Remove from heat.

Quickly make Cream Sauce. Melt butter or margarine, stir in flour smoothly, and add salt and pepper. Stir in cream slowly to make smooth sauce. Let boil 2 or 3 minutes.

Skim oysters out of their hot liquor. Add to cream sauce. Stir and spoon into the potato-bordered platter. Serve at once, spooning mashed potatoes and creamed oysters onto toast strips. Makes 6 or more servings.

The main dish of Sunday-night supper. Serve your favorite tossed salad, a loaf of bread spread with herb butter and made very hot in the oven, and Peaches Marion (page 267), with coffee.

* I have frozen mashed and dehydrated potatoes on hand, always, to avoid potato peeling on busy—or lazy days.

OYSTERS POULETTE

1 quart shelled oysters	½ teaspoon salt
2 tablespoons butter or margarine	¼ teaspoon paprika
	½ teaspoon lemon juice
1 tablespoon flour	1 cup heavy cream, whipped
1 cup light cream	Toast points or pastry cases
4 egg yolks	

Place oysters in saucepan and simmer 2 minutes or until edges curl. Strain and save ½ cup liquid.

Melt butter or margarine in upper part of chafing dish or double boiler over hot water. Stir in flour smoothly. Add oyster liquid and ½ cup light cream, slowly and stirring steadily. Beat egg yolks in remaining ½ cup light cream. Gradually add yolks and cream to sauce. Season with salt, paprika, and lemon juice. Cook, stirring until thickened. Add oysters and heat thoroughly, but do not let boil or it will curdle. Just before serving add garnish of whipped cream to top of creamed oysters. Serve at once on toast points or in pastry cases. Makes 8 servings.

I've never served this without having all my guests ask for the recipe.

OYSTER STEW

⅓ cup butter	1 ½ teaspoons salt
1 pint shelled oysters	½ teaspoon pepper
5 cups milk	1 teaspoon paprika
1 cup cream	

Melt butter in saucepan and add drained oysters. Cook 3 minutes over moderate heat, until edges of oysters curl. Add remaining ingredients except paprika. Let heat almost to boiling point. Serve at once. Add sprinkle of paprika to each serving. Makes 6 servings.

New York Oyster Stew: Heat the butter, 1 tablespoon Worcestershire, the salt, pepper, and paprika in saucepan. Stir in 3 cups clam juice and add oysters. Cook only until edges curl. Add 2 cups milk and 1 cup cream slowly, stirring continually. When steaming hot, serve. Makes 6 servings.

If you're a New Yorker and your husband is late for dinner during the "R" months, he may well be dropping in to have this stew made before his eyes at the Grand Central Oyster Bar. Rx: Get him a chafing dish and all the makings and let him have this as his culinary specialty at home.

See also Soups.

Scallops

When a recipe calls for scallops, the small bay scallops, which measure from 1 to 2 inches across are to be used; or if only deep-sea scallops are available at your fish dealer's, buy the big 2- and 3-inch scallops, cut them in small pieces—the kitchen shears will do it simply—and use according to recipe directions. Large sea scallops are available the year round, the sweet-flavored little scallops in early fall months.

Buy scallops by the pound or pint, or buy quick-frozen scallops.

BROILED SCALLOPS

4 tablespoons butter or margarine	½ teaspoon Worcestershire sauce
1 teaspoon minced onion	1 pint small scallops or 1 (10-ounce) package defrosted quick-frozen scallops
½ teaspoon salt	

Combine butter or margarine, onion, salt, and Worcestershire.

Preheat broiler at moderate heat. Grease shallow baking pan. Pour scallops into pan. Brush with ½ butter mixture. Broil without turning about 4 minutes, until lightly browned. Turn scallops. Brush with remaining butter mixture. Broil 5 to 6 minutes. Makes 4 servings.

Serve very hot, sprinkled with crisp bacon, or with choice of lemon slices, Tartare Sauce (page 524), ketchup, and other condiments. Mashed potatoes, rice or baked macaroni taste good with scallops. Grapefruit-and-orange salad, coffee and cookies complete this menu.

PAN-FRIED SCALLOPS

1 ½ pounds small scallops	⅛ teaspoon pepper
1 egg	¼ teaspoon paprika
½ cup cold water	4 slices bread
½ cup dry bread crumbs	1 tablespoon butter
½ cup butter or margarine	¼ cup white wine
¼ teaspoon salt	1 tablespoon finely cut parsley

Wash scallops, drain, and dry on paper towels. Beat egg slightly and mix with water. Roll scallops in egg, then in crumbs. Let dry a few minutes. Sauté in butter or margarine about 5 minutes, over moderate heat. Sprinkle with seasoning. Turn scallops often to brown evenly.

Toast bread and spread with butter. Place slices on warmed plates. Spoon cooked scallops onto toast. Add wine and parsley to pan in which scallops cooked. Stir with pan fat over heat 1 minute. Pour over scallops and serve. Makes 4 servings.

Serve fruit for dessert, either broiled grapefruit or pears in wine or Cointreau.

CREAMED SCALLOPS IN SHELLS

Coquille St. Jacques

2	pounds small scallops	6 tablespoons butter or marga-
2	cups dry white wine	rine
1	cup water	1 teaspoon lemon juice
1	teaspoon salt	¼ cup flour
2	or 3 celery tops	2 egg yolks
5	sprigs parsley	¼ cup heavy cream
1	bay leaf	¼ cup dry bread crumbs
1	small onion	
2	(3-ounce) cans chopped mush-	
	rooms	

Wash and drain scallops. Combine scallops, wine, water, salt, celery tops, 3 parsley sprigs, and bay leaf in 3-quart saucepan. Cover and cook over low heat about 10 minutes or until scallops are tender. Discard greenery, drain scallops, and save liquid. Chop scallops in small chunks.

Peel onion and dice fine. Combine with mushrooms and the remaining 2 parsley sprigs cut fine. Cook about 10 minutes in 2 tablespoons butter or margarine, then add lemon juice. Mix with chopped scallops.

Melt 3 tablespoons butter or margarine in scallop kettle. Stir in flour smoothly. Gradually add scallop liquid, stirring constantly until sauce thickens, about 5 minutes. Beat egg yolks slightly and add cream to them. Add a little of the hot sauce to yolk mixture. Mix smoothly, then stir all into hot sauce. Cook, stirring, over low heat 4 or 5 minutes or until thick. Stir scallop mixture into sauce.

Spoon into 6 buttered baking shells or individual casseroles. Sprinkle with crumbs, dot with remaining butter, and brown under broiler. Makes 6 servings.

This is a godsend to the help-less hostess. May be made early for popping under the broiler at meal time. A husband-pleaser. As a dinner entrée try extending it with a vegetable as the first course, served separately, French fashion. For example, steamed asparagus with butter sauce, quartered hard-cooked eggs and a sprinkling or grating of nutmeg. Shades of lovely dishes in Amsterdam!

This classic French dish of scallops is meant to be served as a first course at an elaborate, large dinner. But with today's simplified menus, it makes a perfect luncheon or easy dinner main course.

Shrimp

Delicious shrimp are available either fresh, canned, or quick-frozen. Buy fresh shrimp by the pound in the shell, the frozen either in the shell or peeled and deveined. *Never* cook, then shell (see below).

Raw shrimp, or green shrimp, are grayish green. They average 40 very small ones, or 25 to 30 larger shrimp, or 16 to 25 jumbo shrimp to the pound, making 3 to 4 servings, depending on size and the method of cookery.

From the Atlantic, South Gulf, and most Pacific states, shrimp are available the year round but especially plentiful from May to October.

BOILED SHRIMP

2 cups water	1 teaspoon salt
1 small onion, peeled and stuck with clove	1 bay leaf
	½ teaspoon thyme
1 cup dry white wine	½ teaspoon basil
2 slices lemon	2 cloves
1 stalk celery, sliced	2 peppercorns
1 sprig parsley	1 pound raw or green shrimp

Combine water and all ingredients except shrimp in large saucepan. Bring to a boil. Reduce heat and simmer in covered pan for 10 minutes.

This is the way the Chinese (those master shrimp-cooks) prepare shrimp for cooking. Wash under cold running water. Remove shell by holding tail of shrimp. Slip thumb under shell between feelers. Lift off pieces of shell. Ease shrimp out. Make shallow cut down back with sharp knife and remove dark vein. For butterfly shrimp, called for in some recipes, make a little deeper cut and spread shrimp.

Drop cleaned shrimp into simmering stock. Bring to a boil. Reduce heat again, and simmer 3 to 5 minutes or until shrimp are pink. *Over-cooking toughens shrimp and reduces them in size.* Remove shrimp from stock with slotted spoon or strainer. Let cool. Or use as described in recipes, utilizing stock, if possible.

Frozen shelled and cleaned shrimp can be quite simply cooked by merely putting them in a covered saucepan and steaming. The melting ice provides enough moisture.

BROILED BUTTERFLY SHRIMP

1 pound large shrimp	Salt and pepper
4 tablespoons butter	Paprika
1 slice peeled garlic	Lemon sections

Prepare butterfly shrimp. Leave tails on.

Melt butter in saucepan with garlic slice. Add little salt and grind of pepper. Discard garlic. Spread shrimp in shallow pan. Brush generously with garlic butter. Sprinkle with paprika. Broil under moderate heat 3 to 5 minutes, only until shrimp are hot through and barely done. Serve at once with lemon slices. Makes 3 or more servings.

DIXIE FRIED SHRIMP

1½ pounds large raw or quick-frozen shrimp	½ teaspoon baking powder
½ cup sifted flour	1 egg, beaten
¼ cup yellow corn meal	½ cup ice water
½ teaspoon salt	1 tablespoon salad oil
	Fat for deep-frying

Wash and drain shrimp. Defrost if quick-frozen. Peel shells off and remove dark vein, but leave tails on. Let shrimp drain and dry thoroughly while mixing batter.

Sift flour, corn meal, salt, and baking powder together. Combine beaten egg, ice water, and salad oil, beating gently. Mix with dry ingredients just enough to moisten flour.

Dip shrimp in batter. Fry in deep, hot fat (375° F. on frying thermometer) until golden brown. Drain on thick paper towels. Serve at once with Sweet-Sour Shrimp Sauce (page 556). Makes 4 servings as main dish, 6 or more as appetizer.

MEXICAN SHRIMP

1 onion, peeled and cut fine	1 teaspoon Worcestershire sauce
2 tablespoons butter, margarine, peanut oil, olive oil or corn oil	1 teaspoon chili powder
1 sweet red pepper, cut fine	1 green pepper, cut fine
1 clove garlic, peeled and sliced	¼ teaspoon celery salt
1 (7¾-ounce) can tomatoes or 1 cup chopped fresh tomatoes	2 pounds shrimp, cleaned and freshly boiled

Cook onion in butter or margarine until tender. Add remaining ingredients except shrimp. Stir well to mix. Cook 30 minutes, stirring occasionally. If shrimp are freshly boiled and still hot, pour into warm serving dish and pour hot sauce over them. Or add shrimp to sauce. Mix to heat. Pour into serving dish. Serve at once. Makes 6 to 8 servings.

A good dish for rumpus room parties. Prepare a big casserole of macaroni and cheese, a baked ham, or a platter of cold cuts and relishes. This is the night for a fruit cobbler and coffee or a sweetmeat tray of nougat, spiced nuts, and stuffed apricots.

SHRIMP GUMBO

1 pound quick-frozen deveined shrimp	1 ½ teaspoons salt
2 cups sliced fresh okra or 1 (10-ounce) package quick-frozen okra, sliced	½ teaspoon pepper
	2 cups hot water
	1 cup canned tomatoes
⅓ cup shortening	2 bay leaves
⅔ cup chopped green onions and tops	3 drops Tabasco sauce
	1 teaspoon filé powder, if available
2 cloves garlic, peeled and mashed	1 ½ cups cooked rice

Let shrimp defrost as described on package.

Sauté okra in shortening about 10 minutes or until okra appears dry, stirring constantly. Add onions, garlic, salt, and pepper. Stir and cook 2 or 3 minutes. Remove garlic and discard. Add shrimp. Cook about 5 minutes. Add water, tomatoes, and bay leaves. Cover and simmer 20 minutes. Remove bay leaves. Add Tabasco and filé powder. Stir; remove from heat at once. Place ¼ cup hot rice in each of 6 deep soup plates. Fill with gumbo. Makes 6 servings.

This is a meal in itself.

See also Soups.

SHRIMP-CRAB POULETTE

From the Pontchartrain, New Orleans

4 shallots, thinly sliced	1 quart Thick Cream Sauce
1 pound raw frozen, or fresh	(page 557)
shrimp, shelled and deveined	1 pound lump crab meat, care-
4 tablespoons butter	fully boned
½ cup Sauterne wine	8 slices toast
½ cup sherry	

Sauté shallots and shrimp in butter in 2½-quart saucepan, over medium heat, 5 minutes. Add both wines. Bring to a boil. Add sauce and stir to blend well. Add crab meat. Simmer 5 minutes or until just steaming hot. Serve at once on toast strips. Makes 6 to 8 servings.

You'll have this in New Orleans as I do, each delightful trip. It's dramatic done in a chafing dish as a company dinner entrée or as a big moment in a Sunday night supper. Encourage the Chef to make it a specialty.

SHRIMP CREOLE

1 onion, peeled and sliced	1 teaspoon salt
1 green pepper, cut fine	½ teaspoon sugar
½ cup sliced celery	⅛ teaspoon cayenne
½ bay leaf	1½ pounds cleaned cooked
2 tablespoons butter or marga-	shrimp
rine	3 cups hot cooked rice
1 tablespoon flour	
3 cups chopped canned	
tomatoes	

Sauté onion, green pepper, celery, and bay leaf in butter or margarine 8 minutes. Add flour, and stir and mix smoothly 2 or 3 minutes. Add tomatoes, salt, sugar, and cayenne. Mix, and let simmer 15 minutes. Add cooked shrimp. Let simmer only until shrimp are hot. Do not boil. Serve on hot rice. Makes 4 to 6 servings.

Excellent for buffet but also good as main lunch or dinner dish. It can—and does, in my family—go on beach picnics in a covered casserole with salad makings and an ice-cold watermelon.

SHRIMP CURRY

4 tablespoons butter or margarine	2 teaspoons curry powder
1 onion, peeled and sliced	½ teaspoon powdered ginger
2 tablespoons finely cut green pepper	2 chicken bouillon cubes
½ clove garlic, peeled and mashed	2 cups boiling water
3 tablespoons flour	2 (5-ounce) cans deveined shrimp
	4 cups hot cooked rice

Melt butter or margarine. Sauté onion, pepper, and garlic only until onion is tender. Remove garlic and discard. Mix flour, curry powder, and ginger. Stir into onion mixture. Add bouillon cubes and boiling water. Cook, stirring until thickened. Add a little salt and pepper if needed. Add drained shrimp. Heat through, but do not boil. Serve over hot rice. Makes 4 to 6 servings.

If you are hot-curry people, add curry to taste during the sauce-making process. I sometimes add minced, peeled tart apple or a dollop of orange marmalade. The condiments that go with it make an event of this dish—small side dishes of chopped peanuts, chutney, chopped eggs, dried coconut.

SHRIMP JAMBALAYA

2 (4½-ounce) cans deveined small shrimp	1½ cups canned tomatoes
1 cup diced ham	1½ cups shrimp liquid and water
2 tablespoons shortening	1 cup uncooked rice
½ cup chopped peeled onions	¼ teaspoon salt
1 cup finely cut green peppers	1 bay leaf
2 cloves garlic, peeled and mashed	½ teaspoon thyme
	⅛ teaspoon cayenne
	¼ cup finely cut parsley

Drain shrimp and save liquor. Cook ham in shortening in deep heavy skillet about 3 minutes. Add onions, green peppers, and garlic. Cook until onions and peppers are tender. Remove garlic and discard. Add tomatoes, shrimp liquid and water, rice, and seasonings. Cover skillet. Cook slowly 25 to 30 minutes or until rice is tender. Stir occasionally. Add parsley and shrimp. Heat but do not boil. Serve at once. Makes 6 servings.

Serve on toast or with beaten biscuit. Makes a one-dish meal.

SHRIMP, ITALIAN STYLE

1 pound fresh shrimp or 2 (10-ounce) packages quick-frozen shrimp	1 clove garlic
	6 green peppers
6 tablespoons flour	½ cup olive oil
2 tablespoons grated Gruyère or Parmesan cheese	¼ cup dry white wine
	¾ teaspoon salt
1 teaspoon salt	⅛ teaspoon pepper

Rinse shrimp under cold running water and let drain. Peel shrimp and remove dark vein. If deveined quick-frozen shrimp are used, let defrost. Drop into boiling water for 5 minutes then drain.

Mix flour, cheese, and salt in a paper bag. Add shrimp and shake bag to coat shrimp well. Peel garlic and mash it. Remove stem and seeds from green peppers. Cut peppers in strips. Heat oil in large skillet or chafing dish. Add shrimp and garlic and cook about 5 minutes or until shrimp are golden. Remove garlic and discard. Remove shrimp and set aside. Put pepper strips in same skillet or chafing dish. Cover tightly and cook over medium heat 10 to 15 minutes or until tender. Add shrimp, wine, salt, pepper. Stir and heat through, 5 to 8 minutes. Makes 4 servings.

SHRIMP NEWBURG

3 tablespoons butter	⅛ teaspoon paprika
3 tablespoons flour	¼ cup sherry
2 cups light cream	2 tablespoons cognac
¼ teaspoon salt	2 cups cooked cleaned shrimp
⅛ teaspoon pepper	4 to 6 slices buttered toast

Melt butter in upper part of double boiler or chafing dish over hot water. Add flour and stir until smooth. Add cream, stirring as you add, over moderate heat. Continue to cook and stir until thickened. Season with salt, pepper, and paprika. Add sherry and brandy, a little at a time, stirring well after each addition. Add shrimp, mix, and heat through. Serve at once on toast. Makes 4 to 6 servings.

Shrimp à la King: Omit brandy, add 1 or 2 canned pimientos, cut fine, 1 cup cooked peas, ¼ cup sliced ripe olives. Serve over rice as a **Shrimp Risotto.** Shrimp à la King is sometimes served in patty shells as either a first course or as a main dish.

Shrimp Newburg, or à la King, Sandwich: Cover lightly buttered slices of toast with shrimp Newburg or à la King mixture. Sprinkle top lightly with grated Gruyère or Parmesan cheese. Run under broiler heat 2 or 3 minutes, only until top is browning. Serve at once as hot, open-face sandwich. Recipe makes about 6 such sandwiches or 8 smaller ones. Good for Sunday night.

CHAPTER FOURTEEN

Meats and Game

There are a few guides to meat buying which beginner cooks should follow to insure flavorful, tender meat dishes. The first, and most important, is to choose a dealer who handles high-quality meat. He can become a friendly dealer who will discuss cuts with you, advise on cookery, and guide you in selecting specials and seasonal bargains.

A second helper for all cooks is the reminder that less tender cuts, the meat specialties, and many canned and quick-frozen meats and meat products add variety to menus and help whittle down the budget.

The appearance of the meat, the Government inspection stamp which assures meat from healthy animals, slaughtered under exacting sanitary conditions, and packer brand, retailer brand, city or state inspection stamps, and Government grade, which indicates quality of meat, are guides in buying meat. Your dealer will point out any such stamps and brands when cutting roasts or other meats for you.

In choosing self-service meats, look for information on the package and the label, such as name of cut, packer, retailer or Government grade, weight, price per pound or total weight. Such meats, as well as pre-packaged hams and other large cuts, often include cookery directions. Check any such directions against your best recipes, for some of the commercial directions are too general to apply with success. In general it is safe to follow cooking instructions on frozen meats. Some cooks prefer to defrost meat partially before cooking. Others prefer to place frozen meat in a skillet or oven and increase the cooking time accordingly.

Basically, there are two methods of cooking meat: they are with dry heat or moist heat, depending on whether liquid is used in the cooking process. Dry-heat cookery—oven roasting, broiling, pan broiling, and pan frying—is ideal for tender cuts, chops, steaks, and roasts. In moist-heat cookery—braising, stewing, simmering—liquid combines with the meat to create steam to soften tough or less tender cuts.

CUTS OF BEEF

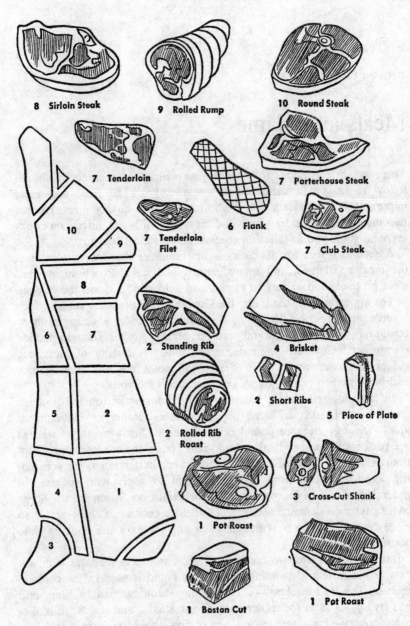

8 Sirloin Steak

9 Rolled Rump

10 Round Steak

7 Tenderloin

7 Porterhouse Steak

7 Tenderloin Filet

6 Flank

7 Club Steak

2 Standing Rib

4 Brisket

2 Short Ribs

5 Piece of Plate

2 Rolled Rib Roast

3 Cross-Cut Shank

1 Pot Roast

1 Boston Cut

1 Pot Roast

CUTS OF VEAL

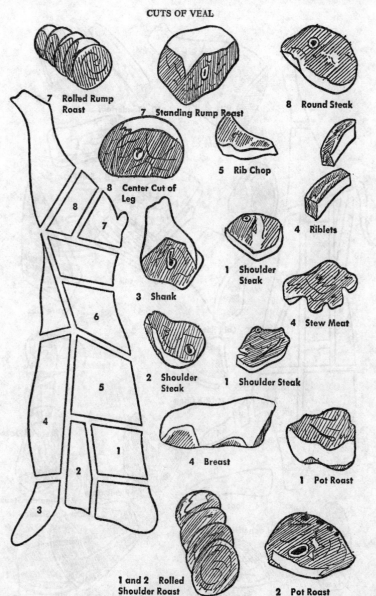

7 Rolled Rump Roast

7 Standing Rump Roast

8 Round Steak

8 Center Cut of Leg

5 Rib Chop

4 Riblets

3 Shank

1 Shoulder Steak

4 Stew Meat

2 Shoulder Steak

1 Shoulder Steak

4 Breast

1 Pot Roast

1 and 2 Rolled Shoulder Roast

2 Pot Roast

CUTS OF PORK

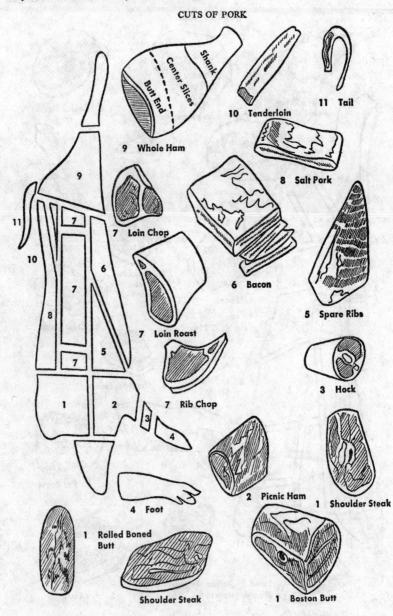

9 Whole Ham
(Shank, Center Slices, Butt End)

10 Tenderloin

11 Tail

8 Salt Pork

7 Loin Chop

6 Bacon

5 Spare Ribs

7 Loin Roast

3 Hock

7 Rib Chop

2 Picnic Ham

1 Shoulder Steak

4 Foot

1 Rolled Boned Butt

Shoulder Steak

1 Boston Butt

CUTS OF LAMB

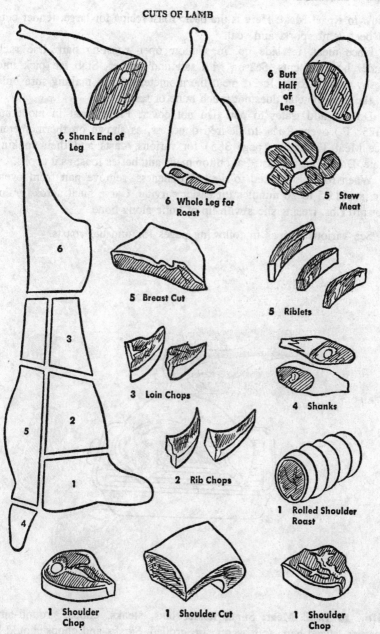

6 Shank End of Leg

6 Whole Leg for Roast

6 Butt Half of Leg

5 Stew Meat

5 Breast Cut

5 Riblets

3 Loin Chops

4 Shanks

2 Rib Chops

1 Rolled Shoulder Roast

1 Shoulder Chop

1 Shoulder Cut

1 Shoulder Chop

How to Roast Meat: Here is the basic roast recipe for large, tender cuts of beef, lamb, pork, and veal.

Place meat, fat side up, in shallow open roasting pan. Use rack under boneless cuts. Season with salt and pepper. Stab ice pick into fleshy part of roast. Insert meat thermometer deeply, making sure bulb of the thermometer does not touch bone or rest in fat.

Do not add water to pan. Do not cover. Place roast in moderate (325° F.) oven. Roast to desired doneness, as shown on thermometer. See Meat Timetable (page 385) for various roasts and their cooking time. Do not baste roast. Fat on top melts and bastes roast as it cooks.

When roast is cooked to desired doneness, remove pan from oven. Let stand 15 to 20 minutes for easier carving. Carve meat across grain, toward ribs, freeing slices with tip of knife along bone.

See various recipes in following pages for unusual roasts.

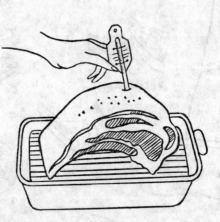

How to Broil Meat: Small tender cuts, steaks, chops, ground-meat patties, sliced ham and bacon, are broiled. Steaks and chops should be cut about 1 inch thick. They may be broiled frozen or partially or completely thawed.

Do not broil fresh pork. It should be cooked at lower temperature for longer time. Do not broil veal. It lacks the essential fat for broiling.

Place steak or chops on greased rack in broiler pan. Slash fat edge of meat at 1-inch intervals to prevent curling. Brush very lean meat with melted fat before broiling.

Follow your range manufacturer's directions for broiling. Place rack so that surface of meat is 2½ to 3 inches from source of heat—greater distance for very thick cuts. Broil about half of time indicated in Broiling Table (page 386). Season meat, turn, and finish broiling. To turn, use tongs. Or if fork is used, insert it in fat, not in the meat where juices would be lost.

Degree of doneness of meat depends on preference. Avoid overcooking. Serve sizzling on hot platter. Add a pat of butter to steaks, or brush with flavored butter or sauce according to recipe.

How to Cook Frozen Meat: For best results, thaw frozen meats in refrigerator. Leave meats wrapped while thawing. Do not immerse meat in water for thawing unless meat is to be cooked in the water after thawing. Cook meat as soon as thawed. Do not refreeze meat after thawing. Follow frozen-food packer's instructions on thawing meat and on the cookery and seasoning.

To Store Fresh Meat: Place meat in refrigerator as soon as it comes from market. Loosen store wrappings or rewrap loosely in waxed paper. Pre-packaged meats should have wrappings loosened before refrigerating.

Steaks, chops, small roasts can be held under good refrigeration for 2 to 3 days. Larger roasts can be held slightly longer. Ground or cubed meat and variety meats should be cooked within 24 hours after purchase.

After cooking, meat should be allowed to stand at room temperature only about half an hour. Then it should be stored in covered dish or wrapped tightly to prevent drying out. Place in very cold part of refrigerator. Meat keeps better in large pieces. Cooked roasts and larger cuts of meat, if unsliced, will hold for 4 days in a good refrigerator.

Beef

BRAISED SHORT RIBS

3 pounds short ribs (cut in 4 serving pieces)	Bay leaf, crumbled
1 ½ teaspoons salt	¼ cup salad oil
½ teaspoon pepper	1 ½ cups beef stock or consommé
¼ cup flour	¼ cup cold water
2 onions, peeled and grated	1 tablespoon flour
¼ cup finely cut celery leaves	2 tablespoons heavy cream or sour cream
	1 teaspoon sugar

Roll and tie each serving with string. Mix salt, pepper, and flour. Dredge meat lightly and place in roasting pan with cover.

Start oven at moderate (375° F.).

Combine onions, celery leaves, bay leaf, and oil. Pour over meat. Brown uncovered in oven about 30 minutes, turning meat frequently. When well browned, add stock or consommé to half cover. Cover pan with lid. Lower heat to moderately slow (300° F.) and continue cooking about 1 hour or until meat is tender. Test with fork and continue cooking if necessary.

Remove meat to warmed platter and keep it hot. Discard string. Skim fat from roasting pan liquid. Stir cold water into flour smoothly. Add slowly to hot liquid in baking pan. Stir steadily over moderate heat until thickened, about 1 or 2 minutes of boiling. Stir in cream, add sugar, and bring to a boil again. Pour over meat and serve at once. Makes 4 servings.

BOILED BEEF WITH VEGETABLES

3 pounds beef brisket or 4-pound piece cross-rib beef	2 tablespoons vinegar
Boiling water	1 teaspoon salt
1 onion, peeled and sliced	12 medium potatoes, pared
2 stalks celery, sliced	12 small onions, peeled
1 bay leaf	12 small carrots, scraped

Place meat in deep stewing kettle or Dutch oven. Cover with boiling water. Add onion, celery, bay leaf, vinegar, and salt. Cover kettle and bring to a boil. Reduce heat and simmer about 3 hours, until meat is tender. Remove any scum which comes to top at the end of 2 hours.

Add potatoes, onions, carrots. Cover pot and continue to simmer 1½ hours, until vegetables are cooked.

Remove meat from kettle to warmed platter. Cut enough slices for all to be served. Surround meat with drained vegetables. Makes 6 servings.

Usually Mustard Sauce (page 553) or Horse-radish Sauce (page 427) is served with boiled beef.

Stock left in kettle should be simmered down to about 5 or 6 cups. Chill overnight in covered bowl in refrigerator. Next day skim off fat. Heat stock, strain, and serve as lunch broth. Garnish with small croutons or cheese croutons.

We always save some broth for a base for split pea soup either making the soup in quantity and freezing what we don't eat up, or freezing stock for the cold winter day when pea soup with croutons, salad, and French garlic bread will warm our cockles. No stale bread ever goes to waste at Daisyfields. It is made into savoury, herb-flavored croutons and stored in glass jars, covered, in the refrigerator to add zing to soups or salads.

RAGOUT, HÔTEL DE GENÈVE

Leftover roast beef or game	Salt and pepper
4 tablespoons butter or margarine	¼ cup currant or cranberry jelly
4 tablespoons flour	1 tablespoon Worcestershire Sauce
4 cups stock or bouillon	1 tablespoon brown sugar

Leftover roast beef, or game such as moose or venison, is the base of this delicious ragout. Cut cold meat into bite-size pieces, making about 2½ cups.

Melt butter or margarine in 2-quart kettle. Stir in flour until lightly browned. Stir in stock or bouillon, continuing to stir and cook until boiling. Add seasoning if needed. Stir in jelly, Worcestershire, and sugar. When mixed, add meat. Cover pot and cook slowly over low heat 30 minutes. Uncover pot, to let cook down a little. Makes 4 servings.

Good flavor and economy are the virtues of this Swiss dish. Try it for a cold night's dinner.

BEEF CURRY

3 ½ pounds top round or sirloin	1 cup seedless raisins
1 cup all-purpose flour	2 apples, pared and cored, or
2 ½ tablespoons curry powder	2 fresh plums, seeded and
¼ pound butter or margarine	halved
2 cloves garlic, peeled and mashed	1 cup diced peeled onion
	Salt and pepper
4 cups hot water	6 or more cups hot rice

Have meat dealer cube meat, or cut it in the kitchen to bite-size pieces. Mix flour and curry powder. Dredge meat thoroughly with mixture. Melt butter or margarine in deep skillet or Dutch oven. Add garlic. Brown the meat, stirring often. When all pieces are browned, discard garlic. Add water, raisins, apples or plums, and onion. Cover, bring slowly to a boil, then reduce heat and cook over moderate heat 1 hour. Taste, and add salt and pepper if needed. Serve at once over hot rice or reheat curry mixture in chafing dish and serve on hot rice. Makes 6 to 8 servings.

Condiments for Curry: These are an important part of its service and the enjoyment of your guests. (See other curry recipes in various chapters.) Use matching Chinese bowls, if possible, for chopped green pepper, scallions, peanuts, and hard-cooked eggs. Minced celery leaves and finely cut candied ginger or pineapple are sometimes served as curry condiments, and the best flavor of all is Bombay duck—dried salt fish—crumbled and sprinkled on top of a plate of hot rice and curry. Also see Serundang (page 555) in relish chapter.

OVEN BEEF STEW

2 tablespoons flour	1 clove garlic, peeled and cut fine
1 ½ teaspoons salt	
⅛ teaspoon pepper	1 bay leaf
1 ½ pounds beef chuck cut in 1-inch cubes	⅛ teaspoon thyme or savory
	1 ½ cups water
2 tablespoons fat	1 tablespoon vinegar
6 carrots, scraped and sliced	1 (10-ounce) package quick-frozen peas
10 small onions, peeled	
1 (6-ounce) can tomato paste	

Combine flour, salt, and pepper and dredge over meat until thoroughly coated. Brown meat in hot fat in flameproof 2-quart casserole or Dutch oven. Add carrots and onions. Mix tomato paste, garlic, bay leaf, thyme, water, and vinegar in saucepan and bring to a boil. Pour over meat.

Start oven at moderate (350° F.).

Bake casserole, covered, about 45 minutes. Add partially thawed peas. Cover casserole. Bake about 45 minutes longer or until meat and all vegetables are done. Makes 4 to 6 servings.

I often make this on Thursdays, the day I run office *and* house and top it all off with a dancing lesson at 5 o'clock. I start it at the lunch hour break and time the final cooking to meet the dinner schedule. My sons always know that on Mother's day at the stove there's always enough for one—or four or five more.

BEEF STEW, DAISYFIELDS

2 pound lean chuck beef cut in 1½-inch cubes
2 tablespoons fat
1 teaspoon sugar
1 tablespoon flour
2 teaspoons salt
¼ teaspoon pepper
1 teaspoon chili powder
1 bay leaf
¼ teaspoon thyme or savory
4 cloves
2 tomatoes, peeled and quartered
1 green pepper, coarsely cut
2 cups meat stock or consommé
2 cups boiling water
6 small potatoes, pared and halved
6 small carrots, scraped and halved
6 small onions, peeled
3 or 4 stalks celery, sliced
1 cup fresh peas

Brown meat slowly in hot fat in Dutch oven or heavy kettle. Sprinkle with sugar and continue browning until all meat is well seared. Dust lightly with flour and continue to brown. Add seasonings, bay leaf, cloves, tomatoes, green pepper, stock or consommé, and boiling water. Cover kettle. Simmer over low heat about 1½ to 2 hours or until meat is tender.

Add vegetables, except peas, and continue to cook 30 minutes longer. Add peas; cook 15 minutes longer or until all are done. Makes 6 servings.

We really dress this up, serving it from a lovely old Meissen onion-ware tureen in Meissen soup plates with Staffordshire service plates beneath. Small buttered baking powder biscuits or orange muffins complement it nicely.

BEEF GOULASH WITH NOODLES

¼ pound salt pork
1½ pounds round steak, cut in
    2-inch pieces
1 tablespoon flour
1 teaspoon salt
½ teaspoon pepper
1 clove garlic, mashed

½ cup finely cut peeled onion
1 cup condensed beef bouillon
1 (8-ounce) can tomato sauce
12 peppercorns
1 tablespoon paprika
1 (6-ounce) package noodles

Dice salt pork. Heat in heavy skillet over low heat until cooked. Remove salt pork and save. Sprinkle steak with flour, salt, and pepper. Brown on all sides in pork fat. Add garlic, onion, bouillon, and tomato sauce, and mix. Stir in salt, peppercorns, and paprika. Cover pan. Cook over low heat about 30 minutes. Remove garlic and discard it.

Continue cooking 1 hour. Add more liquid from time to time if necessary. Sprinkle cooked diced salt pork on top. Serve on bed of hot noodles. Makes 4 servings.

My friend, Harry Elmlark, loves to serve beef goulash with noodles at the big buffet suppers the Elmlarks give in Westport. Mr. Elmlark makes the goulash in quantity the day before and reheats it on the buffet table. He serves it with mixed green salad, garlic bread, macédoine of fruit, perhaps with kirschwasser in it. A nice Burgundy goes well with it or mugs of cold beer.

RIB STEW WITH DUMPLINGS

2 pounds short ribs
¼ cup flour
1 tablespoon salt
¼ teaspoon pepper
2 tablespoons fat
2 (1-pound) cans tomatoes,
    chopped
½ clove garlic, peeled and
    minced

1 tablespoon Worcestershire
    sauce
4 carrots, scraped and sliced
2 medium onions, peeled and
    sliced
1 potato, pared and diced
Parsley Dumplings

Cut ribs into serving pieces. Combine flour, salt, and pepper. Dredge meat on all sides. Brown meat in hot fat in Dutch oven or heavy kettle. Combine tomatoes, garlic, Worcestershire. Pour over meat. Cover kettle and simmer 1½ hours. Add vegetables, cover, and simmer 45 minutes longer or until meat and vegetables are done. Skim fat off top. Taste for seasoning. Add salt and pepper if needed.

Drop Parsley Dumpling mixture from tablespoon on top of bubbling stew. Cover kettle tightly. Increase heat to a rapid boil, then reduce heat and simmer 15 minutes. Do not lift cover during the 15-minute period. Test dumplings for doneness. Continue cooking if necessary. Serve as soon as dumplings are done. Makes 4 to 6 servings.

Parsley Dumplings

1 cup sifted all-purpose flour
2 teaspoons baking powder
½ teaspoon salt
¼ cup finely cut parsley

½ cup milk
2 tablespoons oil or melted butter

Sift flour, baking powder, and salt together, and add parsley. Combine milk and oil or shortening and add to dry ingredients. Stir just enough to moisten dry ingredients. Drop as dumplings on stew, as described above. See also other dumpling recipes.

MY FAMILY'S FAVORITE POT ROAST

6-pounds boned beef rump pot roast
⅓ cup all-purpose flour
2 tablespoons beef fat or shortening
2 teaspoons salt
⅛ teaspoon pepper
¼ teaspoon orégano
¼ cup wine vinegar

2 thin slices lemon
1 large yellow onion, peeled and sliced
1 (No. 2½) can tomatoes
2 cups peeled small whole white onions
8 small carrots, scraped
3 tablespoons flour
½ cup water

Sprinkle beef with flour, coating all sides. Brown 15 to 20 minutes in fat in heavy kettle or Dutch oven over moderate heat. Sprinkle meat with salt and pepper as it browns. Add orégano, vinegar, lemon, onion, and tomatoes. Cover pot tightly and let simmer over low heat. Turn roast occasionally. Cook 3½ hours.

Add onions and carrots. Cover and simmer 1 hour longer or until beef is tender and vegetables done. Add bouillon mixed with white wine or hot water if more liquid is needed. Remove roast to warmed platter. Surround with vegetables. Serve at once. Or, if making gravy, keep roast and vegetables warm in oven. Skim fat from pot broth. Add enough boiling water to broth to make 2½ cups gravy. Stir 2 tablespoons flour into about ½ cup of this broth, then stir into the pot. Let boil 2 or 3 minutes, stirring smoothly. Season as needed. Serve hot with roast and vegetables. Makes 10 servings.

Rump Roast with Noodles: Prepare roast as described on previous page. Cook noodles as described on package. Serve mounds of buttered, seasoned noodles alternating with vegetables on platter around roast.

BEEF STROGANOFF

1 ½ pounds beef fillet	1 teaspoon tomato paste
4 tablespoons butter or margarine	2 tablespoons flour
1 large yellow onion	1 cup stock or bouillon
½ pound fresh mushrooms or 1 (6-ounce) can sliced mushrooms	1 ½ teaspoons salt
	1 teaspoon pepper
	1 cup commercial sour cream
½ teaspoon meat glaze	2 teaspoons finely cut dill

Trim all fat and sinew from beef. Cut against the grain into small strips about 2 inches long and ½ inch thick. Brown in 2 tablespoons butter or margarine in heavy fireproof casserole.

Start oven at moderate or 375° F.

Peel and dice onion, and slice mushrooms. Melt remaining 2 tablespoons butter or margarine in small skillet. Cook onion and mushrooms over moderate heat until onion is tender but not brown. Remove skillet from heat. Stir in glaze and tomato paste. Mix flour smoothly with a little stock or bouillon and stir into mixture. Gradually add remaining bouillon. Return pan to heat, and stir until sauce begins to boil. Add salt and pepper. Stir sour cream, a little at a time, into center of sauce, stirring steadily. Pour over beef in casserole. Sprinkle with 1 teaspoon of dill.

Cover and heat in oven 20 minutes or until hot through. If less expensive cut of beef, such as round, is used, extend oven time to 25 or 30 minutes or until meat is tender. Sprinkle with remaining dill and serve. Makes 4 servings.

This delicious, impressive party dish is often served with noodles.

CHUCK ROAST, FLEMISH STYLE

5 pounds chuck beef
1 cup cider vinegar
Salt
Pepper
2 teaspoons whole allspice
1 blade mace
2 cups bread crumbs
1 egg
1 onion, peeled and chopped
1½ teaspoons mixed dried herbs
 (thyme, marjoram, sage,
 savory)

1 tablespoon melted butter or
 margarine
1 (8 or 9-ounce) can tomato
 paste
2 or 3 tablespoons shortening
 or fat
Boiling water
1 onion, peeled and stuck with
 cloves
Flour

Have roast rolled and larded at meat market. Heat vinegar, 2 teaspoons salt, ½ teaspoon pepper, the allspice, and mace together 5 minutes in glass or enamel saucepan. Pour over meat. Let marinate while preparing dressing.

Combine crumbs with egg, chopped onion, a little salt and pepper, the mixed herbs, melted butter or margarine, and tomato paste. Mix well. Remove meat from spiced vinegar. Gash deeply with sharp knife. Fill slits with crumb dressing.

Brown stuffed roll in fat in Dutch oven or heavy kettle. When well browned on all sides add enough boiling water to cover bottom of kettle and prevent burning. Add onion stuck with cloves. Cover kettle. Let meat simmer 2 to 3 hours or until tender. Add a little more boiling water to kettle from time to time if necessary.

There should be about 1½ cups brown sauce in bottom of kettle when roast is done. Remove meat to hot platter and cut 8 slices. Keep it hot. Thicken sauce with about 1 tablespoon flour. Stir and boil 2 or 3 minutes. Pour over meat and serve hot. Makes 8 or more servings.

This is a good dish for a family-plus-guests dinner with hungry men at your table. Add small baked potatoes, a mixed green salad, brown-and-serve clover rolls, and my Pears and Wine Dessert (page 268) for a well-rounded menu.

FRENCH POT ROAST
Boeuf à la Mode

4 pounds boneless pot roast	½ calf's foot or 1 veal knuckle,
2 tablespoons butter	cracked
3 tablespoons cognac	1 teaspoon salt
1 cup dry white wine	½ teaspoon pepper
1 bay leaf	18 small white onions, peeled
1 sprig parsley	6 large carrots, scraped
½ teaspoon thyme	

Ask meat dealer to lard the roast with thin strips of salt pork. Heat butter in deep flameproof casserole. Brown beef on all sides. Heat brandy in small saucepan or in very large cooking spoon. Ignite with match and pour over meat. Add wine and enough water almost to cover meat. Bring to a boil slowly. Add herbs and calf's foot or veal knuckle. Season with salt and pepper. Cover casserole.

Start oven at moderate (350° F.).

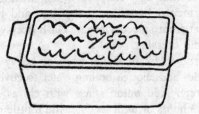

Place casserole in oven and let cook 1½ hours. Add onions and carrots. Cook another hour or 1½ hours, until meat is done and vegetables are tender. To serve, chop meat off calf's foot and discard bone or veal knuckle. Skim fat from top of sauce. Add calf's foot meat and serve very hot in casserole. Or remove beef to hot serving dish and surround with vegetables. Reheat gravy and serve separately. Makes 6 to 8 servings.

This is one of my freezer specialties. I double the recipe and freeze what's left over against a maid's day-out or sudden drop-ins.

SAUERBRATEN

3 pounds boned rump or chuck	2 tablespoons drippings
2 teaspoons salt	3 stalks celery, sliced
½ teaspoon pepper	6 small carrots, quartered
2 tablespoons sugar	½ teaspoon salt
2 bay leaves	2 peppercorns
6 whole cloves	2 cloves
4 peppercorns	¼ cup sugar
2 onions, peeled and sliced	6 gingersnaps, crumbled
1 quart cider vinegar	½ cup commercial sour cream
2 cups water	
1 pint red wine (optional) or cider	

Three or 4 days before a sauerbraten dinner, select a fine rump or chuck pot roast. Rinse meat and pat dry with paper towel. Rub salt and pepper into meat thoroughly. Place in deep earthen dish or crock. Sprinkle with sugar, bay leaves, cloves, peppercorns, and onions. Combine vinegar, water, and wine, and pour over meat. Add more liquid if necessary, since meat must be covered. Cover dish or crock. Let stand in refrigerator 3 or 4 days. Turn meat occasionally and stir vinegar marinade over and around it.

On the day to be cooked, drain meat; save vinegar marinade. Brown meat quickly on all sides in drippings in Dutch oven or heavy kettle, about 20 minutes. Add onions from marinade, celery, carrots, salt, peppercorns, cloves, and about 1½ cups of the marinade. Cover kettle. Cook 3½ hours or longer, until meat is thoroughly tender. Add more marinade from time to time if necessary.

Remove meat to hot platter, slicing some of it. Keep platter hot in open oven. Strain drippings. Skim off fat. Stir ¼ cup sugar into the hot kettle. Let sugar melt and begin to brown. Stir in 2 cups strained drippings. Add gingersnap crumbs. Stir and heat until thickened. Stir in cream. Heat but do not boil. Pour a little hot sauce over the roast. Serve remaining sauce in gravy bowl. Makes 6 or more servings.

This is my favorite German dish. At Lüchow's famous old German restaurant in New York, I learned the secret of using gingersnaps in the sauce.

ROAST TENDERLOIN OF BEEF, DAISYFIELDS

4-pounds beef tenderloin
¾ pound beef suet
1 teaspoon salt
Quick grind fresh pepper
½ cup dry white wine
1 (6-ounce) can sliced mushrooms
3 tablesspoons butter or margarine

1 shallot or green onion, chopped
1 teaspoon meat glaze
1 teaspoon tomato paste
2 teaspoons cornstarch or potato flour
1 cup bouillon or hot water
½ cup Madeira or sherry

Remove fat from meat. Slice fat and extra suet and wrap around meat, tying with strings. Season with salt and pepper.

Start oven at hot (450° F.).

Place roast in shallow open roasting pan. Roast until fat is hot. Reduce temperature to moderate (325° F.). Continue roasting until thermometer registers 160° F. or roast is medium-well done. Or continue roasting to desired doneness.

Remove roasting pan. Pour wine over meat. Keep warm in oven with door left open. Sauté mushrooms in butter or margarine. Sauté shallot or onion in tablespoon fat from roasting pan. Remove from heat and stir in meat glaze. Add tomato paste and mix well. Stir in cornstarch or potato flour until well mixed. Stir in stock or water with wine. Heat and stir until boiling. Add mushrooms. Let simmer 5 minutes.

Remove strings from roast. Place roast on hot serving platter. Cut slices to serve all at table. Spoon a little hot mushroom sauce over cut slices. Serve remaining sauce in warm bowl. Makes 6 to 8 servings.

BROILED STEAKS

See general directions for broiling at beginning of this chapter.

Sirloin or porterhouse steaks are cuts generally used for broiled steaks large enough to serve two or more people. Cooking time depends on thickness and quality of meat and distance from heat. The most accurate test for doneness is to insert paring knife close to bone and see how steak looks.

Tournedos are round cuts of tender, boneless steak about 2 inches in diameter and 1 inch thick. They are cut from the thin end of the beef fillet, trimmed, then surrounded with thin layer of fat.

Filets mignons are similar to tournedos but are cut from the slightly larger center section of beef fillet. These expensive cuts may be imitated by cutting a thick steak into rounds and surrounding each with suet, bacon, or salt pork.

Such cuts are sautéed or broiled. Season lightly. Cook in heavy skillet in plenty of butter over moderate heat. When meat is browned on one side, lower heat, turn tournedo, and cook other side to desired doneness, usually medium rare for such cuts. For broiling, place in preheated greased pan and broil 5 to 7 minutes on each side.

You will live on these in Spain. Delicious at Madrid's Jockey Club, at the Ritz or at Horchers.

Chateaubriand is cut from the thick end of beef fillet. Should weigh between 1 or 2 pounds. It is boneless, serves 2 to 4 people, may be sautéed or broiled.

BROILED STEAK WITH PARMESAN CHEESE

Steak Parmigiana

3 ½ -pounds sirloin or porterhouse steak	½ cup bread crumbs
2 cloves garlic, mashed	1 teaspoon salt
½ cup olive oil	½ teaspoon pepper
1 cup grated Parmesan cheese	½ teaspoon dried orégano
	¼ teaspoon rosemary

Place steak in shallow dish. Add garlic to oil and pour over steak. Let stand covered in cold place, not necessarily in refrigerator, 1 hour. Turn steak a few times during the hour.

Make mixture of cheese, crumbs, salt, pepper, and herbs. Lay drained steak on preheated broiler pan. Broil about 5 minutes. Quickly spread with half of cheese mixture. Return to heat. Broil slowly, until browned. Turn steak. Pour a little of garlic oil over it. Broil 5 minutes. Spread quickly with remaining cheese mixture. Broil slowly to desired doneness. Serve on hot platter. Makes 4 to 6 servings.

This is delicious with those flat, green Italian string beans now available frozen.

BEEF MARROW STEAK

¼ pound beef marrow, diced	1 cup dry white wine
4 tablespoon butter or marga- rine	1½ teaspoons salt Quick grind black pepper
½ cup sliced shallots or young onions	2 teaspoons finely cut parsley 3-pound Delmonico, porterhouse,
½ teaspoon thyme	or sirloin steak
¼ teaspoon minced garlic	

Poach beef marrow 10 minutes in salted water to cover. Drain.

Melt butter or margarine in upper part of double boiler over hot water. Add shallots or onions. Cook over low heat 5 minutes. Add thyme, garlic, wine, salt, and pepper. Stir and cook over medium heat until reduced to half. Add parsley and marrow. Mix. Keep hot until steak is ready.

Broil steak to desired doneness. Remove to hot serving platter. Slice in 6 portions. Pour hot sauce over. Serve at once. Makes 6 servings.

FLANK STEAK WITH VEGETABLES

1½ to 2-pound flank steak	1 large onion, peeled and
2 tablespoons flour	sliced
1 teaspoon salt	1 green pepper, sliced
2 tablespoons beef fat or shortening	1 teaspoon salt
	¼ teaspoon pepper
4 potatoes, scrubbed, pared, sliced	1 (1 pound 3-ounce) can to- matoes chopped

Start oven at moderate (325° F.).

Make shallow cuts in surface of steak diagonally across grain. Mix flour and salt together. Rub into both sides of steak. Melt fat in heavy flameproof casserole. Brown steak well on both sides, over high heat. Heap potatoes, onion, and pepper on top of steak. Season with salt and pepper. Pour tomatoes over all. Cover casserole.

Bake 2 hours or until vegetables are cooked and tender. Makes 4 servings.

This is a great favorite with boys of all sizes. A fine busy-day dish. Pop it in the oven and have time to recover your equilibrium before dinner.

RIB STEAKS, FRENCH STYLE

In France the steaks cut from beef ribs, *entrecôtes,* may be 1½ to 2 inches thick and large enough to make 4 servings as broiled steaks. But in America the *entrecôte* is cut into small steaks called club or Delmonico and is boneless. These small steaks make 1 or 2 servings and are usually sautéed instead of broiled.

When the French cut them small, they make an especially flavorsome dish, combining steak with vegetables. Here is the recipe:

2 pounds potatoes	1 teaspoon lemon juice
7 tablespoons butter	4 slices lean bacon
4 individual rib steaks	½ cup white wine
1 teaspoon salt	2 tablespoons finely cut parsley
Quick grind black pepper	
1 (6-ounce) can sliced mush-rooms	

Scrub and pare potatoes. Cut into small cubes. Cover with ice water and let stand 30 minutes. Drain and let dry in clean towel.

Melt 3 tablespoons butter in skillet. When foaming, stir in potatoes. Cook about 20 minutes or until browned on all sides. Season with salt and pepper.

Sauté steaks in 2 tablespoons butter in another skillet about 5 minutes or until browned on one side. Add another tablespoon butter to pan. Turn steaks and brown other side. Keep hot in skillet in hot oven with its door open.

Drain mushrooms. Sauté 3 minutes in 1 tablespoon butter. Add lemon juice. Cook bacon until crisp and drain.

Remove cooked steaks from skillet to hot serving platter. Add wine to pan, stir, and bring quickly to a boil. Pour over steaks. Surround with mounds of potatoes and mushrooms and garnish with bacon. Sprinkle potatoes with parsley. Makes 4 servings.

JOANNE'S STEAK À LA MILANESE

4 filets mignons or 4 (½ pound) hamburger patties	¼ teaspoon dry mustard
	¼ teaspoon Worcestershire sauce
2 tablespoons butter	1 jigger (3 tablespoons) cognac
½ teaspoon rosemary	

Melt 1 tablespoon butter with rosemary in heavy skillet. Do not let butter brown. When rosemary has flavored butter well, add meat and cook to taste, turning meat from time to time. When meat is done, remove to hot platter. Add remaining tablespoon butter, mustard, Worcestershire sauce, and cognac. Let heat well but do not boil. Pour over meat. Serve immediately. Makes 4 servings.

Good with fresh Asparagus Hollandaise (page 615), baked potato, mixed green salad, and fresh apple or pear with Camembert cheese.

One of the busiest career women I know, Joanne Moonan, makes this gourmet delight in her best party dress as guests stand around goggle-eyed. I can't praise the dish or her culinary *savoir-faire* enough.

PLANKED STEAK

2-pound sirloin steak cut 1 inch thick	2 cups hot mashed potatoes
2 teaspoons Kitchen Bouquet	1 egg yolk, beaten
1 teaspoon powdered ginger	4 very small tomatoes, peeled and stem end cut out
½ teaspoon garlic salt	Cooked seasoned cauliflower
½ teaspoon onion salt	1 (3-ounce) can broiled mushrooms
Seasoned oak steak-plank	

Cut fat edge in 4 or 5 places to prevent curling. Mix Kitchen Bouquet, ginger, garlic salt, and onion salt. Brush mixture over steak in shallow dish. Cover and let season at cool room temperature about 1 hour.

Start oven at hot (425° F.).

Place steak on greased rack in broiling compartment. For *medium rare* broil 4 inches from moderate heat about 5 minutes. Turn and broil other side 5 minutes.

While steak broils, place broiling plank in pre-heated oven. As soon as steak is broiled to desired doneness on both sides, place it on warmed plank. Surround with mounds of mashed potatoes. Brush potatoes with egg yolk. Place seasoned tomatoes at each end of plank. Place plank on cooky sheet in oven. Bake about 10 minutes, until potatoes are browned. Remove plank. Spoon hot, seasoned cauliflower between potato mounds. Garnish with mushrooms heated in their own juice and drained. Place plank on large warmed platter or tray. Serve immediately. Makes 4 servings.

ROLLED STUFFED STEAKS

4 small, thin, tender steaks	Flour
½ clove garlic	2 tablespoons bacon fat
1 teaspoon salt	1 cup red wine
Quick grind black pepper	1 teaspoon tomato paste
¾ cup sausage meat	½ cup sliced olives
3 tablespoons finely cut parsley	
2 tablespoons finely cut peeled onion	

Rub steaks with garlic. Season with salt and pepper. Spread thin layer sausage meat over each. Sprinkle a little parsley and onion over sausage. Roll each steak and fasten with small metal skewer or wooden picks at each end.

Dredge rolls in flour. Brown in hot bacon fat 5 minutes on each side. Add wine to pan. Mix tomato paste with little wine from the pan. Stir into pan. Cover. Cook slowly 1 hour, or a little longer. Sausage must be thoroughly cooked and steak tender and done. Add olives to pan. Stir with pan juices. Continue cooking 15 minutes. Serve hot. Makes 4 servings.

Stuffed Steak Roll: Use 1 large steak cut thin, in same recipe. Steaks should serve 4 people. Increase amount of wine for larger steak, or mix wine with small amount of consommé or bouillon.

STEAK TARTARE

2 pounds finest beef, chopped (no fat)	1 ½ teaspoons freshly ground black pepper
1 ½ large onions, peeled and finely diced	2 teaspoons English mustard
¼ cup chili sauce	½ onion, peeled and chopped
¼ cup Worcestershire sauce	1 tablespoon capers
1 ½ teaspoons salt	1 tablespoon finely cut parsley or chives

Mix well chilled beef, onions, chili sauce, Worcestershire, salt, pepper, and mustard, just enough to distribute seasonings evenly. Heap lightly in bowl. Garnish top with the ½ chopped onion, capers, and parsley or chives. (Some people like a raw egg broken over it, too.) Serve with hot buttered toasted rolls or bread. Makes 3 or 4 servings.

Some men prefer toasted buns with Steak Tartare, and a hot or cold drink, as a supper after tennis or a swim. If you want to add Caesar Salad or a fine-flavored Italian green salad, and pie with cheese, there are usually appreciative hungry males who will eat every crumb and second helpings of pie and cheese.

I know many figure-conscious women who enjoy this too. They and their escorts enjoy tiny balls of steak tartare rolled in minced parsley and speared with toothpicks as protein cocktail snacks.

Warning: Chop or grind the beef for this at home. At the meat dealer's there is a possibility that the beef will be run through a chopper where pork has been ground. So dangerous to eat raw!

TIME AND TEMPERATURE CHART FOR
COOKING MEAT

Roasting—Use oven temperature of 325° F. Or see recipes.

CUT	WEIGHT RANGE	INTERNAL MEAT TEMPERATURE	APPROXIMATE TOTAL TIME (HOURS)	MINUTES PER POUND
BEEF				
Standing Ribs (3)	8–9 lbs.	140° F. rare	2¼–2½	18–20
		160° F. medium	2¾–3	22–25
		170° F. well done	3½–4	27–30
Standing Ribs (2)	6–6½ lbs.	140° F. rare	1¾–2	18–20
		160° F. medium	2¼–2½	22–25
		170° F. well done	3–3¼	27–30
Rolled Rib	4–5 lbs.	(Use times for 3-rib standing rib.)		
Rolled Rump	5–7 lbs.	170° F. well done	2½–3½	35–40
Sirloin Tip	3–3½ lbs.	160° F. medium	2–2½	22–25
VEAL				
Leg (Center Cut)	7–8 lbs.	170° F.	3–3½	30
Loin	4½–5 lbs.	170° F.	2½–3	30
Boned Rolled Shoulder	5–6 lbs.	170° F.	3½–4	30–40
Boned Rolled Shoulder	3 lbs.	170° F.	3	30–40
LAMB				
Leg (whole)	6–7 lbs.	175–180° F.	3½–3¾	30–35
Leg (half)	3–4 lbs.	175–180° F.	3–3½	30–35
Boned Rolled Shoulder	4–6 lbs.	175–180° F.	3–4	40–45
Bone-in, Stuffed	4–5 lbs.	175–180° F.	2½–2¾	30–35
PORK AND HAM				
Smoked Ham	10–14 lbs.	185° F.	3½–5	20–30
Smoked Ham (half)	5–6 lbs.	185° F.	1⅔–2	20–30
Pork Loin	4–5 lbs.	185° F.	2⅓–2⅔	35–40
Pork Loin End	2½–3 lbs.	185° F.	1½–2	35–40
Pork Shoulder Butt	4–6 lbs.	185° F.	2⅓–2⅔	40–45

TIME AND TEMPERATURE CHART FOR
COOKING MEAT

Broiling

CUT	THICK-NESS	WEIGHT	RARE	MEDIUM	WELL DONE
			MINUTES PER POUND		

CUT	THICK-NESS	WEIGHT	RARE	MEDIUM	WELL DONE
BEEF					
Rib Steak	1 inch	1½ lbs.	8–10	12–14	18–20
Club Steak	1 inch	1½ lbs.	8–10	12–14	18–20
Porterhouse	1 inch	1½–2 lbs.	10–12	14–16	20–25
	1½ in.	2½–3 lbs.	14–16	18–20	25–30
	2 inch	3–3½ lbs.	20–25	30–35	40–45
Sirloin	1 inch	2½–3½ lbs.	10–12	14–16	20–25
	1½ in.	3½–4½ lbs.	14–16	18–20	25–30
	2 inch	5–5½ lbs.	20–25	30–35	40–45
Ground Beef Patties	¾ inch	4 oz. each	8	12	15
Tenderloin	1 inch	– – – – – – –	8–10	12–14	18–20
LAMB					
Rib or Loin Chops (1 rib)	¾ inch	2–3 oz. each	– – – –	– – – –	14–15
Double Rib	1½ in.	4–5 oz. each	– – – –	– – – –	22–25
Lamb Shoulder Chops	¾ inch	3–4 oz. each	– – – –	– – – –	14–15
Lamb Patties	¾ inch	4 oz. each	– – – –	– – – –	14–15

Ham

Buy ham by brand to be sure of quality. Select labeled and wrapped ham, or unwrapped name ham from a reliable dealer, in the form best suited to your needs, considering number to be served, method of cookery, and leftover possibilities. Plan several meals around a whole ham purchase. Read labels for information as to product, cookery, and storage. But also ask dealer for information as to cookery. Some hams from reliable packers have vague cookery directions on label, or incorrect information.

Store ham, before and after cooking, in refrigerator. If you live in the country and have a cold-meat shed, hams will keep well in winter in such a shed. Most canned hams, unless otherwise labeled, should be stored in refrigerator before and after opening. Do not keep smoked ham any longer than you would unsmoked meats.

After cooking and serving, cut remaining ham from bone and store in refrigerator. Use bone immediately for soup or seasoning. Keep ham wrapped in foil or waxed paper to prevent drying.

Cured and smoked meats lose flavor rapidly when frozen. So do not freeze ham unless necessary, then use it within 60 days.

Regular smoked hams weigh from 8 to 24 pounds. They are variously prepared as available smoked, to be cooked before eating or as ready to eat or fully cooked, meaning you may serve it cold, at once, or heat and serve. Such hams also are sold in slices to be broiled, or as butt and shank ends, or cut in half and sold as halves.

Canned ham, boneless and fully cooked in large and small sizes, may be served right from the can or heated. Some imported canned hams are prepared with wine and other marinades.

Skinless, shankless ham is boned, skinned, and trimmed of excess fat for fine meaty slices. Sold wrapped, to be cooked, or also as ready-to-eat hams.

Smoked picnic is a shoulder cut, cured and smoked, from 5-to-8-pound sizes, to be simmered and baked, or may be bought fully cooked and ready to serve.

Smoked shoulder butt is a boneless shoulder cut shaped into a roll, cured and smoked, and packaged in transparent casing. These 1½-to-3-pound "hams" are simmered, then baked, or sliced and pan-fried or broiled.

The luxurious boneless and skinless ham, shaped into rolls and packaged in transparent casings, must be cooked before eating. If labeled fully cooked, they may be served without cooking. Meat dealers sell these hams whole or cut to customer's needs.

In general, ham cookery is so simple that it is a favorite with young homemakers, and certainly its deliciousness makes it a favorite with the guests at their tables. See Baked Ham Timetable (page 385) for cooking times, and be guided by recipes which follow.

BAKED PICNIC HAM

4-to-5-pound smoked picnic shoulder with bone
Whole cloves

1 cup dark corn syrup
2 teaspoons dry mustard
½ teaspoon powdered cloves

Start oven at moderate (325° F.).

Scrub meat well with brush. Rinse, drain. Place on rack, fat side up, in shallow roasting pan.

Bake 30 to 35 minutes per pound, about 2½ hours, or until internal temperature registers 170° F. on meat thermometer.

Remove pan from oven. With sharp knife cut rind off ham. Score fat by making diagonal cuts ¼ inch deep across ham. Push whole cloves into fat. Combine syrup, mustard, and powdered cloves. Pour ⅓ over roast. Return pan to oven. Bake 30 minutes. Baste twice during this period with remaining syrup mixture. Makes 8 or more generous servings.

GLAZED HAM

Bake whole ham, according to directions for the type you buy. About 45 minutes before it is done, remove pan from oven. Remove fat drippings from pan and cut rind off ham. Score fat deeply with sharp knife. Mix glaze consisting of 1 tablespoon grated orange peel, ½ cup orange juice, 1 cup honey.

Pour about ⅓ of glaze over scored ham. Return pan to oven. Bake 45 minutes longer, basting ham with remaining syrup at intervals.

Brown Sugar and Honey Glaze for Ham: Combine 1 cup brown sugar, packed, ½ cup honey, ¼ cup ham fat. Spread over scored, skinned ham about 45 minutes before it is done. Repeat basting every 10 minutes until ham is done. Garnish platter with canned peach halves sautéed in butter and honey.

Currant Jelly-and-Horse-Radish Glaze for Ham: Spread currant jelly mixed with a little prepared horse-radish thickly over scored, skinned baked ham. Return pan to oven. Bake 45 minutes longer. Spread melted currant jelly over ham twice in this baking period.

Christmas Glazed Ham: Combine ½ cup honey, 1 cup brown sugar, packed, ¼ cup apricot nectar. Spread on scored, skinned ham as described for other glazes. Baste with same mixture twice during final half hour of baking. Decorate top of ham while hot with groups of green gumdrop or angelica leaves and cinnamon candies, to form holly leaves and berries.

GLAZED SMOKED SHOULDER BUTT

2 ½-pound smoked shoulder butt
Whole cloves
½ cup brown sugar, packed

3 tablespoons cider vinegar
¾ teaspoon dry mustard

Place meat in deep kettle and cover with water. Simmer, do not boil, about 50 minutes per pound, or until tender. Remove from water. Place in baking pan.

Start oven at moderately hot (400° F.).

Stud meat with cloves. Combine sugar, vinegar, and mustard. Spread on meat.

Bake 15 minutes or until top is glazed and very hot. Makes 6 to 8 servings.

JELLIED HAM LOAF

2 envelopes unflavored gelatin	2 tablespoons vinegar
½ cup cold water	2 tablespoons prepared mustard
3 cups finely chopped cooked ham	½ teaspoon salt
	¼ teaspoon pepper
¼ cups finely sliced green onions	1 cup heavy cream, whipped
¼ cup finely diced celery	Water cress
1 cup mayonnaise	Thin slices cucumber

Soften gelatin in cold water. Dissolve over hot water. Let stand until it begins to thicken. Combine remaining ingredients except cream. Stir mixture into gelatin. Fold in whipped cream. Pour into 2-quart mold or loaf pan. Chill until firm. Unmold onto chilled platter. Garnish with water cress and thin slices cucumber. Makes 8 servings.

BROILED HAM WITH PINEAPPLE SAUCE

1 ½-pound ham slice cut ¾ inch thick	2 tablespoons brown sugar
	¼ teaspoon powdered allspice
1 (1-pound 4-ounce) can pineapple chunks	¼ teaspoon powdered ginger
	1 tablespoon vinegar
1 tablespoon cornstarch or potato flour	¼ cup finely diced green pepper
2 tablespoons butter or margarine	

Place ham slice in cold skillet. Let heat and cook until browned on one side. Turn ham to brown other side.

Prepare sauce: drain syrup from pineapple. Combine with cornstarch or flour in small enamel or glass saucepan over moderate heat. Stir until smooth. Add butter or margarine, sugar, spice, vinegar, and green pepper. Stir and heat 1 or 2 minutes. Add 1 cup pineapple chunks. Stir and cook until sauce thickens and is clear. Serve hot over hot ham slice. Makes 4 servings.

This same sauce is delicious over hot sliced baked ham.

Lamb

Loin and rib sections and the leg of lamb are the most expensive cuts. Chops from loin and rib are usually broiled and should be cooked so that the outside is brown and crisp and the inside evenly well done.

Loin roast, called the saddle, and rib roast, called the rack, of lamb are roasted whole.

The leg may be roasted whole or with part of it cut into cubes for dishes such as ragout. The center part of the leg can also be cut into steaks which are broiled like beef steaks, and the shank end may be cubed for curries and stews.

Young lamb should be well done. European cooks prefer a medium-rare roast for older lamb. This taste is not universal in America, however, and most homemakers and their families like lamb evenly cooked and well done.

Moderate cost cuts of lamb are the shoulder, breast, neck, and shank. Shoulder and breast can be boned by the meat dealer and roasted stuffed. Neck and other economical cuts are used in stews and ragouts.

LAMB CHOPS

Broiled Lamb Chops: Have loin, rib, or shoulder chops cut 1 inch thick. Preheat broiler. Place chops on greased broiler rack about 2 inches below heat. Broil until browned. Season with salt and pepper. Turn chops with tongs. Brown other side. Season. Serve hot. Cook chops total of 15 minutes. Slightly less for thinner chops.

Baked Lamb Chops: Have 6 loin chops cut 1½ inches thick. Place skewer through tail end to hold in place. Broil 2 inches from heat 5 minutes or until browned. Season with salt and pepper. Turn chops with tongs to retain juices. Broil until browned. Season.

Transfer to warm baking pan. Set pan in moderately slow (300° F.) oven. Bake uncovered 30 minutes. Remove skewers. Serve hot. Makes 6 servings.

BAKED LAMB CHOPS WITH VEGETABLES

6 lamb shoulder chops	½ teaspoon paprika
1 tablespoon butter	1 (1-pound 3-ounce) can toma-
6 potatoes, pared and sliced	toes, chopped
2 teaspoons salt	1 cup water
½ teaspoon pepper	

Brown chops in hot butter lightly on both sides.

Start oven at moderate (350° F.).

Make layer of 3 browned chops in 2-quart casserole. Cover with potatoes. Season with salt, pepper, and paprika. Spoon half tomatoes over potatoes. Make second layer of 3 remaining browned lamb chops. Cover with remaining sliced potatoes, seasoning, and remaining tomatoes. Pour water over mixture. Cover.

Bake 1 hour. Remove cover and continue baking ½ hour or until meat and potatoes are done. Makes 6 servings.

LAMB CHOPS, HÔTEL CRILLON

Côtelettes D'Agneau de Vin

8 loin lamb chops	3 potatoes, pared and sliced
1 tablespoon flour	12 small onions, peeled
1 teaspoon salt	1 cup dry white wine
¼ teaspoon pepper	3 tablespoons finely-cut chives
2 tablespoons butter	
1 (3-ounce) can sliced mush-	
rooms	

Dust chops lightly with flour, salt, and pepper. Brown chops in butter in heavy flameproof casserole. Place mushrooms, potatoes, and onions on chops. Add wine. Cover casserole. Cook slowly, 45 minutes to 1 hour, or until done. Use wide pancake turner to lift potato-covered chops to hot serving platter or serve from casserole. Add sprinkling of chives. Makes 4 to 8 servings.

CROWN ROAST OF LAMB

Have meat dealer prepare crown roast of 10 to 16 ribs. Wrap each rib end with strip of salt pork or bacon to prevent charring. Season roast with salt and pepper. Place bone ends up on rack in open roasting pan. Fill roast with any preferred stuffing.

Start oven at moderate (325° F.).

Roast 35 minutes per pound. When done, remove pork or bacon from chop bones. Slip decorative paper frill on each bone. Serve hot on large hot platter.

When dressing is not used, do not wrap bone ends but turn this roast upside down, so fat from meat bastes rib ends. When roast is done, turn right side up, fill center with cooked tiny carrots sprinkled with fresh mint or fill with new peas or freshly cooked whole small cauliflower.

Makes 10 to 16 servings.

For those tiny carrots in this recipe, I keep on hand at all times a case of the tiny canned French carrots. They're so good, so decorative. Sometimes, when there is no fresh mint, I sprinkle the carrots with green onion and a few drops of lemon juice.

Save this—it's expensive—for a really impressive meal.

ROAST LEG OF LAMB

Do not remove fell (the thin, papery covering over outside of lamb). Meat cooks better, keeps its shape better, and will be juicier if cooked with fell left in place until serving time.

Start oven at moderate (325° F.).

Place leg, skin side down, on rack in open roasting pan. If fat covering is scant, lay bacon or salt pork strips over cut side. Roast 35 minutes per pound or until meat thermometer registers 180° F. for well done. Remove fell and discard it. Serve roast very hot on warmed platter. Makes 8 to 12 servings.

My Herbed Roast Lamb: Fell must be removed from leg of lamb for this dish. Place lamb in large dish or enameled pan. Peel 1 onion and stud it with cloves. Mix ½ cup salad oil, 2 tablespoons wine vinegar, and 1 pint red wine. Add 1 teaspoon salt, ¼ teaspoon pepper, ½ teaspoon orégano, 1 garlic clove, peeled and mashed. Pour mixture, with clove-studded onion, over lamb. Cover and refrigerate. Let marinate 24 hours. Turn lamb several times, or spoon mixture over meat frequently during marinating period. Drain. Roast as described above for leg of lamb. Makes 8 to 12 servings.

Roast Lamb with Barbecue Sauce: Prepare Roast Leg of Lamb as described above. When half done, slide pan out on oven door. Loosen fell and remove and discard it. Return pan to oven. Prepare barbecue mixture and baste lamb every few minutes during remainder of roasting period. Here is a good mixture for this roast: ½ cup cider vinegar, ½ cup ketchup, ½ cup brown sugar, packed, 1 cup apricot nectar, 2 teaspoons chili powder, 1 cup water. Combine, mix well. Use to baste lamb as it roasts. Makes 8 to 12 servings.

FRENCH RAGOUT OF LAMB

Blanquette of Lamb

4-pound boneless lamb breast or shoulder	1 (6-ounce) can sliced mushrooms
2 tablespoons shortening	2 tablespoons flour
1 teaspoon salt	1 cup milk
⅛ teaspoon pepper	¼ cup dry sherry or light Dubonnet
12 small white onions, peeled	½ cup heavy cream
5 tablespoons butter or margarine	

Have meat dealer cut lamb into small chunks. Brown in melted shortening about 20 minutes, stirring to brown all sides. Season with salt and pepper. Cook slowly 15 minutes longer.

Cook onions in 3 tablespoons butter or margarine in large skillet until almost tender. Add mushrooms. Stir and cook 3 minutes. Melt remaining 2 tablespoons butter or margarine in large saucepan. Stir in flour smoothly. Add milk gradually, stirring constantly. Cook and stir slowly, until thickened and sauce bubbles.

Add lamb to onion-mushroom mixture. Rinse lamb pan with wine and add to lamb-onion mixture. Stir all into sauce. Add cream. Mix. Cook slowly 35 minutes. Makes 6 servings. Serve with hot rice or noodles.

LAMB STEW, CHINESE STYLE

1 ½ pounds boneless lamb stew
    meat
1 green pepper, sliced thin
1 onion, peeled and sliced thin
1 cup diced celery
2 tablespoons peanut oil
1 teaspoon cornstarch or
    potato flour
1 teaspoon soy sauce
2 teaspoons salt
¼ teaspoon pepper
¼ cup cold water
1 (1-pound) can bean sprouts
1 (3-ounce) can sliced mush-
    rooms
1 (5 ¼-ounce) can water chest-
    nuts

Have meat dealer cut lamb into serving-size pieces. Sauté pepper, onion, and celery in oil in large skillet until tender but not brown. Remove from skillet. Brown meat in same skillet. Return sautéed pepper, onion, and celery to skillet. Stir cornstarch or flour and seasonings in cold water and liquid drained from bean sprouts. Mix well. Stir into meat mixture. Cook until meat is tender, about 20 minutes. Stir frequently. Add drained sprouts, mushrooms, and chestnuts. Cover skillet. Continue cooking until meat and vegetables are done and well cooked together. Makes 4 servings.

Serve rice with this, and plenty of scalding tea.

LAMB STEW WITH VEGETABLES

1 ½ pounds boneless lamb
    shoulder
3 tablespoons flour
2 tablespoons salad oil
2 onions, peeled and diced
2 cups hot water
1 teaspoon salt
¼ teaspoon pepper
¾ teaspoon marjoram
6 carrots, scraped and
    quartered
6 small potatoes, pared and
    halved

Have meat dealer cut lamb in serving-size pieces. Dredge meat evenly in flour. Heat oil in Dutch oven or heavy kettle. Brown meat well on all sides. Add onions during last 5 minutes of browning. Stir to mix well. Add water, salt, pepper, and marjoram. Reduce heat. Cover kettle. Let simmer about 1½ hours. Add carrots and potatoes. Cover kettle again. Continue cooking about 30 minutes or until vegetables are done. Makes 4 servings.

Some cooks make lamb stew without browning the meat. Various vegetables may be used in place of potatoes. For instance, small white turnips, sliced parsnips, or kohlrabi.

Various Lamb Dishes

FANCHONETTES OF LAMB

3 shanks lamb
3 whole cloves
1 teaspoon celery seeds
½ bay leaf
1 teaspoon thyme
¼ teaspoon crumbled sage
3 cups well-seasoned mashed potatoes

1 cup cooked or canned small kidney beans
1 cup coarsely chopped cooked cabbage
1 cup sliced cooked carrots
1 egg or
3 tablespoons milk

Place lamb in saucepan and cover with water. Add cloves, celery seeds, bay leaf, thyme, and sage. Bring to a boil. Lower heat and cook slowly about 1 hour or until meat is tender. Drain. Save stock. Remove meat from bones; cut in cubes.

Start oven at hot (450° F.).

Line 6 individual casseroles, using about 2½ cups mashed potatoes. Fill these with lamb and vegetables. Moisten with lamb stock. Top with remaining mashed potatoes. Brush over with beaten egg, or milk.

Brown in oven, about 15 minutes. Makes 6 servings.

This needs no apologies either as a main family dinner dish when the budget is limping. Lamb shanks are sweet in flavor and tender. They should stir the cook's imagination more.

LAMB ON SKEWERS

1 teaspoon powdered ginger
1 teaspoon dry mustard
½ cup soy sauce
¼ cup salad oil
1 tablespoon molasses
2 cloves garlic, peeled and mashed

4 pounds lamb, cut in serving-size cubes
4 green peppers, cut in squares
5 small tomatoes, quartered

Combine ginger, mustard, soy sauce, oil, molasses, and garlic. Let stand at room temperature 24 hours to blend flavors. Remove garlic and discard it. Add meat to marinade mixture. Let stand 2 or 3 hours; turn meat occasionally to flavor all.

To cook, thread meat cube, square of green pepper, meat cube, and tomato quarter on greased metal skewers. Broil 20 to 25 minutes, turning skewers often. Baste occasionally with sauce. Makes 6 to 8 servings.

Various combinations of vegetables and lamb are cooked in Near Eastern countries as a lamb kabob. Tomato and green pepper are favorites. Sometimes cooked artichoke quarters and sections of canned pimiento and ripe olive are added to the skewer. Slide hot cooked meat and vegetables off onto bed of hot wheat or rice pilaf when serving Eastern style.

MINCED LAMB AND PICKLED WALNUTS

1 tablespoon butter	½ pound (2 cups) minced cooked lamb
1 tablespoon flour	1 or 2 tablespoons cream
½ teaspoon salt	4 pickled walnuts, chopped
¼ teaspoon pepper	
1 cup milk	

Melt butter in saucepan. Stir in flour until smooth. Add seasonings and milk, stirring until slightly thickened. Let sauce boil 2 or 3 minutes. Add lamb. Mix. Add a little cream. Heat thoroughly. Serve hot, garnished with chopped pickled walnuts. Makes 4 servings.

This makes a perfect dish for luncheon or supper. Add a hot vegetable, such as lima beans or string beans. Or omit hot vegetable and serve an especially good salad, such as avocado with green pepper and romaine. Apricot tart and coffee make a delicious finish to this menu.

I had this on the *Queen Elizabeth,* but for breakfast! I know, now, what to do with pickled walnuts. Try this on a husband who imagines he's against leftovers.

COTES D'AGNEAU AUX FLAGEOLETS
(Rack of Lamb with Lima Beans)

1 8-chop rack of lamb	1 cup white wine
4 cloves garlic	3 shallots, peeled and chopped
½ cup butter	2 cups cooked Lima beans
1 cup beef bouillon	1 tablespoon minced parsley

Peel the garlic and cut cloves in half lengthwise. Insert a piece of garlic into each chop. Place on rack in roasting pan. Put in butter and bouillon. Cook in 450 degree oven 15 minutes, basting occasionally. Add wine and shallots. Continue basting until meat is done (about 15 minutes longer) or until meat thermometer reaches 140 degrees). Serve on a bed of hot Lima beans. Pour meat juices over all and sprinkle beans with parsley. Serves 4.

Pork

Fresh pork roasting should be long and slow. Pork is always cooked to the well-done stage, and because it is fatty, it is usually improved by serving fruit with it in some form.

Here are some of my favorite pork dishes:

BAKED PORK CHOPS, DUTCH STYLE

4 thick pork chops	½ teaspoon pepper
1 lemon, peeled, cut in 4 slices	½ teaspoon powdered nutmeg
½ cup bread crumbs	Drippings or margarine
1 ½ teaspoons salt	Juice 1 lemon

Start oven at moderately hot (400 ° F.).

Place chops in greased baking pan; top each with slice of lemon. Sprinkle with crumbs, salt, pepper, and nutmeg. Dot with drippings or margarine. Add squeeze of lemon juice to each chop.

Bake 30 minutes to the pound or until well done. Serve with Cauliflower (page 622). Makes 4 servings.

STUFFED PORK CHOPS

4 double loin pork chops cut 1 ½ inches thick	½ teaspoon pepper
	⅛ teaspoon powdered nutmeg
1 onion, peeled and chopped	4 prunes, cooked, stoned, and chopped
1 tablespoon butter or margarine	
½ cup soft bread crumbs	Prune juice
1 teaspoon salt	Juice 1 lemon

Have meat dealer cut slit pocket in each chop.

Sauté onion 5 minutes in butter or margarine. Stir in crumbs and mix. Season with salt, pepper, and nutmeg. Mix in prunes, and if too dry add a little prune juice or other fruit juice. Stuff into pocket in chops. Secure with small skewers or wooden picks.

Start oven at moderate (350° F.).

Place chops in baking pan. Squeeze lemon juice on each.

Bake about 1 hour or until well browned. Baste once or twice during baking with a very little mixed lemon and prune juice. Makes 4 servings.

PAN-COOKED PORK CHOPS WITH SHERRY SAUCE

6 loin pork chops
2 onions, peeled and cut fine
1 (6-ounce) can chopped mushrooms
1 (6-ounce) can tomato sauce
¼ cup chopped cooked ham
¼ cup chopped cooked tongue

¼ cup dry sherry
1 teaspoon salt
Grind of black pepper
Paprika
Major Grey's Indian Chutney for
   garnish

Brown chops on both sides in large heavy skillet over high heat. Reduce heat. Cover skillet. Cook slowly about 25 minutes or until almost done. Add onions. Cook 5 minutes, stirring onions in the pan fat. Add drained mushrooms, tomato sauce, and chopped meats. Mix with fat in pan. If pan mixture seems dry, add small amount of tomato sauce blended with hot water. Stir into pan. Cover and cook 5 minutes. Add sherry, salt, and pepper. Mix. Spoon all over chops. Cover pan and continue to cook 3 minutes. Serve on hot platter. Add light sprinkle of paprika and garnish of Major Grey's Indian Chutney. Makes 6 servings.

This is a delicious dish for a country supper, or for any dinner for family and guests. Makes a fine skillet supper, too, using electric skillet.

PORK CHOPS, POLISH HOUSEWIFE STYLE

4 loin pork chops
3 tablespoons finely cut peeled
   onion
1 (6-ounce) can tomato sauce
½ cup commercial sour cream
1 dill pickle, cut fine

¼ cup dry sherry
1 teaspoon salt
¼ teaspoon pepper
Beet Salad (page 491) as garnish

Brown chops on both sides in heavy skillet over high heat. Reduce heat. Cover. Cook slowly about 25 minutes or until chops are almost done. Add onion. Cover and continue cooking 10 minutes. Add tomato sauce, sour cream, pickle, sherry, and seasonings. Stir in pan and spoon over chops until very hot. Serve on warmed platter. Garnish with small pickled-beet salads on lettuce leaf. Makes 4 servings.

COUNTRY PORK ROAST

5 pounds pork shoulder
Salt and pepper
4 cups dry bread crumbs
1 cup finely diced celery
¼ cup chopped scallions
1 teaspoon salt

½ teaspoon pepper
1 teaspoon orégano
⅓ cup melted butter or margarine
Hot water or lemon juice

Have meat dealer remove bone and make pocket for stuffing. Season inside and out with salt and pepper. Combine remaining ingredients. Add little hot water or juice. Mix well. Tie roast with string to hold stuffing in.

Start oven at moderate (325° F.).

Place meat, fat side up, in open roasting pan. Do not cover. Score meat in a few places with sharp knife.

Roast 40 to 45 minutes per pound, about 3½ hours. Meat thermometer should register 185° F. Make gravy from pan drippings. Makes 8 to 10 servings.

Use any other favorite stuffing, or add 2 tablespoons grated orange peel to this mixture and substitute orange juice for hot water to moisten stuffing.

DAISYFIELDS FRUIT-GLAZED PORK ROAST

3½ to 4-pound pork loin
1 tablespoon flour
1 teaspoon salt
1 teaspoon dry mustard
¼ teaspoon pepper
2 cups drained, sieved, cooked quinces or pears

¼ cup brown sugar, packed
¼ teaspoon powdered cinnamon
¼ teaspoon powdered cloves

Start oven at moderate (325° F.).

Combine flour and seasonings. Rub roast. Place fat side up in open roasting pan. Do not add water. Roast uncovered until meat thermometer registers 185° F., 35 to 40 minutes per pound.

About 2 hours after roast has gone into oven, spread with mixture of sieved fruit, sugar, and spices. Return to oven and continue to roast until well done. Baste often with pan juices. Garnish platter with spiced crab apples or seckel pears. Makes 6 to 8 servings.

PENNSYLVANIA DUTCH PORK

4 pork hocks
2 cups water
1 onion, peeled and sliced
1 carrot, scraped and sliced
½ teaspoon mixed pickling
  spices

1 teaspoon salt
2 (1-pound) cans sauerkraut, 4
  cups
2 or 3 tart plums

Place hocks in large kettle with water, vegetables, spices, and salt. Cook covered, on moderate heat, about 1½ hours or until meat is done.

Start oven at slow (250° F.).

Drain kraut. Place in 2-quart casserole. Place cooked hocks on kraut. Baste with kraut juice. Add halved plums, peeled and seeded.

Bake uncovered about one hour. Baste occasionally with kraut juice. Makes 4 servings.

Some Pennsylvania cooks add chopped apple to the kraut as well as the various spices preferred by the family, such as caraway or celery seed, or both.

PORK RIB ROAST, MEXICO CITY STYLE

3 to 4-pound loin-back ribs
1 cup ketchup
⅓ cup Worcestershire sauce
2 teaspoons chili powder

1 teaspoon salt
¼ teaspoon Tabasco sauce
2 cups water

Start oven at hot (450° F.).

Place in shallow roasting pan, meaty side up. Roast 30 minutes. Combine remaining ingredients in saucepan. Bring to a boil; pour over meat in roasting pan. Lower oven heat to moderate (325° F.). Continue roasting about 1 hour or until meat is tender. Total time should be 40 minutes per pound.

Baste ribs with sauce in pan every 15 minutes. If sauce gets too thick, stir a little hot water into pan. Baste roast. Serve hot. Makes 4 servings.

The combination of pork and chili powder is really inspired. In Mexico City, I found they sometimes went too far afield with the chili. But it *belongs here.*

PORK CROWN ROAST

4-pound pork loin, trimmed	1 teaspoon crumbled sage
½ cup diced peeled onions	1 teaspoon orégano
½ cup diced celery	½ teaspoon salt
2 tablespoons butter or marga-rine	½ cup water
	1 cup currant jelly, melted
2 cups coarse dry bread crumbs	¼ cup orange juice
2 tablespoons finely cut parsley	

Have meat dealer cut chine (back) bone away from roast (roast should weigh 4 pounds trimmed) and slice into 10 chops from fat side almost through to back. Twist loin into crown shape and fasten with skewers or tie with string.

Start oven at moderately slow (325° F.).

Cook onions and celery 5 minutes in butter or margarine in saucepan. Stir in crumbs. Add parsley, sage, orégano, salt, and water. Stir and heat 1 or 2 minutes. Spoon stuffing into center of pork roast. Place on rack in shallow baking pan.

Roast 1½ hours. Baste meat with melted jelly mixed with orange juice. Continue roasting, basting often with jelly and orange juice, an additional 45 minutes or 1 hour, or until meat is glazed, tender, and well done when pierced with fork. If roasting thermometer is used, roast to 185° F. internal temperature.

Serve on warmed platter surrounded by spiced or baked apples, peaches, or seckel pears. Makes 5 to 10 servings.

An impressive holiday roast. The garnish may be minted pears, alternated with cinnamon apples for traditional Christmas colors, or surround with canned apricots or peach halves which have been oven-heated in their own juice 20 minutes in a shallow baking pan.

CANTONESE SWEET-SOUR PORK

2 pounds lean pork shoulder	1 tablespoon soy sauce
2 tablespoons peanut oil	½ teaspoon salt
¼ cup hot water	1 green pepper cut in thin strips
1 (No. 2) can pineapple chunks	¼ cup thinly sliced peeled onion
¼ cup brown sugar, packed	2 cans chow-mein noodles
2 tablespoons cornstarch	(about 5 cups)
¼ cup cider vinegar	

Have meat cut in strips about 2 inches long and ½ inch wide. Brown pork slowly in hot oil. Add water. Cover and simmer about 1 hour or until tender.

Drain pineapple. Save syrup. Combine sugar and cornstarch in glass or enamel saucepan. Add pineapple syrup, vinegar, soy sauce, and salt. Cook, stirring, over low heat until thick and clear. Pour over hot cooked pork. Let stand 10 minutes or longer. Add pineapple cubes, green pepper, and onion. Bring to a boil. Boil 3 minutes, stirring occasionally. Serve over chow-mein noodles made crisp in a hot oven. Makes 6 servings.

We love Chinese cooking at home. It's very easy, actually, but advance preparation takes time—cutting pork and vegetables in strips. Don't ever warm over a Chinese dish. Cook fresh and never *over* cook. Serve *hot* and promptly.

CHINESE BAKED SPARERIBS

3 pounds pork spareribs, cut in serving pieces	3 tablespoons cider vinegar
¼ cup prepared mustard	2 tablespoons Worcestershire sauce
¼ cup light molasses	2 teaspoons Tabasco sauce
¼ cup soy sauce	

Place ribs in shallow baking dish. Combine remaining ingredients and pour over ribs. Chill, covered, 3 hours or longer.

Start oven at moderate (350° F.).

Bake ribs about 1½ hours or until tender and done. Baste frequently with sauce in pan. Turn ribs once during baking. When brown and crusty, serve at once. Makes 3 to 4 servings.

This is a finger food—no holds barred in our house. Forks ruin the fun. Plenty of paper napkins with this one.

Sausage

Shape bulk pork sausage into patties. Pan-fry slowly, using very little fat and starting in cold skillet. Cook 15 to 20 minutes, until sausage is thoroughly cooked through and browned on both sides.

Patties may be dipped in beaten egg and crumbs or crushed corn flakes first. Or sausage may be shaped into roll, then sliced in rounds and cooked as described.

Fry link sausages over low heat, using 2 or 3 tablespoons water in skillet. When sausages begin to cook, cover skillet. Let steam 10 minutes. Drain any liquid. Continue cooking over low heat until well browned on all sides. Do not prick with fork. Sausages must be well done. Serve hot, 1 or 2 as a serving, with scrambled eggs or mashed potatoes.

Sausages in White Wine: Cook 3 sausages for each serving. With 12 sausages in skillet, add 1½ cups dry white wine mixed with ¾ cup water. Cover. Bring to a boil, then simmer 15 minutes. Drain sausages. Continue to heat and cook sausages until well browned on all sides. Serve with mashed potatoes.

Veal

Veal is the meat of a calf. Good veal is light in color, slightly pink, fine-grained, smooth-textured, and softer than beef. There should be a little fat on a veal cut, and what fat is there should be firm and clear.

No matter by what method you cook veal, it must be well done.

The best cuts for roasting are loin, ribs, and leg. The leg may or may not be boned. The boned rolled shoulder is also a good veal roast. Veal breast is stuffed and roasted.

Veal cutlet: whole slices of leg are used as veal chops, and cutlets or schnitzel. Scaloppine and veal birds are cut from sections of the leg. Most other cuts are used for stews and casserole.

Since veal is not as fat as beef, or as richly flavored, veal cookery must include added fat and various vegetables and seasonings, depending on the dish.

ROAST VEAL

In general, to roast veal, rub with salt and pepper. Place skin side up in shallow roasting pan; roast uncovered in moderate oven (325° F.), allowing 30 minutes per pound. If a meat thermometer is used, make a hole with a skewer through the skin side, insert thermometer so bulb will be in center of roast and not on bone if one is present.

Have dealer bone a shoulder roast of veal, but take bone with you and add it to roasting pan with meat.

Serve with brown gravy, either noodles or potatoes, and new green peas or small lima beans. A 6-pound roast makes 8 to 10 servings.

FRENCH VEAL STEW

Blanquette de Veau

2 pounds stewing veal
1 large onion, peeled, studded with cloves
¼ cup chopped, scraped carrot
1 bay leaf
1 sprig fresh thyme or ½ teaspoon dried thyme
4 peppercorns
2 teaspoons salt
1 quart boiling water

12 small onions, peeled
5 tablespoons butter or margarine
¼ cup flour
3 cups veal stock
Juice ½ lemon
2 egg yolks, slightly beaten
1 (6-ounce) can sliced mushrooms
2 tablespoons finely cut parsley

Cut veal in 2-inch pieces or have meat dealer cut it. Combine veal with onion, carrot, bay leaf, herb, peppercorns, and salt in large kettle. Add boiling water. Bring to a boil. Reduce heat; simmer 1 hour or until meat is tender.

Cook small onions in 2 tablespoons butter or margarine in covered heavy saucepan or skillet 20 to 30 minutes, until tender. Drain veal. Measure 3 cups stock. Melt remaining 3 tablespoons butter or margarine. Stir in flour, blend smoothly. Add 3 cups strained stock. Cook, stirring constantly, over moderate heat until mixture thickens and boils. Stir lemon juice and egg yolks into a little of the thickened sauce. Mix. Stir into saucepan. Add mushrooms, veal, parsley. Reheat just to boiling point. Serve on hot platter with mounds of cooked onions. Makes 6 servings.

This is from my French culinary notebook. It was one of the first important dishes I learned to make, and it still has priority among my party-food preferences. So few people know what to do with veal. This is a memorable dish. Your guests will ask for the recipe.

A DELICATE DISH OF VEAL

2	pounds breast of veal	1	bay leaf
3	tablespoons butter or margarine	1	tablespoon finely cut parsley
		2	slices lemon
2	tablespoons flour	¼	teaspoon powdered nutmeg
3	cups water	1½	teaspoons salt
1	onion, peeled	½	teaspoon pepper
4	whole cloves	¼	cup white wine

Cut veal into serving-size pieces. Cream butter or margarine with flour. Add to veal and water in Dutch oven or heavy kettle. Add onion stuck with cloves. Add bay leaf, parsley, lemon slices, nutmeg, salt, pepper, and wine. Cover pot. Cook slowly 1½ to 2 hours or until meat is tender and mixture is thickened. Strain sauce from meat. Pour over veal again. Reheat. Serve with or without hot rice. Makes 6 servings.

Veal is a favorite dish in Europe—a meat staple. Too often here it is pale and tasteless. If you and veal are not yet *en rapport,* try this recipe and change your mind.

FRENCH VEAL CASSEROLE

2	pounds veal leg	3	tablespoons flour
3	tablespoons butter or margarine	1	cup stock or bouillon
		1	cup commercial sour cream
2	tablespoons Marsala or dry sherry	4	tomatoes, skinned and chopped
1	clove garlic, peeled and mashed	1	teaspoon salt
		½	teaspoon pepper
3	mushrooms, sliced	1	bay leaf
1	teaspoon meat glaze	1	tablespoon finely cut chives
1	teaspoon tomato paste		

Cut meat in serving-size pieces. Brown quickly in 2 tablespoons butter or margarine in flameproof casserole. Heat wine in small saucepan. Ignite with match. Pour over veal. Stir. Remove meat from casserole. Add remaining tablespoon butter or margarine to casserole with garlic. Cook 1 minute. Add mushrooms. Stir and cook 2 minutes. Discard garlic. Remove casserole from heat. Stir in meat glaze and blend. Add tomato paste and mix well. Stir in flour and mix until smooth. Return to heat. Add stock or bouillon, stirring and cooking until mixture boils. Add sour cream, stirring continually.

Return veal to casserole. Stir to coat well with sour cream gravy. When well combined, add tomatoes, salt, pepper, and bay leaf, stir. Cover casserole and let cook slowly on top of stove or in moderate (350° F.) oven 45 minutes or until meat is done. Sprinkle with chives and serve. Makes 4 to 6 servings.

JELLIED VEAL

4 pounds veal shank bones, cracked	½ teaspoon pepper
	1 quart water
2 carrots, scraped and quartered	1 egg white
2 onions, peeled and quartered	1 hard-cooked egg
1 stalk celery	½ cup sliced stuffed olives
2 teaspoons salt	

Place meat in large kettle. Add carrots, onions, celery, salt, pepper, and water. Cover. Bring to a boil. Reduce heat. Simmer about 2½ hours or until meat is tender. When meat is done, remove from stock. Cook stock down until reduced to 2 cups. Let cool. Skim fat off top. Dice veal fine. Discard all fat, gristle, bones.

To clear skimmed veal stock, heat to a boil. Add egg white. Cook, stirring constantly, about 10 minutes. Strain through several thicknesses of cheesecloth. Combine strained stock with diced veal.

Oil 1½-quart mold or loaf pan. Arrange slices of hard-cooked egg and olives in bottom. Pour a little veal stock over egg and olives and refrigerate until thick enough to hold decorations in place. Spoon remaining veal mixture into mold. Chill until firm. Unmold on chilled platter. Garnish with small crisp lettuce cups containing Tartare Sauce (page 524) or Lemon Mayonnaise (page 523) and chopped ripe olives. Makes 6 servings.

This is a lifesaver on a hot Sunday night. Do it the day before. It is impressive, delicious, cool-looking, *professional*.

VEAL GOULASH, VIENNA STYLE

2 pounds veal shoulder, cubed	⅓ cup tomato sauce
2 teaspoons salt	2 fresh tomatoes, skinned
1 tablespoon paprika	3 tablespoons commercial sour
4 small onions, peeled and diced	cream
4 tablespoons butter or margarine	

Season veal with salt and paprika. Cook onions in butter or margarine in heavy 2-quart kettle or Dutch oven until browning. Add seasoned veal. Cook, stirring, over moderate heat until veal is lightly browned on all sides. Reduce heat. Add tomato sauce. Cut tomatoes in small cubes into the kettle, stirring juice and tomatoes into the sauce. Cover. Simmer about 1 hour or until meat is done. Stir occasionally. Stir cream into mixture. Cook until very hot. Serve with or without noodles. Makes 4 to 6 servings.

Of course you'll go to Vienna someday. When you do, order this at the Sacher, followed of course by the famous Sachertorte and good resolutions.

WHYTE'S VEAL GOULASH

2 pounds veal shoulder	1½ teaspoons salt
1 clove garlic, peeled and crushed	4 tablespoons drippings or fat
Sprig dried dill	1½ cups boiling water
3 onions, peeled and sliced	2 pounds sauerkraut, drained
1 tablespoon caraway seed	2 cups commercial sour cream
	1 teaspoon paprika

Cut veal in bite-size pieces. Add garlic, dill, onions, caraway, and salt. Brown on all sides in 2 tablespoons fat in Dutch oven, 15 minutes. Add boiling water and remaining fat. Cover. Bring to a boil. Lower heat. Let simmer 2 hours. Mix in sauerkraut. Bring to a boil. Stir in sour cream and paprika. Reheat and serve. Makes 6 servings.

This is a specialty I enjoyed at this fine old New York restaurant, a favorite luncheon place of my father and grandfather.

VEAL POT ROAST

3-to-5-pound boned veal rump
   roast
2 tablespoons beef fat, shortening, or olive oil
¼ cup water
1 teaspoon salt

2 to 4 whole cloves
1-inch piece cinnamon stick
¼ teaspoon powdered nutmeg
1 cup dained canned apricot
   halves

Brown roast 15 to 20 minutes in hot fat, shortening, or oil in heavy kettle or Dutch oven. Add water, salt, spice. Cover. Let simmer 2½ hours. Add apricot halves. Cover. Cook 1 hour or longer, until veal is tender and done. Remove veal and apricot to warmed platter. Serve hot. Makes 6 to 10 servings.

Especially good with hot boiled rice or new potatoes. If gravy is desired, keep meat and fruit garnish hot on warmed platter in oven. Make gravy by adding enough boiling water to liquid in kettle to make 2½ cups. Stir 2 tablespoons flour into a little of the hot liquid, then stir into the kettle. Let boil 2 or 3 minutes, stirring continually. Season if needed. Serve hot with roast.

VEAL CHOPS, PARIS BISTRO

4 veal chops
Salt and paprika
3 tablespoons butter
½ cup dry white wine

2 tablespoons finely cut chives
2 tablespoons finely cut parsley
1 teaspoon finely cut tarragon
2 tablespoons cognac

Dredge chops lightly in flour. Season with salt and paprika. Brown lightly in butter. Lower heat. Cook until chops are done, 20 minutes or longer, depending on thickness. Turn chops with pancake turner.

Place chops on hot plater. Keep them hot. Pour wine into pan, tilt and scrape, mixing with butter and any brown from the chops. Add chives, parsley, tarragon, and brandy. Bring quickly to a boil. Pour over chops and serve immediately. Makes 4 servings.

It's difficult to find poor food in France except, perhaps, in those American-style quick-service places now starting up in Paris. This dish is familiar to Americans who love Paris-as-she-was.

VEAL CUTLET, VIENNA STYLE
Wiener Schnitzel

2 pounds veal cut for schnitzel	1 cup fine dry bread crumbs
Juice 2 lemons	¼ cup flour
Paprika	½ pound butter
2 eggs	12 anchovy fillets
2 tablespoons water	1 lemon, quartered

Have meat dealer cut veal for schnitzel. That is, across the grain on a slight slant, about ⅛ to ¼ inch thick. Place slices between 2 or 3 thicknesses waxed paper. Pound with wooden mallet until thinned down to about 1/16 inch thick.

Place veal in shallow dish. Cover with lemon juice. Sprinkle lightly with paprika. Let marinate about 1 hour. Turn meat several times while marinating.

Beat eggs. Add water. Drain veal. Dip lightly into egg, then into crumbs and flour. Let stand 20 minutes to dry.

Melt 12 tablespoons butter in small saucepan. Mix with mashed and chopped anchovies. Keep this sauce hot.

Melt remaining 4 tablespoons butter in skillet. When hot reduce heat. Add veal. Sauté 1½ minutes. Use pancake turner and turn veal as soon as golden brown and sauté other side 1½ minutes. Schnitzel is done when both sides are browned. Remove to hot serving platter. Sprinkle lightly with lemon juice. Pour hot anchovy butter over. Serve at once with garnish of lemon quarter. Makes 4 servings.

Add one fried egg per portion and it becomes Wiener Schnitzel Holstein. I like mine plain.

BREADED VEAL CUTLETS

4 veal cutlets or chops cut ½ inch thick	1 teaspoon paprika
½ clove garlic	1 egg, beaten
1 cup fine bread crumbs	2 tablespoons water
1 teaspoon salt	4 tablespoons butter or margarine
½ teaspoon pepper	

Rub cutlets with garlic. Dip in crumbs mixed with salt, pepper, and paprika, then into beaten egg mixed with water, and again in crumbs.

Let stand 10 to 20 minutes to dry. Brown in butter or margarine over high heat. Reduce heat, cover skillet, cook over low heat about 30 minutes or until veal is done. Add a little more butter or a little hot water if needed.

Serve with a well-seasoned tomato sauce. The cooked cutlets or chops may be heated in the sauce, or serve hot chops on a warm platter with sauce around them. Makes 4 servings.

This may be done up to the point of browning the night or day before by harried career women—or busy mothers. Or on a dull day make up a double or triple amount for the freezer to be cooked at the appropriate time. You will be grateful for your foresightedness.

VEAL BIRDS, STEPHEN'S FAVORITE

1 ½	pounds veal round, cut very thin	¼ cup seedless raisins
1	cup coarse whole-wheat or rye bread crumbs	Salt
		Flour
4	tablespoons butter or margarine	½ cup milk
		½ cup water
1	small onion, peeled and diced	

Divide cutlet into 8 pieces. Place between several thicknesses of waxed paper and pound with meat mallet or edge of heavy plate until thin.

Combine crumbs with 2 tablespoons butter or margarine in saucepan over moderate heat. Stir. Add onion and raisins; mix.

Spoon about 1½ tablespoons raisin mixture onto each piece of veal. Roll. Fasten with small skewers or wooden picks. Sprinkle rolls with salt. Roll lightly in flour. Brown in remaining 2 tablespoons butter or margarine in skillet. Reduce heat when well browned. Add mixture of milk and water to about half cover rolls. Cover skillet. Cook rolls over moderate heat about ½ hour or until meat is tender. Remove skewers. Makes 4 servings.

Make gravy with pan juices or serve "birds" with tomato sauce. A delicious variation is made by substituting chopped dried apricots for raisins in the stuffing. With apricots add ½ teaspoon basil or marjoram and ¼ teaspoon powdered cinnamon; *omit* onion.

DELICIOUS VEAL PATTIES

2 thick slices white bread
½ cup water
½ cup red wine
½ small onion, peeled and diced
1 pound ground veal

2 teaspoons salt
⅛ teaspoon black pepper
½ cup fine, dry bread crumbs
4 tablespoons butter or margarine

Soak bread in mixture of water and wine. Beat with fork until thick and mushy. Mix with onion, veal, salt, and pepper.

Shape into 12 thin patties. Coat patties with crumbs. Let stand 15 minutes to dry. Brown on both sides in hot butter or margarine. Cook about 20 minutes, until patties are tender as well as brown. Serve hot with or without German Mustard Sauce (page 553). Makes 6 servings.

VEAL SCALOPPINE

1 pound very thin veal cutlets
½ cup flour
4 tablespoons butter
½ cup Marsala wine or sherry

1 teaspoon salt
Quick grind black pepper
1 lemon, thinly sliced

Have meat dealer flatten veal, or place between 2 or 3 thicknesses of waxed paper and pound with wooden mallet or edge of heavy plate until very thin. Cut veal into 4 pieces. Roll lightly in flour. Heat heavy skillet. Melt butter. Brown cutlets quickly, but thoroughly, on both sides. Turn with pancake turner. Add wine, cover pan. Simmer over low heat about 5 minutes or until meat is tender. Season with salt and pepper. Serve at once on hot platter, garnished with lemon slices. Makes 4 servings.

When serving scaloppine for luncheon or dinner have all vegetables and other foods on the menu ready to serve as soon as the veal is done. Scaloppine at its best should be eaten a few minutes after it comes from the skillet.

Veal Scaloppine Parmesan: Combine ¼ cup grated Parmesan cheese with ½ cup flour in which scallops are dipped. Dredge each scallop, coating both sides generously with cheese and flour. Cook as described for plain scaloppine. Superb flavor. Makes 4 servings.

Veal Chops Parmesan: Prepare veal chops, cut ½ inch thick, as described for Veal Scaloppine Parmesan. Chops require longer cooking, about 40 minutes, or until tender and done, over moderate heat. Makes 4 servings.

Mixed Meat Dishes

CHILI CON CARNE

2 tablespoons butter or margarine

1 large onion, peeled and shredded

1 (4-ounce) can pimientos, drained

2 pounds round, rump, or chuck beef, ground

1 cup canned tomatoes, chopped

2 cups beef stock or bouillon

1 tablespoon chili powder

1 teaspoon salt

1 teaspoon sugar

¼ teaspoon black pepper

Melt butter or margarine in large skillet. Add onion and pimientos. Mix and cook until onion begins to brown. Add beef. Stir and cook 10 minutes. Add tomatoes, stock or bouillon, and seasonings. Cover and let simmer 1 hour. Garnish with spoonfuls of hot rice or drained canned kidney beans. Makes 6 or more servings.

MIXED CHILI CON CARNE

2 pounds round steak

1 pound lean pork

3 tablespoons olive oil

1 or 2 cloves garlic, peeled and sliced

1 large onion, peeled and diced

2 tablespoons chili powder

1 tablespoon flour

1 (No. 1 tall) can tomatoes

1 tablespoon salt

1 teaspoon marjoram

2 bay leaves

1 cup chopped stuffed olives

3 cups cooked rice or (9-ounce) package spaghetti

Cut meats into cubes. Heat oil in Dutch oven or heavy kettle. Add garlic and onion. Stir. When onion is golden, stir in chili powder mixed with flour. Mix well. Add meats. Cover kettle and let brown slowly 20 minutes. Stir frequently to coat all meat with oil and seasonings. Add tomatoes, salt, marjoram, and bay leaves. Cover kettle. Let cook gently 2 hours. Add olives. Cook 20 minutes longer. Serve with rice or spaghetti. Makes 6 servings.

CONNECTICUT HAMBURGERS

1 large Spanish onion	¾ cup soft bread crumbs
3 tablespoons drippings	1 ½ teaspoons salt
2 tablespoons butter or marga-rine	½ teaspoon pepper
	1 ½ pounds ground lean beef
1 small onion, peeled and diced	1 egg
	6 slices bacon
3 tablespoons finely cut parsley	Parsley or cut chives

Start oven at moderate (350° F.).

Peel onion. Cut in 6 slices. Arrange slices in shallow baking pan. Pour melted bacon drippings over onion and bake about 20 minutes. Remove from oven and set aside.

Melt butter or margarine. Mix with small diced onion, parsley, crumbs, salt, pepper, meat, and slightly beaten egg. Mix well, shape in 6 plump patties. Wrap each with slice of bacon. Secure with wooden skewer or picks. Place patty on cooked onion slice in baking pan. Brush patties with drippings in pan.

Broil 4 to 5 minutes on each side or to desired doneness. Remove skewers. Garnish each hamburger and its onion base with parsley or chives. Makes 6 servings.

MEAT BALLS WITH BURGUNDY SAUCE

1 pound ground beef chuck or round	1 small onion, peeled and diced
1 large apple, pared, cored, and shredded	¾ cup Burgundy wine
	¼ cup water
1 egg, slightly beaten	2 (8-ounce) cans tomato sauce
1 ¼ teaspoons salt	½ teaspoon basil
¼ teaspoon pepper	¼ teaspoon rosemary
¼ cup flour	¼ teaspoon sugar
2 tablespoons salad oil	

Combine beef, apple, egg, salt, and pepper. Mix lightly and evenly. Shape into small balls. Roll in flour. Heat oil in large skillet. Add meat balls and onion. Cook over low heat about 10 minutes or until lightly browned on all sides. Mix wine and water. Combine with tomato sauce, herbs, and sugar. Pour over meat balls. Cover. Simmer 15 minutes or until meat is done. Makes 4 to 6 servings.

Serve over hot spaghetti, noodles, or other hot pasta. This is an easy dish for electric skillet or large chafing dish.

MEAT BALLS, RUSSIAN STYLE
Dimitri's Bitki

1	large loaf fresh bread	½	teaspoon pepper
1 ½	cups milk (approximate)	1	teaspoon Kitchen Bouquet or
1	pound beef, ground		Worcestershire sauce
1	pound pork, ground	¼	cup water
1	pound veal, ground	¾	cup bread crumbs
4	eggs	3	tablespoons butter or marga-
1	tablespoon finely cut fresh dill		rine
1 ½	teaspoons salt	1 ½	cups commercial sour cream

Remove crust from bread. Break bread coarsely. Moisten with milk and let stand until very soft. Combine meats, mixing thoroughly with the hands. Beat 2 eggs lightly and work into meats.

Add dill, salt, pepper, and Kitchen Bouquet or Worcestershire to the softened bread and combine with meat mixture. Form loose balls the size of a small orange. Beat remaining 2 eggs lightly. Mix with about ¼ cup water. Dip meat balls into egg, then into crumbs. Sauté in butter or margarine in a metal-base casserole on moderate heat 10 minutes. Turn meat balls and brown 10 minutes longer.

Start oven at moderate (375° F.). When meat balls are lightly browned, pour sour cream over them. Cover casserole.

Bake 45 minutes. Makes 6 to 8 servings.

I keep extra copies of this recipe on file cards to fill the inevitable requests. In winter I use dried dill.

MUSHROOM HAMBURGERS

1 (10½-ounce) can condensed cream-of-mushroom soup
1 pound ground beef
⅔ cup dry bread crumbs
2 tablespoons minced peeled onion

1 tablespoon finely cut parsley
1 egg, slightly beaten
2 tablespoons butter or margarine
8 round buns, split, toasted

Combine ¼ cup soup with beef, crumbs, onion, parsley, and egg. Mix lightly but thoroughly. Shape into 8 patties. Brown patties in butter or margarine to desired doneness. Mix ¼ cup water with remaining soup. Pour over patties in frying pan. Cover. Cook 5 minutes or until sauce is boiling. Stir occasionally. Serve on split and toasted buns. Makes 8 servings.

Add garnish of sautéed mushrooms to dress this up and add delicate flavor.

SWEDISH MEAT BALLS

2 eggs
1 cup light cream
½ cup dry bread crumbs
1 onion, peeled and sliced
3 tablespoons butter or margarine
1 pound beef, finely ground
½ pound veal, finely ground

¼ pound suet, finely ground
⅛ teaspoon powdered allspice
1 tablespoon salt
½ teaspoon pepper
2 cups boiling water
¼ cup flour
2 tablespoons finely cut fresh dill

Beat eggs in large bowl. Stir cream into eggs. Add crumbs and let soften 5 minutes. Cook onion in large skillet in 1 tablespoon butter until tender. Add to egg mixture. Add meats and seasonings. Mix well. Shape into 1-inch balls. Melt remaining 2 tablespoons butter in skillet. Brown meat balls lightly. Add boiling water and cover skillet. Bring to a boil, then lower heat and simmer 20 minutes. Remove meat balls to warmed platter.

Skim off excess fat from skillet liquid. Blend flour with little fat from pan, then stir back into skillet until thickened and smooth. If too thick, stir little boiling water into skillet. Let boil 2 or 3 minutes, stirring constantly. Pour over meat balls and sprinkle with dill. Serve hot. Makes 8 servings.

Having a big cocktail party? Make this the hot hors d'oeuvres in a chafing dish or on an electric hot tray and forget everything except the compliments.

Meat Loaves

BEEF-AND-TOMATO LOAF

1 ½	pounds ground beef	1	small bay leaf, crumbled
1 ½	cups dry bread crumbs	¼	teaspoon thyme
⅔	cup diced processed American cheese	½	teaspoon garlic salt
1	onion, peeled and diced	2	eggs, slightly beaten
½	green pepper, diced	1	(10 ½ -ounce) can tomato sauce, 1 ¼ cups
2	teaspoons salt		

Mix beef, crumbs, cheese, onion, green pepper, and seasonings. Combine eggs and tomato sauce. Mix with meat combination.

Start oven at moderate (350° F.).

Shape meat mixture into 2 loaves in buttered shallow pan.

Bake about 1 hour or until browned and done through. Serve hot, with or without tomato sauce. Makes 8 to 10 servings.

To freeze these loaves, let them cool thoroughly when they come from the oven. Wrap them on tray or pan in which they baked, using wrapping according to instructions for your deep freezer. Seal loose ends with freezer tape. Freeze quickly. To serve, unwrap pan, place in moderate (350° F.) oven, and bake about 1½ hours.

THE MCLENNANS' SCOTCH MEAT ROLL

2 pounds top round, ground
½ pound lean bacon or ham, ground
1 cup soft white bread crumbs
1 medium onion, peeled and chopped

2 teaspoons salt
2 teaspoons freshly ground pepper
Boiling water
1 cup dry bread crumbs

Combine all ingredients except boiling water and the dry bread crumbs. Mix well. Form a roll about 10 inches long. Wrap in waxed paper, then in thin cotton cloth. Tie both ends tightly with string. Place in large pot of boiling water. When water returns to a boil, lower heat and let water simmer 3 hours. Let roll cool in water in which it cooked.

Remove cloth and waxed paper. Roll meat in dry bread crumbs. Serve cold, sliced, with salad or hot vegetables. Makes 5 or 6 servings.

MEAT LOAF, ITALIAN STYLE

2 slices Italian whole-wheat bread
2 slices Italian white bread
1 cup water
1 onion
4 sprigs parsley
1 pound ground lean beef
3 tablespoons grated Parmesan or Gruyère cheese

1 egg
1 teaspoon salt
¼ teaspoon pepper
2 tablespoons butter or margarine
1 (8-ounce) can tomato sauce
1 teaspoon orégano

Start oven at moderate (375° F.). Oil shallow baking pan.

Crumble bread in mixing bowl. Pour water over and let soak few minutes. Peel and chop onion. Cut parsley fine. Mash soaked bread with fork. Combine with beef, onion, parsley, and cheese in mixing bowl. Mix with fork lightly and evenly. Add egg, salt, and pepper. Mix. Shape into loaf in prepared pan. Add dabs of butter along top of loaf.

Bake 30 minutes. Pour tomato sauce over loaf and sprinkle with orégano. Bake 20 minutes longer. Serve hot or cold. Makes 6 or more servings.

Meat Pies

CALIFORNIA MEAT PIE

1 medium onion, peeled	⅛ teaspoon cayenne
2 cups cut-up cooked beef, lamb, or veal	¼ cup undiluted consommé
10 pitted ripe olives	1 (No. 2) can cream-style corn
2 hard-cooked eggs	2 eggs, well beaten
1 teaspoon orégano	Salt
½ teaspoon salt	Pepper

Grind onion, meat, olives, and hard-cooked eggs together in food chopper.

Start oven at moderate (375° F.). Grease 9-inch pie plate.

Mix meat combination with orégano, salt, cayenne, and consommé.

Mix corn with beaten eggs and add ¼ teaspoon salt and ⅛ teaspoon pepper.

Use meat mixture to line bottom and sides of prepared pie plate up to rim. Pat mixture in place. Pour corn mixture into meat-lined pan. Bake 45 minutes. Increase oven heat to moderately hot (400° F.) and bake 15 minutes longer. Remove pan from oven. Let cool about 10 minutes. Cut pie in 6 wedges. Makes 6 servings.

A perfect one-dish supper, with a refreshing green salad, chunky French bread, and hot coffee served with a well-filled fruit bowl.

BARDI'S SAUSAGE PIE

Pastry for 2-crust pie	1 teaspoon salt
1 pound sausage meat	½ teaspoon pepper
6 eggs	

Start oven at moderately hot (400° F.).

Line pie plate with pastry and trim edge. Sauté sausage in hot frying pan about 10 minutes, until hot through and beginning to brown. Pour into lined pie plate. Use tablespoon and make 6 hollows in sausage. Break egg into saucer and slip into each hollow. Season all lightly with salt and pepper. Place top pastry over all. Trim edge and crimp as for any pie. Bake 45 minutes. Serve hot or cold. Makes 6 servings.

Wonderful with leftover gravy or Mushroom Sauce (page 553). Or serve with baked zucchini and a broiled tomato half as a one-plate supper.

MARY MANVILLE'S TAMALE PIE

My neighbor, Mary Manville, gave me this recipe, a streamlined version of one which has been a favorite in her mother's family in California for three generations. It has great advantage for party service in that it stretches a small amount of meat a long way and it can be prepared the day before. In fact, it is better so.

3 onions, peeled and chopped	1 cup yellow corn meal
2 tablespoons olive oil	½ cup cold water
2 pounds ground chuck beef	1 teaspoon salt
1 teaspoon salt	3 cups boiling water
3 tablespoons chili powder	1 cup pitted ripe olives
½ teaspoon orégano	½ cup crumbled pepperoni (hot
½ teaspoon basil	Italian sausage)
2 tablespoons sugar	¼ cup grated cheese
1 large can tomato purée or 1 (No. 2½) can tomatoes plus 1 (6-ounce) can tomato paste	

Cook onions in oil until golden. Add meat. Cook and stir until lightly browned. Sprinkle salt, chili powder, herbs, and sugar over meat while cooking. Don't let it cook dry. Add tomato purée or tomatoes and paste. Simmer 1 hour, stirring occasionally. Taste. Add more salt if needed.

Mix corn meal with cold water and salt. Stir into boiling water. Cook, stirring over low heat, about 10 minutes. As it cooks spoon some of the liquid from the meat skillet into the corn-meal mixture so it will have the chili flavor.

Start oven at moderate (350° F.). Grease 2½-to-3-quart casserole.

Put layer of corn-meal mixture in prepared casserole. Add meat sauce and dot with olives. Spread remaining corn-meal mixture on top. Sprinkle with pepperoni and grated cheese. Brown 15 minutes or until bubbly. Makes 8 generous servings.

Best prepared the day before: complete casserole, but do not top with pepperoni and cheese. When cool, refrigerate. Next day, to serve, sprinkle top with pepperoni and cheese, heat 1 hour in moderately slow (300° F.) oven, or use hotter oven until dish is browned and bubbly.

VEAL-AND-HAM PIE

Rich pastry for 2-crust pie
½ cup bread crumbs, soaked in little milk
1 cup chopped cooked ham
1 cup chopped cooked veal
1 egg, beaten
1 tablespoon finely cut parsley

1 teaspoon grated lemon peel
1 onion, peeled and diced
¼ cup veal gravy or bouillon
½ teaspoon basil
½ teaspoon salt
½ teaspoon pepper
Milk

Prepare rich pastry and divide in half. Roll out half to fit shallow oval casserole or pâté form. Fit pastry into dish and let edge extend about 1 inch beyond dish. Trim evenly. Chill remaining half of pastry.

Start oven at moderate (375° F.).

Drain crumbs. Combine in mixing bowl with meats and all remaining ingredients except milk. Mix lightly but evenly with fork. Pour into pastry-lined dish. Add a little more gravy or bouillon if mixture seems too dry. Should be the consistency of hash.

Roll remaining pastry to fit top and gash in 2 or 3 places decoratively. Fit cover on dish. Trim overhang evenly and then crimp top and bottom pastry together into upstanding rim around dish. Brush top pastry with milk.

Bake about 40 minutes or until pastry is golden. Serve hot or cold. Makes 4 to 6 servings.

Leftover gravy, or mushroom sauce combined with gravy, goes well with this pie.

We used to take these, cold, on spring picnics in Switzerland when we went to gather the narcissi. It was almost the *only* time we ever saw sliced, *uncooked* Gruyère cheese (so good with these). It was rationed to us school girls at 1½ kilos each per week, and used in almost all our food, it seemed. No wonder we rounded out.

Specialty Meats

Specialty meats include brains, tongue, sweetbreads, tripe, heart, liver, and kidneys. Beef liver and kidneys are too pronounced in flavor for most of us, but the more delicate calf's liver, lamb's liver and kidneys can make delicious additions to the menus.

Here are some of my favorite dishes made with these meats.

CALF'S LIVER SAUTÉED WITH HERBS

4 tablespoons butter or margarine

8 slices calf's liver

8 slices lean bacon, cooked until crisp

1 tablespoon diced peeled onion

1 tablespoon lemon juice

½ cup dry white wine

3 tablespoons mixed fresh herbs (thyme, parsley, chervil, chives)

or

1 tablespoon mixed parsley and chives and

1 teaspoon mixed dried thyme and chervil

½ teaspoon salt

Freshly ground pepper

Heat 2 tablespoons butter or margarine in heavy skillet. Brown slices of liver quickly on each side. When cooked to desired doneness, place on hot platter. Garnish with grilled bacon. Keep platter hot in hot oven with door left open.

Melt remaining 2 tablespoons butter in pan where liver cooked. Sauté onion 2 or 3 minutes. Add lemon juice, wine, and herbs. Stir. Add salt and pepper. Heat quickly to a boil. Pour over liver on serving platter. Serve at once. Makes 4 servings.

BAKED STUFFED HEART

1 beef heart or 2 calves' hearts

4 cups poultry stuffing

Flour

1 teaspoon salt

½ teaspoon pepper

3 tablespoons bacon fat

Boiling water

Have meat dealer remove fat, veins, and arteries from heart. Wash heart thoroughly under cold running water. Drain and fill cavity with stuffing. Skewer edges together with small metal skewers and tie with string.

Start oven at slow (275° F.).

Mix flour, salt, and pepper. Dredge stuffed heart. Melt bacon fat in flameproof casserole or baking pan. Brown heart on all sides. Add boiling water to the depth of 1 inch. Cover casserole or pan.

Bake about 2 hours or until tender. Remove strings and skewers. Serve on heated platter. Carve in thin slices. Any sauce suggested for smoked beef tongue goes well with baked heart. Makes 4 to 6 servings.

Pickled Beef Heart: Have meat dealer clean heart of all fat, veins, and arteries. Cook like boiled Smoked Beef Tongue (page 426). Add ½ cup vinegar to stock when heart is tender. Let stand in stock several hours. Drain and chill. Serve sliced with any piquant sauce.

This was a wartime standby but as we *liked* it, it stayed in my active recipe files. A real budget balancer.

LAMB KIDNEYS ON SKEWERS
Brochette

8 lamb kidneys	2 green peppers, cut in squares
8 slices lean bacon	1 clove garlic, peeled and mashed
½ pound boiled ham in 1 piece	
8 mushroom caps	Salt, pepper
5 tablespoons butter or marga-rine	4 cups hot saffron rice
	Water cress
8 small white onions, peeled and parboiled	

Wash kidneys and remove outer membrane. Cut kidneys in half and remove white center cores. Rinse under cold running water and drain. Pat dry with paper towel. Cut bacon in half crosswise. Wrap each piece of kidney with bacon strip.

Cut ham in 1-inch cubes. Sauté mushrooms in 2 tablespoons butter or margarine. Add onions and cook slowly 5 minutes or until tender. Sauté green peppers 1 or 2 minutes.

Alternate bacon-wrapped kidney, green pepper, ham, mushroom, and onion on skewers. Melt remaining 3 tablespoons butter or margarine in pan in which onions cooked. Add garlic. Stir and cook 1 minute. Remove garlic and discard.

Start broiler heat at moderate (350° F.).

Place skewers in shallow pan. Pour garlic butter over them and season with salt and pepper. Broil 5 minutes on each side. When kidney is done and bacon well cooked, serve skewered foods by pushing all off onto serving of hot saffron rice. Makes 4 servings.

LAMB KIDNEYS, DIABLE

8 lamb kidneys
4 tablespoons butter
4 teaspoons flour
1 small onion, peeled and diced
½ teaspoon dry mustard
1 tablespoon tomato paste

½ cup meat stock or bouillon
1 tablespoon finely cut chutney
4 slices toast
1 tablespoon finely cut parsley
  mixed with 1 tablespoon
  softened butter

Remove outer membrane from kidneys. Split lengthwise almost in half. Use scissors to remove fat, core, and veins. Wash under cold running water. Dry between paper towels. Insert small skewer in each to keep the two halves flat during cooking.

Sauté kidneys in hot butter in skillet over medium heat about 15 minutes or until tender. Turn them often. Reduce heat and sprinkle kidneys with flour. Stir flour with fat in skillet. Add onion, mustard, tomato paste, stock or bouillon, and chutney at one side. Stir well. Spoon over kidneys. Cover pan and cook over low heat until sauce is boiling and slightly thickened. Lift kidneys out onto toast on warm plates. Remove skewers. Add little parsley butter to each piece of kidney. Stir sauce in skillet and pour over all. Serve hot. Makes 4 servings.

Just right for Sunday brunch or a Saturday-night supper. A tossed green salad or a lemon-aspic ring filled with chopped vegetable salad, baked custard or fruit flambé, and coffee round out the menu for supper.

The English are the best kidney cooks. I enjoyed this dish on Cunard crossings and this recipe is from the *Queen Elizabeth* galley, translated into home cookery terms.

VEAL KIDNEYS, BRANDY SAUTÉE

Rognons de Veau Flambés

3 veal kidneys
3 tablespoons butter or margarine
¼ cup cognac
1 (3-ounce) can sliced broiled
  mushrooms

¼ teaspoon dry mustard
1 cup heavy cream whipped
Salt, pepper
4 slices buttered toast
1 tablespoon finely cut parsley

Remove fat and membrane from kidneys. Split lengthwise almost in half. Use scissors to remove core and veins. Wash under cold running water. Drain and pat dry with paper towel.

Cut kidneys into 1-inch cubes. Heat 1 tablespoon butter or margarine in heavy skillet. Brown kidney cubes quickly all over. Stir once or twice. Heat brandy in small pan. Ignite with match. Pour flaming over kidneys and mix well. Remove kidneys with slotted spoon.

Melt remaining 2 tablespoons butter or margarine in same pan. Heat mushrooms 1 or 2 minutes. Add mustard, mix and stir in whipped cream. Put cooked kidneys back into this sauce. Season to taste with salt and pepper. Cook only until kidneys are heated through again. Serve at once on hot toast. Sprinkle lightly with parsley. Makes 4 servings.

SWEETBREADS CRILLON

2 pairs sweetbreads	1 tomato, peeled and diced
1 quart cold water	2 tablespoons finely cut parsley
1 bay leaf	¼ teaspoon thyme
1 carrot, scraped and sliced	1 teaspoon salt
2 onions, peeled and sliced	½ teaspoon pepper
Juice 1 lemon	1 cup dry white wine
4 slices lean bacon	8 triangles toast
2 tablespoons flour	

Soak sweetbreads in cold water 20 minutes. Drain. Combine 1 quart water, bay leaf, carrot, 1 onion, and lemon juice in enamel kettle and bring to a boil. Add sweetbreads. Simmer 20 minutes. Drain. Cover sweetbreads with cold water 5 minutes. When cool, cut skin, fat, gristle, veins from sweetbreads and break them up into serving-size pieces.

Cook bacon in skillet until crisp. Break with fork in pan. Remove large pieces of bacon, leaving bits and the fat. Roll sweetbreads in flour. Brown in bacon fat 2 minutes on each side over high heat. Lower heat and add remaining onion, tomato, parsley, thyme, salt, and pepper. Add crumbled bacon. Blend all. Cook over medium heat 5 minutes. Add wine. Simmer uncovered 15 minutes. Serve on toast. Makes 4 servings.

SWEETBREADS AU GRATIN

3 pairs large sweetbreads
1 tablespoon lemon juice
5 tablespoons butter or margarine
2 tablespoons Marsala wine or sherry
1 small clove garlic, peeled and mashed
1 (6-ounce) can sliced mushrooms

½ teaspoon meat glaze
3 teaspoons cornstarch
1 cup stock or bouillon
¾ cup commercial sour cream
½ teaspoon salt
¼ teaspoon pepper
¼ teaspoon thyme
¾ cup grated Parmesan or Gruyère cheese

Soak sweetbreads in cold water 1 hour and drain. Place in enamel or glass saucepan with cold water to cover. Add lemon juice and bring slowly to a boil, then lower heat. Simmer 5 minutes and drain again. Put parboiled sweetbreads in ice water a few minutes and drain. Cut off skin, membranes, and tubes. Cut sweetbreads in half lengthwise. Brown quickly on both sides in 2 tablespoons butter or margarine in flameproof shallow casserole.

Heat wine in small pan. Ignite with match. Pour over sweetbreads. Remove sweetbreads and add another 2 tablespoons butter to casserole with garlic and mushrooms. Cook briskly 2 minutes. Discard garlic. Remove casserole from heat and stir in meat glaze. Add cornstarch, stir smoothly into mixture. Return pan to heat and add stock or bouillon, stirring and cooking until boiling. Stir constantly and add sour cream a little at a time. Add salt, pepper, and thyme. Return sweetbreads to casserole. Cover. Simmer over moderate heat 15 to 20 minutes. Sprinkle with grated cheese and dot top with 1 tablespoon butter. Brown under moderate broiler heat 3 to 5 minutes. Makes 6 servings.

Fussy children wedded to franks and hamburgers may be lured into trying these because of the *name* of the meat. Once they taste, they are converts. My youngest was won over in Stockholm.

SMOKED BEEF TONGUE
WITH SWEET-AND-SOUR SAUCE

2-to-5-pound smoked beef tongue
1 teaspoon whole allspice

1 bay leaf, broken
2 or 3 whole cloves

Wash beef tongue. Drain and cover with cold water and let soak several hours or overnight. Drain. Place in large kettle. Cover with cold water. Add seasonings. Cover kettle and bring to a boil. Lower heat and let simmer about 3½ hours or until very tender. Remove tongue from kettle, saving 3 cups stock. Keep stock hot. Let tongue cool slightly. Trim bone and gristle from heavy end. Slit skin on underside, loosen all around with paring knife, then pull skin off.

Sweet-and-Sour Sauce

3 tablespoons chicken or goose fat	¼ cup seedless raisins
2 tablespoons flour	½ teaspoon powdered cinnamon
1 medium onion, peeled and cut fine	2 cloves
3 cups tongue stock	1 teaspoon vinegar
1 lemon, sliced thin and quartered	1 tablespoon maple syrup
¼ cup sliced blanched almonds	4 tablespoons sugar, caramelized (cooked over low heat until liquefied and brown)

Heat fat in large saucepan. Stir in flour smoothly. Add onion and cook, stirring 5 minutes. Add stock gradually. Stir and let boil 5 minutes. Add lemon, nuts, raisins, cinnamon, cloves, and vinegar. Sweeten with maple syrup and caramelized sugar. Cook slowly 30 minutes or until sauce is reduced to about 2 cups. Place tongue in sauce. Cover saucepan and heat slowly 20 minutes. Remove tongue to warmed platter. Slice diagonally in thin slices. Serve with remaining sauce. Makes 6 to 10 servings.

Serve for buffet supper as suggested for Baked Corned Beef.

Smoked Beef Tongue with Horse-Radish Sauce: Cook tongue as described in preceding recipe. Let trimmed, skinned tongue chill about 4 hours in refrigerator. Combine ¼ cup commercial sour cream, ⅜ cup prepared horse-radish, 1 tablespoon drained capers, 1 tablespoon finely cut chives *or* 1 slice peeled garlic. Mix well. Chill. To serve, remove garlic slice. Serve sauce in chilled bowl or heap in small crisp lettuce cups placed around tongue platter. Makes sauce for 4 servings. Double recipe for large tongue.

When using canned whole tongue, follow directions on label about cooking or serving as is.

TRIPE WITH HERB SAUCE

Tripe à la Caen

1 ½	pounds honeycomb tripe	1	bay leaf
1	cracked marrow bone	2	cloves
2	onions, peeled and sliced	4	peppercorns
2	cups sliced carrots	1	teaspoon salt
½	teaspoon thyme	2	cups cider or still champagne

Wash tripe thoroughly under cold running water. Cut in 2-inch pieces. Start oven at slow (275° F.). Butter 2-quart baking dish.

Arrange tripe around marrow bone in center of buttered dish, in layers with vegetables, herbs, and seasoning. Add cider or champagne. Cover casserole. Bake 4 to 5 hours. If necessary, add a little hot water mixed with cider or champagne during cooking. Let cook longer if time permits. According to French cooks, tripe can't be overcooked. Makes 6 servings.

Sautéed Tripe; Creamed Tripe: Wash honeycomb tripe thoroughly. Boil 1 hour or longer, in water mixed with stock or bouillon, until tender. Drain and cut in serving-size pieces. Sauté in butter or combine with well-seasoned cream sauce. Serve Sautéed Tripe with crisp bacon and broiled seasoned tomatoes. Serve Creamed Tripe on anchovy toast or in hollowed-out, toasted loaf of bread.

Luncheon Meats

CREAMED CHIPPED BEEF

¼	pound sliced dried or chipped beef	3	tablespoons flour
		⅛	teaspoon pepper
4	tablespoons butter or margarine	2	cups milk
		6	slices toast

Tear beef in small pieces. Melt butter or margarine in frying pan or saucepan. Add beef. Sauté until beef is hot and turning brown. Sprinkle flour and pepper over beef. Stir to coat meat. Add milk slowly, stirring. Cook and stir constantly over low heat until mixture thickens and boils. Spoon onto hot toast. Makes 6 servings.

Or, make well-seasoned White Sauce. Stir dried beef into sauce and reheat. Serve on toast for luncheon or breakfast.

Frizzled Beef: Sauté chipped or dried beef a few minutes in hot butter. When beef is crisp, drain. Use as garnish on omelet, scrambled eggs, leftover creamed dishes, or corn pudding. Especially good as garnish for cheese-sauce dishes.

This is a Sunday breakfast standby—we don't have Sunday dinner. Sometimes there's time before Sunday School for real cornbread. For us the quick variety is too sweet. Left-over cornbread squares, toasted, make a good foundation, too, for creamed chipped beef.

STUFFED FRANKFURTERS

Besides the well-known frankfurter dishes, which the boys in my family demand regularly as luncheon or supper favorites, we make this stuffed dish:

8 frankfurters	1 teaspoon prepared mustard
¼ cup processed cheese spread	8 slices bacon
¼ cup pickle relish	

Split frankfurters open lengthwise but do not cut all the way through. Combine cheese spread, pickle relish, and mustard. Spread about 1 tablespoon of mixture on each frankfurter. Wind a slice of bacon around each. Secure bacon with wooden picks.

Broil rolls about 6 minutes, turning once. Bacon should be cooked and crisping. Slip these out of broiler pan with pancake turner onto warmed serving plates. Let the boys remove skewers themselves and eat frankfurters with cornbread or split, toasted scones or English muffins. Makes 8 servings.

Variations: Substitute peanut butter for cheese spread. Increase mustard to 1 tablespoon. Blend all. Stuff and broil as described.

Another flavor favorite: use chopped olives in place of pickle relish. Combine flaked tuna with finely cut anchovy fillets in place of cheese spread. Combine fish mixture, olives, and mustard. Add little mayonnaise if needed. Spread frankfurters and broil as described. Serve in split, toasted frankfurter rolls.

NORMA'S BAKED CORNED BEEF
WITH MUSTARD SAUCE

4-to-5-pound piece corned beef | 4 bay leaves
1 or 2 cloves garlic, peeled and halved | 2 tablespoons whole cloves

Sauce

2 tablespoons butter or margarine | 1 tablespoon prepared mustard
⅓ cup brown sugar, packed | ⅓ cup ketchup
| 3 tablespoons cider vinegar

Buy a packaged half brisket of corned beef weighing 4 to 5 pounds or select larger piece and have it rolled and tied. Place in deep large kettle. Cover with cold water. Add garlic and bay leaves. Cover kettle and bring to a boil. Lower heat and let simmer 4 to 5 hours or until beef is tender. Let cool in liquid in which it cooked. Drain meat. Place in shallow baking pan. Decorate top thickly with cloves.

Start oven at moderate (350° F.).

Mix sauce ingredients smoothly together in a small enamel saucepan, adding a little water or liquid from kettle if needed. Heat and stir only until blended. Pour over corned beef.

Bake 30 minutes or until browned, basting occasionally. Makes 8 to 10 servings.

CORNED-BEEF HASH

4 tablespoons butter or bacon fat | 1 onion, peeled and diced
2 cups coarsely ground or finely chopped corned beef | ½ cup milk
| Quick grind black pepper
3 cups finely chopped boiled potatoes

Melt butter or fat in frying pan. Combine beef and potatoes in mixing bowl. Add onion and milk. Mix lightly but evenly with fork. Add pepper. Spread mixture evenly in hot fat in frying pan and cook over low heat. Shake pan occasionally or lift meat at one side with greased pancake turner. When hash is well browned on bottom, fold like omelet and lift onto warmed platter. Serve at once, garnished with scrambled or poached eggs. Makes 6 servings.

For delicious variations, follow label suggestions of packers on best-quality canned corned-beef hash.

Red-Flannel Hash: One cup finely diced cooked and drained beets is substituted for 1 cup potatoes in above recipe.

Roast-Beef Hash and other meat hashes are cooked like Corned-Beef Hash.

Baked Canned Corned-Beef Hash: Chill can of hash. Open. Slice. Surround each slice with strip of bacon. Fasten strips with wooden picks. Bake in moderate (350° F.) oven until bacon is crisp. Serve surrounded with poached eggs or, as a supper dish, surround with stuffed green peppers. Makes 4 servings.

Baked Corned-Beef Hash with Cheese: Heat contents of 1 can corned-beef hash in heavy skillet. Stir and, when thoroughly hot, heap onto 4 pieces toast in shallow baking pan. Top each with spoonful tomato sauce. Cover with very thin slice Mozzarella cheese. Bake 25 minutes in moderate (350° F.) oven. Makes 4 servings.

Dumplings

DUMPLINGS FOR STEW

1 ½ cups sifted all-purpose flour	⅛ teaspoon powdered nutmeg
2 teaspoons baking powder	1 egg
¼ teaspoon salt	½ cup milk
¼ teaspoon celery salt	2 tablespoons finely cut parsley

Mix and sift dry ingredients together. Beat egg. Combine with milk. Stir into dry ingredients. Beat well. Drop mixture by tablespoonful on gently boiling thickened stew. Cook uncovered 15 minutes. Turn dumplings frequently with spoon, basting with the gravy in the stew. When ready to serve stew and dumplings, add sprinkling of parsley. Makes 12 dumplings.

Most people today prefer very small dumplings. Use teaspoon for dropping dough onto stew. This recipe then makes 24 small dumplings.

My family will embrace any meat dish boasting dumplings. Why do women think they're so difficult? Nothing to it.

POTATO DUMPLINGS

2 to 3 cups mashed potatoes	¼ teaspoon pepper
1 egg	⅛ teaspoon powdered nutmeg
½ cup sifted all-purpose flour	24 fried or sautéed croutons
½ teaspoon salt	

Beat potatoes and egg together smoothly. Beat in flour and seasonings. Chill mixture about 30 minutes. Divide into 12 portions or 24 very small portions. Wrap larger portions around 2 croutons. If smaller dumplings are made, enclose 1 crouton in each.

Drop dumplings on gently boiling thickened stew or sauerbraten. Cook uncovered 15 minutes. Turn dumplings frequently with spoon, basting with gravy in stew or sauerbraten. Makes 12 to 24 dumplings.

This is another way I use my refrigerated croutons.

Meat Garnishes

See various recipes for garnishes suited to specific dishes.

In general, a tart, fresh fruit or vegetable goes well with meat. **Cinnamon apples** stuffed with cream cheese mixed with mayonnaise or lemon juice look good and taste fine with pork, ham, almost any roast.

Fried apple slices; canned whole plums, cut in half and dabbed with thick sour cream. Large black cherries, canned or fresh, pitted and stuffed with bleu or Roquefort cheese, are other good flavors to add appetite appeal to a roast or platter of meats.

For baked ham, in addition to garnishes suggested in the ham recipes, these little apricot molds are delicious:

1 (No 2½) can peeled apricot halves	4 inches stick cinnamon
¼ cup cider vinegar	1 package orange-flavored gelatin
¼ teaspoon whole cloves	

Drain apricots. Combine syrup, vinegar, and spices in enamel or glass saucepan and bring to a boil. Add apricots. Simmer 10 minutes. Remove apricots, placing each in 12 small individual molds. Strain syrup mixture. Measure. Add enough hot water to make 2 cups. Pour over gelatin and stir until dissolved. Pour gelatin mixture over apricots in molds. Chill until firm. Use as garnish around roast or meat platter. For variety, place each mold on slice of canned pineapple or cranberry jelly. Makes 6 to 12 molds.

All spiced fruits add flavor appeal to a roast of meat or game. Spiced seckel pears, peaches, and other fruits made at home or bought are served plain, or combined with raisins or other fruits or with cream cheese mixed with chopped candied ginger.

Fruits in season—such as big red strawberries, frosty-blue plums, seedless white grapes, halved peaches or pears filled with chopped fresh fruits or berries—add good flavor to meat platters.

The pickle family contributes a good bit to the garnishing of various meat platters. Mustard pickle, sliced dill pickle, capers, tiny gherkins sliced and "fanned" are favorites. Combine pickle with crisp lettuce or some other green for such garnishing.

Small whole ripe tomatoes, skinned, cored, and stuffed with chopped vegetables and mayonnaise, make a colorful garnish. Or cook the tomatoes and season with salt, pepper, and butter. This adds another hot vegetable to the menu as well as garnish for the roast.

Stuffed green peppers, raw as salad or hot as vegetable, are often used as garnish and so are small **baked, stuffed zucchini and cucumbers.** Or use cucumber raw, pared or scraped, seasoned inside and filled with chopped vegetables in mayonnaise.

Game

HARE, PROVENÇAL STYLE

Large hare, cleaned and ready to cook
1 pound salt pork
24 shallots peeled and chopped
2 teaspoons salt
1 teaspoon black pepper
1 pint dry white wine
½ teaspoon savory
½ teaspoon Worcestershire sauce

Ask meat dealer to tie the hare's head to the hind legs, forming a circle. Cut pork fine. Cook in large heavy skillet or Dutch oven until browning. Sear hare in hot pork, turning to brown all sides. Lower heat. Add shallots, salt, pepper, and wine. Cover skillet or pot. Simmer 1½ hours or until tender and thoroughly cooked. Add more wine with a little hot water or consommé if liquid cooks away.

When cooked, remove string and place hare on hot serving dish. Skim fat off gravy in pot. Stir in Worcestershire. Taste, and correct seasoning as desired. Bring sauce to a boil. Pour over hare. Makes 4 to 6 servings.

I first ate hare on the Union Pacific Railroad en route to Seattle. The game and the fresh-water small salmon steaks of this area remain a culinary dream.

PHEASANT, A GOURMET'S RECIPE

3 small pheasant, ready for cooking
½ cup milk
Salt
Quick grind black pepper
2 apples, pared, cored, sliced
2 thin slices peeled onion
3 tablespoons butter
3 cups commercial sour cream
4 slices toast
Water cress

Start oven at moderate (375° F.).

Brush birds inside and out with milk. Season inside and out with salt and pepper. Stuff cavity with apple slices.

Sauté onion lightly in butter in deep flameproof casserole. Brown birds in this fat. Pour sour cream over birds and season lightly with salt and pepper. Cover casserole.

Cook in oven 1 hour. Baste birds with sauce in casserole every 15 minutes. Serve hot from casserole onto toast. Garnish with water cress. Makes 3 to 6 servings.

Use squab chicken, Rock Cornish hens, or other small game birds or domestic fowl in place of pheasant.

Saffron rice, new asparagus or peas, your favorite green salad go with this dish. And for dessert, peach-and-black-cherry compote, and coffee.

ROAST WILD DUCK

2 ducks
Salt and pepper
4 stalks celery
4 slices peeled onion
½ cup melted butter or margarine

Paprika
¼ cup cognac
Sauce prepared in advance

Start oven at hot (450° F.).

Wash cleaned and dressed ducks. Drain. Salt and pepper insides. Place 2 stalks celery with leaves and 2 slices onion inside each duck. Place in roasting pan. Pour melted butter or margarine over birds. Sprinkle lightly with salt, pepper, and paprika.

Roast 18 minutes for rare, longer for medium and well-done ducks. Remove pan from oven. Pour brandy over birds and ignite. As soon as blaze dies down, place ducks on hot platter and serve with sauce prepared in advance. Makes 4 servings.

Roast Wild Duck Sauce: Four tablespoons butter, 6 mushrooms, chopped, 3 shallots or green onions sliced thin, ⅛ teaspoon thyme, 2 tablespoons browned flour, ½ cup hot consommé, 1 tablespoon tomato paste, ¾ cup red wine, 1/16 teaspoon cayenne, ½ cup green olives.

Melt butter in saucepan. Add mushrooms, shallots or onions, and thyme. Sauté 2 minutes. Stir in browned flour, mixing well. Stir in consommé mixed with tomato paste. Mix well. Add wine, a little at a time, stirring as the sauce cooks. When very hot and bubbling, add cayenne and olives. Stir and cook until thickened. Serve with wild duck. Makes about 2 cups sauce.

F. Van Wyck Mason and many another talented shot insist that wild duck must always be served rare (ruddy), that longer cooking makes it inedible.

BRAISED VENISON, BLACK FOREST STYLE

Noisette of Venison

2 to 3 pounds venison loin	10 whole cloves
Juice 2 lemons	1 bay leaf
1 cup red wine	4 peppercorns
1 cup cider	¼ cup salad oil
1 onion, peeled and sliced	Puréed Chestnuts (page 624)

Have loin of venison cut away from the bone and sliced about 1½ inches thick. Rinse meat. Pat dry with paper towel. Place in dish with cover. Combine lemon juice, wine, cider, onion, cloves, bay leaf, peppercorns, and 2 tablespoons oil. Pour over meat. Cover dish and place in refrigerator 2 days. Turn meat frequently.

To cook, drain meat. Cook in generous amount of hot oil, slowly, until done as desired. Slice thinly onto hot platter. Surround with mounds of Puréed Chestnuts. Makes 4 or more servings.

Wild rice with currant jelly and braised celery are other favorites with this dish.

Venison in Europe is considered better than our American venison. The animals, I am told, are smaller, hence more tender. In Zurich, too, I had a dish similar to this recipe. It was served with lingonberries.

ROAST VENISON

The best parts of venison are the leg and the saddle, to be cut into steaks or cooked whole as a roast. Use shoulder and neck cuts in stew.

The meat dealer who sells venison to you should let the freshly killed meat hang at least 24 hours, or, better still, for several days. When he cuts your piece for roasting, ask him to lard it with strips of salt pork.

Marinate the roast as described in recipe for Braised Venison. Let stand at least 2 days in marinade. Then roast, as for lamb, in open pan at moderate (325° F.) temperature to desired doneness.

SWISS VENISON STEW

3 or 4 pounds venison
¼ cup flour
3 tablespoons drippings
1 ½ cups hot water
1 cup red wine
1 teaspoon mixed dried herbs (thyme, marjoram, basil)
1 teaspoon dried parsley

1 large onion, peeled and sliced
1 ½ teaspoons salt
½ teaspoon pepper
3 carrots, scraped and quartered
3 potatoes, pared and quartered

Cut sinews and bones from venison. Cut meat into bite-size pieces. There should be about 2½ pounds meat. Roll meat in flour. Brown in hot drippings in deep kettle. Add hot water, wine, herbs, onion, salt, and pepper. Cover pot. Bring to a boil. Lower heat and simmer 2 hours. Add carrots and potatoes. Cover and simmer 1 hour, adding a little more hot water if needed. When meat is tender and vegetables done, serve hot. Makes 6 or more servings.

This mountaineer's dish should be served with thickly sliced French bread. A good winter dish.

CHAPTER FIFTEEN

Pastas and Rice

CANNELLONI

2 cups sifted all-purpose flour	¼ pound Italian ham, finely ground
1 tablespoon melted butter	
5 eggs	2 cups Italian tomato sauce
½ teaspoon salt	1 tablespoon chopped fresh basil or 1 teaspoon dried basil
⅔ cup lukewarm water	
1 pound ricotta cheese	½ cup grated Romano cheese

Combine flour, butter, 3 eggs beaten, salt. Add just enough water to form medium-soft dough. Knead dough until smooth on lightly floured board. Roll thin. Cut in rectangles about 4-by-6 inches.

Mix ricotta cheese and ham smoothly together. Beat remaining 2 eggs and work into cheese mixture. Place about 1½ tablespoons cheese mixture in center of each piece of dough. Fold dough over. Moisten all edges and press together to seal, to prevent filling from falling out.

Bring 8 quarts water to a rapid boil in 2½-gallon kettle. Add pastry rolls one at a time so boiling does not stop. Let rolls boil 10 minutes. Remove rolls with flat, broad strainer.

Start oven at moderately hot (400° F.). Rub 3-quart casserole with butter. Place boiled cannelloni in casserole. Pour tomato sauce over all. Sprinkle with basil.

Bake 10 minutes. Add light sprinkling of Romano cheese. Bake 5 minutes longer. Serve hot. Makes 6 servings.

This Italian favorite is served as a luncheon or supper main dish. Antipasto first, a green salad afterwards. The best cannelloni I ever ate was in a famous restaurant in Venice, the Alla Colomba, near the Place San Marco.

Macaroni

BAKED MACARONI PUFF

¼ pound lean bacon	1 teaspoon prepared mustard
3 tablespoons butter	1 teaspoon salt
3 tablespoons flour	¼ teaspoon pepper
1 cup milk	3 eggs
½ cup grated Old English or Cheddar cheese	1⅓ cups cooked elbow macaroni
1 tablespoon prepared horse-radish	Paprika

Cook bacon until crisp. Drain on thick paper towels. Melt butter in heavy saucepan. Add flour and stir until smooth. Add milk slowly, stirring over moderate heat. Cook and stir until thickened. Add cheese, horse-radish, and mustard. Stir until well blended. Season with salt and pepper. Remove from heat.

Start oven at moderate (325° F.). Butter 1½-quart casserole.

Cut bacon in small pieces. Beat egg whites stiff. Beat yolks slightly. Add thick cheese sauce gradually to yolks, beating after each addition. Add macaroni and bacon. Mix well. Fold into egg whites. Pour into prepared baking dish and sprinkle top lightly with paprika. Set dish in shallow pan of hot water.

Bake 45 minutes or until slightly browned and firm to touch. Makes 5 to 6 servings.

MY BEST BAKED MACARONI

1½ cups uncooked macaroni	2 cups shredded sharp cheese
6 eggs	1 cup coarsely cut green pepper
1½ cups milk	1 (4-ounce) can pimientos, chopped, drained
1 teaspoon salt	
½ teaspoon dry mustard	
1½ cups soft bread crumbs	

Cook macaroni as described on package. Drain.

Start oven at moderate (325° F.). Grease 2-quart casserole.

Beat egg yolks. Combine with milk, salt, mustard, crumbs, and cheese. Add green pepper and pimientos. Add macaroni. Beat egg whites stiff, until they stand in points when beater is removed. Fold macaroni mixture into whites. Pour into prepared baking dish. Set dish in shallow pan of hot water.

Bake 1 hour and 15 minutes. Makes 6 servings.

I like to take this in a casserole to night beach picnics. It's also good with glazed ham for a buffet, with a nice tossed green salad.

MACARONI MEAT PIE

1 (8-ounce) package macaroni	¼ teaspoon ground nutmeg
½ cup chopped peeled onions	2 cups meat broth or consommé
¼ cup chopped green pepper	1 teaspoon Worcestershire sauce
½ cup sliced mushrooms	2 cups cubed cooked beef or
2 tablespoons butter or marga-	lamb
rine	1 cup well-drained chopped
2 tablespoons flour	tomatoes
1 teaspoon salt	½ cup grated cheese
¼ teaspoon pepper	½ cup buttered crumbs

Cook macaroni as described on package. Drain. Cook onions, green pepper, and mushrooms in butter or margarine 5 minutes. Add flour, salt, pepper, and nutmeg. Stir, cooking about 5 minutes longer. Add broth or consommé and Worcestershire sauce, stirring constantly and let cook until thickened. Remove from heat.

Start oven at moderate (350° F.). Butter 2-quart casserole.

Line prepared casserole with half the macaroni. Add beef or lamb and sauce. Pour tomatoes over all. Add rest of macaroni. Sprinkle with cheese and cover with crumbs.

Bake about 25 minutes or until top is lightly browned and bubbly. Makes 6 servings.

Feature this dish at a help-yourself supper. Hot muffins or a pan of warm cornbread, a platter of small, individual aspic vegetable salads add to the pleasure. For dessert this is the night for glazed baked apples, perhaps stuffed with nuts and raisins.

THE BOYS' DO-IT-YOURSELF LUNCH

4 frankfurters, sliced
2 tablespoons butter or margarine

2 (15¼-ounce) cans macaroni in cheese sauce
Toasted buns

Sauté frankfurters in butter or margarine until slightly browned. Stir macaroni-and-cheese sauce into frankfurters. Serve at once on split, toasted buns. Makes 4 generous servings.

Good for camp-outs.

For additional macaroni dishes see casserole, cheese, chicken, and fish chapters.

COUNTRY-KITCHEN MUSH

4 cups water
1 cup yellow corn meal
1 teaspoon salt

Additional corn meal
Butter or margarine
Warm syrup

Heat 3 cups water to boiling point in 2-quart saucepan. Combine corn meal, salt, and 1 cup cold water. Stir into boiling water slowly. Cook until mixture thickens, stirring frequently. Cover. Continue cooking over low heat 10 minutes longer.

Pour into greased loaf pan about 8 by 4 by 2½ inches. Let cool. Chill thoroughly. Turn out of pan onto large platter. Cut in ½-inch slices. Dip lightly into corn meal. Sauté lightly in butter or margarine or on greased griddle. Turn when golden brown and brown other side. Serve hot with butter and warmed syrup. Makes 8 servings.

Mush as cereal: Cook mush as described. Serve hot as cereal with cream or top milk, sugar, and a few currants.

Or serve as a buttered "vegetable," especially with ham, smoked tongue, or baked corned beef. I was able to introduce this by calling it "India Meal." "Mush" to children sounds like "mush."

Noodles

TO MAKE NOODLES

3 eggs	2 ½ cups sifted all-purpose flour
1 tablespoon melted butter or margarine	

To make noodle dough for cutting in strips and other forms, use all the flour called for. For making noodle dough to be used in ravioli recipe, use less flour, making a softer dough, just stiff enough to roll out nicely and hold its shape when cut in squares and rounds.

Beat eggs lightly. Add butter or margarine and stir in flour gradually. When using all of the flour, turn stiff dough out on lightly floured board or marble slab. Roll very thin into stiff sheets. Spread out on lightly floured cloths to dry. Before the sheets of dough are too stiff to handle, fold over 2 or 3 times and cut in thin shreds. Toss the shreds apart to dry thoroughly. Keep in tightly closed glass jar until ready for use.

To cook noodles, drop the dry shreds into rapidly boiling salted water (3 quarts). Boil 20 minutes or until noodles are tender and done. Drain in a strainer. Rinse by pouring cold water over them quickly. Reheat with butter and seasoning in upper part of double boiler over boiling water. Makes 4 to 6 servings.

Poppy-Seed Noodles: Add 2 or 3 teaspoons poppy seeds to butter in upper part of double boiler when reheating noodles before serving. Toss lightly with 2 spoons to coat noodles.

Green Noodles: Add ½ cup sieved cooked spinach to beaten eggs in plain noodles recipe. Increase butter to 3 tablespoons. Continue recipe as described. Keep in tightly covered glass jar until ready for use.

Green Noodles with Cream: To cook, drop noodles into rapidly boiling salted water (3 quarts). Boil 20 minutes or until noodles are tender. Drain and rinse with hot water in strainer. Reheat in upper part of double boiler over boiling water, adding 2 cups heavy cream, ¼ teaspoon paprika, ¼ teaspoon powdered nutmeg, ½ teaspoon salt. When hot, pour into buttered shallow baking dish. Sprinkle with 2 tablespoons grated Parmesan cheese. Bake in hot oven (425° F.) 10 minutes or until lightly browned.

Green Noodles with Italian Meat Sauce: Cook noodles in rapidly boiling water as described. Drain. Serve hot, mixed lightly with this sauce from a Bleecker Street Italian restaurant:

¾ pound ground beef	2 (1-pound) cans tomatoes, chopped
1 tablespoon olive oil	
¼ pound pork sausage	2 (6-ounce) cans tomato paste
¼ cup chopped peeled onions	¼ cup grated Parmesan cheese
¼ cup chopped celery	2 tablespoons finely cut parsley
1 clove garlic, peeled and minced	1 ½ teaspoons salt
	1 teaspoon orégano

Brown beef in oil in large, heavy skillet or saucepan. Stir bulk sausage into beef. Cook and stir until all is well browned. Add onions, celery, garlic. Cook and stir 5 minutes. Add tomatoes and tomato paste. Stir and cook few minutes. Add cheese, parsley, salt, and orégano. Mix well. Cover skillet. Let simmer over low heat about 1 hour and 30 minutes. Skim off excess fat from top. Serve hot over hot green noodles or pour noodles into serving dish, make well in center, pour meat sauce into well. Makes 6 servings.

Some Italian cooks turn noodles and meat sauce into shallow baking dish, sprinkle top with Parmesan, and brown a few minutes under moderate broiler heat.

The green noodles with meat sauce make a main dish for luncheon or supper. Serve plain green noodles or the creamed dish, as the Italians do, with fish, chicken, or meat.

GREEN NOODLES, PARMESAN

½ pound green noodles	¼ cup grated Parmesan cheese
¼ pound ham, diced	Freshly ground pepper
¼ cup olive oil	

Cook noodles according to directions on package or follow preceding recipe. Sauté ham in hot oil until ham is lightly browned. Pour ham and oil over drained noodles. Mix lightly. Sprinkle with Parmesan cheese and a little pepper. Serve at once. Makes 4 servings.

Butter or margarine may be used in place of oil. Freshly cut parsley or basil sprinkled on top adds good flavor variation.

NOODLES DE LUXE

Cook noodles as described on package or in recipe (page 443). Drain thoroughly. Add 3 or 4 tablespoons butter and ⅔ cup slivered toasted almonds. Toss lightly to coat noodles with butter. Serve on heated platter around sliced pot roast, chicken, or veal paprika.

EASY-BAKED LASAGNE

½ pound wide lasagne noodles	¼ teaspoon pepper
1 teaspoon salt	½ pound sliced Swiss cheese
1 (10½-ounce) can condensed mushroom soup	½ cup buttered crumbs
½ pound cottage cheese	1½ tablespoons grated Parmesan cheese
½ teaspoon curry powder	

Cook noodles in 3 quarts rapidly boiling water, with 1 teaspoon salt added, about 15 minutes or until tender. Drain.

Start oven at moderate (375° F.). Butter 2-quart casserole.

Mix soup with cottage cheese and seasonings. Make layers of noodles, Swiss cheese, and soup mixture in prepared casserole. Sprinkle crumbs on top. Scatter Parmesan cheese generously over crumbs. If soup-cheese mixture is too dry, pour small amount of milk over filled casserole.

Bake 20 minutes or until bubbly and browned. Makes 4 to 6 servings.

Italian Baked Lasagne: Use ¼ cup olive oil, 1 large onion, peeled and chopped, 2 cups chopped canned tomatoes, ½ teaspoon salt, ½ teaspoon pepper, 1 teaspoon sugar, 1 pound wide noodles, 1 small Mozzarella cheese, thinly sliced, ½ cup grated Parmesan cheese. Heat oil and onion together until onion begins to brown. Add tomatoes and seasonings. Cover pan. Cook very slowly about 1 hour. Stir frequently to prevent burning. Sauce should not cook down too much, but thicken slightly.

Cook noodles in 5 quarts rapidly boiling water with 1 teaspoon salt added. Stir frequently to prevent sticking. At end of 15 minutes, or when tender, drain noodles. Start oven at moderate (375° F.). Make alternate layers of noodles, sauce, sliced cheese, and Parmesan in 2-quart baking dish, with top layer cheese. Bake 20 minutes or until brown and bubbly. Makes 6 servings.

Spaghetti

BAKED SPAGHETTI AND CHICKEN
Chicken Tetrazzini

1 large or 2 small tender chickens for stewing
Boiling water
1 small onion, peeled and sliced
2 sprigs celery leaves
Salt and pepper
1 (8-ounce) package spaghetti
½ pound mushrooms
4 tablespoons butter or margarine

2 tablespoons flour
2 cups chicken stock
Salt and white pepper
1 cup heavy cream, warmed
2 tablespoons sherry
3 tablespoons grated Parmesan cheese

Buy ready-to-cook chickens. Have cut in pieces by poultry dealer. Place in saucepan. Add boiling water to depth of about 1 inch. Add onion, celery leaves, 1 teaspoon salt, ½ teaspoon pepper. Start cooking on high heat so water boils quickly. Reduce heat. Cover pot and simmer 2 hours or until chicken is tender. Remove chicken. Strain stock and measure 2 cups for use in sauce. Cut chicken in very small cubes. There should be 2 to 3 cups cubed chicken.

Cook spaghetti as described on package. In place of spaghetti, you may use narrow noodles or small macaroni. Drain. Wash, drain mushrooms. Peel caps. Slice stems fine. Slice caps coarsely. Sauté mushrooms 5 minutes in 1 tablespoon butter. Combine with spaghetti.

Melt remaining 3 tablespoons butter or margarine. Stir in flour smoothly. Stir in 2 cups chicken stock. Continue to stir and cook until thickened. Remove from heat. Stir in cream, then add sherry a little at a time, stirring slowly.

Start oven at moderate (375° F.). Grease 2-quart baking dish.

Combine ½ sauce with spaghetti mixture. Pour spaghetti into prepared dish. Make hole in center. Combine remaining sauce with chicken. Pour chicken into center of spaghetti. Sprinkle grated cheese over all. Bake about 25 minutes or until top is lightly browned. Makes 8 servings.

For a big buffet party make this recipe twice, using matching casseroles. Also popular when baked in individual baking dishes.

A good green salad with herb dressing and very small anchovy sandwiches are delicious companions for this luxurious dish. Serve hot coffee and a large *bombe* of raspberry, lemon, and pineapple sherbet.

BLEECKER STREET SPAGHETTI

½ cup finely cut parsley
1 slice garlic, peeled and minced
3 tablespoons grated Parmesan cheese
¼ teaspoon salt
3 tablespoons olive oil

1 (3-ounce) package cream cheese
½ cup light cream
1 (8-ounce) package spaghetti, cooked and drained
Extra Parmesan cheese

Combine parsley, garlic, Parmesan cheese, and salt in mortar or heavy bowl. Mash and blend together until smooth paste. Stir in olive oil. Beat in cream cheese, stirring and beating until smooth sauce is formed.

Keep drained spaghetti hot in upper part of double boiler over boiling water. As soon as sauce is smoothly mixed, combine lightly with spaghetti. Heap on warmed platter. Sprinkle with additional Parmesan and serve. Makes 4 servings.

BROAD SPAGHETTI

Linguine

1 pound linguine (flat spaghetti)
½ pound ricotta or cottage cheese
4 tablespoons sweet butter
½ cup grated Parmesan cheese
Freshly ground black pepper

Cook spaghetti according to directions on package. Mix cheese and butter together in saucepan. Simmer about 7 minutes, stirring frequently. Spoon over hot drained spaghetti. Sprinkle with Parmesan and a little pepper. Makes 6 servings.

ROTELLE WITH FRIDAY SAUCE

1 pound rotelle (spiral spaghetti)	½ cup olive oil
1 small can anchovy fillets	¼ cup finely cut parsley
1 onion, peeled and diced	¼ cup grated Parmesan cheese
1 small green pepper, diced	

Cook spaghetti according to directions on package. Drain anchovies. Discard oil. Cut anchovies in fine bits. Mix with onion and green pepper. Sauté in hot oil until onion is golden. Add parsley. Spoon sauce over drained spaghetti. Sprinkle with cheese or serve plain. Makes 6 servings.

This same anchovy-oil sauce is a favorite in Italian restaurants for other forms of spaghetti, especially on Friday when meat sauces are forbidden to some customers.

SPAGHETTI WITH MEAT SAUCE

1 cup olive oil	½ teaspoon pepper
1½ cups minced peeled onions	½ teaspoon basil
3 cloves garlic, peeled and minced	1 (6-ounce) can sliced broiled mushrooms
1½ pounds ground beef	2 (6-ounce) cans tomato paste
1 tablespoon Kitchen Bouquet	⅓ cup minced parsley
4 (No. 303) cans tomatoes	3 pounds uncooked spaghetti
2 tablespoons salt	1½ cups grated Parmesan cheese

Heat oil in large saucepan. Cook onions and garlic until transparent but not browning. Stir frequently. Add beef. Cook until browning. Stir all remaining ingredients, except spaghetti and cheese, into meat mixture. Mix well. Bring to a boil. Lower heat and simmer uncovered 30 minutes. Stir frequently.

Cook spaghetti according to directions on package and drain. Pour hot spaghetti into large tureen. Serve sauce over spaghetti. Sprinkle top with cheese. Serve additional cheese with spaghetti. Makes 12 servings.

This is a popular dish for buffet suppers or for any occasion when large numbers of people are to be served. The recipe can be made two or three times, or with restaurant-size utensils it may be doubled.

The sauce may be made ahead of time, reheated when spaghetti is ready to serve. For large numbers of people, drain cooked spaghetti, leave in kettle in which it cooked. Add sauce and mix lightly. Serve plates from the cooking utensil.

Rice

Usually I cannot improve on the recipes given on the packages of various brands of quick-cooking rice and other kinds of rice. Follow directions exactly the first time you use a new brand of rice. Then make your corrections as to time, and amount of water, if the recipe does not seem right for your needs. I find, however, that quick-cooking rice, which, according to some package recipes, should steam 13 minutes tightly covered, is ready in 10 minutes, all liquid absorbed, the rice grains distinct, tender, the kettle full of fluffy and delicious rice.

Wild Rice: For wild rice, most package recipes do not call for long enough soaking, and in most cases cooking time also is too short. Wash wild rice thoroughly and drain. Cover with cold water and let soak several hours or all day. To cook, drain. Cover with mixture of half hot water and half consommé. Use 2½ cups liquid to 1 cup rice. Add 1 tablespoon grated orange peel or finely chopped mushrooms for each cup rice. Cover saucepan. Bring to a boil. Reduce heat to moderate; cook slowly 45 minutes to 1 hour, until rice is fluffy, tender, and the dark seed shells have opened and softened. All liquid should be absorbed.

The brand of wild rice you use may not call for such long cooking. Watch the saucepan. Test for doneness and adjust cooking time accordingly. This rice, which is now cultivated in certain parts of the country, varies from one section to another. It is so delicious, especially with game and poultry, that it deserves a place in your menus. I always have some cooked, and in the freezer, to dress up meals for unexpected guests. It heats up beautifully in a steamer.

Almond Rice: When cooking rice, either the quick-cooking or long-process variety, add a few tablespoons slivered blanched almonds just before serving. Mix almonds lightly into hot rice, using 2 forks.

BROWN RICE

2 cups brown rice	Grind of black pepper
4 cups consommé	2 tablespoons grated onion
½ teaspoon saffron	

Wash rice and drain. Combine in heavy 2-quart kettle with consommé and saffron. Bring to a boil. Stir rice and cover pot tightly. Lower heat to simmering and let cook 45 minutes or until rice is tender and liquid absorbed. Serve rice in heated serving dish. Sprinkle with pepper and grated onion. Makes 6 servings.

A delicious rice with lamb curry or veal roast. Saffron may be omitted. You may also buy brown rice canned now, too. What little is needed to make left-overs party fare!

CURRIED FRUIT ON RICE

1 cup chicken broth or consommé	4 cups hot rice
	2 ripe bananas, sliced
1 ½ cups white wine	2 canned or fresh peaches, sliced
1 cup seedless raisins, washed and drained	
1 cup pistachio or pignolia nuts	2 canned or fresh apricots, sliced
2 tablespoons curry powder	¾ cup shredded coconut
1 tablespoon cornstarch	

Combine consommé and 1 cup wine in saucepan. Heat to boiling point. Add raisins and nuts. Reduce heat. Simmer 5 minutes. Mix curry powder with cornstarch and remaining ½ cup wine. Add to simmering sauce. Stir and boil 5 minutes or until it thickens and clears. Taste for seasoning. Add little salt if needed.

To serve this curry, which makes an ideal dish for summer luncheon, spoon hot rice into soup plates. Arrange sliced fruit quickly over rice. Pour hot curry sauce over all. Sprinkle with coconut and serve. Makes 4 servings.

RICE-AND-CRAB CROQUETTES

1 cup uncooked rice	1 teaspoon prepared mustard
1 ½ cups boiling water	¼ teaspoon orégano
1 teaspoon salt	1 cup crab meat, cleaned, flaked
¼ cup sifted all-purpose flour	
½ cup melted butter or margarine	2 canned pimientos, drained and chopped
1 cup milk	

Rinse and drain rice. Add to boiling water with salt. Stir and bring to a boil again. Cover pan. Turn heat low. Steam 20 minutes. Drain.

Stir flour into 4 tablespoons melted butter in saucepan. When smooth add milk, stirring continually. Add mustard and orégano. Stir and cook 10 minutes or until thickened. Stir in crab meat and pimientos. Combine with cooked, drained rice. To cool, spread on platter. Shape into 8 small, or 4 large, croquettes.

Start oven at moderate (375° F.). Butter large shallow baking pan. Place croquettes in pan. Dribble remaining 4 tablespoons melted butter or margarine over croquettes.

Bake 30 minutes or until golden brown. Turn croquettes once, using 2 large spoons. Makes 4 or more servings. Serve with Cheese Sauce (page 546) or Mushroom Sauce (page 553).

To deep-fry croquettes: Use frying basket. Heat fat to 390° F. on frying thermometer. Lower 2 or 3 croquettes at a time into hot fat. Fry 2 or 3 minutes or until golden brown. Drain on thick paper towels on pan in hot oven with door left open.

Wild-Rice-and-Mushroom Croquettes: Follow recipe for Rice-and-Crab Croquettes. Substitute boiled wild rice for white rice. Substitute 1 cup sautéed chopped mushrooms for crab meat. Finish recipe as described. Especially good with poultry and game. Serve with garnish of tart jelly.

PAELLA

2	small frying chickens, ready to cook	2 ¾	cups uncooked rice
Olive oil		1	tablespoon salt
¼	pound raw smoked ham, cut in thin strips	4	tablespoons finely cut parsley
2	cloves garlic, peeled and chopped	6	cups boiling water
1	onion, peeled and sliced thin	1	(12-ounce) package quick-frozen deveined shrimp
2	tomatoes, peeled and chopped	¼	pound any whitefish cut in pieces
1	teaspoon saffron	2	canned pimientos, drained and sliced

Cut each chicken in 10 pieces. Wash, drain and pat dry with paper towel. Fry in oil in skillet until well browned on all sides. Remove to large Dutch oven or heavy pot with cover.

Drain excess fat from skillet. Add ham, garlic, onion, tomatoes, saffron, and rice. Stir, cook 5 minutes. Add to chicken in pot. Add salt, parsley, and boiling water. Mix and bring to a boil. Cover and lower heat to moderate. Cook 20 minutes or until rice and chicken are tender, stirring occasionally with fork. Add thawed shrimp and fish. Cook 10 minutes longer. Add pimientos a few minutes before removing from heat. Serve hot, in soup plates. Makes 8 servings.

Serve as main dish for luncheon or supper. A mixed green salad, delicious dessert, and coffee are demanded by this savory Spanish-Argentinian dish.

Some like fresh clams in the shells in this dish, too. For this variation add scrubbed, tightly closed clams—about a dozen steamers—when you add fish and shrimp. Some gourmets soak the saffron in lemon juice.

SAFFRON RICE

1 ½	cups long-grain rice	½	cup melted butter or margarine
2	quarts boiling water		
2	teaspoons salt	2	tablespoons finely cut parsley
½	teaspoon saffron	½	teaspoon white pepper

Cook rice in salted boiling water about 13 minutes or until grains are just tender. Drain any excess water. Pour rice into colander or sieve. Place over kettle of boiling water and steam 10 to 15 minutes.

Crush saffron in about 2 tablespoons hot water, stirring and mashing smoothly. Add melted butter or margarine. Mix into rice with fork. Add parsley and pepper. Serve at once. Makes 4 large servings.

Rice Ring for Vegetables: Cook rice as described on package for simple steamed or boiled rice. Fill warm oiled ring mold with rice. Press firmly. Unmold at once on warmed platter. Fill center with creamed vegetables, or a curry, or a creole mixture of tomatoes and green peppers. Use saffron rice for a ring in which to serve curried shrimp, too. Garnish with mounds of curry condiments.

At the fabulous Hotel Avis in Lisbon they served curried rice with beef hocks, a tasty stew similar to the Italian *ossi buchi,* which the Italians make with veal.

For additional rice recipes see chapters on casseroles, desserts, fish and shellfish cookery.

RICE PILAU
OR PILAFF

½ pound butter
1 large onion, peeled and chopped
2 cloves garlic, peeled and chopped
12 black peppercorns
12 whole cloves
12 whole cardamom seeds
2 (3-inch) cinnamon sticks
½ teaspoon whole allspice

1 pound long-grain rice, washed and drained
1 ½ teaspoons salt
Boiling water
1 cup white raisins, washed and drained
½ cup pignolia or pistachio nuts
Chopped scallions for garnish
Toasted almonds

Melt butter in deep 2-quart saucepan with tightly fitting cover. Sauté onion and garlic until golden. Tie all spices in cheesecloth bag. Add to saucepan. Continue to cook onions and garlic with spices about 5 minutes longer. Remove bag and garlic. Add rice to saucepan. Sauté until golden. Add salt and boiling water to cover rice by about 2 inches. Add spice bag again to pan. Cover saucepan and cook rice until all water has been absorbed.

Watch rice carefully. Toss with spatula or fork occasionally. When nearly done, remove spice bag and discard it. Add raisins and nuts. Cover pan again and continue to cook a few minutes. Heap pilau on hot serving dish. Garnish with mounds of sliced scallions and toasted almonds. Makes 6 servings.

Pilau with Chicken Livers: Cook ½ pound chicken livers in 1 table-spoon butter until done. Drain and slice. Add 1 tablespoon butter to same pan. Sauté 1 diced green pepper and 1 diced peeled yellow onion slowly about 10 minutes, until vegetables are tender. Add 1 (3-ounce) can chopped mushrooms. Sauté and stir. Add cooked livers. Mix. Season lightly with salt and pepper.

When ready to serve, pour hot rice mixture into warmed serving dish. Hollow out space in center. Pour in chicken liver mixture. Garnish top with sliced scallions and almonds. Makes 6 or more servings.

Serve plain pilau with lamb cooked on skewer or with roast lamb, baked tomatoes, and artichoke salad. Also delicious with roast chicken.

GUIDE TO PASTAS

Macaroni. (tubular)	Long. Elbow. *Zita,* large tube cut in inch lengths. *Mezzani,* like zita, but thinner and smaller pieces. *Mezzani rigati,* grooved. *Mostaccioli,* cut diagonally. *Mostaccioli rigati,* grooved. *Ditali,* ½-inch lengths. *Ditalini,* small ditali. *Occhio di lupo,* very large macaroni. *Rigatoni,* large grooved. *Tufoli,* extra large. *Tufoli rigati,* grooved. *Manicotti,* extra-large delicate egg macaroni. *Maccaroncella,* thin macaroni, similar to *bucatini,* which is spaghetti with a hole.
Spaghetti. (solid rod)	*Spaghettini,* very thin spaghetti. *Vermicelli,* extra-thin spaghetti.
Noodles. (and ribbon types)	Regular or folded, fine, medium, or wide. Vegetable-flavored, such as spinach (green) or tomato. *Lasagne,* extra wide. *Fettucelle,* flat, medium. *Linguini,* narrow noodles. *Mafalde,* wide, with curly edge. *Tagliarini,* flat. *Margherito,* medium wide, twisted. *Linguine,* flat spaghetti. *Ravioli,* squares of noodle dough.

Many Shapes. Macaroni shells, such as *maruzze,* which are large. *Maruzzelle,* medium, and *maruzzine,* small. Egg-noodle bow ties, such as *tripolini,* small, *farfalle,* medium, and *farfalloni,* large. Cockscomb shape, called *cresta di gallo. Stelline,* stars. Alphabets, various letters. *Acini pepe,* little dots. *Pastina,* tiny pieces often flavored with vegetable or egg. *Seme di mellone,* seed shape. *Orzo,* oat shape.

CHAPTER SIXTEEN

Pies, Tarts, Turnovers

The continuous improvement in commercial pastry mixes encourages busy cooks, and beginner cooks especially, to use this easy simplified modern method of making pie dough. Directions on the mix packages must be followed exactly, and the results can be all that an old-fashioned cook or a young homemaker might desire.

But many of us like to mix our own pastry when time permits. Here is a recipe for plain pastry for pies, tarts, and turnovers, and for lining and covering a casserole when chicken, fish, or meat pie is baked.

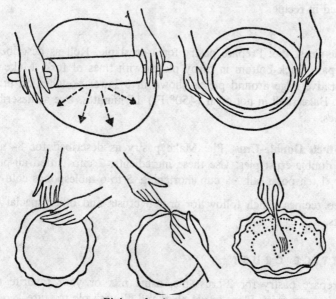

Fixing the lower crust

PLAIN PASTRY

1 ½ cups sifted all-purpose flour   ½ cup shortening
½ teaspoon salt   4 to 5 tablespoons water

Sift flour and salt together into mixing bowl. Cut shortening in with pastry blender or blending fork until mixture is in pieces about the size of peas.

Add cold water, few drops at a time, tossing mixture with fork until all flour-coated bits of fat are barely dampened.

Turn mixture onto square of waxed paper. Gather up corners of paper, pressing from the outside to form a compact ball. Divide dough in two parts, for upper and lower crust. Chill.

Roll ball of pastry out ⅛ inch thick. *Roll lightly* from center to outer edges as shown on page 457. Place pastry in 8- or 9-inch pie pan. Press lightly with fingers to fit into pan. Trim edge flush with rim of pie pan. Moisten edge.

Roll out upper crust. Gash with knife in stem-and-leaf pattern or any other simple design to permit steam to escape. Transfer to *filled pie pan*. Trim upper crust with kitchen scissors ½ inch beyond pan edge. Tuck pastry under edge of lower crust. Crimp the two together between thumb and forefinger to make decorative, protective upstanding finish around pie. This crimped edge seals in juices. Bake as described in recipe.

Single-Crust Pie: Prepare pastry for 1-crust pie. Roll as described. Fit into pan. Prick bottom in many places with tines of fork. Make thick, decorative edge around pie as shown in 3 lower sketches on previous page. Bake shell in hot oven (450° F.) 15 minutes. Use as described in recipes.

Ten-Inch Double-Crust Pie: Make pastry as described for 8- and 9-inch double-crust pies. Use these ingredients: 2 cups sifted all-purpose flour, 1 teaspoon salt, ⅔ cup shortening, 5 to 6 tablespoons cold water.

See recipes which follow for crumb crusts and other special pastry crusts.

LATTICE CRUST

Prepare pastry for 2-crust pie, using mix or your favorite recipe. Roll bottom crust. Place in pie plate and fill with pie mixture.

Roll out remaining dough about ⅛ inch thick. Cut strips ¾ inch wide with pastry wheel or knife. Lay lengthwise strips on top of filled pie about 1 inch apart. Lay additional strips diagonally across these, weaving in and out, over and under. Trim bottom crust and ends of lattice strips even with rim of pie plate. Seal edges by pressing together with fork. Then dampen edge and place extra strip of dough over it, around pie, covering ends of crisscross. Press this covering strip with tines of fork to seal, or crimp edge between thumb and forefinger. Bake pie as described in recipes.

EASY PUFF PASTE

Make your favorite pie pastry for 2-crust pie. Roll out ⅛ inch thick. Dot with bits of butter, using about ⅓ cup firm butter, neither hard nor soft. Fold dough so that two sides meet in center.

Seal by pressing edges with fingers. Fold ends to center and seal. Wrap in waxed paper. Chill thoroughly in refrigerator.

Roll folded pastry out like regular pie pastry. Cut and fit into pie pans, or make tart shells, or use as called for in various recipes.

GRAHAM-CRACKER CRUST
FOR CHEESECAKE AND PUDDING-TYPE PIES

1 ¾ cups fine graham-cracker crumbs

¼ cup finely chopped pecans or almonds

½ teaspoon powdered cinnamon

¼ teaspoon powdered ginger

½ cup melted butter or margarine

Combine ingredients. Mix well together. Reserve 3 tablespoons of mixture. Press remainder in bottom and 2½ inches up sides of 9-inch spring-form pan. Use 8-inch pie pan to press crumbs evenly in the larger pan.

Fill with cheesecake mixture. Use reserved mixture to decorate cheesecake. Bake according to cheesecake recipe. Makes 1 (9-inch) crust.

CRUMB CRUST

20 square graham crackers
¼ cup softened butter or margarine

¼ cup sugar

Start oven at moderate (375° F.).

Roll crackers between two sheets waxed paper. Crumbs should be fine and measure 1⅔ cups. Mix with softened butter or margarine and sugar thoroughly. Pour into 9-inch pie plate. Use 8-inch pie pan to press crumbs evenly against bottom and sides in the larger pan.

Bake 8 minutes. Let cool. Use as described in recipes.

MERINGUE SHELL

4 egg whites
⅛ teaspoon salt
¼ teaspoon cream of tartar

1 cup sifted granulated sugar
1 teaspoon vanilla

Start oven at slow (275° F.). Grease 9-inch pie pan thoroughly.

Beat egg whites with salt until foamy. Continue to beat, adding cream of tartar until they stand in soft peaks when the beater is withdrawn. Add sugar, about 2 tablespoons at a time, beating until meringue is thick and glossy. Stir in vanilla.

Spread meringue thickly over bottom and sides of prepared pie pan. Build meringue up around edge to from rim. Let bottom be about ¼ inch thick, sides about 1 inch thick.

Bake 40 to 45 minutes or until surface is crusty. Do not let brown.

Loosen meringue from pan with spatula while still warm. Let cool before filling with fruit, ice cream, or custard. Filled, the shell makes 6 servings.

I usually call this *Mrs. Durham's Angel Pie*, because the recipe was sent to me in my editorial days and I gave Mrs. Durham a prize for it. She used this meringue crust as a base for tart lemon custard filling and topped it with whipped cream.

ROLLED-OATS PIE CRUST

1 cup rolled oats
⅓ cup sifted all-purpose flour
⅓ cup brown sugar, packed

½ teaspoon salt
⅓ cup melted shortening

Start oven at moderate (375° F.).

Combine oats, flour, sugar, and salt in mixing bowl. Add shortening, mixing until crumbly. Pack mixture firmly in bottom and on sides of 9-inch plate. Set an 8-inch pie plate inside to press evenly.

Bake about 15 minutes. Let stand 5 minutes. Remove smaller pan. Let crust cool in its plate. Fill with pie mixture. Makes 1 (9-inch) crust.

RICH PASTRY

1 cup sifted all-purpose flour	4 tablespoons butter or margarine
½ teaspoon salt	
1 teaspoon baking powder	1 teaspoon lemon juice
4 tablespoons shortening	1 egg yolk, well beaten
¼ cup hot water	

Sift flour, salt, and baking powder together into mixing bowl. Cut in shortening. Pour hot water over butter or margarine and stir until melted. Let cool to lukewarm. Add lemon juice and egg yolk. Stir into dry ingredients and stir only until mixed. Chill thoroughly.

Start oven at hot (425° F.).

Roll chilled pastry out about ⅓ inch thick. Cut in small shapes for canapés and tart shells. Use wide spatula and slip pieces onto ungreased cooky sheet. Bake 10 minutes or until golden. Let cool. Makes 24 or more canapé crackers, 12 or more shells for tarts.

This same delicious pastry may be cut in rounds or wedges, placed on top of chicken casserole or other mixtures, and baked as topping. Or it may be used for larger tart shells and turnovers.

Cheese Straws: Make rich pastry by above recipe. Roll out. Sprinkle with mixed grated Parmesan and Cheddar cheese. Cut in narrow strips. Slip onto ungreased cooky sheet. Bake in hot oven (425° F.) 15 minutes or until golden. Makes 36 or more strips.

Another version of Cheese Pastry: Using this recipe, roll pastry as described. Sprinkle with cheese. Fold pastry and roll again. Cut in strips and bake as described. Or use cheese pastry to make tart shells.

TART SHELLS

Start oven at hot (450° F.).

Mix pastry for 9-inch 1-crust pie. Roll thin. Cut in 5- or 6-inch circles. Fit into large muffin pans. Press evenly into pan and prick surface with tines of fork. Crimp edge into decorative rim.

Bake about 15 minutes. Makes 8 shells.

Also use preceding recipes for puff pastry, rich pastry, and cheese pastry.

APPLE PIE

Pastry for 9-inch 2-crust pie
1 cup sugar
½ teaspoon powdered ginger
1 teaspoon powdered cinnamon
¼ teaspoon powdered nutmeg
¼ teaspoon salt
2 tablespoons flour

3 tablespoons strong tea
1 tablespoon lemon juice
4 cups sliced pared and cored apples (about 8 or 9)
2 tablespoons butter or margarine

Roll out ½ pastry for bottom crust. Fit loosely into 9-inch pie pan. Start oven at hot (425° F.).

Combine sugar, spices, salt, flour, tea, and lemon juice. Mix well. Alternate sliced apples and sugar mixture until pan is filled, heaping slightly in center. Dot with butter or margarine. Roll out top crust and cut slits for escaping steam. Place over apples. Trim pastry and press edges together with tines of fork.

Bake 40 to 50 minutes or until apples are tender and crust is browned. Makes 6 servings.

Serve warm with wedges of sharp American Cheddar.

Apple Pie Variations: Alternate apples, seedless raisins, and sugar when filling bottom crust, until pan is full. Sprinkle lightly with cinnamon. Add dabs of butter. Bake in moderate oven (350° F.) about 1 hour. Let cool. Serve plain or with hard sauce or cream. In some parts of the South the warm baked pie is inverted on a serving plate, cut in wedges, and served with a "dip" or sweet vanilla sauce.

Cheese-Topped Apple Pie: Prepare your favorite apple pie and put it together except for the top crust. Spoon grated Cheddar cheese on top of apples, about 1 generous tablespoon per cut of pie. Adjust top pastry and bake as usual. Cheese melts and permeates whole pie with its sharp tang and good flavor.

Deep-Dish Apple Pie: Prepare apples as for 2-crust pie. Fill buttered pie plate with apples. Season with mixture of 3 tablespoons sugar and ½ teaspoon cinnamon. Dot with 1½ tablespoons butter. Cover with pastry as for Apple Pie. Bake as described.

Deep-Dish Peach Pie: Use fresh or canned peaches. Follow recipe for Deep-Dish Apple Pie. Increase sugar by 2 tablespoons for fresh peaches.

APPLE CHIFFON PIE

Baked 9-inch pastry or Crumb Crust (page 987)
1 envelope unflavored gelatin
¼ cup cold water
3 eggs
½ cup molasses
½ teaspoon salt
1 teaspoon grated lemon peel
2 tablespoons lemon juice
1½ cups thick applesauce

Prepare and bake pastry crust or make Crumb Crust.

Sprinkle gelatin on cold water. Beat egg yolks slightly. Combine with molasses, salt, lemon peel, and juice in upper part of glass or enamel double boiler. Cook over hot water, stirring constantly until thickened. Add softened gelatin and stir until dissolved. Add applesauce. Chill until mixture begins to thicken. Whip egg whites until they stand in stiff points when beater is removed. Fold apple mixture into whites. Pour into pie crust. Chill until firm. Makes 6 servings.

APPLE-RUM PIE

¾ cup sifted all-purpose flour
1 cup sugar
1 teaspoon salt
3¾ cups milk
4 eggs, slightly beaten
¼ cup rum
4 tablespoons butter or margarine
Pastry (see next page)
3 cups thinly sliced, pared apples
Powdered ginger
Sugar
¾ cup apricot jam

Combine flour, sugar, and salt in upper part of double boiler over hot water. Add milk gradually, stirring until well blended. Cook, stirring constantly until thickened. Cover and cook 10 minutes longer, stirring frequently. Add 1 tablespoon of mixture to beaten eggs, stirring well. Then stir eggs into double boiler. Cook 2 or 3 minutes longer, stirring constantly. Remove from heat. Stir in rum and butter or margarine and let cool.

Mix pastry, using following ingredients:

1 cup sifted all-purpose flour
2 tablespoons sugar
⅛ teaspoon salt

4 tablespoons butter or margarine
1 egg yolk

Sift flour, sugar, and salt into mixing bowl. Mix in butter or margarine and beaten yolk until well blended and soft. Shape into ball.
Roll pastry between 2 sheets waxed paper into circle 9 inches in diameter. Fit pastry into bottom of 9-inch spring form or any other loose-
bottomed cake form. Pour rum filling into pastry-lined pan. Smooth top
with spoon.

Start oven at moderate (350° F.).

Arrange apple slices overlapping around top of filled pan. Sprinkle
generously with sugar and lightly with ginger.

Bake 45 minutes or until apples are tender. Remove from oven.
Spread with jam. Let cool. Chill.

To serve, remove sides of pan. Cut in wedges. Serve plain or with
whipped cream. Makes 6 servings.

VERMONT APPLE PIE

Pastry mix for 9-inch 2-crust pie
6 to 8 large, tart apples
1 cup maple sugar, packed
2 teaspoons flour
¼ teaspoon powdered nutmeg

½ teaspoon powdered cinnamon
2 tablespoons butter or margarine
1 egg yolk, beaten

Prepare pastry. Line pie plate. Pare, core, and slice apples. Combine sugar, flour, and spices. Rub a little flour mixture into pastry-lined
pan. Arrange sliced apples in pan and sprinkle with remaining sugar
mixture and dot with butter.

Start oven at hot (425° F.).

Roll out remaining pastry for top crust. Cut small circle out of center.
Place top crust over apples, trim pastry, seal edges of pie. From small
pastry circle cut an apple, using cardboard pattern. Place pastry apple
in hole in center of top crust. Brush pastry with beaten egg.

Bake 40 to 45 minutes or until pastry is browned. Makes 6 servings.

SAN YSIDRO WALNUT PIE

1   unbaked 9-inch pie shell
½ cup brown sugar, packed
½ cup softened butter or marga-
    rine
¾ cup granulated sugar
3   eggs
¼ teaspoon salt

¼ cup light corn syrup
½ cup light cream
1   cup coarsely chopped Cali-
    fornia walnuts
½ teaspoon vanilla
¼ cup walnut halves

Prepare pastry and line pie plate.

Start oven at moderate (350° F.).

Combine brown sugar and butter or margarine in upper part of double boiler. Beat smoothly together. Add granulated sugar and mix thoroughly. Add eggs one at a time, beating after each addition. Add salt, syrup, and cream. Mix well. Cook over boiling water, stirring 5 minutes. Remove from heat. Stir in chopped walnuts and vanilla. Pour into prepared pie shell.

Bake 1 hour. Pull out oven shelf. Scatter walnut halves on top of pie. Return to oven and bake 5 minutes longer. Let cool. Makes 6 servings. A specialty at San Ysidro Ranch, Santa Barbara.

Brown-Sugar Pecan Pie: Pecans are used instead of walnuts.

CHOCOLATE REFRIGERATOR PIE

Meringue Shell (page 460)
¼ pound sweet chocolate
3   tablespoons strongly brewed
    black coffee

1   teaspoon vanilla
1   cup heavy cream
Extra cream for decoration

Make meringue shell and let cool.

Melt chocolate in upper part of double boiler over hot but not boiling water. Stir in coffee. Mix well. Add vanilla. Let cool. Whip cream stiff and fold into cooled chocolate mixture. Pour into cooled pie shell. Refrigerate, lightly covered with waxed paper, 2 to 3 hours.

To serve, use pastry tube and decorate top with whipped cream in ruffles. Makes 6 servings.

Finely chopped pignolia or pistachio nuts may be added to the whipped cream for decorating top.

MARLIN'S CHOCOLATE PIE

Graham-cracker crust for 9-inch
  pie
1 (9-ounce) Hershey almond bar
  or 10¼ (5-cent) bars,
  ⅞-ounce each

⅔ cup milk
12 marshmallows
1 cup heavy cream, whipped

Prepare crust. Melt chocolate bars in top of double boiler over boiling water. Stir in milk and marshmallows. When smooth, remove from heat. Let cool. Fold in whipped cream. Pour into crumb shell. Chill. Serve topped with additional whipped cream if desired. Makes 6 servings.

This is a recipe I swapped with a delightful friend in Madrid. I've passed it along to my Connecticut friends and they are as enthusiastic as I am.

COFFEE COCONUT PIE

⅓ cup all-purpose flour
½ cup sugar
⅛ teaspoon salt
1 cup strongly brewed coffee
1 cup evaporated milk
3 egg yolks, beaten slightly

2 tablespoons butter or margarine
1 teaspoon vanilla
1½ cups shredded coconut
Coffee Coconut Pie Shell
Whipped cream

Combine flour, sugar, and salt in upper part of double boiler over hot water. Add coffee and evaporated milk gradually, stirring continually. Stir little of hot mixture into beaten yolks, then stir yolks into double boiler. Cook 2 minutes, stirring constantly. Remove from heat. Add butter or margarine, vanilla, and 1 cup coconut. Mix. Let cool. Pour into special pie shell. Garnish with whipped cream and remaining ½ cup coconut. Makes 6 servings.

Coffee Coconut Pie Shell

1 (4-ounce) can shredded coconut

Strong, hot coffee
2 tablespoons butter or margarine

Start oven at moderate (350° F.).

Empty can of coconut into bowl. Add enough strong, hot coffee to barely cover. Let stand 5 minutes, then drain. Pat coconut dry between layers of paper towels. Rub butter or margarine on bottom and sides of 9-inch pie pan. Press coconut in buttered pan thickly, to make pie shell.

Bake 10 minutes. Let cool. Use for Coffee Coconut Pie.

CUBAN RHYTHM CHIFFON PIE

Graham cracker crust for 9-inch
pie
1 tablespoon unflavored gelatin
¼ cup cold, strongly brewed
coffee
2 eggs
⅔ cup sweetened condensed
milk

¼ teaspoon salt
1¼ cups strong, hot coffee
3 tablespoons light rum
1½ tablespoons grated or
scraped bitter chocolate

Prepare graham cracker crust. Soften gelatin in cold coffee. Let stand 5 minutes. Beat egg yolks lightly in mixing bowl. Add condensed milk and salt. Dissolve gelatin mixture in hot coffee and rum. Stir gradually into yolk mixture. Place in refrigerator until mixture begins to set.

Whip egg whites until they stand in stiff points when beater is removed. Fold gelatin mixture into whites. Pour into prepared crust. Sprinkle grated chocolate over top of pie. Return to refrigerator until ready to serve.

To serve, cut into 6 pie-shaped pieces and lift carefully with pie server. Makes 6 servings.

This is a delicious and delicate rum pie, which we usually put in a very short crust or else use graham cracker or cooky crumb crust. A good variation is a crust made of chocolate wafers. Follow directions for graham cracker crust (page 459). Approximates the rum pie which is a specialty of "Justines" in Memphis.

CUSTARD APPLESAUCE PIE

1 package pie-crust mix
2 cups thick, unsweetened applesauce
⅛ teaspoon powdered nutmeg
½ cup sugar
4 eggs

3 cups milk, scalded
⅛ teaspoon salt
1 teaspoon vanilla
Extra nutmeg
1 cup heavy cream, optional

Make pastry according to directions on package. Line deep 10-inch pie pan. Flute edge of pastry with thumb and forefinger.

Start oven at hot (425° F.).

Combine applesauce and nutmeg in mixing bowl. Beat sugar with eggs slightly. Add scalded milk slowly to sugar and eggs while stirring. Add salt and vanilla. Pour slowly into applesauce mixture, blending well. Taste for sweetness. If necessary, add more sugar. Pour into pie shell and sprinkle lightly with nutmeg.

Bake 30 to 40 minutes or until knife inserted near center of pie comes out clean. Let cool. Garnish with ruffle of whipped cream if desired. Makes 6 servings.

DEEP-DISH BLUEBERRY PIE

Pastry for 9-inch 2-crust pie
2½ cups blueberries
1 cup sugar
¼ cup flour

⅛ teaspoon salt
1 tablespoon lemon juice
2 tablespoons butter or margarine

Prepare pastry. Roll out about half of it ¼ inch thick. Cut in 6 triangles the right size together to cover the bottom of the pie dish. Place triangles on baking sheet.

Start oven at hot (450° F.). Bake pastry triangles 10 minutes or until lightly browned and crisp.

Wash and drain berries. Look over for discards. Combine berries with sugar, flour, salt, and lemon juice. Place baked triangles of pastry in bottom of deep pie dish. Fill dish with berry mixture and dot with butter or margarine.

Roll remaining pastry about ¼ inch thick. Pierce in several places with tines of fork. Lay over berries. Trim edge around dish. Crimp pastry to dish with thumb and forefinger.

Bake 10 minutes at 450° F. Reduce heat to moderate (350° F.) and bake 30 minutes longer. Serve warm or cold. Makes 6 to 8 servings.

Serve this pie in dessert dishes, rather than on plates, and top each serving with spoonful of vanilla ice cream. Don't wait for the blueberry season for this favorite pie. You can get fine results with canned or deep-frozen berries.

HONEY-CREAM PEACH PIE

Pastry for 9-inch 1-crust pie
½ cup sugar
3 tablespoons flour
¼ cup honey
⅓ cup heavy cream
5 or 6 large ripe peaches, peeled, cut in thick slices

½ teaspoon powdered ginger
¼ teaspoon powdered nutmeg
1 tablespoon butter or margarine

Prepare pastry. Roll out. Line 9-inch pie plate. Sprinkle bottom of pastry evenly with 1 tablespoon each sugar and flour.

Start oven at hot (425° F.).

Combine remaining sugar and flour. Stir in honey and cream, mixing until smooth. Pour over peaches. Mix gently to coat peaches but do not break them. Spoon into pastry-lined pie plate. Sprinkle with ginger and nutmeg. Dot with butter or margarine.

Bake 45 minutes or until pastry is done and peaches are tender and top browned. Makes 6 servings.

HUNGARIAN PEACH PASTRY

Prepare your favorite pie pastry for 2-crust pie. Use puff paste or extra-rich pastry for best results. Chill pastry until ready to use.

Roll or pat pastry out lightly in narrow rectangle about 18 inches long and 4 inches wide. Turn ¾-inch edge up all around pastry strip. Crimp corners together.

Start oven at hot (450° F.).

Heat 1½ cups peach jam in upper part of double boiler over boiling water until slightly softened. Spoon into pastry. Spread evenly to fill corners. Use more jam if necessary. With wide spatula slip jam-filled pastry onto lightly greased baking sheet.

Bake about 10 minutes. Turn oven down to moderate (350° F.) and bake about 20 minutes longer or until pastry is done and browning.

Serve warm or cold. Bring whole pastry to table on long platter or bread-cutting board. Let guests cut their own pieces. Makes 9 2-inch servings or 12 smaller ones.

Double recipe, making 2 pastries for large buffet party.

LEMON MERINGUE PIE

Use blender

Crumb Crust or 9-inch baked pastry shell	1 lemon
1 envelope unflavored gelatin	4 eggs
¼ cup cold water	1 cup sugar
	¼ teaspoon salt

Prepare crust. Bake and let cool.

Soften gelatin in cold water 5 minutes, then dissolve over hot water. Cut peel from half of lemon, lengthwise. Discard this peel. Cut lemon in 8 small pieces and remove seeds. Add few pieces at a time to blender. Cover container and let run. Add pieces of lemon until all have been cut very fine. Stop blender and scrape down sides. Add dissolved gelatin. Start blender. Add egg yolks, one at a time. Add ½ cup sugar and the salt. Blend until sugar is dissolved. Pour mixture into small bowl and chill until partially set.

Beat egg whites in mixing bowl until they stand in soft points when beater is removed. Gradually add remaining ½ cup sugar to whites and beat until stiff peaks are formed. Fold semi-thickened gelatin into egg whites. Pour into pie shell. Chill until firm. Makes 6 servings.

LEMON RAISIN PIE

½ cup seedless raisins	3 tablespoons water
Pastry for 2-crust 8-inch pie	2 tablespoons melted butter
1 ¼ cups sugar	2 teaspoons grated lemon peel
1 tablespoon cornstarch	⅓ cup lemon juice
3 eggs, well beaten	

Cover raisins with warm water, let soak 30 minutes.

Start oven at moderately hot (400° F.).

Roll out half pastry to ⅛ inch thickness. Line 8-inch pie pan and trim edge even with rim of pan.

Drain raisins and spread over pastry. Combine sugar and cornstarch. Stir in eggs. Mix water, butter, lemon peel and juice into egg mixture. Pour over raisins. Roll out remaining pastry and place over filling. Trim edge ½ inch beyond rim of pie pan, turn under, and crimp edge to seal. Slash top crust to allow steam to escape.

Bake 35 minutes. When pie is done, arrange on top of pie lemon and leaf cutouts made from pastry scraps and baked on separate pie pan the last 10 minutes the pie is baking. Let cool before serving. Makes 6 servings.

A Daisyfields specialty developed from Grandmother Vanderbilt's very "lemony" pie.

MINCE CHIFFON PIE

Prepare this pie the day before it is to be served.

22 gingersnaps, rolled into fine crumbs
¼ cup sugar
3 tablespoons butter or margarine

Blend crumbs, sugar, and butter or margarine smoothly together. Pour mixture into 9-inch pie plate. Spread in bottom and press firmly into even layer against sides. Use 8-inch pie plate in the larger plate to get smooth, firm pressure. Smooth edge of crust all around.

1 (9-ounce) box condensed mincemeat
2 envelopes unflavored gelatin
½ cup cold water
½ cup heavy cream, whipped
3 egg whites
6 tablespoons sugar
Extra cream and crumbs

Prepare mincemeat according to directions on package. Soak gelatin in water in a cup about 5 minutes. Set cup in hot water and heat until gelatin dissolves. Blend into mincemeat. Chill until partially set. Fold in whipped cream. Beat egg whites until they stand in soft peaks. Add sugar gradually, beating until mixture stands in stiff points when beater is removed. Fold mincemeat into meringue. Spoon into pie shell. Chill in refrigerator.

To serve, garnish with additional whipped cream mixed with a few gingersnap crumbs. Makes 6 servings.

Much too rich to serve after the traditional Thanksgiving or Christmas dinner. Better to serve it as a specialty, with coffee, some night when friends come in to sing carols or to listen to records or watch television.

MINCE PIE

Pastry for 2-crust pie
2 ½ cups mincemeat
½ cup chopped tart apples

2 tablespoons cognac
Fruit juice, if needed

Prepare pastry; line 9-inch pan. Trim edge.

Start oven at hot (425 ° F.).

Combine mincemeat with apples. Fill lined pan. Roll top crust and place over filled pan. Trim around edge, leaving 1-inch overhang. Turn pastry under edge of bottom crust and press together with fingers. Crimp into upstanding edge. Cut small round hole in center of top crust. Pour brandy in before baking. Add a little fruit juice at same time if mincemeat mixture seems dry. Prick pastry with fork.

Bake 30 minutes. Serve warm.

If stronger brandy flavor is desired, do not pour cognac into pie before baking. Add 1 or 2 tablespoons fruit juice. Bake as described. Remove pie from oven, pour brandy in and let stand a few minutes. Serve. Makes 6 servings.

A cube of American sharp Cheddar is served with this in our house.

MOLASSES RUM PIE

9-inch baked pastry shell
1 envelope unflavored gelatin
½ cup sugar
⅛ teaspoon salt
3 eggs

1 cup milk
⅓ cup molasses
1 ½ teaspoons rum
1 cup heavy cream, whipped

Prepare and bake pastry shell. Let cool.

Mix gelatin, 2 tablespoons sugar, and the salt together in the upper part of a double boiler over boiling water. Beat egg yolks and milk together. Stir into gelatin mixture slowly with molasses. Cook over boiling water, stirring occasionally until mixture is slightly thickened. Remove from heat. Stir in rum. Chill until mixture is slightly thicker than consistency of unbeaten egg white.

Beat egg whites until stiff but not dry. Gradually add remaining 6 tablespoons sugar to whites, beating until they stand in stiff points when beater is removed. Fold gelatin mixture into whites. Fold in whipped cream. Turn mixture into cooled baked pastry shell. Chill.

Serve as is or decorate top with additional whipped cream and sprinkle with instant coffee. Makes 6 servings.

NECTARINE CREAM PIE

9-inch baked pastry or crumb
   shell
1½ cups heavy cream
1 tablespoon sugar
1 teaspoon orange flavoring

4 or 5 ripe nectarines
2 tablespoons apricot jam
2 tablespoons boiling water
3 or 4 tablespoons shredded
   blanched almonds

Prepare and bake pastry shell or make crumb shell. Let cool.

Whip cream and add sugar to taste and orange flavoring. Spread in cooled pie shell. Cream should fill pie shell level with top. Peel ripe nectarines and cut in thin sections. Cover surface of cream thickly with fruit. Mix jam and boiling water. Let cool a little. Brush over surface of fruit. Sprinkle thickly with almonds. Chill 1 hour or longer before serving. Makes 6 to 8 servings.

Apricot Cream Pie: In recipe above, substitute very ripe apricots.

Peach Cream Pie: In recipe above, substitute very ripe peaches.

Other fruits may be used in this recipe: sliced ripe strawberries make a delicious pie. So do crushed ripe currants sweetened and allowed to stand an hour before using. Combine cooked dried fruits, such as prunes with apricots, for another version of this luxurious dessert.

OPEN-FACE FRUIT PIE

Pastry for 9-inch 1-crust pie
2 packages quick-frozen raspberries, blueberries, or sliced
   peaches
¾ cup sugar

2 tablespoons flour
¼ teaspoon salt
2 tablespoons butter or margarine

Prepare pastry to line 9-inch pie plate. Trim around edge and crimp edge decoratively.

Defrost fruit as described on package. If juicy, drain thoroughly. Start oven at hot (425° F.).

Mix sugar, flour, and salt together. Cut butter or margarine in with pastry blender or fork until crumbly. Fill pastry-lined plate with drained fruit. Sprinkle crumbs thickly over all.

Bake 40 to 45 minutes or until edges of pastry are browned. Makes 6 servings.

Open-Face Peach Pie: Use recipe above and No. 2½ can sliced peaches, well drained.

PECAN PIE

Use blender

Pastry for 9-inch 1-crust pie
3 eggs
½ cup heavy cream
½ cup dark corn syrup
⅛ teaspoon salt

1 cup sugar
1 teaspoon vanilla
2 tablespoons butter or margarine
1½ cups broken pecans

Prepare pastry. Line 9-inch pie plate. Trim edge and flute rim into a decorative border.

Start oven at moderately hot (400° F.).

Combine remaining ingredients in glass container of blender. Cover and blend about 10 seconds or until nuts are coarsely chopped. Pour into unbaked pastry-lined plate.

Bake about 35 minutes or until crust is browned and filling puffs up. Remove from oven. Let cool at room temperature. Makes 6 to 8 servings.

GEORGIA PECAN PIE

Pastry for 8-inch 1-crust pie
3 eggs, beaten
¾ cup molasses
¾ cup light corn syrup
½ cup very strongly brewed coffee

2 tablespoons melted butter or margarine
1 teaspoon salt
1 teaspoon vanilla
1 cup chopped pecans
¼ cup sifted all-purpose flour

Prepare pastry and line pie plate. Trim edge and crimp rim into a decorative edge.

Start oven at moderate (375° F.).

Combine eggs, molasses, syrup, coffee, melted butter or margarine, salt, and vanilla. Mix thoroughly. Combine pecans and flour. Add to egg mixture. Stir to mix well. Pour into unbaked pie shell.

Bake 40 to 45 minutes or until firm. Let cool at room temperature before cutting. Makes 6 or 8 portions.

PARK AVENUE PRUNE PIE

Pastry for 9-inch 1-crust pie
 1 envelope unflavored gelatin
 ¼ cup water
 ½ cup prune juice
 ½ cup sugar
 ⅛ teaspoon salt

 1 tablespoon cognac
 1½ cups puréed cooked prunes
     (baby food)
 1½ cups heavy cream
 Toasted slivered almonds

Prepare and bake pastry shell. Let cool.

Soak gelatin in cold water 5 minutes. Heat prune juice. Stir into gelatin until dissolved. Stir in sugar, salt, brandy, and puréed prunes. Mix well. Whip cream stiff. Fold ⅔ of cream into prune mixture. Pour into baked crust. Chill. Garnish with remaining whipped cream and almonds. Makes 6 to 8 servings.

PRUNE CREAM PIE

Use blender

Pastry for 9-inch 1-crust pie
 3 eggs
 ½ cup prune juice
 1 cup milk
 ¼ cup sifted all-purpose flour
 ½ teaspoon salt

 ⅛ teaspoon powdered cinnamon
 1 cup pitted cooked or canned
     prunes, drained
 1 cup sugar
 ½ cup heavy cream

Prepare pastry. Line pie plate. Trim edge. Crimp rim in decorative edge.

Start oven at moderately hot (400° F.).

Combine eggs, prune juice, milk, flour, seasonings, prunes, and sugar in glass container of blender. Cover and blend about 30 seconds or until thoroughly mixed. Pour mixture into unbaked pie shell.

Bake about 35 minutes, until crust is brown and filling is set. Remove from oven. Let cool slightly.

When ready to serve, whip cream and spread over pie. Makes 6 or more servings.

Stir 1 tablespoon currant jelly through the whipped cream before spreading on cooled pie. A delicate and delicious combination of flavors.

PUMPKIN PIE

Use blender

Pastry for 9-inch 1-crust pie
2 eggs
¼ cup evaporated milk
1 cup milk
1 cup sieved cooked or canned pumpkin
½ tablespoon cornstarch

⅓ cup brown sugar, packed
2 tablespoons granulated sugar
½ teaspoon powdered cinnamon
⅛ teaspoon powdered allspice
⅛ teaspoon powdered ginger
¼ teaspoon salt
Powdered nutmeg

Prepare unbaked 9-inch pie shell.
Start oven at moderate (350° F.).
Combine eggs, evaporated milk, milk, and pumpkin in glass container or bowl of electric mixer. Blend at low speed until smoothly mixed. Sift dry ingredients, except nutmeg, together into pumpkin mixture. Blend at high speed until smooth. Pour into prepared unbaked pie shell. Sprinkle lightly with nutmeg.

Bake 30 minutes or until crust is lightly browned and filling is set. Let cool at room temperature in pan. Makes 6 to 8 servings.

Rich Old-Fashioned Pumpkin Pie: Use above recipe. Substitute light cream for both evaporated milk and milk. Increase eggs to 3. If blender is not used, beat eggs in bowl. Combine with cream, pumpkin, and all remaining ingredients except nutmeg. Beat until smooth. Pour into prepared unbaked pie shell. Sprinkle lightly with nutmeg. Bake as described. The additional egg and substituted cream give a lighter and richer pie. Let cool at room temperature in pan. Makes 6 or more servings.

STRAWBERRY CHIFFON PIE

1 recipe Crumb Crust (page 460)
1 pint fresh red-ripe strawberries
¾ cup sugar
1 envelope unflavored gelatin
¼ cup cold water
½ cup hot water

1 tablespoon lemon juice
⅛ teaspoon salt
½ cup heavy cream
2 egg whites
Extra strawberries
Heavy cream

Prepare Crumb Crust and set aside to chill.

Crush berries. Sprinkle with ½ cup sugar. Let stand 30 minutes. Soften gelatin in cold water. Dissolve in hot water and let cool. Add sugared strawberries, lemon juice, and salt. Chill until partially set.

Whip ½ cup cream stiff. Fold into strawberry mixture. Whip egg whites until soft peaks form. Beat remaining ¼ cup sugar into them until stiff peaks form when beater is removed. Fold strawberry mixture into whites. Pour into chilled Crumb Crust. Chill pie until firm.

To serve, garnish with sliced berries and whipped cream or omit cream. Makes 6 servings.

Raspberry Chiffon Pie: Use fresh red raspberries or defrosted and drained quick-frozen red raspberries. Follow recipe above.

SUMMER PEAR PIE

Pastry for 9-inch 2-crust pie	⅛ teaspoon salt
½ cup granulated sugar	6 cups sliced, pared ripe pears
¼ cup brown sugar, packed	2 teaspoons lemon juice
3 tablespoons flour	2 teaspoons grated lemon peel
½ teaspoon powdered nutmeg	1 tablespoon butter or margarine
½ teaspoon powdered cinnamon	

Prepare pastry. Roll out half of it and line 9-inch pie plate. Start oven at hot (425° F.).

Combine sugars, flour, nutmeg, cinnamon, and salt. Mix. Sprinkle over pears in bowl. Toss lightly to coat pears. Pour pear mixture into pastry-lined pan. Sprinkle with lemon juice and peel. Add dabs of butter or margarine. Roll out remaining half of pastry. Gash with decorative slits. Place over pie. Trim and seal. Flute or crimp edges.

Bake 40 to 45 minutes or until pastry top is golden and done.

Serve slightly warm. Makes 6 servings.

A mild cheese makes a fine accompaniment for this pie, or use your favorite cheese pastry as the crust.

SWEET-CHERRY PIE

Pastry for 9-inch 2-crust pie
¾ cup sugar
3 tablespoons all-purpose flour
⅛ teaspoon salt
½ cup juice from canned cherries
¼ teaspoon almond flavoring

Few drops red pure-food coloring
3 cups canned water-pack sweet, red, pitted cherries, drained
1 tablespoon butter or margarine

Prepare pastry. Roll out half and line 9-inch pie plate.

Start oven at hot (425° F.).

Mix sugar, flour, and salt. Add cherry juice gradually, stirring until smooth. Add almond flavoring and red food coloring. Pour mixture over drained cherries. Mix to coat cherries evenly. Pour into pastry-lined pan. Dot top with butter or margarine.

Roll remaining pastry. Cover pie. Trim, seal, and flute the edge. Cut several crisscrosses or stem-and-leaf design into pastry to let steam escape.

Bake 35 to 40 minutes or until juice bubbles and crust is golden brown.

Serve slightly warm, or cold. Makes 6 servings.

When served at end of light luncheon or supper, a spoonful of vanilla ice cream on each piece of pie brings applause from family and guests.

Sour-Cherry Pie: Use above recipe. Substitute 3 cups pitted sour cherries for sweet cherries. Increase sugar to 1½ cups, depending on sourness of fruit. Canned sour cherries are less tart than fresh fruit. Taste mixture. Bake as described.

JUANITA'S SWEET-POTATO PIE

Pastry for 9-inch 1-crust pie
4 eggs
1½ cups mashed boiled sweet potatoes
⅓ cup sugar
2 tablespoons honey
½ cup finely chopped black walnuts or pecans

⅔ cup milk
⅓ cup orange juice
1 teaspoon vanilla
⅛ teaspoon salt
½ cup heavy cream
1 tablespoon grated orange peel
½ teaspoon powdered nutmeg

Prepare pastry. Line 9-inch pan. Trim edge. Make decorative rim around edge.

Start oven at hot (450° F.).

Beat eggs until light. Combine with mashed potatoes and sugar. Beat thoroughly. Stir in honey. Add nuts, milk, orange juice, vanilla, and salt, beating well after each addition. Pour into unbaked pie shell.

Bake 10 minutes. Reduce temperature of oven to moderate (350° F.); bake 30 minutes longer or until pastry is done and knife inserted near center of pie comes out clean.

Let pie cool at room temperature. Whip cream. Mix with orange peel and nutmeg. Spread over pie to serve. Makes 6 or more servings.

Tarts

APPLE MERINGUE TART

½ cup sifted all-purpose flour
2 tablespoons sugar
4 tablespoons butter or margarine
¾ cup thick applesauce or sliced
  cooked apples

½ tablespoon brown sugar
½ tablespoon grated lemon peel
3 egg whites
6 tablespoons sugar
Custard Sauce (page 565)

Start oven at moderate (350° F.).

Sift flour and 2 tablespoons sugar together in small mixing bowl. Chop butter or margarine into flour and sugar with pastry blender until pastry holds together. Turn dough out on lightly floured board. Pat out lightly and cut 6 circles 2½ inches in diameter. Bake on ungreased cooky sheet 10 to 15 minutes.

Remove pastry from oven. Reduce oven temperature to moderately slow (300° F.).

Season applesauce or slices with brown sugar and lemon peel. Place heaping tablespoon of apple mixture on each baked pastry circle.

Beat egg whites. Add sugar gradually, beating until meringue stands in points when whip is removed. Heap meringue on apple-topped pastry. Spread meringue over top and sides thickly. Bake 30 minutes or until golden. Let cool. Serve with or without Custard Sauce. Makes 6 servings.

BLACK-CHERRY TARTS

½ recipe plain or rich pastry

2 cups pitted oxheart cherries, fresh or canned

⅓ cup cherry juice

⅓ cup granulated sugar

⅓ cup brown sugar, packed

3 tablespoons quick-cooking tapioca

1 tablespoon butter or margarine

Prepare pastry. Line 8 muffin pans with pastry. Crimp edge of each into decorative rim.

Start oven at hot (425° F.).

Drain cherries. Combine with juice, sugars, and tapioca. Let stand 15 minutes. Pour into pastry-lined muffin pans. Add dab of butter or margarine to each.

Bake 14 to 20 minutes or until pastry is done and browning. Let cool. Makes 8 servings.

LEMON MERINGUE TARTS

8 baked tart shells

1¼ cups sugar

6 tablespoons cornstarch

⅛ teaspoon salt

2 cups boiling water

1 teaspoon grated lemon peel

4 tablespoons butter or margarine

3 eggs

⅔ cup lemon juice

6 tablespoons sugar

Prepare pastry and bake tart shells. Let cool. Place on baking sheet ready for filling.

Start oven at moderately hot (400° F.).

Mix sugar, cornstarch, and salt together in saucepan. Add boiling water and lemon peel. Stir constantly. Cook over moderate heat until thickened. Continue cooking and stirring about 20 minutes or until clear and no taste of cornstarch remains. Remove from heat. Add butter or margarine.

Beat egg yolks slightly. Mix with lemon juice. Pour hot mixture gradually into yolk mixture. Beat until smooth. Return to heat. Let come just to boiling point, stirring to prevent scorching. Do not boil. Pour into tart shells.

Bake 5 minutes. Remove from oven and cover with meringue made by whipping egg whites until stiff, adding 6 tablespoons sugar. Return tarts to oven. Lower heat to moderate (350° F.). Bake 10 to 12 minutes or until meringue is delicately browned. Makes 8 tarts.

PUMPKIN CHIFFON TARTS

8 baked tart shells
1 envelope unflavored gelatin
¼ cup cold water
3 eggs
1 cup sugar
1⅓ cups sieved canned pumpkin
⅓ cup milk
½ teaspoon salt

½ teaspoon powdered cinnamon
½ teaspoon powdered nutmeg
½ cup heavy cream
2 tablespoons grated lemon or orange peel
Extra powdered nutmeg

Prepare pastry and bake tart shells. Let cool.

Soften gelatin in cold water. Beat egg yolks with ½ cup sugar in saucepan until thick. Add pumpkin, milk, salt, cinnamon, and nutmeg. Mix well. Cook over moderate heat about 5 minutes or until thickened. Stir constantly. Add gelatin. Stir until dissolved. Let mixture cool.

Whip egg whites until soft peaks form. Whip remaining ½ cup sugar into egg whites until mixture stands in stiff peaks when beater is withdrawn. Fold pumpkin mixture into whites. Spoon mixture into tart shells. Let chill until set.

Whip cream stiff. Add grated peel. To serve, add spoonful of whipped cream to top of each tart and sprinkle lightly with nutmeg. Makes 8 tarts.

RAISIN TARTS

8 unbaked tart shells
1½ cups seedless raisins
2 tablespoons chopped pecans

1½ tablespoons lemon juice
2 tablespoons brown sugar

Prepare pastry and line tart pans as described for tart shells.

Cover raisins with water. Let soak 30 minutes. Or heat until boiling. Remove from heat. Let stand until cool. Drain.

Start oven at moderately hot (400° F.).

Combine drained raisins, nuts, lemon juice, and sugar. Fill pastry-lined muffin pans.

Bake 15 to 20 minutes. Serve warm or let cool. Makes 8 tarts.

Use smaller pans and make tiny tarts to serve as finger desserts for buffet party. Delicious with a dab of ice cream, whipped cream, or thick sour cream on each.

RASPBERRY MERINGUE TARTS

4 egg whites	1 pint heavy cream
½ teaspoon vinegar	2 cups canned or defrosted,
1 teaspoon vanilla	drained quick-frozen red rasp-
¼ teaspoon salt	berries
1 cup sugar	
½ cup uncooked quick-cooking	
oatmeal	

Start oven at slow (275° F.). Spread unglazed paper on baking sheet.

Begin beating egg whites. Add vinegar, vanilla, and salt as you beat. Beat until frothy. Add sugar gradually, beating well after each addition. Continue beating until mixture stands in peaks when beater is withdrawn. Fold oats in lightly.

Make 8 mounds of meringue on paper-covered baking sheet. Use spatula or spoon to hollow out centers and build up sides like tart shells.

Bake 45 minutes to 1 hour. Let cool few minutes, then remove from paper to serving platter or tray. Let cool thoroughly.

Whip cream stiff. Combine with berries. Heap into meringue shells. Makes 8 meringue tarts.

Peach Meringue Tarts: The above recipe for meringue shells may be used for various dessert fillings. Sliced fresh or quick-frozen peaches, topped with a dab of vanilla or peach ice cream, make appetizing peach tarts. Or use sliced spiced peaches.

Blueberry Meringue Tarts: Use fresh, cooked, canned, or quick-frozen blueberries. Drain well.

Strawberry Meringue Tarts: Slice fresh berries. Sprinkle with sugar. Let stand 30 minutes. Use in meringue shells. Or use drained, defrosted quick-frozen sliced berries.

Chocolate Ice Cream Meringue Tarts: Fill shells with chocolate ice cream. Sprinkle top with instant coffee and chopped nuts.

Make very small shells to serve as finger desserts at buffet parties.

Turnovers

APPLE TURNOVERS

Rich Pastry (page 461) or Puff
Pastry (page 459)
2 cups finely chopped tart apples
½ cup sugar
2 teaspoons powdered cinnamon

1 tablespoon butter or margarine
Light cream
Sifted confectioners' sugar

Prepare pastry. Roll out about ⅛ inch thick. Cut in 4-inch squares. Place about ¼ cup chopped apple in center of each square. Mix sugar and cinnamon. Sprinkle over apples. Dot with butter or margarine. Brush edge of pastry with cream. Fold over in triangles. Seal edges well by pressing with fingers or with tines of fork. Cut few slits in top to let steam escape.

Start oven at hot (450° F.). Cover baking sheet with aluminum foil. Place turnovers on sheet.

Bake 20 to 25 minutes or until nicely browned. Remove from oven, sprinkle lightly with confectioners' sugar. Serve warm or cold. Makes 8 to 12 turnovers.

Your favorite pastry may be used in place of Rich or Puff Pastry.

Berry Turnovers: Use recipe above. Fill with drained cooked, canned, or defrosted quick-frozen raspberries, strawberries, blueberries, or other small fruits. Cooked gooseberries and ripe currants make delicious turnovers. With berries omit cinnamon. Use a very small amount of powdered ginger and nutmeg, plus sugar to sweeten.

Peach Turnovers: Pear Turnovers: Plum Turnovers: Use recipe above. Remove pits and seeds. Cut large fruits into small pieces. Sweeten and use small amount mixed spices. Serve warm with plain cream, or without, as finger dessert.

FIG TURNOVERS

Steam large dried figs until they are softened. Fill each fig with hard sauce. Place filled fig in circle of pie pastry. Fold pastry over. Seal edges with tines of fork. Prick top in 2 or 3 places with fork.

Bake in hot oven (425° F.) 15 minutes or until pastry is golden. Serve warm with cream, or let cool and serve as finger dessert.

FRIED APPLE TURNOVERS

Prepare your favorite recipe for doughnut dough or use doughnut mix. Roll out ¼ inch thick. Cut in 6-inch rounds. Place 2 tablespoons thick, sweetened, spiced applesauce in center of each round. Moisten edges. Fold over and press edges firmly together with tines of fork.

Fry in fat 2 inches deep, heated to 365° F. on frying thermometer, until puffed and brown. Drain on thick paper towels. Serve with sharp cheese. Makes finger dessert for buffet and terrace parties.

VIENNA TURNOVERS

½ cup butter or margarine	1 egg yolk
1 (3-ounce) package cream cheese	2 tablespoons milk
	½ cup finely chopped pecans
1 cup sifted all-purpose flour	Confectioners' sugar
⅓ cup red currant jelly	

Beat butter or margarine with cheese in mixing bowl. When soft and smooth, stir in flour, mixing evenly and thoroughly. Chill about 1 hour.

Start oven at moderately hot (400° F.).

Roll cheese dough out about ⅛ inch thick on lightly floured board. Cut in 2-inch squares. Spoon small dab of jelly into center of each. Fold dough over jelly to form triangle. Pinch edges together to seal. Pull the two corners of triangle toward each other to form crescent.

Beat egg yolk slightly. Combine with milk. Dip crescents in egg mixture. Roll in chopped nuts. Place on ungreased cooky sheet.

Bake 8 to 10 minutes or until lightly browned. Sprinkle with confectioners' sugar. Let cool. Makes 2 dozen.

A good sweet for the tea or coffee tray. Also fine for lunch box or picnic basket.

CHAPTER SEVENTEEN

Salads and Their Dressings

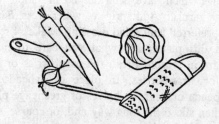

Fruit Salads

APPLE AND GRAPEFRUIT SALAD

24 grapefruit sections	French Dressing (page 518)
4 crisp lettuce leaves	3 red eating apples
16 strips green peppers	¼ cup pecan halves
4 or 5 sprigs fresh mint	2 or 3 tablespoons mayonnaise

Arrange grapefruit sections on lettuce on 4 chilled plates. Add green pepper, mint leaves, a little French dressing. Wash and core apples. Cut in cubes. Mix with pecans and lightly with mayonnaise. Add generous spoonful to each grapefruit plate. Makes 4 servings.

FRUIT LUNCHEON PLATTER

1 ripe pineapple

4 oranges, peeled and sectioned

1 cup sliced large strawberries

1 (8-ounce) container creamed cottage cheese

1 avocado, pared, halved, and cut in rings

2 tablespoons lemon juice

4 fresh dates

4 large pecan halves

Water cress

French Dressing (page 518)

Wash and drain pineapple. Use sharp knife and cut down through spikes and fruit into quarters. Cut core from each quarter, then cut fruit out of each quarter in even wedges.

Refill pineapple shells with alternate pieces of pineapple and orange sections. Place shells on long platter.

Arrange strawberries in mound at each end of platter. Whip cottage cheese lightly and mound it across middle of platter. Garnish cheese with avocado rings which have been dipped in lemon juice. Stuff dates with nuts. Add as garnish. Add sprigs of water cress. Serve with French Dressing or any preferred fruit salad dressing. Makes 4 servings.

Variations on this platter are what you care to make them, with whatever fruits are in season. Fresh red raspberries or blueberries may be substituted for strawberries. In place of avocado rings use thin wedges of ripe peach or pear, or halves of greengage plums, or banana cut in quarters then sliced the long way and, of course, dipped in lemon juice to prevent darkening.

Sour-cream dressing is preferred by some with fruits. It's a good idea to serve two dressings—a chilled bowl of French Dressing and another of sour-cream dressing.

Fruit Salad Bowl: Serve fruits in above recipe in large lettuce-lined salad bowl, keeping pieces large. Add sprigs of fresh mint. Serve with Honey-Lime Dressing, Orlando (page 522).

Vary the combination by using 1 pink grapefruit peeled and sectioned, 3 oranges peeled and sectioned, 2 bananas quartered, 1 pint large whole strawberries or seeded black cherries. Makes 4 to 6 servings.

Honeydew Fruit Platter: Cut chilled honeydew melon in crosswise slices. Pare. Place on salad plates. Fill center of each ring with assorted chilled fruits, such as cubes of fresh peach, banana, plum, apricot, pear. Decorate center with large seeded black cherries or whole strawberries or spoonful red raspberries or blueberries. Trim with mint sprig.

Pass cottage cheese or any preferred fruit French Dressing.

This makes a main dish for luncheon for calorie-counting friends. Add whole-wheat toast or rolls, tea or black coffee.

Or serve this as dessert after a summer luncheon such as soufflé omelet, asparagus, and coffee.

APPLE AND VEGETABLE SALAD

1 cup commercial sour cream	1 teaspoon dry mustard
2 tablespoons lemon juice	1 cup sliced celery
2 tablespoons cider vinegar	2 cups shredded cabbage
2 tablespoons sugar	1 cup shredded scraped carrots
1 teaspoon salt	2 large red apples
¼ teaspoon coarsely ground black pepper	⅓ cup seedless raisins

Combine first 7 ingredients. Beat smooth. Combine vegetables. Wash and core apples. Cut in strips. Add to vegetables with raisins. Combine with sour-cream mixture. Toss to mix evenly. Makes 8 servings.

WALDORF SALAD

According to the Waldorf-Astoria Hotel in New York, the true Waldorf Salad is made by this recipe:

1 ripe eating apple	¼ cup mayonnaise
Juice 1 lemon	Salt and pepper
1 stalk celery, chopped fine	Crisp lettuce leaves

Wash, core, and pare apple. Cut in halves and slice halves. Reserve 4 slices. Cut remainder in narrow strips. All should be doused generously with lemon juice to keep from turning dark.

Mix celery, mayonnaise, and apple strips. Season with little salt, white pepper, or to taste. Arrange on lettuce. Top with apple slices. Makes 1 serving.

A large Waldorf Salad makes a perfect light luncheon. Or serve a small amount as an appetizer salad at beginning of luncheon or dinner.

California Waldorf Salad: Add 1 cup halved and seeded Emperor grapes or seedless white grapes and ½ cup broken California walnuts to celery, mayonnaise, and apple strips. Increase mayonnaise to ½ cup. Complete recipe as described. Makes 2 servings.

STUFFED FIG SALAD

Drain chilled canned figs. Cut out stem end. Stuff with cream cheese. Serve on crisp romaine with thin orange slices and French dressing.

If you can find fresh ripe figs in your market, by all means use them in this salad. Perfect!

PINEAPPLE-STICKS SALAD

Drain chilled canned pineapple spears. Spread each quickly with softened cream cheese which has been mixed with a little sour cream, paprika, and celery salt or curry powder. For each serving arrange 3 sticks on crisp water cress. Add few large whole strawberries or other berries. Serve plain or with French Dressing.

WATERMELON FILLED WITH FRUIT SALAD

1 medium-sized ripe watermelon	3 eating apples
1 pint jar spiced seckel pears	½ cup French Dressing (page
3 ripe peaches or apricots	518)
3 seedless oranges	Fresh mint leaves
1 cup seedless white grapes	

Chill melon. Cut slice about 3 inches deep from end to end. Cut out the red fruit from lid and rest of melon. Remove all seeds. Cut best part of melon into bite-sized cubes. Pile them back into melon shell. Put lid on and return melon to refrigerator.

Drain seckel pears. Save liquid. Remove stems and cores. Slice pears thickly. Wash, peel, and slice peaches. Or cut small apricots in halves. Discard seeds. Peel and section oranges. Wash and drain grapes. Pare and core apples and cut into bite-size cubes. Mix spiced pear liquid with French Dressing made with fruit juice. Pour over fruits.

To serve, add fruits to cubed melon in watermelon shell. Lift and mix lightly with two forks. Serve at once on chilled plates garnished with fresh mint leaves. Makes 6 to 8 or more servings.

Vegetable Salads

ARTICHOKE HEARTS AND RIPE-OLIVE SALAD

12 canned artichoke hearts, drained
16 large ripe olives
Small pickled cocktail onions
Lemon French Dressing (page 518)

2 tablespoons shredded orange peel
Crisp lettuce

Select artichoke hearts canned in olive oil. Drain. Chill. Slice olives coarsely. Drain onions. Combine orange peel and French Dressing. Arrange lettuce leaves on salad plates. Place 3 artichoke hearts on each. Garnish with olive slices and 4 or 5 onions. Add generous spoonful dressing. Makes 4 servings.

Quick-frozen artichoke hearts may be substituted in this recipe. Follow directions on package for cooking. Dress cooked artichoke with a little salad dressing. Chill. Drain and complete recipe as described.

My children love this salad, adore olives and artichokes. Perhaps because no one ever implied they wouldn't!

ASPARAGUS VINAIGRETTE SALAD

Cooked asparagus tips
Vinaigrette Sauce (page 556)
Deviled eggs

Crisp lettuce
Pimiento strips
Bermuda onion rings

Place drained cooked asparagus in shallow dish. Pour Vinaigrette Sauce over. Let chill, covered, 1 hour or longer.

For each serving, arrange 6 or 8 small stalks on individual plates, with deviled egg halves, lettuce, and strip of pimiento for color. Top with onion ring. Serve as salad or as first-course appetizer before barbecue supper.

Additional Vinaigrette Dressing, or mayonnaise, may be served with asparagus.

This is a favorite of mine for spring and summer buffets. My guests are always so amazed and appreciative. I don't know why more people don't serve it. It's so easy to prepare.

AVOCADO SPRING SALAD

1 avocado	6 small radishes
Lemon juice	Lettuce
6 scallions	French Dressing (page 518)

Pare avocado. Dice and sprinkle with lemon juice. Slice washed scallions very thin. Wash radishes. Grate coarsely. Combine avocado, scallions, and radishes lightly, using two forks. Heap on lettuce. Serve with French Dressing. Makes 2 servings.

This is so simple, so good, so Floridian.

AVOCADO LUNCHEON SALAD

2 avocados	½ cup diced cucumber
1 cup diced cooked chicken or crab meat	½ cup mayonnaise
	4 lemon quarters
¾ cup diced celery	Lettuce or water cress

Cut avocados in half lengthwise. Remove seeds. Combine chicken or crab meat, celery, cucumber, and mayonnaise. Mix lightly. Heap in avocado halves. Place on lettuce leaf on salad plate. Garnish with lemon. Makes 4 servings.

Use tuna fish, chopped cooked deveined shrimp or lobster in place of chicken or crab meat in same recipe. Chop 2 or 3 black olives for additional good flavor and color.

Avocado Vegetable Salad: Here's another combination with these delicious fruit-vegetable alligator pears. Combine ⅔ cup diced celery, ⅔ cup diced drained tomato, ¼ cup thinly sliced scallions, ½ cup sliced ripe olives. Moisten with little French Dressing mixed with 1 tablespoon ketchup. Heap into 4 avocado halves. Add dab of mayonnaise or leave plain. Makes 4 servings.

COTTAGE BEAN SALAD

2 cups hot, drained cooked green beans	2 tablespoons ketchup
	1 teaspoon minced peeled onion
¼ cup French Dressing, (page 518)	2 cups cottage cheese
	Crisp lettuce

Toss beans with French Dressing and ketchup. Keep in covered bowl in refrigerator until thoroughly chilled. Just before serving, add onion.

Spoon about ⅓ cup cottage cheese onto each lettuce-covered salad plate, then add spoonful of marinated beans. Makes 6 servings.

Various favorite herbs add interesting flavor to this simple salad: add 1 teaspoon basil or thyme with ketchup, or summer savory—dried or fresh. Or substitute 1 tablespoon finely cut chives for onion.

We use our good home-grown beans in this salad. Beans love our woodsy soil and sometimes grow almost too enthusiastically!

BEET SALAD FOR GARNISHING

Drain chilled canned or cooked whole beets. Slice thin. Combine with same amount of finely cut fresh water cress. Dress lightly with well-seasoned French Dressing. Heap in crisp lettuce leaves. Use as garnish around large salad platter or with cold cuts.

Sometimes I grate a small raw beet and a small sweet onion over romaine, then add French Dressing, when I toss a salad at the table. Delicious flavor, very colorful effect.

BEET AND ENDIVE SALAD

1 (No. 303) can small whole beets	4 heads Belgian endive
½ cup French Dressing (page 518)	Salt and pepper

Drain beets. Slice and pour French Dressing over. Chill in covered bowl in refrigerator until very cold. To serve, wash chilled endive. Cut bunches lengthwise in halves. Place 2 halves on each salad plate. Spoon generous amount of sliced beets across heavy end of stalks. Season lightly with salt. Add quick grind black pepper. Makes 4 or more servings.

To increase number of servings and make small appetizer salads, separate endive leaves. Arrange 4 to 6 slender spears on each salad plate and add few beet slices.

Herbed Beet Salad: Combine drained, sliced cooked or canned beets with thin onion rings. Sprinkle with few grains marjoram or orégano. Add French Dressing made with tarragon vinegar. Let marinate and chill. Drain. Serve on endive spears or lettuce or as garnish around other vegetable salad platters.

CABBAGE SALAD

3 cups finely shredded chilled cabbage	1 tablespoon prepared horse-radish
½ cup diced Cheddar cheese	1 tablespoon prepared mustard
½ cup commercial sour cream	1 teaspoon salt
1 tablespoon vinegar	⅛ teaspoon cayenne

Combine cabbage and cheese, tossing lightly with two forks. Combine remaining ingredients. Mix. Pour over salad. Toss only enough to mix. Serve at once. Makes 4 to 6 servings.

Red-and-White Cabbage Salad: Combine 1½ cups finely shredded chilled red cabbage, 1½ cups finely shredded chilled green cabbage, 1 onion, peeled and diced. Combine ⅔ cup mayonnaise, 1 tablespoon sugar, 3 tablespoons vinegar, 1 teaspoon salt, 1 teaspoon celery seed; stir to dissolve sugar. Pour dressing over cabbage. Toss to mix lightly. Makes 4 to 6 servings.

My Favorite Cabbage Salad: Three cups finely shredded crisp, cold cabbage, ¾ cup finely cut parsley, 2 onions, peeled and grated or diced very fine. Combine vegetables, tossing lightly. Just before serving, combine 3 tablespoons sugar, 1½ teaspoons salt, ¼ cup vinegar, 3 tablespoons salad oil. Shake or stir until sugar is dissolved and dressing is smooth. Pour over vegetables. Makes 6 servings.

Cabbage Salad with Cauliflower: Add about 1 cup sliced raw cauliflower to 2 cups shredded crisp cabbage. Use tarragon vinegar in place of cider vinegar in dressing. Thinly sliced sweet red pepper rings add to color and flavor of this mixture. Makes 4 to 6 servings.

COLESLAW

3 cups cold, shredded cabbage	¾ cup Cooked Salad Dressing (page 515) or mayonnaise or Sour Cream Dressing (page 516)
1 tablespoon minced peeled onion	
¼ cup diced green pepper	Crisp lettuce-leaf cups

Remove wilted leaves from head of cabbage. Let stand head down in pan of cold water half an hour. Drain. Cut in wedges. Slice on slaw cutter or with large sharp knife on cutting board. Mix with onion, green pepper, and dressing. Serve in lettuce-leaf cups. Makes 6 servings.

Red-Cabbage Slaw: Substitute red cabbage for green. Add 1 cup diced celery. Omit green pepper. Substitute ½ cup French dressing for cooked or other dressing.

CAESAR SALAD

1 clove garlic, peeled and mashed	1 teaspoon salt
¾ cup olive oil	Quick grind black pepper
2 cups croutons	1 egg
1 small head lettuce	Juice 1 lemon
1 large bunch water cress	6 fillets anchovies cut in small bits
1 small head romaine	

Combine garlic and oil. Let stand several hours or overnight. Toast croutons or sauté until well browned in a little garlic oil; drain on thick paper towel. Break washed, drained, and chilled lettuce into salad bowl. Add as much water cress as you like. Break romaine into same bowl. Combine garlic oil, salt, and pepper. Scatter over greens. Turn with spoon and fork until all greens are lightly coated. Cook egg in simmering water 1 minute. Break on top of salad. Squeeze lemon juice over egg. Mix into salad, lifting leaves and turning until all are coated. Add anchovy as you mix. Serve at once. Makes 6 or more servings.

There are several California versions of this salad. A simple recipe uses a good French Dressing and Worcestershire, adds croutons and omits anchovies, but tops the finished salad with grated Parmesan cheese. Some add both anchovies and cheese. Some versions include chopped vegetables, such as cucumbers and celery. A New York Caesar salad which I have enjoyed adds 1 cup cottage cheese with the egg and lemon juice, combining all with bowlful of greens.

This is, of course, virtually a meal in itself. Best for lunch or supper alone in its glory.

CHEF'S SALAD

1 quart mixed salad greens, washed, dried, chilled	¼ pound thinly sliced Swiss cheese
1 (12-ounce) can smoked tongue, corned beef, or ham	French Dressing (page 518)

Tear greens into small pieces in chilled salad bowl. Slice meat. Cut in narrow strips. Cut cheese in same size strips. Arrange meat and cheese on top of greens. Add French Dressing, toss, and serve. Makes 3 to 4 servings.

As with the Caesar Salad, many variations on Chef's Salad have developed in different restaurants. Most men prefer this salad made with garlic-flavored French Dressing. Chilled cooked peas, asparagus, or other vegetables are sometimes added. The bowl may be garnished with sliced radishes and deviled eggs. This salad has become a popular one-dish luncheon for businessmen who are watching their waistlines.

Garlic croutons make a good addition to this bowl (I usually have a store of them on hand, kept in covered glass jar). Or I julienne whatever leftover roast may be in the refrigerator—lamb, chicken, ham. Both croutons and meat slivers add flavor and food value to the bowl.

COOKED VEGETABLE SALAD

Use any colorful combination of chilled cooked vegetables, with a French Dressing, and serve on crisp greens. Drained, cooked fresh or quick-frozen asparagus, peas, green beans or wax beans, and cauliflowerettes look good on a salad plate. Make separate mounds of each. Dress lightly with French Dressing. Add mixture of mayonnaise and sour cream to center of plate or serve cottage cheese and any other preferred dressing. Grated raw carrots or turnips add good flavor to the cooked combination. Or garnish with 2 thin young scallions or 2 or 3 slender carrot sticks.

CUCUMBER AND BEAN SALAD

Combine thinly sliced raw cucumbers with drained cooked green beans. Spoon French Dressing over both. Let marinate in refrigerator about 1 hour or longer. Drain. Serve on crisp lettuce. Garnish with finely cut chives or parsley, or both. Add spoonful of mayonnaise.

CUCUMBER AND GREEN PEPPER SALAD

3 large green peppers
2 cucumbers
6 pimiento-stuffed olives
3 tablespoons capers

2 tablespoons finely cut chives
French Dressing
1 head firm lettuce

Wash peppers. Cut off stem end and remove seeds and fibers. Cut in thin rings. Wash cucumbers. Do not pare, but scrape with tines of fork. Slice thinly. Cut olives fine. Combine with capers, chives, and French Dressing. Shake well. Wash lettuce. Discard soft outer leaves. Slice crosswise in 6 pieces. Place lettuce on salad plates. Top with green peppers and cucumbers. Serve dressing with it. Makes 6 servings.

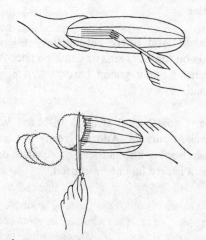

A fork run lengthwise on peeled or unpeeled cucumber neatly scallops slices.

ENDIVE SALAD

Wash and chill Belgian endive. Cut off root end and pull leaves off carefully. Fill center from wide end about ¾ way up the leaf with any of the following mixtures: blended Roquefort and cream cheese. Chive-cottage cheese. Blended Cheddar cheese, chopped walnuts, and Russian Dressing. Pickle relish mixed with cottage cheese and Tartare Sauce. Or finely chopped carrots, onions, and cucumber held together with a little mayonnaise.

For stuffed Romaine Salad use romaine leaves in above recipe.

GREEN SALAD

A green salad may be any combination of greens and vegetables you prefer. Lettuce, romaine, water cress, Chinese cabbage, other greens such as dandelion and specialties of Italian markets which vary from city to city are the favorites. Add quartered, peeled tomatoes, sliced pared avocado, scraped carrots cut in very thin curls or strips. Or keep the salad all green.

One of my favorites is romaine lettuce sprinkled with finely cut water cress, then dressed with tarragon or wine French dressing. So good with chops or roast.

The one essential rule is that all greens used should be crisply cold and dry. They should be broken into or arranged in a chilled bowl just before serving, and dressed at the last moment with whatever kind of dressing you prefer.

Anchovy Green Salad: Add finely cut anchovy fillets to any green salad. Either sprinkle on top of greens or combine anchovy with dressing and pour over greens. Usually grated hard-cooked eggs are added to an anchovy green salad.

Bacon Green Salad: Cook 2 or 3 strips lean bacon very crisp. Drain on thick paper towels. Crumble. Add to greens just as salad is ready for serving. Garnish bowl with quarters of deviled or pickled hard-cooked eggs. Makes a hearty luncheon in itself.

ITALIAN GREEN SALAD

1 head curly endive	8 or 10 small ripe olives
2 or 3 pieces finocchio or fennel	2 tablespoons wine vinegar
1 head escarole	¼ cup olive oil
½ pound dandelion greens	Salt
½ garlic clove	Freshly ground black pepper
2 tomatoes, scalded and peeled	

Look over all greens. Remove wilted or undesirable parts. Wash several times under cold running water. Remove outer leaves of finocchio. Wash thoroughly. Cut in thin slices. Drain greens and finocchio. Wrap in clean towel and place in refrigerator about 20 minutes or longer.

Rub wooden salad bowl with garlic. Discard garlic. Add greens to bowl. Cut tomatoes into quarters and add to bowl with olives. Blend vinegar and oil together. Pour over salad. Add sprinkling of salt and pepper. Toss greens to coat well with dressing. Serve at once. Makes 4 to 6 servings.

Appetizing variations of flavor are possible with an Italian salad by adding various herbs: 1 tablespoon finely cut fresh dill may be added, or a little anise or basil. Thyme is a favorite of some Italian hosts, and added to a green salad, it gives fragrance and flavor. Parsley, orégano, water cress, chervil, chives are other good additions. One famous Italian restaurateur combines 5 or 6 fresh herbs, prepares his salad as usual, adds a few blades of rugola—a delicious, pungent green— in the spring, and after the greens are tossed and mixed with the dressing he adds 2 or 3 tablespoons of the mixed finely cut herbs to the bowl, sprinkling them on lavishly. Subtle fragrance and flavor are the results of this inspiration.

If you decide to gather your own dandelion greens, choose an early spring morning and fare forth, like your Italian neighbors, with a sack or basket, or a generous apron, and a small paring knife. Cut the young leaves close to the root but don't, please, destroy the plant. Only the young spring leaves are good in salad. The old ones are too tough and bitter. Dandelions are now grown commercially and are available at fruit stands and vegetable markets in Italian neighborhoods.

GREEN PEPPER AND ONION SALAD

2 large green peppers
2 large sweet Bermuda onions

Crisp lettuce or romaine
Herbed French Dressing
(page 517)

Wash and chill peppers. When ready to make salad, slice crosswise in thin slices. Remove center core and fiber, leaving large green rings. Cut peeled onions in large thin slices. Separate into rings. Arrange equal amounts of green pepper and onion rings on lettuce or romaine. Dress liberally with Herb Salad Dressing. Makes 4 to 6 servings.

Thin slices boiled potato, marinated in the dressing, then added to this salad, turn it into a heartier dish. Garnish with quartered deviled eggs. Excellent combination of flavors with cold cuts or with baked or browned corned-beef hash.

LEBANESE SALAD

6 small very ripe tomatoes	Quick grind black pepper
12 scallions, sliced	½ cup wine vinegar
1 teaspoon salt	½ cup finely cut fresh mint

Wash, peel, and slice chilled tomatoes into chilled bowl. Add scallions. Sprinkle with salt and pepper. Pour vinegar over. Sprinkle with mint. Makes 3 to 4 servings.

Serve at once, with lamb and pilaff dinner. Delectable. Dieters, note!

If you live near an Armenian or other Near Eastern neighborhood, buy some of their special cracked wheat and scatter a little in your salads. Indescribably good and authentic Near East flavor. If you have no Armenian neighborhood in which to shop, see page 727 for the name and address of a company who will be glad to fill mail orders. Wheat germ is a fair substitute.

POTATO SALAD, CHATEAU STYLE

6 potatoes	3 tablespoons finely cut parsley
1 cup dry white wine	French Dressing (page 518)
10 thin scallions	Mayonnaise

Scrub potatoes. Rinse. Do not pare. Boil until tender. Peel while hot and slice into bowl. Pour wine over at once. Let stand until potatoes are cold. Drain. Chill potatoes. To serve, slice scallions into bowl with potatoes. Add parsley. Add light sprinkling of French dressing made with wine vinegar. Add small amount of mayonnaise and combine lightly. Serve garnished with pimiento, sliced eggs, and spears of Belgian endive. Makes 4 servings.

OLD-FASHIONED POTATO SALAD

6 medium potatoes (about 2½ pounds)	1½ teaspoons salt
Boiling water	⅛ teaspoon pepper
½ cup chopped celery	1 tablespoon poppy seeds
½ cup pared, diced cucumber	¾ cup French Dressing (page 518)
¼ cup chopped peeled onion	¼ cup mayonnaise
	Paprika

Scrub potatoes. Rinse. Pare and cut into halves. Place in saucepan. Cover with boiling, salted water. Cover pan. Cook 20 minutes or until potatoes are tender when pierced with fork. Drain. Shake pan over low heat a few minutes to dry the potatoes. Cut into small cubes. Combine with vegetables and seasoning, tossing to mix well. Combine French Dressing and mayonnaise. Pour over salad. Toss just enough to coat potatoes with dressing. Chill in covered bowl in refrigerator. Sprinkle with paprika before serving. Makes 4 to 6 servings.

POTATO AND SARDINE SALAD

2	(3 ¼-ounce) cans boneless, skinless sardines	3	hard-cooked eggs
½	cup sour cream	4	or 5 cups cubed, cold boiled potatoes
1	teaspoon prepared mustard	½	cup sliced celery
1 ½	teaspoons salt	¼	cup sliced, peeled onion
¼	teaspoon pepper	¼	cup French Dressing (page 518)

Mash sardines from 1 can. Combine with sour cream and seasonings. Chop 2 eggs. Combine with potatoes, celery, and onion. Spoon French Dressing over potato mixture. Pour sardine mixture over. Combine lightly, using two forks. Chill 1 or 2 hours or longer. Garnish with remaining hard-cooked egg, cut in thin slices, and sardines from remaining can. Makes 6 servings.

Danish and Swedish Potato Salad: For those good salads seen on the smörgåsbord tables in Scandinavian restaurants, add a few chopped, cooked beets to the Potato and Sardine Salad. The proportion should be ¼ as much diced beets as potatoes. If you prefer, use finely cut anchovy fillets in place of sardines. Both make delicious but hearty salads.

HOT POTATO SALAD

6 medium potatoes (about 2½ pounds)	1⅛ cups cider vinegar
	1½ tablespoons sugar
12 slices lean bacon	1½ teaspoons salt
1½ cups chopped peeled onions	¼ teaspoon pepper

Scrub potatoes. Rinse. Pare and cut in halves. Place in saucepan. Cover with boiling salted water. Cover pan. Cook 20 minutes or until potatoes are tender when pierced with fork. Drain. Shake pan over low heat few minutes to dry potatoes. Cut potatoes in ¼-inch slices.

Dice and pan-broil bacon until crisp. Drain bacon on thick paper towels. Return 6 tablespoons of drippings to skillet. Add onions and cook, stirring frequently, until transparent. Stir in vinegar, sugar, salt, and pepper. Heat to boiling point. Add bacon and stir. Pour over potatoes. Toss lightly to distribute bacon. Serve immediately. Makes 4 to 6 servings.

This is a favorite German dish, good with all the pork family, with cold roast beef, with hot or cold sliced beef tongue.

STUFFED TOMATO SALADS

4 large ripe tomatoes	2 tablespoons finely cut parsley
Salt and pepper	2 tablespoons lemon juice
½ cup diced cucumber	1½ teaspoons finely cut fresh dill
1½ cups flaked tuna fish	
3 tablespoons finely sliced scallions	¾ cup mayonnaise
	Crisp lettuce leaves

Scald tomatoes. Peel. Chill. Cut tops from tomatoes. Scoop out center deeply. Invert tomatoes to drain. Season centers with salt and pepper. Combine remaining ingredients lightly. Heap into tomatoes. Serve each on lettuce leaf. Makes 4 servings.

Substitute diced cooked chicken for tuna. Omit dill.

Substitute flaked crab meat, sliced cooked and cleaned shrimp, or cubed cooked lobster for tuna.

Substitute all vegetables for tuna, such as mixed cooked and chilled peas, carrots, cut string beans, and baby limas, and substitute 1 teaspoon dried marjoram or basil for dill.

Stuff seasoned tomatoes with chive-cottage cheese or combination of Danish bleu cheese creamed with cottage cheese.

TOMATO AND ASPARAGUS SALAD

4 ripe tomatoes
Crisp lettuce
16 stalks cooked asparagus,
drained and chilled

French Dressing (page 518)
Mayonnaise
2 hard-cooked eggs

Scald tomatoes. Peel. Chill. To serve, arrange lettuce on salad plates. Cut stem end out of tomatoes. Cut each tomato down in quarters but do not cut through to bottom. Spread quarters out. Lay stalk of asparagus between each 2 quarters. Spoon a little French Dressing over all. Add dab of mayonnaise to center of tomato. Sieve a little hard-cooked egg over each plate. Makes 4 servings.

Tomato and Broccoli Salad: Substitute cooked, drained, and chilled broccoli for asparagus in above recipe. Especially good with this combination is French Dressing containing a little curry powder.

Tomato and Cauliflower Salad: Substitute cooked, drained, and chilled flowerettes of cauliflower for asparagus. Garnish with finely cut green pepper.

Tomato and Orange Salad: Substitute thin slices or seeded sections of oranges for asparagus. Garnish with thin rings of sweet onion. Add capers to the French Dressing. Or serve with Anchovy French Dressing (page 518).

VEGETABLE COMBINATION SALAD

1 green pepper
1 red apple
Juice 1 lemon
1 slice boiled or baked ham
2 hard-cooked eggs
2 cold boiled potatoes

2 cooked beets
8 stuffed olives
1 celery heart
Head of curly chicory or romaine
Mayonnaise (page 520)

Cut green pepper in very narrow strips. Core apple. Do not pare. Cut in strips. Cover with lemon juice to prevent darkening. Cut ham in strips. Dice eggs, potatoes, and beets. Slice olives and celery. Combine all with broken chicory or romaine. Add just enough mayonnaise to coat lightly. Toss to mix. Makes 4 servings.

Substitute diced raw turnip for celery for another flavorful vegetable combination.

WATER-CRESS SALAD

Wash cress carefully. Drain. Roll in towel to chill and dry off. Cut leaves from large stems. Discard stems. Sprinkle leaves with lemon juice, salt, pepper. Add a little French Dressing. Toss lightly to coat leaves. Serve at once.

This is one of the most fragrant and best-flavored green salads to accompany roast beef or pork. Delicious with game.

WILTED LETTUCE SALAD

1 head country lettuce or enough leaves to serve 6	2 tablespoons French Dressing (page 518)
¼ cup light cream	2 strips lean bacon

Wash lettuce. Break large pieces. Drain. Combine cream and French dressing. Stir to mix smoothly. Cut bacon in small pieces. Fry until crisp. Pour cream dressing over lettuce. Mix lightly. Pour hot bacon and fat over all. Mix lightly with two forks. Serve at once. Makes 6 servings.

The old-fashioned version of this country salad is made without the cream and French Dressing. Cook bacon. Stir ¼ cup vinegar into skillet. Mix bacon, fat, and vinegar to boiling point. Pour over lettuce. Toss with forks and serve.

This is the *only* way we ever had salad in my Swiss school—*laitue fatigué*.

Chicken, Turkey, and Meat Salads

90° CHICKEN SALAD

5 cups diced cooked chicken	1 teaspoon salt
1 small onion, peeled and grated	¼ teaspoon pepper
1 cup diced cucumbers	1 teaspoon curry powder
1 cup finely cut green peppers	2 tablespoons vinegar
¼ cup light cream	Salad greens
⅔ cup mayonnaise	Blanched whole almonds

Combine chicken, onion, cucumbers, and peppers. Combine cream, mayonnaise, seasonings, and vinegar. Pour over chicken mixture. Mix lightly. Chill in covered bowl in refrigerator. To serve, arrange lettuce or other greens in chilled salad bowl or on chilled plates. Heap salad in bowl or on plates. Garnish with few almonds. Makes 6 to 8 salads.

Curry powder may be omitted. Substitute drained capers for almonds.

90° Turkey Salad: Substitute bite-size pieces of turkey for chicken in recipe above. With turkey, less onion may be used or entirely omitted.

These salads take care of the meal on those hot nights when 90° is the topic of conversation. We have them in Weston too, occasionally.

CHICKEN AND ASPARAGUS SALAD

1 ½ cups diced cooked chicken
1 small onion, peeled and diced
1 cup finely cut water cress
¼ cup finely cut green pepper
1 canned pimiento, drained and finely cut

½ cup mayonnaise
½ teaspoon salt
¼ teaspoon pepper
1 (No. 300) can California white asparagus drained
French Dressing (page 518)
Crisp lettuce or romaine

Combine chicken, onion, cress, green pepper, pimiento, mayonnaise, and seasoning. Toss lightly. Chill in covered bowl in refrigerator. Drain asparagus. Spoon French Dressing over asparagus. Chill in refrigerator. To serve, spoon salad mixture onto lettuce or romaine leaves. Arrange drained asparagus tips as garnish. Makes 4 to 6 servings.

NIGHT-OFF MEAT SALAD

1 cup slivered cooked ham
1 cup slivered cooked chicken
1 cup shredded Cheddar cheese
3 cups broken mixed greens

⅓ cup mayonnaise
2 tablespoons French Dressing (page 518)
⅓ cup crumbled bleu cheese
Crisp lettuce

Combine all ingredients. Toss lightly. Increase amount of dressing if needed. Serve on crisp lettuce. Makes 6 servings.

A few diced cooked potatoes added to this bowl extends number of servings. Add a little more mayonnaise. Season potatoes lightly with salt before adding.

Read a book in the afternoon or go to a movie. Or visit a neighbor, take a long walk, or give yourself a permanent. This dish will take care of a spring, summer, or early fall evening meal. No apologies.

CORNED-BEEF SALAD

4 medium potatoes, boiled, drained, and chilled	2 tablespoons lemon juice
1 (12-ounce) can corned beef	2 teaspoons prepared mustard
4 dill pickles, diced and drained	1 tablespoon Worcestershire sauce
½ cup diced celery	1 teaspoon salt
1 small onion, peeled and diced	Crisp lettuce, endive, or water cress
1 cup French Dressing (page 518)	

Cut potatoes and corned beef into small cubes. Add pickles, celery, onion. Toss lightly with two forks. Combine French Dressing with lemon juice, mustard, Worcestershire, and salt if needed. Pour over meat mixture. Mix lightly. Chill in covered bowl 1 hour or longer. Serve on crisp greens. Makes 4 to 6 servings.

Ham Salad: Substitute boiled or baked ham for corned beef in above recipe. Omit salt from French Dressing.

Roast Beef Salad: Substitute diced well-done roast or boiled beef for corned beef in recipe above. Increase mustard in dressing to 1 tablespoon prepared mustard.

Other meats, such as leftover roast lamb, pork, veal, game meats and game birds, are substituted in this recipe for a hearty, filling salad.

Especially good with beer and toasted buns.

Fish and Shellfish Salads

CRAB-MEAT SALAD

1½ pounds cooked or canned crab meat	Crisp lettuce
6 cooked artichoke hearts	2 hard-cooked eggs
French Dressing (page 518)	Mayonnaise (page 520)
3 ripe tomatoes	Drained capers

Look over crab meat. Remove all fibers and bones. Leave meat in large bite-size pieces. Chill. Cook quick-frozen artichoke hearts as described on package. Drain. Moisten lightly with French Dressing. Chill. Scald tomatoes. Peel. Cut in quarters. To serve, heap crab meat in lettuce leaf. Garnish with 2 tomato quarters and 1 halved artichoke heart. Add slice of egg. Top with favorite dressing or mayonnaise. Add a few capers. Makes 6 servings.

Lobster Salad: Substitute cooked lobster meat for crab meat in the recipe above. Garnishes may be omitted, except capers, which always add good flavor to sea-food salad.

Shrimp Salad: Combine cooked, cleaned, and chilled shrimp with enough mayonnaise to moisten. Chill again. Serve heaped in lettuce leaf. Decorate with sliced stuffed olives or capers. Or combine ⅓ as much sliced celery with shrimp. Add mayonnaise to coat. Serve in lettuce leaf or heaped in hollowed-out seasoned tomato.

Those words "favorite dressing" mean any savory salad dressing which you have tried out on sea food. Try combining ½ cup chili sauce with 1 cup mayonnaise. Add 2 teaspoons curry powder. Mix. Chill. Use as described in recipes above.

CRAB-MEAT PEPPER SALAD

1 cup crab meat, flaked and cleaned	3 tablespoons lemon juice
	⅓ cup mayonnaise
½ cup sliced celery	8 green peppers
¼ cup finely diced green pepper	French Dressing (page 518)
¼ teaspoon salt	Mayonnaise (page 520)
⅛ teaspoon pepper	1 canned pimiento, drained

Combine crab meat, celery, green pepper, and seasoning. Add lemon juice and mayonnaise. Mix lightly. Chill in covered bowl in refrigerator.

Cut tops from green peppers. Remove seeds and fibers. Boil or steam 10 minutes. Drain. Chill. To serve, moisten inside of cooked peppers with French Dressing. Fill with crab-meat mixture. Add dab of mayonnaise to top. Cut pimiento into small stars or circles. Add piece as garnish to top of each pepper. Makes 8 servings.

Lobster Pepper Salad. Shrimp Pepper Salad: Substitute cooked lobster meat or cleaned, cooked shrimp for crab meat in above recipe.

SAN ANTONIO ARGYLE CLUB SALAD

I was served a delicious salad bowl at the San Antonio, Texas, Argyle Club. It consisted of a ring of chopped hard-cooked eggs around whole shrimp, on a base of Julienne ham, Swiss cheese, chicken, and lobster, all on shredded lettuce. Russian Dressing topped the savory combination.

The shrimp were cooked, deveined, and icy cold. The ham, cheese, and chicken julienned, and the lobster in bite-size pieces.

Another salad trick at this club is serving thinly sliced raw summer squash as garnish on vegetable salads.

SHRIMP SALAD IN AVOCADO, MIAMI STYLE

1 cup cooked, cleaned small shrimp	3 tablespoons mayonnaise
	Salt and pepper
½ cup sliced celery	2 avocados
¼ cup diced cucumber	Crisp greens
2 tablespoons sliced scallions	1 lemon, cut in quarters
1 tablespoon lemon juice	

If shrimp are very small, leave whole. Combine with vegetables. Sprinkle with lemon juice. Add mayonnaise. Toss to mix lightly. Add salt and pepper if needed. Chill in covered bowl in refrigerator.

To serve, pare avocados. Cut in halves lengthwise. Remove seed. Place avocado halves on lettuce or other greens. Fill with shrimp salad. Serve with lemon quarter. Makes 4 salads.

Crab-Meat Salad in Avocado and Lobster Salad in Avocado: Substitute cleaned cooked crab meat or lobster for shrimp in above recipe. Omit scallions with crab and lobster.

TUNA AND COTTAGE CHEESE SALAD

1 (7¾-ounce) can chunk-style tuna	½ cup grated raw carrot
	2 tablespoons finely cut chives
2 cups cottage cheese	6 stuffed olives, sliced
1 teaspoon salt	French Dressing or mayonnaise
1 tablespoon lemon juice	Cabbage leaves or salad greens

Drain tuna. Flake. Combine with cheese, seasoning, carrot, chives, and olives. Add small amount French Dressing or mayonnaise if desired. Chill thoroughly. Heap into cabbage or lettuce leaf. Makes 6 servings.

SARDINE SALAD FOR FRIDAY

For each salad place 3 slices peeled ripe tomato on crisp lettuce leaf. Top each with 2 onion rings. Arrange 2 drained boneless and skinless sardines on top. Garnish with olives. Serve with French Dressing.

Gelatin Salads—Chicken and Sea Food

Any gelatin salad can be prepared the day before.

CHICKEN MOUSSE SALAD

8 egg yolks	⅓ cup ground green pepper
4 cups milk	⅓ cup finely cut drained pimiento
5 envelopes unflavored gelatin	½ cup chopped blanched almonds
3 cups chicken consommé or stock	2 cups heavy cream, whipped
5 cups ground cooked chicken	Green pepper and pimiento for mold

Beat yolks in upper part of large double boiler set over hot water. Stir milk into yolks, beating steadily. Cook over hot water until mixture coats metal spoon. Remove from hot water.

Soften gelatin in consommé or stock. Dissolve over hot water. Combine egg mixture with gelatin mixture in large saucepan. Add chicken, pepper, pimiento, and almonds. Heat to just below boiling point but do not boil. Stir from bottom of pan to mix evenly. Let cool. When cold, fold in whipped cream. Pour into oiled 3-quart mold, decorated with strips of green pepper and pimiento. Chill until set. Makes 12 to 15 servings.

Can be chilled in shallow pans, then cut in strips or squares for serving.

Turkey Mousse Salad: Substitute ground cooked turkey for chicken in above recipe.

Sea-Food Mousse Salads: Substitute ground cooked fish, such as tuna or any whitefish, or cooked and cleaned shrimp, flaked and cleaned crab meat or lobster. For any sea-food mousse, add a few ground cooked oysters for flavor.

CRAB-MEAT MOLD

1 teaspoon unflavored gelatin
¼ cup cold water
½ cup mayonnaise
2 cups cleaned cooked crab
   meat
1 cup thinly sliced celery
1 tablespoon finely cut parsley

1 tablespoon finely cut chives
½ teaspoon finely cut tarragon
Crisp greens
4 deviled eggs
8 small, cleaned, cooked shrimp
   dipped in Russian Dressing

Soften gelatin in water 5 minutes. Set saucepan over hot water and let gelatin dissolve. Let cool. Combine with mayonnaise.

Combine crab meat, celery, parsley, chives, and tarragon. Mix with gelatin-mayonnaise. Pour into an oiled 1-quart mold. Chill several hours. To serve, unmold on crisp greens. Garnish with quartered deviled eggs and small shrimp dipped in Russian Dressing. Makes 6 servings.

Sea-Food Molds: Other cooked sea food may be substituted for crab in the above recipe. Especially good made with lobster. If shrimp are used, grind the deveined cooked shrimp. Add 1 or 2 cooked oysters when grinding.

See also Sea-Food Mousse Salads (page 507).

SALMON SALAD MOLD

1 envelope unflavored gelatin
½ cup cold water
½ cup boiling water
2 tablespoons lemon juice
1 (7¾-ounce) can best salmon
¾ cup thinly sliced celery
¼ teaspoon celery salt

2 tablespoons finely chopped
   dill pickle
2 tablespoons finely cut chives
1 teaspoon salt
¼ teaspoon pepper
2 cups cottage cheese
Salad greens

Soften gelatin in cold water about 5 minutes. Add boiling water and stir to dissolve gelatin. Add lemon juice. Drain salmon. Remove skin, any bones. Flake lightly. Combine salmon, celery, celery salt, pickle, chives, salt, pepper, and cottage cheese. Mix lightly but evenly. Pour into oiled 1½-quart mold. Chill several hours or until firm. Serve on salad greens. Makes 6 or more servings.

May be chilled in loaf or square pan and cut in squares or strips.

JELLIED TUNA LOAF

2 envelopes unflavored gelatin
½ cup cold water
1 (10½-ounce) can condensed cream-of-celery soup
¼ cup lemon juice
1 tablespoon prepared mustard
1 teaspoon salt
¼ teaspoon pepper
1 cup mayonnaise
2 (6½- or 7-ounce) cans tuna
1 cup thinly-sliced celery
½ cup grated cucumber
¼ cup finely cut green pepper
Salad greens

Soften gelatin in cold water. Heat soup just to boiling point. Stir in gelatin until dissolved. Stir in lemon juice, mustard, salt, and pepper. Let cool. Chill until partially set. Blend in mayonnaise. Drain tuna. Flake. Fold into mayonnaise mixture with celery, cucumber, and green pepper. Pour into oiled loaf pan, 8½ by 4½ by 2½ inches. Chill several hours or until firm. Unmold on chilled platter with salad greens. Makes 8 servings.

My children will eat tuna in any form, but this tempts their appetites on hot nights, especially with baking-powder biscuits.

Gelatin Salads—Fruit

AVOCADO MOUSSE SALAD, SAN FRANCISCO STYLE

1 cup hot water
1 (3-ounce) package lime-flavored gelatin
2 small avocados
1 (3-ounce) package cream cheese
2 tablespoons mayonnaise
2 tablespoons lemon juice
1 teaspoon salt
¾ cup diced grapefruit sections, drained
Whole grapefruit sections
Water cress

Add hot water to gelatin. Stir until dissolved. Let chill until consistency of unbeaten egg white. Pare avocados. Remove seeds. Mash enough avocado to make ⅔ cup. Slice remainder. Beat mashed avocado, cheese, mayonnaise, lemon juice, and salt together with rotary beater until creamy. Add thickened gelatin mixture. Beat until blended. Fold sliced avocado and diced grapefruit sections into mixture. Pour into 1-quart mold. Chill until firm. Unmold on chilled salad platter. Garnish with grapefruit sections. Makes 6 servings.

CRANBERRY RELISH MOLD

1 tablespoon unflavored gelatin	2 cups ground raw cranberries
¼ cup cold water	1 tablespoon grated orange peel
1½ cups hot water	¼ cup orange juice
½ cup sugar	

Soften gelatin in cold water about 5 minutes. Stir into hot water until dissolved. Add remaining ingredients. Pour into 8 individual molds or into 1-quart mold. Chill until firm. Makes 8 servings.

Serve as garnish for roast turkey or as garnish on salad platter. Or serve on water cress with mayonnaise or Sour Cream Dressing (page 516).

GRAPEFRUIT GELATIN RING

2 tablespoons unflavored gelatin	¼ cup sugar
3½ cups canned or fresh grape-fruit juice	3 cups drained grapefruit sections
¼ teaspoon salt	¼ cup sliced olives

Sprinkle gelatin in 1 cup cold grapefruit juice in upper part of an enamel or glass double boiler. Place over boiling water. Stir until dissolved. Add salt, sugar, and remaining juice.

Place several whole grapefruit sections and olive slices in a design in bottom of 5-cup ring mold. Cover with small amount of the gelatin mixture. Chill until almost firm. Chill remaining gelatin until consistency of unbeaten egg white. Fold half of remaining grapefruit sections into the gelatin with remaining olive slices. Spoon into mold on top of gelatin. Chill until firm. Makes 8 to 12 servings.

Lime Gelatin: Follow above recipe. Use 2½ cups canned or fresh grapefruit juice and 1 cup fresh lime juice. Increase sugar to 6 tablespoons.

This is one of the most adaptable and useful of salad rings. Filled with sea-food salad, it makes an inviting, appetite-stimulating picture.

In place of olives, add sliced candied mint cherries *for a sweeter salad ring*. Perfect for a Waldorf salad or other fruit combination. Or fill center of ring with cottage cheese mixed with chopped fruits and nuts. Garnish platter with cold, crisp lettuce. Water cress is a happy addition.

AVOCADO RING SALAD

2 tablespoons unflavored
  gelatin
½ cup cold water
1 ¼ cups hot water
6 tablespoons lemon juice
1 ½ teaspoons grated onion

2 ¼ teaspoons salt
⅛ teaspoon Tabasco sauce
3 cups sieved avocados
¾ cup mayonnaise
Salad greens
Avocado slices

Soften gelatin in cold water. Dissolve in hot water. Add lemon juice, onion, salt, and Tabasco. Stir into sieved avocado and mayonnaise. Mix evenly. Pour into 8-inch ring mold. Chill until firm. Unmold on greens. Fill center with chicken or sea-food salad. Garnish with sliced avocado. Makes 10 or more servings.

Equally good filled with fresh fruit salad, especially grapefruit sections and green pepper strips.

Gelatin Salads—Meat, Eggs, Vegetable

BEEF-TONGUE MOUSSE

1 tablespoon unflavored
  gelatin
¼ cup cold water
1 ¼ cups boiling beef stock or
  bouillon
½ cup heavy cream
1 teaspoon dry mustard
1 teaspoon salt
¼ teaspoon pepper

2 tablespoons grated onion
2 tablespoons finely cut green
  pepper
2 tablespoons finely cut parsley
2 tablespoons lemon juice
2 cups chopped cooked or
  canned tongue
Greens and sliced tomatoes for
  garnishing

Soak gelatin in cold water 5 minutes. Add to boiling beef stock or bouillon. Stir until dissolved. Let cool in refrigerator until partially set.

Whip cream stiff. Combine with mustard, salt, pepper, vegetables, lemon juice, and tongue. Beat into slightly thickened gelatin. Pour into loaf pan 9 by 5 by 3 inches. Chill until firm, 2 or 3 hours. Unmold on chilled platter. Garnish with crisp salad greens and sliced tomatoes. If desired, serve with Mustard Mayonnaise (page 520). Makes 8 servings.

DEVILED EGGS IN ASPIC

2 Deviled Eggs (page 289)	½ teaspoon paprika
1 tablespoon unflavored gelatin	¼ teaspoon celery salt
1 ½ cups chicken consommé	Crisp romaine or chicory
2 tablespoons vinegar	
½ teaspoon salt	

Prepare deviled eggs. Soak gelatin in ¼ cup cold consommé. Heat another ¼ cup consommé. When boiling, stir in softened gelatin until dissolved. Add to remaining 1 cup cold consommé combined with vinegar, salt, paprika, and celery salt. Pour aspic mixture into small mold. Let chill until almost set. Arrange egg halves, yolk side down, at even intervals around mold. Chill until firm. Turn out on romaine or chicory. Makes 2 servings.

Sliced ripe olives, sliced celery or radishes, or thin slices of pickle may be added with eggs for a more colorful aspic. Mayonnaise or French Dressing is served with this aspic salad.

HAM MOUSSE

1 tablespoon unflavored gelatin	¼ cup finely diced green pepper
¼ cup cold water	2 tablespoons finely cut
2 egg yolks, slightly beaten	pimiento, drained
½ teaspoon salt	½ teaspoon paprika
1 teaspoon dry mustard	2 cups ground cooked ham
1 cup chicken consommé or	½ cup heavy cream, whipped
bouillon	Green pepper rings
1 cup milk	Small celery hearts
1 tablespoon grated onion	
1 teaspoon prepared horse-radish	

Soften gelatin in water. Combine egg yolks, salt, and mustard in top part of double boiler. Stir in consommé and milk. Cook, stirring over boiling water 5 to 6 minutes, until slightly thickened. Remove from hot water. Add gelatin. Stir until dissolved. Fold in onion, horse-radish, green pepper, pimiento, paprika, and ham. Chill until mixture begins to thicken. Fold in cream. Pour into 1½-quart mold. Chill overnight or until firm. Unmold on chilled salad platter. Garnish with green pepper rings, small celery hearts, and, if you like, lettuce-leaf cups containing pickle relish. Makes 6 servings.

Ham-Mousse Ring: Pour mixture into lightly oiled ring mold. Chill until firm. Unmold onto chilled salad platter. Fill center with potato salad or mixed vegetable salad.

This is very good for a wedding reception buffet (growing in popularity). Make the recipe twice, or more times as required. Pretty and hearty.

TWO-LAYER HAM ASPIC

1 tablespoon unflavored gelatin	1 (4½-ounce) can deviled ham
½ cup cold water	1 teaspoon diced onion
¼ teaspoon salt	¼ cup finely cut sweet pickle
2 tablespoons lemon juice	1½ cups finely shredded cabbage
¾ cup mayonnaise	

Stir gelatin into water. Let soften 5 minutes. Place over boiling water and stir until gelatin dissolves. Add salt and lemon juice. Let cool.

Gradually stir in mayonnaise, then mix in remaining ingredients. Turn into lightly oiled 1½-quart mold. Chill in refrigerator until almost firm. Make second layer while first one chills.

Second Layer

1¾ cups tomato juice	⅛ teaspoon Tabasco
1 tablespoon unflavored gelatin	1 tablespoon lemon juice
¼ teaspoon salt	

Pour ½ cup tomato juice into upper part of small glass or enamel double boiler. Stir gelatin into juice. Let soften 5 minutes. Set over hot water. Stir until gelatin dissolves. Stir in remaining ingredients. Mix well. Let cool. Chill in refrigerator until almost stiff.

The first layer should be almost firm by this time. Pour slightly stiffened tomato mixture over it. Chill until whole aspic is firm. Unmold on salad greens. Makes 8 servings.

TOMATO ASPIC RING

1 quart tomato juice	2 tablespoons unflavored gela-
⅓ cup finely diced peeled onion	tin
¼ cup finely cut celery leaves	¼ cup cold water
2 tablespoons brown sugar	3 tablespoons lemon juice
1 teaspoon salt	1 cup thinly sliced celery
2 small bay leaves	Crisp greens
4 whole cloves	

Combine tomato juice, onion, celery leaves, sugar, salt, bay leaves, and cloves in enamel or glass saucepan. Simmer 5 minutes. Strain. Soften gelatin in cold water. Stir into hot tomato mixture. Add lemon juice. Chill until partially set. Add celery. Pour into lightly oiled 1½-quart ring mold. Chill until firm. Unmold on salad greens. Fill center with cold mayonnaise or Russian Dressing or with sliced avocado and mayonnaise. Makes 8 or more servings.

There is no more popular jellied salad than this one made with tomato juice. It may be chilled in a shallow pan and cut in squares to be added to a salad platter, or chilled in a loaf pan and sliced to be served on greens with mayonnaise, or chilled in 6 or 8 small individual molds.

VEGETABLE GELATIN SALAD

2 tablespoons unflavored gelatin	1½ cups finely shredded cabbage
½ cup cold water	1 cup shredded scraped carrots
2 cups hot water	
½ cup sugar	¼ cup shredded drained pimiento
1 teaspoon salt	
½ cup vinegar	½ cup finely cut green pepper
2 tablespoons lemon juice	Salad greens

Soften gelatin in cold water. Dissolve in hot water. Add sugar and salt. Stir until dissolved. Add vinegar and lemon juice. Let cool. When mixture begins to thicken, add remaining ingredients. Except salad greens. Pour into lightly oiled loaf pan, ring mold, or 6 or 8 individual molds. Chill until firm. Unmold on salad greens. Serve with mayonnaise. Makes 6 to 8 servings.

Salad Dressings—Cooked and Cream

These can be prepared in advance.

BOILED DRESSING

1 cup vinegar
4 tablespoons sugar
1 tablespoon flour
½ tablespoon dry mustard
1 teaspoon salt

½ teaspoon black pepper (coarsely ground)
4 egg yolks
1 tablespoon butter or margarine

Heat vinegar. Sift dry ingredients, add to slightly beaten egg yolks and beat well. Pour boiling vinegar over mixture, stirring.

Cook in upper part of double boiler over hot water until mixture thickens, stirring continuously. Add butter or margarine and remove from fire. Cool slightly. Refrigerate. Beaten egg whites or whipped cream may be folded in before serving. Makes about 2 cups of dressing.

CURRANT-CREAM SALAD DRESSING

1 (3-ounce) package soft cream cheese
3 tablespoons currant jelly

2 teaspoons lemon juice
⅓ cup heavy cream, whipped

Blend all ingredients, beating lightly until well combined. Makes about 1 cup dressing.

Just right for certain fruit combinations, such as chilled canned pears combined with black cherries. Also good on salad of mixed fruits, such as apple, banana, fresh pineapple, and white grapes.

DUTCH CREAM DRESSING

⅔ cup mayonnaise
3 tablespoons commercial sour cream

1 teaspoon caraway seeds
¼ cup very thin slivers sharp American cheese

Combine all ingredients. Makes a little more than 1 cup dressing. Delicious on crisp, cold vegetable salad. A surprise dressing for vegetable-stuffed tomato salad or on meat salad in parboiled green pepper shell.

GINGER-CREAM DRESSING

1 cup commercial sour cream
1 teaspoon lemon juice
½ teaspoon salt

¼ to ½ teaspoon powdered
ginger

Combine all ingredients. Makes about 1 cup.

A favorite for melon-ball-and-fruit salads, especially when fresh pineapple is present.

JOANNE'S COLESLAW DRESSING

½ cup commercial sour cream
1 tablespoon vinegar
½ tablespoon lemon juice

½ teaspoon sugar
3 tablespoons finely cut chives
or 1 tablespoon celery seeds

Combine all ingredients. Mix well. Pour over chilled, finely shaved cabbage. Toss to mix. Makes about ¾ cup dressing.

I like this dressing very much. A fine combination of flavors with the cabbage.

SOUR CREAM DRESSING

½ cup commercial sour cream
½ cup mayonnaise or tartare
sauce
1 ½ teaspoons salt

¼ teaspoon white pepper
2 teaspoons prepared mustard
1 tablespoon minced parsley
1 teaspoon poppy seeds

Combine all ingredients in bowl. Stir to mix evenly. Makes about 1⅛ cups. Easily doubled for large salads.

CHIVE-SOUR CREAM DRESSING

1 cup commercial sour cream
½ cup mayonnaise
¼ cup finely cut chives

2 tablespoons tarragon vinegar
½ teaspoon salt
¼ teaspoon white pepper

Mix all ingredients together. Makes about 1¾ cups dressing.

Serve as dip for cucumbers or as dressing to go with tomato and scallion salad and other garden salads.

YOGURT SALAD DRESSING

For calorie-counters

¼ cup diced peeled onion	1 teaspoon salt
½ clove garlic, peeled	2 teaspoons sugar
¼ cup celery leaves	1 tablespoon tomato paste
¼ cup finely cut parsley	1 (8-ounce) container yogurt

Combine all ingredients in glass container of mixer or blender. Cover and blend about 1 minute or until smooth. Makes about 1⅓ cups. Serve over crisp, cold salad greens and on raw or cooked vegetables.

Omit garlic and tomato paste when dressing is served on fruit.

Various French Dressings

HERBED FRENCH DRESSING

½ cup olive oil	1 tablespoon finely minced
3 tablespoons cider vinegar	onion
1 tablespoon lemon juice	¼ teaspoon tarragon
¼ teaspoon orégano	½ teaspoon tomato paste
¼ teaspoon basil	

Combine all ingredients in bottle and shake well. Or beat with spoon in bowl. Makes about ¾ cup dressing.

HERB-WINE DRESSING

¼ cup finely cut chives	Quick grind black pepper
¼ cup finely cut parsley	Olive oil
½ cup dry white wine	Juice ½ lemon
½ teaspoon salt	

Combine chives and parsley. Pour wine over. Let stand about 1 hour. Add salt, pepper, and stir in about ½ cup oil slowly. Taste when ¼ cup oil has been added. Dressing may be right for salad you have planned. Add lemon juice if needed. Makes from 1¼ to 1½ cups dressing. Add to mixed greens. Toss to coat all greens. Add additional lemon juice if needed.

If fresh sweet basil is available, add about 1 teaspoon, finely chopped, when oil is combined with herb mixture.

FRENCH DRESSING

1 cup salad oil	1 teaspoon dry mustard
¼ cup vinegar	½ teaspoon paprika
1 teaspoon salt	½ teaspoon sugar

Combine all ingredients in bottle. Shake vigorously. Or blend 30 seconds in mixer or blender. Makes about 1¼ cups.

This is a controversial dressing: some cooks insist that onion must be added to basic French Dressing either as grated onion or finely cut chives or as onion salt. Others increase amount of sugar to 1 teaspoon or even more. My favorite mixture includes 2 teaspoons Worcestershire sauce, 2 teaspoons sugar or honey, and I use wine vinegar in place of cider or white vinegar. Or, I use lemon juice in place of vinegar, making *Lemon French Dressing*.

Experiment until you find the mixture which is right for your salads. I often add green onion. Add garlic salt or a piece of garlic if you like. But this makes a Garlic French Dressing. See also recipes below for Garlic Salad Dressing and Country Garlic Dressing.

Anchovy French Dressing: Use basic recipe given above. Substitute lemon juice for vinegar. Add 4 to 6 anchovy fillets cut very fine. Makes about 1¼ cups.

Dill French Dressing: Marinate 1 or 2 teaspoons fresh dill in French Dressing several hours. Strain dressing before using.

Mint French Dressing: Add 2 tablespoons finely cut fresh mint leaves to 1 cup French Dressing. Let stand about 1 hour. Especially good on fruit salad or mixtures of lettuce, escarole, and water cress.

GARLIC SALAD DRESSING

½ teaspoon dry mustard	Grated peel and juice 2 lemons
½ teaspoon pepper	2 cloves garlic, peeled and
⅔ cup olive oil	mashed

Combine all ingredients in jar. Shake well. Let stand at least 1 hour. Remove garlic and discard it. Makes about 1 cup.

Country Garlic Dressing: Combine 1 teaspoon salt, ½ teaspoon pepper, ½ teaspoon celery salt, ¼ teaspoon cayenne, ¼ teaspoon dry mustard. Mix with 2 tablespoons cider vinegar, 2 tablespoons tomato juice, and ⅛ teaspoon Tabasco sauce. Combine with 1 cup salad oil. Add 1 clove garlic, peeled and mashed. Shake in covered jar. Let stand 1 hour or longer before using. Discard garlic. Makes about 1¼ cups dressing.

WATCH-HILL SALAD DRESSING

½ teaspoon salt
¼ teaspoon sugar
½ teaspoon dry mustard
3 tablespoons tarragon vinegar
1 teaspoon grated peeled onion

½ teaspoon finely cut parsley
1 clove garlic, peeled and mashed
½ cup plus 1 tablespoon olive oil

Mix salt, sugar, and mustard into smooth paste with vinegar. Add onion, parsley, and garlic. Let stand 1 hour. Discard garlic. Add olive oil slowly, stirring and beating constantly until thickened. Makes about 1¼ cups dressing.

Use just enough dressing to coat each piece of salad lightly, without leaving any surplus dressing in bottom of bowl.

ROQUEFORT SALAD DRESSING

One of the most simple Roquefort dressings is made by crumbling the cheese into your favorite well-seasoned French Dressing. Use about 1 teaspoon crumbled cheese to 1 cup dressing. Here are 2 other versions:

½ cup chili sauce
1 tablespoon lemon juice
½ cup salad oil
½ cup crumbled Roquefort
1 clove garlic, peeled and mashed

½ teaspoon salt
½ teaspoon paprika
1 (8-ounce) can tomato sauce

Combine all ingredients in glass container of mixer or blender. Cover. Blend 30 seconds. Keep in covered glass jar in refrigerator. Makes 1½ cups dressing.
Omit garlic, if preferred.

Blended Roquefort Dressing: One half cup softened cream cheese; 1 cup crumbled Roquefort. Beat together. Add French Dressing, stirring smoothly until of desired consistency.

HONEY DRESSING FOR FRUIT

⅔ cup sugar
1 teaspoon dry mustard
½ teaspoon paprika
¼ teaspoon powdered cloves
¼ teaspoon salt

⅓ cup honey
⅓ cup cider vinegar
1 tablespoon lemon juice
1 teaspoon grated onion
1 cup salad oil

Combine dry ingredients. Mix with honey, vinegar, lemon juice, and onion. Add oil gradually, beating smoothly. Makes about 2 cups dressing.

SHERRY DRESSING FOR FRUIT

¼ cup lemon juice
⅛ teaspoon salt

¼ cup sugar
2 tablespoons sherry

Beat all ingredients together until sugar is dissolved. Makes about ½ cup dressing.

Port Dressing for Fruit: Substitute port wine for sherry in above recipe. Other sweet wines may be used. Marsala and various cordials are favorites, depending on kind of fruits in salad. Cherries, peaches, sweet plums, bananas, seedless grapes are harmonious with wine.

MAYONNAISE AND ITS VARIANTS

1 egg
½ teaspoon dry mustard
1 teaspoon salt

2 tablespoons cider vinegar or lemon juice
1 cup salad oil

Beat egg with mustard and salt in bowl or in glass container of blender. If blender is used, set it at medium speed. Add about 1 teaspoon vinegar, still beating or slowly blending. Add about ¼ cup oil, still beating or slowly blending. Continue until all vinegar and oil are added to mixture. Stop beating or blending when last of oil has been added. Makes about 1¼ cups mayonnaise.

For kitchen perfectionists.

Mustard Mayonnaise: Add 1 tablespoon prepared mustard, beating in alternately with vinegar and oil.

AVOCADO MAYONNAISE

⅔ cup mashed or sieved avo-
    cado
½ teaspoon salt
1 tablespoon lemon juice

¼ teaspoon Tabasco sauce
3 tablespoons mayonnaise
1 tablespoon finely cut chives or
    parsley

Combine avocado with salt, lemon juice, and Tabasco. Beat in mayonnaise. Add parsley or chives. If too thick, add either more mayonnaise or a little sour cream. Makes about 1 cup dressing.

This is a California favorite for sliced tomatoes and cucumbers as well as citrus-fruit salads. It is delicious on chilled cooked shrimp, too.

CUCUMBER DRESSING FOR SEA-FOOD SALADS

1 cup mayonnaise
½ cup finely cut cucumber

1 teaspoon lemon juice
1 tablespoon finely cut chives

Blend all ingredients. Makes about 1½ cups dressing. Serve on seafood cocktail, such as shrimp or crab meat, and on sea-food salads. Or with tray of chilled, cooked lobster and other cold fish.

Have small dishes of sliced scallions or rings of Bermuda onion, small pickled onions, and sliced or chopped olives for those who want to make additions to the salad dressing.

Cucumber Mayonnaise: Add 1 cup finely diced cucumber and 1 teaspoon finely cut fresh mint leaves to 1 cup mayonnaise. Makes about 2 cups dressing. Superb on cold sea food.

Green Mayonnaise (Sauce Verte): Eight spinach leaves, 4 tablespoons finely cut parsley, 6 tablespoons finely cut water-cress leaves. Wash all leaves thoroughly. Drain. Cover with boiling water and let stand 5 minutes. Drain. Chop or press through fine sieve or use blender. Combine with 1 cup mayonnaise. Makes about 1¼ cups dressing.

GARDEN MAYONNAISE FOR CRAB SALAD

1 cup mayonnaise
⅓ cup heavy cream, whipped
¼ cup chili sauce

2 tablespoons finely cut scallions
2 tablespoons finely cut parsley
1/16 teaspoon cayenne

Combine all ingredients. Chill. Makes about 2 cups dressing.
Especially good on crab and other sea-food salads.

GARLIC-HAM MAYONNAISE

1 cup mayonnaise	1 (2 ¼-ounce) can deviled ham
½ clove garlic, peeled and mashed	¼ teaspoon orégano

Add garlic to mayonnaise. Let chill in refrigerator in covered jar 1 hour or longer. Remove garlic and discard it. Combine mayonnaise, ham, and herb. Mix evenly. Makes about 1¼ cups dressing.

Especially good on Belgian endive with greens and tomato, and as dip for crackers or potato chips.

HONEY-LIME DRESSING, ORLANDO

¾ cup mayonnaise	½ cup heavy cream
2 tablespoons honey	1 tablespoon grated lime peel
1 ½ tablespoons fresh lime juice	

Combine mayonnaise with honey and lime juice. Whip cream stiff. Fold into honey mixture. Chill. To serve, fold in lime peel and serve at once. Makes about 1⅔ cups dressing.

HONEY MAYONNAISE FOR FRUIT

½ cup mayonnaise	1 teaspoon grated lemon peel
1 tablespoon honey	2 tablespoons soft cream cheese
1 tablespoon lemon juice	

Chill mayonnaise. Combine honey, lemon juice, peel, and cheese. Mix with mayonnaise. Makes about 1¼ cups dressing.

Just right for fruit salad combinations with avocado or melon balls.

MAYONNAISE GELATIN COATING

Mayonnaise Chaud-Froid

2 tablespoons unflavored gelatin	½ cup cold water
	2 cups mayonnaise

Soften gelatin in cold water 5 minutes. Set bowl over hot water and stir until dissolved. Add to mayonnaise. Blend well. Makes about 2 cups gelatin coating.

Use to coat sea food, meats, chicken, and turkey when creating decorative cold platter for buffet. After coating let stand few minutes to partially set. Add decorations and chill. The gelatin mixture helps hold decorations of green pepper, pimiento, olive, et cetera, in place. Also use to combine with vegetables or other foods in making a molded salad.

MAYONNAISE RAVIGOTE

2 tablespoons each finely chopped capers, chervil, parsley, scallions, and hot onion	1 tablespoon lemon juice
	¼ teaspoon anchovy paste
½ cup dry white wine	1 hard-cooked egg white
	1 cup mayonnaise

Combine capers, herbs, scallions, and onion in small saucepan. Pour wine and lemon juice over. Cook on low heat 15 minutes. Let cool. Add anchovy paste and chopped egg white to mayonnaise. Combine with wine mixture. Chill thoroughly. Makes about 2 cups sauce.

Serve on hot poached or baked eggs, on sea food, such as cold crab meat in scallop shells (a classic), and on delicate chicken dishes, such as breast of chicken in aspic.

SAN BERNARDINO LEMON-CREAM MAYONNAISE

Juice ½ lemon	2 tablespoons heavy cream
1 cup mayonnaise	1 teaspoon grated lemon peel

Add lemon juice to mayonnaise. Fold in whipped cream and peel. Makes about 1¼ cups mayonnaise. Especially good on fruit and vegetable combinations.

RUSSIAN DRESSING

1 cup mayonnaise	1 teaspoon finely cut chives
¼ cup chili sauce	1 teaspoon finely cut green pepper
1 teaspoon finely cut pimiento	

Combine all ingredients. Chill. Makes about 1¼ cups dressing. For sea-food salads, avocado, Belgian endive.

Add ½ cup chili sauce if a stronger coloring and more tomato flavor are preferred.

TARTARE SAUCE

1 cup mayonnaise	1 tablespoon ketchup
1 teaspoon finely cut fresh	1 teaspoon lemon juice
tarragon	1 teaspoon capers, chopped

Combine all ingredients. Chill. Makes about 1⅛ cups sauce. If fresh tarragon is not available, use dried tarragon and tarragon vinegar in place of lemon juice. Delicious on cold salmon, and on many cold seafood dishes.

Tartare Sauce for Lobster: One small sweet red pepper cut very fine, 1 cup mayonnaise, 1 teaspoon finely cut fresh tarragon, 1 teaspoon finely cut chives, ¼ cup tomato sauce. Combine all. Chill. Makes about 1½ cups sauce. Especially good for lobster salad or cold lobster platter.

CHAPTER EIGHTEEN

Sandwiches, Pizzas, Savory-Spread Loaves

When you make sandwiches, for the tea table or for a tray luncheon or any other occasion, do it the easy way: assemble all you need in foods and utensils. Work swiftly. Serve sandwiches at once or cover with a damp towel and chill until served. Sandwiches for the lunch-box or picnic basket should be securely wrapped in waxed paper or foil.

In general: Use fresh or one-day-old bread. Slice thin with a thin-bladed, long knife. Vary breads for flavor, color, texture, size, and shape. Slice the bread across the loaf, unless the recipe demands other cuts. Cut the crusts off for rolled and tea sandwiches and for others which are to be served small.

Soften the butter or margarine for spreading at room temperature or by creaming for a few minutes. Blend the butter or margarine with other spreads such as mayonnaise, mustard, salad dressings. Use special-flavor butters when the recipe calls for them. Arrange the butter and other spreads in bowls on your kitchen table for easy reach.

Follow the recipe instructions and chop or grind, slice, or otherwise prepare fillings. Combine with seasonings and moisteners according to the recipes. Have sliced vegetables, such as cucumber, chilled and drained. Have other green fillings, such as water cress, parsley, and mint, washed and well drained. All should be chilled before using in sandwiches.

When spreading bread, line up matching slices. Spread evenly and quickly with softened butter or other spread clear to the edges of each slice. Trim any sliced filling, such as meat, chicken, cheese, smoked salmon, and others, to fit the sliced bread. And when you want a generously thick filling use 2 or more thin slices in place of 1 thick one.

BAKED SARDINES IN BUNS

3 (3¼-ounce) cans boneless and skinless sardines
1 pound sharp cheese, grated
1 (8-ounce) can tomato sauce
1 tablespoon Worcestershire sauce
2 teaspoons salt
½ teaspoon pepper
¼ cup salad oil
½ cup chopped ripe olives
2 tablespoons minced onion
1 cup finely cut celery
2 tablespoons minced pimiento
12 burger buns

Start oven at moderately slow (300° F.).

Flake and mash sardines with fork. Combine sardines with cheese and remaining ingredients except buns. Split buns ¾ way through. Fill with sardine mixture. Stand buns filled side up in large baking pan with cover.

Cover and bake 30 minutes. Uncover and bake 10 minutes more. Serve hot. Makes 12 servings.

Sardine mixture may be prepared ahead of time and kept in covered glass bowl in refrigerator. Remove it from the refrigerator about 20 minutes before baking time. Buns may be split, heaped on a tray, covered with a towel, and be ready for stuffing and baking—teen-agers can do the work themselves.

So good for a Friday-night school buffet supper. Better make twice as many. Serve with hot chocolate and a choice of desserts, such as maple ice cream with coconut frosted cupcakes or baked apples stuffed with raisins and nuts and topped with whipped cream. And soft drinks, of course!

BROILED LOAF BEEFBURGERS

1 loaf Vienna bread about 12 by 5 inches
Soft butter or margarine
1½ pounds ground beef
½ cup grated onion
2 tablespoons Worcestershire sauce
1¼ teaspoons salt
2 pats butter
Onion rings

Cut loaf in half lengthwise. Spread cut surfaces with butter or margarine. Combine remaining ingredients except butter and onion rings. Spread mixture about ½ inch thick on each half loaf. Build edges up slightly. Place about 6 inches under broiler heat. Broil about 15 minutes or until meat is cooked. Top with pats of butter. Garnish with onion rings. Place on warmed platter. Cut in generous chunks to serve. Makes 8 servings.

A hand-to-mouth supper for teen-agers or anyone. Delicious as the one hot sandwich in a cold-cuts supper.

BUFFET LOAF SANDWICHES

1 (6 to 8-inch) round pumpernickel or dark bread	2 tablespoons hot prepared mustard
1 (4½-ounce) can deviled ham	8 to 12 slices eating apple
1 package soft snappy cheese	Lemon juice
1 (3-ounce) cake cream cheese	

Remove bottom crust from loaf. With thin-bladed long knife slice through loaf in 5 lengthwise slices. Spread one slice with one half the deviled ham, another with all the snappy cheese, the next with all the cream cheese combined with the mustard. Spread fourth slice with remaining deviled ham. Press slices firmly together sandwich style, with unspread slice on top. Wrap in foil or waxed paper. Chill 1 hour or longer.

To serve, cut in wedges but do not separate. Top each wedge with a thin slice or half slice of lemon-dipped apple. Makes 8 to 12 sandwich wedges.

Unseparated, these wedge-shaped sandwiches make an attractive center to a large tray of assorted sandwiches and salads for a buffet meal. Surround them with open-face ham, Swiss cheese, and bologna sandwiches. Provide relishes, dill pickle sticks, radishes, scallions, prepared mustard for help-yourself sandwich makers. Old-fashioned potato salad is good with this assortment. So are small, stuffed whole tomatoes, filled to the brim and overflowing with chicken salad or with a mixture of leftover cooked vegetables and mayonnaise. Add a hot drink, and hungry guests will consider themselves well fed.

BURGER BUNS

1 pound ground beef	1 (8-ounce) can tomato sauce
1 tablespoon fat	¼ cup ketchup
½ cup finely cut peeled onion	1 tablespoon vinegar
¼ cup finely cut celery	1 ½ teaspoons Worcestershire
¼ cup finely cut green pepper	sauce
1 tablespoon sugar	4 hamburger buns
1 teaspoon salt	Dill pickles
⅛ teaspoon pepper	

Brown meat slowly in hot fat. Add onion, celery, and green pepper. Cook until vegetables are tender and meat is almost done. Stir in seasonings and remaining ingredients except buns and pickles. Let simmer 5 to 10 minutes or until well thickened. Split buns. Toast them. Heap with hot filling. Serve on plate garnished with strips of dill pickle. Makes 4 servings.

These buns, with tray of condiments, can be the center attraction of a terrace supper for teen-agers. Cold drinks and a favorite dessert, such as an ice-cream pie (bought), will make everybody happy. Burger mixture can be cooked over barbecue grill and buns can be toasted on same grill.

CHICKEN-ALMOND SANDWICHES

2 cups ground cooked chicken	Mayonnaise
1 cup ground toasted almonds	1 tablespoon finely cut parsley

Combine chicken and almonds. Add enough mayonnaise to make smooth-spreading mixture. Add parsley. Makes 3 cups filling.

Spread on thin slices cheese bread. Cover each slice with thin slice white bread. Trim crusts. Cut each sandwich in 4 strips.

Or use mixture as filling for small split, toasted biscuits or small toasted baker's rolls. A perfect sandwich to garnish a fruit-salad platter. Enough for 12 or more sandwiches.

This is a fine recipe for a wedding reception or an anniversary where refreshments are simple—champagne, or punch, bite-size sandwiches. Ground, toasted almonds are available canned.

COTTAGE-CHEESE SANDWICH FILLINGS

1 cup cream-style cottage cheese mixed with any of these combinations:

1 (5½-ounce) can crab meat, flaked, 1 tablespoon mayonnaise, ½ teaspoon prepared mustard, a little salt.

2 chopped hard-cooked eggs, 2 tablespoons minced anchovies, 1 table-spoon mayonnaise, 1 tablespoon chives or grated onion.

½ cup chili sauce, 1 tablespoon chopped parsley, 1 tablespoon chopped dill pickle.

½ cup finely minced cooked shrimp, 2 tablespoons mayonnaise, 2 tablespoons grated onion, 1 teaspoon orégano.

½ cup finely cut ripe olives, ¼ cup chopped almonds or peanuts, salt to taste. Add a little sour cream if needed for spreading consistency.

HAM-SALAD ROLLS

12 frankfurter rolls	3 small dill pickles
Softened butter or margarine	1 small onion, peeled
1½ pounds cooked or canned	⅓ cup prepared mustard
ham (about 3 cups ground)	⅓ cup mayonnaise
1 pound Cheddar cheese	

Cut lengthwise slice from top of each roll. Butter this slice carefully. Hollow out rolls. Spread hollows with softened butter or margarine. Grind ham, cheese, pickles, onion together in food chopper, using fine blade. Combine mustard and mayonnaise. Mix with ground ham salad. Fill rolls generously with ham mixture. Put top slices back in place.

Start oven at moderate (375° F.). Heat rolls on baking sheet 10 minutes or until very hot. Makes 12 salad rolls.

For barbecue parties, wrap unheated filled rolls in foil. Place in hot coals which have lost their red color. Heat about 30 minutes. Wear barbecue gloves to handle, of course. They are hot. Slit foil wrap to serve.

HOT CREAMED-FISH SANDWICH

1 (7-ounce) can tuna or (7¾-ounce) can salmon
1 teaspoon lemon juice
1 tablespoon butter or margarine
1 tablespoon flour
½ cup milk

Salt and pepper
¼ teaspoon Worcestershire sauce
4 slices bread
1 large tomato, peeled and sliced

Drain tuna or salmon. Fork into flakes. Sprinkle with lemon juice. Melt butter or margarine in saucepan. Stir in flour smoothly. Add milk gradually, stirring continually, and cook over low heat, stirring constantly until sauce is slightly thickened and bubbly. Season with salt, pepper, and Worcestershire. Stir tuna or salmon into sauce. Let simmer until heated.

Butter bread on one side. Toast, buttered side up, until brown. Spoon creamed fish on untoasted side. Broil until sandwich is heated through. Serve on plate with garnish of sliced tomato. Makes 4 servings.

Enough for supper, with a green salad, hot drink, and good dessert, such as fresh fruit pie.

NUT-BREAD LAYER SANDWICHES

Cut loaf of nut bread in thin slices. Spread each 2 slices generously with cream cheese. Layer them, placing both with cheese side up. Top with third slice of unspread nut bread. Press gently together. Trim crusts. Keep sandwiches on platter, under waxed paper and damp towel, until serving time. Cut through each 3-layer stack diagonally, making 2 triangular stacks. Stand on end around large platter of assorted sandwiches.

To vary the spread use mixture of jelly and cream cheese, nuts and softened snappy cheese, marmalade, apple butter, other favorite butter and jams.

PARTY SANDWICH

1 pound fresh asparagus, cooked and chilled
½ cup mayonnaise
½ teaspoon celery seed

4 frankfurter rolls
2 hard-cooked eggs, sliced
Salt and pepper
Paprika

Drain asparagus. Combine mayonnaise and celery seed and mix well. Split rolls. Spread lightly with celery mayonnaise. Arrange egg slices in each roll, then add 2 or 3 stalks asparagus. Sprinkle with salt, pepper, and paprika. Top with a little remaining celery mayonnaise. Makes 4 servings.

A hearty luncheon sandwich. Serve a cup of hot bouillon or jellied Madrilène first, then the sandwich, followed by strawberries and ice cream and hot coffee.

This is very like the hors d'oeuvres on miniature buns that Americans love at Demel's, the marvelous pastry shop in Vienna.

RAW ONION BEDTIME SANDWICH

A man I knew claimed that raw Bermuda onion, properly prepared, made the very best bedtime sandwich and is, according to him, burp-proof. I never dared try. But for the adventurous, here it is:

1 medium-sized Bermuda onion, peeled and sliced	Sweet butter
	Lettuce, if desired
Boiling water	Salt and pepper
Fresh caraway rye bread	

Scald sliced onion with boiling water. Drain slices and dry them on paper towel. Make sandwiches. Serve with beer. Sweet dreams!

REUBEN'S SANDWICHES

The large menu card at Reuben's, the famous New York restaurant, includes an impressive sandwich section. Most of the specialties were thought up by visiting celebrities.

Jack Benny and Mary Livingston always want Reuben's open-face sandwich made of turkey, smoked beef tongue, Swiss cheese on rye bread, with coleslaw and Russian Dressing. Try this on hungry men guests and you'll understand why the Jack Bennys like it too.

Mary Martin's favorite: Virginia ham, Swiss cheese, sliced dill pickle on rye bread.

Ed Sullivan's sandwich: Chopped chicken livers and corned beef on rye bread.

Ethel Merman's favorite at Reuben's: Sliced turkey, sliced tomato, hard-cooked egg, Russian Dressing on whole-wheat bread.

Ginger Roger's Special: Imported caviar and cream cheese on rye or white toast.

Judy Garland's sandwich: Nova Scotia salmon and Swiss cheese on rye bread.

Sliced turkey with cranberry sauce on French toast is another good sandwich on this menu. This is the way my sons like to dispose of the holiday bird, I find. Good served with maple syrup for teen parties.

My own favorite there, though they haven't immortalized it, is crusty rye bread, sliced tongue, Swiss cheese and coleslaw.

SANDWICHES ON WHEELS

At the elegant Argyle Club in San Antonio a sandwich tray is wheeled about, so that guests may help themselves, making their own favorite combinations. I noticed on the tray both dark and light breads and delicious favorites such as thinly sliced Swiss cheese, spiced beef, crisply cooked bacon, and of course lettuce, olives, radishes, sliced tomatoes, and savory relishes of several kinds.

At the same club *Hot Corn-Meal Pancakes* are served as a sandwich, with broiled tomato slices and ham as the fillers, and hot creamed oysters as a sauce over all! What a good idea for any hostess for her Sunday-night supper or for holiday brunch.

Tea Sandwiches

CHECKERBOARD TEA SANDWICHES

Make a 4-layer sandwich, using alternate slices of white and whole-wheat bread. Spread softened butter or smooth, moist filling between slices. Press the stack of slices together, then wrap lightly with foil or waxed paper. Chill several hours. Unwrap and cut the stack into

½-inch slices. Spread cut sides of slices with softened butter or smooth, soft filling. Rebuild in 3-layer stack and wrap and chill again. Unwrap. Cut into ¼-inch slices. Makes 24 checkerboard sandwiches.

Children are especially amused by these. Try them for a birthday party.

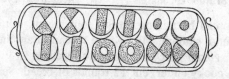

RIBBON TEA SANDWICHES

¼ pound butter or margarine
1 teaspoon prepared mustard
½ tablespoon grated onion
4 tablespoons grated bleu
   cheese

8 slices fresh white bread
8 slices dark whole-grain bread

Combine softened butter or margarine with mustard, onion, and cheese. Beat until smooth. Trim crusts from bread. Spread the butter mixture on 6 slices white and 6 slices brown. Stack slices in 4 piles, alternating brown and white bread and ending with an unspread slice. Wrap tightly in waxed paper, then in damp towel. Chill 1 hour or longer. To serve, unwrap and cut in ½-inch slices from top to bottom. Makes 24 ribbon sandwiches.

Variations for the filling are what you want to make them. Use jam or jelly and butter. Omit mustard, onion, and cheese.

Combine butter, cream cheese, and grated orange peel for another good combination.

Mix apple butter, cream cheese, softened butter for delicious flavor.

Add grated cucumber or 4 tablespoons finely cut water cress in place of bleu cheese for a spread with fresh, sharp flavor welcome with tea or cocktails.

DOUBLE-DECKER TEA ROUNDS

First Spread	Second Spread
1 (3-ounce) package cream cheese	½ (3-ounce) package cream cheese
1 teaspoon sour cream	½ teaspoon sour cream
¼ teaspoon salt	¼ teaspoon salt
¼ teaspoon curry powder	½ tablespoon finely cut pimiento
1 tablespoon grated cucumber	16 slices fresh bread

Blend first spread by mixing cheese, sour cream, salt, curry powder, and cucumber until smooth. Mix second spread in another bowl, blending cheese, sour cream, salt, and pimiento together.

Using 2-inch cooky cutter, cut 12 rounds of bread. Spread these with cucumber mixture. Use 1-inch cutter and cut 12 rounds from remaining slices. Spread these little rounds with pimiento mixture. Put them together, large round on bottom, small round on top. Cover with waxed paper. Lay damp towel on top. Chill in refrigerator 30 minutes or longer. Serve plain or garnished with sprig of water cress, dill, parsley, or toasted nut. Makes 12 double-deckers.

Vary these spreads according to your needs. An all-sweet sandwich for tea can be made by using cream cheese and apricot marmalade for the bottom round, cream cheese and apple jelly for the top round. Add a few chopped nuts to the top.

Delicious when you spread the large rounds with minced chicken salad mixture or finely minced lobster or crab meat blended with mayonnaise and spread top rounds with anchovy butter.

Add still more variety by cutting the large rounds from slices of whole wheat, Boston, or other dark bread and the small top rounds from white bread.

ROLLED ROQUEFORT TEA SANDWICHES

1 (3-ounce) package cream cheese	1½ teaspoons Worcestershire sauce
⅓ pound Roquefort cheese	2 drops Tabasco sauce
3 tablespoons thick commercial sour cream	1 tablespoon sherry or cognac
	1 loaf fresh sandwich bread

Combine all ingredients for filling. Blend smoothly. Cut bread as thinly as possible. Cut off crusts. Spread slices generously with mixture. Roll each sandwich as for jelly roll. Lay rolls seam side down on platter. Cover with waxed paper, then with damp towel. Chill 1 hour or longer. Makes 16 to 18 rolls.

For appetizing **Roquefort Ring Canapés:** Freeze sandwich rolls. When ready to serve, slice in 1-inch pieces. They thaw at room temperature in about 20 minutes. Makes about 4 dozen rings.

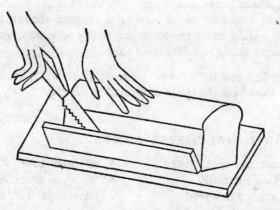

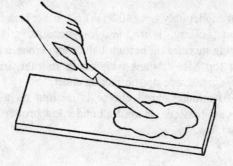

TOASTED BEEF ROLLS

1 cup ground cooked beef	½ teaspoon salt
½ cup shredded sharp American cheese	¼ teaspoon pepper
	12 thin slices fresh bread
¼ cup mayonnaise	Softened butter or margarine

Combine beef, cheese, mayonnaise, salt, and pepper, mixing smoothly together. Cut crusts from bread. Spread slices with softened butter or margarine. Spread with meat mixture.

Roll each slice up as for jelly roll and place seam side down in pan lined with waxed paper. Cover rolls with waxed paper with damp towel on top. Chill 1 or 2 hours. To serve, place rolls in shallow baking pan, brush with melted butter or margarine, broil under moderate heat until lightly toasted. Serve hot. Makes 12 rolls.

An excellent end for leftover pot roast, flank steak, roast beef—the sweet meat cut from the bones of a standing rib roast.

TOASTED TUNA-CHEESE BUNS

1 (7-ounce) can tuna, flaked	6 sandwich buns
½ cup finely cut celery	6 thin slices processed cheese
2 tablespoons pickle relish	2 tablespoons soft butter or margarine
¼ cup mayonnaise	

Start oven at moderately hot (400° F.).

Combine tuna, celery, relish, and mayonnaise, mixing well. Split buns. Spread tuna mixture on bottom halves and cover each with slice of cheese. Spread top half of buns with butter or margarine. Place both halves of buns, spread side up, on baking sheet.

Bake 5 to 10 minutes, until cheese is melting on filled halves and buttered halves are toasted. Or toast all under low broiler heat. Serve hot. Makes 6 sandwiches.

WATER-CRESS SANDWICHES

½ cup butter or margarine, softened	¾ teaspoon Worcestershire sauce
½ cup finely cut water cress	½ teaspoon salt
1 teaspoon grated onion	¼ teaspoon pepper
1 tablespoon finely cut chives	1 loaf fresh sandwich bread

Combine all ingredients for filling. Slice loaf of bread as thinly as possible. Cut in rounds with 1½-inch cutter. Spread half of rounds with water-cress mixture. Cover with plain rounds. Place on platter and cover with waxed paper, then with damp towel. Chill 1 hour. Makes 3 dozen tea sandwiches.

Omit onion and chives for plain water-cress sandwich. Or substitute grated cucumber for onion and chives.

These sandwiches always bring back memories of my summers as a schoolgirl in London. They seem to be an indispensable part of the English tea and are wonderful additions to our own teatime hour.

Pizzas

PIZZAS FOR A PARTY

½ pound bulk sausage	1 ¼ cups tomato paste
2 cups sifted all-purpose flour	1 ½ cups grated sharp Cheddar
2 ½ teaspoons baking powder	cheese
½ teaspoon salt	Crushed fresh orégano, or
⅓ cup shortening or margarine	2 tablespoons powdered
¾ cup milk	orégano

Mash sausage in cold frying pan. Heat slowly. Cook sausage, stirring frequently to cook thoroughly, and break into small pieces. Drain.

Sift flour, baking powder, and salt together into mixing bowl. Cut in shortening until mixture is like coarse meal. Add milk. Blend with fork until dry ingredients are just dampened. Turn out on lightly floured board. Knead dough gently, about ½ minute. Roll out about ¼ inch thick. Cut with 1½-inch or 3-inch round cutter.

Start oven at hot (450° F.).

Place rounds on ungreased baking sheets. Pinch edges up slightly to form rim around each. Spread on each a little tomato paste, then cheese, then sausage. Add a very little crushed fresh herb or a few grains of dried herb. Divide all ingredients evenly among the pizzas.

Bake about 12 minutes, until dough is baked and filling is hot. Serve hot. Makes 60 small pizzas, about 30 larger ones.

This is very fine teen-age party fare, and fine post-teen fare too. Make the full quantity, even for a small party. They freeze well. Pop deep-frozen pizzas into a shallow pan. Heat in moderate oven (350° F.) 15 minutes. Turn oven to hot (425° F.) and finish heating in about 5 minutes.

PIZZA FOR FOUR

⅔ cup milk
2 cups packaged biscuit mix
2 (8-ounce) cans pork sausages
2 cups shredded processed
    American cheese

1 (8-ounce) can tomato sauce
8 anchovy fillets, cut fine
¾ teaspoon orégano

Add milk to biscuit mix in a bowl, stirring only until moistened. Turn dough out onto lightly floured board. Cut dough in half. Roll each half in 10-inch circle. Place on ungreased baking sheet. Pinch edges to form a slight rim.

Start oven at hot (425° F.).

Place opened cans of pork sausages in hot water and let stand 10 minutes. Drain sausages well. Crumble fine with fork and spread over the 2 dough circles. Sprinkle cheese over sausage. Combine tomato sauce, anchovies, and herb. Scatter mixture over cheese.

Bake 18 to 20 minutes or until crust is done and cheese mixture is melted, hot, and bubbly. Cut circles in generous wedges. Makes 8 to 12 servings.

Supply your guests with cold drinks or a cup of hot bouillon while you finish the pizza. Dough may be prepared, placed on baking sheet, and set in refrigerator ahead of time. Remove baking sheet from refrigerator and complete pizzas, baking them after guests arrive.

Give them a salad of water cress, endive, cucumber, and ripe olives with French Dressing. Follow salad with baked caramel custards and hot coffee. Or serve sugared doughnuts, a bowl of apples and nuts, cider, and coffee.

Savory-Spread Loaves

SPREADS FOR SAVORY LOAVES

A loaf of baker's bread, sliced and spread with a savory butter mixture, then heated in the oven until the bread is hot through and crust toasting, can add a gourmet touch to luncheon or supper. The most famous of such loaves is spread with garlic butter, which is nothing more than butter softened at room temperature and blended with crushed peeled garlic, as little garlic or as much garlic as you and your guests like. (I use a garlic press and do not peel cloves. Result: no garlic odor on hands.)

Here is **Daisyfields' Herb Spread:** Melt ¼ pound, or 1 stick, butter. Stir into it 1 teaspoon each dried basil, marjoram, and fresh-cut chives (we grow our own). Add 1 tablespoon fresh-cut parsley. Mix. Spread on sliced French or American-type loaf. Place in loaf pan, or tie string around loaf and place on baking sheet.

Bake in moderately hot oven (400° F.) 15 minutes or until loaf is hot through and beginning to toast around edges.

Instead of slicing loaf, cut in thick slices not quite through to bottom of loaf. Spread slices slightly apart, spread both sides with herb butter. Press loaf back in shape and heat as above.

Curry-Onion Spread: ¼ pound, or 1 stick, butter, melted, ⅓ cup grated onion, 1 teaspoon curry powder, ½ teaspoon celery salt, ½ teaspoon paprika. Use as described for herb spread.

Ginger Spread: ¼ pound, or 1 stick, butter, melted, ¼ cup finely minced candied ginger, 1 tablespoon grated orange peel, 1 tablespoon sugar. Use as described for herb spread.

Parmesan Spread: ¼ pound, or 1 stick, butter, melted, 1 cup grated Parmesan cheese, ⅓ cup grated onion, ½ teaspoon paprika. Use as described for herb spread.

Sage-and-Onion Spread: ¼ pound or 1 stick butter, melted, ½ teaspoon crumbled sage, ½ teaspoon onion salt or grated fresh onion, ¼ teaspoon celery salt. Use as described for herb spread.

Freeze or refrigerate savory spread slices or loaves.

To serve, heat unthawed, as described, extending the heating time 5 or 10 minutes, or enough to make loaf hot and bring it almost to toasting stage.

Additional spreads follow as well as recipes for loaves.

Amy Vanderbilt's Complete Cookbook

ANCHOVY BUTTER

6 tablespoons butter or margarine

2 tablespoons anchovy paste or
6 anchovy fillets, mashed

Combine softened butter or margarine with anchovy paste or mashed fillets. Beat until evenly mixed. Use as spread on rolls or loaves to be heated, or use in sandwiches. Or spread thin slices of bread with the anchovy butter before adding chopped egg salad or similar fillings. Delicious. Makes about ½ cup filling.

Other uses for anchovy butter: Spread on sliced tomatoes, serve as garnish on broiled fish. Also spread anchovy butter on hot broiled fish steaks.

CHEESE BUTTER

½ cup grated Cheddar cheese
4 tablespoons butter or margarine
1 teaspoon dry mustard

½ teaspoon Worcestershire
sauce
Freshly ground pepper

Cream all ingredients together, seasoning with a small grind of pepper. Taste butter. Correct seasoning if necessary. Keep at room temperature for spreading. Makes about ¾ cup spread.

Use for canapés and sandwiches. Delicious on narrow strips of toast, crackers, and tiny hot buttered biscuits.

LOBSTER BUTTER

Shell and coral 1 cooked lobster
3 tablespoons butter or margarine

2 tablespoons water

Crush shell and coral of cooked lobster with butter or margarine. Heat slowly with 2 tablespoons water in upper part of double boiler over hot water. Cook 10 minutes without letting mixture boil. Strain liquid through fine sieve. Chill in refrigerator. Butter rises to top. Makes about ⅓ cup butter.

Another version of lobster butter is easily made by creaming butter or margarine with finely minced or ground cooked lobster claw meat. Combine 2 tablespoons butter to each tablespoon ground lobster. Add few drops lemon juice and light sprinkling of paprika.

540

Use lobster butter in delicate tea sandwiches or to spread toast triangles which garnish creamed shrimp or fish steaks.

SHRIMP BUTTER

½ cup ground cooked shrimp
4 tablespoons butter or margarine

Lemon juice
Powdered nutmeg

Use cleaned, canned, cooked, or quick-frozen shrimp. Grind as fine as possible. Cream with butter or margarine until well blended. Add few drops lemon juice and light sprinkling of nutmeg. Makes about ¾ cup butter.

Use for tea sandwiches, canapés, or spread on buttered toast as base for hot creamed lobster or crab meat.

Keep at room temperature for spreading on toast and sandwiches.

To dress up a simple broiled fish steak, keep the shrimp butter in the refrigerator. When fish is cooked, and on warm serving platter, add a slice of *cold* shrimp butter to each hot steak. Delicious.

CHEESE-AND-SHERRY LOAF

¼ pound Cheddar or snappy cheese
¼ cup sherry
2 tablespoons finely cut chives
4 tablespoons butter or margarine

½ teaspoon paprika
½ teaspoon salt
Long loaf French bread
Extra butter or margarine

Grate cheese. Pour wine over it. Add chives and mix together. Add butter or margarine. Beat until smooth and evenly mixed. Add seasonings.

Start oven at moderate (375° F.).

Slice loaf diagonally, almost to bottom crust. Spread paste on slices. Brush outside of loaf with butter or margarine. Place on baking sheet and set in oven 20 minutes or until hot and top is browning slightly. Makes 8 or more servings.

For cook-out and barbecue suppers, prepare the loaf, wrap in foil, lay on grill over hot coals 15 minutes or until hot. Wear barbecue gloves to unwrap!

FRESH PARSLEY LOAF

1 (1-pound) loaf unsliced sandwich bread
½ cup soft butter or margarine

¾ cup finely cut parsley
1 tablespoon lemon juice
Additional cut parsley

Start oven at moderate (375° F.).

Trim crust from top and sides of unsliced loaf. Cut loaf in half
lengthwise, almost to bottom crust. Then cut crosswise in 12 slices almost to bottom crust. Combine soft butter or margarine, parsley, and
lemon juice, mixing thoroughly (Parsley Butter). Spread on slices.
Place loaf on baking sheet.

Heat in oven 8 to 10 minutes or until hot and crusty. Sprinkle top
with a little finely cut parsley. Makes 12 slices. Let guests break off
their own.

Fresh Chive Loaf: Substitute finely cut chives for parsley in the recipe,
for another delicious loaf. Especially good with barbecued meats, but
equally appreciated with baked ham or any roast or casserole.

ONION LOAF

Start oven at low (275° F.).

Cut loaf of Italian or French bread into 1-inch slices, almost through
to the bottom crust. Spread each slice liberally with butter or margarine. Dust generously with onion salt. Place on baking sheet in low
oven 10 to 15 minutes or until very hot. Serve at once. Makes 8 to
10 servings.

A fragrant loaf to serve with salad or chowder. Or wrap the unheated
loaf in foil and let it heat at the rear of the *barbecue* grill 20 to 30
minutes. Less time if over a hot spot. When foil package is very hot,
open and pass with the spareribs or salad. Handle with barbecue gloves!

TOASTED SWEET LOAF

1 loaf unsliced bread
¾ cup brown sugar, packed
6 tablespoons softened butter or
margarine

¼ cup shredded coconut
3 tablespoons honey
½ teaspoon powdered cinnamon
¼ teaspoon powdered nutmeg

Start oven at moderately hot (400° F.).

Cut crust from top and sides of loaf. Place loaf on greased baking sheet. Make 1 cut lengthwise down center of loaf almost to bottom crust. Then slice bread crosswise, at 1½-inch intervals, cutting almost to bottom crust.

Combine sugar, butter, or margarine, coconut, honey, cinnamon, and nutmeg. Spread between bread squares and all over top. Tie string around loaf to hold it together.

Heat in oven about 10 minutes or until loaf is hot. Remove string. Serve loaf while warm. Makes about 12 servings.

Delicious with coffee or tea. A luxurious dessert bread for brunch or luncheon.

GARLIC SLICES FOR SALAD

½ cup butter or margarine
½ clove garlic, peeled and
  mashed

6 slices French or Vienna bread,
  cut 1 to 1½ inches thick

Start oven at moderately hot (400° F.).

Melt butter or margarine in an 11-by-7-by-1½-inch baking pan. Remove pan from oven. Add garlic. Arrange bread in baking pan, turning slices once to butter both sides. Let stand 10 minutes. Remove garlic. Then heat bread in oven 10 minutes or until very hot and browning. Makes 6 servings.

Bring hot to the table in the baking pan and serve with green salad or with cold cuts, cheese, and potato salad. A fine beer supper idea. Also especially good outdoors with any barbecued meat.

Hot Herbed French Bread: Use recipe above. In place of garlic use 1 tablespoon mixed herbs, chives, basil, marjoram and orégano.

HOT APRICOT-JAM SLICES

1 loaf French bread about 12
  inches long
8 tablespoons softened butter or
  margarine

½ cup apricot jam
Powdered cinnamon

Start oven at moderately hot (400° F.).

Cut bread in 1½-inch slices diagonally through the loaf. Use thin sharp knife. Spread with butter, then with jam. Sprinkle generously with cinnamon. Place slices, jam side up, on baking sheet.

Heat in hot oven about 8 minutes or until hot and toasting. Makes 8 to 10 slices. Serve with tea.

TOASTED SEED ROLLS

Split buns and brush with melted butter or margarine. Sprinkle with sesame or poppy seed. Toast under broiler heat until golden brown. Especially good with salad or soup.

CHAPTER NINETEEN

Sauces and Relishes

AMANDINE SAUCE

½ cup butter or margarine	1 tablespoon lemon juice
¼ cup sliced almonds	¼ teaspoon salt
1 teaspoon onion juice	¼ teaspoon pepper
1 teaspoon finely cut chives	1/16 teaspoon powdered nutmeg

Melt 1 tablespoon butter or margarine in saucepan. Add almonds. Stir until almonds are lightly browned. Add remaining butter or margarine. Stir in onion juice, chives, and lemon juice. Heat to boiling point, stirring gently. Add seasonings. Makes about ¾ cup sauce.

Serve hot over hot fish steaks, broiled chicken or turkey, or reheated leftover roast veal or lamb. Delicious on asparagus, broccoli, cauliflower, new potatoes.

BUTTER SAUCE FOR VEGETABLES

½ cup butter or margarine	2 tablespoons finely cut water cress
2 tablespoons lemon juice	
2 tablespoons finely cut chives	1/16 teaspoon cayenne

Melt butter or margarine in skillet. Heat until butter starts to brown. Stir in lemon juice. Add chives, water cress, and cayenne. Stir. Makes about ¾ cup sauce.

Serve hot over broccoli, green beans, asparagus, cauliflower, new potatoes, carrots, other vegetables.

CHEESE SAUCE

4 tablespoons butter or margarine
¼ cup sifted all-purpose flour
2 ½ cups milk
1 teaspoon salt
½ teaspoon dry mustard

¼ teaspoon paprika
1 tablespoon Worcestershire
  sauce
4 tablespoons grated processed
  American cheese

Combine all ingredients in glass container of mixer or blender. Blend 30 seconds or until smooth. Stop blender and stir down if necessary. Pour into upper part of double boiler over hot water and bring to a boil. Cook and stir continually until smoothly thickened. Makes about 3 cups.

This sauce can be made without blender. Melt butter or margarine in upper part of double boiler over hot water. Stir in flour smoothly. Add milk gradually, stirring continually. Add all remaining ingredients. Stir and cook until smoothly thickened, which should be just as boiling point is reached. Remove from heat. Let stand few minutes.

Use on toasted English muffins, on cauliflower, asparagus, and other vegetables. Pour over casseroles of mixed vegetables and macaroni or rice and in various dishes calling for cheese. Increase amount of cheese by 2 or 3 additional tablespoons for thicker, cheesier sauce.

COCKTAIL SAUCE

1 tablespoon tarragon vinegar
1 teaspoon grated fresh horse-
  radish
1 cup mayonnaise

2 tablespoons ketchup
2 tablespoons chili sauce
⅛ teaspoon cayenne

Mix all together smoothly. Chill in refrigerator in covered glass bowl. Beat again before serving. Spoon over chilled shrimp or crab meat in iced cocktail glasses. Makes a little over 1¼ cups of sauce.

CUBAN COCKTAIL SAUCE

¾ cup chili sauce or ketchup
2 tablespoons prepared horse-
radish
1 tablespoon lemon juice
½ teaspoon salt

⅛ teaspoon pepper
1/16 teaspoon cayenne
½ teaspoon Worcestershire
sauce

Mix all ingredients together thoroughly. Chill. Beat again before serving over iced sea food. Makes about 1 cup sauce.

Serve this sauce with iced shrimp, clams, or crab meat. Delicious with fried oysters. For a variation, mix with equal amount of tartare sauce. Serve with cold fisherman's platter.

Cocktail Sauce with Onion: Add 1 teaspoon grated hot onion and 2 drops Tabasco sauce to above recipe.

Cocktail Sauce with Tarragon: One tablespoon tarragon vinegar, 1 teaspoon grated fresh horse-radish, 1 cup mayonnaise, 2 tablespoons ketchup, 2 tablespoons chili sauce, ⅛ teaspoon cayenne. Mix well together and chill in bowl in refrigerator. Beat again before serving. Makes about 1¼ cups sauce. Especially good with shrimp and crab meat.

CRAB SAUCE FOR PANCAKES

3 tablespoons butter or margarine
3 tablespoons flour
1 cup milk
2 canned pimientos, drained
and chopped

¼ teaspoon orégano
½ teaspoon salt
1 teaspoon prepared mustard
1 cup crab meat, cleaned and
flaked

Melt butter or margarine in saucepan. Stir in flour smoothly. Stir in milk and remaining ingredients except crab meat. Stir and cook until thickened. Add crab meat. Makes about 2 cups thick creamed crab meat.

Serve on pancakes or omelet. Or spoon onto large pancake, roll cake around it, and slice into servings. Garnish omelet or pancake with few chives or parsley. Enough for 8 servings.

Delicious served in hollowed-out toasted loaf of bread as brunch or luncheon dish.

CREAMED CHICKEN SAUCE FOR OMELETS

1 (10½-ounce) can condensed cream-of-chicken soup
1 (3-ounce) can chopped mushrooms and liquid

2 tablespoons each chopped green pepper, pimiento, ripe olives
2 teaspoons chopped chives

Combine ingredients in small saucepan. Stir and heat thoroughly. Makes 4 servings. Serve on omelet, vegetable loaf, or toast.

CUCUMBER SAUCE

¼ cup mayonnaise or sour cream
½ cup chopped cucumber
¼ teaspoon salt

Grind of black pepper
½ teaspoon poppy seed

Combine all ingredients and chill. Makes about ¾ cup. Serve on hot or cold sea food or salads.

CUCUMBER SAUCE FOR CHICKEN

1 teaspoon prepared mustard
1 teaspoon tarragon vinegar
¼ cup drained prepared horse-radish

1 teaspoon confectioners' sugar
½ large cucumber, pared and finely diced
1 cup heavy cream, whipped

Combine seasonings with cucumber. Fold into cold whipped cream. Makes 4 to 6 servings. Serve on hot broiled chicken halves.

Equally good on broiled salmon steaks. It is an unforgettable combination with hot baked stuffed oysters.

CURRANT SAUCE FOR PORK OR LAMB

1 cup currant jelly
¼ cup water
2 teaspoons lemon juice

2 tablespoons finely cut fresh mint leaves or grated orange or lemon peel

Combine jelly and water in small saucepan over low heat. Let jelly melt. Remove from heat and blend in lemon juice and mint or peel. Makes about 1¼ cups sauce.

Also delicious on roast duck and smoked tongue.

CURRY SAUCE FOR LAMB

4 tablespoons butter or margarine	1½ tablespoons curry powder
	2½ cups milk, scalded
¼ cup sifted flour	1½ cups lamb stock or pan gravy

Melt butter or margarine in top part of double boiler. Stir in flour and curry powder smoothly. Stir constantly over direct heat until mixture is smooth. Set pan over hot water. Add milk and stir constantly until thickened. Let boil 1 or 2 minutes. Add meat stock or gravy, stirring until well mixed and smooth. When hot and steaming, pour over hot cooked lamb cut in serving-size pieces, or reheat cold lamb in curry sauce. Makes about 4 cups sauce, enough for 6 or more servings lamb and hot rice.

Lamb is of such assertive flavor we usually have it roasted, hot, and only occasionally serve it cold, sliced, the following day. Instead I cube leftover lamb and deep-freeze it for use on one of those busy days when dinner-getting becomes a problem. To use the frozen lamb cubes in the above recipe, remove from freezer, heat in bouillon (bouillon cube and boiling water) until tender and hot. Drain. Combine with curry sauce.

When this sauce is used for fish (as in my Fish Pilau, page 181), you should, of course, use fish stock or chicken bouillon in place of the lamb stock or gravy.

FILET MIGNON SAUCE

½ cup heavy cream	2 tablespoons chopped canned mushrooms
2 tablespoons cognac	
1 teaspoon dry mustard	2 tablespoons finely cut parsley
1 teaspoon prepared English mustard	

Have cream well chilled. Mix brandy and mustards. Stir into cream. Add mushrooms and parsley. Serve at once on hot fillet. Makes 4 to 6 servings.

FINES HERBES BASE FOR SAUCES

3 tablespoons butter	1 teaspoon finely cut parsley
2 scallions, sliced	1 teaspoon finely cut chervil
½ cup dry white wine	Salt and pepper

Melt butter in saucepan. Add scallions and wine. Heat until scallions are transparent. Add parsley and chervil. Makes about ½ cup for use as topping on baked, creamed fish or on broiled and baked fish. Or add herbs mixture to a *velouté* or cream sauce and serve with fish.

HERB BOUQUET

Bouquet Garni

A bunch of sweet herbs is often called for in flavoring sauces, soups, stews, and other dishes. To make this *bouquet garni* (also called a *faggot*) combine:

6 sprigs parsley	1 bay leaf
1 sprig celery leaves or small stalk celery	9 peppercorns
	2 whole cloves
1 sprig fresh thyme	

Wash fresh herbs and celery thoroughly under cold running water. Tie sprigs together securely with white thread. Press bay leaf, peppercorns, and cloves into the bunch. At the beginning of cookery place bouquet in soup or other mixture, according to recipe. Remove bouquet before serving. Discard bouquet. It is used only once.

HOLLANDAISE SAUCE

3 egg yolks	½ teaspoon salt
2 tablespoons lemon juice	⅛ teaspoon pepper
1 sprig parsley	½ cup butter
1 slice peeled onion	½ cup boiling water

Combine all ingredients, except boiling water, in glass container of mixer or blender. Blend about 5 seconds or until smooth. Add boiling water gradually as blending continues. Pour mixture into top part of double boiler. Cook over hot water, stirring briskly until sauce is consistency of soft custard. Remove from heat. Keep sauce warm over hot water until served. Or store in refrigerator and reheat over warm water when needed. Makes 1 cup sauce.

Easy Hollandaise: Good Hollandaise is easily made without a mixer or blender. About ½ hour before serving, cut ¼ pound butter or margarine into small pieces in upper part of double boiler. Add 3 egg yolks and 3 tablespoons lemon juice. Let stand at room temperature. Just before serving, stir mixture briskly over gently boiling water 2 or 3 minutes or until thickened. Remove at once from water. Use at once. Makes about 1 cup.

This is the popular sauce which is served with artichokes, sprouts, broccoli, asparagus, Eggs Benedict, and in other dishes.

Mock Hollandaise: Blend ½ cup mayonnaise, 2 tablespoons prepared mustard, 3 drops Tabasco sauce in upper part of double boiler. Stir briskly about 4 minutes over boiling water. Spoon over hot or cold vegetables. Makes about ½ cup sauce.

Béarnaise Sauce: This sauce is a highly flavored Hollandaise. Use ¼ cup tarragon vinegar, 2 shallots, chopped, 3 sprigs fresh tarragon, 4 peppercorns, crushed, ¼ cup white wine, 3 egg yolks, slightly beaten, ½ pound melted butter, ½ teaspoon salt, 1/16 teaspoon cayenne, sprig fresh chervil. Mix vinegar, shallots, chopped stems of tarragon, peppercorns, and wine in upper part of glass or enamel double boiler. Cook over low heat until reduced to thick paste. Mix egg yolks with 1 tablespoon water. Stir into vinegar mixture. Whip or stir briskly over hot, but not boiling, water. When creamy, add butter slowly, stirring constantly. Add cayenne and salt. Strain through fine sieve or cheesecloth. Add chopped tarragon leaves and chervil. Serve at once. Makes about 1¾ cups sauce.

Served on broiled steak in some French restaurants. Use like Hollandaise in many recipes.

CHINESE MUSTARD SAUCE

¾ cup ketchup	1½ tablespoons dry mustard
¼ cup water	1 teaspoon salt

Combine ingredients and mix smoothly. Chill. Makes about 1 cup sauce.

Serve with barbecued or baked spareribs, fried shrimp, and fried fish sticks. Usually paired with sweet-sour sauce in Chinese menus.

MADEIRA SAUCE FOR HAM

⅓ cup brown sugar, packed
½ cup seedless raisins
1 tablespoon currant jelly
1 cup ham liquor
¼ teaspoon powdered cloves
Juice ½ lemon

¼ teaspoon dry mustard
½ teaspoon salt
2 teaspoons cornstarch
½ cup Madeira wine
¼ cup chopped almonds

Combine sugar, raisins, jelly, ham liquor, cloves, lemon juice, mustard, and salt in glass or enamel saucepan. Bring to a boil slowly over low heat. Taste for seasoning. Add more salt if needed. Blend cornstarch with 1 tablespoon cold water. Stir into sauce. Cook and stir until sauce thickens and is clear. Add wine and nuts. Do not let sauce boil again. Serve at once. Makes about 2¼ cups sauce.

To serve with baked ham, place roast on warmed platter, cut slices for all at table and spoon a little hot sauce over slices. Serve remaining sauce in warmed sauce dish.

Delicious on cold ham, too, and with smoked beef tongue, ham croquettes, broiled ham slice, and with game birds and meats.

MEAT SAUCE FOR SPAGHETTI

1 (4-ounce) can sliced mushrooms
3 tablespoons butter or margarine
¼ pound ground beef
1 tablespoon chopped peeled onion

1 slice peeled garlic
2 tablespoons flour
1 cup milk
¼ teaspoon basil
⅛ teaspoon pepper
1 (6-ounce) can tomato paste
½ teaspoon salt

Drain and chop mushrooms. Save liquor. Melt 2 tablespoons butter or margarine in large heavy saucepan. Add meat, mushrooms, onion, and garlic. Cook, stirring constantly, over moderate heat until meat is browned and onion is tender. Add remaining butter. Stir in flour smoothly. Pour in milk, stirring vigorously. Add basil. Cook and stir until thickened. Add pepper and tomato paste. Cook and stir continually. Add salt if needed. If sauce is too thick, thin with mushroom liquid. Makes about 2 cups sauce.

Serve over hot spaghetti, macaroni, and other pastas. Sprinkle top with grated Parmesan or finely cut parsley.

This recipe is easily doubled for large spaghetti suppers. Or make the doubled recipe twice or three times. Combine all cooked sauce in large enamel kettle. Keep covered in refrigerator. Reheat at party time, stirring well.

MUSHROOM SAUCE

½ pound fresh mushrooms	½ cup heavy cream
1 onion, peeled and sliced	½ cup commercial sour cream
2 tablespoons butter or margarine	½ teaspoon salt
	¼ teaspoon pepper
2 tablespoons flour	

Wash mushrooms and drain. Slice stems and caps thin. Cook mushrooms and onion in butter or margarine over low heat about 10 minutes or until tender but not browned. Push vegetables to one side. Stir in flour smoothly. Add cream, sour cream, and seasonings. Stir and mix. Heat slowly to boiling point. Mix vegetables evenly into sauce. Serve hot. Makes about 2 cups sauce.

Delicious over various pastry turnovers filled with mixed vegetables and meat. Good on omelet and pancakes. Suggested in many recipes in fish, chicken, and meat chapters.

GERMAN MUSTARD SAUCE

2 tablespoons prepared mustard	3 tablespoons mayonnaise
1 tablespoon prepared horseradish	2 tablespoons ketchup
	¼ teaspoon Tabasco sauce
¼ cup sweet pickle relish	

Combine all ingredients smoothly. Makes about 1 cup sauce.

Serve with frankfurters, German sausages, corned beef, grilled meats, baked and broiled ham.

Fluffy Mustard Sauce: Whip 1 cup heavy cream stiff. Fold into German Mustard Sauce. Heap in chilled bowl. Delicious with cold meats, meat salads, and aspics.

NUTMEG CREAM SAUCE
FOR CAULIFLOWER

2 tablespoons butter or margarine	¾ cup milk
2 tablespoons flour	¼ cup water from cauliflower kettle
⅛ teaspoon pepper	¼ cup buttered crumbs
½ teaspoon salt	Extra nutmeg
½ teaspoon powdered nutmeg	

Melt butter or margarine in saucepan over low heat. Stir in flour smoothly. Add seasonings and mix until well blended. Stir in milk and cauliflower liquid slowly. Cook, stirring constantly, until smooth and thickened. Pour over hot cauliflower in serving dish. Sprinkle with buttered crumbs. Sprinkle with few grains of nutmeg. Makes 1 cup cream sauce. If mixed with crumbs, makes 1¼ cups sauce.

RAISIN SAUCE FOR MEATS

2 tablespoons butter or margarine	1½ cups water
1 onion, peeled and diced	2 tablespoons brown sugar
⅓ cup orange juice	⅛ teaspoon powdered cinnamon
1 tablespoon grated orange peel	⅛ teaspoon powdered cloves
1 small lemon, sliced and seeded	¼ teaspoon dry mustard
1 tablespoon cornstarch	½ cup seedless raisins
	½ teaspoon Kitchen Bouquet

Combine butter or margarine, onion, orange juice, peel, and lemon in glass container of mixer or blender. Cover and blend about 1 minute or until lemon is finely cut. Add remaining ingredients and blend about 30 seconds or until raisins are coarsely cut. Pour into saucepan. Bring to a boil. Stir constantly. Makes about 1½ cups sauce.

Serve hot with boiled beef tongue, baked or broiled ham, roast duckling, game birds and meats.

Port-Wine Raisin Sauce: Combine 1 cup port wine, ¼ cup wine vinegar, ½ cup seedless raisins, 1 tablespoon cornstarch, ½ cup sugar,

½ teaspoon powdered allspice, and 1 teaspoon dry mustard in glass container of mixer or blender. Blend 15 seconds. Pour into enamel or glass saucepan. Cook over moderate heat and stir continually until thickened. Let boil 3 or 4 minutes, stirring constantly. Makes about 2 cups sauce.

Serve hot with duckling, ham, beef tongue, game meats and birds.

ONION SAUCE

12 medium onions, peeled and diced fine
¼ cup butter or margarine
1 teaspoon salt
¼ teaspoon orégano
1 tablespoon Kitchen Bouquet
½ cup hot water

Cook onions in butter or margarine 15 minutes. Stir occasionally until just tender. Add salt, orégano, and Kitchen Bouquet. Mix well. Pour mixture into glass container of mixer or blender. Add hot water and cover. Blend 3 seconds or until onions are finely minced. Reheat and serve hot. Makes about 3 cups sauce.

Serve with hamburgers, sautéed liver, steak, and other meats. Delicious over small meat pastries, such as ham turnovers, and with reheated roast beef, lamb, or ham.

SERUNDANG

Condiment to serve with curry

1 4-ounce can shredded coconut
4 tablespoons butter
4 tablespoons brown sugar
1 8-ounce can salted peanuts, or less
1 teaspoon powdered coriander
½ teaspoon powdered cumin

Brown coconut lightly in butter. Add sugar. Stir and mix well. Add seasonings and peanuts. Stir to make all hot. Let cool. Serve as one of the many condiments which add flavor to a curry of chicken or lamb. This recipe makes 8 or more heaping tablespoons, enough for 8 servings.

Double for large party. Use ground peanuts if you prefer.

SWEET-AND-SOUR SAUCE

9-ounce can (1 cup) crushed pine-apple	½ cup cider vinegar
½ cup sugar	¼ cup water
½ cup chopped green pepper	2 tablespoons soy sauce
¼ cup chopped pimiento	10 drops Tabasco
½ clove garlic, mashed	2 tablespoons cornstarch
	¼ cup cold water

Use 1-quart glass or enamel saucepan. Combine pineapple, sugar, green pepper, pimiento, garlic, vinegar, ¼ cup water, the soy sauce, and Tabasco. Mix and heat slowly 5 minutes. Remove garlic. Stir cornstarch into ¼ cup water until smooth. Stir into hot mixture. Cook, stirring constantly, until thickened and clear, about 5 minutes' boiling. Makes 4 main-dish servings or 6 or more appetizer servings.

Serve with deep-fat fried shrimp. In Chinese restaurants a spicy, hot mustard sauce, or a bland fruit sauce, such as stewed, sieved plums, is served with the sweet-and-sour sauces. Fried shrimp held by the tail are dipped first into one and then the other and eaten with the fingers.

VINAIGRETTE SAUCE

½ cup French Dressing	1 teaspoon finely cut parsley
3 tablespoons chopped India relish	

Combine all ingredients. Makes about ¾ cup sauce.

Recipe is easily doubled or tripled. Spoon over cold asparagus or broccoli. Cover dish and let marinate in refrigerator an hour or longer before serving. To serve, drain vegetable, arrange on crisp lettuce, pour marinade over again. This is a favorite of mine over cold asparagus.

WALNUT-BUTTER SAUCE FOR VEGETABLES

A delicious variation of the butter sauce which is poured over hot asparagus tips, broccoli, and other green vegetables is made by adding 1 or 2 tablespoons ground walnuts to melted butter. Season with a little salt, pepper, and paprika.

Almond-Butter Sauce: Substitute ground or finely chopped toasted almonds for walnuts.

WHITE SAUCE

Thin

1 tablespoon butter or margarine	½ teaspoon salt
1 tablespoon flour	⅛ teaspoon pepper
	1 cup milk

Medium

2 tablespoons butter or margarine	½ teaspoon salt
2 tablespoons flour	⅛ teaspoon pepper
	1 cup milk

Thick

3 tablespoons butter or margarine	½ teaspoon salt
3 tablespoons flour	⅛ teaspoon pepper
	1 cup milk

Melt butter in saucepan. Stir in flour and seasoning smoothly. Add milk slowly. Cook and stir continually over moderate heat until boiling and cooked to desired thickness. Remove from heat. Use as described in various recipes. Makes a little more than 1 cup.

Additional seasonings, such as garlic salt, celery salt, sliced onion, Worcestershire, or Tabasco may be added. For *Cream Sauce* use half milk and half light cream, or all light cream, or whole evaporated milk.

Barbecue Sauces

FOUR-HERB BASTING SAUCE

½ cup salad oil	1 teaspoon salt
½ cup lemon juice	½ teaspoon black pepper
½ cup wine vinegar	1 teaspoon each basil, thyme, marjoram, savory
¼ cup soy sauce	

Combine all ingredients. Shake or stir and pour into glass jar with screw top. Keep covered in refrigerator until needed. Stir again before using. Makes about 2 cups sauce.

Use to baste lamb or chicken while roasting. Delicious on broiled butterfly shrimp.

See also barbecue chapter.

FISH BARBECUE SAUCE

1 cup ketchup or chili sauce
½ cup water
¼ cup olive oil
½ cup lemon juice
1 teaspoon paprika
⅛ teaspoon cayenne

⅛ teaspoon pepper
2 tablespoons grated onion
2 tablespoons Worcestershire
sauce
1 tablespoon sugar

Combine all ingredients in saucepan. Stir and simmer about 15 minutes. Keep pan warm on grill until fish are cooked. Makes about 2½ cups sauce. Serve with cooked fish.

KABOB BARBECUE SAUCE

⅔ cup vinegar
3 cups tomato juice
¼ cup brown sugar, packed
¼ cup prepared mustard
2 teaspoons garlic salt
2 teaspoons salt

½ teaspoon pepper
2 small onions, peeled and sliced
½ cup ketchup
2 tablespoons Worcestershire
sauce

Combine all ingredients in a 1½-quart agate or enamel saucepan. Stir, heat to boiling point, then lower heat and simmer 20 minutes. Keep hot on grill until kabobs are ready. Makes about 4½ cups sauce. Brush kabobs while cooking. Serve remaining sauce with cooked kabobs and rice.

TOMATO BARBECUE SAUCE

2 (8-ounce) cans tomato sauce
½ cup chopped peeled onion
½ teaspoon salt
¼ teaspoon pepper
2 teaspoons sugar

1 tablespoon vinegar
1 teaspoon Worcestershire sauce
½ teaspoon Tabasco sauce
Finely chopped onion for garnish

Combine tomato sauce with chopped onion, salt, pepper, sugar, vinegar, Worcestershire and Tabasco sauces in enamel or glass saucepan. Cover. Cook over low heat 30 minutes or until onion is tender and almost absorbed into sauce. Makes about 2 cups sauce.

Use to baste pork chops, burgers, franks, steaks. Serve any extra sauce, warm, with chopped onion on top of sauce bowl, as accompaniment for barbecued meat.

Fish Sauces

BÉCHAMEL SAUCE

1 cup milk	½ small peeled onion, minced
1 cup Fish Stock (page 302)	fine
4 tablespoons butter	4 tablespoons flour

Heat milk and Fish Stock together. Do not boil. Melt butter in saucepan. Add onion. Stir and cook 5 minutes. Add flour, stirring smoothly. Add hot milk and Fish Stock. Stir and cook over low heat until smooth and thickened. Let boil 2 or 3 minutes. Strain through fine sieve. Reheat. Makes about 2 cups sauce.

Serve with fish fillets, steaks, and baked whole stuffed fish.

CAPER SAUCE FOR FISH

½ cup melted butter	1 tablespoon lemon juice
1 tablespoon capers	Thin slice lemon

Combine melted butter, capers, and lemon juice. Place lemon slice in bottom of warmed sauce dish. Pour in butter sauce and serve. Makes about ⅝ cup, enough for 4 fish steaks.

DILL SAUCE FOR FISH

2 cups finely cut peeled onions	½ cup finely diced dill pickle
2 tablespoons butter or margarine	1 teaspoon finely cut fresh dill
	2 tablespoons finely cut parsley
1 tablespoon flour	½ teaspoon salt
1 cup milk	¼ teaspoon pepper

Add 2 or 3 tablespoons water to onions in saucepan. Simmer 6 or 7 minutes or until tender. Drain. Melt butter or margarine in another saucepan. Stir in flour smoothly. Add milk gradually, cooking and stirring until slightly thickened. Add onions and remaining ingredients. Stir and heat to boiling point. Makes about 2½ cups sauce.

Serve on baked stuffed whole fish, fish steaks, fried fish, fried oysters.

EGG SAUCE FOR BROILED FISH

2 cups Fish *Velouté*
2 teaspoons lemon juice

2 tablespoons butter
2 hard-cooked eggs

Add lemon juice and butter to hot *Velouté*. Dice eggs very fine. Stir into sauce. Makes 2½ cups sauce.

Serve with plain boiled, broiled, or baked fish.

FISH VELOUTÉ

2 tablespoons butter
2 tablespoons flour

2 cups Fish Stock (page 302)
Salt and pepper

Melt butter in saucepan. Stir in flour until smooth and golden. Stir in Fish Stock gradually. Cook, stirring continually, until sauce is smooth and thickened. If stock is well seasoned, no additional salt and pepper are needed. Taste, and season accordingly. Makes about 2 cups sauce. Use in various fish-sauce recipes as described.

For instance, *Sauce Cardinal:* Add 2 or 3 tablespoons Fish Stock to 2 cups hot Fish *Velouté*. Stir in 1 tablespoon chopped truffle, a little truffle juice, and 4 tablespoons Lobster Butter (page 540). A light sauce for sole or for any delicate fish fillet or steak. Makes about 2½ cups sauce.

GARLIC SAUCE FOR FISH

2 cups Fish *Velouté*
1 clove garlic
1 tablespoon diced green pepper
1 teaspoon diced peeled onion
1 teaspoon curry powder

1/16 teaspoon turmeric
1/16 teaspoon powdered cloves
1/16 teaspoon powdered cinnamon
1 tablespoon butter

Prepare *velouté*. Peel garlic, mash. Combine with remaining ingredients and stir and heat 3 minutes over low heat. Discard garlic. Stir remaining mixture into *velouté*. Bring to a boil. Makes about 2 cups sauce. Serve at once with grilled, broiled, or baked fish, with baked oysters or a barbecue of fish and oysters.

LEEKS SAUCE FOR FISH

2 tablespoons sliced leeks or scallions	1 teaspoon lemon juice
¾ cup dry white wine	2 tablespoons softened butter
2 cups Fish *Velouté (page 560)*	Salt and pepper

Heat leeks or scallions and wine in saucepan until liquid is reduced to about 3 tablespoons. Stir in *velouté*. Cook over low heat 5 minutes. Remove from heat. Blend lemon juice and soft butter together and stir into sauce. Add seasoning if needed. Makes about 2¾ cups sauce.

Serve on fish steaks, baked fillets, boiled or broiled salmon.

LOBSTER CREAM SAUCE

3 cups Medium Cream Sauce (page 557) (using 2 cups milk, 1 cup cream)	¼ teaspoon white pepper
	1 cup lobster meat, cut fine
½ teaspoon salt	2 tablespoons butter
	¼ cup dry sherry

Make Cream Sauce. Season with salt and pepper. Cut lobster in fine pieces or grind. Sauté lobster 3 minutes in butter. Add lobster and butter to sauce. Heat in upper part of double boiler over hot water about 15 minutes, stirring occasionally. Just before serving, stir in sherry. Makes about 4 cups sauce. Nice for Sunday night supper.

Serve over omelet, pancakes, toasted English muffins. Also serve on baked stuffed fish, fillets, fish steaks.

Crab Cream Sauce: Substitute 1 cup finely flaked, cleaned, cooked crab meat for lobster in above recipe.

Shrimp Cream Sauce: Substitute 1 cup finely minced, cooked and cleaned shrimp for lobster in above recipe.

OYSTER SAUCE FOR FISH

1 dozen shucked oysters	½ cup heavy cream
Oyster liquid	½ teaspoon salt
½ cup white wine	¼ teaspoon pepper
3 tablespoons butter	2 tablespoons finely cut parsley
2 tablespoons flour	1 tablespoon lemon juice

Heat oysters in saucepan over low heat 2 or 3 minutes or until steaming and edges begin to curl. Drain. Measure juice. Add enough wine to juice to make 1 cup. Melt butter in saucepan. Stir in flour smoothly. Add oyster-wine liquid, stirring steadily until slightly thickened. Add cream, a little at a time, stirring steadily as sauce thickens. Season. Add parsley and lemon juice. Makes about 2 cups sauce. Serve hot over fish steaks or broiled fillets.

PIMIENTO SAUCE FOR SHRIMP

½ cup Tartare Sauce (page 524)	½ cup commercial sour cream
3 whole canned pimientos, drained and cut fine	

Combine ingredients and mix thoroughly. Makes 1¼ cups sauce. Serve with iced shrimp as cocktail sauce, or on shrimp salad, or as dip.

Popular as sauce for the cold meats platter at our house.

REMOULADE SAUCE

1 clove garlic	1 cup mayonnaise
1 teaspoon dried tarragon	1 tablespoon capers
2 tablespoons finely cut parsley	½ teaspoon anchovy paste
1 hard-cooked egg, grated	½ teaspoon dry mustard

Peel garlic. Crush or dice fine. Mix with tarragon, parsley, egg, and mayonnaise. Mix remaining ingredients into sauce. Chill. Makes 1½ cups.

This is the sauce which is so essential to hot or cold fish, as a garnish or accessory to the fish flavor. Should be chilled for hot fish or as a garnish for cold salmon or a sea-food aspic.

Remoulade Sauce, Nino: Combine 2 cups mayonnaise, ½ cup finely chopped sour pickles, 2 tablespoons finely chopped capers, 1 tablespoon prepared mustard, 1 tablespoon mixed finely cut parsley, tarragon, and chervil. Makes about 2¾ cups sauce.

Other versions of this popular sauce include *Remoulade Sauce, Indienne,* which means 1 teaspoon curry powder is added, with 4 anchovy fillets, mashed, and about 1/16 teaspoon cayenne. A small amount of concentrated tomato paste may be added for color and flavor.

SAILOR'S SAUCE
Sauce Marinière

1 tablespoon butter or margarine	2 egg yolks
2 shallots or onions, finely chopped	Juice ½ lemon
¾ cup cream	Cooked mussels, small shrimp, oysters, or oyster crabs
½ cup Béchamel Sauce (page 559)	

Melt butter or margarine in saucepan. Add shallots. Stir and cook 2 minutes. Stir in ½ cup cream. Cook mixture until reduced to half the original amount. Stir in Béchamel Sauce. Bring to a boil. Taste for seasoning. Add little salt and pepper if needed. Beat egg yolks with remaining ¼ cup cream. Stir into sauce. Cook over low heat, stirring briskly until thickened. *Do not let boil.* Stir in lemon juice. Serve at once. Makes about 1½ cups sauce.

Traditionally this sauce is served with boiled or broiled fish garnished with a few cooked mussels, tiny shrimp, chopped cooked oysters, or oyster crabs. This sauce is also fine for spaghetti.

Dessert Sauces

BRANDY SAUCE

2 cups water	4 tablespoons butter
1 cup sugar	¼ cup cognac
1 tablespoon cornstarch	Juice ½ lemon

Combine water and sugar in saucepan. Heat until clear. Stir cornstarch into small amount of mixture, then into saucepan. Bring to a boil. Boil 2 minutes. Remove from heat. Add butter, brandy, and lemon juice. Mix. Serve slightly warm. Makes about 2½ cups sauce.

Delicious over spongecake, angel cake, rice pudding, other puddings.

BUTTERSCOTCH SAUCE

1 ¼ cups brown sugar, packed
½ cup light cream
2 tablespoons light corn syrup

4 tablespoons butter or margarine
1 teaspoon vanilla

Combine all ingredients except vanilla in small saucepan. Heat to boiling point. Boil 1 minute. Remove from heat. Stir in vanilla. Makes about 2 cups sauce.

Serve slightly warm over cupcake, ice cream, custard, and other desserts. If sauce becomes too thick on standing, reheat over hot water.

CARAMEL PECAN SAUCE

½ pound caramels
   (28 caramels)

½ cup light cream
¼ cup chopped pecans

Combine caramels and cream in upper part of double boiler over hot water. Stir and heat until candy is melted and smooth. Remove. Stir in nuts. Makes about 2 cups sauce.

Serve on ice cream, sponge pudding, spongecake.

CHOCOLATE ALMOND SAUCE

½ cup sugar
½ cup water
¼ cup light corn syrup
1 ½ (1-ounce) squares unsweetened chocolate

½ teaspoon vanilla
⅓ cup toasted slivered almonds

Combine sugar, water, and syrup in saucepan. Cook to thread stage or 230° F. on candy thermometer. Remove from heat. Add chocolate. Stir until melted. Add vanilla and almonds. Makes about 2 cups.

Delicious on ice cream, angel cake, poundcake, chilled canned or wine-cooked pears.

CHOCOLATE MARSHMALLOW SAUCE

½ pound (32) marshmallows
2 (1-ounce) squares unsweetened chocolate

½ cup evaporated milk
1 teaspoon vanilla

Combine marshmallows and chocolate in top part of double boiler over hot water. Stir and heat until mixture is smoothly melted. Stir in milk gradually. Add vanilla. Makes about 2 cups sauce.

Use on spongecake, ice cream, rice pudding.

UNCOOKED CHOCOLATE SAUCE

2 (1-ounce) squares unsweetened chocolate, grated
½ cup sugar
⅜ cup light cream, warmed

1 tablespoon butter or margarine
½ teaspoon vanilla
¹⁄₁₆ teaspoon salt

Combine all ingredients in blender. Blend 30 seconds or until smooth. Makes about 1 cup.

FUDGE SAUCE

½ cup light corn syrup
1 cup sugar
1 cup water

3 (1-ounce) squares unsweetened chocolate
1 teaspoon vanilla

Combine syrup, sugar, and water in saucepan. Bring to a boil. Add chocolate and stir until melted. Reduce heat. Simmer 10 to 15 minutes, until smooth. Stir occasionally. Add vanilla and let cool. Makes about 1½ cups.

CUSTARD SAUCE

3 egg yolks
3 tablespoons sugar
¹⁄₁₆ teaspoon salt

1½ cups milk
½ teaspoon vanilla

Beat yolks slightly in small saucepan. Stir in sugar and salt. Set pan over low heat. Stir in milk and cook, stirring constantly, until sauce thickens and coats metal spoon. Add flavoring. Remove from heat and set aside to cool. Makes about 2 cups sauce.

Serve this sauce over squares of spongecake or wherever a custard-type sauce is called for. Delicious on pears cooked in white wine and on various puddings.

Called Vanilla Sauce by some cooks. See also custards in dessert chapter.

HARD SAUCE

⅓ cup butter
¾ cup sifted confectioners' sugar
1 teaspoon vanilla or lemon extract or

2 tablespoons brandy, rum, or sherry

Cream butter. Add sugar gradually. Continue creaming until light and fluffy. Beat in flavoring. Serve on hot puddings. Makes 6 servings.

Fluffy Hard Sauce: Whip ¼ cup heavy cream. Fold into hard sauce after flavoring has been added. Increases number of servings to 8 or more.

Brown-Sugar Hard Sauce: Substitute ¾ cup brown sugar, packed, for confectioners' sugar. Beat in 1 egg yolk after butter and sugar have been creamed together. Fold in ½ cup chopped toasted almonds after flavoring has been added. Makes 8 servings.

MOLASSES HARD SAUCE

5 tablespoons butter or margarine
2 ¼ cups sifted confectioners' sugar

1 tablespoon milk
2 tablespoons molasses

Cream butter or margarine. Add sugar alternately with milk and molasses. Makes 2⅔ cups.

Delicious variation: add ¼ cup chopped toasted almonds or pecans. Makes almost 3 cups.

Delectable on hot pancakes and waffles and on almost any fruit pudding.

HONEY LEMON SAUCE

1 cup honey
½ cup water

1 tablespoon lemon juice
½ teaspoon powdered nutmeg

Combine all ingredients in saucepan. Heat only until very hot. Do not boil. Makes about 1½ cups sauce.

Serve hot over pancakes, plain cupcakes, gingerbread, rice pudding or other pudding. Also delicious over warm apple or peach turnover. Old-fashioned cooks served it over warm peach pie—that's a New England and Ohio tradition.

MACAROON CREAM SAUCE

1 cup heavy cream   ½ cup crumbled macaroon
                                         crumbs

Whip cream until stiff. Fold in crumbs. Makes about 1½ cups cream.

Serve with jellied fruit. Especially good with Coffee Jelly (page 273).

MOCHA SAUCE FOR SOUFFLÉS

2 egg yolks   ⅔ cup triple-strength, freshly
½ cup sugar   brewed coffee
⅛ teaspoon salt   1 cup heavy cream, whipped

Beat egg yolks slightly in upper part of double boiler. Add sugar, salt, and coffee. Cook over hot, not boiling, water until thickened and smooth. Stir constantly. Let cool. Fold whipped cream into mixture. Makes 6 servings.

Serve on chocolate and lemon, orange, or other fruit soufflés.

MOLASSES SAUCE FOR PANCAKES

1 cup butter or margarine   2 tablespoons New Orleans
2 teaspoons sugar or brown sugar   molasses

Soften butter or margarine. Combine with sugar and molasses. Makes about 1 cup sauce.

Serve on waffles, pancakes, toast, and for after-school snack spread on bread.

NUTMEG SAUCE

1 tablespoon cornstarch   1 teaspoon grated lemon peel
½ cup sugar   3 tablespoons lemon juice or
¼ teaspoon salt   sherry
½ teaspoon powdered nutmeg   1 tablespoon grenadine
1 cup boiling water   2 tablespoons butter

Mix cornstarch, sugar, salt, and nutmeg. Stir into boiling water gradually. Continue to stir over low heat until mixture thickens and boils. Boil 2 or 3 minutes, until sauce is clear. Beat in lemon peel, juice or sherry, and grenadine. Serve hot with Suet Pudding (page 682). Makes 6 servings.

SHERRY CREAM SAUCE

2 eggs	2 tablespoons sherry
1½ cups powdered sugar	⅛ teaspoon salt
1 teaspoon vanilla	1 cup heavy cream, whipped

Beat yolks until thick and lemon-colored. Beat ¾ cup sugar into yolks. Beat whites until they stand in stiff points when beater is removed. Beat remaining ¾ cup sugar into whites. Combine whites and yolks. Add vanilla, sherry, and salt. Just before serving, fold in whipped cream. Makes about 3 cups sauce.

Delicious on orange, lemon, or chocolate soufflé and on fruit puddings.

EASY STRAWBERRY SAUCE

1 pint fresh strawberries	½ cup confectioners' sugar

Clean berries. Combine with sugar in glass container of mixer or blender. Blend about 5 minutes or until smooth. Serve immediately over ice cream or cake, or chill in refrigerator until ready for use. Makes about 1½ cups sauce.

Substitute 1 (12-ounce) package quick-frozen berries for fresh strawberries.

Kirsch Strawberry Sauce: Flavor the sauce with 1 teaspoon kirsch. Add kirsch few drops at a time in last minute of blending.

Easy Raspberry Sauce: Easy Blueberry Sauce: Easy Blackberry Sauce: Substitute fresh or quick-frozen berries for strawberries in recipe above.

CHAPTER TWENTY

Skillet Suppers

A skillet supper is another name for an informal, happy occasion when a heart-warming dish satisfies hunger. Because it is cooked on the table it makes a conversation piece for a family or guest meal.

Terrace, play room, back porch luncheons and suppers, almost any meal planned for leisurely, easy service, may be highlighted by a skillet-cooked main dish—which means a dish either cooked in its entirety in an electric skillet at the table or completed in this manner. Many of my chafing dish recipes can be prepared in an electric skillet. So can many, many other dishes in the eggs, fish, meats, poultry, and vegetable chapters. Read the recipes through, prepare sauces and various mixtures ahead of time, and, as with chafing dish cookery, arrange on a tray all foods, seasonings, and accessories used in making the dish.

Try out any new appliance on the family before attempting a supper for guests. Follow the manufacturer's directions with an electric skillet (or any other appliance) and adapt the recipe's general preparation and cookery instructions to the appliance. Of course these recipes also may be cooked in a non-electric skillet set on an electric hot plate or Sterno on a tray at the table.

Most of the skillet recipes are for hearty main dishes. You may want to serve a tossed salad, hot bread, and a fruit or other dessert with them. I find that guests at this kind of informal party like to help in the cooking and serving, so instead of setting a table I arrange plates and silver as I do for buffet meals and let everybody have a share in the work as well as in the enjoyment of the hot dish.

BEEF AND CHINESE NOODLES

1 onion, peeled and chopped	1 ¼ cups leftover gravy or 1
1 green pepper, sliced	(10 ½ -ounce) can condensed
1 (4-ounce) can sliced mush-rooms	mushroom soup
	2 cups cubed cooked beef
2 tablespoons butter or marga-rine	4 cups canned Chinese noodles, crisped in oven

Sauté onion, green pepper, and drained mushrooms in butter or margarine about 5 minutes or until vegetables are tender. Stir frequently. Add gravy or mushroom soup. Thin a little, if necessary, with a very small amount of hot water or consommé. Stir and mix. Add beef. Continue to stir and heat until boiling. Serve on mounds of oven-crisped Chinese noodles. Makes 4 servings.

BEEF BALLS AND ONION RINGS

12 large onion rings	1 egg, beaten
3 tablespoons butter or marga-rine	¼ cup raw quick-cooking rice
	¼ cup bread crumbs
1 ¼ cups leftover gravy or 1 (10 ½ -ounce) can condensed mushroom soup	1 small onion, peeled and diced
1 pound ground beef	1 teaspoon salt
	½ teaspoon pepper

Fry onion rings in butter or margarine until almost tender. Drain and keep hot. Combine ¼ cup gravy or mushroom soup, the meat, egg, rice, crumbs, and diced onion. Mix evenly, using two forks. Add seasonings. Mix and shape into 12 small balls. Brown in same fat in which onion cooked. When meat balls are browned on all sides, add remaining 1 cup gravy or soup. Cover skillet. Simmer 25 to 30 minutes, on low heat, until meat is cooked. Serve garnished with hot onion rings. Makes 6 servings.

Additional vegetables give color and good flavor to this skillet dish: try adding 3 sliced, scraped carrots, or 1 chopped green pepper, or 3 cubed new potatoes. Cover and simmer 30 minutes. Add more gravy if needed for good consistency.

BACON-WRAPPED FRANKS WITH BEANS

8 frankfurters
8 strips lean bacon
2 tablespoons molasses

2 tablespoons prepared mustard
2 tablespoons cider vinegar
2 (1-pound) cans kidney beans

Wrap each frankfurter with bacon strip. Place in cold skillet and turn heat high. Cook until bacon is crisp all over. Turn franks carefully with pancake turner. Remove franks and keep them hot. Pour off most of fat. Mix molasses, mustard, and vinegar. Stir into kidney beans. Mix well. Pour into skillet. Cook over medium heat until slightly thickened and very hot. Place franks on top and continue to heat 5 minutes. Makes 4 servings.

An assortment of pickle relishes adds to the enjoyment of this skillet favorite. Mustard, mustard pickle, red-pepper relish, green-pickle relish, sliced sweet pickles in serving dishes on a relish tray are favorites at Daisyfields. We toast rolls and serve a tomato aspic salad with romaine with this dish. Fresh fruit or cake and coffee finish the supper.

FRANKFURTERS IN SPANISH SAUCE

8 frankfurters
¼ cup butter or margarine
½ green pepper, sliced
1 onion, peeled and sliced
1 (5-ounce) package quick-cooking rice

1 ¾ cups hot water
2 (8-ounce) cans tomato sauce
1 teaspoon salt
¼ teaspoon pepper
2 tablespoons finely cut parsley

Brown franks in a little butter or margarine in skillet on medium heat. Remove cooked franks. Melt remaining butter or margarine in skillet. Add green pepper, onion, and uncooked rice. Cook and stir on high heat 5 minutes or until vegetables are lightly browned. Add hot water, tomato sauce, salt, and pepper. Mix well. Bring to a boil. Cover. Lower heat and simmer 15 minutes. Slice frankfurters into hot sauce. Simmer 5 minutes longer. Sprinkle top with parsley. Makes 4 servings.

KABUTOYAKI

Japanese Beef Dinner

1 cup shoyu sauce	2 or 3 cubes bean curd (*tofu*)
½ cup dry sherry or *sake*	2 green peppers, cut in strips,
½ cup olive oil	parboiled
¼ cup cider vinegar	1 small eggplant, cut in thin
¼ teaspoon chili powder	slices
Beef fat for skillet	6 carrots, scraped, boiled, cut in
1 pound sirloin steak, cut in thin	strips
strips	

Mix shoyu sauce, sherry or *sake*, oil, and vinegar. Season with chili powder to taste. Pour about half mixture into shallow dish. Pour remaining mixture into 4 small dishes for guests.

Add just enough fat to skillet to sizzle evenly all over cooking surface. Dip strips of steak into shoyu mixture. Lay on hot cooking surface. Cook at high heat, turning meat once, until beef is done. Serve at once or push to one side in skillet. Add vegetables. Cook in very little fat until tender and browning. Serve all at once onto warmed dinner plates. Guests use fork or chopsticks to dip meat into sauce. Makes 4 servings.

Beef Sukiyaki: The best-known Japanese skillet dinner is sukiyaki, which is delicious and easily prepared at the table. Ask meat dealer to give you the most tender cut of beef. Cut it in thin slices about 1 inch wide and 2 or 3 inches long, or have meat dealer do this for you.

1 small piece beef suet	8 washed, drained spinach
1 pound beef	leaves
4-ounce pieces of bean curd (*tofu*)	8 scallions, or 4 leeks, sliced
1⅓ cups consommé or bouillon	4 thin slices Chinese lettuce or
½ cup shoyu sauce	head lettuce
¼ cup sugar	4 mushrooms, sliced
2 tablespoons *sake*, sherry, or	
whiskey	

Heat a large skillet slightly. Rub the cooking surface with small piece beef suet. Spread the slices of beef over greased surface. Cook until browned. Add more suet and curd to skillet while meat cooks tender and done. Gather beef at one side of skillet. Remove remaining suet or curd. Mix consommé or bouillon, shoyu sauce, sugar, and *sake*, sherry, or whiskey and pour into skillet. Add spinach, scallions or leeks, lettuce, and mushrooms. Cover skillet and let cook. Stir with long chopsticks frequently. Uncover after 5 minutes. When vegetables are done, which is about 10 minutes cooking, each guest immediately helps himself to meat and vegetables. Makes 4 servings.

At Japanese restaurants the skillet for sukiyaki is put on the table on a gas ring or electric plate and the cooking is started. Then a clear soup is served. When the soup is eaten, cold, crisp vegetables, such as carrots, white turnips, radishes, and green peppers, decoratively sliced, are brought to the table and then hot rice in a covered bowl. By this time the delicate greens added to the beef in the skillet are ready. These are served with meat from the skillet to your plate, the waiter using long chopsticks. Some Japanese restaurants serve a thin macaroni or vermicelli in place of rice, and offer a raw egg for the Japanese-trained gourmet who likes to eat the hot meat after dipping it into beaten egg.

Other dishes served with either of these Japanese skillet dishes include grated raw radishes, chopped pickled melon rind, shrimp sautéed and to be dipped by guests into shoyu sauce, preserved fruits, fresh fruits, tea, sherry or dry wine or *sake,* and almond cookies.

KRAUT SAUSAGE SKILLET

1 pound sausage meat	1 (No. 2) can sauerkraut
1 (14-ounce) can pineapple chunks	¼ cup pineapple syrup
1 large apple, cored and sliced	1 tablespoon brown sugar

This dish should be started before guests arrive, since it calls for long, slow cooking. Cook sausage slowly over low heat, 15 minutes. Stir with fork from time to time to brown all. Drain off all but about 2 tablespoons drippings.

Drain pineapple. Save ¼ cup syrup. Add pineapple and apple slices to sausage. Continue cooking 5 minutes. Add kraut, pineapple syrup, and sprinkle with sugar. Cover skillet. Let cook over low heat 40 minutes. Makes 4 to 6 servings.

A good winter night's supper dish. Serve small boiled potatoes with this dish, hot corn bread, and prune or peach open-face pie for dessert.

PABLO'S SPANISH RICE

½ cup bacon drippings	1 ¾ cups water
1 pound ground beef	1 (8-ounce) can tomato paste
½ green pepper, diced	1 (8-ounce) can tomatoes
1 large onion, peeled and sliced thin	1 teaspoon salt
4 ripe olives, sliced	¼ teaspoon pepper
1 ⅓ cups raw quick-cooking rice	1 teaspoon prepared mustard

Heat drippings in skillet. Brown beef 5 minutes or longer. Add green pepper, onion, olives, and rice. Stir and cook 10 minutes. Add all remaining ingredients. Mix and stir. Bring to a boil. Cover tightly. Reduce heat and let simmer 10 minutes. Makes 4 or more servings.

Corn bread is good with this one, too, or toasted English muffins, buttered and served with grape jelly or currant jam.

Hot coffee and dessert, such as a smooth, cold chocolate mousse, make this an easy and delicious supper.

FU'S PEPPER STEAK

1 pound sirloin, cut ¼ inch thick	1 (1-pound) can tomatoes, chopped
2 tablespoons beef suet	1 large green pepper, cut in thin strips
¼ cup chopped peeled onion	2 tablespoons cornstarch
1 slice peeled garlic	¼ cup cold water
1 teaspoon salt	2 tablespoons soy sauce
¼ teaspoon pepper	4 cups hot cooked noodles
1 bouillon cube	
1 cup hot water	

Cut beef in serving pieces or narrow strips. Brown slowly in hot beef fat about 15 minutes. Add onion and garlic. Season with salt and pepper. Stir and cook 1 or 2 minutes longer. Dissolve bouillon cube in hot water. Add to meat. Cover skillet and let simmer until meat is almost done, 20 to 30 minutes. Add tomatoes and green pepper. Cook 10 minutes longer. Remove garlic slice. Uncover skillet. Add combined cornstarch, water, and soy sauce stirred together. Mix and bring to a boil. Cook, stirring constantly, 5 minutes longer or until sauce is thickened and clear. Serve with hot noodles. Makes 4 servings.

Our Chinese houseman, Fu, sometimes omitted tomatoes. He added tender young Chinese pea pods or increased the amount of green pepper after his trips to Chinatown for supplies.

PORK AND BEANS, SICILIAN

2	tablespoons olive oil	1 ½	teaspoons salt
1	clove garlic, peeled and mashed	¼	teaspoon pepper
		½	teaspoon thyme
1	cup sliced peeled onions	2	cups diced cooked pork
2	tablespoons flour	1 ½	to 2 cups yellow wax beans, broken
1	(No. 303) can tomatoes		
½	cup water	4	cups hot saffron rice
½	cup ketchup		

Heat oil in skillet. Add garlic and onions. Cook until onions are tender. Blend in flour. Stir smoothly and cook 4 or 5 minutes, stirring steadily. Add tomatoes, water, ketchup, salt, pepper, thyme, and pork. Cover skillet and bring to a boil; turn heat low. Simmer 15 minutes. Remove garlic and discard it. Stir beans into mixture. Cover and continue to cook 20 minutes or until beans are done. Serve on mound of hot saffron rice, spooning gravy from skillet over the top. Makes 6 servings.

PORK CHOPS, SAN FRANCISCO STYLE

6	loin pork chops	2	tablespoons cornstarch
Salt and pepper		½	teaspoon rosemary
1	tablespoon bacon drippings	1 ¼	cups hot water
½	peeled garlic clove	3	tablespoons lemon juice
2	tablespoons sugar	6	thin slices lemon

Season chops with salt and pepper. Brown in hot fat in skillet with garlic 15 minutes on medium heat. When chops are browned on both sides, remove garlic and discard it. Move chops to 1 side.

Add sugar, cornstarch, and rosemary to skillet. Reduce heat. Stir to mix with fat in skillet. Add water slowly, stirring to mix. Cook and stir until thick and clear. Stir in lemon juice. Place 1 lemon slice on each browned chop in sauce. Cover skillet and simmer at low heat about 40 minutes. Uncover. Cook 10 minutes or until fork-tender. Makes 6 servings.

Start this dish before guests come to the table for their appetizer first course, which may be a colorful California salad. Taste the sauce before placing the chops in it, and add salt or more herb if needed.

If salad is not the first course, serve a big fruit-platter salad after this main dish. Hot coffee, of course. If dessert is wanted, poundcake or a delicate soufflé will taste good.

SKILLET MEAT-AND-NOODLES

1	(8-ounce) package noodles	2	teaspoons salt
3	tablespoons butter or margarine	⅛	teaspoon pepper
2	onions, peeled and sliced	6	tablespoons grated Parmesan cheese
1	cup thinly sliced celery	1½	cups undiluted evaporated milk
2½	cups cut-up leftover pot roast of lamb, veal, beef, or chicken	2	tablespoons finely cut parsley

Cook noodles according to directions on package and drain. While noodles are cooking, sauté onions and celery in butter or margarine in large skillet. Cook 5 minutes or until vegetables are beginning to brown. Push vegetables to one side. Add meat and heat slowly.

Season drained noodles with salt and pepper. Add cheese and milk. Stir into meat and vegetables in skillet. Let all heat 5 minutes, mixing lightly with two forks. Sprinkle top with parsley. Makes 6 servings.

STEAK-ROLL SKILLET SUPPER

1	onion, peeled and cut fine	30	crackers, crumbled
1	green pepper, cut fine	1	teaspoon salt
1	clove garlic, peeled and cut fine	½	teaspoon pepper
¼	pound butter or margarine	4	cube steaks
1	(7-ounce) can tomato paste	¾	cup hot water

Sauté onion, green pepper, and garlic in half the butter or margarine in large skillet, or electric skillet at 250° F., until golden brown. Combine half tomato paste with cracker crumbs, salt, and pepper. Add to onion mixture. Spoon mixture onto steaks. Roll each and fasten with small skewer. Brown rolls on all sides in remaining butter or margarine. Blend remaining tomato paste with ¾ cup hot water. Pour over steaks and cover skillet. Simmer covered over low heat 40 to 50 minutes, electric skillet at 150° F. to 180° F. Remove skewers before serving. Makes 4 servings.

Washed, drained, cut string beans may be cooked with steaks. Add to skillet for last 20 minutes of cooking. Increased liquid may be necessary. Add a little hot water.

Cube steaks are small, thin, not-so-tender steaks, usually from the round or chuck. The meat dealer scores them or "cubes" them, cutting the fibers to make the meat more tender. If minute steaks are used in this recipe, pound them lightly, season with salt and pepper before stuffing and rolling.

For dinner, serve a sardine-cheese canapé and vegetable-juice cocktail, raisin bread or muffins, a cucumber salad, and sherbet with coffee.

WONDERFUL-FLAVOR VEAL

2 pounds tender veal cutlet	2 tablespoons finely cut parsley
Flour	¾ cup dry vermouth
6 slices lean bacon	½ cup chopped pecans
1 ½ teaspoons salt	4 cups hot cooked noodles or
Paprika	rice
2 tablespoons finely cut chives	

Cut veal in bite-size cubes and dredge well with flour. Cook bacon in skillet until crisp. Drain on thick paper towels. Crumble bacon or cut in small pieces. Cook veal in hot bacon drippings over high heat. Add salt, paprika, chives, parsley, and bacon. Heat ½ cup vermouth and pour over meat mixture. Stir well. Cover skillet and lower heat. Let sauce cook down. Add remaining ¼ cup heated vermouth, and nuts. Cook 2 or 3 minutes. Serve with hot noodles or rice. Makes 4 to 6 servings.

CHAPTER TWENTY-ONE

Soufflés

A controversy on soufflés among home economists and homemakers centers on whether to grease the soufflé dish or not. Some of my favorite recipes, given to me by hostesses in the South, in the West, as well as around New England and the Middle West, call for a greased deep dish. Others specify an ungreased casserole. I follow *their* recipes and my soufflés are airy and light, do not fall in a crumpled heap, and are a pleasure to serve as well as a satisfyingly handsome and delicious part of my menus.

As a general rule, a basic white sauce or cream sauce, or other smooth and slightly thickened sauce, is essential to good soufflé results. The sauce mixture is folded into stiffly beaten egg whites. Fold gently. Lift up and over in high strokes.

Pour mixture at once into soufflé dish, whether greased or ungreased, according to recipe instructions. Bake in a slow or moderately slow oven, but again, follow the recipe as to oven temperature and time. Do not open oven to observe the soufflé's progress. If you *must* open the oven, do not close the door with a bang. Leave the soufflé alone to gently rise and bake. Remove it from the oven to the table. Serve at once!

"Serve tenderly," one famous chef told me. Break soufflé apart into servings, using fork and spoon or two forks, and onto waiting dessert dishes or plates only seconds from the oven.

Cheese Soufflés

"SUNNYBANK" CHEESE SOUFFLÉ

1 cup milk	1/16 teaspoon paprika
3 tablespoons butter or margarine	1/16 teaspoon soda
1/4 cup flour	1/4 pound sharp processed cheese, chopped
1/2 teaspoon salt	4 eggs
1/4 teaspoon black pepper	

Scald milk in small saucepan. Melt butter or margarine in upper part of 1-quart double boiler over hot water. Stir in flour smoothly. Add hot milk, salt, pepper, paprika, and soda. Stir and cook until smooth and thickened. Stir cheese into sauce until melted and smooth. Remove pan from hot water. Let stand at kitchen temperature 30 minutes.

Start oven at moderately slow (300° F.).

Beat egg yolks until light and lemony. Beat egg whites until they stand in stiff points when beater is removed. Beat yolks into cheese mixture, then fold into whites. Turn into ungreased 1½-quart casserole. Set casserole (if oven glass or any ware but very heavy pottery) in shallow pan of hot water.

Bake 1 hour and 15 minutes. Do not open oven door while soufflé is baking. Serve at once. Makes 4 to 6 servings.

This has been my standard cheese soufflé recipe for nigh onto twenty years, with never a failure. It was the standard of "Sunnybank," beloved home of my old often remembered friend, Albert Payson Terhune.

See also cheese chapter.

CHEDDAR SOUFFLÉ SAN YSIDRO

3 tablespoons butter or margarine	1/4 teaspoon curry powder
3 tablespoons flour	1 teaspoon Worcestershire sauce
1 teaspoon grated peeled onion	1 cup milk
1 teaspoon prepared mustard	1 cup grated Cheddar cheese
1/2 teaspoon salt	4 eggs, plus 1 egg white

Start oven at moderately slow (300° F.).

Melt butter or margarine in small saucepan. Stir in flour smoothly. Add onion, mustard, salt, curry powder, and Worcestershire sauce. Stir in milk slowly. Cook, stirring constantly, over low heat until mixture thickens and boils 1 minute. Add cheese. Stir until cheese melts. Remove from heat.

Beat egg whites until they stand in stiff points when beater is removed. Beat yolks until thick and lemon-colored. Stir cheese sauce into yolks slowly. Fold into whites gently and lightly.

Pour at once into ungreased 1½-quart deep baking dish. Make circle in top of soufflé with tip of spoon about 1 inch from rim of dish. Set dish in shallow pan of hot water.

Bake 50 minutes to 1 hour or until top is puffy and browned. Serve at once. Makes 6 servings.

Serve with or without rarebit sauce, the specialty of San Ysidro Ranch, Santa Barbara. Leftover or canned chicken gravy heated with a little curry powder for seasoning makes a delicious sauce on this soufflé as does tomato sauce.

CHEESE-AND-MUSHROOM SOUFFLÉ

1 (3-ounce) can chopped broiled mushrooms
½ teaspoon salt
1 thin slice peeled onion
1 tablespoon quick-cooking rice
2 tablespoons butter or margarine
¼ cup grated processed American cheese
¼ teaspoon paprika
3 eggs, plus 1 egg white

Drain mushrooms. Grind fine. Add water to mushroom broth to make ½ cup liquid. Heat, with salt and onion added, in saucepan. When boiling, add rice. Stir until thickened. Cover and simmer over low heat 3 minutes. Remove from heat. Add butter or margarine, cheese, and paprika. Mix smoothly.

Start oven at moderate (325° F.).

Beat egg yolks until thick and lemon-colored. Add to rice mixture, stirring until thickened. Add mushrooms. Let cool. Beat egg whites until they stand in stiff points when beater is removed. Fold mushroom mixture into whites. Pour at once into ungreased 1-quart deep baking dish. Set dish in shallow pan of hot water.

Bake about 35 minutes or until puffed and browned. Serve at once. Makes 4 servings.

Cheese-and-Vegetable Soufflés: Substitute 6 tablespoons any mashed, cooked vegetable, such as peas, green beans, limas, asparagus, broccoli, zucchini, or carrots, for mushrooms in above recipe. A good way to use leftover cooked green vegetables. Mash or grind. If dry, moisten with a little hot water or consommé. Add to rice mixture in place of mushrooms, as described.

See also cheese chapter.

Chicken, Fish, and Meat Soufflés .

CHICKEN SOUFFLÉ

3 tablespoons butter or margarine	⅛ teaspoon pepper
	¼ teaspoon paprika
1 thin slice peeled onion	1 cup milk
3 tablespoons flour	3 eggs
½ teaspoon salt	1 cup cubed cooked chicken
⅛ teaspoon powdered ginger	

Start oven at moderate (375° F.).

Combine all ingredients except egg whites in glass container of mixer or blender. Cover and blend about 15 seconds or until barely mixed. Pour into saucepan. Cook over moderate heat, stirring constantly until thickened. Remove from heat. Whip egg whites until they stand in peaks when beater is removed. Gently fold cooked mixture into whites.

Pour at once into ungreased 1-quart deep baking dish. Set dish in shallow pan of hot water.

Bake about 35 minutes or until puffy and brown. Serve at once. Makes 4 servings.

Serve as main dish of luncheon or Sunday supper. Needs only a hearty salad or a cooked vegetable, such as broccoli or asparagus, as accompaniment. Dessert after this delicate main dish may be a good fruit pie or favorite cake, with coffee.

See also chicken, fish, and meat chapters.

CRAB-MEAT SOUFFLÉ, BALTIMORE STYLE

¼ cup flour
¼ teaspoon salt
¼ teaspoon pepper
½ cup mayonnaise
¼ cup milk

¼ teaspoon basil
¼ teaspoon tarragon
1 ¼ cups flaked, cleaned crab meat
4 egg whites

Start oven at moderate (325° F.). Grease deep 7-inch casserole.

Combine flour, salt, pepper, and mayonnaise. Do not beat. Stir only to mix. Add milk slowly, stirring gently. Add herbs. Stir only until smooth. Stir in crab meat. Beat egg whites until they stand in stiff points when beater is removed. Fold crab mixture gently into whites. Pour at once into prepared baking dish. Set dish in shallow pan of hot water.

Bake 40 to 45 minutes. Makes 4 servings. Serve with hot mushroom sauce.

A good Sunday luncheon dish. A delicate salad, such as Belgian endive, or new potatoes with parsley-butter sauce, and very small currant muffins add up to a good menu. Serve fresh strawberries or red raspberries for dessert.

HAM SOUFFLÉ

4 tablespoons butter or margarine
¼ cup all-purpose flour
¾ cup milk
4 egg yolks

1 cup ground cooked ham
1 teaspoon dry mustard
⅛ teaspoon pepper
6 egg whites
½ teaspoon cream of tartar

Start oven at moderate (375° F.). Grease narrow, deep 2-quart baking dish or casserole.

Melt butter or margarine in saucepan. Stir in flour smoothly. Add milk gradually, stirring and cooking until mixture thickens and boils. Remove from heat. Beat egg yolks slightly. Stir into cream sauce. Add ham, mustard, and pepper. Mix. Beat egg whites until foamy. Add cream of tartar and beat until they stand in stiff points when beater is removed. Fold ham mixture into egg whites. Pour at once into prepared baking dish. Set dish in shallow pan of hot water.

Bake 35 to 40 minutes, until puffy and browned. Serve immediately. Makes 4 servings.

CRAB-MEAT SOUFFLÉ, HOTEL PIERRE

2 tablespoons finely cut green peppers	4 eggs, plus 1 extra egg white
1 teaspoon finely cut peeled onion	2 cups cleaned, flaked, cooked crab meat
1 tablespoon butter	½ teaspoon salt
2 cups cream sauce	¼ teaspoon pepper
	⅛ teaspoon dry mustard

Start oven at moderate (350° F.).

Sauté peppers and onion in butter until vegetables are tender. Combine with cream sauce. Beat egg yolks until thick and lemon-colored. Add cream sauce. Mix gently to blend. Add crab meat and combine evenly but gently. Add seasonings. Whip 5 egg whites until they stand in points when beater is removed. Fold crab mixture into whites gently. Pour at once into straight-sided 2-quart baking dish. Set dish in shallow pan of hot water.

Bake 40 minutes or until soufflé rises and is well browned. Makes 6 servings.

May be served with hot mushroom sauce or with a delicate cheese sauce. Succotash tastes good with this. So does a tossed green salad. Small fruit tarts, or a sherbet with cookies or layer cake, round out a menu featuring this soufflé.

Lobster Soufflé: Substitute 2 cups flaked, finely cut cooked or canned lobster meat for crab meat in above recipe. Add 1 or 2 truffles, finely minced. Serve with any fish sauce. Makes 6 servings.

Shrimp Soufflé: Substitute 2 cups ground cooked or canned shrimp for crab in above recipe. Add 1 teaspoon anchovy paste or 1 tablespoon finely cut anchovies to mixture before folding into beaten whites. Serve with any fish sauce. Makes 6 servings.

FISH SOUFFLÉ

1¼ cups flaked cooked fish	3 eggs, plus 2 egg whites
1 tablespoon butter	½ teaspoon salt
⅔ cup thick Béchamel Sauce (page 559)	¼ teaspoon pepper

Start oven at moderate (350° F.). Butter deep 1½-quart soufflé baking dish.

If fish seems dry, moisten with little hot water or Fish Stock. Cook in butter 6 to 7 minutes, stirring to break up fish. Add Béchamel Sauce. Mix lightly.

Beat egg yolks until thick and lemon-colored. Fold fish mixture into yolks. Add salt and pepper. Whip 5 egg whites until they stand in stiff points when beater is removed. Fold fish-and-yolk mixture into whites. Pour at once into prepared baking dish. Set dish in shallow pan of hot water.

Bake 30 to 40 minutes or until soufflé is risen and browned. Makes 6 servings.

A cucumber salad and either new peas and carrots with butter sauce or green beans go well with this soufflé. Small hot rolls, with a sweet jam, such as strawberry, and to finish, a cool dessert such as a sherbet or quick-frozen berries.

Oyster Soufflé: Cook 1½ cups small shelled oysters in their own juice 3 or 4 minutes or only until edges curl. Let cool. Grind very fine and then put through sieve. Combine with Béchamel Sauce. Complete recipe as given above. Makes 6 servings.

Serve with garnish of crisp bacon or thin strips of broiled or baked ham.

A tomato salad, or broiled tomato halves, and baked zucchini are vegetables which round out the flavors in an oyster soufflé. Small mince tarts, a raisin pie, or a luxurious compote of brandied fruits to finish.

Soufflés for Dessert

SOFT CHOCOLATE SOUFFLÉ, FRENCH STYLE

5 egg whites
½ cup sugar
⅛ teaspoon salt
2 (1-ounce) squares bitter chocolate, melted

½ cup ground pecans
Mocha Sauce for Soufflés
   (page 567)

Beat egg whites until they stand in points when beater is removed. Beat sugar and salt into whites. Fold melted chocolate and nuts into whites. Pour into top part of 2-quart double boiler and cover. Cook over hot water 45 minutes without lifting cover. Turn out on warmed platter. Serve at once with the Mocha Sauce. Makes 6 servings.

CHOCOLATE SOUFFLÉ

2 tablespoons butter
2 (1-ounce) squares unsweetened chocolate
2 tablespoons flour
½ teaspoon salt
⅓ cup sugar
2 tablespoons quick-cooking tapioca

2 cups milk
⅛ teaspoon powdered mace
⅓ cup chopped nuts
3 eggs, plus 1 egg white
1 cup heavy cream

Melt butter and chocolate together in upper part of 1-quart double boiler over hot water. Blend well. Mix flour, salt, sugar, and tapioca together. Stir into chocolate mixture to make thick paste. Add milk gradually, stirring constantly. Cook about 20 minutes or until thick. Remove pan from water and let cool to lukewarm.

Start oven at moderate (325° F.). Butter deep 2-quart casserole.

Add mace and chopped nuts to chocolate mixture. Beat yolks until thick and lemony. Fold into chocolate mixture. Whip 4 egg whites until they stand in peaks when beater is removed. Fold chocolate mixture into whites. Pour at once into prepared casserole. Set casserole in shallow pan of hot water.

Bake 1 hour and 15 minutes or until soufflé is firm. Do not open oven door during baking. Serve immediately with whipped cream. Makes 6 servings.

This can bake happily through an attenuated company dinner. If its finish doesn't synchronize with the removal of the salad course, we just explain what is coming and everyone quite understands. Sometimes we omit the whipped-cream topping and serve a thinned marshmallow sauce. The children, and all males at the table, adore it. Having to wait adds to their anticipation.

APPLE SOUFFLÉ

⅓ cup quick-cooking tapioca
½ cup sugar
½ teaspoon salt
2 cups milk
2 tablespoons butter or margarine
¼ teaspoon powdered cinnamon

⅛ teaspoon powdered nutmeg
1½ tablespoons lemon juice
1 cup grated raw apple
Butter and powdered sugar for baking dish
3 eggs
1 cup heavy cream, whipped

Combine tapioca, sugar, salt, and milk in top part of double boiler. Place over rapidly boiling water. Bring to scalding point, 3 to 5 minutes, and cook 5 minutes longer, stirring frequently. Add butter or margarine, spices, lemon juice, and apple. Mix. Let cool slightly.

Start oven at moderate (350° F.). Rub deep 1½-quart soufflé baking dish lightly with butter, then dust lightly with powdered sugar.

Beat egg yolks until thick and lemon-colored. Whip egg whites until they stand in peaks when beater is removed. Add yolks to apple mixture. Blend well. Fold into whites. Pour at once into prepared baking dish. Place in shallow pan of hot water.

Bake 50 to 60 minutes or until soufflé is firm. Serve at once with whipped cream. Makes 6 servings.

PRUNE SOUFFLÉ

1 cup prune purée
½ cup sugar
¼ teaspoon salt
1 teaspoon lemon juice

1 teaspoon grated lemon peel
5 egg whites
Whipped cream

Grease upper part of 2-quart double boiler with butter.

Use glass jar prune baby food for the purée or put stewed prunes through the blender or sieve. Combine sugar with purée. Stir well. Add salt, lemon peel, and juice. Whip egg whites until they stand in stiff points when beater is removed. Fold prune mixture into whites. Pour into prepared boiler. Set over hot water. Cover soufflé. Cook 1 hour. Do not uncover during cooking period. Turn out on warmed serving plate. Serve with whipped cream. Makes 4 to 6 servings.

Apricot Soufflé: Substitute apricot baby food, or the mixture of apricots-and-applesauce prepared by some baby-food packers, in place of prune purée or blend your own. Serve with whipped cream or an apricot or orange sauce.

MOCHA SOUFFLÉ

⅓ cup all-purpose flour
3 tablespoons cocoa
¼ teaspoon salt

1 cup strongly brewed coffee
4 eggs, plus 1 egg white
½ cup sugar

Start oven at hot (425° F.). Grease 1-quart deep casserole with softened but not melted butter. Dust greased surface lightly with granulated sugar.

Mix flour, cocoa, and salt in saucepan. Stir in coffee slowly until well blended. Cook over low heat, stirring vigorously until mixture boils and is very thick. Beat in one egg yolk at a time. Stir in sugar. Whip 5 egg whites until they stand in peaks when beater is removed. Fold coffee mixture into whites. Pour at once into casserole. Set dish in shallow pan of hot water.

Bake about 25 minutes, until well risen and top is crusty. Serve at once. Makes 6 servings.

Chocolate sauce is a rich addition to this dessert and so is whipped cream or lemon custard sauce. I like to dust powdered sugar lightly over each serving instead of adding a calorie-laden sauce.

LIQUEUR SOUFFLÉS

4 tablespoons butter or margarine
¼ cup sifted all-purpose flour
¼ teaspoon salt
¼ cup sugar

1 ¼ cups scalded milk
4 eggs, plus 1 egg white
¼ cup liqueur, such as cherry cordial or apricot brandy
Any favorite sweet sauce

Start oven at hot (425° F.). Butter 1-quart deep baking dish. Dust all greased surface heavily with granulated sugar.

Melt butter or margarine in saucepan. Stir in flour, salt, and sugar smoothly. Add hot milk slowly, stirring continually. Cook over moderate heat, stirring constantly until mixture thickens. Beat egg yolks until thick and lemon-colored. Add a little hot sauce to yolks. Mix, then stir yolks into sauce. Remove from heat. Add liqueur slowly, mixing gently. Whip egg whites until they stand in stiff points when beater is removed. Fold yolk mixture into whites. Pour at once into prepared baking dish. Set in shallow pan of hot water.

Bake 20 to 25 minutes or until puffed and lightly browned. Serve at once. Makes 4 or more servings.

ORANGE SOUFFLÉ

½ cup sifted all-purpose flour	1 tablespoon lemon juice
1 cup orange juice	1 tablespoon grated orange peel
4 eggs, plus 1 egg white	Whipped cream or favorite sauce
½ cup sugar	

Start oven at moderately hot (400° F.). Butter 2-quart deep casserole generously with butter. Coat greased surface heavily with granulated sugar.

Combine flour and a little orange juice in saucepan, stirring until smooth. Set over low heat. Add remaining orange juice a little at a time, stirring constantly. Cook and stir until slightly thickened. Remove from heat. Add unbeaten egg yolks, one at a time, beating well after each addition. Add half the sugar. Mix. Stir in lemon juice and orange peel. Whip egg whites until they stand in stiff peaks when beater is removed. Fold remaining sugar into egg whites, then fold orange mixture into whites. Pour at once into prepared baking dish. Set dish in shallow pan of hot water.

Bake about 30 minutes. Serve at once. Makes 6 servings.

Lemon Soufflé: Use the above recipe. Substitute ½ cup lemon juice for half the liquid, that is, use ½ cup lemon juice, ½ cup orange juice. Increase the ½ cup sugar to ¾ cup. Use 2 tablespoons grated lemon peel in place of the orange peel.

SOUFFLÉ ROTHSCHILD

8 tablespoons (¼ pound) butter	8 eggs
1 cup sifted all-purpose flour	¼ cup sugar
1 cup milk, scalded	¼ cup chopped crystallized fruits

Start oven at moderate (350° F.). Rub deep 2-quart casserole or soufflé dish lightly with butter. Dust greased surface lightly with powdered sugar.

Melt butter in saucepan. Stir in flour until smooth. Add hot milk, stirring continually until sauce boils 1 or 2 minutes and is slightly thickened. Beat yolks with sugar. Stir into milk mixture slowly, mixing well. Remove from heat.

Whip egg whites until they stand in peaks when beater is removed. Fold yolk mixture with chopped fruits into whites. Pour at once into prepared casserole. Set casserole in shallow pan of hot water.

Bake 30 to 35 minutes, until soufflé is risen and firm on top. Serve at once. Make 8 servings.

This is more of an English pudding than a real soufflé. It is good with a simple fruit sauce made of 1½ cups apricot jam heated in the upper part of a double boiler over hot water to thin it. It may also be served with hot chocolate sauce. It is attractive served in individual casseroles which take approximately 15 minutes. A light dusting of powdered sugar is a pleasing adjunct.

CHAPTER TWENTY-TWO

Soups

Many excellent soups are available in canned, quick-frozen, dried, and other easily prepared forms. The household which enjoys soup in its menus need never be without a flavorful, interesting hot or cold bowl of it, even though a stock pot has never been heard of in the family. The stock pot was a joy and delight in the old days when women had more time for stirring and mixing, and kitchen stoves were fueled with wood or coal and could stay pleasantly warm all over the top from morning to night, providing the perfect low temperature for a stock pot.

The modern range does not adapt to the old earthen *marmite* or French soup kettle. Many of my friends, however, pride themselves on their authentic French and English soups made with stock, using a modern soup pot of enamelware or heavy aluminum and modern, short-cooking recipes. Bought meat glaze, bouillon cubes and other concentrates, and canned bouillon and consommé can contribute to delicious soups. Also the cooking liquid from a stewed chicken is excellent stock and should be kept and used. It can be boiled down a little after the chicken is removed from the kettle, then stored in refrigerator. Or it may be quick-frozen in amounts suitable to family recipes. See also fish chapter for Fish Stock (page 302).

591

Broths and Consommés

BEEF STOCK

Veal knuckle, cracked by meat dealer
1 or 2 large beef bones
1 gallon water
2 pounds beef brisket
1 large onion, peeled and sliced
1 large carrot, scraped and sliced
2 or 3 leeks, sliced
Few celery leaves
2 tablespoons parsley
1 tablespoon tomato paste
Herb bouquet
6 peppercorns

Wash veal knuckle and beef bones under cold running water. Drain. Put in large kettle. Add water and bring slowly to a boil. Skim carefully. Add beef, vegetables, and tomato paste. Add herb bouquet and peppercorns. Cover and simmer slowly 3 hours or longer. Taste stock for seasoning. Add salt if needed. Strain stock. Let cool. Spoon off any fat which has risen to top. Place in covered bowl or jar in refrigerator until used. Makes about 2 quarts stock.

CELERY AND CHICKEN CONSOMMÉ

2 (10½-ounce) cans chicken consommé
4 tablespoons finely diced celery
¼ teaspoon thyme
¼ teaspoon basil

Prepare consommé according to instructions on can, but do not dilute as much as label suggests. Consommé should be richly concentrated. Add celery and heat to boiling point. Add herbs. Cover saucepan and let heat 2 or 3 minutes. Do not boil. Serve in warmed bouillon cups. Makes 4 or 5 servings.

A pleasing garnish for a thin soup is a lemon slice sprinkled with minced parsley or paprika, or with dried chopped green onion, an indispensable item on my extensive spice shelf.

EGG DROP SOUP

2 (10½-ounce) cans consommé   2 eggs

Heat consommé to boiling point. Beat eggs until very light. Stir soup rapidly with fork and pour egg slowly into boiling soup until egg is shredded and cooked in long strings. Serve into warmed bowls. Makes 2 or 3 servings.

When I serve this soup I use Chinese chinaware soup spoons and Chinese soup or rice bowls (with the rice pattern). And don't forget the soy sauce on the table.

LUNCHEON CONSOMMÉ

Consommé Bellevue

3 cups chicken consommé   ½ cup heavy cream
3 cups clam broth   Celery salt
Salt and pepper   Paprika

Heat consommé and clam broth separately. Combine, stir. Taste for seasoning and add salt and pepper as needed. Whip cream with few grains celery salt and paprika added. Serve consommé very hot in warmed cups. Add dab of seasoned whipped cream to each. Makes 6 servings.

RUBY CONSOMMÉ

3 cups tomato juice   1 teaspoon lemon juice
1 cup beef bouillon   ⅛ teaspoon pepper
1 teaspoon soy sauce   ½ teaspoon salt
1 teaspoon finely cut chives   1 egg white, beaten stiff

Combine tomato juice and bouillon in enamel or glass saucepan. Bring to boiling point. Add soy sauce and chives. Reduce heat and simmer 5 minutes. Add lemon juice, pepper, salt. Remove from heat. Add gradually to beaten egg white. Stir. Leave a little of the egg white as foam on top of soup. Pour into warmed bouillon cups. Makes 4 servings.

For a delicious variation add ½ teaspoon port or sherry to each warmed cup before pouring in consommé.

Serve hot piroshkis with this soup, or cheese-stuffed celery.

WINE SOUP

A little white wine added to soup, bisque, creamed soup, or consommé in the cooking will enhance flavor and give a subtle, appetizing aroma, both much appreciated by gourmet guests.

Or suggest to your family and guests that they add a little red wine to the last few spoonfuls of soup in their bowls, as the French do.

Another way to add a little wine to a soup is a spoonful in the warmed bowl before any hot consommé or bouillon is poured in. Serve at once.

Cream Soups

CREAM-OF-ASPARAGUS SOUP

1 (12-ounce) package quick-frozen asparagus, or 1 bunch fresh asparagus

2 cups rich milk, light cream, or undiluted evaporated milk

1 tablespoon butter or margarine

1 ½ teaspoons salt

⅛ teaspoon black pepper

Cook asparagus until tender in small amount of boiling water. Drain. Save liquid. Cut short tips off 4 stalks and save for garnish. Combine 1 cup milk and asparagus liquid in blender with remaining asparagus. Start blender slowly. Blend until asparagus is smoothly cut and mixed with liquid. Add remaining milk. Pour into saucepan and heat just to boiling point, stirring frequently. Add butter or margarine, salt, and pepper. Pour into warmed cream-soup cups or bowls. Add reserved asparagus tip to each as garnish. Makes 4 servings.

Serve oven-crisp whole-wheat crackers with this soup, or spread Melba toast very lightly with a savory butter such as chive or anchovy.

CREAM-OF-CHICKEN SOUP WITH SHERRY

1 (10½-ounce) can condensed cream-of-chicken soup

1 soup can milk, or half milk and half consommé

1 tablespoon sherry

Few small croutons

Combine soup, milk, or mixture of milk and consommé in saucepan over low heat. Stir to mix smoothly. Bring to boiling point. Lower heat at once and simmer 3 to 4 minutes. Add sherry. Serve immediately in warmed soup cups or bowls. Add a few croutons to top of each serving. Makes 2 or 3 servings.

Heat celery crackers or cheese straws a few minutes in oven. Serve with soup.

To give croutons zesty flavor, sauté in butter or margarine until lightly browned. Sprinkle with celery salt or a very small amount of dried thyme.

CREAM-OF-CURRY SOUP

2 ½ tablespoons flour	Cayenne
2 tablespoons melted butter or margarine	1 teaspoon curry powder
1 quart chicken stock or consommé	2 egg yolks
	½ cup light cream
Salt	¾ cup croutons, fried in butter or margarine

Blend flour and melted butter or margarine. Heat stock or consommé in 1½-quart saucepan or kettle. Stir flour and butter mixture slowly into stock. Let boil 15 minutes. Taste, and add salt as needed, and few grains cayenne. Moisten curry powder with little hot stock. Add to beaten yolks. Blend with cream. Stir into soup and continue to heat but do not let soup boil again. Serve at once in warmed soup bowls. Garnish each with a few croutons. Makes 4 or 5 servings.

A perfect luncheon soup. Serve lamb chops, new peas, compote of Bing cherries and sliced peaches, with coffee or tea.

I try to have croutons on hand, not only for soups, but for creamed spinach, fresh turnip greens, and certain salads. It hurts me to see stale bread wasted. (This is sound French-cookery psychology.) So, before bread becomes too stale to cut, I cut it in cubes and sauté them in butter, margarine, chicken fat, or olive oil well flavored with garlic or garlic salt. If I don't use them immediately, I store them in the refrigerator in a tightly covered jar. I always have some on hand.

CREAM-OF-VEGETABLE SOUP

2 ½ cups milk
1 tablespoon flour
2 tablespoons butter or margarine

1 teaspoon salt
1/16 teaspoon pepper
1 cup diced raw or cooked vegetables

Combine milk, flour, butter or margarine, salt, and pepper in glass container of mixer or blender. Add vegetables and any special seasonings such as herb or curry powder. Cover container. Blend 1 to 3 minutes, until smooth. Raw vegetables need longer blending for smooth mixture.

Pour blended mixture into saucepan. Bring to a boil over low heat, stirring constantly. Let boil 2 or 3 minutes. Pour into warmed cream-soup bowls or cups. Makes 3 or 4 servings.

Cooked asparagus, peas, lima beans, string beans are favorites for this cup. Use one kind, or combine two or more kinds of vegetables.

Add light sprinkling of powdered nutmeg, paprika, or onion salt, or few finely cut celery leaves, parsley, chives, water cress, or thinly sliced scallions.

QUICK CELERY SOUP

1 (10½-ounce) can condensed cream-of-celery soup
1 ½ cups milk
½ teaspoon salt

1 tablespoon finely cut celery leaves
1 hard-cooked egg, sieved

Combine soup and milk in saucepan. Stir to blend well and heat to boiling point, stirring constantly. Remove from heat. Add salt, celery leaves, and egg. Serve at once in warmed cream-soup cups or bowls. Makes 3 or 4 servings.

For color, add minced parsley or chives to each serving.

Fish and Shellfish Soups

CLAM BISQUE

1 (10½-ounce) can minced clams
1 cup water
½ cup white wine
2 tablespoons butter

½ teaspoon salt
¼ teaspoon pepper
½ cup light cream
1 or 2 egg yolks
Paprika

Combine clams and their juice with water in upper part of double boiler. Add wine, butter, salt, and pepper. Stir over low heat 5 or 6 minutes, to just below boiling point. Set pan over boiling water. Add cream which has been beaten with egg yolks. Stir constantly until mixture begins to coat spoon and thicken. Remove from hot water at once. Pour into warmed bowls or cups; add paprika to each serving. Makes 4 servings.

Canned minced clams are always on my emergency shelf. I use them in this bisque, for quick chowders, in iced clam-and-vegetable juice drinks, and in eggplant cookery. Canned mussels, too, plain, and pickled in oil and spice. Great stand-bys!

BRAZILIAN FISH CHOWDER

¼ cup minced peeled onion	3 teaspoons salt, or to taste
3 cloves garlic, peeled and mashed	¼ teaspoon cayenne or chili powder
2 tablespoons finely cut green pepper	½ teaspoon Beau Monde seasoning
2 tablespoons olive oil	1 cup white wine
¼ cup flour	2 pounds fillets whitefish
2 cups water	1 pound fresh or quick-frozen haddock or cod, cleaned and cubed
4 cups canned tomatoes, chopped	
1 tablespoon tomato paste	3 tablespoons finely cut parsley

Cook onion, garlic, and green pepper in oil in heavy 3-quart pot or Dutch oven until onions are golden. Sprinkle with flour. Stir and cook 2 or 3 minutes. Add water, tomatoes and paste, seasonings and wine. Stir and bring to boiling point. Add fish. Lower heat and let simmer 1 hour or until fish is done but still firm. Serve in warmed chowder bowls, topped with parsley. Makes 6 or more servings.

Garlic French bread goes well with this chowder. Actually it's essential! People who imagine they don't like fish love this soup. It makes a hearty one-dish meal. In fact, that's the only way I ever serve it. The "makings" are always on hand. Sometimes I dress it up by serving it in a treasured Meissen tureen (I first warm it carefully with warm water) with its six antique matching soup plates. Fruit is the obvious finish for the meal—a big bowl of iced, assorted fruits.

See also fish chapter.

LOBSTER BISQUE

2 cups milk	2 tablespoons flour
1 cup light cream	½ teaspoon salt
1 slice onion	½ teaspoon paprika
1 stalk celery, sliced	⅛ teaspoon white pepper
2 sprigs parsley	1 (5-ounce) can lobster or meat
1 small bay leaf	from small boiled lobster or
3 tablespoons butter	quick-frozen lobster tails

Scald milk and cream with onion, celery, parsley, and bay leaf. Strain. Melt butter in 1½-quart saucepan. Stir in flour gradually until smooth. Add scalded milk slowly, stirring. Add salt, paprika, pepper, and flaked drained lobster meat. Stir and cook over low heat until thickened. Serve in warmed cream-soup bowls. Makes 4 servings.

Crab-Meat Bisque: Follow same recipe. Use 1 (6½-ounce) can crab meat in place of lobster. Clean and flake crab meat before adding to soup.

Codfish Bisque: Haddock Bisque: Fish Bisque: Be sure all bones are removed from cooked fish and substitute 1 cup flaked fish for lobster in above recipe. Add ¼ teaspoon curry powder.

Interesting as a winter luncheon soup. Follow it by an omelet or vegetable soufflé or ham mousse, with rolls and hot beverage, and you have a guest menu to please men as well as women. A brandied fruit or sherry-flavored gelatin dessert makes a perfect ending for this luncheon.

SAVORY CREAMED FISH SOUP

1½ pounds clean whitefish	2 tablespoons finely cut parsley
1 quart water	6 cloves
1 onion, peeled and chopped	1 bay leaf
1 clove garlic, peeled and chopped	⅛ teaspoon saffron
	¼ teaspoon white pepper
3 tablespoons butter or margarine	Salt to taste
	½ cup heavy cream
1 cup chopped canned tomatoes	

Cut fish in small pieces. Place in 3-quart saucepan, add water and bring to a boil. Boil gently 10 minutes. Sauté onion and garlic (use less garlic, or omit) in butter or margarine 5 minutes. Add to fish. Add tomatoes, 1 tablespoon parsley, cloves, bay leaf, saffron, and pepper. Reduce heat. Cook slowly 30 minutes. Strain soup. Season with salt if needed. Reheat. Add cream, stirring slowly. Let simmer 10 minutes longer. Serve with remaining chopped parsley sprinkled on top. Makes 4 or more servings.

Toasted bread is especially good accompaniment for this soup. A small salad, a fruit platter, hot popovers or raisin muffins make a complete luncheon when this soup is featured.

SCALLOP CHOWDER

2 medium onions	1 tablespoon finely cut chives
2 medium potatoes	1 pound small scallops
3 tablespoons butter	2 cups milk, or 1 cup milk and
3 cups water	1 cup light cream
¼ teaspoon basil	2 teaspoons salt
1 bay leaf	½ teaspoon pepper

Wash vegetables and drain. Peel onions. Slice or chop. Pare potatoes. Cut in small chunks. Cook onions in hot butter in a 2½-quart kettle. When limp, add potatoes, water, basil, bay leaf, and chives and bring to a boil. Reduce heat. Cover and cook slowly 15 to 20 minutes or until potatoes are soft.

Wash and drain scallops. Cut in small pieces. Add with milk and cream to onion-potato mixture. Add seasoning. Cover and bring to a boil again. Reduce heat and cook gently 5 minutes. Serve in warmed deep bowls. Makes 4 or more servings.

The availability of quick-frozen scallops has made it possible to serve this delicacy now anywhere in the country.

This chowder makes a good main dish for lunch or a Sunday supper. Recipe may be doubled and soup made in an electric soup kettle, right at buffet table, for guests to help themselves. Have bowls warming near by on an electric tray.

TOMATO OYSTER BISQUE

1 dozen canned or quick-frozen oysters	2 soup cans milk
2 tablespoons butter or margarine	¼ teaspoon salt
	¾ cup oyster liquor
2 (10½-ounce) cans condensed tomato soup	

If frozen oysters are used, defrost. Cook oysters in butter or margarine slowly, until edges curl. Combine soup, milk, salt, and oyster liquor. Heat, but do not boil. Add oysters to soup. Heat just to boiling point. Do not boil. Pour into warmed cream-soup cups or bowls. Makes 4 to 6 servings.

Various Vegetable Soups

BAKED ONION SOUP

6 tablespoons butter or margarine	Salt
8 onions, peeled and sliced	Quick grind black pepper
1½ quarts boiling water	1 cup dry white wine
7 beef or chicken bouillon cubes	6 thick slices French bread, toasted
	½ cup grated Parmesan cheese

Start oven at hot (425° F.).

Melt butter or margarine in 2-quart saucepan. Cook onions 10 minutes or until soft and transparent. Stir once or twice. Dissolve bouillon cubes in boiling water or use 6 cups stock or canned bouillon. Taste and add salt and pepper if needed. Stir. Add to onions. Cook uncovered over low heat about 10 minutes. Add wine. Stir and cook about 10 minutes. Pour soup into deep earthenware soup casserole. Place toast on top. Sprinkle toast with cheese.

Bake in oven about 20 minutes or until very hot and cheese melts. Serve soup into warmed bowls. Spoon pieces of toast on top of each serving. Makes 6 servings.

Can be baked in 6 individual soup casseroles. Serve with additional grated Parmesan cheese.

This is a great midnight favorite after a dance or theater, when there's a little nip in the air. We may want it even on an August night in Weston. For this kind of service, I make it in advance, then bake it when we gather around the fireplace, usually the large one in the family kitchen.

CUBAN BLACK-BEAN SOUP

Use imported black turtle beans

3 cups black beans
2 quarts water
2 tablespoons beef extract
1 stalk celery, sliced
1 bay leaf, broken
½ pound ham
1 tablespoon ground parsley
1 teaspoon *fines herbes*
1 teaspoon paprika

1 green pepper, finely chopped
2 medium onions, peeled and chopped
1 clove garlic, peeled and mashed
⅓ pound salt pork
1 cup good chianti or full-bodied red wine

Wash beans. Look over for discards. Rinse and drain. Cover with cold water and let soak overnight. To cook, drain beans. Add to large soup pot with 2 quarts of cold water. Add beef extract, celery, bay leaf, ham, parsley, *fines herbes,* and paprika. Cook green pepper, onions, and garlic in skillet with salt pork 5 minutes or until all are hot and browning. Add contents of skillet to soup pot. Stir to mix. Cover and bring to a boil. Lower heat and let simmer slowly 4 hours.

Stir mixture vigorously every half hour. Before serving, add wine. Reheat just to boiling point. Serve in warmed deep bowls. Makes 4 to 6 servings.

This is the famous bean soup of The Argyle Club of San Antonio, Texas. At the club the soup is served with separate bowls of hot rice, finely cut chives, and crisp bacon for each person, much as curry is served surrounded with accessories. It's a meal in itself.

Canned black-bean soup can be made up according to directions on the can. Serve with slice of lemon in each cup.

BUTTERMILK BEET SOUP

8 large cooked or canned beets, peeled and sliced	Salt
	Pepper
1 large onion, peeled and sliced	1 quart buttermilk
3 cups water	Sour cream
4 cloves	Finely cut parsley
¼ teaspoon celery seed	

Combine beets, onion, water, and seasonings except parsley, in 2-quart saucepan or kettle. Bring to a boil. Reduce heat and let simmer 2 hours. Strain soup and reheat. Stir buttermilk slowly into soup. Do not let boil. When hot and steaming, serve at once in warmed soup bowls. Add spoonful of sour cream and light sprinkling of parsley to each bowl. Makes 6 to 8 servings.

Serve a meat pie or meat baked in pastry rolls after this soup. Then a good dessert, such as a chocolate mousse, and your guests will bless you for a different—and satisfying—menu.

This is my own version of this famous dish. People who think they dislike borsch love this.

GRANDMOTHER VANDERBILT'S MEAL-IN-ONE SOUP

2 pounds rump steak in 1 piece	2 tablespoons diced celery
2 to 3 quarts water	1 cup diced peeled onions
2 cups chopped fresh or canned tomatoes	2 teaspoons salt
	½ teaspoon pepper
2 cups diced scraped carrots (optional)	½ teaspoon chili powder

Remove excess fat from beef. Place meat in soup kettle. Pour water over. Cover kettle and bring to boiling point. Reduce heat and simmer 2 hours. Skim occasionally to remove scum and fat. At end of 3-hour cooking period add vegetables and seasonings. The meat should be almost ready to fall apart. Cover kettle again. Cook 30 minutes or until all vegetables are done.

Remove meat to warmed platter. Slice into hot soup at table. Makes 6 to 8 servings.

The chili powder is my contribution. Grandmother didn't know about it. It helps this hearty soup stick to the ribs.

SAN YSIDRO CHOWDER

¼ pound lean salt pork, diced
1 large onion, peeled and sliced
1 cup sliced celery
2 tablespoons butter or margarine
4 cups finely diced raw potatoes
1 cup water
2 (1-pound) cans cream-style corn

2 cups milk
1 (14½-ounce) can evaporated milk
1 teaspoon salt
Quick grind black pepper
¼ cup finely cut parsley

Cook pork slowly in kettle 15 minutes or until crisp. Remove pork and drain fat from kettle. Sauté onion and celery in butter or margarine in same kettle 5 minutes. Add potatoes and water. Cook over low heat 10 minutes or until potatoes are done. Stir in corn. Add fresh and evaporated milk and salt pork. Add salt and pepper. Heat just to boiling point. Serve in warmed bowls with parsley sprinkled on top. Makes 8 or more servings.

A good buffet party soup. It is served from the buffet at the famous San Ysidro Ranch in Santa Barbara.

NAVY BEAN SOUP

2 pounds navy beans
1½ pounds smoked ham hock
4 quarts hot water
1 onion, peeled and sliced

1 tablespoon butter or margarine
Salt and pepper

Wash beans in hot water and drain. Combine in large kettle with ham hock and 4 quarts hot water. Cover and cook slowly 3 to 4 hours or until beans are tender but not mushy. Toward end of cooking time sauté onion in butter or margarine 5 minutes. Add with fat in pan to beans. Taste mixture for seasoning. Add salt and pepper if needed. Cook over moderate heat 10 minutes or longer. Serve in warmed bowls. Makes 6 servings.

So good reheated next day and served with toasted French bread or corn bread. Protein rich.

POTATO-AND-CHEESE SOUP

1 large potato	½ pound processed Cheddar cheese, grated
3 cups hot water	
2 cups potato water	1 tablespoon grated onion
2 beef bouillon cubes	⅛ teaspoon paprika
2 cups milk	⅛ teaspoon Worcestershire
1 cup light cream	sauce
3 tablespoons flour	1 ½ teaspoons salt
2 tablespoons softened butter or margarine	1 tablespoon finely cut parsley

Scrub, rinse, and pare potato. Dice fine into 3-quart saucepan. Add hot water and cook until potato is soft. Drain off 2 cups potato water and save. Drain any remaining water and discard. Put potato through ricer or sieve. Combine potato water, sieved potato, bouillon cubes, milk, and cream in saucepan. Heat, stirring a few minutes. Blend flour and butter or margarine together. Stir into potato mixture. Stir constantly and cook until mixture thickens and is smooth. Let boil 2 or 3 minutes. Add cheese and onion. Reduce heat. Stir until cheese is melted. Add seasonings and parsley. Serve in warmed bowls. Makes 4 servings.

VEGETABLE AND CHICKEN SOUP

1 roast-chicken carcass	½ teaspoon poultry seasoning
6 cups water	¼ teaspoon pepper
1 (No. 2) can tomatoes, chopped	⅔ cup raw rice
½ cup finely cut celery leaves	1 (9-ounce) package quick-frozen mixed vegetables or succotash
1 large onion, peeled and quartered	
1 tablespoon salt	½ green pepper, finely diced

Combine all ingredients except rice and quick-frozen vegetables in large kettle. Cover. Simmer about 3 hours or until all meat has fallen from bones. Remove bones. Strain soup. Let cool. Skim surface. Add rice and quick-frozen vegetables. Simmer 30 minutes or until rice and vegetables are tender. Serve in warmed bowls. Garnish with green pepper. Makes 4 to 6 servings.

THE KING OF SWEDEN'S SOUP

1 pound dried split peas	¼ pound fat salt pork
1 small onion, peeled	1 ½ quarts water
1 carrot, scraped	1 ½ tablesoons salt
2 leeks	1 ½ teaspoons sugar
3 lettuce leaves	

Wash and drain peas. Cover with water and bring to a boil. Cook 5 minutes. Remove from heat. Let peas soak overnight in water in which they cooked. Drain.

Chop onion, carrot, leeks, and lettuce coarsely together. Cook 1 or 2 minutes with salt pork, stirring until hot fat coats all. Remove pork. Pour vegetables and fat into drained peas. Add water, salt, and sugar. Cover. Cook slowly 2 hours. If soup is too thick, add little hot water or consommé. Serve in warmed bowls. Makes 4 to 6 servings.

According to my Swedish friends, some version of this famous old soup was served every Thursday to the late Gustaf V, whether he was in residence at the palace in Stockholm or at his summer place in the country. Thursday is pea soup day throughout Sweden among rich and poor.

I make it a household rule never to discard the water in which ham or tongue has been cooked, and that's what I use as a base for any dried pea, lentil, or bean soup. I always have frozen stock in my freezer. I freeze it in waxed-paper freezer cartons, of course. The special yellowish-green split peas are on sale at Swedish grocery stores and in some supermarkets.

VEGETABLE AND CHEESE SOUP

1 (10 ½-ounce) can condensed vegetable soup	2 tablespoons grated mild processed cheese
1 soup can milk	2 or 3 pieces parsley

Combine soup with milk in saucepan. Heat just to boiling point. Reduce heat and simmer 10 minutes. Do not boil. Add cheese. Stir until it melts. Pour into warmed bowls. Garnish with parsley. Makes 2 to 3 servings.

Sometimes, on a winter day, I greet the children with this as an after-school snack, to keep them out of the cookies.

Chilled Soups

CHILLED TOMATO BOUILLON

2 beef bouillon cubes	1 teaspoon sugar
1 cup hot water	½ teaspoon salt
3 cups tomato juice	⅛ teaspoon powdered cloves
1 green pepper, finely chopped	⅛ teaspoon pepper
2 tablespoons lemon juice	½ garlic clove, peeled
1 teaspoon Worcestershire sauce	

Combine bouillon cubes with water in 2-quart enamel or glass saucepan. Add tomato juice and all ingredients except garlic. Cover and bring to boiling point. Reduce heat and simmer 8 minutes or until green pepper is tender. Strain soup. Add garlic. Let cool. Chill about 3 hours. Remove garlic and discard. Serve in chilled cups. Makes 4 servings.

Hot Tomato Bouillon: Serve hot after straining soup. Omit garlic.

Jellied Tomato Bouillon: Follow above recipe. While bouillon is simmering, soften 1 tablespoon unflavored gelatin in ¼ cup cold water. Let stand 5 minutes. Add to strained hot bouillon. Stir until gelatin is completely dissolved. Let cool. Chill in refrigerator about 5 hours, until set. Beat lightly with fork before serving in chilled cups. Garnish each serving with slice of lemon or sliced scallions, chives, or parsley. Makes 4 or more servings.

FROSTED CREAM-OF-TOMATO SOUP

4 cups tomato juice	¼ teaspoon Tabasco sauce
1 cup light cream	½ teaspoon salt
1 tablespoon grated peeled onion	½ cup commercial sour cream
	3 tablespoons finely cut parsley

Combine tomato juice, cream, onion, Tabasco, and salt in mixing bowl. Chill 2 hours or longer. Serve in chilled bowls or cups. Add spoonful sour cream to top of each serving. Sprinkle with parsley. Makes 4 or more servings.

Vary the flavor to suit your taste. A small amount of curry powder or a little celery seed, or a few grains of basil, orégano, or thyme, add freshness to this cold soup.

FROSTED CURRY SOUP

2 teaspoons curry powder	2 egg yolks
2 (10½-ounce) cans chicken consommé	Avocado and tart apple or Water cress and
1 consommé can cold water	Parsley
½ cup heavy cream	

Combine curry powder, consommé, and water in saucepan. Bring to a boil. Stir occasionally. Reduce heat and cook gently 8 minutes longer.

Heat cream until film forms on top. Beat egg yolks slightly and stir into cream very slowly. Mix into curry combination thoroughly. Let cool. Chill several hours. Beat soup with rotary beater before serving. If too thick, add a little very cold milk. Serve in chilled bowls. Garnish with thin slice avocado and few thin apple sticks. Or, just before serving, stir ½ cup finely cut water cress or 3 tablespoons finely cut parsley into soup. Makes 4 servings.

Another good addition to this soup, to make it a one-dish meal, is ½ cup cubed cooked chicken. Add chicken to soup just before serving. Serve hot toasted rolls with soup and a fruit salad platter for dessert, with hot or cold coffee.

GAZPACHO

Spanish Cold Vegetable Soup

1 garlic clove	1 can condensed consommé
1 onion, peeled	¼ cup wine vinegar
2 cucumbers	⅓ cup olive oil
2 tomatoes, peeled	¼ teaspoon Tabasco sauce
½ green pepper, seeds removed	1 teaspoon salt
2 (8-ounce) cans tomato sauce	Quick grind black pepper

Have all vegetables washed and well chilled. Cut garlic in half. Rub inside of chilled glass or pottery bowl. Combine vegetables and chop very fine. Pour into seasoned bowl with tomato sauce, consommé, vinegar, oil, Tabasco, salt, and pepper. Mix well. Serve in chilled soup dishes. Makes 8 or more servings.

A friend of mine lived on this in Spain, she says, all of one lovely September! But her husband insisted it tasted like salad dressing and would have no part of it. *"Chacun à son goût,"* as the French say.

JELLIED MADRILÈNE

1 (No. 2) can tomatoes	⅓ cup beet juice
1 quart beef bouillon or con- sommé	4 teaspoons grated peeled onion
1 envelope (1 tablespoon) un- flavored gelatin	4 paper-thin slices lemon

Crush tomatoes as fine as possible. Press through sieve. Cook in a large enamel saucepan over high heat until cooked down about one half. Add bouillon. Stir and heat slowly. Soften gelatin in beet juice about 5 minutes. Add little hot bouillon to beet juice and stir until gelatin is almost dissolved. Stir into hot tomato mixture until completely dissolved. Let cool. Chill in refrigerator until set. Beat jelly with fork to break it up. Serve in chilled bouillon cups with little grated onion on top and slice of lemon. Makes 4 or 5 servings.

Was there ever a better dieter's friend than this? Serve it as an appetite-appeaser and your friends will cheer!

DAISYFIELDS VICHYSSOISE

3 cups diced raw potatoes	1½ cups light cream or rich milk
2½ cups bouillon or consommé	½ teaspoon salt
⅓ cup finely minced peeled onions	⅛ teaspoon pepper
1 teaspoon prepared yellow mustard	

Scrub potatoes. Rinse. Pare and dice. Cover with bouillon or consommé in saucepan. Boil 10 minutes. Add onions. Continue cooking until potatoes are tender. Put mixture through ricer or sieve. Stir in mustard. Add cream or milk, salt, and pepper. Let cool. Then chill thoroughly. Serve in chilled soup cups. Makes 4 to 6 servings.

Garnish each filled cup with finely cut chives or few bits of young scallion or small fried croutons.

This is my own version, a little different from the standard. And I am taking the stump to get waiters to pronounce the French word properly—Vichy*swaz*—honest!

WATER-CRESS BISQUE

1 can quick-frozen cream-of-
potato soup
1 soup can milk

2 cups washed, drained finely
cut water cress

Thaw soup a little by placing opened can in pan of hot water. Pour into glass container of electric mixer or blender. Add milk and water cress. Blend until smooth. Refrigerate until well chilled. Just before serving, pour into blender again and blend few seconds. If too thick, add little cold milk or cream. Serve in chilled soup cups. Makes 3 or 4 servings.

Go-Together Canned Soups

Combine canned soups to make delicious hot or chilled first-course or whole-meal dishes. And don't forget that any canned soup, diluted according to directions on its label, can have heightened flavor and appetite appeal if 1 teaspoon sweet basil or marjoram, or ½ teaspoon orégano, is added a few minutes before serving. Stir herb into soup just as it reaches the ready-to-boil point. Cover soup kettle. Turn off heat. Let stand 3 or 4 minutes. Serve in warmed cups or bowls.

Here are flavorful combinations: Condensed cream-of-chicken and cream-of-mushroom soups, diluted with milk, combined and heated to boiling point, then flavored with 1 tablespoon freshly cut parsley.

Condensed tomato soup heated with chicken-with-rice soup, diluted with little hot water or bouillon, ¼ teaspoon saffron added.

Cream-of-asparagus soup heated with cream-of-celery soup, diluted with milk, topped with sprinkling of finely cut chives, croutons, or minced ham or tongue.

Vegetable and beef-noodle soups heated together, diluted a little if directions say so, thin slices scallion or celery added as garnish.

Boola Boola: Combine equal amounts of strained green turtle soup, condensed pea soup, (my friend, Effie Heyn, puts fresh cooked peas in the blender) and bouillon. For 3 cups soup mixture add ¼ teaspoon *each* dried basil, marjoram, rosemary, and thyme; add small piece bay leaf and 3 cloves. Add smallest possible pinch of anise. Heat to steaming. Makes 3 servings.

At Trader Vic's restaurant in New York they put their version of this soup (made with purée of spinach and oysters) in individual pottery casseroles, top it with whipped cream and pop it under the broiler for a few minutes.

Chicken-Avocado Soup

1 (10½-ounce) can condensed cream-of-chicken soup	1 ripe avocado
Milk	¼ teaspoon powdered nutmeg
	Salt and pepper, if needed

Dilute soup as directed on can, using milk. Cut avocado in half, remove seed; pare avocado and grate it. Stir into soup with seasoning. Stir until steaming hot. Makes 2 or 3 servings.

Ready Purée Mongol: Combine 1 (10½-ounce) can condensed tomato soup, I can condensed green pea soup, 1½ soup cans water. Heat to boiling point. Stir to blend well. Garnish with finely cut chives or parsley or paprika dipped lemon slices. Makes 3 or 4 servings.

A good addition to this old-time favorite is ½ to 1 teaspoon curry powder. Do as Chinese cooks do. Heat the curry powder in the kettle first, stirring it a little. Pour the mixed soups and water into the kettle over the hot curry powder. Continue to stir until boiling point is reached. Serve at once.

CHAPTER TWENTY-THREE

Vegetables

With quick-frozen, canned, dried, dehydrated, and, usually best of all, fresh vegetables now available, almost without regard to the gardener's calendar, our menus need never lack these essential foods.

A general reminder: cook only as much vegetable as needed for one meal unless you are planning a specific use for the leftover. If you are fortunate enough to have a garden or to buy vegetables from nearby gardens, cook them as soon after they are picked as possible. Wash and prepare them for cooking, then cook them. Don't let them stand in cold water or in the refrigerator, since freshness, both as to flavor and vitamin and mineral content, begins to go as soon as vegetables leave the garden.

Follow recipes. But, in general, use a small amount of salted boiling water for cooking. For a simple, seasoned and buttered vegetable, add butter and seasonings to the cooking water. Cover the pan. Bring to a boil over high heat. Reduce the heat. Cook the minimum of time called for. Stir only once or twice. Serve as soon as done. Save any excess cooking water to use in soups and sauces or add to your pets' food. Most leafy vegetables may be steamed in this way: Use small amount of salted water or none at all. Just 1 tablespoon of butter, margarine, corn or olive oil in washed spinach and desired seasonings, for example. When the pot is tightly covered enough steam is produced for cooking.

For glass-canned peas, green beans, limas, carrots, asparagus, and other vegetables, drain off liquid into saucepan; boil down to about one half original volume. Add vegetable. Reheat. Season and serve.

Seasoning is important. Salt and pepper are added to most vegetables with butter, cream, or sour cream. For variety add a little celery salt, onion salt, or curry powder. Or, just as vegetable finishes cooking, add ½ to 1 teaspoon dried thyme, basil, or marjoram to saucepan. Cover. Remove from heat and let steam "awaken" the herb. After 5 minutes stir herb into vegetable. Serve in warmed vegetable dish. Delicious.

With other vegetables a spoonful of prepared horse-radish creamed with butter adds tangy flavor. Grated lemon peel, lemon juice, and butter is another combination to add to almost any cooked green vegetable. A few sautéed scallions or sliced young onions make a fragrant springtime combination with new peas. I also add Aćcent to all but strong-flavored vegetables.

TO OVEN-COOK FROZEN VEGETABLES

While a roast or a casserole of meat cooks, a frozen vegetable also will cook deliciously in the oven. Break the frozen block of spinach or other vegetable into four or five pieces or use a frozen-vegetable knife. Place in 1-quart casserole with 2 tablespoons butter or margarine. Season with ½ teaspoon salt. Cover. Cook according to time given below. If oven is set at moderate, or 325° F., for roast, add 10 minutes to vegetable's required time. If oven is 375° F. for meat, subtract 10 minutes from the required vegetable baking time.

Frozen Vegetable	350° F. Oven
Asparagus, cut or spears	55 to 60 minutes
Broccoli, chopped	45 to 50 "
Broccoli, spears	40 to 45 "
Brussels sprouts	40 to 45 "
Cauliflower	50 to 55 "
Corn, whole kernel	45 to 50 "
Green beans	55 to 60 "
Limas	45 to 50 "
Mixed vegetables	50 to 60 "
Peas	45 to 50 "
Peas-and-carrots	55 to 60 "
Spinach	45 to 50 "
Squash	45 "
Succotash	55 to 60 "
Wax beans, cut	55 to 60 "

For large lima beans, add 2 tablespoons water.

If sauce or additional seasoning, such as teaspoon of dried herb, is to be added, stir into the vegetable just before serving.

Marjoram is especially good with the large limas. One tablespoon finely cut parsley adds fine flavor to green beans, as does summer savory, Beau Monde seasoning or shredded fresh or dried scallions.

Add ½ teaspoon powdered nutmeg to spinach.

Use a grind of fresh black pepper over the top of oven-cooked squash. I like chopped green onion added to summer squash.

Stir 1 tablespoon finely cut fresh or dried mint into peas-and-carrots.

ARTICHOKES

To clean artichokes, plunge them up and down in cold running water. Let stand head down 30 minutes in cold water. Drain. Trim stem close. Strip off tough outer leaves. Cut tough leaf tops off right across the artichoke, using scissors.

Steamed Artichokes: Tie string around each artichoke. Place in steamer above boiling salted water or mixture of white wine and water. Cover steamer tightly. Steam 45 minutes to 1 hour, until leaves are tender. Remove. Drain. Discard string. Serve hot or cold, with melted butter, mayonnaise, or Lemon French Dressing (page 518).

Also, steamed artichokes are cooled then may be stuffed with seafood or vegetable salad mixtures such as ground cooked shrimp, crab meat, lobster, or tuna with Lemon Mayonnaise (page 523). Spread center leaves of hot, steamed artichoke slightly apart. Remove choke and insert about 2 teaspoons salad mixture Also use cooked chicken or cooked mixed vegetables. Roquefort Cheese Dressing (page 519) combines well with vegetables for this topping. Serve 1 artichoke, or 2 small ones, on small salad plate with accompanying small dish of sauce.

To eat whole steamed artichokes, pluck the leaves off, one at a time, dip into sauce, eat tender base of leaf by pulling leaf through the teeth. Discard remaining tough end. When all leaves have been eaten, remove fuzzy choke with fork to one side of your plate; eat base or heart of the artichoke with fork, dipping bite-size pieces into melted butter or sauce.

Near-Eastern Artichokes: Mix 2 tablespoons finely cut ripe olives into onion-seasoned French dressing. Combine with equal amount dry white wine. Marinate drained, steamed artichokes in this dressing several hours in refrigerator. Serve with additional dressing.

ARTICHOKE HEARTS WITH LEMON BUTTER

1 (9-ounce) package quick-frozen artichoke hearts

½ teaspoon salt

1 cup water

3 tablespoons butter or margarine

1 tablespoon lemon juice

Quick grind black pepper

Place quick-frozen artichoke hearts in saucepan. Add salt and water or mixture of water and vinegar or white wine. Cover and bring quickly to a boil over high heat. Reduce heat. Boil gently 12 minutes or until just tender. Drain if excess liquid remains. Dress with melted butter or margarine and lemon juice. Add quick grind of black pepper. Makes 4 servings.

These artichoke hearts make delicious additions to the salad plate and appetizer tray. Cook as described on package or in above recipe. Drain. Marinate in French Dressing in refrigerator 1 hour or longer.

ASPARAGUS

1 pound asparagus

Boiling water

1 teaspoon salt

6 tablespoons melted butter

2 tablespoons lemon juice

Wash asparagus under cold running water several times. Sand sticks in the scales on the stalks and must be loosened and washed away.

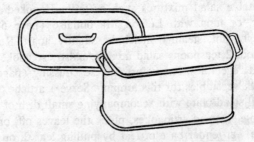

Asparagus Steamer

Better to remove scales where sand is lodged with a vegetable knife. Cut off tough stem ends. Place stalks in covered steamer over rapidly boiling salted water, or tie asparagus in bunch and stand upright in bottom of double boiler containing about 2 inches of boiling water with a little salt added. Invert top part of double boiler over asparagus, being careful not to break tips. Let steam 20 minutes or longer, until tender.

Drain. Remove string. Serve hot asparagus, 3, 4, or more stalks as a serving, with melted butter combined with lemon juice. Makes 3 or 4 servings.

Asparagus Hollandaise: Cook fresh asparagus as described. Add spoonful Hollandaise Sauce (page 550) over each serving.

Asparagus Parmesan, Little Italy: At Barbetta's famous Italian restaurant in New York City, the asparagus Parmesan has long been a featured specialty on the menu. Clean and cook asparagus as described above. Drain. Lay stalks in shallow baking dish. Pour melted butter over. Add squeeze of lemon juice and sprinkle generously with grated Parmesan and Romano cheese. Broil under moderate heat until cheese is lightly browned.

Other good asparagus ideas: Place drained hot asparagus on serving dish. Sprinkle with melted butter, chopped toasted almonds, and crisp bacon bits. Or add few sautéed mushroom slices and a little powdered nutmeg with melted butter.

See also appetizer and salads chapter for additional ways of serving asparagus.

DAISYFIELDS ASPARAGUS

2 (9-ounce) packages quick-frozen cut-up asparagus	¾ cup undiluted evaporated milk
3 tablespoons butter or margarine	½ teaspoon salt
1½ tablespoons flour	¼ teaspoon pepper
¾ cup liquid from asparagus	Sprinkling of nutmeg
	Buttered toast

Cook asparagus as described on package. Drain. Measure liquid and add water to make ¾ cup.

Melt butter or margarine in saucepan. Stir in flour smoothly. Add asparagus water, stirring until smooth. Add milk. Stir and cook 1 or 2 minutes; add seasonings. Cook and stir until thickened. Add asparagus. Heat just to boiling point. Serve on toast. Makes 4 servings.

Asparagus au Gratin: Prepare asparagus as described above. Pour asparagus and cream sauce into shallow baking dish. Sprinkle generously with grated Cheddar cheese. Add dusting of paprika. Heat in moderate oven (375° F.) until cheese is melting and browned. Serve at once.

GREEN BEANS AND MUSHROOMS

1 pound green beans	½ teaspoon salt
1 slice bacon, or 2 tablespoons butter or margarine	Quick grind fresh pepper
	¼ teaspoon powdered nutmeg
1 small onion, peeled and cut fine	⅓ cup light cream
1 (3-ounce) can chopped mushrooms	

Wash and string beans. Cut slantwise into 1-inch lengths. Cook bacon in skillet. When crisp, remove and drain on paper towels. Pour off all but 2 tablespoons fat. If butter or margarine is used in place of bacon, add to skillet. Add beans, onion, mushrooms and their liquid, salt, pepper, and nutmeg. Cover. Turn heat low; cook slowly 20 to 25 minutes. If more liquid is needed, add 2 or 3 tablespoons water. When beans are tender pour cream over. Heat 3 or 4 minutes. Serve at once, sprinkled with bacon. Makes 4 servings.

Green Beans, Peasant Style: Substitute for mushrooms 3 peeled, chopped tomatoes. Add 2 diced pared potatoes, omit nutmeg. Increase salt as desired. Cook as described, 25 minutes, or until potatoes are tender. Makes 5 servings.

GREEN BEANS, HOFBRAU STYLE

Cook one (9-ounce) package quick-frozen green beans as described on package. When tender, remove from heat. Sprinkle with 1 teaspoon dried or fresh dill or 1 tablespoon freshly cut chives. Add 2 or 3 tablespoons butter. Cover saucepan and let steam from beans melt butter. Stir. Add ½ cup commercial sour cream. Cover pan again. Let stand few minutes. Stir and serve. Makes 2 or 3 servings.

Green Beans with Almonds: Cook two (9-ounce) packages quick-frozen French-style green beans as described on package. Season with 2 tablespoons butter or margarine, ¾ teaspoon salt, ½ teaspoon pepper. When done, turn into warmed serving dish. Sprinkle with ⅓ cup slivered toasted almonds. Makes 5 to 6 servings.

BAKED LIMA BEANS WITH TOMATOES

1 cup dried lima beans	1 cup water
¼ pound diced salt pork	2 tablespoons finely cut parsley
½ cup sliced peeled onions	
1 (10½-ounce) can condensed tomato soup	

Wash and look over beans. Drain. Cover with 1 quart cold water. Let soak overnight or all day. Drain. Cover with fresh water. Cook about 2 hours or until tender. Drain. There should be about 3 cups cooked beans. Cover and keep in refrigerator until next day or whenever baked dish is to be prepared.

Start oven at moderate (350° F.).

Cook salt pork 5 minutes in heavy frying pan. Add onions. Cook 5 minutes longer. Add drained cooked lima beans. Mix well. Pour into greased one-quart baking dish. Mix tomato soup and water. Pour over beans.

Bake 30 minutes or until hot and bubbly. If beans are not tender, continue baking until beans are entirely cooked. Sprinkle top with parsley and serve hot. Makes 4 or more servings.

CHEESED LIMAS

1 (9-ounce) package large quick-frozen lima beans	1 tablespoon butter or margarine
¼ cup grated processed American cheese	⅓ cup light cream
	Salt and pepper

Cook beans as described on package. Lower heat. Add cheese, butter or margarine, and cream. Mix lightly with fork. Cover. Let steam melt cheese. Season with salt and pepper. Serve at once. Makes 3 or 4 servings.

Lima Beans in Potato Ring: Make thick ring of hot, well-seasoned mashed potatoes on warmed serving dish. Pour lima beans, cooked as described in above recipe, into ring. Serve at once. Or make small mashed-potato nests. Fill with lima beans. Place as garnish around roast turkey, chicken, or veal.

SPANISH LIMAS

Cook quick-frozen or fresh limas as usual. When half done, add 2 tablespoons grated onion. Continue cooking. About 5 minutes before serving add 2 tablespoons chopped canned pimiento.

Herbed Lima Beans: Another delicious variation on plain buttered limas: add 1 teaspoon dried thyme, ½ teaspoon orégano, stir herbs through hot beans. Cover and let stand 2 or 3 minutes. Serve at once.

BAKED BLACK OR KIDNEY BEANS

4 cups cooked or canned black, or kidney, beans	1 cup commercial sour cream
1 cup thinly sliced celery	1 teaspoon dry mustard
1 sweet red pepper, cut fine	1 tablespoon brown sugar
½ cup finely cut cooked ham	1 ½ teaspoons salt
1 (10-ounce) can condensed cream-of-celery soup	¼ teaspoon rosemary

Start oven at moderate (350° F.).
Combine all ingredients in 2-quart casserole or bean pot. Bake about 30 minutes. Uncover and let top brown a little. Makes 6 servings.

BAKED NAVY BEANS

3 cups navy beans	2 teaspoons dry mustard
½ pound salt pork	½ cup molasses
1 teaspoon salt	1 cup boiling water
3 tablespoons sugar	

Wash beans. Look over. Drain. Soak beans overnight in water to cover. Next morning drain. Cover with fresh cold water. Bring to a boil. Reduce heat. Cover tightly and cook slowly about 30 minutes. Drain again.

Start oven at moderately slow (300° F.).

Cut salt pork in half. Put one piece in bottom of bean pot or 2-quart casserole. Pour beans in; push other piece of pork into top of beans. Mix remaining ingredients. Pour over beans. Add additional water to just cover beans. Cover bean pot or casserole tightly.

Bake about 8 hours. Look at beans every hour. Add little more water if beans seem dry. When baking time is nearly completed, remove cover and let top brown. Makes 6 servings.

For crusty top. When cover is removed to let beans brown, sprinkle 2 or 3 tablespoons buttered crumbs and sugar on top.

BEETS

Wash 4 or 5 large fresh beets or 8 small ones thoroughly. Rinse. Drain. Pare. Slice thin or cut in sticks. Cook in small amount of salted boiling water in covered saucepan until tender. Add any one of these seasonings: 1 tablespoon lemon juice. Two or three tablespoons sautéed chopped onion. One fourth teaspoon powdered cloves or allspice. 1 tablespoon prepared horse-radish with 1 cup commercial sour cream or ½ cup mild vinegar. With sour cream or vinegar, reheat beets a few minutes. Serve hot. Makes 4 servings.

Beets are the one vegetable in my opinion *nearly* as good canned as fresh—and much less trouble.

SAVORY BUTTERED BEETS

6 beets
½ teaspoon salt
½ teaspoon celery salt

⅛ teaspoon pepper
2 tablespoons butter or margarine

Wash and scrub beets thoroughly. Rinse and drain. Pare. Grate on medium grater into saucepan. Sprinkle with seasonings. Dot with butter or margarine. Cover. Simmer over low heat about 30 minutes or until tender. Serve with a little vinegar or lemon quarters. Makes 4 to 6 servings.

This vegetable is especially appetizing heaped in lettuce leaf. May be garnished with dab of Hollandaise or mayonnaise.

BROCCOLI

Cook quick-frozen or fresh broccoli in small amount of salted boiling water in covered saucepan until stalks are just tender. Season with butter, salt, pepper, and lemon juice.

Or serve with hot cheese sauce or Hollandaise. Also delicious sprinkled with melted butter and grated cheese and browned a few minutes under broiler heat.

See asparagus recipes.

BROCCOLI ITALIAN STYLE

1 ½ pounds broccoli	⅓ minced peeled onion
¼ cup olive oil	¼ teaspoon chili powder
1 clove garlic, peeled and mashed	2 tablespoons water
	1 teaspoon salt

Wash broccoli. Look over carefully. Trim stalks. Remove all large coarse leaves. Cut stalks and flowerets into large pieces.

Heat oil in large skillet. Add garlic, onion, and chili powder. Stir and heat until onion is soft. Remove garlic and discard. Add broccoli, water, and salt. Cover skillet. Cook 12 to 15 minutes or until just tender. Serve immediately. Makes 4 servings.

BRUSSELS SPROUTS

Remove imperfect leaves from 1 quart sprouts. Look over carefully. Cut away any spoiled parts. Wash. Drain. Soak in salted water to cover about 30 minutes. Drain. Cook covered in small amount of salted boiling water 10 to 20 minutes or until tender. Drain. Dress with melted butter. Add 1 tablespoon lemon juice. Makes 6 servings.

Creamed Brussels Sprouts: Dress cooked sprouts with well-seasoned cream sauce.

Brussels Sprouts with Chestnuts: Add 1 cup sliced cooked chestnuts to cooked sprouts before dressing with melted butter or cream sauce.

If sprouts are large, slice each in half lengthwise for quicker cooking.

A little grated onion added to seasoning or sauce adds good flavor to sprouts.

Cooked, drained, and chilled, sprouts are delicious additions to vegetable salads.

CABBAGE

Wash cabbage. Drain. Discard damaged or coarse leaves. Cut in wedges or slices. Cook in small amount salted boiling water in covered saucepan until tender. Drain.

To serve, add well-seasoned cream sauce with chopped crisp bacon added, or cheese sauce, or cream sauce flavored with sour cream and prepared mustard.

Cream sauce, with 1 or 2 tablespoons finely cut chives added, makes a good topping for cabbage.

Scalloped Cabbage: Cook 4 cups shredded cabbage as described in above recipe. Drain. Combine in buttered 1½-quart baking dish with ⅓ cup chopped canned tomatoes and 1 cup medium white sauce. Sprinkle top generously with ½ cup bread crumbs and ½ cup grated Cheddar cheese, mixing some of crumbs and cheese down into cabbage mixture. Bake in moderate oven (350° F.) about 25 minutes or until top is bubbly and browned. Makes 4 to 6 servings.

STUFFED CABBAGE LEAVES

6 large cabbage leaves	1 cup shredded sharp Cheddar
Boiling water	cheese
1 (9-ounce) package quick-frozen	1 teaspoon salt
spinach, thawed and chopped	1 cup cooked long rice
1 egg	1 teaspoon grated onion

Pour boiling water over cabbage leaves. Let stand 10 minutes. Drain and pat dry. Cut each leaf in half lengthwise. Remove center rib. Combine remaining ingredients. Spoon 1 tablespoon spinach mixture on each piece cabbage. Roll up, folding edges in and ends under. Fasten with wooden picks.

Cook in steamer over rapidly boiling water 30 minutes or until cabbage is tender. Or add cabbage rolls to pot of boiling beef tongue or chicken 30 minutes before meat is done. Serve hot with meat. Makes 6 servings. A great favorite with men, especially. It may also be baked covered with tomato sauce—40 minutes at 350°.

CARROTS

Wash carrots. Scrape. Grate or slice thin. Cook in small amount boiling water in covered saucepan until tender. Mash. Whip lightly with small amount of cream or sour cream, salt, and pepper. Heap in warmed serving dish to serve.

A small amount of finely cut chives, parsley, mint, or dried savory makes a good seasoning for carrots.

CARROTS WITH ORANGE

1 pound carrots
½ teaspoon salt
⅛ teaspoon powdered ginger
1 teaspoon sugar
1 tablespoon butter or margarine

¾ cup orange juice
2 tablespoons grated orange peel

Wash and scrub carrots. Rinse. Drain. Scrape. Cut in ½-inch slices. Combine with seasonings, sugar, butter or margarine, and orange juice in enamel or glass saucepan. Cover. Bring to a boil; lower heat and simmer 15 to 20 minutes or until carrots are tender. Sprinkle with orange peel. Makes 4 servings.

CAULIFLOWER

Wash cauliflower. Drain. Cut away any damaged parts. Cut apart into flowerets or leave whole. Cook covered in small amount boiling water until tender. Drain. Place on warmed serving dish. Dress with lemon juice and melted butter, or Hollandaise, or melted butter with chopped walnuts, or curry sauce, cheese sauce, or buttered bread crumbs. Or dress with Nutmeg Cream Sauce (page 554).

Chinese cooks add butter, a little heavy cream, parsley or chives, and paprika to cauliflower after it has been sliced and braised until tender. It is delicious.

Overcooking of cauliflower destroys texture, flavor, and appearance.

CAULIFLOWER SCALLOP

2 eggs
1 (10½-ounce) can cream-of-celery soup
2 (9-ounce) packages quick-frozen cauliflower, thawed, coarsely chopped
½ cup grated processed American cheese

½ cup bread crumbs
¼ cup finely cut parsley
2 canned pimientos, finely cut
2 tablespoons diced onion
1 teaspoon salt
⅛ teaspoon pepper

Start oven at moderate (375° F.). Butter 1½-quart baking dish. Beat eggs slightly in large bowl. Stir in remaining ingredients. Turn into prepared baking dish. Set dish in shallow pan of hot water.
Bake about 50 minutes or until firm. Serve hot. Makes 4 to 6 servings.

BRAISED CELERY AND TOMATOES

2 tablespoons butter or margarine	⅛ teaspoon pepper
	1 teaspoon sugar
2 cups celery, cut in 1-inch pieces	¼ teaspoon onion salt
	1 (No. 2) can tomatoes
¾ teaspoon salt	2 tablespoons finely cut parsley

Melt butter or margarine in covered 1½-quart saucepan. Add celery and seasonings. Mix. Drain tomatoes, add juice to celery. Cover, bring to a boil. Lower heat and let simmer 10 minutes or until celery is tender.

Cut tomatoes in quarters and add with parsley to celery. Cover. Cook 5 minutes or until mixture is boiling. Makes 4 servings.

DUTCH STUFFED-CELERY AU GRATIN

1 cooked celery heart per person	2 cups or more cheese sauce, slightly flavored with nutmeg
1 thin slice boiled or baked Virginia ham per person	Additional grated cheese

Fold ham slices around drained, cooked celery hearts. Arrange bundles in greased baking dish. Cover with cheese sauce. Sprinkle with grated cheese. Bake 20 minutes or until bubbly and browned.

Celery hearts now come packed in glass.

Braised Celery Hearts: To cook celery hearts, wash celery. Trim off leaf end of stalks. Slice large, bulky celery hearts in half lengthwise. Cook smaller ones whole. Cover with mixture of equal amounts of water and consommé. Cook covered over low heat 15 minutes. Uncover pan and continue cooking until most of liquid is absorbed. Celery heart should be tender through. Drain if any liquid remains. Serve as vegetable, with or without sauce, or use as described in recipe.

Braised Celery with Almonds: Cook sliced celery hearts as described in water and consommé. Let all liquid cook away, absorbed by the celery. Add small amount of butter or margarine to pan. Sauté cooked celery about 5 minutes. Add 2 tablespoons slivered toasted almonds. Serve hot.

Celery Root: Cook knob or root celery in boiling water to cover until tender but not too soft. Drain. Cool and peel. Dice or slice. Allow ⅓ to ½ pound per serving. Dress with a little cream or melted butter.

CHESTNUTS AS VEGETABLE

Wash ½ pound chestnuts. Drain. Use short, sharp knife to cut 2 gashes on flat side of each nut. Cook in 2 tablespoons olive oil or butter in heavy skillet. Shake over low heat until shells loosen. Let cool. Remove shells and skins with knife. Slice nuts and add to Brussels sprouts or onions, or use in stuffing for poultry. If chestnuts are not tender after skillet cooking, steam them for 20 minutes or longer. Use creamed or with butter sauce or as a salad—or to flavor one.

Chestnut Purée: Use recipe above for cooking chestnuts. Remove shells and skin. Leave nuts whole. Cover with salted boiling water. Cook 20 minutes, until nuts are very soft. Put through potato ricer or use blender. Season with salt, pepper, butter or cream. Beat and reheat in upper part of double boiler over boiling water, whipping mixture lightly as it heats. Allow ⅓ to ½ pound chestnuts per serving.

Makes a delicious accessory to roast fowl or game.

CORN ON THE COB

The perfect summer corn dish is made of freshly gathered corn, husked and cooked all within 30 minutes from corn patch to dinner table. But if you have to depend on corn bought at roadside or market, do the next best thing—give it a very short cooking time and serve at once.

Remove husks and silk from sweet corn. Place corn in vigorously boiling water for 3 to 5 minutes. Salt or sugar need not be added for really fresh corn.

If corn looks and feels mature, add 1 or 2 teaspoons sugar to boiling water. Drain cooked corn. Place on warmed platter. Cover with folded napkin to keep steam in. Serve with butter, salt, and pepper. Or mix butter, salt, pepper, and paprika. Pack in individual small dishes or in one round small dish. Decorate the top by making small gashes around the rim with a knife—looks very much like the spokes of a wheel—and pass with a butter knife.

THELMA'S CORN FRITTERS

3 eggs	⅛ teaspoon pepper
1 ⅔ cups cooked or canned whole-kernel corn	¼ cup sifted all-purpose flour
½ teaspoon salt	6 tablespoons fat

Beat egg yolks well. Add corn, salt, pepper, and flour. Mix thoroughly. Whip egg whites until they stand in stiff peaks when beater is withdrawn. Fold corn mixture into whites. Drop by tablespoon into hot fat in skillet. Cook on both sides until brown and done. Makes 6 servings.

A brunch favorite at our house. Especially good with Canadian bacon or pot roast. Sometimes served at breakfast with real Vermont maple syrup and crisp brown sausages.

CORN PUDDING

4 or 5 ears (2 cups) fresh sweet corn or	3 tablespoons flour
1 cup canned cream-style corn and	1 tablespoon sugar
	1 teaspoon salt
1 cup canned whole-kernel corn	¼ teaspoon pepper
4 eggs	1 cup milk
2 tablespoons finely cut green pepper	1 tablespoon melted butter or margarine

Start oven at moderate (325° F.). Grease 1½-quart casserole.

If fresh corn is available, slit center of kernels with sharp knife. Scrape into bowl. Measure 2 cups. Or use the two kinds of canned corn. Beat eggs until thick. Add corn and green pepper. Combine flour, sugar, salt, and pepper in mixing bowl. Stir milk into dry ingredients. Blend in melted butter or margarine. Combine with corn mixture. Beat well. Pour into prepared casserole.

Bake about 1 hour and 20 minutes, until knife inserted comes out clean. Makes 5 or 6 servings.

A small amount of cut sweet red pepper may be added, or 2 tablespoons chopped mushrooms. Also 2 or 3 tablespoons grated Cheddar cheese sprinkled on top of pudding before it goes in the oven adds flavor and color.

EGGPLANT

Wash eggplant. Pare. Cut into thick "fingers." Dust lightly with seasoned flour and melted butter. Broil under moderate heat until golden on all sides. It is *not* necessary to soak eggplant!

Or cut into slices. Season. Dredge lightly with flour. Brown in hot olive oil. Serve on warmed platter, alternate slices of broiled eggplant and broiled seasoned tomatoes.

EGGPLANT, COUNTRY SUPPER STYLE

1 medium-size eggplant, pared and cubed	1 tablespoon finely cut parsley
	1 teaspoon sugar
3 tablespoons bacon drippings or butter	½ teaspoon chili powder
	1 teaspoon salt
½ cup diced peeled onions	⅛ teaspoon pepper
1 (No. 2½) can tomatoes, chopped	1 cup buttered coarse crumbs
	½ cup coarsely grated cheese

Start oven at moderate (350° F.). Grease 2-quart baking dish.

Sauté eggplant 5 minutes in drippings or butter in large frying pan. Pour mixture into prepared baking dish. Sauté onions 2 minutes in same pan. Stir in tomatoes. Add parsley, sugar, chili powder, salt, and pepper. Stir and let come to a boil. Pour over eggplant. Sprinkle generously with crumbs and cheese.

Bake 45 minutes or until top is browning and bubbly. Makes 6 servings.

EGGPLANT PARMESAN

1 large eggplant	2 teaspoons orégano
3 eggs	½ pound sliced Mozzarella cheese
1 cup dry bread crumbs	
¾ cup olive oil	3 (8-ounce) cans tomato sauce
½ cup grated Parmesan cheese	

Start oven at moderate (350° F.). Grease 2-quart casserole.

Wash eggplant. Pare. Cut in thick slices. Dip each slice into beaten eggs, then into crumbs. Sauté in hot oil in skillet until golden on both sides. Place layer of browned eggplant in prepared casserole. Add sprinkling of Parmesan, orégano, and Mozzarella. Cover with tomato sauce. Repeat layers until all eggplant is used, topping last layer of sauce with Mozzarella.

Bake, uncovered, 30 minutes or until sauce is bubbly and cheese is melted. Makes 4 to 6 servings.

Very small eggplants make a delicious variation of this dish. Wash. Do not pare. Cut in thin slices. Continue preparation as described. The small, thin slices sauté crisply, and the flavor of the finished dish is different than when it's made with thicker, larger slices of the vegetable.

BRAISED ENDIVE

6 heads Belgian endive
2 cups consommé

1 tablespoon butter or margarine
Quick grind pepper

Rinse endive in cold water. Remove any damaged outside leaves. Trim base, but do not cut so far that leaves fall apart. Cut each head of endive down through center, making two pieces. Place in large shallow pan. Cover with consommé.

Simmer gently about 20 minutes or until tender. Broth should cook away. Serve endive with spoonful of any remaining broth in pan. Or broth can be used to make thickened cream sauce to pour over endive. Or serve endive plain, which I like best. Makes 6 servings.

Salt and pepper are not needed, since consommé is seasoned, but for garnish, a few grains black pepper or teaspoon finely cut parsley adds to the appearance. Another delicious garnish for each serving is a teaspoon of sautéed chopped mushrooms.

Braised cucumbers: Pare and slice 8 large cucumbers. Cook as described for endive. Makes 8 servings.

KOHLRABI

The best kohlrabi I have ever tasted was cooked with boiled beef by a French friend who had always had it prepared that way in her childhood home.

Remove leaves and stems from kohlrabi. Wash thoroughly. Pare. Remove woody portions. Dice or cut in thin strips. Cook covered in pot with beef, allowing 45 minutes, since beef will be simmering and not boiling rapidly. Drain beef and vegetable. Save broth.

Serve beef sliced hot on warmed platter with spoonful of vegetable and broth.

Creamed Kohlrabi: Clean and prepare vegetable for cooking as described in above recipe. Cook covered in *small* amount of salted boiling water 20 to 30 minutes or until tender; drain. Dress with well-seasoned cream sauce. About 3 bunches kohlrabi make 6 servings.

MUSHROOMS

Buy commercially grown mushrooms from grocer or market. *Don't buy them from countryside stands or pick them in the fields unless you are a mushroom expert.* Many poisonous varieties resemble the edible mushrooms. Young homemakers will do well to rely on the labeled baskets of commercially grown mushrooms at the market and to use quality canned varieties.

To cook fresh mushrooms, wash them well. Drain. Peel caps of large mushrooms. Slice stems and caps or leave whole. Sauté few minutes in butter. Season with lemon juice. Serve on toast or use as described in recipes.

Creamed Mushrooms on Toast: A favorite luncheon dish. Add sautéed mushrooms to medium cream sauce. Or heat drained canned mushrooms and add to sauce. Heat 2 or 3 minutes together, but do not boil. Serve on toast, split corn bread, waffles, or omelet. One pound of mushrooms makes 4 or 5 servings sautéed, 6 or more servings creamed.

STUFFED MUSHROOMS

1 pound mushrooms	½ teaspoon salt
4 tablespoons butter or margarine	⅛ teaspoon pepper
	Melted butter
¼ cup finely cut onion	¼ cup grated processed American cheese
¼ cup finely sliced celery	
1 teaspoon Worcestershire sauce	

Wash mushrooms. Drain. Remove stems. Chop or slice stems fine. Heat butter or margarine in large skillet. Add onion, celery, mushroom stems. Simmer until celery is tender. Stir in Worcestershire, salt, and pepper.

Brush mushroom caps with melted butter. Fill caps with onion mixture.

Start oven at moderate (350° F.).

Arrange stuffed caps, stuffed side up, in greased shallow baking pan. Sprinkle caps with cheese.

Bake 15 minutes or until cheese melts. Makes 4 or 5 servings.

Vary the stuffing: Substitute flaked, boned crab meat for celery. Mix crab with little mayonnaise.

BAKED STUFFED ONIONS

6 large yellow onions
Boiling water
1 cup cooked baby lima beans

4 tablespoons butter or margarine
3 tablespoons crumbs

Wash onions. Cook in small amount of boiling water 20 minutes or until nearly tender. Drain. Peel. Slice tops off. Scoop centers out and save. Fill onions with lima beans. Dot with 3 tablespoons butter.

Start oven at moderately hot (400° F.). Grease 1½-quart baking dish.

Place stuffed onions in prepared baking dish. Bake 15 minutes, or longer, until tender.

Sauté scooped-out onion centers with crumbs in remaining 1 tablespoon butter. Spoon over onions. Continue to bake 5 minutes or until tops are browned. Makes 6 servings.

Vary the stuffing: Leftover cooked beef, lamb, veal, chicken, or fish makes delicious stuffing for baked onions. Substitute for lima beans. Also mixture of leftover cooked vegetables, such as peas, chopped spinach, cooked or raw tomatoes combined with little grated cheese, makes good stuffing for onions.

ESCALLOPED ONIONS AND CHEESE

4 tablespoons butter or margarine
¼ cup sifted all-purpose flour
2 cups milk
¼ teaspoon paprika
1 teaspoon salt

¼ teaspoon celery salt
1 teaspoon prepared mustard
½ cup finely cut Cheddar cheese
2 cups small boiled peeled onions

Melt butter or margarine in top part of double boiler. Add flour and stir until smooth. Add milk slowly, stirring constantly. Add seasonings. Stir to mix. Add cheese and cook until creamy, stirring constantly.

Start oven at moderate (350° F.). Butter 1½-quart baking dish.

Pour drained onions into prepared baking dish. Pour cheese sauce over.

Bake 20 minutes or until hot and bubbly. Makes 4 or more servings.

PAPRIKA ONIONS

4 tablespoons butter or margarine	Paprika
¼ cup honey	½ teaspoon salt
2 tablespoons water	4 large sweet onions, peeled and cut in half

Start oven at moderate (350° F.). Butter shallow baking dish.

Melt butter or margarine with honey, water, 1 teaspoon paprika, and salt in saucepan. Place onion halves, cut side up, in prepared baking dish. Pour honey mixture over. Cover.

Bake 1½ hours or until onions are tender. Baste 2 or 3 times. Sprinkle with additional paprika few minutes before taking from oven. Makes 4 to 8 servings.

BOILED PARSNIPS

Wash parsnips thoroughly. Scrape. Rinse and drain. Cut in halves or quarters. Cook uncovered in large amount of salted boiling water 30 to 50 minutes, until tender. Drain. Slice. Remove any woody core. Dress with hot melted butter mixed with little lemon juice.

Creamed Parsnips: Dress drained boiled parsnips with well-seasoned cream sauce. About ¼ pound parsnips makes 1 serving.

Sautéed Parsnips: Boil parsnips as described. Drain. Slice lengthwise. Sauté in hot butter or bacon fat until brown on all sides. Season with salt, pepper, and a little sugar.

My father used to contend parsnips weren't fit to eat until the first frost which "sweetened" them. Try them sliced, raw in a vegetable dunk.

PEAS AND SCALLIONS

2 cups fresh peas or	2 teaspoons flour
1 (9-ounce) package quick-frozen peas	½ teaspoon salt
	1 teaspoon sugar
¾ cup liquid drained from peas	⅛ teaspoon pepper
12 to 14 scallions, sliced	¼ teaspoon powdered nutmeg
2 tablespoons butter or margarine	

Cook peas in a little salted boiling water until tender. Drain. Reserve liquid. Sauté scallions in butter or margarine 3 minutes. Stir flour, salt, sugar, pepper, and nutmeg into scallions. Add liquid from peas. Cook, stirring until thickened. Add peas. Makes 4 servings.

PEAS PARISIENNE

1 can very small French peas

2 tablespoons butter or margarine

3 or 4 very thin slices onion

½ teaspoon salt

1 tablespoon sugar

2 or 3 tablespoons boiling water

3 or 4 tender lettuce leaves, shredded

2 sprigs parsley or chervil, or 1 teaspoon dried chervil

Drain peas. Combine with butter or margarine in saucepan. Add onion, salt, sugar, and boiling water. Lay lettuce leaves over top. Add herb. Cover. Heat slowly and cook gently until lettuce wilts and is so soft it cooks into peas. Makes 2 to 4 servings.

Some French cooks add 1 tablespoon butter creamed with 1 teaspoon flour to peas before removing from heat. This *beurre manié* must be stirred in, and mixture must boil 1 or 2 minutes before serving.

HASH-STUFFED PEPPERS

4 medium-sized green peppers

1 (1-pound) can corned-beef hash

1 onion, peeled and chopped

2 tablespoons butter or margarine

¼ cup sliced stuffed olives

3 tablespoons buttered bread crumbs

Remove core and seeds from peppers. Steam peppers 10 minutes. Start oven at moderate (350° F.).

Break up hash with fork. Heat with onion in saucepan in butter or margarine. Sauté 5 minutes. Add olives. Mix. Stuff peppers. Top with crumbs. Place peppers in baking pan. Add 2 tablespoons hot water to pan or enough to barely cover bottom.

Bake 30 minutes or until tops are browned and peppers tender. Makes 4 servings.

Any leftover gravy, heated, thinned with milk or light cream, goes well with these peppers. And for extra goodness, flavor the gravy with ¼ to ½ teaspoon curry powder. Stir smoothly and heat to boiling point. Serve hot with the peppers. A budget-helper. Easy, too.

Mushroom-Ham Stuffed Peppers: Substitute 2 (3-ounce) cans chopped broiled mushrooms for hash in above recipe. Add 1 cup ground or diced cooked ham. Complete recipe as described. Before stuffing peppers moisten mixture with little consommé if needed.

Sardine-Stuffed Peppers: Substitute 1 can boneless, skinless sardines for hash. Break up sardines with fork. Heat with onion in saucepan with butter or margarine. Combine with 1½ cups cooked rice, 1 egg well beaten, and ½ cup tomato sauce. Stuff peppers. Top with crumbs. Complete recipe as described.

GREEN PEPPERS STUFFED WITH CHEESE
Chiles Rellenos Con Queso

This recipe was given to me by friends at the Chilean Embassy in Washington. It is an excellent luncheon dish, is suitable for Lent, and makes an interesting vegetable to serve at a buffet supper.

6 green peppers	Sugar
6 small slices Mexican cheese or any other mild, sliceable cheese, such as Münster	3 tablespoons fat
	1 large onion
	1 (6-ounce) can Italian tomato purée
Flour	
2 eggs	1 cup water
Salt and pepper	

Wash and drain peppers; place in shallow baking pan.

Start oven at moderate (350° F.).

Bake peppers about 30 minutes, until tender but not shapeless. When done, wrap peppers in napkin or towel about 15 minutes or until cool enough to handle. Peel. Cut slit in one side of each pepper. Scoop seeds out but leave heart of pepper intact. Insert cheese. Fasten pepper with wooden picks. Sprinkle with flour.

Beat egg whites until stiff. Beat yolks. Combine with whites. Add ¼ teaspoon salt, ⅛ teaspoon pepper, and 1 teaspoon sugar. Dip stuffed peppers carefully into this batter. Sauté in fat in skillet until egg covering is browned on all sides. Drain. Serve hot with sauce. Makes 6 servings.

Sauce: Peel and slice onion. Sauté in fat remaining in skillet in which peppers cooked. Add tomato purée, water, ½ teaspoon salt, and 1 teaspoon sugar. Let simmer 10 to 15 minutes, stirring frequently. Spoon over hot peppers.

BAKED POTATOES

Start oven at moderate (350° F. to 375° F.).

To bake potatoes perfectly, scrub well. Rinse. Drain. Rub skin with oil or fat. Bake in preheated oven 1 hour or longer. Potatoes are done when they pierce easily with fork or feel soft when squeezed gently. To squeeze them, protect fingers with folded towel.

Long, slow baking helps give potatoes dry, mealy texture.

As soon as potatoes are done, slash skin of each with sharp knife in an X, then gently squeeze each potato to free steam. Add butter or margarine, a little salt, pepper, and paprika. Serve hot, 1 potato as a serving.

Stuffings and flavorings: Sprinkle cut, seasoned potato with finely cut fresh parsley, chives, or water cress. Or spoon tablespoon sour cream into each potato. Or add few finely cut scallions. Or add grated Parmesan or other cheese and place potatoes under broiler heat 2 minutes. Or crumble crisp bacon into each opened potato.

Stuffed Baked Potatoes: Cut slice from top of freshly baked potatoes; scoop out insides. Mash. Add hot milk, butter, and seasonings. Beat. Heap into potato shells. Sprinkle with grated cheese. Brown 2 or 3 minutes under broiler heat.

BAKED SLICED POTATOES

4 potatoes	Salt and pepper
¼ cup melted butter or margarine	Paprika

Wash, scrub, and pare potatoes. Cut in ⅛-inch slices. Cover with cold water. Let stand few minutes or chill in refrigerator.

Start oven at moderate (350° F.). Grease shallow baking dish.

To cook, drain potatoes. Pat dry between paper towels. Spread in thin layer in prepared baking dish. Brush with melted butter. Season with salt, pepper, and paprika. Cover dish.

Bake 45 minutes. Remove cover and bake 15 minutes longer. Makes 4 servings.

FRENCH-FRIED POTATOES

Scrub and rinse potatoes. Pare. Cut into strips about ⅜ inch thick. Dry between paper towels. Fry in deep hot oil or fat at 375° F. on frying thermometer until light brown. Drain on paper towels in shallow pan in hot oven with door left open. Sprinkle potatoes lightly with salt. Serve hot. In estimating servings, allow 1 large potato or 2 smaller ones per serving.

FRIED WHOLE POTATOES

Scrub small potatoes. Rinse, drain. Cut slice from each end. Drop whole into deep hot oil or fat at 375° F. on frying thermometer. Fry 20 to 30 minutes, according to size. Drain. Serve with roast or other meats.

HASHED-BROWN POTATOES

4 cups diced raw potatoes	Salt and pepper
¼ cup butter or bacon fat	

Cook potatoes in butter or bacon fat until lightly browned on bottom. Do not stir. Shake pan occasionally to prevent sticking. Season potatoes as they cook. Turn potatoes with pancake turner. Fold and serve on warmed platter. Makes 4 servings.

Hashed-Brown Onion Potatoes: Sauté potatoes in butter until lightly browned on all sides. Season lightly as they cook. Add 1 (10¾-ounce) can condensed onion soup. If too thick, thin with little consommé. Cover skillet. Simmer 10 minutes. Remove cover. Continue to cook until liquid is absorbed and potatoes are browned and done. Fold over with pancake turner. Serve on warmed platter. Makes 4 servings.

MASHED POTATOES

6 potatoes	Butter or cream
4 tablespoons butter	Salt and pepper
⅓ to ½ cup hot milk	

Scrub potatoes. Rinse thoroughly. Drain. Cook covered in small amount of salted boiling water 20 to 30 minutes or until tender. Drain. Peel potatoes. Return to pan. Shake pan over low heat few minutes to dry potatoes. Put through ricer. Beat butter or cream and enough hot milk into potatoes to make them creamy and light. Add seasonings as you beat mixture. Serve heaped in warm serving dish with additional piece of butter or spoonful of warmed cream on top. Makes 6 servings.

Chantilly Potatoes: Fold ½ cup shredded processed American cheese into 4 cups hot mashed potatoes. Spoon into buttered 1-quart baking dish. Add ⅛ teaspoon salt to ½ cup heavy cream. Whip until stiff. Spread over top. Bake in moderately hot oven (400° F.) 15 minutes or until golden. Makes 6 servings.

Potato Puffs: Add 1 beaten egg to 2 cups cold, seasoned mashed potatoes. Form into balls. Roll in corn flakes. Fry until golden brown in deep hot oil or fat at 375° F. on frying thermometer. Drain on thick paper towels in shallow pan in hot oven with door left open. Makes 4 servings.

Potato Patties: Add 1 beaten egg to 2 cups cold, seasoned mashed potatoes. Form into patties. Dip lightly in seasoned flour. Brown in little hot fat on both sides. Makes 4 servings.

Add ¼ cup sliced scallions to the patty mixture. Cook as described. Delicious!

NEW POTATOES

Scrub and rinse very new, small potatoes. Scrub again, removing most of skin from potatoes. Rinse. Cover with salted boiling water and boil 3 minutes. Drain.

For each cup potatoes, heat 2 tablespoons butter, margarine, or chicken fat. Cook potatoes in fat until tender and golden. Drain. Pour fat off. Return potatoes to pan. Add 1 tablespoon butter for each cup potatoes. Cook, shaking and tilting pan so potatoes roll and coat themselves with butter as it melts. Season lightly with salt. Add little finely cut parsley. Allow 3 or more small potatoes as a serving.

New Potatoes in Chive Butter: Add for each cup cooked new potatoes, grated peel ½ lemon, 2 tablespoons lemon juice, and 1 tablespoon finely cut chives to butter in pan when cooked potatoes are added. Complete recipe as described.

Parsley New Potatoes: Substitute finely cut parsley for chives in chive-butter recipe.

DILL-CREAMED NEW POTATOES

1 ½	pounds small new potatoes	½	teaspoon salt
1	cup commercial sour cream	½	teaspoon dill seed

Wash, scrub, and scrape potatoes or pare strip around each. Cook in salted boiling water about 20 minutes or until done. Drain. Combine sour cream, salt, and dill seed. Pour over hot potatoes. Heat 1 or 2 minutes longer, turning potatoes to coat each. Makes 4 servings.

Chive-Creamed Potatoes: Substitute 2 tablespoons finely cut chives for dill seed in above recipe.

Mustard-Creamed Potatoes: Cook potatoes as described in above recipe. Combine 1 cup medium white sauce or cream sauce with 1 tablespoon prepared mustard and 4 tablespoons finely cut parsley. Pour over potatoes; heat 1 or 2 minutes and serve.

Peas and Potatoes Creamed Together: For this old-time favorite, combine 1 cup cooked fresh or quick-frozen peas, 1½ cups medium white sauce or cream sauce. Heat 1 or 2 minutes with hot potatoes. Makes 5 or more servings.

POTATOES AU GRATIN

1 ¾	cups medium white sauce	1	cup grated sharp processed
2	tablespoons minced peeled		American cheese
	onion		
5	cups sliced or diced boiled		
	potatoes		

Start oven at moderately hot (400° F.). Grease 1½-quart baking dish.

Combine sauce and onion. Make layer of potatoes in prepared casserole; cover with sauce. Add layer of cheese. Repeat until all are used, making sauce and cheese top layer.

Bake 30 minutes. Makes 6 or more servings.

Less cheese may be used. Make layers of potatoes and sauce as described. Sprinkle top lightly with cheese. Bake as described.

POTATO CAKES

2 cups grated raw potato	1 ½ teaspoons salt
2 eggs, well beaten	⅛ teaspoon pepper
1 tablespoon grated onion	½ cup fine bread crumbs
1 tablespoon finely cut scallion tops	½ teaspoon baking powder

Let grated potatoes drain in sieve. Beat eggs. Combine with onion, scallion tops, salt, and pepper. Mix with drained potatoes. Combine crumbs and baking powder. Stir into potato mixture. Drop from tablespoon onto greased griddle or skillet. Cook over low heat until brown on one side. Turn and brown the other. Makes 12 or more cakes.

If necessary, add more crumbs, or a little flour, to make mixture the right consistency.

See also Potato Patties (page 635).

POTATO CROQUETTES

5 medium-size potatoes	Flour
2 eggs	Bread crumbs
2 tablespoons butter	Fat for deep frying
Salt and pepper	
2 tablespoons grated orange peel	

Scrub potatoes. Rinse thoroughly. Pare. Boil in large amount of salted boiling water 20 minutes or until tender. Drain. Return potatoes to pan. Shake over low heat few minutes to dry potatoes. Put through ricer. Beat in 1 egg, butter, seasoning, and orange peel. Form into small croquettes. Roll lightly in flour. Brush with beaten egg. Roll in crumbs.

Fry in deep hot fat at 375° F. on frying thermometer until golden brown. Remove with slotted spoon or with frying basket. Drain on thick paper towels in shallow pan in hot oven with door left open. Makes 4 to 6 servings.

See also Potato Puffs (page 635).

ROAST POTATOES

Scrub, rinse, and pare medium potatoes. Cook in salted boiling water 15 minutes. Drain. When a roast of lamb, beef, veal, or fowl is nearly done, add potatoes to roasting pan. Baste potatoes few times with drippings in roasting pan. They should roast about 45 minutes. Turn them occasionally. Sprinkle lightly with salt before serving around roast platter or in a separate warmed serving dish. Allow 2 or more for each serving.

SCALLOPED POTATOES

8 medium potatoes, pared and sliced	1 ¾ cups medium white sauce
¼ cup finely cut green pepper	2 teaspoons salt
¼ cup minced onion	¼ teaspoon pepper

Start oven at moderate (350° F.). Grease 2-quart baking dish.

Make alternate layers of potatoes, green pepper, and onion in prepared baking dish. Combine sauce and seasoning. Pour over potatoes. Cover dish. Bake about 1 hour. Uncover and continue baking 30 minutes, until top has browned. Makes 8 servings.

The old-fashioned version of this delicious dish is made without green peppers and onion. The well-seasoned sauce is poured over potatoes, and additional seasoning added to potatoes if needed. Bake as described in recipe. Top should have areas of brown where sauce is thickest.

SWEET POTATOES

To bake, brown, or mash sweet potatoes follow recipes for white potatoes.

Also, cut sweet potatoes in julienne strips or little larger and fry in deep hot fat at 365° F. on frying thermometer until golden brown and crisp. Drain as described for French-Fried Potatoes (page 634). Sprinkle lightly with salt while still hot.

For seasoning mashed sweet potatoes, add few chopped walnuts sautéed in little butter, or add sprinkling of powdered nutmeg or cinnamon, or add little crushed pineapple. Decide on which seasoning in relation to other foods on menu.

CANDIED SWEET POTATOES

8 sweet potatoes	2 tablespoons honey
¼ cup butter or margarine	1 teaspoon grated orange peel
1 cup brown sugar, packed	½ cup orange juice

Start oven at moderate (375° F.).

Scrub potatoes; rinse; pare. Cut in halves or thick slices lengthwise. Brown well in butter or margarine in 2-quart flameproof baking dish. Sprinkle sugar over. Add honey, peel, and juice. Cover dish.

Bake 30 minutes. Uncover. Continue baking 20 to 30 minutes or until potatoes are tender. Baste often with juices in dish or with additional melted butter or margarine mixed with little brown sugar. Makes 8 servings.

SWEET-POTATO PUFF

4 sweet potatoes	2 tablespoons brown sugar
1 egg, beaten	¼ teaspoon powdered nutmeg
3 tablespoons cream	⅛ teaspoon powdered cloves
⅛ teaspoon salt	16 marshmallows

Scrub potatoes. Rinse. Drain. Pare. Cover with water. Bring to a boil and boil 20 minutes or until tender. Drain potatoes and mash. Beat egg, cream, salt, sugar, and spices together, then beat into mashed potatoes; whip until fluffy.

Start oven at moderate (350° F.). Butter a 1½-quart baking dish.

Pile whipped potatoes in baking dish. Press marshmallows lightly into potato mixture.

Bake uncovered about 30 minutes or until marshmallows are puffy, melting, and browned. Makes 5 or 6 servings.

This is a standard with us at turkey time. But it's good with baked ham, roast chicken or, of course, goose.

SWEET-POTATO SOUFFLÉ

2	cups hot, mashed, boiled sweet potatoes	1/16 teaspoon cayenne
1/2	cup hot milk	1/8 teaspoon powdered nutmeg
1/4	cup sherry	1/2 teaspoon salt
6	tablespoons butter	1 teaspoon grated lemon peel
		4 eggs

Start oven at moderately hot (400° F.). Butter deep 1½-quart baking dish.

Beat potatoes with hot milk, sherry, and butter in bowl until smooth; add seasonings, lemon peel, and egg yolks. Mix. Whip egg whites until they stand in stiff points when beater is removed. Fold potato mixture into whites. Turn into prepared baking dish. Set dish in shallow pan of hot water.

Bake 25 to 30 minutes or until well puffed and slightly browned on top. Serve at once. Makes 4 to 6 servings.

This may also be made with an equivalent amount of canned sweet potatoes, a staple of our grocery shelves.

SPINACH WITH CROUTONS

2	pounds fresh spinach or	1 tablespoon flour
2	(9-ounce) packages quick-frozen spinach	1 teaspoon salt
5	tablespoons butter or margarine	1/4 teaspoon pepper
		1/8 teaspoon powdered nutmeg
1	small onion, peeled	1/2 cup heavy cream
		2 cups bread cubes

Wash fresh spinach thoroughly through many waters. Drain. Remove thick stems. Pile into large saucepan. Cover and cook in its own moisture over medium heat 5 minutes. Or cook frozen spinach as described on package. Remove from heat. Chop very fine.

Melt 3 tablespoons butter or margarine in saucepan. Stir in onion and cook until golden. Add spinach. Sprinkle with flour. Mix well. Stir in seasoning and cream and mix.

Sauté bread cubes in remaining butter and margarine with a little garlic salt, if desired, until crisp and golden. Pour hot spinach into warmed serving dish. Garnish with croutons. Makes 6 servings.

HOT SPINACH VINAIGRETTE

2 (9-ounce) packages quick-frozen spinach

1 teaspoon minced peeled onion

6 tablespoons butter or margarine

½ teaspoon prepared mustard

2 tablespoons lemon juice

¾ teaspoon salt

⅛ teaspoon pepper

2 hard-cooked eggs, chopped fine

Cook spinach as described on package. Drain. Chop. Sauté onion in 1 tablespoon butter or margarine until tender. Add remaining butter or margarine, mustard, lemon juice, salt, and pepper. Heat to boiling point. Pour over spinach. Add half of chopped eggs. Toss lightly with two forks to mix. Pour into warmed serving dish. Add remaining chopped egg as top garnish. Makes 6 servings.

ACORN SQUASH

Wash squash. Cut in halves lengthwise. Remove seeds. Cook in small amount of salted boiling water 25 minutes or until tender. Drain. Mash well in shell. Add seasoning, such as little brown sugar, honey, or orange juice. Or minced onion, with small amount of salt, pepper, and butter. Serve 1 or 2 halves as a serving, depending on size.

Baked Acorn Squash: Halve, seed, and cook 3 acorn squash as described in above recipe. Drain well. Scoop squash out of shells. Mix with 6 tablespoons minced onion sautéed in butter, 1½ teaspoons salt, ¼ teaspoon pepper, 2 tablespoons light cream. Beat well. Heap back into squash shells. Sprinkle lightly with paprika. Place shells in shallow pan. Add 2 or 3 tablespoons water to pan to prevent burning bottom of squash.

Bake 10 to 20 minutes in moderate oven (375° F.). Makes 3 to 6 servings.

Broiled Acorn Squash: Halve, seed, and cook squash as described. Drain. Place in shallow pan. Season each cooked half with salt, pepper, little brown sugar, and dabs of butter. Broil under moderate heat 3 to 5 minutes or until very hot. Makes 3 to 6 servings.

Fu, a former Chinese houseman of mine, used to bake the squash halves (after slight parboiling) with a filling of snippets of bacon, brown sugar and sticky raisins. It's still a favorite of ours as is he wherever he is.

BAKED SQUASH, ENGLISH STYLE

1 quart thinly sliced peeled Hubbard squash	¼ cup sugar
	½ cup heavy cream
2 teaspoons salt	1 teaspoon powdered cinnamon

Start oven at slow (250° F.). Butter 1½-quart baking dish.

Pour sliced squash into dish. Sprinkle with salt and sugar. Pour cream over. Sprinkle with cinnamon; cover dish.

Bake about 50 minutes or until squash is tender. Makes 6 or more servings.

BAKED MASHED SQUASH

Defrost two (9-ounce) packages quick-frozen mashed squash. Place in buttered casserole. Top with layer of very thin onion slices. Sprinkle with brown sugar, salt, and pepper. Dot with butter. Bake 20 minutes in moderate oven (350° F.). Makes 4 or more servings.

This converted the children to squash.

BAKED SUMMER SQUASH

Zucchini

Start oven at moderate (325° or 350° F.). Grease shallow baking dish.

Scrub squash thoroughly to remove all sand. Cut into quarters. Place in prepared baking dish. Dot with butter, margarine, or little olive oil. Season lightly with salt and paprika. Add generous grind of fresh black pepper. Add 2 or 3 tablespoons water to bottom of dish.

Bake while meat or chicken is roasting, allowing 30 to 45 minutes. Squash should be tender, with edges beginning to brown. Allow 1 small squash per serving, or 2 large squash make 4 servings.

Baked Zucchini with Cheese: When baked zucchini is half done, add light sprinkling soy sauce and generous amount grated Parmesan cheese to each piece. Continue to bake as described. Delicious. Makes 4 servings.

FRIED ZUCCHINI

3 zucchini squash	1 tablespoon lemon juice
2 tablespoons flour	¾ cup bread crumbs
½ teaspoon salt	4 tablespoons butter or marga-
¼ teaspoon pepper	rine
1 egg	

Wash zucchini thoroughly, scrubbing gently to loosen all sand. Slice blossom and stem ends from each squash. Cut in lengthwise strips about ½ inch thick. Cut strips in pieces about 2½ inches long.

Coat pieces with flour seasoned with salt and pepper. Dip floured strips in slightly beaten egg and lemon juice. Coat thoroughly with crumbs. Fry in butter or margarine until crisp. Add extra fat if necessary. Drain on thick paper towels. Serve very hot. Makes 4 servings.

Fried Zucchini, Italian Style: Slice scrubbed, washed, and drained zucchini crosswise into ½-inch slices. Sauté in hot olive oil or peanut oil 3 minutes or until lightly browned around edges. Sprinkle with salt and pepper. Serve lightly sprinkled with grated Romano cheese and finely cut parsley. Makes 4 or more servings.

COUNTRY FRIED TOMATOES

6 large tomatoes	1 ½ cups milk
3 tablespoons flour	1 ½ teaspoons sugar
1 ½ teaspoons salt	2 tablespoons ground cooked
¼ teaspoon pepper	beef
¼ cup butter or margarine	1 ½ teaspoons prepared mustard
10 small toast strips	

Cut stem end from tomatoes. Cut tomatoes in thick slices crosswise. Combine 1 tablespoon flour with half of salt and pepper; dredge slices. Sauté in butter or margarine until golden on both sides.

Remove all but 2 slices to hot toast-covered platter. Mash remaining 2 slices into skillet juices. Stir remaining 2 tablespoons flour into them. Add milk, stirring well. Add remaining ¾ teaspoon salt, the sugar, ground meat, and mustard. Stir and cook until boiling and slightly thickened. Pour over tomatoes and toast. Serve at once. Makes 5 or 6 servings.

When frost threatens the last tomatoes in the garden, we do some of the green ones this way.

STUFFED ZUCCHINI

1 pound ground beef or beef
   and lamb mixed
1 small onion, peeled and cut
   fine
¼ cup quick-cooking rice
¼ cup milk

2 teaspoons salt
½ teaspoon pepper
½ teaspoon thyme
8 small zucchini
2 (8-ounce) cans tomato sauce

Start oven at moderate (350° F.).

Combine meat, onion, rice, milk, and seasonings. Wash and scrub squash. Cut ends off. Use apple corer to hollow out squash. Fill each squash loosely with meat stuffing. Heat tomato sauce in flameproof shallow baking dish. Stir scooped-out squash centers into sauce as well as any leftover meat mixture. Mix and bring to a boil. Lay stuffed zucchini in sauce.

Bake, covered, about 1 hour or until squash is tender. Uncover for last 10 minutes of time. Stir sauce occasionally. Makes 4 to 8 servings.

Grated Parmesan cheese makes a good addition to this Italian favorite. Also a small amount of herb, such as thyme, basil, or orégano, stirred into the sauce during last half hour of baking adds interest.

HERBED TOMATO SLICES

2 large tomatoes
Salt and pepper
Sugar
¼ cup fine crumbs

1½ tablespoons mixed dried
   herbs
3 tablespoons butter or margarine

Wash and skin tomatoes. Cut each in 3 or 4 thick slices, depending on size of tomato. Place slices in greased shallow baking pan. Sprinkle each lightly with salt, pepper, and sugar. Add crumbs, herbs, and dabs of butter or margarine. Broil under moderate heat, 3 inches from flame, about 3 minutes or until crumbs are brown. Makes 2 to 4 servings.

Substitute crumbled Roquefort or bleu cheese for herbs. Omit sugar. Voilà! A "new" vegetable.

TURNIPS

Wash, scrub, and drain white turnips. Pare. Cut in quarters or slices. Cook in small amount of salted boiling water until just barely tender. Overcooking darkens turnips and spoils flavor.

Dress boiled turnips with well-seasoned cream sauce. Add onion salt and lemon juice to sauce. Or dress drained, cooked turnips with melted butter, salt, and pepper. Or add little light cream, grated cheese, and freshly ground pepper. Serve hot.

Scalloped Turnips: Cook turnips as described in above recipe. Slice hot turnips into buttered baking dish. Cover with medium white sauce or cream sauce. Add sprinkling chopped green pepper and grated onion. Add 2 or 3 tablespoons grated cheese. Cover dish. Bake in moderate oven (375° F.) only until cheese melts. Uncover dish. Bake 5 minutes longer. Allow 1 or 2 medium-sized turnips per serving.

Other Vegetable Ideas: Sliced, green, red or yellow tomatoes dipped in seasoned bread crumbs or floured and fried in hot fat or oil.

Sliced, seeded green or sweet red peppers (or both varieties together) cooked like any other green vegetable and served with butter or in a cream sauce. Almost calorie-free, served plain.

Fresh or canned peas served with tiny pickled cocktail onions.

Canned or fresh peas cooked with garlic and a little fine olive oil.

Menus for All Occasions

Some of my favorite menus are presented here as a guide for you in meal planning and entertaining. Menus also are suggested elsewhere in the book with recipes in the casserole, chafing-dish, and other main-dish chapters.

Most of my luncheon and supper menus may be served as dinners by extending them a little, either with a first course added or by including an additional vegetable or a salad.

Some of the menus in the dinner menu section may be served as a buffet supper or as a gala luncheon. All menus given are intended to serve as guides, to offer ideas and suggestions for your own menu-making. You should feel free to shorten or enlarge, change, develop, and otherwise modify them to suit your needs.

In many dinner menus hot bread is suggested. But your family and friends may be calorie-counting, so that Ry-Krisp, Norwegian paper-thin flatbröd, or gluten or starch-reduced bread will please them more. Or you may want to omit dessert from certain menus or substitute fresh fruit for the dessert I have suggested.

So-called formal meals follow a traditional pattern. But since only the household with two or more servants can approximate a formal luncheon or dinner, our daily home luncheons, suppers, and dinners take on the form and content which is easiest for us to prepare and which please our families and guests.

Many a good luncheon or supper is impromptu—made up of what is in the refrigerator, freezer, and pantry, then served on a tray on the terrace or by the fireplace, or on a bridge table by a window. Enjoyment of such a meal or of a long-planned, handsomely served guest dinner depends on the same qualities: good food prepared to perfection served by a relaxed hostess.

BREAKFAST SETTING

*At breakfast the first course, fruit juice or stewed fruit, is placed on
the breakfast plate. Dry cereal is placed above the plate but hot cereal
is served from the kitchen. Coffee spoon may be at the right of the knife
or placed on the saucer as shown.*

HOT OATMEAL WITH RAISINS, TOP MILK

BROILED HAM (page 390)

HERBED SCRAMBLED EGGS (page 295)

POPOVERS (page 92)

COFFEE

❋   ❋   ❋

CRANBERRY-AND-GRAPEFRUIT JUICE

CODFISH CAKES (page 305)

HASHED-BROWN POTATOES (page 634)

SOUR-CREAM MUFFINS (page 90)

ALMOND-BAKED APPLES (page 261)

COFFEE

SLICED ORANGES

BROILED CANADIAN BACON AND SCRAMBLED EGGS (page 295)

TOASTED CORN MUFFINS

COFFEE

⌘ ⌘ ⌘

HALF GRAPEFRUIT

KIPPERED HERRING

POTATOES AU GRATIN (page 636)

TOASTED CRACKED-WHEAT BREAD APPLESAUCE

COFFEE TEA

⌘ ⌘ ⌘

RAISIN BRAN WITH TOP MILK

FRIED APPLE SLICES CORNED-BEEF HASH (page 430)

TOASTED SCONES (page 92) MARMALADE

COFFEE TEA

⌘ ⌘ ⌘

HOT COOKED FARINA, TOP MILK OR CREAM

PLAIN OMELET (page 297)

BROILED CANADIAN BACON

TOASTED ENGLISH MUFFINS (page 77–78) CHERRY JAM

BOWL FRESH FRUITS

COFFEE

⌘ ⌘ ⌘

SLICED PEACHES CRISP CEREAL CREAM

CREAMED MUSHROOMS ON TOAST (page 628)

CRISP BACON CURLS

COFFEE OR CAFÉ AU LAIT (page 52)

SLICED ORANGES-AND-STRAWBERRIES

BROWNED MEAT PATTIES (page 412)

(LEFTOVER ROAST BEEF, LAMB, OR VEAL)

OR

POTATO CAKES (page 637)

CORN STICKS (page 91)   GOOSEBERRY JAM

COFFEE

✵ ✵ ✵

GRAPE JUICE

BROWNED RICE PATTIES (use left-over rice, page 449)   APPLE JELLY

BACON   OR   CANADIAN BACON

HOT BRIOCHES (page 77)

COFFEE

✵ ✵ ✵

STEWED CHERRIES, SHREDDED WHEAT, TOP MILK

SPANISH OMELET (page 299)

TOASTED ENGLISH MUFFINS   PLUM JAM

COFFEE

✵ ✵ ✵

SLICED BANANAS, RICE FLAKES, TOP MILK

DAISYFIELDS CREAMED EGGS (page 181) ON ANCHOVY TOAST (page 540)

BROILED LUNCHEON MEAT

COFFEE

MIXED ORANGE-AND-GRAPEFRUIT JUICE

COUNTRY PANCAKES (page 100) WITH CRAB-MEAT SAUCE (page 334)

COFFEE

✖   ✖   ✖

GRAPEFRUIT JUICE

ROAST-BEEF HASH (page 431)   BROILED HERBED TOMATO SLICES (page 644)

HOT BISCUITS (page 82)   HONEY

COFFEE   TEA

✖   ✖   ✖

MIXED ORANGE-AND-APRICOT JUICE

COUNTRY PANCAKES (page 100)   MOLASSES HARD SAUCE

CRISP BACON CURLS

COFFEE

✖   ✖   ✖

CHILLED HONEYDEW MELON

DIXIE WAFFLES (page 102)   HONEY BUTTER

SMALL BROWNED SAUSAGE PATTIES (page 404)

COFFEE   CAFÉ AU LAIT (page 52)

✖   ✖   ✖

SLICED ORANGES

SUNDAY-BRUNCH FINNAN HADDIE

ON TOASTED ENGLISH MUFFINS (page 77–78)

JELLY DOUGHNUTS

COFFEE

RED RASPBERRIES, CREAM

TOAST   HONEY BUTTER

GRILLED SAUSAGES (page 404)   OR   CODFISH CAKES (page 305)

COFFEE

❊   ❊   ❊

SLICED CANNED APRICOTS

ORANGE MUFFINS (page 90)   APPLE BUTTER

CLAM PATTIES (page 328)

HASHED-BROWN POTATOES (page 634)

COFFEE

❊   ❊   ❊

HOT OATMEAL, TOP MILK OR CREAM

CANADIAN BACON   POACHED EGGS (page 295)

TOAST   BLACKBERRY JAM

COFFEE

❊   ❊   ❊

CRISP RICE CEREAL, SLICED BANANAS, MILK

BACON AND SCRAMBLED EGGS (page 295)

TOASTED ROLLS

COFFEE

❊   ❊   ❊

ALMOND-BAKED APPLES

CORNED-BEEF HASH (page 430)

HOT BISCUITS (page 82)   ORANGE MARMALADE

COFFEE

BROILED HALF GRAPEFRUIT (page 263)

HAM OMELET (page 297)

BUTTERED TOAST   STRAWBERRY JAM

COFFEE   OR   TEA

❦   ❦   ❦

WARM COMPOTE PRUNES AND APRICOTS

ASSORTED DRY CEREALS

BROILED HAM (page 390)

POPOVERS (page 92)   PEACH JAM

COFFEE

❦   ❦   ❦

CRANBERRY JUICE

BROILED SHAD ROE (page 322) WITH CRISP BACON

BROILED APPLE   OR   PINEAPPLE RINGS

MUFFINS (page 89) AND BUTTER

COFFEE

❦   ❦   ❦

MELON SLICE

SAUSAGES IN WHITE WINE (page 404)   POTATOES AU GRATIN (page 636)

TOASTED ENGLISH MUFFINS (pages 77–78)

BUTTER AND JAM

COFFEE

CHILLED GRAPEFRUIT SECTIONS

MASHED POTATO PATTIES (page 635)   GRILLED BACON

TOASTED ROLLS   MARMALADE

COFFEE CAKE WITH CHEESE TOPPING (page 87)

COFFEE

❇   ❇   ❇

HALF LARGE ORANGE

SCRAMBLED EGGS WITH CHIVES (page 295)

HASH PATTIES (page 431)

DANISH PASTRY   OR   HONEY BUN

COFFEE

❇   ❇   ❇

CANTALOUPE

COUNTRY KITCHEN MUSH (page 442)   CURRANT JELLY

CHEESE-PIMIENTO BISCUITS (page 83)

COFFEE

❇   ❇   ❇

GRAPEFRUIT JUICE

POACHED EGGS (page 295) ON

DEVILED-HAM TOAST

ORANGE-MARMALADE COFFEE CAKE (page 75)

COFFEE

BLUEBERRIES AND CREAM

TOMATO OMELET (page 299)

FRENCH-FRIED POTATOES (page 634)

SALLY LUNN (page 80)   MARMALADE TRAY

COFFEE

❀   ❀   ❀

SLICED STRAWBERRIES, CRISP CEREAL, CREAM

BROILED CHICKEN HALF (page 203)

POTATO PATTIES (page 635)

BLUEBERRY MUFFINS (page 90)   CRANBERRY JELLY

COFFEE

❀   ❀   ❀

SLICED PEACHES AND CREAM

KIPPERED HERRING

BROILED HERBED TOMATO HALVES (page 644)

BUTTERED TOAST

COFFEE   OR   CAFÉ AU LAIT (page 52)

❀   ❀   ❀

FRESH FRUIT BOWL

SCRAMBLED EGGS WITH ANCHOVIES (page 295)

BROILED HAM (page 390)

ORANGE MUFFINS (page 90)   JELLY

COFFEE

655

GRAPES   PLUMS   CHERRIES

COUNTRY KITCHEN MUSH (page 442)

TASTY LINK SAUSAGES (page 404)

HOT BRIOCHES (page 77)   OR   CROISSANTS

COFFEE

❋   ❋   ❋

MIXED FRESH FRUIT JUICES

EGGS BENEDICT (page 290)   TOASTED ENGLISH MUFFINS (pages 77–78)

CINNAMON RING (page 71)

COFFEE

❋   ❋   ❋

FROSTY TOMATO JUICE

CODFISH CAKES (page 305)   FRIED WHOLE POTATOES (page 634)

JELLY DOUGHNUTS

COFFEE

❋   ❋   ❋

CORNED-BEEF HASH (page 430) WITH POACHED EGG (page 295)

TOASTED WHOLE-GRAIN BREAD

CHERRY JAM

BOWL FRESH FRUITS

COFFEE

CRANBERRY-AND-ORANGE JUICE

VERY SMALL LAMB CHOPS (page 391) FRIED APPLE RINGS

PECAN ROLL (page 72)

COFFEE

⌘ ⌘ ⌘

SLICED ORANGES AND BANANAS

COUNTRY PANCAKES (page 100) WITH CREAMED CHICKEN (page 178)

WHOLE-WHEAT TOAST BLUEBERRY JAM

COFFEE

⌘ ⌘ ⌘

ASSORTED CRISP CEREALS, CREAM, APPLESAUCE

HAM OMELET (page 297)

RAISIN-BREAD TOAST CHERRY JAM

COFFEE

⌘ ⌘ ⌘

SHREDDED WHEAT, RAISINS, TOP MILK

BAKED EGGS IN TOAST CUPS (page 296)

BACON CURLS

ORANGE-MARMALADE COFFEE CAKE (page 75)

COFFEE

⌘ ⌘ ⌘

FROSTY GRAPES CHERRIES

CREAMED SCRAMBLED EGGS (page 295)

BUTTERED TOAST

COFFEE

HOT MUSH AND TOP MILK (page 442)

ORANGE MUFFINS (page 90)   PEACH BUTTER

ALMOND-BAKED APPLES (page 261)

COFFEE

❈   ❈   ❈

RICE CEREAL AND SLICED BANANAS, TOP MILK

BROILED HAM (page 390)   SMALL POTATO CROQUETTES (page 637)

SALLY LUNN (page 80)   BLUEBERRY JAM

COFFEE

❈   ❈   ❈

Diet Special

I eat this every morning except Sunday and never tire of its calculated calories.

½ CUP POT CHEESE   OR   PLAIN COTTAGE CHEESE

1 TABLESPOON STRAWBERRY JAM

4 WHOLE NORWEGIAN FLATBRÖD

*1 PAT BUTTER

BLACK COFFEE

❈   ❈   ❈

*Or omit butter and consume later in the day.

Luncheons or Suppers

INFORMAL LUNCH AND SUPPER

The optional placement of dessert silver above the plate is convenient when service is limited or when the hostess is doing the serving herself.

FORMAL LUNCHEON SETTING

First course may be in place as the guests are seated. Iced-tea spoon is here placed above the service plate but may also be placed to the right of the knives. Salad may also be served with the entree.

RUBY CONSOMMÉ (page 593)   PIROSHKIS (page 11)

BROILED LAMB CHOPS (page 391)

NEW ASPARAGUS TIPS (page 614)   LEMON BUTTER

NEW POTATOES, CHIVE BUTTER (page 635)

SLICED TOMATOES WITH RED ONION RINGS, FRENCH HERB VINEGAR (page 517)
OR FRENCH DRESSING (page 518)

HOT ROLLS

MELON

COFFEE

✳   ✳   ✳

FRESH FRUIT CUP IN MELON SHELL (pages 18–19)

HAMBURGERS WITH BURGUNDY (page 414)

FRENCH-FRIED POTATOES (page 634)

BAKED ONIONS STUFFED WITH LIMA BEANS (page 629)

COLESLAW (page 492) WITH GRATED RAW CARROT OR GRATED RED CABBAGE

COFFEE

✳   ✳   ✳

CRISP CELERY   YOUNG RADISHES   TOMATO JUICE REFRESHER (page 24)

ROAST SADDLE OF LAMB (page 391)

RICE RING WITH PEAS (page 453)

BROWN-AND-SERVE ROLLS

PEARS COINTREAU (page 268)   CHOCOLATE OATMEAL BARS (page 132)

COFFEE   TEA

660

ROMAINE-AND-ALLIGATOR-PEAR APPETIZER SALAD

PUFFY OMELET (page 298) WITH CHICKEN À LA KING (page 178)
SMALL ROLLS

COFFEE JELLY (page 273)   SHERRY SAUCE (page 568)
COFFEE

❊   ❊   ❊

CELERY   SCALLIONS   RADISHES

BAKED LAMB CHOPS (page 391)
OVEN-BAKED SLICED POTATOES (page 633)
BUTTERED BROCCOLI (page 619)
MIXED GREEN SALAD (page 496)
HOT CORN STICKS (pages 89, 91)

COFFEE ICE CREAM (page 250)   LEMON COOKIES (page 137)
COFFEE

❊   ❊   ❊

GRAPEFRUIT-AND-ORANGE CUP

BROILED CHICKEN HALVES (page 203)   SPICED CRABAPPLE GARNISH
TINY HOT BISCUITS (page 83)

LEMON MERINGUE PIE (page 470)
COFFEE   TEA

❊   ❊   ❊

CREAM-OF-ASPARAGUS SOUP (page 594)
SMALL ANCHOVY CANAPÉS

HAM MOUSSE SALAD (page 512) WITH SALAD GREENS (page 496)
FRENCH DRESSING (page 518)

HOT POPPY-SEED ROLLS

BROILED SHERRIED GRAPEFRUIT (page 263)
COFFEE

661

NEW FRIED CHICKEN (page 211)

NEW CORN-ON-COB (page 624)

VEGETABLE GELATIN SALAD (page 514)
FRENCH DRESSING (page 518)

SMALL BLUEBERRY MUFFINS (page 90)

CAKE AND ICE-CREAM LOAF (page 260)

COFFEE   OR   ICED TEA (page 57)

❋   ❋   ❋

BAKED ONION SOUP (page 600), POPPY-SEED CRACKERS

COLD ROAST CAPON, CHICKEN, TURKEY

HOT HERBED FRENCH BREAD (page 543)

ENDIVE SALAD (page 495)

NEUFCHÂTEL   OR   CREAM CHEESE WITH GUAVA JELLY

COFFEE

❋   ❋   ❋

MIXED VEGETABLE JUICE COCKTAIL (page 24)   CELERY CRACKERS

CHICKEN SOUFFLÉ (page 582)

BUTTERED LIMA BEANS

GRAPEFRUIT AND LETTUCE SALAD, PAPRIKA FRENCH DRESSING (page 518)

SMALL MUFFINS   OR   BISCUITS (page 83)

MELON-BALL COMPOTE

TEA   COFFEE

CANTALOUPE RING FILLED WITH MELON BALLS

WAFFLES WITH CHICKEN À LA KING (page 178)

WATER-CRESS SALAD (page 502)

CHOCOLATE ICE-CREAM MERINGUE TARTS (page 482)

ICED TEA (page 57)   ICED COFFEE (page 50)

❊   ❊   ❊

SHRIMP CREOLE (page 356)   HOT RICE (page 449)

ASSORTED SMALL SANDWICHES

MIXED GREEN SALAD—ESCAROLE, ROMAINE,
GARDEN LETTUCE WITH MINCED PARSLEY, FRENCH DRESSING (page 518)

RASPBERRY SHERBET (page 256)   PETITS FOURS (page 116)

CAFFÈ ESPRESSO (page 50)

❊   ❊   ❊

CHICKEN CURRY (page 206)

SAFFRON RICE (page 452)   OR   PILAU (page 453)

ASSORTED CURRY CONDIMENTS

SEEDLESS GRAPES   RAISINS   PLUMS

TEA   COFFEE

❊   ❊   ❊

FRUIT CUP WITH FRESH MINT GARNISH (page 18)

BEEF AND TOMATO LOAF (page 417)

CARROTS AND PEAS COOKED TOGETHER

SLICED PICKLED BEETS (page 619)   MINCED PARSLEY GARNISH

RAISIN BREAD (page 88)   CURRANT JELLY

MOCHA SOUFFLÉ (page 588)

COFFEE

MELON BALL CUP (page 266)

CHICKEN TETRAZZINI (page 446)

GRAPEFRUIT GELATIN RING (page 510)
FILLED WITH GREEN-PEPPER-AND-WATER-CRESS SALAD (page 497)
FRENCH DRESSING (page 518)

SPICE COOKIES (page 135)

TEA

✳   ✳   ✳

BROILED GRAPEFRUIT (page 263)

PUFFY OMELET (page 298) WITH CREAMED TUNA FISH (page 530)

RADISH ROSES, CARROT CURLS (page 22)

TOAST STRIPS

BLUEBERRY AND PEACH SHORTCAKE (page 262)

COFFEE   TEA

✳   ✳   ✳

CUP OF VEGETABLE AND CHICKEN SOUP (page 604)
SESAME-SEED CRACKERS

CHEESE SOUFFLÉ (page 580)

BROILED CANADIAN BACON

PASCAL CELERY AND FENNEL STICKS

BROWN-AND-SERVE ROLLS

SWEETMEAT TRAY (page 139ff.)

COFFEE

CRAB-MEAT COCKTAIL (page 28)

BLACK OLIVES   CELERY HEARTS

VEAL SCALOPPINE (page 412)

BUTTERED ZUCCHINI (page 642)

LETTUCE AND TOMATO SALAD WITH TARRAGON VINEGAR AND
SHREDDED SPANISH ONIONS

HOT HERBED FRENCH BREAD (page 543)

PEARS IN COINTREAU (page 268)

COFFEE

❋   ❋   ❋

ANTIPASTO (page 24)   TOMATO JUICE COCKTAIL

EASY-BAKED LASAGNE (page 445)

PIMIENTO AND GREEN PEPPER RINGS ON LEAF LETTUCE,
TART DRESSING

TOASTED ITALIAN BREAD

SUNDAY NIGHT WINE-JELLY RING (page 274)
FILLED WITH LEMON SHERBET

ANGEL FOOD CAKE (page 106)

COFFEE

❋   ❋   ❋

JELLIED TOMATO BOUILLON (page 606)

PRETZEL STICKS

CHICKEN-LEFTOVER PIE (page 172)

FRUIT SALAD IN PINEAPPLE SHELL

BROWN SUGAR PECAN COOKIES (page 132)

COFFEE

BUTTERMILK BEET SOUP (page 602)

PAPRIKA CRACKERS

HAM MOUSSE (page 512)   TOSSED GREEN SALAD (page 496)

HOT CORN STICKS (pages 89, 91)

CRÈME BRULÉE (page 241)

COFFEE

⌘ ⌘ ⌘

FRUIT JUICE   HOT CHEESE CANAPÉS (pages 6–7, 9, 11)

CALF'S LIVER SAUTÉ (page 422)

CRISP BACON

CORN PUDDING (page 625)

ROMAINE SALAD BOWL WITH GRATED RAW BEET, THINLY SLICED SCALLIONS,
DUTCH CREAM DRESSING (page 515)

BREAD AND BUTTER

PRUNE CREAM PIE (page 475)

COFFEE

⌘ ⌘ ⌘

PURÉE MONGOL (page 610)

WHOLE-WHEAT CRACKERS

CHICKEN SALAD (page 502)

SMALL ROQUEFORT CHEESE SANDWICHES (page 534)

CUCUMBER FINGERS

PINEAPPLE SHERBET (page 257)

SPICE COOKIES (page 135)

COFFEE

CLAM CHOWDER CRACKERS

TOASTED CHEESE-AND-TOMATO SANDWICHES
MADE AT TABLE BROILER

APPLE MERINGUE TARTS (page 479)

COFFEE

❋ ❋ ❋

CREAM-OF-ASPARAGUS SOUP (page 594)

SMALL STUFFED CELERY

CALIFORNIA MEAT PIE (page 419)

TOMATO ASPIC RING (page 514)

CARAMEL-BAKED APPLES (page 261)

COFFEE

❋ ❋ ❋

BAKED LIMA BEANS WITH TOMATOES (page 617)

GRILLED FRANKFURTERS TOASTED FRANKFURTER ROLLS

APRICOT BAVARIAN (page 272)

TEA COFFEE

❋ ❋ ❋

RUBY CONSOMMÉ (page 593) CELERY PINWHEELS (page 22)

SHRIMP SALAD (page 505)

VERY SMALL HAM SANDWICHES

FRESH PEARS CAMEMBERT

TEA OR COFFEE

VICHYSSOISE (page 608)   CELERY CRACKERS

CRUSTY-TOPPED BAKED FISH (page 306)

BAKED LIMA BEANS (page 617)

RED CABBAGE SLAW

SMALL TOASTED ROLLS

WINE JELLY (page 274)   CUSTARD SAUCE (page 565)

TEA   OR   COFFEE

✳   ✳   ✳

FRESH FRUIT CUP IN PINEAPPLE SHELL

STUFFED FLOUNDER FILLETS (page 308)

CORN-TOMATO-CASSEROLE (page 158)

CHEESE BREAD   OR   MUFFINS (page 89)

MARLIN'S CHOCOLATE PIE (page 466)

COFFEE

✳   ✳   ✳

WELSH RABBIT (page 184)   BUTTERED TOAST

TOSSED GREEN SALAD (page 496)

PECAN PIE (page 474)

COFFEE

✳   ✳   ✳

TURKEY SALAD (page 503)

ANCHOVY-BUTTER SANDWICHES (page 540)

RASPBERRY ICE (page 256)   HOLIDAY FRUITCAKE (page 118)

ICED TEA (page 57)

SMALL APPETIZER SALAD (page 27)

SALMON WITH SHRIMP SAUCE (page 315)
NEW POTATOES (page 635)   PARSLEY BUTTER
TOASTED ROLLS

WINE-CHERRY MOLD (page 274)   SOUR CREAM
COFFEE

    ❊   ❊   ❊

CUP FROZEN SHRIMP BISQUE   CELERY CRACKERS

LAMB ON SKEWERS (page 396)
HOT RICE (page 449)
SALAD BOWL WITH ROQUEFORT DRESSING (page 519)

COFFEE

    ❊   ❊   ❊

ICED MIXED VEGETABLE JUICE (page 24)   CHEESE CRACKERS

INDIVIDUAL HOT CHICKEN OR TURKEY PIES (page 172)
ARTICHOKE HEARTS (page 21) WITH FRENCH DRESSING (page 518)
WHOLE-WHEAT BREAD (page 70)

CHOCOLATE MOUSSE (page 340)
COFFEE

    ❊   ❊   ❊

JELLIED MADRILÈNE (page 608)
CHEESE STICKS (page 461)

SAVORY LEFTOVER LAMB (page 397)
COUNTRY-FRIED TOMATOES (page 643)
LEBANESE SALAD (page 498)
HOT ROLLS   GRAPE JELLY

COMPOTE BLACK CHERRIES AND SLICED PEACHES
COFFEE

CALIFORNIA MEAT PIE (page 419)

COLESLAW (page 492)

COUNTRY CORN STICKS (page 91)

BAKED CUSTARD WITH COCONUT TOPPING (page 238)

COFFEE

❊　❊　❊

CREAM-OF-CORN SOUP　SMALL ONION BISCUITS (page 84)

CHICKEN MOUSSE SALAD (page 507)
WITH WATER CRESS (page 502) AND FRENCH DRESSING (page 518)

SPICED PEARS COMPOTE (page 270)

COFFEE

❊　❊　❊

HOT TOMATO BOUILLON (page 606)

THIN SMOKED-SALMON SANDWICHES

CHEESE SOUFFLÉ (page 580)

DUTCH STUFFED-CELERY AU GRATIN (page 623)

LEMON-ORANGE SHERBET (page 258) WITH FRESH RED RASPBERRIES

COFFEE

❊　❊　❊

CUP OYSTER STEW (page 350)　CRACKERS

COLD CUTS: HAM, CHICKEN, SARDINES, ITALIAN CHEESE

RAW CARROT STICKS　OR　CAULIFLOWERETTES

POTATO SALAD (page 498ff.)

BUTTERED BLACK WALNUT BREAD SANDWICHES (page 86)

COFFEE

BUTTERMILK BEET SOUP (page 602)

BUTTERED PUMPERNICKEL

HAM MOUSSE (page 512) GARNISHED WITH CELERY HEARTS

CHOCOLATE POUNDCAKE (page 120)   CHERRY PRESERVES

HOT TEA

❊   ❊   ❊

PURÉE MONGOL (page 610) PAPRIKA CRACKERS

TUNA FISH- BACON-LETTUCE SANDWICHES

ANGEL CAKE (page 106)
CUSTARD SAUCE (page 565)

COFFEE

❊   ❊   ❊

CREAM-OF-CHICKEN SOUP WITH SHERRY (page 594)

THIN HAM SANDWICHES

CUCUMBER-TOMATO-ROMAINE SALAD BOWL

RIPE OLIVES

ASSORTED CAKE TRAY

ICED COFFEE (page 50)

❊   ❊   ❊

CREAMED MUSHROOMS ON TOAST (page 628)

NEW POTATOES WITH CHIVE BUTTER (page 635)

TOSSED LETTUCE-RADISH-GREEN-PEPPER SALAD

ASSORTED BREAD TRAY

WINTER COMPOTE (page 271)

COFFEE

TURKEY-LEFTOVER PIE (page 172) WITH CHEESE CRUST (page 461)

SMALL BAKED SLICED POTATOES (page 633)

ASPARAGUS TIPS WITH LEMON BUTTER (page 545)

CHICORY SALAD WITH CANNED ARTICHOKE HEARTS,
FRENCH DRESSING (page 518)

WATERMELON

ICED COFFEE (page 50)

❊　❊　❊

CELERY　ENDIVE SALAD (page 495)

COCKTAILS　FRUIT JUICE

TOMATO ASPIC RING (page 514) WITH SHRIMP OR CRAB SALAD (page 504)
MAYONNAISE　RUSSIAN DRESSING (page 523)
ROQUEFORT DRESSING (page 519)

SMALL HOT CHEESE BISCUITS (page 82)

BLACK-CHERRY TARTS (page 480)　SOUR CREAM

COFFEE

❊　❊　❊

HASH-STUFFED PEPPERS (page 631)

MUSHROOM SAUCE (page 553)

GRILLED TOMATOES WITH CHOPPED PARSLEY

ENDIVE WITH PIMIENTO STRIPS, SLICED SCALLIONS,
FRENCH DRESSING (page 518)

TOASTED ENGLISH MUFFINS

CHEESE TRAY　APPLES AND PEARS

COFFEE

SCRAMBLED EGGS COOKED IN CHAFING DISH (page 295)

GREEN SALAD WITH HOT BACON DRESSING (page 502)

BUTTERED HOT HOLLAND RUSKS

BROILED CANNED PEACH HALVES   SPICE COOKIES (page 135)

COFFEE   OR   TEA

ˣ   ˣ   ˣ

OYSTER COCKTAIL (page 28)

ROAST CHICKEN (page 216)   SAFFRON RICE WITH RAISINS (page 452)

INDIAN CHUTNEY   SMALL ROLLS, CURRANT JELLY

CELERY HEARTS AND BLACK OLIVES

BISQUE TORTONI   OR   DAISYFIELDS MARBLE LOAF CAKE (page 122)

COFFEE   TEA

ˣ   ˣ   ˣ

LIME GELATIN APPETIZER FRUIT SALAD (page 510)

BAKED MACARONI PUFF (page 440)

GRILLED SALAMI

BROWN-AND-SERVE ROLLS

COFFEE

ˣ   ˣ   ˣ

ANTIPASTO (page 24)

GREEN NOODLES WITH ITALIAN MEAT SAUCE (page 444)

ITALIAN CHEESE   FRESH FRUIT BOWL

CAFFÈ ESPRESSO (page 50)

BAKED ONION SOUP (page 600)   TINY ONION BISCUITS (page 84)

STUFFED MUSHROOMS WITH BROWN SAUCE (page 628)

FRUIT SALAD   SMALL JELLY SANDWICHES

COFFEE

❆   ❆   ❆

SARDINE CANAPÉS   MIXED VEGETABLE JUICE COCKTAIL (page 24)

ROTELLE WITH FRIDAY SAUCE (page 448)

TOSSED GREEN SALAD (page 496)
FRENCH DRESSING WITH WINE VINEGAR (page 517)

COFFEE SPUMONI (page 225)   SMALL RUM CAKE

COFFEE

❆   ❆   ❆

CURRIED FRUIT ON RICE (page 450)
FINGER SANDWICHES OF WHITE BREAD
WITH CHEDDAR CHEESE, JELLY, PÂTÉ, WATER CRESS

COFFEE

❆   ❆   ❆

FRESH STRAWBERRY-AND-BANANA FRUIT CUP

CRAB CAKES (page 333)

NEW PEAS

COLESLAW (page 492)

CHEESE BISCUITS (page 82)   JAM

COFFEE

JELLIED MADRILÈNE (page 608)

SMALL HOT PIROSHKI (page 11)

LOBSTER THERMIDOR (page 339)

FRESH FRUIT SALAD PLATTER (page 486)

COFFEE

❊ ❊ ❊

TOSSED GREEN SALAD (page 496)
CHOICE OF DRESSINGS

HOT HERBED LOAF OF BREAD (page 543)

LEMON-ORANGE SHERBET (page 258)   MARBLE CAKE (page 122)

TEA   OR   COFFEE

❊ ❊ ❊

SWEETBREADS AU GRATIN WITH HAM SPREAD TOAST (page 426)

QUARTERED ICEBERG LETTUCE, RUSSIAN DRESSING (page 523)

COFFEE PARFAITS (page 254)
COUNTRY CRISP SUGAR COOKIES (page 132)

COFFEE

❊ ❊ ❊

CRAB-MEAT-STUFFED MUSHROOMS (page 628),
MUSHROOM SAUCE (page 553)

NEW PEAS   BEET AND ENDIVE SALAD (page 491)

CHEESE BISCUITS (page 82)

HONEYDEW MELON

COFFEE

FORMAL DINNER SETTING

The usual number of glasses include: water, sherry (for the soup course), red wine for the entree, dessert wine. White wine of course is served for fish. It is possible also to serve champagne as the only wine throughout the dinner.

Important Guest Dinners

DRY SHERRY   PÂTÉ DE FOIE GRAS   TOAST TRIANGLES

CELERY AND CHICKEN CONSOMMÉ (page 592)   FLAVORED WITH
CELERY SALT

QUAIL, SQUAB, OR SQUAB CHICKEN ALEXANDRA (page 223)

JELLIED CRANBERRY SALAD MOLDS WITH LETTUCE HEARTS,
THINNED MAYONNAISE

WILD RICE (page 449)   BRAISED BELGIAN ENDIVE (page 627)

LEMON SOUFFLÉ WITH LEMON SAUCE (page 589)

COFFEE

COCKTAIL   OR   DRY VERMOUTH APÉRITIF   OR   CHAMPAGNE

SMOKED STURGEON CANAPÉS

CAVIAR   THIN TOAST STRIPS

RUBY CONSOMMÉ (page 593)

FILET MIGNON (page 379)
WITH FILET MIGNON SAUCE (page 549)

BROILED TOMATO HALF   PEAS PARISIENNE (page 631)

SLICED AVOCADO ON LETTUCE, LIME FRENCH DRESSING (page 517)

RED BEAUJOLAIS WINE
*(or champagne, especially if champagne was
served in place of cocktails, et cetera)*

RIPE CAMEMBERT (page 197)   THIN ROUNDS CRUSTY FRENCH BREAD

PEARS AND APPLES

COFFEE

❅   ❅   ❅

MELON BALLS IN WHITE WINE

BAKED SHAD ROE (page 321) WITH SAUCE BÉARNAISE (page 551)

SMALL MASHED-POTATO CROQUETTES (page 637)

FRESH ASPARAGUS WITH BUTTER SAUCE (page 545)   OR   STRING BEANS

CHICORY SALAD, FRENCH DRESSING (page 518) BRIE CHEESE

DINNER ROLLS

CRÊPES SUZETTE FLAMBÉ (page 100)

COFFEE

TOMATO JUICE   CRANBERRY JUICE   CELERY PINWHEELS (page 22)

SMOKED BEEF TONGUE WITH HOT RAISIN SAUCE (page 554)

CAULIFLOWER AU GRATIN (page 622)

CRUSTY DINNER ROLLS

CHOCOLATE SOUFFLÉ (page 585)

COFFEE

❊   ❊   ❊

HOT CRAB-MEAT BALLS (page 10)

CHILLED MIXED VEGETABLE JUICE COCKTAIL (page 24)

PATTY QUINLAN'S DRUNKEN CHICKEN (page 214)

GRILLED CANNED FRESH PEACH HALVES

NEW POTATOES WITH CHIVE BUTTER (page 635)

SCALLIONS AND CARROT CURLS

BROWN-AND-SERVE ROLLS

GREENGAGE PLUMS DELUXE (page 264)
WITH ANGEL CAKE (page 106)
OR CUSTARD SAUCE (page 565)

COFFEE

❊   ❊   ❊

HALF AVOCADO WITH LEMON QUARTER

FRIED OYSTERS (page 347)   SCALLOPED POTATOES (page 638)

BUTTERED BROCCOLI (page 619)
SLICED TOMATOES ON LETTUCE
FRENCH DRESSING (page 518)

HOT ROLLS   PEACH JAM

CHEESE TRAY   FRESH FRUIT

COFFEE

BROILED HERBED SALMON STEAKS (page 313)

BAKED SLICED POTATOES (page 633)

CREAMED SPINACH WITH CROUTONS (page 640)

BELGIAN ENDIVE-AND-GRAPEFRUIT SALAD (page 495)

CHEESE BISCUITS (page 82)

CHILLED BAKED CUSTARD (page 238)

COFFEE

❋   ❋   ❋

GARLIC-SHRIMP CASSEROLE (page 161)

NEW POTATOES WITH PARSLEY BUTTER (page 635)

WATER-CRESS-AND-ROMAINE SALAD (page 502)
HERB FRENCH DRESSING (page 517)

BEST CHEESECAKE (page 235)

COFFEE

❋   ❋   ❋

FROSTY TOMATO JUICE (page 23)   EMBASSY DIP (page 15)
POTATO CHIPS

FRIED CHICKEN (page 211)   CORN PUDDING (page 625)

BROCCOLI WITH BUTTER SAUCE (page 619)

PEELED, DICED TOMATOES WITH THINLY SLICED CUCUMBERS,
MINCED PARSLEY, HERB VINEGAR

CRUSTY ROLLS

WATERMELON,   OR   WHOLE STRAWBERRIES
SERVED WITH POWDERED SUGAR

COFFEE

INFORMAL DINNER SETTING

Usually the first course is in place—in this case crab-meat cocktail—when the guests are seated. If not, the napkin may be on the plate instead of at the left of the forks as in the illustration. Note the placement of the sea-food fork. This is one of three accepted ways of placing it. Salad is frequently served with the entree to make serving more simple.

DEVILED-EGG APPETIZER (page 289) WITH GARNISH OF ANCHOVIES
AND TOAST STRIPS

TURKEY OR CHICKEN-LEFTOVER PIE (page 172)

HOT HERBED FRENCH BREAD (page 543)

PEAS PARISIENNE (page 631)

GRAPEFRUIT AND ORANGE SALAD ON CHICORY NEST,
ROQUEFORT DRESSING (page 519)

OLD-FASHIONED BURNT-SUGAR CAKE (page 112)

COFFEE

SMALL BOWL OYSTER STEW (page 350)

BAKED HAM (page 388)   BUTTERED LIMA BEANS

INDIVIDUAL SPICED PEACH SALADS

SPOON BREAD (page 93)

FRESH FRUIT   EDAM CHEESE

COFFEE

❋   ❋   ❋

BAKED ONION SOUP (page 600)

MEAT LOAF, ITALIAN STYLE (page 418)   GREEN BEANS

CELERY HEART   OLIVES

CRUSTY FRENCH BREAD

ALMOND-BAKED APPLES (page 261)

COFFEE

❋   ❋   ❋

COCKTAILS   PÂTÉ WITH CHOPPED SCALLIONS   TOAST STRIPS

BAKED WHITEFISH WITH OYSTERS (page 324)

LIMA BEANS WITH TOMATOES (page 617)

BAKED SLICED POTATOES (page 633)

COCONUT ICE CREAM (page 250)   OLD FRENCH CAKE (page 114)

COFFEE

❋   ❋   ❋

STUFFED PORK CHOPS (page 398)

BUTTERED TURNIPS (page 645)

FRUIT SALAD

CRUSTY ROLLS

LEMON SOUFFLÉ (page 589)

COFFEE

ROAST LEG OF LAMB (page 393)

NEW PEAS WITH FRESH MINT (page 645)

COUNTRY-FRIED TOMATOES (page 643)

STUFFED CELERY

BROWN-AND-SERVE ROLLS

NECTARINE CREAM PIE (page 473)

COFFEE

❈   ❈   ❈

BROILED CHICKEN HALVES (page 203)

GREEN BEANS AND MUSHROOMS (page 616)

BAKED SQUASH, ENGLISH STYLE (page 642)

TOSSED SALAD WITH CROUTONS AND CUBES OF ANY FIRM, DRY CHEESE

HOT ROLLS

CHOCOLATE MOUSSE (page 340)

RAISIN ORANGE LAYER CAKE (page 123)

COFFEE

❈   ❈   ❈

MIXED VEGETABLE JUICE COCKTAIL (page 24)

BAKED HAM (page 388) WITH SPICED APPLE GARNISH

SWEET-POTATO PUFF (page 639)

CAULIFLOWER AU GRATIN (page 622)

WATER-CRESS SALAD

BREAD AND BUTTER

CUBAN RHYTHM CHIFFON PIE (page 467)

COFFEE

BRAISED PORK CHOPS

HARVARD BEETS (page 619)

BROWN RICE (page 450)

LETTUCE-TOMATO-AND-CHIVE-CHEESE SALAD

SMALL FINGER ROLLS

FRUIT COMPOTE

COFFEE

❋   ❋   ❋

CREAM-OF-CHICKEN SOUP WITH SHERRY (page 594)

COUNTRY CORN STICKS (page 91)

FRIED OYSTERS (page 347)   SCALLOPED POTATOES (page 638)

COLESLAW (page 492)   SMALL HAM-HASH PATTIES (page 431)

HONEY-CREAM PEACH PIE (page 469)

COFFEE

❋   ❋   ❋

COCKTAILS   SARDINE CANAPÉS

VEAL SCALOPPINE (page 412)

BUTTERED NOODLES (page 443)

TOMATO ASPIC RING WITH AVOCADO (page 514)
FRENCH DRESSING (page 518)

CHOCOLATE MOUSSE (page 340)

COFFEE

EMBASSY DIP (page 15)

TOASTED CRACKERS

BROILED STEAK (page 378)

CREAMED NEW POTATOES-AND-PEAS (page 636)

SPOON BREAD (page 93)

FRUIT BOWL   ROQUEFORT OR BRIE CHEESE

COFFEE

※　　※　　※

TOMATO JUICE   PAPRIKA CRACKERS

BRAISED SHORT RIBS (page 368)

WILD RICE (page 449)

ENDIVE SALAD (page 495), FRENCH DRESSING (page 518)

DINNER ROLLS

DRUNKEN FIGS (page 263)   SPICE COOKIES (page 135)

COFFEE

※　　※　　※

BROILED SHERRIED GRAPEFRUIT (page 263)

BOILED BEEF WITH VEGETABLES (page 368)

SLICED TOMATOES WITH MINCED PARSLEY,
CHIVE SOUR-CREAM DRESSING (page 516)

PUMPERNICKEL (page 70)

PEACH MERINGUE TARTS (page 482)

COFFEE

FRUIT JUICE   OR   COCKTAILS   PASADENA CANAPÉS (page 11)

BEEF STROGANOFF (page 374)

POPPY-SEED NOODLES (page 443)

GREEN SALAD (page 496)

PEARS COINTREAU (page 268)

COFFEE

❈   ❈   ❈

SHRIMP COCKTAIL (page 29)

FRENCH RAGOUT OF LAMB (page 394), WATER-CRESS GARNISH

NEW PEAS   OR   ASPARAGUS (page 614)

BROWN-AND-SERVE ROLLS

BRANDIED EDAM CHEESE (page 189)   CRACKERS

COFFEE

❈   ❈   ❈

TOMATO ASPIC-VEGETABLE SALAD APPETIZER (page 514)

FRENCH VEAL STEW (page 405)

HOT HERBED FRENCH BREAD (page 543)

CUSTARD AND FRUIT DESSERT (page 239)

COFFEE

❈   ❈   ❈

GAZPACHO (page 607)   CHUNKY FRENCH BREAD

ROAST LEG OF LAMB, GRAVY (page 393)   NEW POTATOES (page 635)

ASPARAGUS WITH CHOPPED MUSHROOMS BUTTER SAUCE (page 614)

STRAWBERRIES WITH POWDERED SUGAR AND WHITE WINE, FOR DUNKING
SPICE COOKIES (page 135)

COFFEE

HALF AVOCADO PEAR WITH LEMON JUICE

RIB STEAKS, FRENCH STYLE (page 381)

SLICED GRILLED TOMATO WITH CRUMBLED ROQUEFORT CHEESE

BUTTERED SNAP BEANS

DATE SQUARES HOLT-WILSON (page 133)
WITH COFFEE ICE CREAM (page 250)

COFFEE

✣　✣　✣

CRAB-MEAT COCKTAIL (page 28)

BROILED HAM WITH PINEAPPLE SAUCE (page 390)

CANDIED SWEET POTATOES (page 639)

BUTTERED ASPARAGUS (page 614)

ROMAINE-AND-GRAPEFRUIT SALAD WITH FRENCH DRESSING (page 518)

BREAD AND BUTTER

COFFEE

✣　✣　✣

BROILED HALF TURKEY (page 224)

HERBED LIMA BEANS (page 618)

CARROTS WITH ORANGE (page 622)

GREEN PEPPER AND ONION SALAD

FRENCH BREAD

LEMON MERINGUE TARTS (page 480)

COFFEE

SMALL SALAD APPETIZER

BAKED WHITEFISH WITH OYSTERS (page 324)

NEW PEAS IN BUTTER

BAKED SLICED POTATOES (page 633)

SMALL CABBAGE SALAD WITH CAULIFLOWER (page 492)

PINEAPPLE SHELL FILLED WITH PINEAPPLE SHERBET (page 257)

COFFEE

* * *

FRUIT COCKTAIL

SMOKED BEEF TONGUE (page 426) WITH RAISIN SAUCE (page 554)

NOODLES (page 443)

CREAMED CABBAGE (page 620)

MIXED GREEN SALAD (page 496)

BLACK CHERRY TART (page 480)

COFFEE

* * *

COUNTRY PORK ROAST (page 400)

BAKED ZUCCHINI (page 642)

SLICED PICKLED BEETS (page 619)

HOT ROLLS   CHERRY JAM

SPICED PEACHES   ANGEL CAKE (page 106)

COFFEE

FROSTY TOMATO APPETIZER (page 23)

CELERY CRACKERS

BROILED LAMB CHOPS WITH PINEAPPLE RINGS (page 391)

SMALL MASHED-POTATO PUFFS (page 635)

BEET AND ENDIVE SALAD (page 491)

DINNER ROLLS

SUNDAY-NIGHT WINE JELLY (page 274)

WHIPPED CREAM   OR   CUSTARD SAUCE (page 565)

COFFEE

❋   ❋   ❋

ANTIPASTO (page 24)

CHICKEN CACCIATORA (page 207)

ROTELLE WITH FRIDAY SAUCE (page 448)

TOSSED GREEN SALAD (page 496)

SPUMONI (page 255)

CAFFÈ ESPRESSO (page 50)

❋   ❋   ❋

Foreign Menus

Indian Supper

COLD HONEYDEW MELON (page 265)   ASSORTED FRUITS

CHICKEN CURRY (page 206)   SAFFRON RICE (page 452)

CURRY CONDIMENTS

SWEETMEAT TRAY (page 139ff.)

HOT TEA

Chinese Dinner

EGG ROLLS   BROILED BUTTERFLY SHRIMP (page 354)
(bought quick-frozen)

SWEET-SOUR SAUCE (page 556)   MUSTARD SAUCE (page 551)

EGG FOOYOUNG OMELET (page 297)

FRIED RICE OR STEAMED RICE (page 449)   SOY SAUCE

PRESERVED FRUITS

QUICK COCONUT MACAROONS (page 137)

TEA

✾   ✾   ✾

(For two additional Chinese dinners, substitute CANTONESE SWEET-SOUR PORK
(page 402) OR CHINESE BAKED SPARERIBS (page 403) FOR EGG FOOYOUNG.)

Italian Luncheon or Supper

ANCHOVIES AND OLIVES

OR BOUGHT ANTIPASTO ASSORTMENT

SPAGHETTI (page 446)   OR   RAVIOLI (page 192)

CHICKEN CACCIATORA (page 207)

CELERY-ROOT SALAD WITH WINE VINEGAR DRESSING

FRESH PEAR   OR   APPLE

MANTECA CHEESE WITH BLACK PEPPER (page 199)

CAFFÈ ESPRESSO (page 50)

MANICOTTI (page 194)

TOSSED GREEN SALAD (page 496)
WITH TARRAGON FRENCH DRESSING (page 517)

ITALIAN BREAD STICKS

SPUMONI (page 255)   COOKIES   OR   CAKE

CAFFÈ ESPRESSO (page 50)

❊   ❊   ❊

Italian Dinners

DRY SHERRY   OR   COCKTAILS   ANTIPASTO (page 24)

EASY-BAKED LASAGNE WITH TOMATO SAUCE (page 445)

CHICKEN SAUTÉE ITALIANO (page 209)

BROCCOLI MORNAY (page 156)

DARK ITALIAN BREAD

BISQUE TORTONI

FRESH FRUITS   NUTS   COINTREAU

COFFEE

❊   ❊   ❊

ROTELLE   OR   MACARONI WITH FRIDAY SAUCE (page 448)

VEAL BIRDS (page 411)

BRAISED ENDIVE   OR   CELERY (page 627)

FENNEL AND BLACK OLIVES

ITALIAN BREAD

ZABAGLIONE (page 242)

FRUIT, NUTS

CAFFÈ ESPRESSO (page 50)

CHILLED DRY WHITE WINE   ANTIPASTO (page 24)

HERB-FRIED CHICKEN (page 211)

BAKED OR FRIED EGGPLANT (page 626)

ITALIAN BREAD

MIXED GREEN SALAD (page 496) WITH HERB DRESSING (page 517)

FRESH FIGS, PEARS   CAMEMBERT (page 197)

COFFEE

❅   ❅   ❅

Japanese Luncheon or Supper

CLEAR CLAM BROTH

(WITH VERY THIN SLICED GREEN-PEPPER BITS)

BEEF SUKIYAKI (page 572)

STEAMED OR BOILED RICE (page 449)   SCALLIONS   RADISHES

PRESERVED KUMQUATS

ALMOND WAFERS

JAPANESE GREEN TEA

❅   ❅   ❅

Swedish Dinner

HERRING IN SOUR CREAM   CHEESE   CELERY   RADISHES

SMOKED SALMON WITH MUSTARD SAUCE (page 551)

THE KING OF SWEDEN'S SOUP (page 605)

SWEDISH RY-CRISP

BOILED BEEF WITH VEGETABLES (page 368)

PLÄTTAR WITH LINGONBERRIES (page 98)

COFFEE

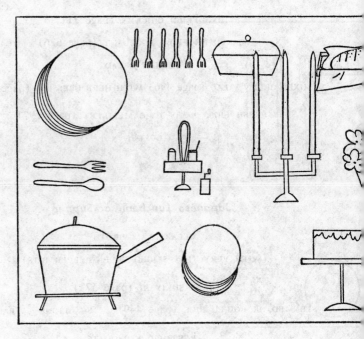

DRINKS TRAY   CHEESE GARLIC DIP (page 14)

POTATO CHIPS AND CRACKERS

BAKED HAM (page 388)   HOT SAFFRON RICE (page 452)

BAKED ZUCCHINI (page 642)

BREAD-AND-BUTTER SANDWICHES

AVOCADO SPRING SALAD (page 490)

CHOCOLATE GOLD CAKE (page 108)   ICE CREAM (page 247ff.)

COFFEE

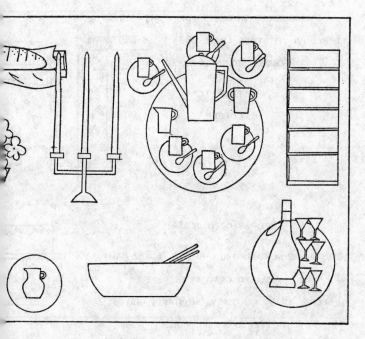

COLD ROAST CHICKEN   HAM   BOLOGNA   SALAMI

WATER CRESS

CHEESE TRAY: CHEDDAR, CREAM CHEESE, SMOKY WISCONSIN

ASSORTED BUTTERED BREADS: PUMPERNICKEL, CHEESE BREAD,
RYE, CRACKED WHEAT

OLIVES   SMALL PICKLES

DEVILED NUTS (page 141)   HOLIDAY FRUITCAKE (page 118)

COFFEE

COLD DRINKS   HOT ASSORTED CANAPÉS (page 5ff.)

BARBECUE BURGERS (page 34)

BAKED SLICED POTATOES (page 633)   SALAD BOWL

CRUSTY FRENCH BREAD

WATERMELON

COFFEE

❊   ❊   ❊

ANTIPASTO (page 24)

CASSEROLE MACARONI-AND-CHEESE (page 440)

SLICED COLD CUTS

RELISH TRAY: CHUTNEY, MUSTARD, OLIVES

BUTTERED SMALL ROLLS

PECAN PIE (page 474)

COFFEE

❊   ❊   ❊

COLD ROAST PORK WITH HOT BROILED SLICED PEACHES

SWEET POTATOES (page 638)

CELERY HEARTS AND RADISH ROSES

TOASTED SMALL ROLLS

LEMON-ORANGE SHERBET (page 258)

SHAGGY-TOP CAKE (page 124)

COFFEE

HOT DEVILED SHRIMP PREPARED IN CHAFING DISH (page 184)

MEAT LOAF (pages 417, 418)   BROILED HERBED TOMATO HALVES

CARROT STICKS SPRINKLED WITH SALT

BUTTERED BROWN BREAD

FRESH STRAWBERRIES   CHOCOLATE POUNDCAKE (page 120)

COFFEE

❊   ❊   ❊

SUNDAY-SUPPER SCRAMBLED EGGS WITH GREEN PEPPERS (page 184)

AVOCADO RING SALAD (page 511)

SMALL HAM SANDWICHES

SLICED FRESH PEARS IN ORANGE JUICE

COFFEE

❊   ❊   ❊

CUBAN BLACK-BEAN SOUP (page 601)

TOASTED FRENCH BREAD

DEVILED EGGS IN ASPIC (page 512)   RUSSIAN DRESSING (page 523)

COLD SLICED BOILED TONGUE (page 426)   CHEESE TRAY

SMALL LEMON MERINGUE TARTS (page 480)

COFFEE

❊   ❊   ❊

DELICIOUS CRAB PIE (page 333)

ASPARAGUS VINAIGRETTE SALAD (page 489)

OLIVES   CHERRY PINWHEELS (page 22)   CARROT STICKS

HOT ROLLS

BRANDIED PEACHES AND PEARS

MRS. MOLNAR'S MOCHA TORTE (page 112)

COFFEE

BEEF STROGANOFF IN CHAFING DISH (page 374)

FRENCH BREAD

VEGETABLE COMBINATION SALAD (page 501)

DAISYFIELDS MARBLE LOAF CAKE (page 122)

TEA   OR   COFFEE

✼   ✼   ✼

GRAPEFRUIT GELATIN RING (page 510)
WITH SHRIMP SALAD (page 505) MAYONNAISE

HOT TINY BISCUITS (page 83)   JELLY

CHOCOLATE GOLD CAKE (page 108)

COFFEE

✼   ✼   ✼

SLICED TONGUE, HAM, CHICKEN
SERVED WITH LETTUCE LEAF UNDERNEATH

CAESAR SALAD (page 493)   ORANGE MUFFINS (page 90)

SUMMER PEAR PIE (page 477)

COFFEE

✼   ✼   ✼

CHICKEN À LA KING (page 178) ON CORN BREAD

HERBED TOMATO SLICES (page 644)

RELISH TRAY: PICKLES, OLIVES, DEVILED EGGS (page 289)

STRAWBERRIES ROMANOFF (page 271)

COFFEE

DRINKS TRAY   PÂTÉ AND FRENCH BREAD

CHICKEN   OR   TURKEY SCALLOP (page 158)

TOSSED SALAD (page 496)   BUTTERED SMALL ROLLS

FIG TURNOVERS (page 483)

COFFEE

✼   ✼   ✼

CHAFING-DISH LOBSTER NEWBURG (page 338) TOAST

TOMATO ASPIC SALAD (page 514)

SLICED COLD TURKEY   TARTARE SAUCE (page 524)

BROWN-AND-SERVE ROLLS

BROWN SUGAR WALNUT PIE (page 465) SOUR CREAM

COFFEE

✼   ✼   ✼

Winter TV Party

TURKEY SALAD (page 503)   JELLIED CRANBERRY GARNISH

SMALL SMOKED-TONGUE SANDWICHES (pages 531, 532)

HOT MULLED CIDER (page 65)   SWEETMEAT TRAY (page 139ff.)

✼   ✼   ✼

Teen-Agers' Saturday Night

CASSEROLE FRANKFURTERS-AND-BEANS

RED AND WHITE CABBAGE SALAD (page 492)

LONG FRENCH BREAD, SLICED AND BUTTERED
SPREAD WITH DEVILED HAM, MAYONNAISE AND LETTUCE

DILL PICKLES   HOT COCOA (page 47)   OR   HOME-MADE SODAS

Buffet Supper
(important)

ASSORTED HORS D'OEUVRES (page 24ff.)

SALMON MOLD (page 314)   MAYONNAISE WITH DILL
CUCUMBERS

SMOKED TURKEY

TINY BAKING-POWDER BISCUITS (page 83)

TOMATO ASPIC RING (page 514) WITH WATER CRESS

MUTTI'S CHOCOLATE MOUSSE (page 240)

COFFEE

✳   ✳   ✳

Buffet Supper
(easy)

CARROT STICKS   RAW CAULIFLOWER

CHEESE-GARLIC DIP (page 14)

BAKED LIMAS (page 617)   BAKED HAM (page 388)

SPICED PEACHES   PEARL ONIONS

PEELED SLICED TOMATOES WITH MINCED CHIVES
(BOTH YELLOW AND RED TOMATOES)

CHARLOTTE RUSSE (page 238)

COFFEE

Tree-Trimming Supper

TOMATO JUICE REFRESHER (page 23)

SARDINE-CHEESE SPREAD (page 16)

ASSORTED CRACKERS

GARLIC-SHRIMP CASSEROLE (page 161)   COLESLAW (page 492)

HOT MUFFINS (page 89)   COCONUT CHOCOLATE CAKE (page 110)

COFFEE

❊   ❊   ❊

Christmas-Week Supper

OYSTER STEW (page 350)

CRISP CELERY CRACKERS

GRAPEFRUIT AND WATER-CRESS SALAD, FRENCH DRESSING (page 518)

HOT SCONES   CHERRY JAM

SWEETMEAT TRAY (page 139ff.)

COFFEE

❊   ❊   ❊

Christmas Eve Supper

LOBSTER STEW (page 340)

THIN FINGER SANDWICHES OF HAM AND MINCED WATER CRESS

DEEP DISH PEACH PIE (page 463)   HARD SAUCE (page 556)

COFFEE

Christmas Open-House

RUBY CONSOMMÉ (page 593)
(GARNISHED WITH PAPRIKA WHIPPED CREAM)

GRAPEFRUIT GELATIN RING (page 510)
WITH CHICKEN-TONGUE-AND-WATER-CRESS SALAD
FRENCH DRESSING (page 518)
ROQUEFORT CHEESE DRESSING (page 519)

TOASTED FRENCH BREAD

MINT SHERBET (page 258) HOLIDAY FRUITCAKE (page 118)
COFFEE

⌘ ⌘ ⌘

Christmas Eve Buffet

BUFFET-PARTY SEA-FOOD CASSEROLE (page 176)

HONEY-GLAZED HAM (page 388)

TOMATO ASPIC RING SALAD (page 514)

SMALL BUTTERED ROLLS LINZERTORTE (page 283)
COFFEE

⌘ ⌘ ⌘

Christmas Dinner

TOMATO-AND-CUCUMBER APPETIZER SALAD

BAKED HAM (page 388)

STUFFED ONIONS WITH LIMA BEANS (page 629)
HOT ROLLS CRANBERRY JELLY

HOLIDAY FRUITCAKE (page 118) ICE CREAM CHRISTMAS MOLD

COFFEE

Christmas Day Late Supper

LEFTOVER COLD HAM AND TURKEY PLATTER

ASSORTED ROLLS

ROMAINE-AND-LETTUCE SALAD, HERB FRENCH DRESSING (page 517)

DEVILED EGGS (page 289)

WINTER COMPOTE (page 271)

ALMONDS   RAISINS   PECANS   WALNUTS

COFFEE

❈   ❈   ❈

New Year's or Other Holiday Dinner

BAKED OYSTERS IN SHELL (page 345)

ROAST TURKEY (page 226), CHICKEN (page 216) OR DUCK (page 218)
WITH STUFFING AND GRAVY

BAKED HALF ORANGES AS GARNISH

ASSORTED SMALL HOT BREADS

PURÉE OF CHESTNUTS (page 624)

SLICED AVOCADO, OLIVE, AND ONION SALAD
FRENCH DRESSING (page 518)

PLUM PUDDING FLAMBÉ WITH RUM   OR   BRANDY

COFFEE

New Year's or Holiday Dinner

DEVILED ALMONDS (page 26) CRANBERRY JUICE COCKTAIL CELERY HEARTS

CHAMPAGNE-BASTED TURKEY (page 229)

CORN-BREAD STUFFING (page 232)

BRUSSELS SPROUTS (page 620) BAKED ACORN SQUASH (page 641)

HOT BISCUITS OR ROLLS

PICKLE RELISH WATERMELON PICKLE BLACK CURRANT JELLY

GEORGIA PECAN PIE (page 474)

COFFEE

⁂

Thanksgiving Dinner

CELERY HEARTS OLIVES RADISHES SMALL CHEESE CANAPÉS

ROAST TURKEY WITH FAVORITE STUFFING (page 226)

SWEETBREAD AND OYSTER PIE (page 170)

HASHED-BROWNED POTATOES (page 634)

BROCCOLI, HOLLANDAISE (page 619)

HOT ROLLS CRANBERRY JELLY

TIPSY PEACHES (page 267) PUMPKIN PIE (page 476) OR

ICE CREAM

COFFEE

Thanksgiving Supper

SLICED ROAST TURKEY GARNISHED
WITH CRANBERRY JELLY CIRCLES (page 226)

TOSSED GREEN SALAD (page 496)

TOASTED ROLLS

ICE CREAM   OR   SWEETMEAT TRAY

COFFEE

✶   ✶   ✶

Easter Dinner

DEVILED EGGS APPETIZER (page 289)

ROAST LEG OF LAMB (page 393)   NEW PEAS

ASPARAGUS WITH BUTTER SAUCE (page 614)

HOT ANCHOVY-BUTTERED LOAF OF BREAD (page 540)

LEMON ICE CREAM EASTER MOLD   HONEY ORANGE CUPCAKES (page 113)

COFFEE

✶   ✶   ✶

Fourth-of-July Luncheon on Porch

CHILLED TOMATO BOUILLON (page 606)

SMALL WATER-CRESS SANDWICHES (page 536)

CHAFING-DISH CHICKEN À LA KING (page 178)   TOAST

WATERMELON

LEMONADE   COFFEE

Festive Birthday Luncheon for Grownups

SMOKED SALMON
WITH SOUR-CREAM CUCUMBERS

BROILED STEAK

SAUTÉED MUSHROOM CAPS (page 628)

PEAS PARISIENNE (page 631)

GREEN SALAD WITH ANCHOVIES (page 496)
AND HARD-COOKED EGG

MINT SHERBET RING WITH FRESH STRAWBERRIES (page 258)

CAKE WITH CANDLES

COFFEE

❊   ❊   ❊

Birthday Party for Youngsters
(Takes the place of their supper at home)

CHICKEN SCALLOP IN INDIVIDUAL CASSEROLES (page 158)

CARROT STICKS

SMALL FANCY SANDWICHES, HAM, AND CREAM CHEESE

ICE CREAM   TINY CUPCAKES (page 115)
GINGERBREAD MEN (page 134)   OR   CAKE WITH CANDLES AND
ICE-CREAM FANCY MOLDS

PINK LEMONADE WITH STRIPED SIPPER STRAWS

St. Patrick's Day Dinner

WATER-CRESS BISQUE (page 609)   PAPRIKA CRACKERS

NORMA'S BAKED CORNED BEEF (page 430)

O'BRIEN POTATOES (CUBED AND FRIED WITH ONION AND PIMIENTO)

SALAD OF GREEN PEPPER, ENDIVE, FRENCH DRESSING (page 518)

DEEP-DISH PEACH PIE (page 463)

IRISH COFFEE (page 53)

❋ ❋ ❋

Picnics

Old-Fashioned Basket Picnic

OLD-FASHIONED POTATO SALAD (page 498)   HAM SANDWICHES

COLD FRIED CHICKEN (page 211)

PICKLES, OLIVES, CELERY HEARTS

SMALL LOAF CAKE (page 120ff.)   FRESH PEACHES AND CHERRIES

VACUUM BOTTLE HOT OR COLD DRINKS

❋ ❋ ❋

VACUUM JAR COLD DRINKS

OLIVES   MIDGET PICKLES   COCKTAIL SNACK CRACKERS

BAKED STUFFED CHICKEN BREAST (page 202)

SMOKED BEEF TONGUE SANDWICHES (page 531)

VERY SMALL STUFFED-TOMATO SALADS (page 500)   STUFFED CELERY

ASSORTED FRUIT TARTS (page 479ff.)

HOT COFFEE

GIANT CHEESEBURGERS   GRILL-TOASTED BUNS

BOSTON BAKED BEANS

TOMATO AND ONION SLICES   MUSTARD PICKLES

SMALL FROSTED CUPCAKES (page 116)

PEPPERMINT CANDY ICE CREAM (page 250)

HOT COFFEE

❊   ❊   ❊

VACUUM JUG SAN YSIDRO CHOWDER (page 603)

BUTTERED ROLLS   OR   SANDWICHES

SMALL STUFFED ROMAINE SALADS (page 495)

APPLE MERINGUE TARTS (page 479)   OR   APPLE PIE (page 462)

CHEESE WEDGES

COFFEE

❊   ❊   ❊

HAMBURGERS ON THE GRILL

ROAST CORN IN HUSKS (page 43)

CUPS OF JELLIED FRUIT SALAD (page 485ff.)

SLICED BLACK WALNUT BUTTERED BREAD (page 86)

WATERMELON

COFFEE   LEMONADE

❊   ❊   ❊

BUTTERED BUNS   SLICED HAM, CHEESE, BOLOGNA, SALAMI

HOT CASSEROLE FRANKFURTERS-AND-BEANS

OLD-FASHIONED POTATO SALAD (page 498)

TOMATO WEDGES

HOT COFFEE   COLD FRUIT DRINKS

VACUUM BOTTLE COLD FRUIT JUICES

BROILED STEAKS (page 378)

(T-bone, cubed, or hamburger)

SCALLIONS   STUFFED ENDIVE (page 495) OR

CELERY WITH ROQUEFORT CHEESE

CASSEROLE OF SCALLOPED POTATOES (page 638)

ASH-ROASTED POTATOES (page 43)

CHOCOLATE ICE CREAM (page 250)

COCONUT MACAROONS (page 131)

HOT COFFEE

✳   ✳   ✳

BLEU CHEESE SANDWICHES (page 13)

WATER-CRESS SANDWICHES (page 536)

ASSORTED COOKIES   THIN NUT WAFERS

ANGEL CAKE (page 106)

MOLDED ICE-CREAM FLOWERS

ROASTED PECANS, WALNUTS, AND ALMONDS

HOT TEA   SHERRY   COFFEE

✳   ✳   ✳

THIN BREAD AND BUTTER

THIN CUCUMBER SANDWICHES, WHITE BREAD

THIN ROQUEFORT CHEESE SANDWICHES, BROWN BREAD

PETITS FOURS (page 116)   CHOCOLATE POUNDCAKE (page 120) OR

FRUITCAKE (page 118)

TEA   SUGAR   CREAM   MILK   LEMON SLICES

BUTTERED BLACK WALNUT BREAD (page 86)

ASSORTED SMALL SANDWICHES

CINNAMON TOAST

TEA   SUGAR   CREAM   MILK   LEMON SLICES

COFFEE

❋   ❋   ❋

WAFFLES WITH MAPLE SYRUP (page 101)

SWEETMEAT TRAY (page 139ff.)

TEA   COFFEE

❋   ❋   ❋

ORANGE-BREAD-AND-CREAM-CHEESE SANDWICHES

THIN BUTTERED ROUNDS FRENCH BREAD

THIN CUCUMBER-AND-MAYONNAISE SANDWICHES (page 520)

MIXED COOKIES (page 130ff.)

TEA   CREAM   MILK   LEMON SLICES

❋   ❋   ❋

TOASTED ENGLISH MUFFINS (pages 77–78)   OR   SCONES (page 92)

MARMALADE

SMALL HAM SANDWICHES

SMALL PUMPERNICKEL-AND-ROQUEFORT-CHEESE SANDWICHES

CHOCOLATE POUNDCAKE (page 120)

TEA   CREAM   SUGAR   LEMON SLICES

ASSORTED FANCY TEA SANDWICHES (pages 532–37)

JELLY TEA ROUNDS (page 534)

HOT PIROSHKI (page 11)

DEVIL'S FOOD CAKE (page 107)   BRICK ICE CREAM

CANDIED NUTS (page 142)   MINTS

TEA   CREAM   SUGAR   MILK

ORANGE AND LEMON SLICES

✳   ✳   ✳

THIN BUTTERED TOAST

HAM-AND-CHEESE CANAPÉS

TINY CHICKEN-SALAD ROLLS (page 502)

DARK CHIFFON CAKE (page 110)   CHOCOLATE MOUSSE (page 252)

ASSORTED SWEETMEAT TRAY (page 139ff.)

CANDIED ORANGE PEEL (page 140), MINTS, DIVINITY (page 146)

TEA   MILK   LEMON SLICES   COFFEE   CREAM   SUGAR

✳   ✳   ✳

Important Tea Reception

ASSORTED SMALL SANDWICHES: CUCUMBER, WALNUTS-WITH-MAYONNAISE,

CREAM-CHEESE-WITH-ANCHOVY, SLICED CHICKEN

HOT CHEESE CANAPÉS (page 6ff.)

SMALL COOKIES   PETITS FOURS (page 116)

LORD BALTIMORE CAKE (page 109)   ICE-CREAM MOLDS

TEA   COFFEE

Wedding Menus

Bridesmaids' Luncheon

CELERY CHICKEN CONSOMMÉ (page 592)
GARNISHED WITH CURRY-FLAVORED WHIPPED CREAM

AVOCADO FILLED WITH CRAB-MEAT SALAD (page 506)

SMALL CHEESE BISCUITS (page 83)

FRESH SLICED PEACHES WITH CURAÇAO

ANGEL CAKE (page 106)

TEA   COFFEE

✻   ✻   ✻

Bridesmaids' Tea

SMALL CHICKEN SANDWICHES

SMALL WATER-CRESS SANDWICHES (page 536)

PETITS FOURS (page 116)   CHOCOLATE POUNDCAKE (page 120)

TEA   SUGAR   CREAM   LEMON SLICES   COFFEE

✻   ✻   ✻

Wedding Breakfast or Luncheon

LUNCHEON CONSOMMÉ (page 593)

LOBSTER MOUSSE (page 507)   SQUAB (page 223)

ENDIVE-AND-ARTICHOKE-HEART SALAD (page 489)

ASSORTED SMALL SANDWICHES

BRIDE'S CAKE (page 108)   WEDDING FRUITCAKE (page 119)

CHAMPAGNE   OR   WEDDING CUP (page 63)   COFFEE

CONSOMMÉ WITH
THIN CUCUMBER SANDWICHES

CREAMED MUSHROOMS ON TOAST (page 628)

TINY CHEESE EGG PUFFS (page 5)

CHICKEN LIVER PÂTÉ IN ASPIC (page 14)

BRIDE'S CAKE (page 108)   PETITS FOURS (page 116)

WEDDING FRUITCAKE (page 119)

WEDDING CUP (page 63)

COFFEE

✳ ✳ ✳

Simple Reception Repast

BRIDE'S CAKE (page 108)   WEDDING FRUITCAKE (page 119)

ICE CREAM BOMBE   WEDDING CUP (page 63)

COFFEE

✳ ✳ ✳

Groom's Dinner

COCKTAILS   ANCHOVY CANAPÉS   SARDINE-AND-CHEESE SPREAD (page 16)
TOAST AND CRACKERS

BROILED STEAK (page 378)   BAKED POTATOES (page 633)

TOSSED GREEN SALAD (pages 496, 497)

HOT HERBED FRENCH BREAD (page 543)

DEEP-DISH APPLE PIE (page 463)

COFFEE

Dinner for Family and Clergyman

(After bride and groom have left and there has been no reception.)

MIXED VEGETABLE JUICE COCKTAIL (page 24)
ASSORTED CANAPÉS (page 5ff.)

FRIED OYSTERS (page 347)   HOT CORN PUDDING (page 625)

TOSSED GREEN SALAD (pages 496, 497)

CHEESE BISCUITS (page 82)

PLUM TURNOVERS (page 483)
OR ASSORTED ICE CREAMS OR MOLDS

COFFEE

✻   ✻   ✻

Warm Weather Menus

Luncheons, Suppers, or Dinners

GRAPEFRUIT GELATIN RING (page 510)
FILLED WITH SHRIMP SALAD (page 505)

SMALL CREAM-CHEESE SANDWICHES

HONEYDEW MELON

ICED TEA   ICED COFFEE

✻   ✻   ✻

DAISYFIELDS WELSH RABBIT (page 184)

TOAST MADE AT TABLE

TOSSED GREEN SALAD (page 496)

SHERBET FROM FREEZER (page 257)   COOKIES (page 130ff.)

HOT COFFEE   OR   ICED TEA

HOT TOMATO BOUILLON (page 606)   CHEESE CRACKERS

AVOCADO MOUSSE SALAD (page 509)

SLICED, BUTTERED NUT BREAD

ICED TEA   ICED COFFEE

✼   ✼   ✼

GAZPACHO (page 607)   ITALIAN BREAD STICKS

BEEF-TONGUE MOUSSE (page 511)   SALAD GREENS
MUSTARD MAYONNAISE (page 520)

TOAST MADE AT TABLE

HOT COFFEE   ICED TEA

✼   ✼   ✼

CREAM-OF-ASPARAGUS SOUP (page 594)
PAPRIKA CRACKERS

CRANBERRY RELISH MOLD SALAD (page 510)

SMALL TONGUE SANDWICHES

HOT COFFEE

✼   ✼   ✼

QUICK CELERY SOUP (page 596)

ASSORTED WHOLE-WHEAT CRACKERS

DEVILED EGGS IN ASPIC (page 512)   SLICED TOMATOES AND LETTUCE

MINT SHERBET (page 258) AND COOKIES (page 130ff.)

COFFEE

✼   ✼   ✼

HAM MOUSSE RING (page 512)
FILLED WITH OLD-FASHIONED POTATO SALAD (page 498)   GREENS

SMALL ROLLS FILLED WITH BLEU CHEESE

STRAWBERRIES AND CREAM

COFFEE

713

TOASTED CHEESE SANDWICHES MADE AT TABLE

TOMATO ASPIC RING FILLED (page 514)
WITH VEGETABLE SALAD (page 489ff.)

FRESH FRUIT BOWL

COFFEE

❄   ❄   ❄

ASSORTED COLD CUTS   VEGETABLE SALAD (page 489ff.)

CHEESE TRAY   CONDIMENTS

WHOLE-WHEAT BREAD   RYE BREAD

WATERMELON

COFFEE

❄   ❄   ❄

HOT CREAMED-FISH SANDWICH (page 530)

TOSSED GREEN SALAD (pages 496, 497)

OPEN-FACE FRUIT PIE (page 473)

COFFEE

❄   ❄   ❄

CHAFING-DISH MEAT BALLS (page 177)

ICE-CREAM SANDWICHES

ICED TEA

❄   ❄   ❄

BACON-WRAPPED FRANKS WITH BEANS, COOKED AT TABLE (page 571)

ROLLS TOASTED AT TABLE

TOMATO ASPIC RING WITH ROMAINE (page 514)

FRESH FRUITS

ICED TEA AND COFFEE

SLICED COLD MEAT LOAF (page 417ff.)   CONDIMENTS

HOT ASPARAGUS (page 614)   OR   STRING BEANS

SMALL WALDORF SALADS (page 487)

BREAD AND BUTTER

BEST CHEESECAKE (page 235)

ICED COFFEE

✖   ✖   ✖

CHICKEN À LA KING ON HOLLAND RUSK,
MADE AT TABLE (page 178)

PICKLED BEETS WITH MINCED PARSLEY AND RED ONION RINGS

PARFAIT OF COFFEE ICE CREAM (page 250)
AND MINT SHERBET (page 258)

COOKIES (page 130ff.)   HOT AND ICED COFFEE

✖   ✖   ✖

BUTTERFLY SHRIMP SAUTÉED AT TABLE (page 184)
CHINESE MUSTARD SAUCE (page 551)
SWEET-AND-SOUR SAUCE (page 556)

THINLY SLICED CUCUMBERS AND DILL FRENCH DRESSING (page 518)

BREAD WITH DAISYFIELDS' HERB SPREAD (page 539)

PINEAPPLE SHERBET (page 257)   ALMOND MACAROONS

ICED TEA

✖   ✖   ✖

HERBED SALMON STEAKS (page 313)

NEW POTATOES WITH PARSLEY BUTTER (page 635)

WATER CRESS AND SLICED RED OR YELLOW PLUM TOMATOES WITH
TARRAGON VINEGAR

CHEESE BREAD

BLUEBERRIES AND CREAM

ICED TEA

PART II
A Word to the Successful Cook

Quick and Easy

In many of the preceding chapters, I have added time-saving suggestions with many of the recipes. Occasionally I inserted a special, or easy, or new way of preparing a dish. Sometimes I've included a trick or simplified step which I learned from friends or remember from my childhood home, from my European school, and from the many homes, clubs, and hotels I have visited here and abroad.

Some suggestions are familiar or prosaic, but if you are a new homemaker, you may not have heard them. And they will add just a little more ease, a little more pleasure to your kitchen activities. For instance, today's aluminum foil—something unheard of in old-time kitchens—will ease the cleanup period if you remember to line the broiling pan with this modern invention. Discard the used foil. Then wash, rinse, and dry the broiler pan. How much easier without the scrubbing and scouring usually necessary.

Another thing I have learned is to wash up utensils—the egg beater, measuring cups, bowls, and cooking spoons—as I cook, instead of piling them in the sink to be done after dinner with the dishes. This keeps the kitchen orderly and clean, and actually saves time. And if your guests are like mine—trooping into the kitchen to help or to ask for ice—you'll find the wash-as-you-go method will bring flattering compliments on your housekeeping.

Here are some other things I've learned:

Keep a mixture of flour, salt, and pepper handy in a large shaker, for flouring meats, poultry, and fish.

Make crumbs easily by placing cookies and crackers in a paper bag and crushing with rolling pin, or rolling them between two thicknesses of waxed paper.

For summer drinks, you may want to make frosty-rim glasses. Dip the glasses to about ¼ inch in lemon juice, then in fine granulated sugar or confectioners' sugar. Chill in refrigerator about 1 hour. Fill glasses with iced beverages, being careful to pour into middle of glass without touching rims. (I use an antique Dutch brass funnel.) Good idea, too, for fruit cups and sherbet glasses.

After using your deep-fat fryer for fish or chicken, cook French fries in the same fat at 350° F. for 1½ minutes. Drain on thick paper towels. Serve hot, or store for future use and reheat in very hot oven to serve.

Use your fryer basket to wash and drain salad greens or cooked foods and to blanch vegetables for freezing.

You need an egg slicer in your kitchen. This small, seemingly unimportant device cuts uniform slices of a hard-cooked egg for casseroles and garnishes with one stroke. Then turn the sliced egg the other way on the slicer, bring slicer knife down, and you have chopped egg.

Another small kitchen device which saves time and aids in the appearance of a dish is a vegetable parer. Use it to scrape carrots for carrot curls, to pare potatoes and other vegetables.

For table cooking, which is more popular every year, there is an electric pancake griddle which has ring outlines on the griddle surface. Pour the batter into the rings, bake, and pancakes come off perfectly round, smooth, and professional-looking.

Have several sizes of muffin pans. I use small ones not only for small muffins but to make individual gelatin molds of fruits or vegetables. The muffin pan goes easily onto a refrigerator shelf. When gelatin is firm, turn the pan upside down on a large platter or tray and unmold all at once by placing a Turkish towel wrung out in hot water on the back of the pan. Baked stuffed peppers or onions hold their shape better if cooked in greased muffin pans. Bake according to recipe. Do the same with baked apples if they are juicy, tender McIntoshes and you want them to hold their shape.

There are many ways to vary biscuit dough. I give several in the biscuit recipes and the appetizer chapter. But a friend passed this idea along to me: add a small pinch of crumbled dried sage to baking-powder biscuit dough. Roll dough as usual; cut with the smallest possible cutter. Bake and serve hot with soup, salad, or as appetizer tidbit. Do the same with other dried herbs, especially basil.

Curry dishes I've eaten in many parts of the world contain either apples or plums. In Hawaii some cooks add thickly sliced banana to the curry. Try that with curry recipes you find in the chapter on chicken and in other chapters.

Renew your herb and spice assortment frequently. For effective seasoning, herbs and spices must be fresh. Buy small amounts at a time from reliable herb growers, use up in daily cookery, or discard after a few months and replace with fresh supply.

Try serving the breakfast or brunch fruit juice in a handsome glass or crystal pitcher, frosty with ice cubes and inviting with sprays of fresh mint.

Almost any fruit may be broiled and served as garnish with meat or poultry. Familiar favorite is halved peaches, but try canned whole apricots, halved blue plums, seedless oxheart cherries.

Ready-to-bake breads and rolls are a boon to the hostess who likes a hot bread with luncheon or any other meal. Watch the grocer's counters and try out new arrivals of the varieties which are refrigerated too. These can be delicious, are certainly time-savers, and can be kept on hand in refrigerator or kitchen to dress up an emergency salad-and-cold-cuts supper. Follow directions on the wrapper for heating. I brush ready-to-bake rolls with thinned marmalade and bake according to directions, to serve sweetened, for tea. To flavor ready-to-bake rolls for a salad supper, I brush an herbed butter over the rolls before they go into the oven. Be sure to read my other suggestions for spreads and herbed loaves in the sandwich chapter. Nothing adds more pleasure and good flavor to a luncheon or supper than one of the breads.

Every good kitchen needs and uses a pair of kitchen scales. Weigh the roast before it goes into the oven; consult the roasting chart and roast accordingly.

A meat thermometer takes the guessing out of meat cookery; insert it away from the bone, first making an incision with a meat skewer or ice pick. Good thermometers for meat cookery, syrups, jelly, candy making, and deep-fat frying are essential to accurate and successful cooking for the beginner. Experienced cooks use them, too, to insure even results day after day.

It's fun to pronounce foreign words correctly, the names of foreign dishes found in cookbooks and on menus. Why not a French-English dictionary on the kitchen bookshelf? And maybe others in German and Italian too. You can "travel" without leaving your stove! Dramatize your work. Tell your family what they are eating. My etiquette book has a glossary of French cookery terms, too.

There are many foods which the experienced housekeeper likes to have readily available, either to dress up a menu because of unusual quality or flavor or to supply a main dish in an emergency guest meal.

I like to shop for unusual preserved fruits, pickled peaches, fine jellied fruits, jams, and preserves and have a few jars on hand.

From foreign-grocery companies I usually buy a few items which make an amusing and delicious luncheon or supper. The list of such shops is given elsewhere in this book, and you will find throughout the cookery sections, and in the menu section, reference to Chinese, Japanese, Scandinavian, Italian, and other menus in which such foods are used.

You can buy sauces, such as Béarnaise and Hollandaise, in jars. Fine mint sauce, delicious mixed and prepared mustards from France and elsewhere are available in good grocery shops. And of course a supply of quick-frozen soups and famous frozen sauces from Maxim's and other great-name restaurants will give you a gourmet reputation if you have them on hand for dressing up a featured guest dish.

I like to use fine Spanish and Italian olive oil, and the good peanut oil which is American is also in my kitchen, and essential, it is, for Chinese cookery.

Many dessert sauces, candied fruits, crystallized fruits, and ready-mix sauces are also to be had.

The list of delicacies which are quick-frozen grows daily, so that your refrigerator storage-freezer or your deep-freezer can be of immediate and handsome assistance in meal planning if you will study your grocer's supply and keep a few of the specialties on hand.

I have added information on care of vegetables, fruits, and other foods to the recipe instructions in many cases. And, as with fine appliances and equipment, read labels, follow food packer's instructions, and when in doubt ask your grocer. The modern grocer keeps up with the continually increasing supply of quick-frozen foods and with other new items as well. He may have leaflets and recipe booklets available, too, which will add to your cookery accomplishments.

Where to Buy Foreign Foods

There was a time in the United States—and not long ago—when foreign foods were all too often considered exotic delicacies for the gourmet. Americans had a sturdy confidence in native dishes—most of them, of course, *naturalized* foods, foods which had been brought over by new settlers—and an equally firm distrust of unfamiliar flavors. Even those who had developed a taste for foreign foods found it difficult to get the necessary ingredients, except, perhaps, in little side-street stores in metropolitan centers where foreign-born people shopped for their native foods.

But in recent years there has been a startling change, particularly since World War II. Whether because of the increase in travel abroad or simply because of the increasing sophistication of American taste, foreign foods have become an important and interesting part of our menu. Undoubtedly, G.I.'s have brought home new food enthusiasms, too.

Quite naturally, too, the supply has grown with the demand. Hundreds of supermarkets all over the country feature gourmet sections filled with a variety of foreign foods. The large national food packers have enlarged their lines to include many such items, and frozen-food concerns in particular have introduced a great variety of prepared foreign foods to the American public. In many of the larger cities, department stores have set up well-stocked food departments with excellent selections of foodstuffs from all over the world, and fine-food shops specializing in unusual and hard-to-find foreign foods now thrive in good shopping areas all over the country.

But even if you live where none of these sources is convenient, you can still indulge your taste for foreign foods, for most of them are also available by mail order. The shopper's columns of all the large household and decorating magazines list sources not only for foreign foods but also for scarce and elusive American products, such as water-ground corn meal, smoked hams, and old-fashioned whole-grain hominy.

The gourmet magazines, naturally, are filled with information about foreign foods in both their editorial and advertising columns.

If you have been having difficulty finding the kinds of foreign foods that you would like to serve, here are some suggestions that may prove helpful. Most of the suppliers listed here are located in New York City—not, of course, because they are necessarily better than others which may be nearer you, but simply because I happen to know them from personal experience. I welcome your own shopping suggestions.

French. French foods are now available in delicacy shops and bakeries in almost every large American city, and their number continues to increase. Ask for snails, the special very small sweet French peas, large chestnuts called *marrons,* truffles, and other delicacies. *Charles and Co.,* 340 Madison Avenue, New York 17, and *Maison Glass,* 52 East 58th Street, New York 22, *Vendôme Table Delicacies Inc.,* 15 East 48th Street, New York 17, are three such shops. The grocery departments of *R. H. Macy and Co.,* 34th Street and Broadway, New York 1, *Bloomingdale's,* 59th Street and Lexington Avenue, New York 22, and *B. Altman,* 34th Street and Fifth Avenue, New York 1, N.Y., also carry a variety of French foods.

German. *Bremen House,* 218 East 86th Street, New York 28, offers German sausages of all types, imported cheese, and, for cool summer drinks, favorite German syrups, such as raspberry. They also have cans of the blanched asparagus which Europeans prefer to our green asparagus. Philadelphia stores and shops feature many such German specialties as well as canned and packaged Pennsylvania Dutch specialties. And of course Milwaukee and Chicago specialize in them.

Irish. Charles and Co., 340 Madison Avenue, New York 17, is the place to go or send for Irish soda bread and such delicacies as Irish oatmeal, bacon, hams, honey, marmalade, and dulse, or seaweed. But Irish Soda Bread Mix now has national distribution.

Italian. In all cities where the Italian population is sizable you will find excellent Italian markets, fruit and vegetable stands, and grocers who import native delicacies. New York has many such fine shops. One especially equipped to handle mail orders in *Manganaro's,* 488 Ninth Avenue, New York 18. They carry a variety of Italian cheeses, salamis and other sausages, as well as anchovies, olives, olive oil, and many other Italian and bottled foods. Tomato sauce and paste are in stock in large and small cans. *Trinacria Importing Co.,* 415 Third Avenue, New York 16, is another Italian grocery which also has other European foods, such as hot Spanish sausages, Indian spice mixtures and curry powders, chutneys, French *pâté de foie gras,* green olives, and Hungarian paprika.

Middle European. *Paprikas Weiss,* 1504 Second Avenue, New York 21, imports fine paprika (sweet, semi-sweet, hot) and other essentials of Hungarian cookery, such as poppy seed and prepared strudel dough rolled into thin sheets and ready to fill. Their catalogue also lists Polish, German, Swiss, and French imports. At *H. Roth and Son,* 1577 First Avenue, New York 28, foods of Hungary and Germany are well represented. Brindza, a sheep's-milk cheese, lekvar (plum butter), and buckwheat, used so much in Middle European cookery, are available there.

Near Eastern. *A. Sahadi,* 187 Atlantic Ave. Brooklyn, New York, is prepared to ship the foods of Syria, Lebanon, Persia, Greece, Turkey. Sesame seed (which is now found in many American drugstores, herb shops and some grocery shops) is sold here, as are the oil, paste, and candies made from the seed. Pickled grape leaves for stuffing, ingredients for baklava, the rich many-layered pastry of the Near East, and other specialties are also available. They ship everywhere.

Oriental. *Oriental Food Shop,* 1302 Amsterdam Avenue, New York 27, offers the ingredients necessary for Japan's sukiyaki. These include tinned bean curd, bamboo shoots, and Japanese shoyu sauce. Thin vermicelli, another sukiyaki ingredient, and other Japanese foods are also listed in that shop's catalogue. *Katagiri,* 224 East 59th Street, New York 22, is another good source for the foods from Japan. Many canned, ready-to-eat Oriental delicacies are on the shelves there, including pickled radish slices and scallions in shoyu sauce, as well as Japanese canned crab meat, lobster, and tangerines (which they call oranges). Katagiri is also a good place to buy the decorative small dishes, chopsticks, and other accessories which make a Japanese party so attractive.

Chinese foods are now available in most large grocery stores and supermarkets all over America. Several Chinese food packers have for some years distributed canned bean sprouts, Chinese noodles, soy sauce, water chestnuts, rice, mushrooms, and other specialties on a nation-wide scale. In New York and San Francisco many shops in the Chinatown districts can supply fresh and canned Chinese delicacies. The restaurants in these neighborhoods will also usually prove to be excellent sources of canned and packaged Chinese delicacies.

Scandinavian. *Scandia Delicatessen,* 224 Flatbush Avenue, Brooklyn, New York 11217, offers a catalogue, available on request, listing anchovies, smoked eel, several kinds of sardines and stockfish. Among other featured items are crisp bread, meat balls in cans, lingonberry jams, and other specialty fruits. *Old Denmark,* 135 East 57th Street, New York 10022, carries Danish hams, jams, cheese, and rugbröd (a delicious dark loaf made of whole-grain rye) as well as many other Scandinavian delicacies. (Note to New Yorkers who can pick up their orders: this shop makes famous Danish open-face sandwiches and canapés, salads, and other Danish foods to carry home.) New York's most modern Swedish Delicatessen is *Nyborg & Nelson, Incorporated* at 937 Second Avenue, New York 10017. No doubt you will find anything you need there.

A Guide to Herbs, Seeds, and Spices

Allspice   Dried ripe fruit of *pimento* tree (not *pimiento,* which is a red pepper). Also known as *Jamaica pepper.* Sold whole and ground. Flavor resembles blend of cinnamon, nutmeg, and cloves. Use in baking, and in seasoning some meat cookery.

Anise seed   Fruit of plant of parsley family. Small, oval, usually greenish-brown. Flavor suggests licorice. Used in Italian meat cookery, salads, in many oriental dishes and pastries. A Mexican favorite, too.

Basil   Leaf of herb plant of mint family. Also known as *sweet basil.* Sold fresh or dried. Flavor is slightly sweet with pungent undertone. Used in soups, salads, many vegetable and meat combinations.

Bay leaf   Aromatic leaf of evergreen sweet-bay or laurel tree. Also known as *laurel leaf.* Sold dried, whole, or broken. Used to flavor soups and many sauces, fish, poultry, meat dishes. One of the oldest and most familiar herbs.

Caraway seed   Fruit of plant of parsley family. Slightly sharp but sweet-undertone flavor. Popular in breads, such as rye; used in many German and Middle European meat and vegetable dishes. Also used in cheese, sauerkraut, mixed pickling spice. Is principal ingredient of kümmel cordial.

Cardamom (*also cardamon*) **seed**   Dried fruit of plant of ginger family. Aromatic and pungent flavor. Seeds used in coffee cups in Near East. Also used (ground) to flavor Danish pastry, coffee cake, and other pastries. Ground with other ingredients in curry powder and in various sausages.

Cassia Spice made of bark of evergreen tree of laurel family. Related to cinnamon and *used as cinnamon* in this country. Stronger flavor than cinnamon; agreeable, aromatic odor and sweet pungent taste. Sold whole in stick form and ground. A favorite for baked products, fruit, and confections.

Cassia buds Dried immature fruits of cassia tree. Flavor is like cassia or cinnamon. Used to give cinnamon flavor to pickling spice mixtures and marinades where whole spice is preferred.

Cayenne pepper Small-fruited species of capsicum. Also known as *chili pepper*. Dried fruit is dark to light red, with yellow seeds; pods vary greatly in size from less than 1 inch to 2½ inches long. Ground, the pepper is hot and pungent, the color bright red. Called for in small amounts to add hotness as well as color to sauces, Spanish-type dishes, and various meat, egg, fish, and vegetable dishes. Used as ingredient of curry powder and in seasoning some sausages. Small peppers used whole in mixed pickling spices. Gourmets use a little pinch in *all* soufflés.

Celery salt Combination of ground fruit of celery plant and table salt. Used in soups, biscuit dough, tomato juice, oyster stew, potato salad, salad dressings, and many other dishes.

Celery seed Seed of member of parsley family *not identical with the celery* we serve as vegetable. Flavor almost identical with celery, warm and slightly bitter. Used to season sauces, salads, pickles, soups, vegetables, and many dishes.

Chervil Delicate, fern-like leaves with a pleasant aromatic flavor, more subtle than tarragon. They are used in salad dressings, sauces, stuffings—especially for fish—also in soups and omelets.

Chili powder (Also called *chile powder*.) A *blend* of chilies, cumin seed, and orégano, all of which are native to Mexico. Other spices may be added to the blend. Used to season Mexican dishes such as chile con carne, also eggs, omelets, sea-food cocktail sauces, stews, soups, hamburgers. Used commercially to season frankfurters and other prepared meats.

Chives Tender young green tips of a delicate member of the onion family. Only the tops are used. Chives are used to flavor cheese spreads. They are also popular on salads, Vichyssoise, and in sauces for fish, chicken, beef.

Cinnamon See Cassia.

Cloves Dried, unopened bud of an evergreen tree. Whole clove is nail shape—word clove comes from French *clou,* meaning nail. Strong, pungent, sweet flavor. Rich brown color. Sold whole and ground. Used in meat cookery, pickling, syrups, stews, baking, confections.

Coriander seed Dried, ripe fruit of herb of the parsley family. White or yellowish brown, almost round seed with a mild, distinctive, fragrant odor. Pleasant, aromatic taste, suggesting combined lemon peel and sage. Used commercially in making frankfurters. Used whole in mixed pickling spice and ground in curry powder. Used to flavor pastry, cookies, buns, and cakes.

Cumin seed (Also known as *cummin and comino seed.*) Dried fruit of herb of parsley family. Somewhat like caraway seed in flavor. Used whole or ground commercially in preparation of meats, pickles, cheese, sausages, curry powder, chili powder, and chutney. Popular as seasonings for soups, stews, bread, rice.

Curry powder Blend of numerous spices, seeds, herbs, depending on manufacturer. Used to flavor sauce, stews, sea food, rice, eggs, vegetables, soups. Characteristic hot spicy flavor and color, varying from very hot to mild, from deep brown to mustard yellow.

Dill seed Dried fruit of dill plant, an herb of parsley family. Small tan, oval seed with a faint caraway flavor. Used in northern Europe to flavor sauces served with fish, also added to potato salad. Used whole and ground in making dill pickles and also in soups, salads, many seafood dishes. Used commercially in making liverwurst, frankfurters, sausages, and bologna.

Fennel seed Dried seed of fennel plant, also of parsley family. Seed has licorice-like flavor similar to anise. Sold whole and ground. Used in making Italian pastries, breads, and rolls. Used in pickles, and in seasoning soups, salads, sauces.

Fenugreek seed Seed of plant of pea family. Pleasantly bitter with flavor something like burnt sugar. Sold whole and ground. Used in chutney, imitation maple extract, and various spice blends.

Garlic powder Ground, dried garlic cloves. (Garlic belongs to lily family.) Powder has commercial use in making various prepared meats. Powder may be used in place of garlic clove to season meats, sauces, many other dishes.

Garlic salt Commercial mixture of table salt and garlic powder. Use like garlic powder.

Ginger Root of tropical plant, dried and sun-bleached. Aromatic, with spicy-sweet, pungent flavor. Sold whole, broken, or ground. Has many uses, including the flavoring of commercial ginger ale and ginger beer. Also used as spice in confections, pastry, cakes, cookies and as seasoner for many meats, pickling, and sauces. Also used in blends of curry powder and in oriental cookery.

Mace The skin which covers the nutmeg seed. Both mace and nutmeg are part of fruit of an evergreen. Whole mace is sold as blades of mace, usually deep orange color. When ground, mace turns to yellowish-orange. Flavor is similar to nutmeg, although softer and less pungent. Used in cakes, also as seasoning for fish, sauces, meat stuffings, vegetables, pumpkin and apple pie. Delicious in whipped cream topping and in egg and chicken dishes in cautious amounts.

Marjoram Leaf of herb of mint family. Gray-green in color. Sold fresh and dried, whole and ground. Used in vegetable, lamb, and mutton dishes, commercially in liverwurst, bologna, headcheese.

Mint Leaf of herb called mint, which includes many varieties, such as spearmint and peppermint. The strong, sweet flavor has tang and a cool aftertaste. Used fresh in summer drinks, and fresh and dried in desserts, with meat cookery, in salads, in flavoring jellies, sauces, confections.

Mixed pickling spice Usually consists of eight to ten or more whole spices in combination, balanced to create distinctive flavor. Used for pickling, but also in meats, stews, soups, and vegetable combinations.

Mustard   The seed of plant of mustard family. Two varieties are commonly used. Each is known by two names, black or brown, white or yellow. Flavor is hot, sharp, pungent. Available in seed and used whole for pickles and other products. It is used as garnish with kraut, boiled cabbage, salad dressings.

Also available in prepared mustard, a mixture of ground seed with salt, vinegar, spices, and various condiments, and as dry mustard, also known as ground mustard, and mustard flour. Used in many dishes, sauces, salad dressings.

Nutmeg   See Mace. Available ground, and whole to be grated by homemaker. Used in breads, cakes, cookies, in puddings, sauces, vegetables, in spice blends for other cookery.

Onion powder   Finely ground dried onions.

Onion salt   A commercial mixture of table salt and onion powder.

Orégano   Leaf of herb of mint family. Also known as Mexican orégano, wild sweet marjoram, and Mexican sage. (Orégano is Spanish for marjoram.) Strong, aromatic, pleasantly bitter undertone, similar to marjoram. Sold fresh, and dried, rubbed, and ground. Used in chili powder, in chile con carne, many Mexican dishes and in soups, salads, sauces, egg dishes.

Paprika   Ground, dried pod of varieties of capsicum. Paprika has mild, pleasant odor and agreeable, slightly sweet taste. The color is bright, rich red. Used as garnish for color and flavoring for salad dressing, seafood dishes, both hot and chilled, soups, eggs, vegetables. Used commercially in ketchup and chili sauce.

Pepper   Dried, ripe berry of perennial climbing vine. Berries are called peppercorns. Marketed dried whole or ground. Black pepper is ground, dried, underripe peppercorns. White pepper is ground, dried inner centers of peppercorns. Both have penetrating odor and hot, biting, pungent flavor. White pepper may be more delicate, but aromatic and pungent, less biting than black pepper. There are many varieties of pepper and they vary in color from yellowish-white through brown and black, light gray and tan, depending on country of origin as well as methods of drying, grinding, etc. Pepper is one of the two most famous seasoners in the Western world, the other, of course, being salt. Both black and white pepper are used in many foods.

Poppy seed Seed of annual plant of poppy family. Has pleasant, crunchy, nutlike flavor. Used whole as topping on rolls, bread, cakes, cookies, pastries, and as filling in Hungarian pastry, coffee cake, and various sweets. Used to flavor and garnish salads and noodles.

Poultry seasoning Blend of sage, thyme, marjoram, and savory, with rosemary and other spices sometimes added. Use to flavor stuffing as well as roast and other dishes.

Pumpkin-pie spice Blend of cinnamon, cloves, and ginger ground together to make smooth, pungent flavoring for cooked pumpkin fillings in pies and tarts.

Rosemary Leaves of evergreen herb of mint family. Also known as *Rosa Maria*. Distinctly fresh, sweet flavor. Sold fresh and dried, whole and ground. Excellent in stews, lamb cookery, many vegetables, and soups.

Saffron The dried stigma of a plant of the crocus family; delicate yellow-orange filaments picked by hand. It takes 225,000 stigmas to make a pound of saffron, hence the high price of this spice. Sometimes ground, or may be sold as stigmas. Pleasantly bitter, yet fragrant. Used for color as well as flavor in rice, soup, sauces. Used commercially in some curry powders.

Sage Dried leaf of herb of mint family. Sold as leaf or ground. Strong, fragrant, aromatic, a little bitter. Used in stuffings for roast fowl, with meat cookery, also in chowder, sauces, aspics.

Savory Leaf of herb of mint family. Also known as *summer savory*. Warm, aromatic. Sold fresh and dried. Used in meat cookery, with chicken soups, salads, sauces, scrambled eggs.

Sesame seed Seed of plant in Sesamum family. Also called *benne* or *bene seed*. Faintly nutty flavor. Used by Near Eastern bakers in breads and on top of breads and rolls. Used by Chinese cooks to flavor many dishes and in making the Oriental candy, halvah, and other confections. Sold hulled or unhulled, small, oval-shaped, shiny seed, pearly white in color. (Sesame oil, made from the seed, is used in very small amounts by Chinese cooks to flavor peanut oil in deep-fat frying.)

Tarragon Leaves and flowering top of herb plant. Flavor similar to licorice or anise. Used fresh or dried to flavor vinegar; used in small amounts to flavor pickles, prepared mustard, and sauces, aspics, chicken, egg and meat dishes.

Thyme Leaf of herb plant of mint family. Used fresh or dried for its warm, aromatic flavor as seasoning in clam chowder and juice, in tossed salads, in dressing for fruit salads, and other dishes.

Turmeric Aromatic root of plant of ginger family. Has clean, fresh odor and distinctive flavor. Not like ginger except in origin. Sold whole and ground. Used in curry powder, prepared mustard, mustard pickle, and other pickle and relish mixtures. May be used to replace saffron as coloring agent. Attractive when used lightly in creamed egg dishes.

Special note on some herbs. **Borage,** for instance, is very good with string beans, with green or cucumber salad. Has cucumber flavor. Add **burnet** to vinegar for a fine-flavored salad dressing. I use such herbs, too, in summer flower arrangements. Delicious smell!

Geranium leaf, added to apple and other delicate jelly. Try mixing some of the jelly with cake filling for a delicate white cake.

Lovage is delicious addition to tomato-juice cocktail, in cream soups; has strong celery flavor.

Nasturtium Use tender young leaves in salads. Place a few seeds in vinegar to flavor it. Remove after 24 hours and discard seeds. Add flowers to fruit punch.

Rue The fresh leaves make good addition to salad; fine in cheese mixtures for dip or sandwiches.

Rugola A green grown by Italian gardeners. Resembles dandelion leaf in general shape, but without the points and angles. Strong, pungent, delicious addition to salad bowl. Can be bought at Italian vegetable stands in spring.

Knives and Carving

Knives

The best cook I know says that she owns just six kitchen knives, without which she could not prepare meals or carve the various roasts and meats served at her table. Her six knives are:

Paring knife, with blade 3 to 3½ inches long.

Utility knife, with blade 5 to 7 inches long, like a long paring knife. Used for halving grapefruit, tomatoes, other vegetables, small melons.

French cook's knife, a heavy blade. It is used like a chopper to mince and cube. Or hold point of knife on chopping board and move handle up and down to cut celery and other foods fine.

Carver, a knife she uses for roast fowl, roasts of meat, and steaks. Blade of such a knife comes in varying widths. See carving suggestions which follow.

Slicer, with a thin blade 8 to 10 inches long. This cuts a smooth, clean slice of meat or anything else. Used for bread, too.

Serrated knife, or saw-tooth blade, for bread, cake.

Many varieties of the basic knives are available in good kitchenware and cutlery departments. When buying the first essential equipment for a new home, select knives, cookery forks, large cookery spoons, spatulas, slotted spoons, pancake turners, and all such pieces for their quality first, then for the feel in your hand. Some women can never get used to the French cook's type knife and prefer to use a small paring knife for all mincing and fine cutting. I find that two paring knives, one with very short blade, one a little longer, do all the small kitchen cutting jobs with ease. And the other knives, listed above, complete any kitchen carving and cutting I want to do as well as carving at the table.

Knives should be stored carefully to protect their blades. Keep them in a slotted box or block, sharp edge down, handles toward you for easy and safe access.

Some households include in the essential tools of the kitchen a carving set. This consists of a knife with an 8- or 9-inch semiflexible blade, a 2-pronged fork with protective guard, and the steel.

In addition, a second set for steak and poultry, consisting of a carving knife with 5½- to 6-inch stiff blade and matching fork for use with steaks, small roasts, and birds, may be needed. Some carvers ask for poultry or game shears, which, with their strong handles and short curved blades, separate joints and small bones better than a knife. There is also a carver's helper or stabilizer. This is a wide, strong fork sometimes used with large roasts or turkey to give greater control and hold the roast securely on the platter while it is being carved.

For slicing hams the perfect knife is a 9½-inch to 10-inch straight, narrow, flexible blade with rounded end. The shape of the blade permits a steady slicing motion without sawing and allows perfect control of the slicing when approaching the bone.

Care of Carving Knives: These special knives and sets will probably arrive as wedding presents. If not, select only those which are essential to your cookery and menus. Let the man of the house practice carving for the family before he must perform at a guest dinner. In practice he learns which knives are best for the various roasts. These should be set aside, kept sharpened (ground occasionally by an expert) and ready for carving only, not used daily in the kitchen. The steel of the carving set does not sharpen. It is used, preferably in the kitchen, to true up the edge of carving knives. When serving a large fish never use a steel knife and fork, as contact with steel may damage flavor and color of fish. Use silver or silver-plated fork, or fork and spoon, and if a knife is needed, use a thin-bladed silver knife to separate servings.

Where carving is done in the kitchen, a carving board is a very useful piece of equipment. In many cases this board fits into a large silver tray or platter on which roast turkey or meat is brought to the table. In any case, no carving should be done on a silver platter or fine china platter without the carving board, since knife scratches and other damage will result.

Technique of Carving

When carving is done at the table by host or hostess, place the meat or poultry platter directly in front of the carver. The carving knife, the tip of which may be on a silver or glass knife rest, should be at the carver's right, the sharp edge turned inward, the fork at the carver's left. One warmed serving plate will be near the right of the platter, the rest of the warmed plates at the left or brought in just as the carver is ready.

Sometimes, especially with a turkey, an extra, small warmed platter is placed at the left of the carver. He uses this plate on which to divide the second joint of the bird for serving. After carving, the carving knife and fork are laid on the platter.

With practice, the hostess can decide whether she wants carving done in the kitchen or at the table or at a buffet or serving table in the dining room. And the question of whether to remove the platter to the kitchen after the carving, so the roast may be kept hot, must also enter into your dinner plans. I often simplify this by using an electrically heated tray on the buffet or on a serving table.

Don't put a silver platter or fine china platter in the oven. Remove the roast from the platter, return it to its pan, wash the platter and keep it warm. When seconds are in order, the hot roast is restored to the platter and returned to the dining table.

Roast Beef: All carving of roast beef should be across the grain of the meat, in thin slices. If the roast is heavy enough (two or three rib), place it upright on the platter, which it will touch only with the tip ends of the ribs and the section of backbone. This brings the browned fat on top. Below this crisp fat is a thin strip of lean meat, which is not especially tender, and between this and the rib bones are the choice cuts of the roast.

Place the platter on the table with the heavy end of the roast to the left of the carver. If the joint has been properly prepared by the butcher, the end (back) bone will have been removed. If it has not been removed before cooking, the knife must be inserted between meat and bone, as close to the bone as possible, and the meat cleanly separated from the bone.

Insert fork or carver's helper firmly in the top of the meat, pressing it in deeply to hold the joint steady. Beginning at the heavy end, carve thin slices from one end to the other, from left to right, cutting through the outer crispy fat, the less tender upper lean layer, and through the tender meat down to the rib bone.

Carve as many slices as are needed for service before releasing the fork. It may be necessary after cutting several slices to turn the knife so the blade is horizontal and, cutting parallel with the ribs, draw the knife along the bone to separate the cut slices from it.

With a roast which is not broad enough (one or two light ribs) to stand firmly upright, place it on its side on platter, ribs toward carver, then cut horizontal slices, loosening these from the bone, where necessary, by holding knife vertically.

The rolled roast is exactly the same joint as the preceding with the bones removed and meat compactly tied or skewered into shape. Stand roll up on platter.

Rolled Roast

To carve, thrust fork firmly into side of roll, inserting it about halfway through on left-hand side, with fork guard up. Then cut thin slices right across the surface of the meat, from right to left, parallel with platter. Lift off each slice as cut. *Avoid skewers.* These cannot be taken out before serving or the roast loses shape, but as you arrive at a skewer remove it by inserting prong of fork into the ring at the end of metal skewer. Wooden skewers must be removed by hand or carefully loosened with carving knife. If the roast is tied with string instead of fastened with skewers, only one cord should be cut at a time, as it is reached.

A rolled roast may also be placed on the platter fat surface uppermost. This makes an easy job for the carver. Insert fork at the left, then carve down vertically from the top to the platter, beginning at the right side of the roast.

To carve a roast fillet or tenderloin insert fork in roast at about the center and hold firmly. Carve in even slices about ½ inch thick, beginning at heavier end, at the right of the carver.

A solid pot roast from the rump is carved in similar manner, in even slices across the grain, but much thinner than the fillet slices.

A rolled pot roast is placed flat side on platter, larger end to right of carver. Insert fork firmly into meat toward upper left, then cut thin slices, beginning at right, straight down through roast across the grain. The strings cannot be removed until the carver reaches them, one at a time, since they hold the roast in shape.

Steak: Steaks are carved with the grain instead of across it. Hold the knife at a slight angle and slice at an angle. Such slices help retain the juices and prevent meat drying out. A thick steak is cut in moderately thin slices, a smaller steak in wider pieces.

A porterhouse or T-bone steak is placed on the platter so that tenderloin is nearest carver. Insert fork in meat, run tip of knife carefully alongside each bone, both sides of center bone, severing meat completely from it. Some carvers like to remove the bone entirely and place it at one side of the platter before slicing steak. Then cut steak down crosswise into slices about ¾ inch wide, serving a portion from below and from above the bone to each person.

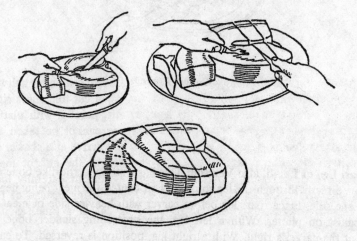

Porterhouse

Other Roasts

Crown Roasts of Lamb and Pork: These are easily carved. These roasts stand upright on platter. Cut down between each two ribs, allowing one chop, or two very small ones, as a serving.

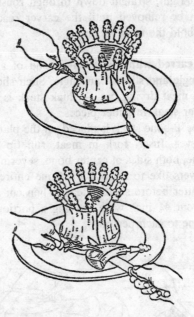

Crown Roast

Roast Leg of Lamb, also Venison: This has a straight, rod-like bone running, directly through the leg somewhat off center, the meat being heavier on one side. Place roast leg before carver with heavier side of meat uppermost on platter. With a left leg, the protruding slender bone will be at the carver's right. With a right leg, position is reversed. To carve, insert fork firmly in meat at left, then, beginning near center, cut several vertical slices from the outer (rear) surface through the heavy side of the meat right down to the bone. Turn the blade of the knife and slip under cut slices, parallel with bone, to separate cut meat from it. Lift slices out on blade of knife to serve.

Roast Stuffed Shoulder of Lamb: This is usually a rolled and tied roast and comes to the table with strings still around it to hold it in shape. This roast usually lies on its side. Insert fork to left of roast. Begin at right end and cut through from top to bottom in vertical slices about ⅓ inch thick. Cut cord when knife comes to it and remove. If shoulder of lamb is plain roasted without rolling and stuffing, it is more difficult to carve, owing to formation of bone. Fibers run in several directions.

Roast Loin of Veal and Pork: These should have rib bones severed from each other at the backbone by the meat dealer, to expedite carving; also back, or chine, bone should be removed by meat dealer. To carve, place roast on platter with rib ends up and meat side nearest carver. Insert fork at the left in heavy part of meat between ribs; begin at right and cut down between each two rib bones. Allow one rib or chop for each serving. If the kidney has been cooked with the loin, slice it and add a small portion to each serving of meat.

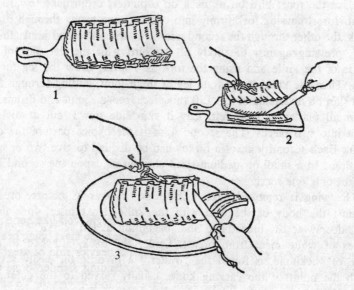

Roast Loin of Pork

743

Baked Whole Fresh and Smoked Hams: As with leg of lamb, there will be a right or a left for the carver. The bone runs right through the ham, but a little off center. The broad or heavier side gives the best cuts, so the ham should be placed on the platter fat side uppermost, broad side away from carver. With a left ham this brings the shank bone to the right. Insert fork firmly in the ham at whatever point gives the firmest and best control, usually near the point at which the carving begins.

Cut three or four thin slices parallel to the length of the ham on the side nearest you, then tip the ham up slightly on the platter so it rests on the cut surface. Hold the ham firmly with the fork. Cut a small thick slice or wedge near the shank bone and lay it aside. Then carve right down from the top to the bone and at right angle to the bone, holding the knife slantwise. Cut several slices. If necessary, run the knife along the bone parallel to it to release these for service. A little of the rich, crisp fat should be served with each slice.

When the ham has been carved right across to the thick end, it should be turned over and the other side carved in the same way. The lower slices will be smaller than the first ones.

Fowl

Place the roast bird on its back on a platter, drumsticks toward the right. Insert carving fork firmly into one leg, one prong through drumstick, the other through the second joint. Cut around second joint (thigh) and, pressing against the body of the bird with the flat part of the blade of the knife and using the fork as a lever, draw the leg toward you. Then use knife to separate leg at thigh joint, cutting through flesh and skin on underside of leg. Lift this piece, second joint and drumstick, to small platter at your left. Lay it skin side down; cut at dividing joint into two pieces. The second joint is the choice part of the dark meat. Each second joint of a turkey can be divided to give two or more portions. In a small or medium-sized chicken or capon the second joint makes only one serving.

The wing is removed next, using fork as lever as before, pressing against the body of the bird with the knife. Next insert fork firmly and deeply across breastbone and, beginning at left, carve long, even slices of white meat from breast. Under the back, attached to each side of backbone, is found the "oyster," a favorite bit easily severed with the point of the carving knife, usually served to the guest who asks for it.

If there are so many guests that most of the bird will be eaten, you will remove both legs and wings before beginning to carve the breast, then slice all meat, dark and light, from one side of the bird before carving the second side. Serve a spoonful of dressing with each portion of meat.

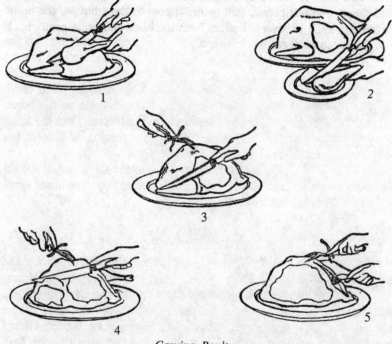

Carving Poultry

Roast Goose and Duck: Place these roast birds before the carver with wing end to left. Insert fork firmly with one prong on each side of the ridge of breastbone. Beginning at left, work from side nearest carver toward center. Hold knife with blade slightly slanted outward, cutting thin parallel slices entire length of breast until bone is reached. Slip knife under meat close to bone. Sever meat. Carve second side of bird in the same way. To separate legs from body, tip bird over slightly on platter with fork. Thigh joint lies nearer backbone than in turkey and chicken. It is more difficult to carve. Both legs and wing may be severed before serving breast meat. There is no white meat. The choice breast meat is dark. Next in preference is the leg of the flying bird or the wing of the swimmer.

Turkey or Capon for the Buffet Table: The buffet bird is pre-carved and pressed back together *before* it reaches the table. Use a sharp, thin-bladed knife. Carve from the lower breast to the upper part, in slices about ⅛ inch thick, cutting almost to the bone. From the breast, go to the leg and thigh and sever the pieces so they will be easy to serve. If the bird is to be served cold, wrap it in foil or heavy waxed paper, to hold shape, and refrigerate. Just before it goes to the table use the tip of the carving knife to sever the slices from the bone and press gently back with fingers to preserve whole shape.

Cookery Terms You Should Know

À la king   Food prepared in a rich cream sauce.

À la mode   "In the manner of." For desserts it means "with ice cream."

Amandine   With almonds.

Antipasto   Assortment of Italian appetizers, such as sardines, anchovies, peppery sausage, canned pimiento, tuna fish, etc.

Aspic   Clear, savory jelly used in moulds (molds) to garnish cold dishes; made with gelatin or from meat bones, etc.

Au beurre   French term meaning cooked in or with butter.

Au gratin   French term meaning a creamed dish with broiler-browned or oven-browned topping of buttered crumbs or crumbs-and-cheese.

Bain-marie   French cooking utensil similar to double boiler. Consists of one utensil for heated water, in which other utensils are set to keep food warm.

Bake   To cook by dry heat in oven.

Barbecue   To broil or roast on grill or spit over coals or other heat. To cook with highly spiced sauce. Also means the picnic or meal of barbecued foods.

Bard   To cover meat or game with sliced bacon or salt pork. See *Lard*.

Baste   To drip or spoon fat or liquid of pan juices over food which is roasting, broiling, etc.

Batter Semi-liquid mixture of flour, water, milk, eggs, etc. A coating for food to be fried. A cake, waffle, or pancake mixture before baking.

Beat To blend or whip with spoon, rotary hand beater, or electric mixer to combine foods or to incorporate air, as in egg whites.

Beignets French for deep-fried sweet fritters and other foods.

Beurre manié French term. Flour and butter worked together, formed into small balls to add to stews, etc., for thickening.

Beurre noir French for "black butter": butter heated until dark brown, to be added to sauce, etc.

Bind To make a mixture hold together by adding liquid, beaten eggs, cream, etc.

Bisque Thick cream soup. Also frozen cream dessert.

Blanch To steep nuts, fruits, etc., in hot or boiling water to loosen skins for removing. Also, to reduce strong flavor or color of foods by immersing briefly in water at boiling point, off the fire.

Blaze To pour warmed brandy or liqueur over food and ignite.

Blend To combine ingredients, mixing until smooth.

Boil To cook in liquid at boiling temperature, when bubbles break the surface.

Bombe Ice cream combined with fruit, custard, or other centers in mould (mold), bombe, or melon shape, held at freezing temperature until serving time.

Bone To remove bones from fish, meat, or poultry. This is best done by fish or meat dealer. A special, short, sharp-pointed boning knife is used.

Bouillon A clear, strained soup of stock made from beef, veal, or fowl cooked with seasonings and vegetables.

Bouillon cube   Concentrated, dehydrated form of bouillon. With boiling water added, cubes make bouillon for sauces, etc.

Bouquet garni   See Faggot.

Braise   To brown in fat gently, with small amount of liquid added. Pan is covered to preserve juices.

Bread   To roll cutlet, croquettes, or other foods in crumbs.

Bread crumbs   Soft bread crumbs, made by crumbling fresh bread, are used for stuffings and to increase bulk of mixtures. Dry crumbs are used for *breading,* to coat foods for frying, etc.

Brine   Strong salt-and-water solution used for pickling vegetables and other foods.

Brioche   Sweet-dough French roll, very light in texture.

Brochette   The skewer and the method of cooking. To cook small pieces of meat, vegetables, fish, chicken, etc., on long metal skewer, under broiler heat or over barbecue grill. See barbecue chapter and meat recipes.

Broil   To cook over or under direct heat. See meats chapter.

Brown   To cook in a little fat at high heat until brown, sealing juices in; to place under broiler heat, or in oven, to brown top, as casserole or *au gratin* dishes.

Brûlé, Brûlée   French word meaning burnt: as for caramelized sugar, cream dessert, New Orleans coffee, Café Brûlé.

Brush   To spread light coating of sauce, butter, other liquid on surface of meat, etc., using pastry brush or other brush.

Canapé   See appetizers chapter.

Capers   Flower buds from shrub (also from nasturtiums) preserved in vinegar, used as condiment and in sauces. Usually imported in bottles.

Capon   Chicken emasculated to increase size and tenderness.

Caramel   Liquid burnt sugar used for coloring and flavor.

Chapon   Small cube of French bread rubbed with garlic to be tossed with green salad.

Chervil   See A Guide to Herbs, Seeds, and Spices.

Chill   To keep in refrigerator or on ice until cold but not frozen.

Chives   See A Guide to Herbs, Seeds, and Spices.

Chop   To cut into small pieces with chopper or knife. Also a cut of veal, lamb, mutton or pork.

Choux paste   Cream-puff pastry made in saucepan over heat.

Clarified butter   Melted butter, strained or skimmed.

Clarify   To clear clouded liquid, such as aspic, bouillon, stock, by heating gently with raw egg white added, stirring, then straining through fine sieve or cheesecloth.

Coat   To dip in flour, crumbs, other mixtures before frying.

Coat the spoon   The liquid mixture is thick enough to adhere in thin layer to the stirring spoon.

Cocottes   Small porcelain dishes, similar to ramekins, used for baking.

Combine   Mix two or more ingredients together.

Compote   Cooked, sweetened fruits.

Consommé   Clarified bouillon or stock.

Core   To remove seed center of fruit or vegetables, leaving rest intact.

Court bouillon   Simmered stock of white wine, water, herbs, fish bones, or vegetables, used in poaching fish and in making fish sauces.

Cream   To work or beat shortening, butter, other fats until light and airy, with or without addition of sugar or flour, etc.

Crêpes   Thin French pancakes.

Crisp   To restore texture of vegetables by covering with ice water for short period; to heat bread, crackers, dry cereals, etc., in oven few minutes.

Croissants   Rich, flaky, crescent-shaped French rolls.

Croquettes   Chopped or ground cooked foods, bound with sauce or beaten egg, formed into rolls, balls, or other shapes, coated with crumbs or flour, and deep-fat fried.

Croûte   French for pastry crust in which casserole mixture is baked.

Croûtons   Fried or toasted bread cubes, used as garnish on fish, meats, poultry, etc.

Crumble   To break into small pieces or crumbs with the fingers.

Cube   To cut into small square pieces.

Cure   To preserve meat, game, etc., with salt, liquid, smoking, etc.

Cut and fold   To blend mixture with liquid by first turning spoon sideways in a cutting motion as the two are combined, then lifting mixture from bottom and folding over top with spoon until all is mixed.

Cut in   To combine shortening with flour and dry ingredients by chopping motion, using pastry blender or two spatulas.

Deep fry   Same as French fry.

Deglaze   To remove the dark clinging particles from pan in which meat has browned, by adding hot liquid and stirring.

Devil   Use hot seasoning or sauce to flavor mixture.

Dice   Cut in small squares.

Dilute To thin by adding liquid. To diminish strength or flavor of liquid.

Dissolve To melt or liquefy.

Dot To scatter small pieces of butter or other food over surface of mixture before cooking.

Dough Spongy mixture of flour, other dry ingredients, and liquid, thick enough to knead.

Drain To strain liquid from solid food.

Draw To remove entrails of poultry, game, etc. To eviscerate.

Drawn butter Clarified butter.

Dredge To coat with flour, sugar, or dry mixture.

Drippings Fat which liquefies during cooking of meat, etc., and runs to bottom of pan.

Dust To sprinkle lightly with flour, sugar, dry mixtures.

Duxelles Finely chopped mushroom garnish used in fish cookery and with certain delicate poultry dishes.

Éclair See recipe.

En brochette See Brochette.

En papillotte Baked in paper. Oiled paper sacks are used, foil, and in some cases waxed paper although the latter chars quickly.

Essence Concentrated flavoring.

Eviscerate See Draw.

Faggot Three to 4 sprigs parsley, 1 or 2 small stalks celery, 1 leek, ½ bay leaf, 1 or 2 sprigs dry thyme tied together in small bundle added to cooking stew, sauce, other foods. Also called *Bouquet garni.*

Farce   Forcemeat; stuffing.

Fat   Butter, margarine, lard, vegetable shortening, rendered drippings from meats, also fatty sections of meats.

Fennel   See A Guide to Herbs, Seeds, and Spices.

Filé powder   Ground root used by Southern Indians and Creoles in fish and meat stews and soups.

Fillet, filet   To remove the bone from meat, fish, etc. Also the boneless piece of meat, fish, etc.

Filter   To strain liquid through several thicknesses of cheesecloth or a special paper filter.

Fines herbes   Mixture of chopped fresh or dried herbs, such as parsley, chives, basil.

Flake   To separate chunks of fish, other foods, lightly into thin pieces with fork.

Flambé   See Blaze.

Foie gras   Goose-liver *pâté*.

Fold   To lift mixture with spoon in an overlapping motion from one side of bowl to the other.

Fold in   To incorporate one mixture into another by blending with a spoon, using an up-and-over motion.

Fondue   See recipe.

Forcemeat   Seasoned stuffing, finely minced, pounded, ground, or combined in mixer or cooked separately and served as garnish.

Frappé   French for frozen. Also a cordial served over cracked or shaved ice, or other beverage shaken with or poured over shaved ice. Also lightly frozen fruit or vegetable juice, to be served as appetizer.

Freeze   To chill in freezing compartment until solid.

French fry To cook in deep hot fat until brown and crisp.

Fricassée To cook by braising with slightly more liquid than in braising. This is usually chicken or veal stewed in cream sauce, with seasoning and white wine added, or in brown sauce or stock.

Fritters Batter-dipped, French-fried food.

Frizzle To fry in hot fat until edges curl: frizzled chipped beef.

Frost To cover cake with icing. To coat rim of glass by dipping it in orange juice or other liquid, then into sugar.

Fry To cook in hot fat or oil in frying pan.

Fumet Concentrated fish or meat stock. See recipe.

Garlic A bulb with pungent odor and flavor, used raw and cooked. The bulb consists of a cluster of smaller ones, *each called a clove*. Should be peeled for use or crushed unpeeled in a handy garlic press.

Garnish To decorate a dish. See recipes.

Giblets The edible small parts of dressed birds: liver, heart, gizzard, etc.

Glacé French word for iced, glazed, or frozen foods.

Glace de viande Concentrated meat glaze made by reducing strong brown stock to jelly-like consistency. Used to flavor and color sauces and dishes.

Glaze Coating of syrup, gelatin, or aspic for hams, roast chicken, etc. Also, brown particles left in pan in which meat or poultry roasted. Also means to brown the top sauce which has been poured over a dish set under broiler or in oven.

Grate To reduce foods to small particles by rubbing over grater or using a grinder-grater.

Gravy   Sauce made in pan in which meat, fish, or poultry was cooked. It includes pan drippings, usually flour, seasonings, cream or milk, or stock.

Grill   To cook under broiler heat or over direct heat. Same as broil.

Grind   To put food through chopper, or grind by hand with mortar and pestle.

Grease   To rub inside of pan, mold, baking dish, with fat to prevent food sticking to it. Also means the cold fat left in frying pan or kettle. Should be reheated, clarified by filtering and stored in refrigerator for second use.

Hang   To age meat or game by hanging in cool unrefrigerated place.

Hors d'oeuvres   French appetizers. See appetizers chapter.

Ice   To chill over ice. Also a smooth, frozen fruit-juice dessert made without milk. Also, to cover a cake, cookies, etc., with frosting.

Icing   Frosting for cakes.

Infusion   Liquid drawn off tea, coffee, herbs which have steeped in boiling water.

Julienne   Food cut in thin strips.

Knead   To work dough with the hands, using a folding and pressing motion until it is smooth and spongy.

Lard   To insert thin strips of bacon or salt pork or suet into lean meat to make it more moist as it cooks. Meat dealers usually will do this. Or lay strips of fat bacon or salt pork over lean meats for roasting.

Leaven   To lighten a mixture by adding yeast, baking powder, eggs.

Leeks   Long, cylindrical onion-like vegetable; usually served cooked.

Legumes   Dried pod vegetables such as peas, beans, lentils. In French it means any vegetable.

Line To cover inside of baking dish with paper, pastry, crumbs, flour, sugar, according to recipe.

Liquor Liquid from shellfish. Liquid from food as it cooks.

Macédoine Mixture of fruits or vegetables.

Macéré French word. Steeped in wine, or pickled.

Marinade Mixture of seasoned liquids in which food is soaked to tenderize or add flavor.

Marinate To soak in a marinade.

Marmite An earthenware cooking utensil usually taller than it is round. A soup casserole. Also used for stews and long, slow-cooking dishes.

Marrons glacés Candied chestnuts, dry or in syrup, whole or chopped.

Marrow Soft fatty substance from cavity of meat bones.

Mash To reduce to pulp with fork or potato masher.

Mask To cover completely with sauce, mayonnaise, gelatin, etc.

Meat glaze See Glace de viande. Commercial versions today are Bovril and B-V.

Melt To liquefy by heat.

Meringue Egg whites beaten stiff, combined with sugar; may mean small or large baked rounds or other forms of the egg white and sugar mixture, or soft, uncooked mixture.

Mill To beat to a froth with a whisk beater, as in the preparation of hot chocolate and other milk drinks. Also, small mixers, choppers, and similar devices are called mills.

Mince To chop finely or put through chopper. Also means the resulting food mixture from such chopping.

Mirepoix French for chopped vegetables, fat, and seasoning added to the casserole or dish in which poultry and some meats are to be braised.

Mix To blend different ingredients by stirring or using electric mixer. Also, commercial preparation for pastry, cakes, and other dishes.

Moisten To add small amount of liquid.

Mortar Deep, heavy bowl of wood, marble, ceramics, in which spices, herbs, etc., are crushed or ground by hand with pestle.

Mould, or mold To shape gelatin-stiffened mixture, or ice cream or other dessert.

Mousse Frozen dessert of heavy-cream mixture. Also, gelatin mixture of finely ground fish, ham, chicken, etc., combined with cream and chilled, or served hot.

Mull To heat beverage, such as cider or wine, with sugar and spices; should be slow heat to bring out flavors.

Pan broil To cook uncovered in skillet, with little or no fat, pouring off fat as it emerges.

Pan fry To cook in skillet in small amount of fat.

Parboil To boil a few minutes, or until partially cooked, in preparation for next step of recipe.

Pare Also peel. To remove skin of fruit and vegetables with knife or parer.

Parfait Rich, frozen dessert, served in tall glass with long-handled spoon.

Pasta Cereal products such as macaroni, spaghetti, noodles.

Paste Mixture of flour and liquid. Also, ground nuts and fruits or combinations of these with sugar; also other ground foods.

Pastry See pies chapter.

Pastry Bag   A cornucopia made of heavy white cotton cloth, with small end having an opening just large enough to hold various metal tubes. Used for shaping doughs, making decorations of mashed potatoes, whipped cream, etc.

Pâté   Seasoned liver paste.

Peel   See Pare. To remove outer soft skin of tomatoes, peaches, etc., with fingers or knife.

Pickle   To preserve in brine or vinegar. Also, pickled vegetables and fruits.

Pinch   An amount of seasoning which is about 1/16 teaspoon, or as much as can be taken up between thumb and forefinger.

Pipe   To decorate with mixture forced through tube of pastry bag.

Pit   To remove kernel of fruit.

Poach   To simmer in liquid just below boiling point.

Potato starch   Flour made from potatoes. It can be used in place of flour or cornstarch as thickener for gravies and sauces.

Pound   To beat with heavy implement, such as mallet for meat or pestle for herbs, etc.

Prick   To pierce surface with fork or sharp knife.

Purée   Food forced through food mill or pulped in blender.

Quenelles   See recipe.

Ragoût   Rich brown stew.

Ramekin   Small individual baking dish.

Reduce   To cook until mixture is diminished in quantity or concentrated.

Render   To cook or heat meat until the fat liquefies and can be strained off.

Rice   To force cooked food through a ricer or sieve.

Roast   To cook uncovered in hot oven or in embers or ashes.

Roe   Fish eggs.

Roll out   To spread dough thin, lightly, with rolling pin.

Roux   Mixture of butter and flour cooked to smooth paste, either cooked only until thickened or until lightly browned. Used for thickening sauces.

Sauté   To brown quickly in small amount of oil or fat.

Scald   To pour boiling water over food. To heat liquid, such as milk, to just under boiling temperature when tiny bubbles start to form around edge.

Scallop   To bake in cream sauce, topped with crumbs or crumbs-and-cheese. Also, a shellfish.

Score   To cut gashes in surface of meat. Also to cut gashes in fat edging ham steak or cuts of beef, to prevent curling.

Scrape   To remove outer skin of vegetables by scraping with blade of paring knife.

Sear   To brown surface of meat at high temperature to hold juices in.

Season   Add salt, pepper, and other seasonings called for in recipe.

Seed   To remove seeds from such vegetables as tomatoes, peppers, cucumbers and certain fruits, such as grapes and pomegranates.

Shallot   Brown onion with strong but mellow flavor.

Sherbet   Frozen fruit-juice mixture containing milk or white of egg, or both.

Shirr   To cook whole eggs with cream and crumbs in dish.

Shortening   Fat used in breads, cakes, pastries, doughs. Also, any fat used in cooking, but especially lard and the hydrogenated vegetable fats.

Shred   To slice in small strips.

Sieve   To put food through strainer or sieve.

Sift   To shake dry ingredients, such as flour, seasonings, baking powder, together in a sieve or special sifter.

Simmer   To cook in liquid below boiling point. Liquid should move gently, with bubbles forming below surface.

Singe   To burn off the down or hairs from plucked game or fowl over a flame.

Skewer   Long wooden or metal pin used to hold fowl or meat in position for cooking. Also, metal rod used for barbecue and broiling small pieces of meat, fowl, fish, vegetables, etc. See Brochette.

Skim   To remove fat and other floating matter from surface of cooking liquid with spoon, strainer spoon, or skimmer.

Slivered   Cut in thin, small pieces.

Soak   To cover food with large amount of liquid to soften.

Spatula   Flexible metal knife, used to remove food from one dish to another or to turn certain foods in cookery. Wooden spatula, used with flour mixtures and sauces by some cooks.

Spice   To add spice and seasonings to a mixture. See also A Guide to Herbs, Seeds, and Spices.

Spit   For barbecuing and roasting. A pointed metal rod on which poultry and meat are fastened for cookery.

Steam To cook food in steam in colander or perforated steamer over boiling water, or by pressure cooker, or in double boiler over steam.

Steep To heat food in water, below boiling point, to extract juices, flavor, color.

Sterilize To kill bacteria by rapidly boiling water or steam, dry heat, or repeated boilings, as for jelly glasses and fruit jars.

Stew Cook in liquid, at slow boiling.

Stir Blend with spoon in circular motion around mixture.

Stock Liquid strained from cooked meat, fish, poultry, vegetables.

Strain To remove liquid from solid food. Also, to purée food through strainer.

Stud To force cloves or other flavoring into surface of food.

Stuff To fill with forcemeat or other mixture.

Stuffing Seasoned filling.

Suet Hard, fatty tissue surrounding certain cuts of beef.

Tenderize Marinate, pound, use commercial tenderizer on meat.

Thicken Flour, cornstarch, potato starch, cream, egg, added to mixtures to give more body.

Thin See Dilute.

Toast To brown by direct heat. Usually bread or bread products browned in oven or electric toaster.

Tomalley Fatty, soft, so-called liver of lobster, greenish gray in color when raw, turning to bright green when cooked. Used to thicken sauces for lobster. Cannot be boiled after tomalley is added or sauce will curdle.

Toss To combine lightly, using two forks or fork and spoon. Usually for salad, stuffings, crumbed mixtures.

Trim To cut away excess fat, dangling ends of meat, before or after cooking. Also applied to vegetables.

Truss Method of preparing dressed chicken or other fowl for roasting pan. Tie wings and legs of bird to body by skewers and string so bird holds shape during roasting.

Try out See Render.

Vanilla bean Use to flavor hot liquid. Split bean and cook piece in liquid. To flavor dish which does not contain hot liquid, split bean, scrape out seeds and pulp, and add to dish. Amount to use for recipe to serve four, about ⅛ teaspoon.

Vanilla sugar After using vanilla beans, wash and dry them. Add to jar of granulated sugar. Cover tightly and let stand few days. Use vanilla sugar in making custards, ice cream, other desserts.

Whip To beat rapidly by hand or in mixer, to incorporate air in egg whites, cream, gelatin mixture for fluffiness and increased bulk.

Work To knead or mix slowly.

Zest Citrus-fruit skin contains oil in its colored exterior. Used for flavoring drinks, desserts, many dishes.

Useful Reference Tables

WEIGHTS AND MEASURES

3 teaspoons	equal	1 tablespoon
4 tablespoons	"	¼ cup
5⅓ "	"	⅓ "
8 "	"	½ "
16 "	"	1 "

2 tablespoons	equal	1 liquid ounce
1 cup	equals	½ pint
2 cups	equal	1 pint
2 pints	"	1 quart
4 cups	"	1 "
8 quarts	"	1 peck
4 pecks	"	1 bushel

OVEN TERMS AND TEMPERATURES

Recipes in this book give both *temperature* and *corresponding term*. This chart will guide you when using other recipes, perhaps those given you by friends, when one term or the other may be omitted.

Also, remember that insulation of your oven, gas pressure, altitude, the quality of the oven-regulator device, et cetera, may affect cooking time. Follow recipe guidance as to setting oven temperature and observing cookery time, then as you go along make any necessary changes in time for baking, browning, and other cookery.

Slow Oven	200° to 275° F. (varying from extremely slow at 200° to 225° and 250° F. for less extreme temperatures).
Moderately Slow	300° F.
Moderate	325°, 350°, 375° F. (see recipe for exact temperature called for).
Moderately Hot	400° F.
Hot	425° to 450° F.
Very Hot	475° to 525° F.

EQUIVALENT MEASURES

Butter or Margarine............... 1 ounce equals 2 tablespoons fat
    ¼ pound equals ½ cup fat (or 1 stick)
    ½ pound equals 1 cup fat
    1 pound equals 2 cups fat

Cheese..... American............... 1 pound equals 5 cups grated
    cream (3 ounce)......... 1 package equals 6⅔ tablespoons

Chocolate....................... 1 square equals 1 ounce equals 3½ tablespoons dry cocoa plus 1 tablespoon butter

Crumbs .... saltine crackers......... 7 coarsely crumbled equal 1 cup (9 finely crumbled)
    graham crackers......... 9 coarsely crumbled equal 1 cup (11 finely crumbled)
    small vanilla wafers ......20 coarsely crumbled equal 1 cup (30 finely crumbled)
    zwieback.............. 4 coarsely crumbled equal 1 cup (9 finely crumbled)

Eggs........................... 12 to 14 egg yolks equal 1 cup
    8 to 10 egg whites equal 1 cup

Flours..... all-purpose........... 1 pound sifted equals 4 cups
    cake.................. 1 pound sifted equals 4½ cups
    graham............... 1 pound unsifted equals 3½ cups
    corn meal.............. 1 pound equals 3 cups

Fruits and nuts................... 1 lemon equals 3 to 4 tablespoons juice
    1 orange equals 6 to 8 tablespoons juice
    1 package seedless raisins equals 3 cups (15-ounce)
    ¼ pound shelled nuts equals 1 cup chopped

Rice.............................. 1 pound equals 2⅓ cups raw rice

Sugar..... granulated...............1 pound equals 2¼ cups

           brown, firmly packed...... 1 pound equals 2¼ cups

           confectioners'............ 1 pound equals 3½ cups

HOW MUCH IN A CAN?

Net Weight on Label	Approximate Cups	Products Such As
8-oz. can	1	Fruits, vegetables, Chinese foods, etc.
10½-oz. can	1¼	Condensed soups, meat, and fish, etc.
12-oz. can	1½	Vacuum-packed corn.
1-lb. No. 300 } can	1¾	Pork and beans, baked beans, cranberry sauce.
16- to 17-oz. No. 303 } can	2	Fruits, vegetables, ready-to-serve soups.
1-lb. 4-oz., or 20-oz., or 18 fl.-oz. No. 2 } can	2½	Juices, fruits, ready-to-serve soups. specialties.
1-lb. 13-oz. or 29-oz. No. 2½ } can	3½	Fruits, some vegetables, pumpkin, sauerkraut, tomatoes.
3-lb. 3-oz. or 46 fl.-oz. } can	5¾	Fruit and vegetable juices, whole chicken, pork and beans.

Index

Á la King, defined, 747
Á la Mode, defined, 747
Acorn squash, 641
    baked, 641
    barbecued, 43
    boiled, 641
    broiled, 641
Alcoholic beverages, 61
Allspice, 729
Almond
    -baked apples, 261
    -bleu cheese spread, 13
    -butter sauce, 556
    -chicken sandwich, 528
    -chocolate pudding, 278
        sauce, 564
    cookies, 134
    custard, 237
    frosting, 124–25
    ice cream
        -brittle, 251
        burnt-, 250
        coconut-, 259
    mousse, chocolate, 253
    paste, buying, 150
    with rice, 449
    -rice stuffing, 234
    sauce, 545
        butter-, 556
        chocolate-, 564
Almonds
    with celery, 623
    glazed, 142
    and green beans, 616
    in stuffing, 232
Amandine sauce, 545
American cheese
    -bacon rolls, 9
    with baked eggs, 288
    croquettes, 192

equivalent measures,
    764
and lima beans, 617
in Noches, 12
in potatoes au gratin,
    636
in rabbits
    tomato, 191
    Welsh, 184
sage dip, 15
sauce, 546
soufflé, 581
Anchovy
    -broiled chicken, 203
    butter, 540
    and eggs, 18
    French Dressing, 518
    green salad, 496
    in Friday sauce, 448
Angel cake, 106–7
Anise seed, 729
Antipasto
    defined, 747
    see also Hors d'oeuvres
Appetizers, 3–30
    canapés, 5–12
    dips and spreads, 13–17
    egg, 17–18
    fruit and vegetable,
        18–24
    hors d'oeuvres, 24–27
    salad, 27
    shellfish, 27–30
Apple
    Charlotte, 262
    crisp, 275
        molasses, 266–67
    fritters, 246
    grapefruit salad, 485
    pies, 462–64
        chiffon, 463

Index

mayonnaise, 523
pies
apricot, 473
nectarine, 473
prune, 475
puffs, 244
sauce, 557
crab-, 561
lobster-, 561
macaroon-, 567
nutmeg-, 554
sherry-, 568
shrimp-, 561
soups
asparagus, 594
celery, 596
chicken, 594
curry, 595
tomato, frosted, 606
vegetable, 596
taffy, 144
torte, lemon-, 284
Creaming, defined, 751
Crème Brulée, 241
Crème de Menthe
in sherbet, 258
Crêpes
defined, 751
Suzette, 100
Crescent, braided, 76
Crisping, defined, 751
Crisps
apple, 275
molasses-apple, 266
Spanish-fritter, 247
Croquettes
cheese, 192
potato, 637
rice-crab, 451
salmon, 317
Croûte, defined, 751
Croûtons
defined, 751
for soup, 595
with spinach, 640
Crumb
pastry, 237
pie crust, 460
Crumbs
equivalent measures, 764
making, 719
Crunch, hazelnut, 149
Cucumber
-bean salad, 494
dip, 16

dressing, 521
-pepper salad
sauce, 548
Cucumbers
braised, 627
as meat garnish, 433
Cumin seed, 731
Cupcakes, 115–17
fruit, 116
honey-orange, 115
New Orleans, 117
petits fours, 116
Cups
fruit, 18, 266
hot, 64–65
Curing, defined, 751
Currant jelly
-and-horse-radish glaze, 389
in salad dressing, 515
sauce, 548
-raspberry, 269
in Vienna turnovers, 484
Curry
baked chicken, 212
beef, 370
chicken, 206
condiment for, 555
egg, 291
fruit, 450
lobster, 338
-and-onion spread, 539
powder, 731
sauce, for lamb, 549
serundang with, 555
shrimp, 357
skate, 325
soup
cream of, 595
frosted, 607
tuna, 182
whitefish, 325
Custard
almond, for dieters, 237
applesauce- pie, 468
baked, 238
cheese, 195
banana- pudding, 276
Charlotte Russe, 238
chocolate, 239
crème brulée, 241
for dieters
almond, 237
frozen, 252
filling

Index

Sukiyaki, 572
Summer
    drinks, 57–61
    menus, 712–15
    squash, 642
Sunday Brunch buns, 73
Supper menus, 659–75
    buffet, 698
    holiday, 699, 701, 702
    Indian, 688
    Italian, 689–70
    Japanese, 691
    warm-weather, 712–15
Suppers, skillet, 569–77
Suprême de pulet Marjolaine, 210–11
Swedish
    cornets, 245
    dinner menu, 691
    foods, buying, 728
Sweet loaf, toasted, 542–43
Sweet-potato
    pie, 478–79
    puff, 639
    soufflé, 640
Sweet potatoes, 638–40
    barbecued, 43
Sweet-sour sauce
    for shrimp, 556
    for tongue, 427
Sweetbread-oyster pie, 170
Sweetbreads, 425–26
    au gratin, 426
    Crillon, 425
Sweetmeats. *See* Candy
Swiss cheese, 200
    bacon canapés, 6–7
    custard, 195
    green beans with, 157
    pie, 196
    salad, 506
    sandwiches, 531, 532
Syrup, chocolate, 58–59

Tables, reference, 763–65
Taffy, cream, 144
    honey, 145
Tamale pie, 420
Tarragon, 735
    in cocktail sauce, 547
Tart shells, 462
Tartare sauce, 524
Tarts, 479–82
    apple meringue, 479
    blueberry meringue, 482

California bite, 6
cheese-jam, 190
cherry, 480
chiffon, pumpkin, 481
chocolate ice cream
    meringue, 482
ice cream meringue, 482
lemon meringue, 480
meringue, 482
    apple, 479
    blueberry, 482
    ice cream, 482
    lemon, 480
    peach, 482
    raspberry, 482
    strawberry, 482
peach meringue, 482
pumpkin chiffon, 481
raisin, 481
raspberry meringue, 482
shells for, 462
strawberry meringue, 482
Tea, 54–57
    evening, 57
    iced, 57
Tea menus, 707–9
    bridesmaids', 710
    reception, 709
Tea sandwiches, 532–37
    beef rolls, toasted, 536
    checkerboard, 532
    double-decker rounds, 534
    Roquefort, 534
    tuna-cheese buns, 536
    water-cress, 536
Teen-agers' Saturday night menu, 697
Temperatures, oven, 763
Tenderizing, 761
Thanksgiving menus, 702–3
Thermometer
    candy, 139
    meat, 722
Thickening, 761
Thyme, 735
Tilsit cheese, 200
Toasting, 761
Tomalley, defined, 761
Tomato
    -asparagus salad, 501
    aspic ring, 514
    barbecue sauce, 558
    beef loaf, 417
    bisque, oyster-, 600
    bouillon, 606
    broccoli salad, 501

Index

Index